MASS COMMUNICATIONS

MASS

COMMUNICATIONS

A BOOK OF READINGS SELECTED
AND EDITED BY THE DIRECTOR OF THE
INSTITUTE FOR COMMUNICATION RESEARCH
AT STANFORD UNIVERSITY, **WILBUR SCHRAMM**

University of Illinois Press, Urbana, 1960

SECOND PRINTING, 1963

SECOND EDITION

© 1960 BY THE BOARD OF TRUSTEES
OF THE UNIVERSITY OF ILLINOIS.
MANUFACTURED IN THE
UNITED STATES OF AMERICA.
LIBRARY OF CONGRESS
CATALOG CARD NO. 60-8343.

This volume is dedicated to three pioneers in the study of mass communications through the social sciences:

PAUL F. LAZARSFELD • HAROLD D. LASSWELL • CARL I. HOVLAND

FOREWORD TO THE SECOND EDITION

TEN YEARS ago, when *Mass Communications* first appeared, we intended it to be a pioneering reader for the study of mass communications through the windows of the social sciences. We hoped it would prove useful to college and university classes studying mass communications and would stimulate scholars to write integrated books to supplement or replace it.

It appears that only half those hopes were realized. The book did indeed prove useful to students and teachers, and was responsible for introducing the study of mass communications from the viewpoint of the social sciences into many universities in several countries. But when we tried to treat it as a pioneering rather than a continuing book, and therefore resisted the temptation to make a second edition and finally let the first edition go out of print, we discovered that nothing had been written which quite replaced this book as an introductory volume. When in one week we received requests from four foreign countries asking the publishers to "please find us a used copy somewhere," and when the sale of used copies was reported at three times the original price of the book, then we reconsidered and decided to bring out a second edition.

Like the first edition, this one brings together anthropologists, psychologists, sociologists, political scientists, economists, teachers of mass communication, and professional mass communicators, combining diversity of approach with unity of target. However, in the years since the first edition, there have been important developments in the field.

So far as the media are concerned, the great event has been the phenomenal growth of television. The first edition hardly mentioned television; in this volume, it has its proper place.

In scholarship there have been equally important, though less spectacular, developments. For one thing, there has been a salutary emphasis on the mass media as organizations, to reflect which we have put in a new section on the structure and function of mass communications, with Harold Lasswell's famous essay on "Structure and Function," descriptions of the day-to-day operations of press, film, and television, a memorandum on gatekeepers, and Warren Breed's sociological study of the newsroom. There has also been a healthful and general realization that the emphasis on "mass" audience—meaning an audience of individuals in lonely and direct contact with mass communication—was never accurate. The publication of Katz and Lazarsfeld's *Personal Influence* dramatized the fact that personal communication in the audience must now be considered in its relation to mass communication, and that the activity within the audience at the end of the communication chain is as important in bringing about the "effect" of the mass media as are the media themselves. We present in this volume one of the best-known ideas within this concept—"the two-step" flow of mass communication. Since the first edition, there has been a most welcome emphasis on responsibility in mass communication, including not only penetrating criticism from the outside but also a newly self-critical attitude on the part of some media men, and the publication of the first major book on communication ethics in thirty years. This chain of development we have also represented here by an entirely new section. There has also been a notable development in the study of mass communication in other countries and between countries, stimulated by the work of UNESCO in mass communication and by such projects as the international communication study at M.I.T. We have included Dr. Lerner's article on countries in transition from oral to media communication, and an appendix on mass communication in other countries. Finally, the statistics of mass communication are in better shape than they were ten years ago (although still far from optimum) and we have been able to include more and better tables than in the first edition.

The selections in the first edition were tried out in the Institute of Communications Research at the University of Illinois, of which the editor was then director. Academic mobility being what it is, it is now possible to report that the selections in the second edition have been used and tested in the Stanford Institute for Communication Research. I believe I can speak for both institutes in saying that they are glad to share their experiences with these readings and to make them available for wider use.

WILBUR SCHRAMM

Center for Advanced Study
in the Behavioral Sciences

December, 1959

CONTENTS

THE DEVELOPMENT OF MASS COMMUNICATIONS

WHEN DID mass communications begin? The date usually given is that of the beginning of printing from movable metal type, in Western Europe in the fifteenth century, but the roots are much earlier and the flowering much later.

The mass media are the resultant of forces set in motion when groups of manlike animals first huddled together against the cold and danger of primitive times. The tool of language came before history, and the tool we know as the alphabet came in the very dawn of history. Sometime between the beginning of language and the invention of the alphabet, man developed highly ingenious ways of storing knowledge and transmitting information. Smoke signals and drum beats were the first broadcasts, and the first libraries were collections of cut stone tablets. The Romans published a sort of wall newspaper, and during the Middle Ages many books and shorter documents were printed from wood blocks. On the eastern edge of Asia there was printing from metal type a long time before men printed from metal on the western edge of Europe. In Korea, where they had paper, ink, and metal type first, conditions were not ripe for the growth of mass communication; in Western Europe, when Gutenberg began to print, society was more nearly ready to develop the new device.

But it was many years after Gutenberg before Western Europe developed anything which we should recognize today as mass media. As soon as the first books and documents came off the presses, however, the new tool of print was caught up in social use. It became a weapon of the men in power and a weapon of revolution. The first news sheets became tools of commerce; the first books became tools of education. Magazines and pamphlets argued out the politics of the sixteenth and seventeenth century. The British, the American, the French revolutions would have been unlikely, if not impossible, without mass communication. When political freedom had been won for the common man, mass

3

communications were able to reach, over the heads of the specially privi-leged and the specially educated, to the great masses of men who had need of information in order to play their proper parts in democracy and to take advantage of the opportunities they were being offered. Political democracy, economic opportunity, free public education, the Industrial Revolution, and mass communication were woven together in the nineteenth and twentieth centuries to make a great change in human life and national relations.

The significance of what happened on the printing presses of the fifteenth century was that a machine had been developed to duplicate an idealized version of man's handwriting. The significance of what happened in the nineteenth century in the laboratories of Daguerre, Edison, Bell, Marconi, and others was that a machine had been de-veloped to see and hear for man at great distances. These are the two kinds of mass communication, and so interwoven are they now in our lives that it is hard to imagine what life would be without them.

The following pages begin with a brief chronology of mass communi-cations. Then comes Professor Park's thoughtful account of the growth of the newspaper in the midst of the social forces with which it inter-acted. This is followed by accounts of some of the newer media: motion picture, radio, modern telecommunication, and the great news agencies. Finally there is a chapter on the growth of the newest medium, tele-vision. Notice also the table on the growth of literacy in the United States. Literacy is at once a cause and an effect of the growth of mass media. Without mass media, there is less reason for people to learn to read; without widespread literacy, there is little market for printed media. This is why the growth of public education was parallel to the growth of mass communications in this country, and also why the first great growth of mass communications in illiterate countries at the present time is usually by means of radio and film.

A BRIEF CHRONOLOGY OF
MASS COMMUNICATIONS

By 105 A.D. Chinese had made paper and ink.

By 450 Block printing practiced in Asia.

868 Oldest preserved block-printed book, *The Diamond Sutra.*

900–1450 Book scribes developed high skill. Movable type developed in China, and cast metal type in Korea. Just before the middle of the fifteenth century, Gutenberg and others apparently perfected the system of casting metal type, and applied it to bookmaking with a practical hand press and oil varnish ink.

1456 The 42-line "Gutenberg" Bible.

1450–1550 Beginning in Germany, printing swept over Europe. Caxton established an English press in 1476. Aldus was operating his famous press in Italy in 1494.

1539 First press in Western Hemisphere—Mexico.

1621 First coranto (news sheet) printed in Amsterdam (first English coranto, 1622).

1638 First press in American colonies. The oldest extant book printed in America—*The Bay Psalm Book*—published in 1640.

1665 First English newspaper, *London Gazette.*

1690 First American newspaper, *Publick Occurrences,* Boston. It lasted one issue.

1702 First daily newspaper in English, *The Daily Courant,* London.

1704 First continuously published American newspaper, *The Boston News-Letter.*

1731 First magazine, in present meaning of that term—*The Gentleman's Magazine*, London.

1741 First magazine in America, *American Magazine*, Philadelphia.

1784 First successful daily newspaper in America, *The Pennsylvania Packet, and Daily Advertiser*, Philadelphia (first issued tri-weekly, then daily).

1805 Stereotyping process developed.

1807 Fourdrinier brothers perfected system for making paper.

1814 Steam power applied to printing press, and cylinder press developed.

1833 First penny paper, *The New York Sun*, opened the way to mass circulation.

1839 Daguerre developed practical method of photography (daguerrotype).

1844 Morse transmitted first telegraph message.

1848 First press association in America.

1853 Paper made from wood pulp.

1857 First transatlantic cable.

1867 First practical typewriter.

1868 First web perfecting press.

1872 Process of photoengraving developed (halftones in 1880).

1873 First daily illustrated paper.

1876 Bell transmitted the first telephone message by overhead wire.

1877 Edison invented the phonograph.

1886 Mergenthaler introduced the Linotype.

1894 Motion picture projector perfected and first films shown the public.

1895 Marconi sends and receives wireless messages.

1897 Motion pictures of Corbett-Fitzsimmons fight. First motion picture which told a story, "The Great Train Robbery," made in 1903.

1904 Telephone wirephoto sent from Munich to Nuremberg.

1906 Fessenden transmitted human voice by radio.

1920 Beginning of regularly scheduled broadcasting—8MK (later WWJ), Detroit, and KDKA, Pittsburgh.

1923 Picture televised between New York and Philadelphia.

1923 *Time* started new fashion in news magazines.

1924 Tabloid newspaper.

1926 Beginning of book clubs.

1926 First radio network, NBC. Blue (ABC) and CBS, 1927. MBS, 1934.

1927 "Jazz Singer" started vogue of talking pictures.

1928 First Disney animated cartoon.

1928 Regular television schedule begun by WGY, Schenectady.

1935 Major E. H. Armstrong developed FM.

1936 *Life* started new fashion in picture magazines.

1938 Daily facsimile broadcasts started by KSD, St. Louis.

1941 Full commercial television authorized.

1948 Beginning of great expansion of television. From 100,000 sets in the U.S. at the beginning of that year, total increased more than one million during 1948, and thereafter in rapidly rising curve.

1952 End of television "freeze," permitting new stations to be licensed and television to spread across the continent.

1954 Beginning of color television broadcasts on regular and continuing commercial basis.

THE NATURAL HISTORY OF THE NEWSPAPER

BY ROBERT E. PARK

The author was a professor of sociology at the University of Chicago.
This essay appears as a chapter in Park, Burgess, and McKenzie's *The
City,* copyrighted by the University of Chicago Press, 1925. It is re-
printed by permission of the publisher.

THE STRUGGLE FOR EXISTENCE

THE NEWSPAPER has a history; but it has, likewise, a natural history.
The press, as it exists, is not, as our moralists sometimes seem to assume, the willful product of any little group of living men. On the
contrary, it is the outcome of a historic process in which many individuals participated without foreseeing what the ultimate product
of their labors was to be.

The newspaper, like the modern city, is not wholly a rational
product. No one sought to make it just what it is. In spite of all the
efforts of individual men and generations of men to control it and
to make it something after their own heart, it has continued to grow
and change in its own incalculable ways.

The type of newspaper that exists is the type that has survived
under the conditions of modern life. The men who may be said to
have made the modern newspaper—James Gordon Bennett, Charles
A. Dana, Joseph Pulitzer, and William Randolph Hearst—are the
men who discovered the kind of paper that men and women would
read and had the courage to publish it.

The natural history of the press is the history of the surviving

8

species. It is an account of the conditions under which the existing newspaper has grown up and taken form.

A newspaper is not merely printed. It is circulated and read. Otherwise it is not a newspaper. The struggle for existence, in the case of the newspaper, has been a struggle for circulation. The newspaper that is not read ceases to be an influence in the community. The power of the press may be roughly measured by the number of people who read it.

The growth of great cities has enormously increased the size of the reading public. Reading, which was a luxury in the country, has become a necessity in the city. In the urban environment literacy is almost as much a necessity as speech itself. That is one reason there are so many foreign-language newspapers.

Mark Villchur, editor of the *Russkoye Slovo*, New York City, asked his readers how many of them had read newspapers in the old country. He found that out of 312 correspondents only 16 had regularly read newspapers in Russia; 10 others from time to time read newspapers in the Volast, the village administration center, and 12 were subscribers to weekly magazines. In America all of them were subscribers or readers of Russian newspapers.

This is interesting because the immigrant has had, first and last, a profound influence on the character of our native newspapers. How to bring the immigrant and his descendants into the circle of newspaper readers has been one of the problems of modern journalism.

The immigrant who has, perhaps, acquired the newspaper habit from reading a foreign-language newspaper is eventually attracted to the native American newspapers. They are for him a window looking out into the larger world outside the narrow circle of the immigrant community in which he has been compelled to live. The newspapers have discovered that even men who can perhaps read no more than the headlines in the daily press will buy a Sunday paper to look at the pictures.

It is said that the most successful of the Hearst papers, the *New York Evening Journal*, gains a new body of subscribers every six years. Apparently it gets its readers mainly from immigrants. They graduate into Mr. Hearst's papers from the foreign-language press, and when the sensationalism of these papers begins to pall, they acquire a taste for some soberer journals. At any rate, Mr. Hearst has been a great Americanizer.

In their efforts to make the newspaper readable to the least-instructed reader, to find in the daily news material that would thrill the crudest intelligence, publishers have made one important discovery. They have found that the difference between the high-brow and the low-brow, which once seemed so profound, is largely a difference in vocabularies. In short, if the press can make itself intelligible to the common man, it will have even less difficulty in being understood by the intellectual. The character of present-day newspapers has been profoundly influenced by this fact.

THE FIRST NEWSPAPERS

What is a newspaper? Many answers have been given. It is the tribune of the people; it is the fourth estate;[1] the Palladium of our civil liberties, etc.

On the other hand, this same newspaper has been characterized as the great sophist. What the popular teachers did for Athens in the period of Socrates and Plato the press has done in modern times for the common man.

The modern newspaper has been accused of being a business enterprise. "Yes," say the newspaper men, "and the commodity it sells is news." It is the truth shop. (The editor is the philosopher turned merchant.) By making information about our common life accessible to every individual at less than the price of a telephone call, we are to regain, it is urged—even in the complicated life of what Graham Wallas calls the "Great Society"—some sort of working democracy.

The advertising manager's notion is again something different. For him the newspaper is a medium for creating advertising values. The business of the editor is to provide the envelope which incloses the space which the advertising man sells. Eventually the newspaper may be conceived as a sort of common carrier, like the railway or the post office.

The newspaper, according to the author of *The Brass Check*, is a

---

[1] The three "estates of the realm" were kings, lords, and commons in the seventeenth century; later they were designated as the lords spiritual, the lords temporal, and the commons. In the eighteenth century the army was sometimes referred to as a "fourth estate," and at least once "the mob" was thus named. Probably Macaulay was the first to give this designation to "the gallery in which the reporters sit," in his essay on Hallam's *Constitutional History* in 1828, though Carlyle in his "Hero as a Man of Letters" ascribes the *bon mot* to Burke. It is not found in Burke's printed works.

crime. The brass check is a symbol of prostitution. "The brass check is found in your pay envelope every week—you who write and print and distribute our newspapers and magazines. The brass check is the price of your shame—you who take the fair body of truth and sell it in the market place, who betray the virgin hopes of mankind into the loathsome brothel of big business."

This is the conception of a moralist and a socialist—Upton Sinclair.

Evidently the newspaper is an institution that is not yet fully understood. What it is, or seems to be, for any one of us at any time is determined by our differing points of view. As a matter of fact, we do not know much about the newspaper. It has never been studied.

One reason we know so little about the newspaper is that as it exists today it is a very recent manifestation. Besides, in the course of its relatively brief history, it has gone through a remarkable series of transfigurations. The press today is, however, all that it was and something more. To understand it we must see it in its historic perspective.

The first newspapers were written or printed letters; news-letters they were called. In the seventeenth century, English country-gentlemen used to employ correspondents to write them once a week from London the gossip of the court and of the town.

The first newspaper in America, at least the first newspaper that lasted beyond its first issue, was the *Boston News-Letter*. It was published by the postmaster. The village post office has always been a public forum, where all the affairs of the nation and the community were discussed. It was to be expected that there, in close proximity to the sources of intelligence, if anywhere, a newspaper would spring up. For a long time the position of postmaster and the vocation of editor were regarded as inseparable.

The first newspapers were simply devices for organizing gossip, and that, to a greater or less extent, they have remained. Horace Greeley's advice to a friend who was about to start a country paper is as good today as it was then.

Begin with a clear conception that the subject of deepest interest to an average human being is himself; next to that, he is most concerned about his neighbors. Asia and the Tongo Islands stand a long way after these in his regard. It does seem to me that most country journals are oblivious as to these vital truths. If you will, so soon as may be, secure a wide-awake, judicious correspondent in each village and township of your county, some young lawyer, doctor, clerk in a store, or assistant in a post-office who will promptly send you whatever of moment occurs in his vicinity, and will make up at least half of your journal of local matter thus collected, nobody in the county can long do without it. Do not let a new church be organized, or new members be added to one already existing, a farm be sold, a new house be raised, a mill be set in motion, a store be opened, nor anything of interest to a dozen families occur, without having the fact duly though briefly chronicled in your columns. If a farmer cuts a big tree, or grows a mammoth beet, or harvests a bounteous yield of wheat or corn, set forth the fact as concisely and un-exceptionally as possible.

What Greeley advises friend Fletcher to do with his country paper the city editor of every newspaper, as far as it humanly is possible, is still trying to do. It is not practicable, in a city of three million and more, to mention everybody's name. For that reason attention is focused upon a few prominent figures. In a city where everything happens every day, it is not possible to record every petty incident, every variation from the routine of the city life. It is possible, however, to select certain particularly picturesque or romantic incidents and treat them symbolically, for their human interest rather than their individual and personal significance. In this way news ceases to be wholly personal and assumes the form of art. It ceases to be the record of the doings of individual men and women and becomes an impersonal account of manners and life.

The motive, conscious or unconscious, of the writers and of the press in all this is to reproduce, as far as possible, in the city the conditions of life in the village. In the village everyone knew everyone else. Everyone called everyone by his first name. The village was democratic. We are a nation of villagers. Our institutions are fundamentally village institutions. In the village, gossip and public opinion were the main sources of social control.

"I would rather live," said Thomas Jefferson, "in a country with newspapers and without a government than in a country with a government and without newspapers."

If public opinion is to continue to govern in the future as it has in the past, if we propose to maintain a democracy as Jefferson conceived it, the newspaper must continue to tell us about ourselves. We must somehow learn to know our community and its affairs in the same intimate way in which we knew them in the country villages. The newspaper must continue to be the printed diary of the home community. Marriages and divorce, crime and politics must continue to make up the main body of our news. Local news is the very stuff that democracy is made of.

But that, according to Walter Lippmann, is just the difficulty. "As social truth is organized today," so he says, "the press is not constituted to furnish from one edition to the next the amount of knowledge which the democratic theory of public opinion demands. . . . When we expect it to supply such a body of truth, we employ a misleading standard of judgment. We misunderstand the limited nature of news, the illimitable complexity of society; we over-estimate our own endurance, public spirit, and all-round competence. We suppose an appetite for uninteresting truths which is not discovered by any honest analysis of our own tastes. . . . Unconsciously the theory sets up the single reader as theoretically incompetent, and puts upon the press the burden of accomplishing whatever representative government, industrial organization, and diplomacy have failed to accomplish. Acting upon everybody for thirty minutes in twenty-four hours, the press is asked to create a mystical force called 'public opinion' that will take up the slack in public institutions."

It is evident that a newspaper cannot do for a community of one million inhabitants what the village did spontaneously for itself through the medium of gossip and personal contact. Nevertheless, the efforts of the newspaper to achieve this impossible result are an interesting chapter in the history of politics as well as of the press.

THE PARTY PAPERS

The first newspapers, the news-letters, were not party papers. Political journals began to supersede the news-letter at the beginning of the eighteenth century. The news with which the reading public was most concerned at that time was the reports of the debates in Parliament.

Even before the rise of the party press certain prying and curious individuals had made a business of visiting the Strangers' Gallery during the sessions of the House of Commons in order to write up from memory, or from notes taken down surreptitiously, accounts of the speeches and discussions during an important debate. At this time all deliberations of Parliament were secret, and it was not until one hundred years later that the right of reporters to attend the sessions of the House of Commons and record its proceedings was officially recognized. In the meantime reporters were compelled to resort to all sorts of subterfuges and indirect methods in order to get information. It is upon this information, gathered in this way, that much of our present history of English politics is based.

One of the most distinguished of these parliamentary reporters was Samuel Johnson. One evening in 1770, it is reported, Johnson, with a number of other celebrities, was taking dinner in London. Conversation turned upon parliamentary oratory. Someone spoke of a famous speech delivered in the House of Commons by the elder Pitt in 1741. Someone else, amid the applause of the company, quoted a passage from this speech as an illustration of an orator who had surpassed in feeling and beauty of language the finest efforts of the orators of antiquity. Then Johnson, who up to that point had taken no part in the discussion, spoke up. "I wrote that speech," he said, "in a garret in Exeter Street."

The guests were struck with amazement. He was asked, "How could it have been written by you, sir?"

"Sir," said Johnson, "I wrote it in Exeter Street. I never was in the gallery of the House of Commons but once. Cave had interests with the doorkeepers; he and the persons employed under him got admittance; they brought away the subjects of discussion, the names of the speakers, the side they took, and the order in which they rose, together with notes of the various arguments adduced in the course of the debate. The whole was afterward communicated to me, and I composed the speeches in the form they now have in the 'Parliamentary Debates,' for the speeches of that period are all printed from Cave's magazine."

Someone undertook to praise Johnson's impartiality, saying that in his reports he seems to have dealt out reason and eloquence with an equal hand to both political parties. "That is not quite true," was Johnson's reply. "I saved appearances tolerably well; but I took care that the Whig dogs should not have the best of it."

This speech of William Pitt, composed by Johnson in Exeter Street, has long held a place in school books and collections of oratory. It is the famous speech in which Pitt answered the accusation of the "atrocious crime of being a young man."

Perhaps Pitt thought he delivered that speech. At any rate there is no evidence that he repudiated it. I might add that Pitt, if he was the first, was not the last statesman who is indebted to the reporters for his reputation as an orator.

The significant thing about this incident is that it illustrates the manner in which, under the influence of the parliamentary reporters, something like a constitutional change was effected in the character of parliamentary government. As soon as the parliamentary orators discovered that they were addressing not only their fellow-members but, indirectly, through the medium of the press, the people of England, the whole character of parliamentary proceedings changed. Through the newspapers the whole country was enabled to participate in the discussions by which issues were framed and legislation was enacted.

Meanwhile, the newspapers themselves, under the influence of the very discussions which they themselves instigated, had become party organs. Whereupon the party press ceased to be a mere chronicle of small gossip and came to be what we know as a "journal of opinion." The editor, meanwhile, no longer a mere newsmonger and humble recorder of events, found himself the mouthpiece of a political party, playing a rôle in politics.

During the long struggle for freedom of thought and speech in the seventeenth century, popular discontent had found literary expression in the pamphlet and broadside. The most notable of these pamphleteers was John Milton, and the most famous of these pamphlets was Milton's *Areopagitica: A defence of the Liberty of Unlicensed Printing*, published in 1646; "the noblest piece of English prose" it has been called by Henry Morley.

When the newspaper became, in the early part of the eighteenth century, a journal of opinion, it took over the function of the political pamphlet. The opinion that had formerly found expression in a broadside was now expressed in the form of editorial leading articles. The editorial writer, who had inherited the mantle of the pamphleteer, now assumed the rôle of a tribune of the people.

It was in this rôle, as the protagonist of the popular cause, that the newspaper captured the imagination of our intelligentsia.

When we read in the political literature of a generation ago references to "the power of the press," it is the editor and the editorial, rather than the reporter and the news, of which these writers are thinking. Even now when we speak of the liberty of the press, it is the liberty to express an opinion, rather than the liberty to investigate and publish the facts, which is meant. The activities of the reporter, upon which any opinion that is relevant to existing conditions is likely to be based, are more often regarded as an infringement of our personal rights than an exercise of our political liberties.

The liberty of the press for which Milton wrote the *Areopagitica* was the liberty to express an opinion. "Give me the liberty," he said, "to know, to alter, and to argue freely according to conscience, above all liberties."

Carlyle was thinking of the editorial writer and not of the reporter when he wrote: "Great is journalism! Is not every able editor a ruler of the world, being a persuader of it?"

The United States inherited its parliamentary government, its party system, and its newspapers from England. The rôle which the political journals played in English politics was re-enacted in America. The American newspapers were a power with which the British government had to reckon in the struggle of the colonies for independence. After the British took possession of New York City, Ambrose Serle, who had undertaken to publish the *New York Gazette* in the interest of the invaders, wrote as follows to Lord Dartmouth in regard to the patriot-party press.

Among other engines which have raised the present commotion, next to indecent harangues of the preachers, none has had a more extensive or stronger influence than the newspapers of the respective colonies. One is astonished to see with what avidity they are sought after, and how implicitly they are believed by the great bulk of the people.

It was nearly a century later, in the person of Horace Greeley, editor of the *New York Tribune* during the anti-slavery struggle, that the journal of opinion reached its highest expression in America. America has had better newspapermen than Horace Greeley, although none, perhaps, whose opinions exercised so wide an influence. "The *New York Tribune*," says Charles Francis Adams, "during those years was the greatest educational factor, economically and morally, this country has ever known."

THE INDEPENDENT PRESS

The power of the press, as represented by the older type of newspaper, rested in the final analysis upon the ability of its editors to create a party and lead it. The journal of opinion is, by its very nature, predestined to become the organ of a party, or at any rate the mouthpiece of a school.

So long as political activities were organized on the basis of village life, the party system worked. In the village community, where life was and still is relatively fixed and settled, custom and tradition provided for most of the exigencies of daily life. In such a community, where every deviation from the ordinary routine of life was a matter of observation and comment and all the facts were known, the political process was, at any rate, a comparatively simple matter. Under these circumstances the work of the newspaper, as a gatherer and interpreter of the news, was but an extension of the function which was otherwise performed spontaneously by the community itself through the medium of personal contact and gossip.

But as our cities expanded and life grew more complicated, it turned out that political parties, in order to survive, must have a permanent organization. Eventually party morale became a greater value than the issues for the determination of which the parties are supposed to exist. The effect upon the party press was to reduce it to the position of a sort of house organ of the party organization. It no longer knew from day to day just what its opinions were. The editor was no longer a free agent. It was of this subjugated *Tribune* that Walt Whitman was thinking when he coined the phrase, "the kept editor."

When, finally, the exigencies of party politics, under conditions of life in great cities, developed the political machine, some of the more independent newspapers revolted. This was the origin of the independent press. It was one of the independent papers, the *New York Times* of that day, that first assailed and eventually overthrew, with the aid of a cartoonist, Thomas Nast, the Tweed Ring, the first and most outrageous of the political machines that party politics in this country has so far produced. Presently there was a general breaking away, particularly by the metropolitan, as distinguished from the country, papers, from the domination of the parties. Party loyalty ceased to be a virtue.

Meanwhile a new political power had arisen and found expression in the press. This power was embodied, not in the editorial and the editorial writer, however, but in the news and the reporter. In spite of the fact that the prestige of the press, up to this time, had rested on its rôle of champion of popular causes, the older newspapers were not read by the masses of the people.

The ordinary man is more interested in news than he is in political doctrines or abstract ideas. H. L. Mencken has called attention to the fact that the average man does not understand more than two-thirds of what "comes from the lips of the average political orator or clergyman."

The ordinary man, as the *Saturday Evening Post* has discovered, thinks in concrete images, anecdotes, pictures, and parables. He finds it difficult and tiresome to read a long article unless it is dramatized and takes the form of what newspapers call a "story." "News story" and "fiction story" are two forms of modern literature that are now sometimes so like one another that it is diffcult to distinguish them. The *Saturday Evening Post,* for example, writes the news in the form of fiction, while the daily press frequently writes fiction in the form of news.

When it is not possible to present ideas in the concrete, dramatic form of a story, the ordinary reader likes them stated in a short paragraph. It is said that James E. Scripps, founder of the *Detroit News* and one of the owners of several afternoon papers in secondary cities, built up his whole string of papers upon the basis of the very simple psychological principle that the ordinary man will read newspaper items in the inverse ratio to their length. His method of measuring the efficiency of his newspapers, therefore, was to count the number of items they contained. The paper that had the largest number of items was the best paper. This is just the reverse of Mr. Hearst's methods; his papers have fewer items than other papers.

The old-time journalist was inclined to have a contempt for news. News was for him simply material upon which to base an editorial. If God let things happen that were not in accordance with his conception of the fitness of things, he simply suppressed them. He refused to take the responsibility of letting his readers learn about things that he knew ought not to have happened.

Manton Marble, who was editor of the *New York World* before Joseph Pulitzer took it and made it yellow, used to say there were not eighteen thousand people in New York City to whom a well-conducted newspaper could offer to address itself. If the circulation of the paper went above that figure he thought there must be something wrong with the paper. Before Mr. Pulitzer took it over, the circulation had actually sunk to ten thousand. The old *New York World* preserved the type of the old conservative high-brow paper down to the eighties. By that time in the larger cities the politically independent newspapers had become the accepted type of journal.

Long before the rise of what was later to be called the independent press, there had appeared in New York two journals that were the forerunners of the present-day newspapers. In 1833 Benjamin Day, with a few associates, started a paper for "mechanics and the masses generally." The price of this paper [the *Sun*] was one cent, but the publishers expected to make up by larger circulation and by advertising the loss sustained by the lower price. At that time most of the other New York papers were selling for six cents.

It was, however, the enterprise of James Gordon Bennett, the founder of the *New York Herald*, which set the pace in the new form of journalism. In fact, as Will Irwin says in the only adequate account that has ever been written of the American newspaper,[2] "James Gordon Bennett invented news as we know it." Bennett, like some others who have contributed most to modern journalism, was a disillusioned man, and for that very reason, perhaps, a ruthless and cynical one. "I renounce all so-called principles," he said in his announcement of the new enterprise. By principles he meant, perhaps, editorial policies. His salutatory was at the same time a valedictory. In announcing the purposes of the new journalism he bade adieu to the aims and aspirations of the old. Henceforth the editors were to be news-gatherers, and the newspaper staked its future on its ability to gather, print, and circulate news.

What is news? There have been many answers. I think it was Charles A. Dana who said, "News is anything that will make people talk." This definition suggests at any rate the aims of the new journalism. Its purpose was to print anything that would make people talk and think, for most people do not think until they begin to talk. Thought is after all a sort of internal conversation.

A later version of the same definition is this: "News is anything that makes the reader say, 'Gee Whiz!'" This is the definition of Arthur McEwen, one of the men who helped make the Hearst papers. It is at the same time the definition of the latest and most successful type of journal, the yellow press. Not all successful journals are, to be sure, yellow. The *New York Times*, for example, is not. But the *New York Times* is not yet a type.

THE YELLOW PRESS

There seems to be, as Walter Lippmann has observed, two types of newspaper readers. "Those who find their own lives interesting"

---

[2] Irwin's *The American Newspaper* was published serially in *Collier's* in 1911, but never appeared in book form.

and "those who find their own lives dull, and wish to live a more thrilling existence." There are, correspondingly, two types of newspapers: papers edited on the principle that readers are mainly interested in reading about themselves, and papers edited upon the principle that their readers, seeking some escape from the dull routine of their own lives, are interested in anything which offers them what the psychoanalysts call "a flight from reality."

The provincial newspaper with its record of weddings, funerals, lodge meetings, oyster suppers, and all the small patter of the small town represents the first type. The metropolitan press, with its persistent search in the drab episodes of city life for the romantic and the picturesque, its dramatic accounts of vice and crime, and its unflagging interest in the movements of personages of a more or less mythical high society represents the latter type.

Up to the last quarter of the nineteenth century, that is to say, up to about 1880, most newspapers, even in our large cities, were conducted on the theory that the best news a paper can print is a death notice or a marriage announcement.

Up to that time the newspapers had not yet begun to break into the tenements, and most people who supported a newspaper lived in homes rather than in apartments. The telephone had not yet come into popular use; the automobile was unheard of; the city was still a mosaic of little neighborhoods, like our foreign-language communities of the present day, in which the city dweller still maintained something of the provincialism of the small town.

Great changes, however, were impending. The independent press was already driving some of the old-time newspapers to the wall. There were more newspapers than either the public or the advertisers were willing to support. It was at this time and under these circumstances that newspaper men discovered that circulation could be greatly increased by making literature out of the news. Charles A. Dana had already done this in the *Sun*, but there still was a large section of the population for whom the clever writing of Mr. Dana's young men was caviar.

The yellow press grew up in an attempt to capture for the newspaper a public whose only literature was the family story paper or the cheap novel. The problem was to write the news in such a way that it would appeal to the fundamental passions. The formula was: love and romance for the women; sport and politics for the men.

The effect of the application of this formula was enormously to increase the circulation of the newspapers, not only in the great cities, but all over the country. These changes were brought about mainly under the leadership of two men, Joseph Pulitzer and William Randolph Hearst.

Pulitzer had discovered, while he was editor of the *St. Louis Post-Dispatch*, that the way to fight popular causes was not to advocate them on the editorial page but to advertise them—write them up— in the news columns. It was Pulitzer who invented muck-raking. It was this kind of journalism which enabled Pulitzer, within a period of six years, to convert the old *New York World*, which was dying of inanition when he took it, into the most talked-about, if not the most widely circulated paper in New York City.

Meanwhile, out in San Francisco, Mr. Hearst had succeeded in galvanizing the old moribund *Examiner* into new life, making it the most widely read newspaper on the Pacific Coast.

It was under Mr. Hearst that the "sob sister" came into vogue. This is her story, as Will Irwin told it in *Collier's*, February 18, 1911:

Chamberlain (managing editor of the *Examiner*) conceived the idea that the city hospital was badly managed. He picked a little slip of a girl from among his cub reporters and assigned her to the investigation. She invented her own method; she "fainted" on the street, and was carried to the hospital for treatment. She turned out a story "with a sob for the unfortunate in every line." That was the professional beginning of "Annie Laurie" or Winifred Black, and of a departure in newspaper writing. For she came to have many imitators, but none other could ever so well stir up the primitive emotions of sympathy and pity; she was a "sob squad" all by herself. Indeed, in the discovery of this sympathetic "woman writing," Hearst broke through the crust into the thing he was after.

With the experience that he had gained on the *Examiner* in San Francisco and with a large fortune that he had inherited from his father, Hearst invaded New York in 1896. It was not until he reached New York and started out to make the *New York Journal* the most widely read paper in the United States that yellow journalism reached the limit.

Pulitzer's principal contribution to yellow journalism was muck-raking. Hearst's was mainly "jazz." The newspaper had been conducted up to this time upon the theory that its business was to instruct. Hearst rejected that conception. His appeal was frankly not to the intellect but to the heart. The newspaper was for him first and last a form of entertainment.

It was about the time the yellow press was engaged in extending the newspaper habit to the masses of people, including women and immigrants—who up to this time did not read newspapers—that the department store was beginning to attract attention. The department store is, in a sense, a creation of the Sunday newspaper. At any rate, without the advertising that the Sunday newspaper was able to give it, the department store would hardly have gained the vogue it has today. It is important in this connection that women read the Sunday paper before they did the dailies. The women are buyers.

It was in the Sunday newspaper that the methods of yellow journalism were first completely worked out. The men who are chiefly responsible for them are Morrill Goddard and Arthur Brisbane. It was Goddard's ambition to make a paper that a man would buy even if he could not read it. He went in for pictures, first in black and white and then in colors. It was in the *Sunday World* that the first seven-column cut was printed. Then followed the comic section and all the other devices with which we are familiar for compelling a dull-minded and reluctant public to read.

After these methods had been worked out in the Sunday paper, they were introduced into the daily. The final triumph of the yellow journal was Brisbane's "Heart-to-Heart Editorials"—a column of predigested platitudes and moralizing, with half-page diagrams and illustrations to re-enforce the text. Nowhere has Herbert Spencer's maxim that the art of writing is economy of attention been so completely realized.

Walter Lippmann, in his study of public opinion, calls attention to the fact that no sociologist has ever written a book on news-gathering. It strikes him as very strange that an institution like the press, from which we expect so much and get so little of what we expect, should not have been the subject of a more disinterested study.

It is true that we have not studied the newspaper as the biologists have studied, for example, the potato bug. But the same may be said of every political institution, and the newspaper is a political institution quite as much as Tammany Hall or the board of aldermen is a political institution. We have grumbled about our political institutions; sometimes we have sought by certain magical legislative devices to exorcise and expel the evil spirits that possessed them. On the whole we have been inclined to regard them as sacred and to treat any fundamental criticism of them as a sort of blasphemy. If things went wrong, it was not the institutions, but the persons we elected to conduct them, and an incorrigible human nature, who were at fault.

What then is the remedy for the existing condition of the newspapers? There is no remedy. Humanly speaking, the present newspapers are about as good as they can be. If the newspapers are to be improved, it will come through the education of the people and the organization of political information and intelligence. As Mr. Lippmann well says, "the number of social phenomena which are now recorded is small, the instruments of analysis are very crude, and the concepts often vague and uncriticized." We must improve our records, and that is a serious task. But first of all we must learn to look at political and social life objectively and cease to think of it wholly in moral terms. In that case we shall have less news, but better newspapers.

The real reason that the ordinary newspaper accounts of the incidents of ordinary life are so sensational is because we know so little of human life that we are not able to interpret the events of life when we read them. It is safe to say that when anything shocks us, we do not understand it.

THE RISE AND PLACE OF
THE MOTION PICTURE

BY TERRY RAMSAYE

Mr. Ramsaye has been editor of *Motion Picture Almanac* and *Motion Picture Herald*. This article appeared in the *Annals of the American Academy of Political and Social Science* for November, 1947, and is reprinted by permission of the author and the Academy, which holds copyright.

THE SCREEN has arrived at the middle of the twentieth century, with a swift fifty years of evolving experience behind it, as a dominant form of expression. Among the masses it shares with the printed word and the radio, somewhat remotely related instruments of communication, and exceeds them both in effective penetration, especially in the great illiterate and semiliterate strata where words falter, fail, and miss.

Being a basic, primitive implement, the film reaches low and deep, with an order of authority to the senses enjoyed by no other form of expression.

It is estimated that there are between seventy-five and eighty thousand motion picture theaters functioning around the world. The weekly attendance is calculated to be in the vicinity of 235,-000,000. Statistics of the motion picture industry, especially world statistics, are not to be viewed as records of extreme precision.

Somewhat indirect evidence of the effective penetration and high competence among the media is afforded by the rising and long continuing pother about the screen from politicians of all lands and the fierce nationalistic film movements to be observed around the world.

RELATION TO OLDER ARTS

The motion picture is anomalously anachronic. While it is the newest of the major media, it is in fact a belated arrival at the primary purpose of man seeking to communicate and to re-create events of interesting, exciting, and enjoyable impact. It may be contended that man became intricately articulate, and with alphabets, because of his inadequate capacity to make pictures as facile instruments of narration. So it has come that the ancient quest, after the centuries, has been empowered by involved technologies of optics, kinetics, photochemistry, and materials. The simple function is, and must be, complexly performed.

Both artists and scholars have come to confusion about the motion picture by seductively automatic endeavors to relate it to the older arts. The picture is in very truth at once the belated predecessor and the successor to the older media of pageant, dance, drama, and such relatively minor devices of communication as sculpture, painting, and opera.

Those older media down the centuries have developed their special sophistications and elaborations of culture, fenced about with conventions and orthodoxies maintained and protected by their priestly zealots of the rituals of art. The motion picture, by reason of unique opportunity, has come to strike its roots into and take its nurture directly from the fundamental soil of the human wish, largely escaping the confusions of derived and interdependent older forms of record and narration.

THE KINETOSCOPE

The history of the motion picture, unlike that of any of the other arts, having covered so short a span of years, is so immediately available for examination that the processes can be seen with clarity. After more than a century of conscious striving toward the motion picture, it was achieved in October of 1889. The machine was the peep-show kinetoscope, invented by Thomas A. Edison, building on the endeavors of the prior workers, and empowered especially by George Eastman's film for "roller photography," made available in September of that year.

The world was not consciously waiting for the motion picture.

Mr. Edison was not much concerned about it, either. He had supervised it into being with desultory attention across two years, apparently mostly because of an assignment to himself to make a machine to do for the eye what his phonograph did for the ear. He was of the pioneer culture of the Middle West, concerned with work—not play, not entertainment. The phonograph had been evolved to be a robot stenographer, and was developing as an entertainment device, with problems and commercial headaches. He let the kinetoscope stand in the corner of his laboratory at West Orange, gathering dust. He did not trouble to patent it in Europe.

By the enterprise of promoters impelled by showmanship, the kinetoscope presented the first film pictures to the public the night of April 14, 1894, after five years, at the Kinetoscope Parlor, 1155 Broadway, New York, with a battery of machines. The pictures were brief snatches and shards of vaudeville acts, boxers in fractional rounds, trivia which had challenged the interest of the shop mechanics who had custody of the new mechanism. One customer at a time could peek into each machine. The little show in Broadway was a moderate success. The invention drew a ripple of Sunday supplement attention. Meanwhile, the machine went into export sales and carried the seeds of film technology to the capitals of the Old World.

THE SCREEN

Within months the pressures of showmanship demanded a union of the kinetoscope's moving pictures with the magic lantern, so that a screen could entertain a whole audience at once. In less than two years that was achieved, and by the spring of 1896 the career of the film in the theater had begun. The pictures immediately and automatically found their place as a component of the variety shows, just then beginning to reach for the pretentious name of "vaudeville." Also black tent theaters became attractions with traveling carnivals and at the amusement parks with which electric traction companies were creating car-ride traffic. The screen was certainly starting at the bottom of the ladder.

The production function continued in the hands of the tinkerers and mechanics and the flotsam of the backwaters of showmanship. The screen was not finding anything to say beyond the level of the dime museum interest.

The screen sensation of 1898 in London was a subject in Charles

Urban's endeavor at a scientific series in which he presented some microscopic studies of life in a Stilton cheese, thereby bestirring the British cheese industry into a demand for censorship. Indicative of the cultural status of the art, the American Mutoscope and Biograph Company of New York, competing with the Edison enterprise, made a brave step by interesting the famed Joseph Jefferson and presenting some excerpts from his Rip van Winkle performances. That classic material aroused no interest, but the Biograph subject entitled "Girl Climbing Apple Tree" became a hit and keynoted a policy.

The industry was beset by patent wars, infringements, piracies, and all the devices of chicane the pitchmen vendors of movies could invent. The business was at low tide. In the vaudeville theaters the pictures had been moved to the end of the bill, to tell the audience the show was over and to clear the house. The films had come to be called "chasers." The Battle of Santiago was pictured with models in a Brooklyn bathtub, and the Boer War was fought for the screen in Flatbush with glimpses of the metropolis in the background.

Here and there appeared some timid steps toward giving the screen a story to tell. For instance, Edwin S. Porter, Edison cameraman, experimented with a bit of a tale to give excuse for that perennial picture of the fire engine making a run. It was a race for life in which the fire chief saved his own child, and then fell from his chair and found it was a dream. The title was "The Life of an American Fireman." Enough interest and print sales resulted to encourage the production of "The Great Train Robbery," that now historic classic known as "the first story picture." It was made in 1903. Moving through the tedious, unorganized distribution of the time, this primitive drama of bandits, bravery, fast riding, and excitement was two years becoming a hit. It also incidentally highlighted the program of the Nickelodeon, a little house casually opened to a film program for the lack of other entertainment, by John P. Harris in Pittsburgh about Thanksgiving time in 1905. With a five-cent admission the theater played to standing room for weeks on end.

THE EARLY AUDIENCE

The five-cent theater of the movies had arrived. In a wildfire wave, imitative nickelodeons rose across the land, all of them in centers, like Pittsburgh, with a high content of foreign-born polyglottic population. Immigration was at high tide. American industry was bringing in labor for mines and mills. Steamship and labor agents were plastering the ports of the Mediterranean with posters of the United States as a land of golden promise, with life made gay with buffaloes, Indians, excitement, and natural wonders.

The workers came over, high of hope, poor in pocket, and finding workaday life dull and demanding. They brought none of their native arts, and they were not literate enough to enjoy their feeble foreign-language press. As for American amusements, there was the language barrier, besides the price. The motion picture's new theater, with a five-cent admission and the silent films of the big open places and excitement, romance, thrills, and success on the spot, made good in a fashion on the promises they had read in Trieste.

Meanwhile, the petty tradesmen of the foreign-labor quarters, shrewd, nimble, anxious, behind the counters of their candy shops, soda fountains, banana stands, and pawnshops, saw the new interest of their customers. They became vendors of the new entertainment. Within a year of that opening in Pittsburgh, there were nearly five thousand of the little five-cent shows.

Demand took production off the roofs and out of the back yards of Manhattan into studios on Long Island, in the Bronx, at Fort Lee over in New Jersey, in the suburbs of Chicago and Philadelphia. Cameramen and some of Broadway's idle actors became directors of the "story pictures." Also, the demand for "story suggestions" rose to the point that $15 was a standard price for "a suggestion." A typical story sale was a plot summary of "Enoch Arden" which one author sold repeatedly. That went on until the Kalem company was required by court order to pay $25,000 for making "Ben Hur" without consulting either the estate of General Lew Wallace or Harper's, the publishers.

In that period the budding industry had everything to learn. It had no recognizable precedents, and its accidentally acquired personnel brought little knowledge of any other businesses. Procedure was on the general assumption that anything could be done until forbidden, specifically, positively by law—and thereafter only in the cover of the Jersey highlands.

Somewhat marginally, as the pictures reached up into middle-class levels of consciousness, some eyebrows were raised at the Mediterranean tastes manifest on the screen. The protest began with the peep show "Dolorita in the Passion Dance" in Atlantic City in 1894, and got really articulate in the New York papers about 1906 when the Children's Society went to court about exhibition of pictures on the Thaw case. Regulations of sorts, including censorships by various cities, resulted.

A new order of discipline was brought into the industry with the arrival of an iron-handed businessman. Jeremiah J. Kennedy, retired engineering expert, was sent uptown by the Empire Trust Company to see what was to be done for the bondholders of the fading American Mutoscope and Biograph Company. He was expected to order liquidation. Instead, he decided to reorganize the whole industry. Out of that decision came the Motion Picture Patents Company, licensing as partners all reputable producers and ending the patent wars, also seeking to end all manner of competitive abuses, such as making "duped" versions of competitive product.

The while, a socially minded organization known as The People's Institute was engaged in trying to be a friend of the struggling art of the common people in its ordeals with the law and the political forces mustered by the jealous New York stage. The Patents Company substantially underwrote the resultant National Board of Censorship, in recent years known as the National Board of Review. It began as a friendly advisory body, and with its internal support, functioned with an authority and power now long since departed. Its authority could not long outlive the Patents Company, soon to be swept into history by evolutions in the industry.

Prosperity came with order. Profits improved swiftly; the product improved slowly.

The Kennedy-Patents Company control movement went into the next phase, the organization of the distribution arm, the General Film Company with a national system of film exchanges. More order came into film rentals to theaters, and more profits to the membership of the big combine.

DEVELOPING AUDIENCE AND ART

It began to be apparent that the audience was developing selectivity. Each of the major contributors to the General Film program had for awhile a designated day. When the little one-sheet poster out in front said "Biograph Day," the attendance was better. That was presently traced to story and picture quality, and that in turn traced the work of one "Larry" Griffith, ex-actor, who had left the stage in 1906 in a "resting" period to essay a job in the humble art of the films. He was due presently to come to fame as D. W. Griffith, later David Wark Griffith. Some of those rather able but anonymous persons in his little Biograph dramas had names like Walthall, Lawrence, Pickford, and Gish.

The audience was expanding. The screen was seeping up into the middle class with neighborhood houses of considerably more comfort and pretense than the little nickelodeons of the labor districts. A ten-cent admission price became a commonplace. "Nickelodeon" began to give way to fancies like "Bijou Dream" and such invitations as "The Family" and "The Cozy."

The old stage institution of the road show, with its "direct from Broadway" melodramas—remember "Sag Harbor," "Way Down East," "East Lynne," "Under Southern Skies," "Cameo Kirby"—was feeling competition. Also the town opera house was venturing a try at movies. The motion picture was bringing drama within walking distance of most of urban America; and the stage was trying to live from the carriage trade. At the peak of this development, in the period 1913–16, there were probably twenty-eight thousand motion picture theaters of all sorts in the United States.

Meanwhile, the art of storytelling on the screen was acquiring skill, quality, and fluidity. The principal influence was Griffith, who with his cameraman extraordinary, William Bitzer, was first to explore the narrative uses of the close-up, the cutback, and the development of parallel lines of action—invaluable to the Griffith suspense technique of "relief on the way." The dramas were still in single reels.

Also, the audience was growing up with its art. The original immigrant audience was acquiring an improving buying power, and by experience was evolving an order of taste. Its exhibitors who started with it were keeping pace, and keeping a step ahead, learning the melting-pot populace as it was simmering into the new America.

Over in Europe the film had come upon no such fertile opportunity of a land and an economic era in the making. The motion picture planted there by the Edison Kinetoscope fell mostly into scientific hands and tended to become an ineffective medium for pursuit of the patterns of the older arts. Its address was at no time so focused on the masses of the community as in the United States. The European screen's ambition was addressed to spectacles and ancient classics. And yet that, too, was to have an influence in America, homeland of the screen.

By 1912 the American motion picture was close to a ceiling. Its horizontal development across the land and its audiences had neared a saturation. The next move had to be a break-through. Again, as ever, the situation found its instrument—in this instance Adolph Zukor, born in Hungary, educated in the American industrial scene, beginning as a furrier's apprentice, and becoming incidentally an investor in a penny arcade enterprise which he had to take over to save the investment. So he came to the amusement world with evolving interests in exhibition. By 1912 he had come to a parting of the ways in his associations. He found inspiration and opportunity in the availability of the American rights to a foreign-made four-reel picture entitled "Queen Elizabeth" with Sarah Bernhardt in the title role. The time had come, considered Mr. Zukor, for the screen to take its place along with the stage in offering a whole evening's entertainment. He also arrived at the line "famous players in famous plays" to keynote a policy. Thereby the "feature" era was born, meaning the rise of the hour-long picture taking over against the established program of short pictures.

The public gave encouragement by patronage of the longer pictures and responding to the promotion which presented them. A signal success was had from road-show type presentations of "Quo Vadis," a long spectacle production made in Rome and vastly more successful in America than in Europe. D. W. Griffith, irked by Biograph's reactionary adherence to the short-picture policy with which it had risen, went off into an independent project which delivered "The Birth of a Nation," which by its success gave powerful impetus to the feature movement in 1915.

A new and ever-growing public was becoming aware of the screen. There were growing pains and problems. The exhibition plant was not adequate for the delivery of the expanding pictures. A new order of more pretentious screen theater was initiated in 1914 with the opening of the Strand Theater on Broadway, soon to be followed by others equally ambitious in the larger centers.

Concurrently, manifestations of the increasing impress of the screen on a larger public came from the field of publication. Scatteringly magazines began to discover the new art of the people. Out in Chicago the *Tribune* pioneered recognition of the motion picture with participation in the promotion of serials, parallel on screen and printed page, as a device to encourage circulation, and succeeded. Joseph Medill Patterson, a *Tribune* editor, became a daily patron of the movie houses, the more lowly the better. That was some years before he became the dominant factor in the founding and operation of *The Daily News,* New York picture newspaper, with the greatest circulation in the nation. Out in Buffalo, Norman E. Mack, publisher, eyed the *Tribune's* serials with interest and became the producer of one entitled "The Perils of Our Girl Reporters." In New York, Robert McAlarney, city editor of the old *Tribune,* summed up the situation in a notice to the staff, which he tacked on the bulletin board in that venerable office down in Nassau Street, saying: "Remember you are in competition with the movies now." He demanded graphic writing. William Randolph Hearst went into serial picture production and newsreel enterprises.

The public was hearing about the screen as it never had heard before. The printed word was carrying the interest up from the proletariat into the reading classes.

THE INDEPENDENTS

Along with that, the feature development was rapidly improving the quality of the product, lifting it to the tastes of new audiences. An amazing order of new competition arose among a new sort of picture makers, the oncoming "independents."

The decisive turn had come for a complex of reasons back in 1912–13, when Adolph Zukor had brought over "Queen Elizabeth." It had been produced in Europe outside the pale of patent protection. Jeremiah J. Kennedy of the Patents Company, supported by Henry Norton Marvin of Biograph, took authority in his hands and issued a license for its exhibition in license-controlled theaters, customers of General Film. The success of the picture and the unfolding picture movement aroused jealous protest among the contributors to the General Film program, and unhappily encountered more than whispered racial bias. Sigmund Lubin of Philadelphia, a first-wave pioneer, was the only Jewish member of the Patents group.

The majority of the General Film producers, prosperous beyond any anticipation, sat in haughty assurance condemning "the feature craze." They had some interior alarms about the costs and the labors of the new order of production. It was uncomfortable, disturbing. "We have the know how," they told themselves and all else who would listen.

Frank N. Dyer, president of General Film and attorney for Thomas A. Edison, observing the vast display of diamonds and emeralds worn by the members of his board, one day whimsically appeared to preside wearing smoked glasses.

When Mr. Zukor appeared seeking a license for his second picture, an American production, he sat waiting for hours on end at the office of the Patents Company in New York, and was refused. He went out entirely on his own. As a lone man he could have been defeated. As the exponent of a development rooted in the service of the great American majority, he was armed with an unrecognized but real authority. Quickly other independents took courage and went into production. They too had all to gain and little to lose, and knew the customers better than their complacent predecessors. There was litigation, of course, but as it threaded through the courts the racing development of the art defeated the Patents Company control by sheer force of product long before final adjudication was had. The Patents group fell apart with dissensions and scattered while issues were pending.

GROWTH OF THE INDUSTRY

The very American process of swift obsolescence with expanding replacement, under the same order of pressures and laws of development all across the industrial scene, was in demonstration as the motion picture, becoming somewhat more of an art, also became very much more of an industry. It was on the final authority of the consumers.

A minor statistical indication of the swiftness of the upturn was afforded in the case of Charles Chaplin. In 1913 he left a vaudeville act to take employment in Keystone's slapstick comedies at $150 a week. In the autumn of 1915 he signed a contract to appear in twelve two-reel comedies in one year at a salary of $10,000 a week, plus a bonus of $150,000. In turn The Lone Star concern sold the British Empire rights to the comedies for the total of Chaplin's salary, $670,000. The deals all made money. By 1916 the patrons of the lowly cinema were willing to pay real millions at the box office for one comedian.

The motion picture made its own order of fame. When Adolph

Zukor had launched his Famous Players company, he presented a schedule of attractions in three classes—A, B, and C. Class C was to present famous *picture* players in famous plays. Bernhardt was typical of Class A. Mary Pickford was Class C. Brief experience showed that the public which the screen had assembled knew nothing about and cared nothing for the great ones of stage and opera, and cared very much for their own people, the stars of the movies. The older arts obviously were without status in melting-pot America.

As the films grew up and their theater with them, the number of houses tended to diminish while seating capacities increased. In part this represented improved and wider drawing power for better theaters, but very considerably it was connected with the new mobility of the customers brought about by the coming of the inexpensive automobile. That encouraged shopping for entertainment and it removed the limitation of walking-distance locations. In 1914–15 the neighborhood theaters played continuously to the same audiences week after week, as reflected by the extraordinary success of serial pictures, requiring repeating attendance. In 1918 the most ambitious serial of them all came to abysmal failure. There was irony in the fact that its first conspicuous fall was in Detroit, the motor center.

Imposing and luxurious theaters of large seating capacities began to rise in outlying residential districts of high buying power and at suburban centers. Downtown districts were left to the houses of the dying art of the stage and its fading gilt and dusty plush.

INFLUENCE OF WORLD WAR I

Starting with and continuing across this period the American motion picture became a special beneficiary of the First World War. The war shut down the studios of Europe and England in 1914, just as the feature era came to flower, and delivered the screens of the world to the American product. That product was almost automatically attuned to a diverse world market by reason of the foreign heritages from many lands of both the initial film audiences and the producers which their patronage encouraged. The American motion picture born to serve a vast polyglottic patronage was born international in its own home market. It took the world's screens without opposition and with few problems of adjustment. The American motion picture came to occupy something like 80 per cent of the world's screen time.

The prosperity of the pictures in World War I, as through World War II, was lavishly supported by the eager buying of the free-spending workers temporarily rich on war wages. The box-office-admissions curve inevitably follows the pay-roll graphs. And sometimes the doles, too. The only exception in history was the onsweep of the nickelodeon wave through the "stringency" of 1907, when the industry was too small to figure in national reactions. The people's art lives out of the people's pocket.

The American industry continued to fortify its world position by the acquisition of the outstanding talent of production abroad as rapidly as it appeared, adding continually to the great talent pool of Hollywood. This enhanced and enriched the product for the markets both at home and abroad, and incidentally reduced competitive development. Britain contributed able players, and from Germany and France came notably skilled technicians and directors.

ENTER THE TALKING PICTURES

In 1926 the art of the motion picture came to revolutionary change with the arrival of electronic sound recording and reproduction, a by-product of telephone and radio. The personal instrument was the late Sam Warner, one of the four sons of Benjamin Warner who had come to these shores and the land of opportunity nearly a generation before. Contemporaries in the industry of the screen looked askance and doubtingly on the talking picture, but demonstration by Warner Brothers prevailed. The silent esperanto of pantomime of nickelodeon days was no longer an asset. By 1926 the audiences all spoke American. So in the next three years the industry was made over with pictures laced with words and music. Importantly, the American talking picture was still to be dominant on the screens of the great market of the English-speaking lands. In fact, the English understood American perfectly, despite the fact that there has been found to be a lot of English that most Americans cannot understand.

When the screen acquired its voice, a new order of material was required. The silent picture had become a hybrid art of mingled pantomime and printed word presented in the subtitles. Some pictures, incidentally, required a capacity for swift reading. They did not do so well.

Seeking talking picture play material, the screen turned to the stage and its playwrights, and thereby reaped a reaction in direct retribution for what it had done to the stage when it swept the road shows out of the hinterlands. The stage, driven back from that contact with the larger public, had taken refuge in the service of sophisticated, metropolitan minorities. In direct consequence came sometimes painfully sophisticated drama and dialogue of candor that would never be tolerated by Dubuque, Bad Axe, or Abilene. Translated to the screen and taken out to the provinces, and even a few squares from Broadway, this material gave rise to protests, threats and acts of censorship, and movements toward federal regulative legislation.

Back in 1922 the industry, confronted with a wave of public disapproval pertaining mostly to conduct of players and other more official figures in the public eye, had organized the Motion Picture Producers and Distributors of America, Inc., and installed Will H. Hays as president and titular "czar of the movies." He became in effect a super public relations counsel. By 1928–29 it was not personnel but product that was out of hand.

REGULATION

Now to the rescue came Martin Quigley, publisher of journals of the industry since 1915, a Catholic layman of prominence, with the device of self-regulation entitled the Production Code, a document of guidance to picture makers calculated to help keep the pictures in line with common decency and American mores. It began and continues essentially as a formula intended to apply the principles of the rather nonsectarian and accepted Ten Commandments to picture production. It is convenient, and accurate enough for the moment, to say that the code requires that a picture, while portraying sin for dramatic purposes, shall not become the Devil's advocate. It was formally adopted by the organized industry in March 1930—forty-six years after "Dolorita in the Passion Dance" got the pictures into trouble on the Boardwalk in Atlantic City.

The public has apparently accepted the product made under the code with equanimity, and probable unawareness, with few further threats of censorship. In 1946, 98 per cent of the product on the American screen bore the seal of code approval. Objections to the code continued to dot the published discussion of the screen, emanating mainly from professionally articulate persons in the Hollywood production community inclined to ask for the American family theater the viewpoints of the art museum and the medical clinic.

Regulative pressures of sorts from government, taking their origins mainly from minority complaints in the field of exhibition, against the trade practices arising from acquisition of theaters by distributor-producer interests, began early in the history of the Federal Trade Commission. They came to flower for apparently special reasons of political design early in the New Deal administration. There was a program, under long and careful consideration at the White House, which looked to profound control of both the screen and the radio. In sequel came the National Recovery Administration and the setting up of an elaborate, and allegedly co-operative, control of the trade practices of the industry under the wings of the NRA Blue Eagle.

After the famed "Chicken Case" decision ended the NRA there was a pause until the filing of the antitrust case, the *U.S. v. Paramount et al.* on July 20, 1938. [Note: After many years of litigation, ownership of theaters was ordered separated from ownership of film studios.]

NATIONALISTIC BARRIERS

While the United States was New-Dealing at home, the new world war was in the making in Europe. Along with that, the walls of nationalism were rising, and in the lands of the Left those walls were raised to varying heights against the American film. Russia would have none of the pictures of this land of luxury, showing a happy and exciting life of capitalism. Germany let in, under assorted and varying restrictions, enough pictures to take a share of screen time. Italy put up dollar barriers by which the American pictures could play but not pay. In Japan the American product was interlarded with government-controlled exhibition to draw in the people for Japan's propaganda injections. England established trade quotas, only partly enforceable by reason of the inadequacy of domestic production and the preference of exhibitors and patrons for the American product.

When World War II swept across the global scene the American industry sustained important invasions of foreign revenue and there were piercing cries. However, the war-enriched masses at home so besieged the box office that it entered into a period of unprecedented prosperity.

In sequel to the end of the shooting aspects of World War II, sometimes called the peace, the walls of nationalism and the issues of nationalism became even more sharply defined. Additionally the fringes of the Russian iron curtain were extending over the screen in lands of Soviet influence. Every nation, great and small, strove for a motion picture industry of its own, mainly for propaganda reasons of its own.

The motion picture has thus become a stuff of empire, a concern of statesmen and national economies. The film takes a place in history along with amber, salt, spices, gold, steel, and oil—also uranium.

MASS SUPPORT NECESSARY

Clearly, the motion picture, in coming of full estate, seeks to serve all peoples and all classes. That is a wide straddle. Its costs are such that it can be generally supported only by the massed buying power of majorities. Inevitably, many minorities cannot be served as they are by the less expensive stage or the relatively inexpensive printed word. Some of those minorities include the most erudite, critical, and articulate persons. From that condition of limitation arises much of the impatient, often militant, criticism of the screen. Some censorship requirements and many projected movements actually represent only areas of unsatisfied demand. Few indeed of the militants who would influence the course of screen development are aware of anything beyond superficial aspects and casual observation. The screen has done little and continues to do little to tell its own story. Few are interested. The people who pay for the pictures want to see them as emotional experience, not as subjects of study. [Editor's Note: Since the writing of this paper, one of the chief developments in the motion picture industry has been the impact of television, which has reduced theater audiences, helped to reduce the number of feature films made in the United States, and taken over many of the studios for its own film-making needs. The movie industry sold a large number of old films to television, and the repeated showing of these has made television a still more formidable competitor to the theaters.]

THE GROWTH OF AMERICAN RADIO

BY LLEWELLYN WHITE

Mr. White, an experienced newspaper, magazine, and press association man, was assistant director of the Commission on Freedom of the Press. This material is from his book, *The American Radio,* and appears here by permission of the University of Chicago Press, which published Mr. White's volume in 1947 and holds copyright.

A NEW FIELD of science and industry was opened in 1895 when Guglielmo Marconi succeeded in transmitting a message by wireless across his father's Bolognese estate. Two years later the enterprising young Italian organized a British company for wireless point-to-point and ship-to-shore communication. In 1899 this company, later known as the Marconi Wireless Telegraph Company, Ltd., incorporated an American subsidiary.

Meanwhile, other inventors were striving to transmit the sounds of the human voice by wireless. In the United States, where the chief rivalry was between the Navy and the American Marconi Company, the first established successes in this direction were achieved by Reginald A. Fessenden and Dr. Lee De Forest, in each case about 1906. Their experiments first attracted wide attention when, on January 20, 1910, the sound of Enrico Caruso's magnificent tenor voice was broadcast from the stage of the Metropolitan Opera in New York.

By the end of World War I, General Electric had acquired the patents on the Alexanderson alternator; American Telephone & Telegraph had bought all the De Forest rights, including his audion tube; and Westinghouse had developed important new transmission equipment, all vitally important to the future of wireless, yet none complete without the others and without devices controlled by American Marconi. The infant industry faced a wasteful patent war, in which the British might come off winners.

To meet this threat, Navy Secretary Daniels proposed government ownership. The Army, the Navy "brass," and a majority in the Congress opposed such a step, but they agreed that the patents should be secured to the United States. Owen D. Young, chairman of the board of General Electric, had a solution: Let the three American firms directly involved pool their resources and buy out American Marconi. Pursuant to Young's suggestion, on October 17, 1919, the Radio Corporation of America (RCA) was formed.

But while the new RCA set about building the world's largest and most powerful wireless station at Port Jefferson, New York, to step up American participation in the expanding point-to-point dot-dash news and private-message market then beginning to parallel that of the cables, Dr. Frank Conrad, of Westinghouse, and other quasi-amateurs relentlessly pursued the elusive goal of voice broadcasting. As early as 1919, Conrad had begun amusing a few friends by playing phonograph records in his garage in East Pittsburgh, Pennsylvania, and broadcasting them from a homemade antenna. Soon a Pittsburgh department store was urging its customers to join the charmed circle by purchasing the crude Westinghouse-made crystal sets which it had in stock. To Westinghouse Vice-president H. P. Davis this was an omen: "If there is sufficient interest to justify a department store in advertising radio sets for sale on an uncertain plan of permanence, I believe there would be sufficient interest to justify the expense of rendering a regular service, looking to the sale of sets and the advertising of the Westinghouse Company for our returns."

On November 2, 1920, having sold a good many sets in anticipation of the event, Westinghouse broadcast from KDKA (Pittsburgh) the Harding-Cox election returns; and others were venturing. Commerce Secretary Hoover had designated 300 meters as the band in which anyone could try his hand at broadcasting if so licensed. By January 1, 1922, thirty licenses had been issued. Fourteen months later, no fewer than 556 broadcasting stations were making the ether crackle with strange sounds.

This tremendous expansion was due in no small part to the fact that the other members of the Big Three that had formed RCA were catching the Davis fever. In 1922, RCA became part owner of Westinghouse's WJZ (Newark, New Jersey), which, two years later, it took over entirely and moved to New York City. General Electric built WGY (Schenectady, New York); Westinghouse itself expanded to Chicago, Philadelphia, and Boston.

In that same year, A.T. & T. decided to withdraw from the RCA consortium and erect two powerful broadcasting stations in New York, to be supported by leasing time to all who had wares to sell. On August 16, 1922, A.T. & T. opened WEAF for business as the first advertising-supported station in the world.

It soon became apparent, both to the station and to those sponsors with more than the New York metropolitan market in mind, that more outlets would bring more listeners, more sales, and higher tolls for the broadcaster. How could this be achieved? In 1921, KDKA, wishing to broadcast a church service, had called on the telephone company for a line to carry it from downtown Pittsburgh to the Westinghouse studio in East Pittsburgh. Encouraged by the results, WEAF brought the 1922 Chicago-Princeton football game from Stagg Field, Chicago, to New York. On January 4, 1923, WEAF and WNAC (Boston) were linked for a special program lasting three and a quarter hours. During the following summer, Colonel Edward Green, who had built a station at Salter's Point, Massachusetts, but who had no programming facilities, made arrangements with A.T. & T. to connect him directly with WEAF by telephone long-lines. When A.T. & T.'s new Washington station, WCAP, was completed, it, too, was linked to WEAF. In October, 1923, WJAR (Providence) was admitted as the first "independent affiliate." By the end of 1924, A.T. & T. had added Worcester, Boston, Philadelphia, Pittsburgh, and Buffalo. Within another year, it was able to boast a chain of 26 stations, reaching as far west as Kansas City in what was to be known for many years as the "Red Network."

Unable to use its rival's telephone lines, RCA countered as best it could by linking WGY, WJZ, and WRC (Washington) with Western Union and Postal Telegraph wires, which, because they had never been designed to carry the sound of the human voice or music, proved inferior. Fortunately for RCA, however, as we shall see in the next chapter, A.T. & T. by 1926 was eager to step out of broadcasting. In September of that year, the National Broadcasting

Company was incorporated as a subsidiary of RCA, and two months later it acquired WEAF for $1,000,000. Thus the Red Network was added to that already launched by RCA, which came to be known as the "Blue Network." During the following year the Columbia chain came into being. Network broadcasting was firmly established by the turn of the depression decade.

Obliged for nearly twenty years to work within the standard broadcast band (550 to 1,500 and, after 1937, to 1,600 kilocycles), the engineers performed wonders. Range was increased by improvements in the location and structure of transmitters and by a gradual stepping-up of power from a few watts to 50,000 and more. Reception quality was raised by the substitution of vacuum-tube sets for the early crystal models and by refinements in the construction of microphones and studios. Interference was reduced by wider separation of the bands of contiguous stations and by the use of directional antennae to concentrate the impact of signals within specified arcs. A portion of the spectrum which some in the early twenties had thought would not accommodate 300 stations was made to support more than a thousand, 800 of them connected with one or another of four great national networks and/or some thirty regional chains.

RAGTIME TO RICHES

THE FOUNDERS of the Radio Corporation of America consortium had been less concerned with what would come out of the magic receiving sets than with who would sell them. A natural division of the whole vast new equipment market suggested itself: Westinghouse and General Electric would manufacture sets, RCA would distribute them, and American Telephone and Telegraph would build and lease or sell transmitters, which, thanks to the patent concentration, all would-be broadcasters would be obliged to use.

Meantime, a public which during the earphones stage had been delighted to hear almost any disconnected series of recognizable sounds was demanding better programs, better continuity, better signals, now that it was buying receiving sets costing anywhere from twenty-five to several hundred dollars. It had had a taste of grand opera, of prize fights and baseball games, of market and weather reports. It wanted more. Where was the money to pay for it?

David Sarnoff, onetime American Marconi engineer, who had come over to RCA and was now a vice-president, explored several avenues. He wrote in a memorandum of June 17, 1922:

> The cost of broadcasting must be borne by those who derive profits directly or indirectly from the business resulting from radio broadcasting: manufacturer, national distributor, wholesale distributor, retail dealer, licensee. I suggest that the Radio Corporation of America pay over to the Broadcasting Company [no such company had yet been formed] 2 per cent of its gross radio sales, that General Electric and Westinghouse do likewise, and that our proposed licensees be required to do the same. We may find it practicable to require our wholesale distributors to pay over a reasonable percentage of their gross radio sales. It is conceivable that the same principle may even be extended in time to the dealers.

43

And, as though he divined that even this arrangement might not prove adequate for long, he added:

It is conceivable that plans may be devised whereby it will receive public support. There may even appear on the horizon a public benefactor who will be willing to contribute a large sum in the form of an endowment. I feel that with suitable publicity activities, such a company will ultimately be regarded as a public institution of great value in the same sense that a library, for example, is regarded today.

Expenses were mounting the while. If the listening public wanted more recognized stars, the recognized stars wanted something more substantial in the way of remuneration than their carfare to New Jersey and the realization that they were participating in the making of history. In the fall of 1922, the American Society of Composers, Authors, and Publishers (ASCAP) decided that broadcasters should pay royalty fees on phonograph records. As the majority of broadcasters were on the verge of bankruptcy, this was a real blow. A number of them organized the National Association of Broadcasters (NAB) to fight ASCAP. Some signed royalty contracts meekly. Others simply dropped transcribed music, falling back on news bulletins, market and weather reports, and amateur skits. Still others appealed to their listeners for contributions. Among these latter was the A.T. & T's WEAF (New York City), which returned to a handful of donors the less than $200 its pleas had brought forth.

The truth was that for some time A.T. & T. had been eyeing RCA's rich manufacturing profits with undisguised envy. The power to force broadcasters to use A.T. & T. transmitting equipment at fees ranging from $500 to $3,000, in addition to the price of the apparatus, had seemed to the telephone corporation's executives, at the time that the bargain with RCA, GE, and Westinghouse had been made, to offer a fair share of the spoils. But it soon became apparent that the number of broadcasting stations could not expand so rapidly or so far as the number of listeners, who, every few years, would want new receiving sets. Moreover, A.T. & T. felt that RCA and the others had got off on the wrong track: a radio broadcast, like a telephone conversation, should be paid for by the person originating it; those who were using the new medium simply to promote their own products, far from performing a public service, were "exploiting a popular craze."

Two weeks after A.T. & T. put WEAF on the air, a real estate firm on Long Island paid $100 for a 10-minute talk which resulted in the quick sale of two apartments. In September a second customer tried the new medium. By March, 1923, WEAF boasted twenty-five sponsors, including the R. H. Macy department store, the Metropolitan Life Insurance Company, the Colgate Company, and I. Miller Shoes. At first, the advertisers contented themselves with what today would be called "spot announcements." Before 1923 was many months old, however, Gimbel Brothers and Browning King were sponsoring hour-long programs of dance music.

The companies deriving their revenues from the sale of sets— RCA, GE, Westinghouse, Philco, Zenith, Stromberg-Carlson, and others—protested that broadcasting was being "debased." Under the prodding of their delegates, the First Radio Conference passed resolutions denouncing "direct sales talk." Secretary of Commerce Hoover, who was responsible for radio "regulations," viewed the trend with "alarm." But the public showed itself ready to accept the "nuisance" in return for better programs and other improvements, among which were regular, scheduled broadcasting and "networks," making it possible for the listeners of one community to hear the talent of another, miles away.

The competition of advertising had been met by RCA with an offer of free time to anyone who would pay for the talent and other "program charges." Even this subterfuge strained the tripartite agreement, which gave A.T. & T. the exclusive right to charge advertising tolls. Independent stations were effectively discouraged from accepting advertising by A.T. & T's monopoly in transmitters. As we have seen, RCA countered the telephone long-lines monopoly by linking WGY (Schenectady), WJZ (New York), and WRC (Washington) by Western Union and Postal Telegraph wires. This, too, proved a feeble gesture, for A.T. & T's long-lines had been refined in the Bell Laboratories for the express purpose of carrying the human voice, whereas Western Union and Postal, interested only in dot-dash, were able to offer only inferior connective service.

Master of the situation, A.T. & T. should have been content, but it was not. It longed to break the tripartite agreement and start producing its own vacuum tubes. It was not popular with the independent broadcasters, who wanted to see it prosecuted as a trust. Within the corporation there were many who questioned the wisdom of staying in the radio broadcasting business: A.T. & T., they argued, was (1) a telephone company, (2) a manufacturer of electronic devices. If it contented itself with leasing telephone long-lines to, and

manufacturing equipment for, the broadcasters, it could draw down
a substantial income from the new industry without incurring any
of its mounting risks.

Even more obvious were RCA's sources of discontent. In the
summer of 1925 a committee, headed by Sarnoff, reported to the
directors that (1) RCA could never be assured of adequate financial
underpinning unless it went into advertising, and (2) it should do
this through a broadcasting subsidiary rather than directly because
(a) listeners wanted good programs with little or no advertising
and (b) the sponsor expected a type of program which RCA would
be "embarrassed" to give him.

In May, 1926, stealing Sarnoff's thunder, A.T. & T. incorporated
a subsidiary, the Broadcasting Company of America. The move was
designed to frighten RCA into making further concessions, for
A.T. & T. already had decided to get out of the broadcasting business. In July, WEAF and WJZ were united under the management
of RCA. In September the National Broadcasting Company was incorporated as a subsidiary of RCA, with RCA, GE, and Westinghouse holding 50, 30, and 20 per cent of the stock, respectively. In
November, exercising its option, RCA paid A.T. & T. $1,000,000 for
WEAF, in return for which A.T. & T. agreed not to re-enter the
broadcasting field for seven years, on pain of refunding $800,000,
and to lease its telephone long-lines to NBC. At the close of the year,
NBC issued advertising rate cards for the Red Network, with WEAF
(since October, 1946, WNBC) as the key station, and for the Blue
Network, headed by WJZ. In the network field they had, for the
moment, no rival.

But broadcasting was not the only, or even the major, concern of
RCA. Although NBC's time sales of $3,000,000 in 1928 were en-
couraging, they had to be compared with a traffic in receiving sets
which, as early as 1924, had reached the proportions of a $50,000,000
business. Meantime, RCA sought new fields. In March, 1929, it acquired a majority of the stock of the Victor Talking Machine Company. In December of the same year it persuaded GE and Westinghouse to permit it to manufacture, as well as distribute, receiving
sets and tubes and to set up the RCA-Victor Company to do it. Two
years earlier, it had set up another subsidiary, the Radiomarine
Corporation, to handle ship-to-shore and aviation traffic. In 1928 it

incorporated RCA Communications, Inc., to operate a world-wide point-to-point radiotelegraph system. In May, 1930, RCA bought out the GE and Westinghouse interests in NBC. Previously, the corporation had acquired a toehold in the motion picture industry through the formation in 1928 of the Radio-Keith-Orpheum (RKO) Company. By 1932, RCA had acquired a better than 60 per cent interest in this production-distribution firm, which also controlled more than two hundred theaters; but in 1935 it sold half its holdings to the Atlas Corporation, and, by the spring of 1943, it was out of the movie business.

Minor subsidiaries, organized or acquired by RCA, included the Photophone Company, organized in April, 1928, and merged with Victor in January, 1932; RCA-Radiotron, formed in 1929; and the Audio Vision Appliance Company, which was incorporated into the RCA-Victor Company in 1929. All these units were brought under unified management in 1934 in the RCA Manufacturing Company, a wholly owned subsidiary. In December, 1942, this company was consolidated with RCA and became the RCA Victor Division of the company, which produces radio sets, tubes, records, Victrolas, transcriptions, and electronic and communications equipment.

On May 13, 1930, the government brought an antitrust action against RCA, GE, A.T. & T., and Westinghouse, as a result of which GE and Westinghouse were forced to dispose of their RCA stock and terminate all exclusive cross-licensing agreements; but RCA continued to control the patents on tubes used in the manufacture of receiving sets, and, in 1931, this was held to be in violation of the Clayton Act. Since then, the percentage of tube business controlled by RCA has declined.

Shortly after the formation of NBC, a rival network was organized. At the fourth annual meeting of the NAB in September, 1926, a promoter, George A. Coats, incensed over the rights and royalties demanded by ASCAP, proposed setting up a great radio program bureau. The idea appealed to Arthur Judson, manager of the Philadelphia Symphony Orchestra, who was apprehensive of the threat to talent booking inherent in the vast plans of RCA. A corporation known as the Judson Radio Program Corporation was organized to book talent and develop radio programs. After an unsuccessful attempt to place talent on NBC, the two men, in January, 1927, incorporated the United Independent Broadcasters (UIB), for the purpose of contracting for radio time, selling it to advertisers, and furnishing programs to broadcasters. In April, UIB became affiliated with the Columbia Phonograph Company, and an operating company was formed, the Columbia Phonograph Broadcasting System, Inc. (CPBS), with UIB remaining as the holding company.

The new network succeeded in signing sixteen stations, with a standard contract which obligated CPBS to pay them $500 a week for 10 specific hours. Owing to unexpected difficulties, the chain was not able to begin broadcasting until September, when the first program went out over the sixteen stations. Meantime, heavy financial losses had piled up, and the following month the Columbia Phonograph Company felt obliged to withdraw. At that time a controlling interest in UIB was acquired by three men, two of them owners of WCAU (Philadelphia), one of the contracted stations. Shortly thereafter, UIB acquired all the outstanding stock of the Columbia Phonograph Company, and the name of the network was changed to the Columbia Broadcasting System, Inc.

The WCAU interests continued to lose money in the company, which was finding it hard to contract sufficient business to cover its expenses. But rich new blood was in the offing. William S. Paley, impressed with the effect on sales of his La Palina cigars of advertising over the new chain, became interested in radio. In September, 1928 he and his family bought 50.3 per cent of the stock of CBS. The new owner set out to turn it into a profitable business. In December, 1928, he bought WABC (New York) (since October, 1946, WCBS), one of the original outlets and still one of the key CBS stations. Although at the close of the year CBS still was in the red, the books showed a profit of $474,203 by December, 1929.

Like Sarnoff, Paley had expansionist ideas. In 1929 he made a deal with the Paramount Publix Corporation, whereby 58,832 shares of Paramount were traded for 50,000 shares (roughly 50 per cent of its stock) of CBS, with the proviso that if the latter averaged earnings of a million during each of the next two years, the motion-picture company would buy back its shares at a premium. But CBS did better than the stipulated amount and bought back its shares instead, thus dissolving the short-lived merger.

In December, 1938, CBS purchased from Consolidated Film Industries, Inc., the capital stock of the American Record Corporation and its subsidiaries, changing the name to the Columbia Recording Corporation, still the opposite number to RCA's Victor Division and sharing with the latter a major portion of the lucrative phonograph record and transcription market.

From the earliest days of broadcasting, the pull from every direction has been such as to make the rapid expansion of networks inevitable. The listeners wanted to hear the "finished" programs from New York and other talent centers. Independent broadcasters wished not only to please their listeners but also to claim a share in the national advertiser's dollar. The networks themselves naturally worked to expand that dollar by putting themselves in position to offer more and more stations.

The irresistible tide flowed slowly. On November 1, 1926, NBC had 19 stations in its Red and Blue networks. By the end of 1927, the number had increased to 48. Ten years later, it stood at 138. As of December, 1946, the chain (meantime divested of the old Blue Network) boasted 159. Meanwhile, CBS, from a start of 16 in 1927, had 28 within a year and 113 by 1939. At the close of 1946, it had 162. By 1938, roughly 38 per cent of the 721 standard stations were either owned by, or under contract to, one of the two big companies. As of the end of 1946, approximately 800 of the more than a thousand on the air were divided as follows:

MBS 384
ABC 238
NBC 162
CBS . . . . .162[1]

As network broadcasting developed, business relationships changed. In the early days, A.T. & T. had asked for no binding contracts with the member stations that formed the nucleus of its 1923–24 network. When NBC was organized, it continued these informal understandings, making special contracts only with those stations that demanded them for protection. In general, it was agreed that the affiliates would receive $45 an hour for commercial programs and pay NBC $45 an hour for sustaining service. No option on time was taken by the network, which had to clear on each occasion with each station before making definite arrangements with the sponsor. On the other hand, CBS wrote individual contracts with its affiliates from the start, agreeing to pay $50 an hour for commercial time and charging the same rate for sustainers.

---

[1] As of July 1, 1959: MBS, 441 radio stations; ABC, 305; NBC, 211; CBS, 202. Television stations: ABC, 203; NBC, 192; CBS, 246 (including affiliates outside continental U.S.A.).

After Paley bought into CBS, payments for sustaining programs were eliminated, and, in return, the stations waived compensation for the first five hours a week of commercial time. In August, 1929, CBS adjusted its rates according to the power, popularity, physical coverage, market, and spot rate charged national advertisers. Hourly rates ranged from $125 to $1,250 for commercial programs, which stations were required to carry, although they were free to take or refuse sustaining programs. In 1932, NBC abolished hourly rates for sustainers, and the stations began paying the network a flat sum of $1,500 a month. By 1935 the older network had changed its contracts to conform to CBS's option policy.

In that year CBS paid affiliates 24.09 per cent of gross network time sales, and NBC paid 22.02. The stations got, for nothing, sustaining programs which cost the networks an average of $387 an hour to produce. Affiliates joining CBS after 1927 were forbidden by an "exclusivity" clause to make their facilities available to any other broadcasting chain. In 1937, at the insistence of some of the stations, a clause was added to prevent CBS from offering to rival stations in the affiliate's territory any network program, whether the affiliate desired to air it or not. A year earlier, NBC had introduced similar clauses, and in both instances the contracts were made binding upon the affiliates for a period of 5 years, though upon the networks for only 1 year.

Meanwhile, the networks were acquiring stations by ownership as well as by affiliation. Many independent stations did not wish to be bound by the rigid contracts of the national networks. Others were primarily interested in coverage on less than the national scale. Still others could not get an NBC or a CBS affiliation. The obvious advantages of limited network operation were not lost on these. In the late 1920's, groups of two or more independent stations began to exchange programs and quote advertising rates based on the combined markets. In the thirties some of these smaller chains expanded and became quite powerful in their regions, using their dominant positions in the markets to bargain collectively with the national networks. Others were content to go quietly along on a statewide basis. Not a few of the earlier ones failed to survive.

It was perhaps inevitable that the radio advertising boom of the thirties should bring NBC and CBS face to face with controlling factors quite outside the realm of government regulation. A number of powerful stations had resisted the networks' offers of affiliation and had succeeded so well as community stations serving large market areas that they could not be ignored by the advertisers. At the same time, a number of the advertisers were beginning to complain that NBC and CBS charged them for more stations than they needed. In 1934 several advertising agencies offered WOR (New York) and WGN (Chicago) contracts based on the regular card rates to local advertisers charged by these two stations if they would link themselves for simultaneous broadcasting at certain hours. WOR and WGN agreed to divide the line charges involved, and soon WXYZ (Detroit) and WLW (Cincinnati) joined the "co-operative" on the same basis. In October, 1934, the Mutual Broadcasting System was incorporated, the capital stock being divided between the Bamberger Broadcasting Service, Inc., licensee of WOR, and WGN, Inc., a subsidiary of the *Chicago Tribune*, licensee of WGN. Each of the four co-operating stations originated programs and received the local card rates, less 5 per cent commission for the time salesmen and the line charges.

In September, 1935, WXYZ left MBS to join NBC as an affiliate and was replaced by CKLW (Windsor, Ontario), which also served the Detroit area, thus lending an international flavor to the new venture. The next year, Don Lee and Colonial joined the MBS fold. By January, 1939, there were 107 "co-operating" stations, 25 of which were able, thanks to the very loose arrangements with MBS, to retain affiliation with NBC, and 5 with CBS. In January, 1940, the original incorporators issued stock to five additional companies: the Don Lee Broadcasting Company, the Colonial Network, Inc., the Cincinnati Times-Star Company (licensee of WKRC), the United Broadcasting Company (a subsidiary of the *Cleveland Plain Dealer* and licensee of WHK [Cleveland] and WHKC [Columbus]), and the Western Ontario Broadcasting Company, Ltd., licensee of CKLW.

It had been decided, however, that the original formula of loose, voluntary mutuality would not enable the new network to compete successfully with the older chains. In 1938, MBS began to ask for options from its affiliates, although it did not, as a network, maintain a programming organization or originate programs. In 1941 the stockholders elected a paid president, who undertook to turn a necessity into a virtue: since MBS had only two of the powerful 50-kilowatt clear-channel stations as full-time affiliates (WOR and WGN), he went after local stations, especially in one-station communities, and managed to convince a number of important national advertisers that such a system offered them a better total audience than those claimed for NBC and CBS. Though the advertising inroads made upon the older networks were not so great as to shake their hold on the cream of the business, MBS did succeed in winning three types of sponsor: those who objected to the rates charged by NBC or CBS; those who wished to test their programs and products in a few selected markets before embarking on a nation-wide campaign; and those who desired intensive regional coverage, either in conjunction with major network advertising or independently.

MBS's intensive drive soon brought it to the top in the number of affiliations. But the figures were misleading; NBC and CBS at the close of the 1930's were interested not only in all but 2 of the 30 powerful 50-kilowatt clear channels but in 53.4 per cent of the regional stations as well.

Moreover, as the Federal Communications Commission was to disclose, NBC and CBS had what amounted almost to a stranglehold on radio talent. The former had set up an Artists' Service in 1926. In 1935 it acquired the Civic Concert Service, Inc. In 1937 the gross talent bookings of the merged unit were $6,032,274. CBS presented a similar situation, having set up Columbia Artists, Inc., and having acquired 55 per cent of the stock of the Columbia Concerts Corporation in 1930.

Moves in the early forties had the effect of breaking up these talent monopolies, relaxing affiliation contracts, and limiting ownership of broadcasting stations to one to a market area, and (by gentleman's agreement) eight over-all. They also were responsible for NBC's having to dispose of one of its networks. The choice was not difficult. In 1938, NBC had paid the seventeen "basic" Red Stations $2,803,839 for airing network commercial programs; Blue's eighteen "basics" got $794,186. In October, 1943, RCA sold the Blue Network to Edward J. Noble, candy manufacturer and licensee of WMCA (New York), and since the summer of 1945, the network has been officially known as the American Broadcasting Company.

Several attempts subsequently were made to launch a fifth national network. In November, 1939, Elliott Roosevelt, onetime president of Hearst Radio, Inc., announced the formation of the Transcontinental Broadcasting System. It never took the air, largely because it failed to secure in advance sufficient promises of revenue to hold in line the 100 stations involved. In July, 1945, Leonard A.

Versluis, a Michigan broadcaster, managed to get the Associated Broadcasting System operating on the basis of a very loose arrangement with a dozen independent stations. Associated threw in the sponge on February 11, 1946.

With the coming of the first two big national networks, the demand for radio sets and broadcasting equipment naturally increased. Even by the end of 1927, the 5-year-old "novelty" had become a $425,000,000 business in terms of gross receipts for apparatus. By 1938 there were 40,000,000 receiving sets in use in the United States. The original cost to the public of the nearly 100,000,000 receiving sets (excluding FM, television, and facsimile receivers) turned out between 1921 and mid–1946 has been estimated at almost $5,000,-000,000.

. . . .

THE NEWSPAPER-RADIO FEUD

As a matter of fact, the publishers have more reason to be on their guard now than they had in the early twenties. Then radio was tolerated as something of a toy, and, although several newspapers owned stations, they did not regard them as competitors. In 1922, the Associated Press warned its members that the broadcasting of its news was contrary to AP by-laws; but, as the United Press and International News Service were supplying news to broadcasters, those warned felt obliged to strain the by-laws. So little did the newspaper owners fear radio that they cheerfully accorded the broadcasters a courtesy long denied (in effect) by most periodicals to motion picture exhibitors, theatrical producers, and book publishers: free announcement of scheduled attractions without the usual *quid pro quo* of paid advertisements.

With the rapid expansion of NBC and CBS in the early thirties, however, the picture rapidly changed. Newspaper advertising lineage fell as radio time billings soared. Radio news coverage, which had dealt a death blow to the afternoon "extra," was utilizing the press association reports—the very raw material of newspapers—to beat the publishers at their own game, and with a decided advantage in timing. The dormant radio committee of the American Association of Newspaper Publishers sprang into action. By 1933 it had persuaded AP, UP, and INS to suspend the service of news to broadcasters.

The response of at least one network was immediate and initially effective. In October, CBS News Chief Paul W. White, a former UP editor, quietly began to organize his own news-gathering staff. Newspapers in areas where CBS had outlets promptly withdrew the network's program listings, and the publishers' committee urged newspapers to accord like treatment to all listings, as a means of bringing concerted broadcaster pressure to bear on CBS.

The broadcasters lost their nerve. They had managed their relations with the press badly, especially in the matter of failing to accompany requests for free space with paid advertisements. Most of them stood in awe of the older medium, insisting that radio needed the support of the press (which, since 1933, it has never received). The network front cracked when NBC decided to play both ends against the middle instead of supporting its news chief in his move to follow White's lead by building up NBC's own news-gathering staff.

A few days of going without printed program logs convinced all but a handful of broadcasters that they could not win in a showdown. The spirit of panic swept CBS up in its tide, and in December, 1933, representatives of both networks met with spokesmen for the ANPA, AP, UP, and INS in the Hotel Biltmore, New York, and signed a ten-point "agreement," which later, perhaps for legal reasons, became known as "the Biltmore program."

A sweeping victory for the publishers, the "agreement" provided for the setting-up of a special news bureau, to be supported wholly by the networks, which was to "edit" the files of the three press associations and release a small distillate to the broadcasters for two daily newscasts of not more than 5 minutes each, one after 9:30 A.M. and one after 9:00 P.M., and for "occasional" broadcasts of special bulletins involving news of "transcendental [sic] importance," which were to be followed by the admonition to "see your local newspaper for further details." Commentators were not to dabble in spot news, and newscasts were, under no circumstances, to be sponsored. Finally, CBS was to suppress its burgeoning news service, and both networks were solemnly to promise never again to attempt anything of the sort—a promise which, fortunately, has not been kept.

Two contributing factors to this curious pact should be noted in passing. One, of particular interest in view of the 1946 newspaper campaign against "government interference" with the broadcasters (touched off by issuance of the FCC's famous "Blue Book"), was the subtle press agitation just prior to the Biltmore conference for congressional legislation more strictly regulating the radio industry, accompanied by some kind words for the British system of government ownership and operation. The other was the broadcasters' mounting coolness toward frequent interruptions of commercial programs by news bulletins, a practice which distressed the sponsors and their advertising agencies. The two time periods selected for newscasts happened fortuitously to fall in "optional" segments which normally produced little or no advertising revenue.

The new clearing house, known as the Press Radio Bureau, began operating on March 1, 1934. It never met with any great success, although the networks obligingly supported it for three years. Its failure stemmed in part from the refusal of certain stations to abide by its provisions and the ineffectiveness of measures taken by the press and the two networks to punish them for their temerity. Even more serious, however, was the rise of Trans-Radio Press, an independent news-gathering agency founded by Herbert Moore, former UP and CBS news editor, which sold news directly to radio advertisers for sponsorship. So well did Trans-Radio succeed that UP and INS, never very enthusiastic about the Biltmore "solution," gave way to envy, and in May, 1935, on the pretext that they were making nothing more than a temporary excursion to squelch the "upstart" news service, persuaded the die-hard ANPA radio committee to modify the agreement to the extent of permitting UP and INS to sell news on the side. AP soon liberalized its news policy for members and, in 1940, removed the no-sponsorship restriction. In the same year Press Radio passed quietly out of existence. The war appeared to be over.

The extent to which the outcome was a Pyrrhic victory for the broadcasters, as well as a missed opportunity for their listeners, may not even today be fully realized. A 1939 *Fortune* survey indicated that 70 per cent of Americans relied on the radio for news and that 58 per cent thought it more accurate than that supplied by the press. A survey by the Survey Research Center of the University of Michigan in 1947 substantiated these findings very dramatically. On many occasions during the war, at subsequent international conferences, and in the midst of numerous strikes which kept newspapers off the stands for days and weeks, listening America might well have wished that radio's handful of reporters had been an army.

Actually, the wartime cessation of hostilities between press and radio may have marked not so much a victory, Pyrrhic or otherwise, as a long armistice. The aggressive reappearance of radio newsmen during the war, together with a succession of time-beats over the newspapers, all the more galling because they usually involved news gathered by and for the press, caused the AP management to "re-examine" the situation, with a view to exploring the possibility of trying to reinforce restrictions on the broadcasters' use of press-association material.

Moreover, facsimile has offered a brand-new source of possible friction. True, virtually all the pioneering in facsimile has been done by newspapers, notably the *New York Times*, the *Chicago Tribune*, the *St. Louis Post-Dispatch*, the *Louisville Courier-Journal*, and *Times*, and the *Columbus Dispatch*. But this may indicate simply that certain publishers had taken steps to attain a position in which they could better control the adaptation of the new medium to news dissemination. There is also the factor of pressure from publishers not eager to see facsimile developed, which was graphically illustrated when West Coast AP members forced that agency to withdraw leased wire facilities over which the *New York Times* was delivering its invaluable facsimile edition to the San Francisco conference in 1945.

"KING CANUTE" PETRILLO

It was radio's peculiar misfortune that it was obliged to rely from the first on many well-intrenched groups other than the publishers and that it developed in a period when some of these were coming to the height of their power. The first such group to waylay the hopeful youngster and levy toll was the American Society of Composers, Authors, and Publishers.

As we have seen, even in the crystal-and-headpiece days, long before the broadcasters had got an inkling of where their revenue was to come from, ASCAP, which controlled the bulk of copyrighted sheet and recorded music, saw a chance to exact tribute from a medium that could not live without copyrighted music. In 1922 stations were presented with formal demands for royalties to be paid every time a piece of music was played, whether by "live" musicians operating in front of a microphone or on phonograph records. Some broadcasters promptly went out of business, others merely continued to pirate copyrighted music, but a few of the

talent for the initial playing, neither training pianists to weave baskets nor expecting them to eke out an existence on the wages of two or three days' employment each month appears to be the answer for radio musicians. The coming of talking motion pictures, catching less resolute AFM leaders without a plan, had thrown 8,300 movie-theater musicians on the human scrap-heap. Radio would not repeat the performance if Petrillo could help it.

Moved by a sense of timing that has characterized his actions ever since, Petrillo in 1935 calmly ordered all broadcasting stations to hire "stand-by" musicians to the number of those used in the making of any recording or transcription every time a "platter" was played more than once, on pain of seeing the musicians walk out of the Chicago recording studios. Early in 1936 he made good his threat. Locals in other cities promptly brought pressure on Joseph Weber, then president of the AFM. Weber extended the stand-by order to the entire country, advising the networks to bring pressure on their affiliates. This the networks declined to undertake. But it was apparent that they would lose, whatever they did; and so, on September 15, 1937, they formally capitulated. Affiliated and independent stations, as well as record manufacturers, had, of course, to follow suit.

Petrillo had outdone the WPA in creating "make-work," but meanwhile the engineers had not been idle. The coming of the automatic record-player or "juke box" presented both a new problem and a new opportunity: the recording companies were making a mint of money, but the 1937 agreement provided no way for the musicians to tap the major portion of it, even indirectly. In June, 1942, having failed to persuade the record-makers to agree to a formula whereby the AFM would receive a graduated scale of fees on all records to be played in public, the new boss threatened to forbid his musicians to make recordings. In August he carried out his threat. Congress stormed. The War Labor Board stepped into the picture, held lengthy hearings, and ordered Petrillo to end his strike. In October, 1944, President Roosevelt personally appealed to the AFM chief to send his men back. But Petrillo turned a deaf ear to all. Decca and WOR had broken the united front by signing in September, 1943. In November, 1944, despairing of any help from the government, Columbia Recording and RCA-Victor gave in.

In the midst of this exhilarating skirmish, Petrillo waded into two more. In 1943, professedly alarmed by the number of "amateur" musicians playing over the air, the leader blew a loud blast on his trumpet: AFM members playing with nonmembers would lose their cards. Dr. Joseph E. Maddy, president of the National Music Camp for school children at Interlochen, Michigan, stuck by his youngsters and lost his card. Again Congress acted. Senator Vandenberg and Representatives Dondero and Hoffman introduced bills, Petrillo shrugged, later graciously "exempted" the Cleveland Public Schools from his ruling.

Meantime, his eagle eye had long since noted that more and more radio stations were employing staff (usually announcers) or mechanical record-changers. Having organized the manual "platter-turners" of Chicago, Petrillo moved in the spring of 1944 to require all stations to employ hand labor, thus providing work for an additional 2,000 AFM scale laborers. This brought him into collision with the National Association of Broadcasting Engineers and Technicians (NABET), an independent union which had organized most of the "disk-jockeys" outside Chicago. Afraid of Petrillo, NBC and ABC hesitated about signing new contracts with NABET, who in turn, took the case to the National Labor Relations Board. The latter upheld NABET, directing NBC and ABC to sign new contracts with the anti-Petrillo union. There, as of the close of 1946, the matter rested. No one supposed that Petrillo, with CBS and a number of independent stations whose "platter-turners" were members of the International Brotherhood of Electrical Workers rather than NABET in his pocket, would let it rest for long.

In February, 1945, "Little Caesar" forbade his musicians to appear on television programs until he had had an opportunity to examine the probable effects of the new medium on employment. In October, he set FM development back at least a year by banning dual AM-FM programming of music unless the full complement of stand-by of musicians was hired. In December he proscribed the airing of foreign musical broadcasts other than those originating in Canada. In January, 1946, he ordered the networks to take the lead in forcing stations throughout the country to employ an "adequate" number of full-time musicians.

Congress whipped through a bill sponsored by Representative Lea of California to amend the Communications Act so as to outlaw "featherbedding" and virtually every type of "coercion" that Petrillo had practiced against the broadcasters. President Truman signed it in April. The AFM chief promptly ordered WAAF (Chicago) to employ three additional musicians as "librarians," announcing that he would fight all the way up the line to the

Supreme Court and would refuse to obey such a law even if the highest tribunal ruled it constitutional. At the AFM annual convention in June, 1946, Petrillo spoke bluntly.

When I became president of the American Federation of Musicians, I made sure that the contracts with the locals in the three cities where network shows originate . . . New York, Chicago, and Los Angeles . . . would all expire on one day. That day is coming next January 31. If the Supreme Court rules the Lea Act constitutional, the small stations won't get any music, because the three locals will make agreements to play locally only.

And if the government attempted to prevent his collecting a fee on each record sold?

We'll just send out a little letter. We'll just say, "Gentlemen, on such and such a date, members of the AFM will not be permitted to perform in the making of recordings or transcriptions."

As a thousand delegates rose to their feet cheering, James Caesar Petrillo put a flourish on his theme song:

Now, Congressmen: dream up a law to make us go to work!

At the end of the year Petrillo had his test case in the judicial wringer. Behind him stood the American Federation of Radio Artists, affiliated through the Associated Actors and Artists of America with Actors Equity, the American Guild of Musical Artists, and the American Guild of Variety Artists; the Radio Directors Guild; the Screen Actors Guild; the United Office and Professional Workers of America; the International Brotherhood of Electrical Workers; and a half-dozen other unions, any one of which could disrupt the broadcasting industry on a moment's notice. In December the United States District Court in Chicago dismissed a criminal information against Petrillo in the WAAF case, ruling the Lea Act unconstitutional on five counts involving the First, Fifth, and Thirteenth amendments. The federal government moved to appeal directly to the Supreme Court. Meanwhile, however, in October, the transcription manufacturers had agreed to meet the AFM "czar's" 50 per cent "across-the-board" wage increase. Once again, the wall had been breached.

THE ADVERTISING MEN MOVE IN

It will be recalled that, when broadcasting took its first halting steps in the early 1920's, it was thought by RCA, GE, Westinghouse, and the other manufacturers that the sale of equipment would support the new medium indefinitely; and that, when A.T. & T., which had virtually no equipment to sell, failed in its appeal to the public for contributions, it turned to the merchants. But potential advertisers were skeptical. For more than a century, they had been dealing with the written word. Those who controlled the print media were loath to see the advertiser's dollar split. Weighing the bird in hand against the rumored two in the bush, the advertising agencies that got their 15 per cent from the print media hesitated to break with old friends.

The rising generation in the advertising-agency field took the longer view. It seemed apparent to them that radio was the ideal medium for certain firms which made package sales that depended on constant iteration of their brand names and which, therefore, naturally desired maximum impact; that maximum impact meant network hookups to bring the number of those "exposed" to a single advertisement well above the top figure for any grouping of newspapers, magazines, outdoor posters, or car-cards.

They began with prospects whose sales graphs were going down despite heavy advertising in the older media: brand coffee, which was feeling the pinch of the cheaper, chain-store lines of coffee "ground before your eyes"; canned soups, which were suffering from the elimination of the soup course and, along with packaged desserts, from the growing American habit of eating out; cigarettes, which were beginning to find pretty-women symbols a drug on the market and had a story to tell about "scientific tests" of "doctors" and tobacco auctioneers which nobody would read in type; pipe tobacco, which had become a sideline because pipe smoking was on the wane; automobile fuel, which was just going into the "ethyl" and "high-test" grading phase.

Corporations in these and other lines were worried. In a nation of "experts," they took it for granted that these impetuous young advertising men knew what they were talking about. By the mid-thirties, radio shows that had creaked along on budgets of $25,000 a year were giving way to variety and comedy shows like "Maxwell House Showboat" and Ed Wynn's "Texaco Fire Chief," running to a quarter-million and employing as many as a hundred and fifty entertainers. By 1935 the net incomes of NBC and CBS had soared to $3,656,907 and $3,228,194, respectively; by 1940, to $5,834,772 and $7,431,634. Meanwhile, the sponsors were making money, too.

And advertising agencies dealing almost solely with the new bo-
nanza were springing up overnight.

That this was a fateful step for the advertising industry was at
once apparent. The official historian of the N. W. Ayer Company
offers some interesting testimony on what sweeping decisions had
to be faced and made:

The Ayer agency . . . believed that radio advertising was particularly
open to abuse which might alienate public opinion. It therefore adopted
the policy that it would maintain direct control over the arrangement and
production of all programs for which it was responsible, instead of leaving program production to the stations. Gradually it developed a staff
of workers especially trained and experienced in this work; and in 1928,
when the possibilities of radio advertising were clearly established, this
staff was separated from the firm's other publicity work and organized as
an independent department. Its duties were to assemble information
about all phases of broadcast advertising, build up programs, hire talent,
direct production, and handle the leasing of station time and all other
details connected with broadcast programs. . . .

It was, perhaps, both natural and inevitable that the purpose of,
and attitude toward, programming should change significantly. The
horse, as the Ayer historian explains, had to follow the cart:

. . . Until 1930, all agencies tended to look for attractive programs and
then to seek advertisers who would take a fling at broadcasting. After
1930, much of the original glamor and mystery of radio had vanished,
and men had to take a more realistic approach. The Ayer firm rapidly
developed the view that an agency must start with the client's sales
problems, determine whether radio can help, and then devise a program
which will achieve specific ends in terms of sales. The complete reversal
of the method is significant.

How significant may be gathered from the following wistful
historical note in the December 8, 1945, issue of *Billboard*:

The networks have always tried to get a firmer foothold in the production field . . . a position they lost to advertising agencies in the early
days of radio.

Soon the agencies were not only building programs and hiring the
talent but also choosing the times at which their shows would be
broadcast and the cities in which they would be heard. How much
further could they go? As Niles Trammell, president of NBC, told
the Senate Interstate Commerce Committee in December, 1943:

The argument is now advanced that business control of broadcasting
operations has nothing to do with programming control. This is to forget

that he who controls the pocketbook controls the man. Business control means complete control, and there is no use arguing to the contrary.[2]

This is not to say that Trammell and all his colleagues were entirely happy about the situation. Indeed, on several occasions during the late thirties, William S. Paley, then president and now chairman of the board of CBS, suggested that the broadcasters ought to take steps to free themselves from advertiser domination. The reaction he got was very much the same as that which usually greets the timid householder attempting to quiet a noisy party across the hall. The feeling was general that what the advertising agencies had given, the advertising agencies could take away. "Why shoot Santa Claus?" the cynics asked.

The sponsors and agencies were building up a solidarity entirely unmatched by the broadcasters. By 1944, CBS had thirteen customers who bought more than $1,000,000 worth of time each, and three who spent more than $4,000,000 each,[3] while NBC had eleven million-dollar-plus clients, ABC nine, and MBS three. But advertising-agency concentration had become even more pronounced. J. Walter Thompson bought $13,470,003 worth of time from CBS, ABC, and MBS in 1944; Young and Rubicam, $10,034,721; Dancer, Fitzgerald, $7,062,811. In other words, three agencies bought nearly a fourth of the time on three of the four networks. In 1945, seven sponsors and six agencies furnished almost half of CBS's $65,724,362 billings; twelve sponsors and five agencies contributed more than 40 per cent of ABC's $40,045,966; six sponsors and five agencies accounted for a third of MBS's $20,637,363.

What this could mean in the way of "pressures" should be apparent even to the layman. It is equally apparent that the small independent stations, operating sometimes on a "shoestring," have no effective way of resisting such pressures. But the networks are not immune, for, obviously, an advertising agency responsible for as much as 10 per cent of a chain's business can wield a good deal of influence over not only the network but also the scores of stations that rely largely on the chains for their livelihood.

The merest suggestion from a courageous network executive that

---

[2] It is perhaps only fair to say that Trammell was speaking of evils he detected in the Chain Broadcasting Regulations rather than in advertiser domination.

[3] General Foods, $5,537,409; Lever Brothers, $4,842,781; Proctor and Gamble, $4,348,795.

he might set aside a choice hour in the evening for a brave new venture in public service could bring a reminder from half-a-dozen agencies of the fact that they could easily take their business next door—and his listeners with it. What would happen if the broadcasters, or even the four networks, moved in unison is a matter for conjecture. They have never tried it.

"LOVE THAT SOAP!"

That this concentration of advertising power should have had its effect on programming tastes is hardly to be wondered at. Once the decision had been made, shows began to stress a more "popular" appeal. Commercial "plugs" became more frequent and more direct. The broadcasters' "rules" against direct advertising, "relaxed" as early as 1927, gradually disappeared altogether. Radio became "show business."

The new pattern formed and hardened swiftly. In 1929, Rudy Vallee, sponsored by Fleischmann's Yeast, expanded the dance-band-with-plugs formula by introducing "radio personalities." The same year saw the beginnings of the "Amos 'n Andy" and Goldberg shows, the latter among the first of the afternoon dramatic serials, forerunners of the "soap operas" of today. Housewives, the advertisers said, found such dramas a relief from "the grim reality of housework." Certain it is that the serials were easy to produce, cost little, and were found to be very successful in selling their sponsors' products. Soap companies like Proctor and Gamble and Lever Brothers flocked to the new standard, and soon this type of program had a generic name to vie with the "horse opera" of the screen.

The logbooks of WEAF and WJZ, at that time both NBC stations, show no prominent commercial sponsors before 6:00 P.M. during 1932 and 1933. By 1936 the daytime hours were filled with 15-minute shows, sponsored primarily by Oxydol, Ivory, Best Foods, Chipso, and Climalene. By 1939 the serial was well established, and such clients as Kolynos, Phillips, Dr. Lyons, and Camay had mounted the bandwagon.

Costs of evening programs, paradoxically, rose steadily through the years from 1935 to 1946. At first, this trend alarmed the sponsors and advertising agencies; for, although there was no doubt about the existence of radio audiences, there was considerable about the radio market: that listeners were purchasing radio-advertised products had not yet been "conclusively" demonstrated. The sponsors, still to be introduced to corporate and income-tax schedules which were to make "good-will" advertising the cheapest commodity on the market, wanted results. Led by the American Tobacco Company's George Washington Hill, with his "unprecedented" Cremo contest and strident Lucky Strike program, they had shaken off all the old network inhibitions against "direct" advertising, except the one about specifying the price. That this taboo to which the broadcasters clung was meaningless was made clear in practice: Eno Fruit Salts described a trial bottle costing "a little less than two packs of cigarettes"; another sponsor announced that his product could be purchased for "the smallest silver coin in circulation"; Richman Brothers boasted that "men who pay $45 for their suits can now get them . . . for half that." The dropping of such "subtleties" was now only a question of time.

Even though it often seemed like sending good money after bad, the advertising agencies eventually went after Hollywood names to "hypo" fading music-and-variety shows. At first, the film capital resented this "exploitation," but the producers soon discovered that radio appearances enhanced the popularity of their stars, as well as the box-office pull of their pictures. The actors, delighted to stumble onto new sources of revenue beyond the reach of the California income-tax collectors, soon learned to demand what the market would bear. During the 1930's, Eddie Cantor, Ed Wynn, Burns and Allen, Jack Benny, Fred Allen, Stoopnagle and Bud, Jimmy Durante, and many another veteran of vaudeville strode to the microphone as the popularity of variety shows steadily increased. Rarer were those who, like Marian and Jim Jordan ("Fibber McGee and Molly"), started more modestly, since they lacked the convenient Hollywood-Broadway springboard, but eventually got to the top.

The first strictly "dramatic" program of the type now common, "First-Nighter," was launched in 1930. It was soon followed by the "Lux Radio Theatre." From this point it was only a step to the dramatization of mystery and murder stories: "The Shadow," "Bulldog Drummond," "The Green Hornet." The Kellogg Company gave the formula a new emphasis with "The Singing Lady," a presupper-hour children's program. Soon all the breakfast-food people were combining cowboy or G-man derring-do and package-top prizes to persuade young Americans to hound their mothers into buying new "taste sensations." The "sealed-in vitamin" fillip was to come later.

By 1938, *Fortune* observed, radio entertainment was becoming "increasingly complicated." Major Bowes had pointed the way for amateur shows, which enjoyed a brief reign and then gave way to quiz and other audience-participation programs, the more extreme types of which proved so popular that thousands of citizens still clamor weekly for the chance to make themselves ridiculous.

Henry Ford and General Motors each had a symphony program. The sponsoring of "serious" music was felt to be a matter of "prestige," as well as a completely noncontroversial form of "public service"; and soon CBS had the New York Philharmonic and NBC its own symphony with Toscanini conducting. The public, *Fortune* feared, "still preferred swing to symphony, comedy to uplift. Program-makers had accustomed the listener to the Big and the New, and now had a self-created mandate to produce it over and over again." Unconvinced, the Blue Network (now ABC) clung to the Metropolitan Opera broadcasts it had begun in December, 1931, occasionally finding a prestige-hungry (or tax-ridden) sponsor for it (American Tobacco in 1933–34, Lambert Pharmaceutical in 1934–35, Texas Company from 1941 to 1943). Symphonies became fixtures. And many a lesser orchestra found a place on a local station.

As early as 1931, broadcasters began to experiment seriously with forum and other "discussion" programs. The oldest of the forums was the "University of Chicago Round Table," launched on NBC's WMAQ (Chicago) in February of that year. "America's Town Meeting of the Air" was for years a Blue Network (ABC) feature, beginning May, 1935, sometimes sponsored, sometimes sustaining. The "American Forum of the Air" was started by MBS in January, 1939. CBS introduced "People's Platform" in July, 1938. The latter's "American School of the Air" and NBC's "University of the Air" were for years sustaining features.

As with the "serious" music programs, most broadcasters have been content to let the networks hold the "forum franchise" for them with one each, and these four coming later and later in the evening or on Sunday afternoon. Unrehearsed discussion of controversial public issues by "outsiders" has been frowned on by the NAB, as we shall see. Such expansion as there has been under the heading of "news and discussion" since the outbreak of World War II, therefore, has been in the direction of a quantitative increase in straight news bulletins and the development of one-man commentaries. The latter device, which made its appearance shortly after Munich and probably reached a peak before V-J Day, brought to the microphone a wide variety of speakers, a handful of them well qualified by experience for the work.

The table on p. 68 will give some indication of the trends between 1932 and 1945. The spectacular rise under the heading "Drama" should be noted with the reservation that it coincides with the development of the "soap opera" and children's serial; bona fide experimentation in the theater arts, symbolized by the "Columbia Workshop" and the outstanding contributions of such men as Orson Welles, Arch Oboler, Norman Corwin, and Archibald MacLeish, represents only a small fraction of the total and, indeed, for a time declined. In connection with the figure for "news," it should be borne in mind that interest reached a peak during the war and has since receded somewhat.

It should be noted in conclusion that the radio advertising situation was changing very rapidly during the summer and fall of 1946. Three factors were cited for a diminution of interest on the part of many wartime broadcast sponsors: (1) the easing of the newsprint shortage, which allowed them to take more space in the print media; (2) the new tax law, which, after January 1, 1946, enabled corporations to pocket profits formerly spent on advertising because 90 cents on the dollar would have gone for taxes if it had not been used in advertising; (3) the high cost of talent; (4) labor stoppages and materials shortages.[4]

This trend, in turn, affected the agencies in more ways than one. Some of them had urged their stars to incorporate themselves, as a device to save the agencies the few dollars for social security deductions which they would otherwise have had to pay; and the stars had found that they rather enjoyed dealing directly with sponsors, with whom they shared the 15 per cent service charge formerly paid to the agencies. Far more serious from the agency standpoint was the trend toward "package" firms, often consisting of a writer and a salesman, who sold finished shows either to the stars or to the sponsors, in either case by-passing the agencies.

How these trends would affect the broadcasters themselves remained to be seen. Having been denied the cream of the agency

---

[4] One might add another: the American businessman's extra-sensory knowledge of the precise moment when the customers have had enough.

Analysis of Program Classifications (in Percentages)

	NBC *			CBS †			MBS ‡
	1933	1939	1944	1933	1939	1944	1944
Music:							
Classical and semi- classical	26.9	14.1	12.2	8.8	6.2	7.3	6.9
Dance and light. . .	40.4	43.1	20.5	45.4	30.8	25.8	32.4
Drama	11.2	20.1	26.7	18.1	26.6	28.6	7.2
News	2.0	3.8	20.4	4.7	10.9	16.5	22.5
Variety and quiz.	2.6	2.9	14.0	7.9	8.4	13.6	8.7
Talks and discussions	7.0	9.6	2.4	7.2	4.8	6.2	12.8
Sports	1.0	1.2	1.1	1.5	7.0	0.8	0.9
Children's §	3.6	2.9	0.4	5.3	3.1	. . . . .	4.6
Religious	1.8	1.3	1.1	1.1	2.2	1.2	4.0
Physical training ‖ . . .	2.3	. . . . .	. . . . .	. . . . .	. . . . .	. . . . .	. . . . .
Total	100.0	100.0	100.0	100.0	100.0	100.0	100.0
Sustaining	76.4	70.3	50.6	77.1	51.3	52.2	69.0
Commercial	23.6	29.7	49.4	22.9	48.7	47.8	31.0

* The 1933 and 1939 figures for NBC are the combined Red and Blue networks—1944 are the figures for NBC (formerly the Red) alone.

† CBS figures in 1933 and 1939 for dance music, drama, and variety were combined into one class ("Popular Entertainment"); whereas it was possible to reclassify the commercial programs, such figures on sustaining were unavailable, hence the figures in the table are an estimate.

‡ Although MBS was already organized in 1934, its sustaining programs in 1939 were broadcast on a mutual basis, and no record was kept to make the figures complete.

§These figures should be compared very approximately, since the networks differ not only on the methods of classification but in degree of change since 1933. CBS no longer classifies children's programs.

‖ A program of setting-up exercises that was popular at the time and was broadcast as much as an hour a day. Such programs are no longer significant.

business and therefore obliged to scratch for new ideas long ago, ABC and MBS may have found a partial solution in the co-operative sponsorship idea, whereby several-score local merchants in various communities help to defray the expense of such $100,000-plus attractions as Raymond Swing and Elmer Davis. Some affiliates had built up enough local business to cushion the shock, and, of course, the independents for the most part always had been, vis-à-vis the networks, national advertisers, and agencies, just what the word implies.

So much for the historical development of a business whose gross time sales grew from a few thousand dollars in 1925 to $100,000,000 in 1935 and to more than $400,000,000 in 1945. For the most part, it has been a natural phenomenon, a case of a hidden spring producing a brook that became a stream and then a torrent, making its own bed as it swept along.

[Editor's Note: This was written, of course, before the impact of television on radio became apparent. The tables in this volume will suggest the extent to which the newer medium has cut into radio listening and radio advertising support.]

THE GROWTH OF
INTERNATIONAL COMMUNICATIONS

BY LLEWELLYN WHITE
AND ROBERT D. LEIGH

This is a part of one of the reports from the Commission on Freedom of
the Press. Mr. Leigh was director of that Commission, and Mr. White a
staff member. Mr. Leigh was for fourteen years president of Bennington
College, and during the war served as director of the Federal Broadcast
Intelligence Service. Mr. White has had twenty-nine years of newspaper,
magazine, and press association experience. This material is reprinted
from their book, *Peoples Speaking to Peoples,* by special permission of
the University of Chicago Press, which published the volume in 1946 and
holds copyright. The reader will notice, of course, that a few of the 1946
details in this selection no longer apply to the present time.

THE TELECOMMUNICATION SERVICES

IN CONTRAST to the United States, the governments of virtually all
countries are directly involved in the business of furnishing telecommunications services. Almost all own and operate their domestic
telegraph systems exclusively and, with the exception of Latin
America, where foreign operators have moved in, the telephones
as well. As to external facilities, the ratio of government interest
varies; Japan, Norway, and Switzerland own and operate all telecommunications; the governments of Belgium, Sweden, and Finland
own some cables and all wireless facilities; the British government
nationalized all cable and wireless facilities; in Greece, Egypt,
Portugal, and most Latin-American countries neither the govern-

ment nor national industry controls the telecommunications links with the outer world, enterprising foreigners (usually either the International Telephone and Telegraph Company or Cable and Wireless, Limited, with Radio Corporation of America appearing also as part of various combinations of foreign groups) having taken over such services by long-term lease.

Two nations clearly dominate the international field: Britain, with 190,000 nautical miles of cables, 63,000 miles of point-to-point wireless circuits, and a potential for broadcasting voice radio, dot-dash, and facsimile to literally every part of the globe; and the United States, with 94,000 miles of cables, 236,000 miles of point-to-point wireless telegraph, and a broadcast potential limited only by the lack of suitable permanent relay points to circumvent the Auroral Zone about the North Pole—a natural phenomenon that does not plague the more fortunately located British, over whose empire the radio signals never fade. The comparison is at once significant and misleading; it indicates that wireless is rapidly surpassing cables, which is true, and that America's predominance in the newer medium has challenged Britain's long-time leadership in international telecommunications, which is also true; but it might be taken as prima facie evidence that America's leadership itself will go unchallenged, and that depends upon what America does to consolidate its position. Our improved position was largely a wartime phenomenon.

The United States has missed the boat on at least two previous occasions. The first was when Cyrus Field, Peter Cooper, and other wise Americans proposed a submarine cable to link America with Europe. It was not the United States government but the British, long aware of the value to a nation with global political and economic interests of rapid, reliable communications, which guaranteed the pioneers a 5 per cent profit for as long as their venture functioned. After that Britain combed the empire for investors willing to lay cables under government guaranties. When that did not work, the government laid them itself, notably the All Red Route from London to Australia, which embraces the two longest submarine cable spans in existence. Guglielmo Marconi, suffering substantially the same fate in his homeland that Field and Cooper had encountered in theirs, found a welcome in England, where his privately owned Wireless Telegraph Company soon established a radiotelegraph network embracing most of the empire. British trade undoubtedly gained in consequence of these two moves. And during World War I the unquestioned dominance of London as the center of world communications proved of incalculable military, news, and propaganda value.

The rapid development of wireless communication by our engineers virtually thrust upon Americans a second opportunity to take the lead in global telecommunications. This, too, was lost, and for a variety of reasons. To begin with, much of the pioneering in radiotelegraphy from the United States was done by RCA, which was interested primarily in the development of a domestic voice radio broadcast network. The other big company in the field, I.T. & T., had invested heavily in cables and still could not believe that the newer device would ever offer anything more than a supplementary "feeder" service.

Wireless telegraph circuits, like cables, require terminal facilities. Like cables, radio to reach around the globe needs automatic relay points to "boost" the signal as it begins to fade. Both requirements, in the case of the United States, involve treaties with foreign powers, because we lack Britain's conveniently placed stepping-stones around the globe. Such treaties were not sought at the Versailles peace table. Given breathing space, the British government spun its own wireless web—a web which soon assumed the characteristics of monopoly in that it denied to rivals the right to operate circuits directly from their own countries to British Empire points. Meantime, but for the swift intervention of our Navy Department, the British in 1919 might have obtained exclusive control of the Alexanderson "alternator," a General Electric product, and the De Forest tube, which would have set American wireless (and domestic radio) development back a decade.

If the efficiency and economy of radiotelegraph did not impress cable-minded Americans with the need to seize early leadership, it made a very deep impression on their British counterparts. Faced with the double threat of rate and service competition from the British Post Office and the Marconi companies and with the ever present rivalry of the American cable companies, British cable owners saw their revenues dwindling and their stocks falling off. Without hesitation, they determined to save their investments by using government aid to subdue their wireless competitors. As neither the War Office nor the Admiralty was completely sold on wireless, the government reacted promptly to their proposal, and according to expectation. An Imperial Wireless and Cable Conference was hurriedly summoned. The result was the formation, in 1929, of two "chosen instruments," one a holding and the other an operating corporation, but both known as Cable and Wireless. Into the consolidation went the private companies' 165,000 miles of cables and practically all of the government's 25,000, the point-to-point radio stations and manufacturing interests of the British Marconi company, and some of the radiotelegraph facilities of the British Post Office. The offer of shares to the public was accompanied by newspaper stories mentioning an expected 6 per cent profit.

Actually the 6 per cent was never approached, and in 1936 the government was obliged to step in again. Rentals of government facilities amounting to a quarter of a million pounds a year were canceled in exchange for government ownership of 9 per cent of the stock; dividends were cut sharply; the company's license was extended to insure greater monopoly benefits; and a uniform maximum empire rate of 1s. 3d. was inaugurated for messages between any two points in the Commonwealth, as a means of meeting foreign wireless competition, chiefly from the Royal Netherlands Post Office. Two years later there was instituted a uniform press rate of a penny (then 2 cents, now 1.17 cents, American) a word between any two points in the Commonwealth. Cable and Wireless seemed on the way to a secure, if somewhat limited future, although the Dutch and the French also, despite their heavy investment in cables, were expanding the wireless links with their own far-flung empires. Indeed, telecommunications had become one of the integral elements of colonial development.

Eighteen months after the new arrangement had been solemnized in the Imperial Telegraphs Act, Hitler attacked Poland. Official government telecommunications traffic immediately assumed such proportions as to assure Cable and Wireless of steady dividends, and at the same time to obscure temporarily the handwriting on every cable-owner's wall.

The British cable-owners had thought so little of international broadcasting that they had left the British Post Office in possession of a few transmitters for experimental multiple-address newscasting and marginal services, and the thriving BBC in command of its own voice-broadcasting facilities. Before the war, BBC began a vigorous program of international broadcasting of news and comment in Italian, Spanish, and Arabic, mainly to counteract Mussolini's radio broadcasting propaganda to the Arab world. To the British Ministry of Information and Reuters, the powerful worldwide press association which operated virtually as a wartime arm of MOI, certain elementary facts soon became apparent: (1) Cable and Wireless, Limited, never very much impressed with the need for speed in handling press dispatches, was becoming, thanks to its monopoly position and the exigencies of wartime, even more dilatory in handling press copy; (2) the broadcasting of news (newscasting) by dot-dash on what is known as the multiple-address principle would bring the unit cost very much lower than Cable and Wireless' 1-penny empire press rate; (3) medium- and short-wave voice radio broadcasts could reach places (occupied Europe, for example) with news beyond the practical reach of dot-dash.

Accordingly, MOI supplied BBC bountifully with news for voice broadcasts and encouraged the Post Office to build new transmitters so that Reuters could reach literally all the world with dot-dash. The results were spectacular in winning friends for a beleaguered nation and contributed powerfully to the Allied cause in occupied countries. But the fact that much of the world was seeing America's war effort through British eyes disturbed many Americans, notably the senators who, in 1943, toured the Mediterranean and Pacific battle-fronts. Assuming that Reuters' advantage stemmed from the Cable and Wireless monopoly which Reuters virtually had ceased to use (Cable and Wireless carried only 2½ per cent of Reuters' file in 1944), these senators returned to join in the clamor for a merger of this country's competing telecommunications companies.

The American telecommunications structure during the years of its rapid development following World War I assumed a form quite different from the British and, indeed, from those of all other countries. There developed actually nine American-owned but not government-owned telecommunications companies, most of which are competing for the same business. There are five major corporations, one of which competes directly with the other four in only a small marginal field confined to the point-to-point transmission of voice radio programs for rebroadcast; and four lesser ones, none of which handles much normal commercial message traffic. The five major corporations are the International Telephone and Telegraph Corporation (cable and wireless circuits); Western Union (cables and domestic telegraph circuits); Radio Corporation of America (chief radiotelegraph operator); American Telephone and Telegraph Company (telephone circuits); and Press Wireless (news circuits).

THE INTERNATIONAL NEWS-GATHERERS

PRIOR TO THE INVENTION of printing type, news traveled by word of mouth and by letter, with the choicest bits of court scandal and international intrigue reserved for the safety and embellishment of conversation. The advantages of the confidential courier were preserved long after the coming of the newspaper. In part, this was because editors appreciated that their news-gatherers were protected in the disguise of a bank clerk or a ship's captain. In part, it was because the original purchaser of the news was not an editor at all but an enterprising businessman who let the editor have it only when he could extract no further profit from its exclusiveness. In any event, although governments created the most important news, they could not control it in a society in which every other traveler might be a part-time reporter.

I. REUTER, THE PRESS ASSOCIATIONS, AND THE CARTEL

Among the most enterprising businessmen of the pretelegraph period in Europe were the Fuggers and later the Rothschilds, who had discovered early that palace-scullery gossip could sometimes be turned to account in the money mart. In the 1840's a no less enterprising German, named Paul Julius Reuter, found that homing pigeons could beat the Rothschilds' couriers. In 1851, on the advice of the Rothschilds, Reuter took his pigeons to London, where he used them to link the newfangled telegraph lines that could span everything in Europe but the Skagerrak and the English Channel.

Three things immediately became apparent to Reuter: (1) copper wire was going to revolutionize and standardize the whole news-gathering operation; (2) because this would give governments the opportunity to interfere with what was said, the wise news merchant would seek to make himself a partner and confidant of government; and (3) newspapers were becoming so numerous and so bulky that they were better wordage-volume customers than brokerage houses. Armed with such wisdom, Reuter approached the *Times* with a proposition to furnish English newspapers with Continental coverage by his staff of foreign observers. The *Times* was skeptical, but the editor of the *Advertiser* closed a shrewd bargain with him.

Within twelve months Reuter was serving a dozen newspapers in the British Isles and making money at it. But his sights were aimed higher: If the government would permit him to use the new submarine cables that were beginning to link the empire's outposts, the global news service he proposed to develop would cement British ties and help to fill the holds of British merchantmen. He may have added as an afterthought, that such a plan already had occurred to a Frenchman named Havas.

In any event the British government was quick to see the point. Reuter became a British citizen, a trusted servant without portfolio. Needless to add, Reuter's news service was careful to say at crucial points what the British government wished it to say.

Meantime, Havas, who had been rounding up Continental news for French newspapers since 1835, was also dreaming of world empire. Havas fought Reuter for a year, but the favorite of Westminster held the high trumps—the cables. Then as now, limited facilities argued limited competition. So Havas persuaded Wolff, a German agency founded in 1849, that prudence dictated dividing the world into three parts. Reuter got the British Empire, North America, a number of "suzerain" states along the Mediterranean-Suez lifeline, and most of Asia; Havas got the French empire, southwestern Europe, South America, and parts of Africa; Wolff got what was left in Europe, including Austria-Hungary, Scandinavia, and the Slav states.

Reuter soon discovered that he was in for trouble in the United States, where a number of newspaper publishers in 1848 had decided to husband their limited facilities by organizing a co-operative news-gathering agency which they styled the "Associated Press." The British government did not want trouble with America over anything touching United States sovereignty so closely and for such relatively small stakes; so Reuter convinced Havas larger stations like A.T. & T.'s WEAF elected at the outset to comply with ASCAP's demands. After a good deal of haggling and some litigation, NBC in February, 1930, signed an agreement covering WEAF, WJZ, WRC (Washington), KOA (Denver), and KGO (San Francisco), which protected the network and all its affiliates but had the effect, naturally, of discouraging the origination of musical programs by stations other than those specified.

By 1935 the sums being paid in royalties by the networks were so staggering that the National Association of Broadcasters (NAB), a trade-group formed specifically to fight inroads of this sort, began looking about for ways to lower the cost. When ASCAP in 1937 announced a rise in royalty scales, NAB redoubled its efforts to line up the industry solidly behind the networks. In September, 1939, the broadcasters decided to take a step from which they had shrunk in their feud with the press: they approved a $1,500,000 NAB war chest with which they set up Broadcast Music, Inc., to develop their own music. Meantime, ASCAP became embroiled with the Department of Justice. But when the government accepted a consent decree, the broadcasters in October, 1941, signed new contracts, based on a 1940 ASCAP offer considerably more moderate than the ultimatum of 1937: BMI had done its job. Record 1940 ASCAP royalties of $5,000,000 plummeted to $300,000 in 1941 and did not reach $3,000,000 in 1942. By 1946 the figure had climbed back to $5,000,000, but only on the basis of a much larger gross volume. For once, the industry appeared to have won a victory destined to benefit all concerned.

While they were winning that battle, however, the broadcasters were assailed from flank and rear. The spearhead of the new hosts was James Caesar Petrillo, at that time president of the Chicago local of the American Federation of Musicians (AFM). To Petrillo two things were apparent: the gains registered by the authors of popular music did not benefit the men who played it; and "live" musicians would always be indispensable to the broadcasters.

Petrillo has been denounced as a "Canute" who is determined to stay the tides of technology. His critics, both in and out of Congress, where he has been made the subject of special legislation, have never bothered to suggest what better course might be followed with respect to the 100,000 artists who entertain America nightly. Buggy-makers could be taught to turn out automobiles. But, as records and transcriptions of music cannot be made without "live" that the original partners would benefit by letting AP into the cartel, since its inclusion would enable them to cover the news of the distant republic without spending a farthing. Even so, AP was not formally admitted until 1887.

During the succeeding years there were changes and modifications of the original four-trust agreement. Smaller news agencies, such as Italy's Stefani and Belgium's Belga, sprang up, only to be forced to become satellites of Reuter or Havas. Here and there, as in the Caribbean and in Central America, Reuter and Havas agreed to share a market. AP was confined to continental United States until after the turn of the century, when it was permitted to venture into Canada and Mexico, and, toward the close of the first World War, into Central and South America. Thus it was that, from 1858 to the first World War, reporting, save in the United States, was never quite free of the taint of government propaganda.

A good many editors, particularly in America, writhed in their straitjackets. They themselves traveled abroad enough to know that they were not getting the facts. Some of the more enterprising, like James Gordon Bennett the elder, sought to gain a measure of independence from the cartel by sending special correspondents to roam the world, as the pre-Reuter couriers had done and as the individual British newspaper correspondents did. AP itself was able to place some of its correspondents in foreign capitals with the right of filing their reports directly to the United States. But it was not until a new enlargement of the telecommunications bottleneck coincided with the development of cheap newsprint and high-speed presses to focus a widespread demand for better news coverage that the cartel got its first serious warning of doom.

The break came during the first decade of the present century. The Commercial Cable Company was challenging the Western Union–British stranglehold on the Atlantic cables and preparing to buy into the new Pacific links. Radiotelegraphy was blossoming as a cheap alternative carrier, capable of carrying many thousands of words a day. The improved Hoe high-speed rotary press was shifting the balance of interest to afternoon newspapers, with their multiple split-second editions for street sales. Among the most vigorous of these afternoon papers were those of the midwestern and far western chains owned by the Scripps family, which, because of AP's exclusive-franchise agreements, could not buy that agency's service. In 1907 the Scripps organized the United Press Associations.

UP soon was joined in the anticartel fight by Hearst's International News Service. By 1914, noncartel correspondents dotted the globe, for UP and INS were not alone. Although for political reasons they would not formally break with the monopoly, venturesome British, Dutch, French, Scandinavian, and Japanese editors could and did send their own reporters forth to "supplement" the cartel's coverage. In Canada, Australia, and Japan cooperative news associations were formed, with the partial object of eliminating governmental dominance.

By dint of considerable energy and some good luck, UP by 1920 had broken the cartel front at what had been regarded as its strongest point: the non-United States news-buying market. A fortuitous friendship between a UP executive and the owners of *La Prensa* of Buenos Aires led, despite Havas' protests, to UP contracts with a number of Latin-American newspapers. At about the same time, AP extended its membership to include a number of leading South and Central American newspapers. And the forthright demand of several English provincial newspapers for something better than Reuters resulted in the formation of British United Press, an entirely British-owned association having close ties with UP, with which it exchanged news items. [Note: In 1958, UP and INS joined to form a single service, United Press International, or UPI.]

II. DIVERSIFICATION IN FOREIGN NEWS-GATHERING

Although Germany's defeat in 1918 gave Wolff's share of the cartel to Havas and Reuters, the old arrangement was finished. Struggling new agencies like Exchange Telegraph in England and Agence Radio in France had followed the UP–INS example. One-paper special correspondents were becoming commonplace in the world's principal cities. Soon their newspapers, singly or in groups, organized syndicates to sell their global coverage to less venturesome editors. Thus, such newspapers as the *London Daily Mail,* the *London Daily Express,* the *Manchester Guardian,* the *Stockholm Tidningens,* the *Berliner Tageblatt,* the *Züricher Zeitung,* *La Prensa* and *Nación* of Buenos Aires, the *Frankfurter Zeitung,* the *Petit Parisien,* the *Tokyo Nippon Dempo,* the *Philadelphia Public Ledger,* the *New York Evening Post,* the *New York World,* the *New York Herald Tribune,* the *New York Times,* and the *Chicago Daily News* branched out as small press associations in the news-selling, as well as the news-gathering, market.

During the late twenties and early thirties, foreign coverage made rapid strides both in the number of observers roaming the world and in the quality of the best of them. Magazine correspondents joined the ranks of newspapermen. As the importance of pictures increased, news photographers and newsreel cameramen began to apply for admission to the correspondents' corps. In the late thirties, radio newsmen and commentators added their eyes and voices.

The very rapid development of wireless and aviation had made possible a flow of words and pictures such as Paul Julius Reuter had never envisioned. The expansion in size and scope of existing periodicals and the creation of many new ones offered a ready outlet for the increased flow. The best of the correspondents departed from time-honored press association methods and began to dig deeply into the social patterns of the countries to which they were assigned. The invention of the "candid" camera and the perfection of fine-screen photographic printing on improved calendar magazine stock called forth a host of first-class photographers, whose art was brought to the home news desk by wire and wireless photo in a matter of minutes. Better book publishing and merchandising methods invited those who roamed the world in search of knowledge to put between the covers the best of what they found.

Again, as in Reuter's time, newer and better facilities inspired newer and better uses of the means of international communication; newer and better uses spurred a popular demand for their continuance and improvement. The independent observer and the wireless telegraph had outmoded Reuter's methods, just as Reuter's news network and the cable had outmoded the methods of his predecessors. In the early thirties, AP broke away completely from the cartel. In 1940 Havas vanished with the French armies. A year later, British newspaper proprietors took over Reuters. In 1942 Mussolini's puppet, Stefani, disappeared, to be succeeded by the Agenzia Nazionale Stampa Associata, modeled along the lines of AP and the new Reuters; and the co-operative association, Agence France Presse, rose from the ruins of the venal Havas. The fall of Deutsche Nachrichten Buro and the Japanese Domei in 1945 left only Spain's EFE and the Russian agency Tass in the field of openly government-controlled news services.

[Note: Five wire news agencies can now (1960) be classified as world agencies. These are Agence France Presse (France), Associated Press and United Press International (U.S.A.), Reuters (U.K.), and Tass (U.S.S.R.). In addition to these, over fifty national news agencies aid in distributing news.]

There is every reason to suppose that the development of wireless multiple-address press and voice broadcasting, together capable of carrying tens of thousands of words and scores of pictures daily to literally every corner of the globe at a fraction of a cent a word, will encourage a quantitative flow of information such as the world has never known. It is now possible, mechanically at least, for any publication to receive the equivalent of a hundred thousand words of foreign news daily. The ideal of trained observers roaming the universe, writing freely and fully of what they see and feel, presses impatiently against political barriers which, ironically, bid fair to stifle the flow of information in some areas at the precise moment that science has elected to make the widest flow physically practicable. Will the "irresistible" ideal shatter against the "immovable" barriers? There will be times in the near future when it will seem to in certain areas. But there will be more times and more areas where the barriers will give way. As with any other, this particular ideal will prevail to the extent that men persist through disappointment and compromise.

III. BARRIERS IN TRANSMISSION

What are the artificial barriers that impede the flow across national borders of informational raw materials? The shortcomings of the present telecommunications systems have been stressed. Obviously, the most reliable news service in the world cannot reach those who are not reached by cable or wireless; the finest magazines and books and pictures cannot reach those who are not reached by fast plane.

Virtually every nation now forbids foreign radiotelegraph companies the right to maintain their own receiving facilities within its borders. The result is that local companies, usually government owned or controlled, supply reception and internal distribution facilities at whatever rates they can command, with further delays in transmission. Although this situation does not involve multiple-address newscasts or short-wave voice broadcasts (except for automatic relay points) and although radiotelephone has worked out relatively satisfactory reciprocal arrangements for international traffic, it is a serious handicap not only to "trunk-line" news transmissions between two points but also to commercial-message traffic. *What is indicated here is a multilateral agreement, binding all nations to permit authorized wireless telegraph and cable companies (and airlines as well) to maintain suitable terminal facilities wherever they are required, subject only to the regulations binding domestic companies, or to maintain nondiscriminatory two-way connections between its own and foreign companies, as has been developed for wireless telephony.* The Bermuda agreements marked a step in this direction.

The need for automatic wireless relay points has been mentioned. These could be obtained through year-to-year leasing of foreign-owned facilities. But wartime experience with this device has shown that long-time control of the relay transmitters by the sender is the only completely satisfactory solution short of the setting-up of international relay points to be operated under the control of an international telecommunications union. Pending the more ideal solution, which does not appear to be immediately realizable, *a sound proposal would seem to involve bilateral treaties giving those nations which require relay points extra-territorial privileges under long-term lease.*

IV. ACCESS AT THE SOURCE

Meantime, there are other and more serious barriers to the free flow of informational raw materials across national frontiers. Discrimination and censorship are the two broad headings that cover those evils of which foreign correspondents (and natives, too, for that matter) most often complain. What do newspapermen mean by these terms?

In Nazi Germany reporters could not wander about at will, writing of what they saw and felt. Doktor Goebbels and his press section gave them stereotyped handouts, took them on stereotyped trips. The parts of Germany and German-occupied lands that they did not see were the special province not merely of German newsmen but of "reliable" German newsmen. The defeat of Germany brought an end to Goebbels; but correspondents may face precisely the same type of discrimination, in varying degree, for a long time to come in Russia and the Russian "spheres" in Europe and Asia and in Spain, China, various Latin-American countries, Saudi Arabia, and certain parts of the British, French, Belgian, and Netherlands empires.

It is characteristic of the one-party type of government to fear criticism and to make provisions to exclude it, on the pious ground that not all reporters have the mental capacity to criticize fairly. This is the antithesis of the democratic view. Experience in the United States, Canada, the United Kingdom, Australia and New Zealand, France, Belgium, the Netherlands, Denmark, Norway, Sweden, and Switzerland has built up a reassuring body of evidence that unfair critics sooner or later defeat their own purposes. It may be useless to try to convince Russia and the others that this is so. The Russians already have made it clear that they think Americans and Britons are foolish to permit newsmen so much freedom, and they can quote more than one recent instance of our newsmen's harmful irresponsibility. Reminders from friendly British and American newspapermen that secrecy in itself is likely to breed unwarranted suspicion and give rise to imaginative "news stories" about Russia of the familiar type which, in the twenties and thirties, usually bore Riga datelines apparently do not move the Narkomindell.

In pre-1939 Britain, France, and many another land by tradition devoted to the principle of a free press, it was not uncommon for government officials to show marked preference to a few hand-picked native reporters and even fewer foreigners. The London papers, for instance, felt the pressure of the Chamberlain government during the appeasement period and responded to it to some extent. The Germans made an effort to systematize this practice. Prior to World War I, a Foreign Office press chief named Hammann was permitted to organize a loose affiliation to a few chosen German newspapermen to "interpret" German foreign policy to the German people. The plan does not appear to have been an unqualified success, in part because newspapers which were left out tended to become even more critical and also because the favored few, which happened to include liberal opposition papers, frequently declined to follow the official line.

The Hammann technique per se will not be tolerated by most newspapermen. But favoritism for individuals (and sometimes even for groups) is widely practiced not only by all governments (including our own) but by private corporations and individuals as well. Actually, newspapermen connive at forming such useful contacts. Indeed, one suspects that the clamor against discrimination of this sort is loudest from those who have been outwitted by it. It becomes impressive only when, as in Russia, it affects all foreigners equally and thus becomes an instrument of anti-internationalism. It is less impressive when newspapermen roll the phrase "equal and unhampered access to all" off their tongues; for every newspaperman must know that equal access would reduce every story to a mass press conference or a mimeographed handout.

What newspapermen really want is what Kent Cooper, former executive director of AP, calls "the right to roam the world at will, writing freely of what they see and feel." This is quite a different thing. It means that what they want is an equal opportunity to use their wits to create *unequal* access. Within that rather broad framework, they want assurances that certain areas will not be open habitually to the few and closed to the many; that news-givers will carefully distinguish between timely news breaks and background material and will confine their special favors to the latter field; and that in the case of "hold-for-release" stories the release date will be scrupulously respected. Newsmen are not always sure even of these things, for in essence these things represent a compromise between the ever warring considerations of security and opportunity that beset anyone engaged in highly competitive private industry. Sorely tempted, a *New York Times'* Raymond Daniell will join a pool to receive Army favors; a *New York Herald Tribune's* Theodore Wallen will beseech a Calvin Coolidge to make an "I do not choose to run" news break exclusive; an AP's Edward Kennedy will double-cross his colleagues by breaking a release date. In sum, carte blanche is the maximum that newsmen dream about, equality of opportunity the minimum for which they will settle.

Either is, of course, more difficult of achievement than mere equal access. Both suggest the need for a degree of organized responsibility on the part of newsmen from which they shrink, using the excuse that freedom of the press does not permit of much self-discipline. The apparent paradox has been shrewdly remarked by the Russians; and there is reason to believe that, as long as it persists, it will be a convenient barrier for Moscow to raise against the democracies in the field of international communication. To press for mass interviews and stereotyped handouts, simply because Russia would be more likely to grant such a demand than any other, would be a disservice alike to the correspondents and to their readers. One is tempted to conclude that any deviation from the expressed ultimate goal of "the right to roam the world at will" would lend credence to Moscow's charge that what the newsmen of the democracies are after is simply a chance to make a little more money. A more honorable strategy would appear to be to hold out for the maximum while admonishing the correspondents to grow up to it and, at the same time, frankly recognize that unsettled conditions during the next few years will not be conducive to achievement of the maximum. *This would seem to involve urging a multilateral accord guaranteeing equality of access as between nationals and foreigners*—knowing that the more enterprising in both categories would use that type of equality to get ahead of their fellows.

How, in the meantime, could those who wish to roam the world and write (or photograph) meet the objection of irresponsibility? *One way might be to tighten the foreign correspondents' corps; adopt a code of professional behavior; and require all newsmen, magazine writers, radio people, authors, and photographers who join the corps to observe its code. Appeals from decisions of a government could be taken by the whole corps rather than by an individual, either to the foreign diplomatic corps or to an appropriate unit of the United Nations Economic and Social Council.* A resolute move in this direction might dispose of the contradiction of newsmen asking for group protection while at the same time declining to organize group responsibility.

V. CENSORSHIP

The right to roam the world at will, writing freely, would seem to imply also the right to get what is written to the market. Here we run into another barrier—censorship. Actually, censorship begins at the level of discrimination at the source. But in general usage it is taken to mean the emasculation or total suppression of written and printed matter, pictures and films, and words spoken over a microphone or telephone.

Here, again, the authoritarian powers have been the worst offenders. Before the war, Russia, China, Spain, Portugal, Italy, Germany, Japan, and a number of Latin-American countries openly practiced deletion and suppression. But they did not practice it in the same way. Whereas in Russia correspondents were summoned to discuss cuts and suppressions with the censor who had made them and on occasion were even able to argue him into restoring some of them, in Italy they never knew until they had a chance to check with their home offices from outside what had got through.

More than frank and open censorship itself, newsmen detest the subtler forms. In a sense they have become hardened to a degree of the forthright variety (when a government or corporation official says "Now that's strictly off the record, boys," he automatically becomes a censor); but the honest, conscientious ones will never become resigned to a mixture of censorship, evasion, intimidation, and deceit. They do not like being visited by police who want to "check their papers." They do not like being beaten up in dark alleys. They do not like having their dispatches lie around in telegraph offices until, like ripe fruit, they have lost all market value. They do not like having their houses searched, their families annoyed or terrorized. They do not like clumsy offers of bribes or subtle hints that they might last longer if they were "more correct." But what they like least of all is being forever in the dark, never knowing what the "rules" are, always wondering when they go to work in the morning what they will be able to "get away with" on that particular day.

What can be done to abolish, or at any rate curb, censorship? *A logical first step might be to press for a multilateral agreement pledging the signatories to keep newsmen informed of the rules by which they expect to operate and to abide by them.* If such an agreement could be reached, the climate might encourage *a second and simultaneous step: agreement to limit censorship wherever and as long as it exists to the open deletion or suppression of dispatches in the presence of the writer.* There is little reason to suppose that Russia, which appears to be the key to any multilateral agreement of this sort, would refuse to adhere to either of these provisions. At a favorable moment Moscow might even subscribe to *a third condition: right of appeal by the writer to the correspondents' corps and through it to the United Nations Economic and Social Council.* Meantime, with the ultimate goal of complete abolition of censorship always before us, we could whittle away at the Russian variety, *either through limited multilateral agreement or through a series of bilateral treaties*—although it must be obvious that the former would almost certainly be interpreted by Russia as a revised manifestation of the *cordon sanitaire.*

VI. BARRIERS IN DISTRIBUTION

The right to roam and write would seem to imply not only the right to get to the market what is written but also the right to sell it there without unjust discrimination. This brings us to another barrier: insistence on interposing a middleman (usually government-controlled) between the wholesaler (press association, news-picture agency, or feature syndicate) and the retailer (newspaper, magazine, or radio station). AP, UP, INS, Reuters, ANSA, and AFP announced that henceforth [after 1946] they would deal only with reputable individual newspapers, magazines, and radio stations or with bona fide associations of reputable newspapers, magazines, and radio stations. *Except for bilateral pacts, which would have the effect of blessing such arangements,* it is difficult to see what might be accomplished by formal convention at this time, since obviously, those who wish to do business in Russia and China will be obliged to deal with government agencies, as AP and Reuters are doing. One factor which ought to do much to discourage middleman monopolies is multiple-address newscasting, which will bring uncensored news to the very borders of monopoly-ridden countries—and even enable the more daring publishers there, by listening in, to check what their governments give them against what the rest of the world is getting.

What of finished products in international communication, as distinguished from the raw material and semifinished goods? How are newspapers, magazines, books, short-wave radio programs, and motion pictures to be circulated across national frontiers in greater numbers? What are the barriers that presently limit this useful flow?

THE PRINTED WORD

The circulation of printed newspapers across national frontiers dates back to the very beginning of newspaperdom, when every ship brought weeks-old copies from foreign ports which were eagerly scanned by government bureaus and liberally borrowed from by editors who had no better way of getting foreign news. Except for limited areas divided by political but not language barriers or as between mother-countries and their colonies, newspapers were not designed for or shipped in sufficient numbers to reach mass audiences directly. With the development of press agencies, editors began to watch for them less eagerly. In the latter part of the nineteenth century a handful of ambitious publishers founded foreign editions, notably James Gordon Bennett's *New York Herald* and Lord Northcliffe's *London Daily Mail*, both in Paris. But these were edited for, and distributed among, nationals of the countries of origin living abroad; and those natives who deciphered them in the hope of improving their knowledge of other peoples were not usually repaid for their pains. After 1900 a number of independent papers like the *Japan Advertiser*, the *Shanghai Post and Mercury*, and the *Manila Times* were launched by and for aliens of the countries in which they were published. Not until the mid-1930's did it occur to governments to try to reach foreign mass audiences directly through the press—and even then the Germans, Italians, Russians, and Japanese preferred the time-honored technique of hiding behind the mastheads of local organs.

The interchange of printed magazines followed much the same pattern. In the 1920's, however, a number of British, American, and German magazine publishers went into the foreign market with the idea of reaching foreigners rather than expatriates. Their publications fell into two classes: women's magazines like the British Amalgamated group's *Woman's World*, which tried a Paris edition; Condé Nast's British and French *Vogue* and French *Jardin des Modes* (German and Spanish *Vogues* were launched in the thirties, quickly scuttled when they did not pan out); Hearst's British editions of *Good Housekeeping, Harper's Bazaar,* and *Connoisseur*; the German *Die Dame*, which circulated widely in Switzerland and eastern Europe—and "pulps" like Macfadden's British, French, German, and Swedish editions of *True Story*.

The war and a number of technical developments have wrought many changes in the techniques of circulating printed newspapers and magazines. Governments were brought into the international publishing business on a scale hitherto undreamed of—thanks, in no small part, to the amazing recent improvements in aviation and offset printing. The German *Signal* at one time boasted a circulation of 7,000,000 outside Germany. Up to 1945 the OWI's *Victory*, by then jointly sponsored by *Collier's*, had sold 26,000,000 copies in fifteen languages in forty-six countries. The OIAA's *En Guardia* had sold 8,000,000 in two languages in sixteen countries. A score of British and Russian publications had reached comparable totals. Moreover, the war (as well as technological improvements) supplied the spur to a number of private publishers. Thus, at the beginning of 1946, *Reader's Digest* was printing British, Spanish (for Spain), Spanish (for Latin America), Portuguese (for Portugal), Portuguese (for Brazil), Swedish, and Finnish-language editions. *Time, Life,* and *Newsweek* had fourteen, one, and five foreign editions, respectively. *Magazine Digest,* a rapidly growing Canadian monthly, seven-eighths of whose 1,250,000 readers live in the United States, was going forward with plans for several foreign-language editions. The *New York Herald Tribune* and the *London Daily Mail* had revived their Paris editions. The *London Times* was flying a pony edition (greatly reduced in size and printed on thin stock) around the world.

But there were evidences of contraction as well as expansion. The *New York Post,* which entered the Paris afternoon field in August, 1945, was withdrawing for want of American readers. And the *New York Times* apparently was not pushing plans for worldwide facsimile circulation, although its experiments with a facsimile edition at the San Francisco United Nations Conference were mechanically successful and of great value to the conference. [Note: The *New York Times* is now publishing an edition in Amsterdam.]

The immediate future for international circulation of newspapers and magazines is far from clear. Government publications (in the United States, at any rate—although the State Department has continued *Amerika,* published especially for Russia) did not survive the war. On the other hand, there is an embarrassment of mechanical alternatives which clouds the picture. The sheer bulk and weight of standard-size publications makes their shipment in large quantities by air impracticable. Thus publishers must choose between flying pony editions and printing abroad. Those who elect to print abroad will have a variety of means for getting their copy and pictures to the plant. Whole pages in as many as four colors and in any desired language can be dispatched by wireless in a few minutes. Time, Incorporated, has developed a secret mat of the color and consistency of cellophane, which compresses an entire issue of *Time* or *Life* into a packet which a plane pilot could store in his cap. Printing plates for rotary or flat-bed presses can be pulled with equal facility from facsimile prints or the *Time* mats.

Thus the ease with which periodicals now can be whisked across national borders opens up a prospect of lively competition in this field. What barriers are the enterprising publishers likely to encounter? And how seriously should we take them?

One may eliminate the normal problems that beset foreign-owned business in any country: taxes, licensing, labor troubles, the complicated mechanics of nonpostal distribution which sometimes even in this country involve the payment of premiums to handlers and dealers, local laws requiring the hiring of a certain percentage of natives, and the like. Publishers have somehow got around such obstacles in the past. It is possible that here and there they will be treated worse than native publishers. When that happens, the wise publisher will set up a native subsidiary, with a few prominent native leaders on its board, as Condé Nast did in Paris and London before the war; or publish in a smaller but conveniently located country where the attitude toward business is benevolent, as *Reader's Digest* did in several countries.

. . . .

The flow of books across national frontiers has followed a discernible pattern for the last century, with Britain, Germany, France, and Spain vying for leadership and the United States trailing far behind even such smaller countries as Sweden, Switzerland, and the Netherlands. . . . In general this has reflected a combination of language advantages (the Swiss, Swedes, and Dutch have worked extensively in German) and a spirit of enterprise. The Germans believed that if they bombarded school children with scientific and technical books, the children would grow up thinking of Germany as the logical supplier of the types of goods advertised therein. The British, for two centuries blessed with a virtual monopoly of the market for books originally written in English, were a little slow to see the literal truth of the Leipzig *Börsenverein's* slogan, "Trade follows the book," but are rapidly making amends for their omission. Both British and American publishers were slow to match Spain's traditional cultural ties with Latin America and France's cultural ties with the whole literate world by launching their campaign to make English the lingua franca of the twentieth century. Indeed, it might fairly be said that American publishers were slow to see the value of book exports from any standpoint. No other satisfactory reason can be found for the fact that they allowed themselves to be maneuvered into a position with respect to reprint and translation rights which returns them less than an equitable share of the republisher's profit or for their failure to obtain United States adherence to some equitable international copyright agreement.

The explanation for the adverse reprint situation may have been at one time historically sound. In the early days of our country, we were almost wholly dependent on Europe for books. Until toward the close of the last century the number of books by American authors wanted in Europe was so small compared to the number of books by European authors wanted in America that publishers in this country readily agreed to terms that injured both them and their writers. When the tide began to change, American authors took matters into their own hands and extracted royalty arrangements from the British which made them quite independent of any action by American publishers. The publishers, in consequence, took no action, since they regarded the export business as a "2 per cent nuisance" anyway. Moved by this same spirit of indifference, American publishers for many years have permitted the objections, first of the Typesetters Union and latterly of the radio-broadcasting industry, to keep the United States almost alone among leading nations from adhering to the Berne Convention—with the result that American publishers have lost tangible tens of thousands of dollars through the wholesale pirating, notably by the Dutch and Chinese, of books entirely without legal protection outside the United States and its possessions, and with the further result that the United States has permitted the pirating of foreign authors—a circumstance which seriously dilutes American claims to morality and a respect for culture. The Berne Convention is a model of the kind of international agreement which eliminates barriers in a whole area of mass communication. It provides simply that books copyrighted in any signatory country are protected by the copyright in all other signatory countries.

The coming of the cheap paper-bound reprint edition in this country, which has already lowered the forbidding price barrier to mass circulation of books in many countries, may make it possible for more books to flow across national borders than ever before.

. . . .

INTERNATIONAL BROADCASTS

The projection across national boundaries of voice broadcasts is, as has been noted, largely a phenomenon of the thirties, although amateurs experimented with short wave for much longer. International broadcasting does not necessarily connote direct broadcasting, as nations can exchange programs by mail, cable, radiotelegraph, or radiotelephone for rebroadcast over local facilities. Before the war, American stations concentrated on this method for reaching Latin America, leaving Germany, Britain, Russia, France, and Japan to bring direct short- or medium-wave broadcasting to a peak never approached in the Western Hemisphere. . . .

[Note: In the 1950's international shortwave broadcasting reached a new peak. In particular, the United States, Britain, and the Soviet Union were active in this field, but more than fifty countries were pouring regular broadcasts into other countries. Heavy "jamming" by the Iron Curtain countries was a feature of the radio "war."]

MOTION-PICTURE EXPORTS

The history of the international flow of motion pictures is unique. From the end of the first World War, when earlier bids for mastery by the Swedes and later the British had subsided, until recently, the flow was almost entirely one way: from Hollywood to every habitable part of the globe. From the early 1920's until the mid-thirties, a score of countries seeking to establish their own infant industries fought Hollywood's domination without success. The most obvious government subsidy and protection could not obscure the fact that Hollywood had the most successful writers, the most skillful directors, the ablest cameramen, the best-known stars, and, because it paid the highest salaries, the best chance of picking off foreign stars as soon as they began to show promise. In vain did governments raise import duties and taxes on the operations of those distributing agencies they could reach, institute quotas which required that a certain number of homemade pictures be shown for every American import, devise elaborate fees for the dubbing-in of sound-track in the language of the country by native artists, and extend loans to their own producers. The foreign public wanted Hollywood films and was prepared to make trouble for any government that sought to shut them off altogether. Foreign exhibitors wanted full houses so they could pay their rent, and their landlords wanted the rent. As an example of how a uniquely popular product can override the stiffest protectionism, Hollywood's success was to be compared with that of the French dressmakers and perfume manufacturers.

The coming of talking pictures proved to be a turning-point. Pantomimists like Charlie Chaplin and Buster Keaton, who had been the idols of all the world, dropped from their pinnacles. The emphasis in Hollywood shifted from gesturing to fast-paced dialogue, much of it in an idiom that defied translation. Musical pictures became practicable for the first time. And for the first time Hollywood's rivals found themselves able to compete on something approaching equal terms. Who could sing German *lieder* better than a German? Who could tickle Gallic risibilities better than a Frenchman? It remained only to learn how to produce better pictures mechanically; and in the thirties British and French cameramen and directors who had been concentrating on national audiences began to switch to Hollywood's tried and true formulas to win international favor. Rising young stars like Michael Redgrave, Ralph Richardson, Googie Withers, Esmond Knight, Jean Gabin, and Michele Morgan and veterans like Raimu and Louis Jouvet turned their backs on Hollywood gold (it was the fall of France, not the lure of riches, that brought Gabin and Mlle. Morgan to this country).

The result was better pictures. But the trend was established so shortly before the outbreak of war that few persons even in Hollywood realized the extent to which it was likely to accelerate after the war. Russian and Swedish, as well as British and French, pictures are improving. Mexico has built up a thriving industry which already is giving American distributors some trouble in Latin America. There is little question that Hollywood is in for a type of competition that will make discriminatory government edicts all the more burdensome. The Department of Commerce listed fifty-eight separate legal restrictions adversely affecting Hollywood's export business at the outset of the war. Few have since been rescinded. Indeed, in the United Kingdom, France, and the Netherlands they have been added to and stiffened. The United Artists' general manager for South Africa, returning in August, 1945, from a fifty-thousand-mile tour of Africa, the Middle East, India, and China, reported that, although American films still were received enthusiastically, new and complex barriers were being raised against them. He discovered that the Russians were financing construction of theaters in several countries through "extremely lenient long-term loans" made with the condition that the theater-owners devote at least 15 per cent of their programs to Soviet pictures.

From the standpoint of promoting the circulation of motion pictures as instruments of understanding, it is difficult to see what can be done—or should be done—to arrest this righting of the balance. The effect of the present trend may very well be to give

Americans and others a chance to see more British, Canadian, Swedish, French, Russian, and Latin-American films; and it could scarcely be argued that this would be a bad thing for international understanding. Moreover, the American film industry cannot boast, as can the American press associations, for example, that it leads the world in informational quality. Whatever Hollywood may say about our being admired throughout the world because we have not consciously tried to put our best foot forward in films, the consensus of Americans who lived and traveled abroad during the period between the wars seems to be that American movies have hindered more than furthered an understanding of us. Finally, the United States is hardly in a position to lead a crusade for free trade.

THE GROWTH OF TELEVISION

BY LEO BOGART

Dr. Bogart, a sociologist, is director of marketing research for Revlon, Inc., in New York. This is the first chapter in his book *The Age of Television* (New York: Frederick Ungar, 1958). It is reprinted here by permission of the author and publisher, who holds copyright.

ON THE EVENING of March 7, 1955, one out of every two Americans was watching Mary Martin play "Peter Pan" before the television cameras. Never before in history had a single person been seen and heard by so many others at the same time. The vast size of the audience was a phenomenon in itself as fantastic as any fairy tale. The age of television had arrived.

In the stream of history, a great invention is always both effect and cause. It arises from the existing base of knowledge and technology, and from the kinds of questions which the challenges of life in his place and time suggest to the curious mind of the inventor. Once it has come into being, the invention acquires a dynamism of its own, merging with a thousand other forces and events to set in motion new ways of action and thought.

Television broadcasting as it exists in America today is not merely the product of a science which has mastered mysteries of light and sound and electronics. It is also the creature of an economy capable of producing and distributing goods on a massive scale and of a society so complex that its business cannot be handled by face-to-face communication.

THE MASS MEDIA AND THE GREAT SOCIETY

America in the mid-twentieth century is the supreme embodiment of what social philosophers since Adam Smith have characterized as the Great Society, and which they have contrasted with the simpler life of our ancestors or "primitive" contemporaries. This is a society in which people assemble in large aggregations, in which wealth grows through the increased productivity made possible by a division of labor. But as work becomes specialized, and as the tempo of life is speeded, the relations between human beings change their character.

It is no accident that the invention of the printing press and the discovery of America were products of the same half-century. There is also no cause for surprise in the fact that television and controlled atomic fission came as parallel discoveries. As the world acquires new vistas it becomes more intricate. There is more being done and a consciousness of more to be done: more information needed and more information to communicate. Modern industrial technology has made possible the reproduction of communications on a massive scale. The linotype, the rotary press, the motion picture camera, and the vacuum tube all provide a basis for reaching vast audiences.

In a more complex world of specialized tasks and lessening distances, the ties between a man and his next-door neighbors may be less important than those which bind him to fellows of his own profession or hobby or taste. As the social bonds of traditional community living have weakened, the mass media have created a new set of common interests and loyalties. They offer a new kind of shared experience, in which millions can laugh at the same jokes, feel the same thrills and anxieties, and respond to the same heroes.

Mass media are possible only where mass-produced symbols are meaningful. In a world of standardized goods, it is to be expected that entertainment should be dispensed through impersonal commercial agencies rather than through the intimate channels of conversation and play that prevail in more simple communities. With no other form of impersonal communication has the sharing of experience been possible on so universal a scale and to so intense a degree as with television.

TOWARD A MIDDLE-CLASS SOCIETY

In the last century, technological growth has brought about far-reaching changes in the American economy and in the American style of life. The United States is today a "middle-class" country not only in its income but in its values.

While the 1930 census showed 30% of the population in white-collar jobs, the figure had grown to 37% in 1950. In the last twenty-five years the number of professional men has more than doubled; managers and proprietors have grown in numbers by one-half. Proportionately fewer people run small family businesses; more work for big companies. Less than half the work force is engaged in making or growing things.

Whereas only one person in five had a middle-class standard of life or better in 1929, one in two had achieved this by 1952. (*Fortune* magazine estimates 20% of all U.S. families had an income of $4000 or over after taxes in 1929; 49% were in this bracket in 1952—using constant 1952 dollar values.) Real income—in purchasing power—is about 50% higher per person today than it was just before World War II. Between 1929 and 1957, real disposable income per household grew from $4373 to $4900 (in 1947 dollars), while households grew smaller (from 4.1 to 3.3 persons apiece). Women in ever-increasing numbers have entered the labor force, raising the total income of millions of families.

Americans today are better educated than their parents. Children stay in school longer, and succeeding generations have become constantly better educated. By 1950, 52% of the adult population had been to high school or college; before the war only 39% had gone this far in their education. Today, of every three persons of college age, one is actually attending college.

Improved education, like higher income, carries the implication of a change in outlook. So does the changing distribution of the population. Americans are more heavily concentrated in large metropolitan areas than they ever were in the past, but increasingly they move to the suburbs rather than the central cities. By 1956, a fifth of the total population was living in the suburbs of metropolitan areas, with an additional 8% in semi-suburban communities. Between 1940 and 1950, the proportion of families who owned their own homes went from 44% to 55%. While population grew by one-fourth in the last quarter-century, the number of households grew by one-half.

To a greater extent than ever before, the distinctions in income between white-collar and manual workers have been diminishing under labor union pressure, and the distinctions in style of life are also tending to disappear. Studies made by Macfadden Publications show few differences in the buying patterns of wage-earner and white-collar households in the same neighborhoods. This point has been well described by Frederic Dewhurst and his associates of the Twentieth Century Fund:

The banker or well-to-do businessman of the 1890's dressed and acted the part. He rode in his own carriage, driven by a hired coachman. The man of modest income, whether farmer or mechanic, also dressed and acted the part. Although the farmer drove to town with his own horse and buggy, the bicycle was the only form of personal transportation the city worker could afford—as it is today even in the more advanced European countries. Today American farmers and city dwellers, those well-off and those in modest circumstances, drive their own cars. The debutante of half a century ago was distinguishable at a distance from her unfortunate sister who had to work for a living. Today they both wear nylon stockings and fur coats and although there may still be a big difference in the cost of their wardrobes, it takes a discerning feminine eye to tell them apart.

As to the typical products that have transformed the household during the past half-century, the upper and lower income groups both use the same vacuum cleaners, refrigerators, deep-freezers, oil burners, gas and electric stoves, radios and television sets. Their homes may have much the same kind of bathroom equipment and plumbing and lighting fixtures. They read the same newspapers and magazines, go to the same movies, listen to the same radio and television programs. They smoke the same brands of cigarettes, drink the same frozen orange juice, eat the same canned, frozen or out-of-season fresh food, bought at the same supermarket.

The far-reaching changes which have taken place on the American scene have prepared the way for the growth of television:

1. The expansion of purchasing power, and the creation of a vast demand for the amenities of life made it possible for people to acquire television sets rapidly and on an enormous scale—41,000,000 in a dozen years.

2. The vast growth of the American economy also made possible a huge advertising investment in the new medium, and provided commercial backing for its high programming costs.

3. The concentration of population into metropolitan areas made it economically possible to bring television quickly to great numbers of people, in spite of the short range of TV signals (compared to radio) and in spite of the financial and legal obstacles to the rapid construction of stations in outlying smaller towns.

4. The levelling of social differences is part of a standardization of tastes and interests to which the mass media give expression, and to which they also contribute. The ubiquitous TV antenna is a symbol of people seeking—and getting—the identical message.

THE GROWTH OF LEISURE

The increased fruitfulness of the American economy has made life more pleasant by bringing more of its comforts within the budgetary reach of the average man; it has also given people more time to spend at their own discretion. Until relatively most recent times, life for most people in Europe and America was a steady alternation of work and sleep, with little time for the luxuries of art or entertainment.

Over the last century, both the conditions and philosophy of work have changed. "Honest toil" is no longer accepted as the principal mission of man on earth. A hundred years ago, woman's work was never done and men sweated in farm, factory, and office virtually from dawn to dusk. Today leisure gives signs of replacing work as the main focus of living. The great growth in leisure has meant a rising demand and an increasing opportunity for the mass media. It has given Americans the many hours which they now spend watching television.

There are two principal reasons why people today have more free time on their hands:

1. They are spending fewer and fewer hours at work, because of a steady decline in the average length of the work week and a constant increase in vacation and holiday time. A century ago the average work week was 70 hours. It will be 37½ hours by 1960. For every waking hour the average American worker spends at his job each week he has two to spend at his discretion. Part of this must go for transportation, eating, and life's necessary tasks, but the bulk of it is free for him to follow his own bent.

2. Apart from work, life in mid-twentieth century America is more convenient for most people than it ever was in most other times and places. Labor-saving gadgets and devices have reduced

the modern housewife's burdens. Her chores are more quickly done, even though she is less likely to have the aid of a domestic servant than was her mother or grandmother.

A few examples will illustrate the extent of the transformation: By 1950 four American homes in every five had mechanical refrigerators; seven in ten had a gas or electric range; seven in ten had electric washing machines (and an additional 12% used self-service laundries); three in five had vacuum cleaners. These proportions are greater now, and are still growing.

Thermostats and automatic stokers make furnace-tending less painful (and time-consuming) for the head of the household. The power lawnmower and the automatic dishwasher have lightened even the children's chores.

Fashions in eating have changed, as popular recipes stress rapid preparation, and as prepackaged and frozen foods have made cooking easier and more efficient. And actually, more meals are being eaten in restaurants. Self-service stores now account for nine dollars of every ten spent for groceries. (They represented three dollars in five in 1946, three in ten in 1939.) Shopping in supermarkets is quicker than the old style of personal service, and the self-service principle is being constantly extended beyond the grocery field. The development of suburban shopping centers has saved still more time for millions of families.

One woman in every five is working today—and the majority of the women who work are married. A study made by the General Electric Company shows that these working housewives manage to spend nearly three-fourths as much time on their household chores as the full-time housewives do, and they spend nearly as much time in social activity. However, they spend only half as much time on personal maintenance and in relaxation.

The increase of leisure, it should be noted, has not set limits for the growth of the media. Radio, and to some extent television, can claim more than free time; they get into the hours of work. Radio follows the housewife as she does her chores and brightens the hours of the worker or shop clerk at his job.

The rise of the mass media cannot be explained merely as an effect of the growth of the leisure time. There has also been a reciprocal effect. The mass media have themselves spread popular awareness of what constitutes a good life. By making the good life familiar, they have made it seem possible (as well as desirable) for the great masses of people. They have offered glimpses of a life apart from work, a life more genteel or interesting than most of the audience knows first-hand, but one into which it can readily project its imagination. To varying degrees, people model themselves after the idealized characters who figure in TV or film dramas, in magazine short stories and in cigarette ads. The mass media have thus supported a system of values which encourages striving for greater achievement, which is expressed in more wealth and more leisure.

With more people, more money to spend and more free time, all the media have shown a phenomenal growth, and this growth has continued for a generation, apart from a setback during the Depression years. Today four Americans in five read magazines and daily newspapers, and they read more copies of both than were ever before published. The number of newspapers sold every day is greater than the number of households. In total, magazines sell almost as many copies per issue as there are people to read them.

. . . .

Radio is now in virtually every home in America, in two-thirds of the 54,000,000 passenger cars on the road, and in 10,000,000 public places. Television, when it first arrived, rode in on the crest of a rising wave of interest in the existing media.

THE GROWTH OF TELEVISION

Television today is a firmly established feature of American life. It is present in four out of five U.S. homes, and within reception range of all but 3%. Because of the increase in population, there are actually more homes with television sets today than there were homes with radios just before the beginning of World War II. This entire growth has taken place in less than a decade.

Television's history goes back much further than the post-war era. It was first developed in the '20s and '30s. Its real development did not begin until the perfection of an electronic scanning device and picture tube by Vladimir Zworykin in 1931 eliminated the need for a cumbersome scanning disc. In an address before the Radio Manufacturers' Association in October, 1938, David Sarnoff declared that "television in the home is now technically feasible."

Not everyone agreed. The magazine Radio Guide sent its friends a century plant seed wrapped in cellophane, with a note that read: "Plant it in a pot, water it carefully, expose it to the sunlight. When it blossoms, throw the switch on the new television cabinet that your grandson will have bought and you may expect to see telecasts offering program quality and network coverage comparable to that of our broadcasts of today."

The following year the National Broadcasting Company began telecasting from the New York World's Fair, and the Columbia Broadcasting System and Allen B. DuMont laboratories went on the air soon afterwards. The Federal Communications Commission approved commercial television for July 1, 1941. By the end of the year there were half a dozen commercial television stations in the United States (three in New York) and approximately 10,000 television sets, half of them in New York. Department stores began to advertise sets and assembly kits were on sale to radio enthusiasts who wanted to put them together themselves.

Development of television was interrupted by the war, with the heavy diversion of electronic parts and equipment to military use. During this period no new television sets were sold, and production got off to a slow start after hostilities ended. By January, 1948, there were 102,000 sets in the nation, two-thirds of them in New York. By April the number of sets had more than doubled. During that year nearly a million television sets were manufactured, compared with 179,000 in 1947, and 6500 in 1946.

Television broadcasting developed swiftly under the aegis of the major radio networks who invested millions of dollars in what was destined to be an unprofitable enterprise for its first few years. There were 24 stations on the air in 15 cities. The first television network linked New York, Schenectady, and Philadelphia for nightly sponsored shows.

The expansion of television was interrupted in September, 1948, by the Federal Communications Commission, which ordered a "freeze" on new station permits. The purpose of this move was to allow time to study and work out the problems of allocating enough channel assignments to make the medium truly national in scope. To avoid interference in transmission, F.C.C. rules permitted no two stations closer than 190 miles apart to broadcast on the same channel. With only 12 channels available, this set very tight limits on the number of possible stations. During the period of the "freeze," which lasted until July, 1952, television was confined to 63 major metropolitan areas, and was within reception range of nearly three-fifths of the U.S. population. In these areas the number of sets grew steadily as mass production brought prices down and as program quality improved. This improvement in turn reflected the growth of the audience, which made the medium more attractive to advertisers. It also was helped by the spreading system of co-axial telephone cables linking stations in different cities and thus bringing entertainment of national network caliber directly to local stations.

The lifting of the "freeze" brought about a new boom in television as seventy new channels in the ultra-high frequency (U.H.F.) band were added to the original twelve in the very-high frequency (V.H.F.) range. Movies, newspapers, magazines, and radio had made television familiar even to those parts of the country which had never seen it. As a result, television did not have to go through the slow stages of growth it had undergone in the areas where it had first been introduced. Cities caught "TV fever" as new stations opened up. Elaborate promotional efforts stimulated a high degree of popular excitement and enthusiasm, and many sets were sold even before the stations came on the air.

Unlike AM radio signals, which can be received over considerable distances, television coverage is limited to a radius of somewhere between thirty and one hundred miles of the transmitting antenna. The reception range is affected by such things as the height of the antenna, the power of the transmitter, the channel on which the signal is broadcast, and the character of the terrain. Since a station can only serve a limited territory in the vicinity of the city in which it is located, the smaller cities and more sparsely populated areas had no television long after the major metropolitan centers had a number of stations.

The equipment required to set up a station is expensive. Operation and programming are far more costly for television than for radio. A station supported by advertising must necessarily have a substantial number of potential viewers within range of its transmitter in order to produce sufficient revenues to pay for its high construction and operating costs. Nonetheless, the number of stations has continued to grow, though the growth has shown signs of tapering off.

In its short life, commercial television has risen to about the same dimensions (in number of homes) that radio had achieved by the end of World War II. About fifteen years after the beginning of commercial radio broadcasting, three-fourths of the homes in the

TABLE 1. Growth of Homes Owning Radio and Television

	Total U.S. Homes	Radio Homes *(in millions)*	TV Homes	Per Cent in TV Coverage Area	Per Cent Owning Radio	TV
1925	27.4	2.7	–	–	10%	–
1930	30.0	13.8	–	–	46	–
1935	31.9	21.5	–	–	67	–
1940	34.8	28.5	–	–	82	–
1945	37.6	33.1	–	–	88	–
1950	42.9	40.8	3.1	56%	95	7%
1951	44.2	41.9	10.0	60	95	23
1952	44.7	43.3	16.0	62	97	37
1953	45.6	45.2	21.2	67	99	46
1954	47.6	46.6	27.7	95	98	58
1955	47.8	47.0	32.0	97	98	67
1956	48.0	47.0	35.1	97	98	73
1957	50.0	48.5	41.0	97	98	82

Source: A. C. Nielsen Co., NBC, CBS.

United States were radio-equipped. Television has reached the same proportion in less than a decade. By 1950, radio had reached a virtual saturation point; it was present in 95 homes out of a hundred. But television will probably arrive at this level long before another fifteen years have passed.

Television's growth in the near future will not continue as rapidly as in the recent past. There are two reasons for this:

1. Television grew fast as it came to new parts of the country. But the stations just starting up, and those which will start in the future, are mostly in smaller cities already within range of TV transmitters in other places.

2. The initial growth of television took place most slowly among families who were least able to afford it, and also in very small families, especially childless ones, where there was least demand for it. Many of these families will continue to get along without TV for a while.

In the dozen years since the end of World War II, 51,00,000 television sets were manufactured in the United States, according to estimates made by the Sylvania Electric Company. Of these, all but 9,000,000 scrapped or discarded units were in use in the middle of 1957.

By 1956, the U.S. public invested $15.6 billions in its television sets—$10.4 billions for the sets themselves, $2.4 billions for servicing, $1.7 billions for antennas and other components, and $1.1 billions for replacement tubes. (The cost of electric power consumption is not included in this estimate.)

Of the 42,000,000 sets in use, the great majority are large-screen sets of relatively recent vintage. 55% have 19-21-inch-wide tubes (4% are even wider), 29% are 16-18-inch models, and only 12% have screens 15 inches or smaller in width. 2,250,000 are portables.

A necessary prerequisite to the growth in the number of television sets has been the expansion of the television coverage area. Before the lifting of the TV "freeze," about 56% of the nation's homes were within reception range of a TV station; today the figure is 97%. This expansion of coverage in turn reflects the soaring number of television stations, located in an increasingly large number of viewing areas (see Table 2).

More stations have not only brought more new people within range of television; they have also broadened the range of choice of the television owner, bringing more channels within his reach. Only 4% of the viewers are within range of only a single station. Seventy-two per cent of television homes can today receive four stations or more; even though only eighteen cities have four or more channels operating, stations located in other nearby cities are often within viewing range.

The increased opportunity for programming choice on the part of the viewer was spurred also by the beginnings of multiple set ownership (which included 6% of all TV homes by mid-1957). As

TABLE 2. Growth of U.S. Television Reception

	Number of Television Areas	Number of Television Stations
January 1949	28	48
1950	56	96
1951	61	106
1952	62	108
1953	73	120
1954	192	309
1955	239	395
1956	243	459
1957	251	502

Source: Television Bureau of Advertising.

the early, small-screen sets became obsolescent, many of the original TV owners acquired new sets with wider screens. In many cases the old set was neither discarded nor traded in, but moved out of the living room and into some other part of the house, giving the individual viewer even greater freedom to select what he wants to see.

By January, 1958, there were 521 stations on the air in the United States, and forty in Canada. Thus television has gradually come to approach some of the potentialities for individual choice and selectivity that existed in radio. As smaller cities acquired their own TV transmitters, wider areas were brought within reach of stations in nearby cities as well as those in their own. Nearly four hundred community antenna systems, operating on a subscription basis, provide television service to many homes whose reception might otherwise be faulty because of unfavorable terrain.

TV AND NON-TV HOMES: THE CHANGING PATTERN

In television's early days, or in its early days in a new television area, sets were acquired first by those of above-average income, like any other expensive consumer goods. Unlike many other similarly expensive commodities, television quickly spread to the lower income levels.

An early TV survey in New Brunswick, New Jersey, conducted by Rutgers University under CBS sponsorship, found that the pioneer set owners who had acquired TV before July 1947 were considerably higher in social status than those who bought sets during the year 1947-48. Of the pioneer owners, 19% were semi-skilled or unskilled, 36% were white-collar or skilled workers, and 45% were proprietors and professionals. Of the latter purchasers, 37% were semi-skilled and unskilled, 45% white-collar and skilled workers, but only 18% proprietors and professionals.

The broadened base of television ownership may be clearly seen by a reanalysis of data collected annually, since 1949, by the Market Research Corporation. Their sample may be divided into equal quarters on the basis of income. If television ownership were evenly distributed regardless of income, it too would naturally be divided into four equal parts. In 1949, the bottom fourth of the sample population owned only 13% of the sets, while the two top quarters owned a disproportionately heavy 30% apiece. Today the bottom quarter is up to 19% of the sets, and the two top quarters have dropped correspondingly in their share of the total.

· · · · · · · · · · · · · · · ·

A number of surveys made throughout television's history could document the change in the composition of the TV-owning public. Because the Market Research Corporation has maintained the same methods of measurement year after year, its findings show the trends much more clearly than would be the case if unrelated surveys were compared.

Table 3 shows the percentage of TV ownership in households of differing characteristics, for the years 1949-1956. Each figure shown under a given year represents the proportion of television-owning households in the particular category.

The most striking feature of the trend figures shown in Table 3 is the steady narrowing of the differences in the proportion of TV ownership among various sub-groups of the population. This is an inevitable by-product of the fact that more and more people have acquired TV, and that the rate of growth has been most rapid where the opportunities for growth were greatest—namely, in groups where ownership has been below average.

For a long while the college-educated lagged behind the high-school educated in TV ownership, though the gap has now virtually disappeared. The least-educated (those who have been only to grade school) are still behind in ownership.

In the last four years alone, TV ownership has spread from one farm family in four to over half. Of the rural non-farm families, two-thirds now have sets. Small families, childless families, and families where the housewife is older, have been, from the start, below average in TV ownership. They, too, are edging up to the average.

TV AND NON-TV HOMES: A COMPARISON

Although the differences are diminishing, as TV penetration grows, the four homes in five which have television are still not identical with their non-television neighbors. The most accurate recent information on the subject is provided by a survey made in June, 1955, by the U.S. Bureau of the Census. At a time when 76% of U.S. households owned at least one television set (and 7% of the total had two or more sets), substantial differences (shown in Table 4) were found to exist in set ownership, by region, size of family, and city size.

Television ownership is heavily concentrated in urban areas, and particularly in the large metropolitan centers. There are several reasons for this. It is in these areas that television was first estab-

TABLE 3. Growth of TV Penetration in Different Segments of the U.S. Market, 1949-1956

	Sept. 1949	Oct. 1950	July 1951	July 1952	July 1953	July 1954	July 1955	July 1956
U. S. Total	6%	18%	27%	37%	49%	58%	68%	76%
Region								
Northeast	13%	35%	45%	59%	69%	77%	85%	88%
South	1	4	13	17	30	37	54	64
North Central	4	15	27	39	50	61	70	79
Mountain, Southwest	*	3	10	16	31	40	52	62
Pacific	5	19	26	34	47	56	66	76
City Size								
Farm	*	3%	7%	12%	23%	28%	43%	54%
Under 2,500	*	5	9	16	26	41	56	67
2,500 to 50,000	*	9	16	18	31	39	53	65
50,000 to 500,000	*	17	28	37	51	64	75	82
500,000 & over	14%	40	53	69	77	81	87	89
Income								
Upper Fourth	7%	24%	33%	45%	58%	70%	81%	87%
Next Fourth	7	19	32	41	55	63	76	85
Next Fourth	6	18	28	40	50	59	69	76
Lowest Fourth	3	12	18	23	32	41	48	58
Education								
Grade School	4%	16%	23%	31%	43%	51%	62%	70%
High School	7	22	34	45	57	65	75	83
College	6	17	24	38	48	61	73	79
Family Size								
1 & 2 Members	4%	12%	19%	28%	38%	48%	59%	69%
3 Members	6	18	30	41	52	65	73	81
4 & 5 Members	7	22	35	45	58	69	78	85
6 & More Members	6	19	27	39	53	55	66	74
Age of Housewife								
Under 35	8%	23%	36%	44%	58%	65%	75%	82%
35 through 44 Years	8	23	37	48	60	68	74	82
45 Years & Over	3	12	19	28	40	49	61	70
Presence of Children								
5 Years & Under	7%	23%	36%	48%	54%	65%	75%	81%
6 to 12 Years	7	22	35	46	56	65	76	83
13 to 20 Years	6	18	28	39	49	58	71	78
No Children	4	13	21	29	37	50	61	70

Source: Market Research Corporation reports.
  *No Data.

lished; they still enjoy a better quality of reception and, typically, can receive a larger number of stations than most rural areas. They are better able to afford television, since their family income is above the national average. Cities of a quarter-million or more inhabitants have the highest concentration of households with television—about four in every five.

Farm dwellers, last to come within range of television, and below average in income, are lowest in ownership. Accessibility is one explanation. In December, 1952, a mail survey conducted among 300 farm families subscribing to *Successful Farming* magazine found that among the 22% who then owned television sets, the average distance from the nearest TV station was 43 miles. Of every ten farmers who were television owners, four lived over 50 miles from the nearest television station.

Families with children were from the start under especially heavy pressure to acquire television. In families of three, four, and five persons, television ownership is substantially higher than in two-person households. It is also higher than in households of six or

TABLE 4. Penetration of Television, June, 1955

	Per Cent of Households Owning TV
By Urban and Rural Location	
Total Urban	74%
Inside urbanized areas of:	
3,000,000 inhabitants or more	81
1,000,000 to 3,000,000 inhabitants	82
250,000 to 1,000,000 inhabitants	79
50,000 to 250,000 inhabitants	74
Outside urbanized areas, in urban places of:	
10,000 inhabitants or more	62
2,500 to 10,000 inhabitants	52
Rural Non-Farm, Total	61
Rural Farm, Total	42
By Size of Household	
1 person	36
2 persons	64
3 persons	73
4 persons	79
5 persons	78
6 persons or more	66
By Census Regions	
Northeast	80
North Central	72
South	53
West	62
U.S. Total	67%

Source: U.S. Bureau of the Census.

TABLE 5. A Comparison of Women in TV and Non-TV Homes

Per cent of homes in each category	TV Homes	Non-TV Homes
Children under 18 years	60%	48%
Under $3,000 Income	20	53
Professional, semi-professional,		
managerial occupation (head of house)	23	14
Grade school education or less (housewife)	24	39
Own automobile	77	63
Own home	58	51
Live in single-family dwelling	63	72
Metropolitan areas	77	37
55 and older (housewife)	18	28
Married (housewife)	80	71
Employed outside the home (housewife)	35	28
White	93	84

Source: NBC-Simmons "Daytime TV" 1954 Study.

more persons—probably because these are more often found in rural areas than anywhere else. People who live alone are least apt to own a television set (though paradoxically, they might be able to profit most from its companionship). This may be because their income is lower, or because they spend less time at home and generally lead more mobile lives.

Urban areas—and TV ownership—are geographically concentrated most heavily in the Northeastern states. The Rocky Mountain and Midwestern states, with their relatively sparse distribution of population, and the South, with its lower income level, lag behind the rest of the country in TV penetration.

The characteristic differences, in family size and city-size location, were also found when television and non-television homes were compared by the National Broadcasting Company in a survey of women's daytime television viewing habits. (This study was made by Willard R. Simmons and Associates in January, 1954, at a time when 57% of the households had TV.)

As Table 5 shows, this study also confirmed that television is more often found in homes where there are children under 18, where family income is higher, where the head of the house has an occupation of higher status, and where the housewife herself is younger and better educated. The television families are more apt to own a car, and to be home-owners. In the television home, the woman of the house is more apt to be married, and to be employed outside the home. Because Negroes enjoy a lower average income than whites, and because a sizable proportion of them are rural Southerners, relatively fewer Negroes than whites are television owners.

An analysis by Daniel Starch shows that among families without children, 19% purchased new television sets in the years 1952-54. Among families with children aged 14-17, 23% purchased a set in this period. The proportion increased as the age of the children decreased, with the heaviest proportion of new purchasers (32%) found among parents of children under 2.

In a study of religious broadcasting in New Haven (1952), Everett Parker and his associates found that religion (and presumably ethnicity) were strongly related to television set ownership, independently of social class (which by itself is related to religious affiliation). In a cross-section of 3559 interviews, it was found that at every social class level, TV ownership was lower among Protestants than among Catholics or Jews. The difference was particularly noticeable at the upper and upper-middle social level. Thus in the highest social category (the wealthy families whose heads were leaders in the community) TV was owned by 82% of the Catholics, by 82% of the Jews, but by only 34% of the Protestants. At the next level, the "well-to-do" who lack inherited wealth, 75% of the Catholics, 78% of the Jews, but only 51% of the Protestants, had TV. By contrast at the lowest level, among the tenement dwellers, TV was found in 81% of the Catholic homes, in 63% of the Jewish homes, and in 61% of the Protestant homes. In the words of the authors, "something in the nature of a 'Protestant culture,' vague as it might be, influenced Protestant families in New Haven against the purchase of television sets and this made the proportion of Protestants in the general television audience smaller than the proportion of Protestants in the total population." There is no evidence as to whether this fascinating observation applies to other places than New Haven. In any case, as television ownership approaches saturation, such differences among different population groups have naturally tended to disappear.

Charles Swanson and Robert Jones, interviewing a probability sample of 202 Minneapolis adults in the spring of 1950, found that the TV owners did not differ from non-owners in income, education, social activity, or average intelligence level; however, they showed greater variability in intelligence, and tended to know less about government affairs.

THE GROWTH OF LITERACY IN AMERICA

Percentage of Literacy among Americans 10 or Older

	Population 10 or Older	Per cent Literate
1890	47,413,559	86.7
1900	57,949,824	89.3
1910	71,580,270	92.3
1920	82,739,315	94.0
1930	98,723,047	95.7
1940	110,442,000	96.5
1950	150,700,000	97.5

Source: U.S. Census.

THE STRUCTURE AND FUNCTION
OF MASS COMMUNICATIONS

MASS COMMUNICATIONS came into being because they are the most efficient means yet found to meet some of the pressing needs of society. Man has always needed something to watch over his environment and report to him on dangers and opportunities; something to circulate opinions and facts, help a group make decisions, and then circulate the decisions; something to help pass on the lore and wisdom and expectations of society to the new members of society; something to entertain people on a broad scale; something to broaden trade and commerce. Primitive tribes assigned individuals to these tasks: watchmen, members of the tribal council, parents and later teachers, bards and jesters, and itinerant traders. In our society the jobs have grown too big for individuals, and are given chiefly to great organizations which we call the mass media.

A mass medium is essentially a working group organized around some device for circulating the same message, at about the same time, to large numbers of people. That is, the newspaper is a group made up of men concerned with news and editorial comment, men concerned with selling advertising and handling the business of the paper, men concerned with printing the paper, and men concerned with circulating the paper—organized around the high-speed printing press. A television station is a group made up of men concerned with programs, with the business of the station, and with the electronics of the station—organized around the TV transmitter. When such an organization is a metropolitan newspaper or a television network, it is a very large and complex organization indeed. A large newspaper may have correspondents in many countries, maintain news wires that bring information from all over the world, own paper mills of its own, deliver with its own trucks and airplanes, and do more than ten million dollars worth of business a year. A television network may supply a number of hours daily of programs to 250 stations throughout the country, maintain connections with all branches of professional entertainment, and sell upwards of one hundred million dollars worth of advertising a year. The news that comes to you from Asia may pass through a hundred hands and a dozen large organizations. The entertainment that flickers on your television tube may have required the cooperation of several advertising agencies, one or more film studios, forty or fifty expert entertainers, one hundred or more expert television employees, the telephone company, and the electric company.

Communication in modern society, therefore, has come a long way from the time when an individual could serve as the watchman, and a ballad singer could furnish the entertainment. Because these modern organizations of communication are so large, complicated, and potent, it becomes important to know what they are trying to do, and how. It is much harder to check up on the mass media than on the watchman or the ballad singer. That is why the kind of work you will see in the following pages is of importance.

The section begins with Professor Lasswell's classic essay which did so much to delineate the place the mass media occupy in society. Then comes an article by Dr. Lerner which considers the problem of change in social communication. All through the world at this time are young, developing countries, passing from the stage of oral communication to that of mass communication. This is the process which Dr. Lerner considers. This is followed by accounts of what happens in a typical day in three mass media: the newsroom of a newspaper, a film lot during the making of a feature motion picture, and a television station during the making of a commercial. There is a memorandum on that highly important phenomenon of large-scale communication, the gatekeeper. Then comes Dr. Breed's study of how social control is exerted over a mass medium—in this case, who has the right to say what news goes into a newspaper, and how the employees "get the word." And finally there are a number of tables on the size of mass communications in the United States, and their rate of growth.

THE STRUCTURE AND FUNCTION
OF COMMUNICATION IN SOCIETY

BY HAROLD D. LASSWELL

Dr. Lasswell is a professor of law at Yale, and long a distinguished contributor to the literature of communication studies. This paper was published in *The Communication of Ideas,* edited by Lyman Bryson, published and copyrighted by the Institute for Religious and Social Studies, of New York City, in 1948. It is here reprinted by permission of author and publisher.

THE ACT OF COMMUNICATION

A CONVENIENT WAY to describe an act of communication is to answer the following questions:

> Who
> Says What
> In Which Channel
> To Whom
> With What Effect?

The scientific study of the process of communication tends to concentrate upon one or another of these questions. Scholars who study the "who," the communicator, look into the factors that initiate and guide the act of communication. We call this subdivision of the field of research *control analysis.* Specialists who focus upon the "says what" engage in *content analysis.* Those who look primarily at the radio, press, film, and other channels of communication are doing *media analysis.* When the principal concern is with the persons reached by the media, we speak of *audience analysis.* If the question is the impact upon audiences, the problem is *effect analysis.*

Whether such distinctions are useful depends entirely upon the degree of refinement which is regarded as appropriate to a given scientific and managerial objective. Often it is simpler to combine audience and effect analysis, for instance, than to keep them apart. On the other hand, we may want to concentrate on the analysis of content, and for this purpose subdivide the field into the study of purport and style, the first referring to the message, and the second to the arrangement of the elements of which the message is composed.

STRUCTURE AND FUNCTION

Enticing as it is to work out these categories in more detail, the present discussion has a different scope. We are less interested in dividing up the act of communication than in viewing the act as a whole in relation to the entire social process. Any process can be examined in two frames of reference, namely, structure and function; and our analysis of communication will deal with the specializations that carry on certain functions, of which the following may be clearly distinguished: (1) The surveillance of the environment; (2) the correlation of the parts of society in responding to the environment; (3) the transmission of the social heritage from one generation to the next.

BIOLOGICAL EQUIVALENCIES

At the risk of calling up false analogies, we can gain perspective on human societies when we note the degree to which communication is a feature of life at every level. A vital entity, whether relatively isolated or in association, has specialized ways of receiving stimuli from the environment. The single-celled organism or the many-membered group tends to maintain an internal equilibrium and to respond to changes in the environment in a way that maintains this equilibrium. The responding process calls for specialized ways of bringing the parts of the whole into harmonious action. Multicelled animals specialize cells to the function of external contact and internal correlation. Thus, among the primates, specialization is exemplified by organs such as the ear and eye, and the nervous system itself. When the stimuli receiving and disseminating patterns operate smoothly, the several parts of the animal act in concert in reference to the environment ("feeding," "fleeing," "attacking").[1]

In some animal societies certain members perform specialized roles, and survey the environment. Individuals act as "sentinels," standing apart from the herd or flock and creating a disturbance whenever an alarming change occurs in the surroundings. The trumpeting, cackling, or shrilling of the sentinel is enough to set the herd in motion. Among the activities engaged in by specialized "leaders" is the internal stimulation of "followers" to adapt in an orderly manner to the circumstances heralded by the sentinels.

Within a single, highly differentiated organism, incoming nervous impulses and outgoing impulses are transmitted along fibers that make synaptic junction with other fibers. The critical points in the process occur at the relay stations, where the arriving impulse may be too weak to reach the threshold which stirs the next link into action. At the higher centers, separate currents modify one another, producing results that differ in many ways from the outcome when each is allowed to continue a separate path. At any relay station there is no conductance, total conductance, or intermediate conductance. The same categories apply to what goes on among members of an animal society. The sly fox may approach the barnyard in a way that supplies too meager stimuli for the sentinel to sound the alarm. Or the attacking animal may eliminate the sentinel before he makes more than a feeble outcry. Obviously there is every gradation possible between total conductance and no conductance.

ATTENTION IN WORLD SOCIETY

When we examine the process of communication of any state in the world community, we note three categories of specialists. One group surveys the political environment of the state as a whole, another correlates the response of the whole state to the environment, and the third transmits certain patterns of response from the old to the young. Diplomats, attachés, and foreign correspondents are representative of those who specialize on the environment. Editors, journalists, and speakers are correlators of the internal response. Educators in family and school transmit the social inheritance.

Communications which originate abroad pass through sequences

---

[1] To the extent that behavior patterns are transmitted in the structures inherited by the single animal, a function is performed parallel to the transmission of the "social heritage" by means of education.

in which various senders and receivers are linked with one another. Subject to modification at each relay point in the chain, messages originating with a diplomat or foreign correspondent may pass through editorial desks and eventually reach large audiences.

If we think of the world attention process as a series of *attention frames*, it is possible to describe the rate at which comparable content is brought to the notice of individuals and groups. We can inquire into the point at which "conductance" no longer occurs; and we can look into the range between "total conductance" and "minimum conductance." The metropolitan and political centers of the world have much in common with the interdependence, differentiation, and activity of the cortical or subcortical centers of an individual organism. Hence the attention frames found in these spots are the most variable, refined, and interactive of all frames in the world community.

At the other extreme are the attention frames of primitive inhabitants of isolated areas. Not that folk cultures are wholly untouched by industrial civilization. Whether we parachute into the interior of New Guinea, or land on the slopes of the Himalayas, we find no tribe wholly out of contact with the world. The long threads of trade, of missionary zeal, of adventurous exploration and scientific field study, and of global war reach far distant places. No one is entirely out of this world.

Among primitives the final shape taken by communication is the ballad or tale. Remote happenings in the great world of affairs, happenings that come to the notice of metropolitan audiences, are reflected, however dimly, in the thematic material of ballad singers and reciters. In these creations faraway political leaders may be shown supplying land to the peasants or restoring an abundance of game to the hills.

When we push upstream of the flow of communication, we note that the immediate relay function for nomadic and remote tribesmen is sometimes performed by the inhabitants of settled villages with whom they come in occasional contact. The relayer can be the school teacher, doctor, judge, tax collector, policeman, soldier, peddler, salesman, missionary, student; in any case he is an assembly point of news and comment.

MORE DETAILED EQUIVALENCIES

The communication processes of human society, when examined in detail, reveal many equivalencies to the specializations found in the physical organism, and in the lower animal societies. The diplomats, for instance, of a single state are stationed all over the world and send messages to a few focal points. Obviously, these incoming reports move from the many to the few, where they interact upon one another. Later on, the sequence spreads fanwise according to a few to many pattern, as when a foreign secretary gives a speech in public, an article is put out in the press, or a news film is distributed to the theaters. The lines leading from the outer environment of the state are functionally equivalent to the afferent channels that convey incoming nervous impulses to the central nervous system of a single animal, and to the means by which alarm is spread among a flock. Outgoing, or efferent impulses, display corresponding parallels.

The central nervous system of the body is only partly involved in the entire flow of afferent-efferent impulses. There are automatic systems that can act on one another without involving the "higher" centers at all. The stability of the internal environment is maintained principally through the mediation of the vegetive or autonomic specializations of the nervous system. Similarly, most of the messages within any state do not involve the central channels of communication. They take place within families, neighborhoods, shops, field gangs, and other local contexts. Most of the educational process is carried on the same way.

A further set of significant equivalencies is related to the circuits of communication, which are predominantly one-way or two-way, depending upon the degree of reciprocity between communicators and audience. Or, to express it differently, two-way communication occurs when the sending and receiving functions are performed with equal frequency by two or more persons. A conversation is usually assumed to be a pattern of two-way communication (although monologues are hardly unknown). The modern instruments of mass communication give an enormous advantage to the controllers of printing plants, broadcasting equipment, and other forms of fixed and specialized capital. But it should be noted that audiences do "talk back," after some delay; and many controllers of mass media use scientific methods of sampling in order to expedite this closing of the circuit.

Circuits of two-way contact are particularly in evidence among the great metropolitan, political, and cultural centers of the world. New York, Moscow, London, and Paris, for example, are in intense two-way contact, even when the flow is severely curtailed in volume (as between Moscow and New York). Even insignificant sites become world centers when they are transformed into capital cities (Canberra in Australia, Ankara in Turkey, the District of Columbia, U.S.A.). A cultural center like Vatican City is in intense two-way relationship with the dominant centers throughout the world. Even specialized production centers like Hollywood, despite their preponderance of outgoing material, receive an enormous volume of messages.

A further distinction can be made between message controlling and message handling centers and social formations. The message center in the vast Pentagon Building of the War Department in Washington, D.C., transmits with no more than accidental change incoming messages to addressees. This is the role of the printers and distributors of books; of dispatchers, linemen, and messengers connected with telegraphic communication; of radio engineers and other technicians associated with broadcasting. Such message handlers may be contrasted with those who affect the content of what is said, which is the function of editors, censors, and propagandists. Speaking of the symbol specialists as a whole, therefore, we separate them into the manipulators (controllers) and the handlers; the first group typically modifies content, while the second does not.

NEEDS AND VALUES

Though we have noted a number of functional and structural equivalencies between communication in human societies and other living entities, it is not implied that we can most fruitfully investigate the process of communication in America or the world by the methods most appropriate to research on the lower animals or on single physical organisms. In comparative psychology when we describe some part of the surroundings of a rat, cat, or monkey as a stimulus (that is, as part of the environment reaching the attention of the animal), we cannot ask the rat; we use other means of inferring perception. When human beings are our objects of investigation, we can interview the great "talking animal." (This is not that we take everything at face value. Sometimes we forecast the opposite of what the person says he intends to do. In this case, we depend on other indications, both verbal and non-verbal.)

In the study of living forms, it is rewarding, as we have said, to look at them as modifiers of the environment in the process of gratifying needs, and hence of maintaining a steady state of internal equilibrium. Food, sex, and other activities which involve the environment can be examined on a comparative basis. Since human beings exhibit speech reactions, we can investigate many more relationships than in the non-human species.[2] Allowing for the data furnished by speech (and other communicative acts), we can investigate human society in terms of values; that is, in reference to categories of relationships that are recognized objects of gratification. In America, for example, it requires no elaborate technique of study to discern that power and respect are values. We can demonstrate this by listening to testimony, and by watching what is done when opportunity is afforded.

It is possible to establish a list of values current in any group chosen for investigation. Further than this, we can discover the rank order in which these values are sought. We can rank the members of the group according to their position in relation to the values. So far as industrial civilization is concerned, we have no hesitation in saying that power, wealth, respect, well being, and enlightenment are among the values. If we stop with this list, which is not exhaustive, we can describe on the basis of available knowledge (fragmentary though it may often be), the social structure of most of the world. Since values are not equally distributed, the social structure reveals more or less concentration of relatively abundant shares of power, wealth, and other values in a few hands. In some places this concentration is passed on from generation to generation, forming castes rather than a mobile society.

In every society the values are shaped and distributed according to more or less distinctive patterns (*institutions*). The institutions include communications which are invoked in support of the network as a whole. Such communications are the ideology; and in relation to power we can differentiate the political *doctrine,* the political *formula,* and the *miranda.*[3] These are illustrated in the United States by the doctrine of individualism, the paragraphs of the Constitution, which are the formula, and the ceremonies and

---

[2] Properly handled, the speech event can be described with as much reliability and validity as many non-speech events which are more conventionally used as data in scientific investigations.

[3] These distinctions are derived and adapted from the writings of Charles E. Merriam, Gaetano Mosca, Karl Mannheim, and others. For a systematic exposition see *Power and Society* (New Haven: Yale University Press, 1950) by Harold D. Lasswell and Abraham Kaplan.

legends of public life, which comprise the miranda. The ideology is communicated to the rising generation through such specialized agencies as the home and school.

Ideology is only part of the myths of any given society. There may be counterideologies directed against the dominant doctrine, formula, and miranda. Today the power structure of world politics is deeply affected by ideological conflict, and by the role of two giant powers, the United States and Russia. The ruling elites view one another as potential enemies, not only in the sense that interstate differences may be settled by war, but in the more urgent sense that the ideology of the other may appeal to disaffected elements at home and weaken the internal power position of each ruling class.

SOCIAL CONFLICT AND COMMUNICATION

Under the circumstances, one ruling element is especially alert to the other, and relies upon communication as a means of preserving power. One function of communication, therefore, is to provide intelligence about what the other elite is doing, and about its strength. Fearful that intelligence channels will be controlled by the other, in order to withhold and distort, there is a tendency to resort to secret surveillance. Hence international espionage is intensified above its usual level in peacetime. Moreover, efforts are made to "black out" the self in order to counteract the scrutiny of the potential enemy. In addition, communication is employed affirmatively for the purpose of establishing contact with audiences within the frontiers of the other power.

These varied activities are manifested in the use of open and secret agents to scrutinize the other, in counterintelligence work, in censorship and travel restriction, in broadcasting and other informational activities across frontiers.

Ruling elites are also sensitized to potential threats in the internal environment. Besides using open sources of information, secret measures are also adopted. Precautions are taken to impose "security" upon as many policy matters as possible. At the same time, the ideology of the elite is reaffirmed, and counterideologies are suppressed.

The processes here sketched run parallel to phenomena to be observed throughout the animal kingdom. Specialized agencies are used to keep aware of threats and opportunities in the external environment. The parallels include the surveillance exercised over the internal environment, since among the lower animals some herd leaders sometimes give evidence of fearing attack on two fronts, internal and external; they keep an uneasy eye on both environments. As a means of preventing surveillance by an enemy, well-known devices are at the disposal of certain species, *e.g.*, the squid's use of a liquid fog screen, the protective coloration of the chameleon. However, there appears to be no correlate of the distinction between the "secret" and "open" channels of human society.

Inside a physical organism the closest parallel to social revolution would be the growth of new nervous connections with parts of the body that rival, and can take the place of, the existing structures of central integration. Can this be said to occur as the embryo develops in the mother's body? Or, if we take a destructive, as distinct from a reconstructive, process, can we properly say that internal surveillance occurs in regard to cancer, since cancers compete for the food supplies of the body?

EFFICIENT COMMUNICATION

The analysis up to the present implies certain criteria of efficiency or inefficiency in communication. In human societies the process is efficient to the degree that rational judgments are facilitated. A rational judgment implements value-goals. In animal societies communication is efficient when it aids survival, or some other specified need of the aggregate. The same criteria can be applied to the single organism.

One task of a rationally organized society is to discover and control any factors that interfere with efficient communication. Some limiting factors are psychotechnical. Destructive radiation, for instance, may be present in the environment, yet remain undetected owing to the limited range of the unaided organism.

But even technical insufficiencies can be overcome by knowledge. In recent years shortwave broadcasting has been interfered with by disturbances which will either be surmounted, or will eventually lead to the abandonment of this mode of broadcasting. During the past few years advances have been made toward providing satisfactory substitutes for defective hearing and seeing. A less dramatic, though no less important, development has been the discovery of how inadequate reading habits can be corrected.

There are, of course, deliberate obstacles put in the way of communication, like censorship and drastic curtailment of travel. To some extent obstacles can be surmounted by skillful evasion, but in the long run it will doubtless be more efficient to get rid of them by consent or coercion.

Sheer ignorance is a pervasive factor whose consequences have never been adequately assessed. Ignorance here means the absence, at a given point in the process of communication, of knowledge which is available elsewhere in society. Lacking proper training, the personnel engaged in gathering and disseminating intelligence is continually misconstruing or overlooking the facts, if we define the facts as what the objective, trained observer could find.

In accounting for inefficiency we must not overlook the low evaluations put upon skill in relevant communication. Too often irrelevant, or positively distorting, performances command prestige. In the interest of a "scoop," the reporter gives a sensational twist to a mild international conference, and contributes to the popular image of international politics as chronic, intense conflict, and little else. Specialists in communication often fail to keep up with the expansion of knowledge about the process; note the reluctance with which many visual devices have been adopted. And despite research on vocabulary, many mass communicators select words that fail. This happens, for instance, when a foreign correspondent allows himself to become absorbed in the foreign scene and forgets that his home audience has no direct equivalents in experience for "left," "center," and other factional terms.

Besides skill factors, the level of efficiency is sometimes adversely influenced by personality structure. An optimistic, outgoing person may hunt "birds of a feather" and gain an uncorrected and hence exaggeratedly optimistic view of events. On the contrary, when pessimistic, brooding personalities mix, they choose quite different birds, who confirm their gloom. There are also important differences among people which spring from contrasts in intelligence and energy.

Some of the most serious threats to efficient communication for the community as a whole relate to the values of power, wealth, and respect. Perhaps the most striking examples of power distortion occur when the content of communication is deliberately adjusted to fit an ideology or counterideology. Distortions related to wealth not only arise from attempts to influence the market, for instance, but from rigid conceptions of economic interest. A typical instance of inefficiencies connected with respect (social class) occurs when an upper class person mixes only with persons of his own stratum and forgets to correct his perspective by being exposed to members of other classes.

RESEARCH IN COMMUNICATION

The foregoing reminders of some factors that interfere with efficient communication point to the kinds of research which can usefully be conducted on representative links in the chain of communication. Each agent is a vortex of interacting environmental and predispositional factors. Whoever performs a relay function can be examined in relation to input and output. What statements are brought to the attention of the relay link? What does he pass on verbatim? What does he drop out? What does he rework? What does he add? How do differences in input and output correlate with culture and personality?' By answering such questions it is possible to weigh the various factors in conductance, no conductance, and modified conductance.

Besides the relay link, we must consider the primary link in a communication sequence. In studying the focus of attention of the primary observer, we emphasize two sets of influences: Statements to which he is exposed; other features of his environment. An attaché or foreign correspondent exposes himself to mass media and private talk; also, he can count soldiers, measure gun emplacements, note hours of work in a factory, see butter and fat on the table.

Actually it is useful to consider the attention frame of the relay as well as the primary link in terms of media and non-media exposures. The role of non-media factors is very slight in the case of many relay operators, while it is certain to be significant in accounting for the primary observer.

ATTENTION AGGREGATES AND PUBLICS

It should be pointed out that everyone is not a member of the world public, even though he belongs to some extent to the world attention aggregate. To belong to an attention aggregate it is only necessary to have common symbols of reference. Everyone who has a symbol of reference for New York, North America, the Western

Hemisphere, or the globe is a member respectively of the attention aggregate of New York, North America, the Western Hemisphere, the globe. To be a member of the New York public, however, it is essential to make demands for public action in New York, or expressly affecting New York.

The public of the United States, for instance, is not confined to residents or citizens, since non-citizens who live beyond the frontier may try to influence American politics. Conversely, everyone who lives in the United States is not a member of the American public, since something more than passive attention is necessary. An individual passes from an attention aggregate to the public when he begins to expect that what he wants can affect public policy.

SENTIMENT GROUPS AND PUBLICS

A further limitation must be taken into account before we can correctly classify a specific person or group as part of a public. The demands made regarding public policy must be debatable. The world public is relatively weak and undeveloped, partly because it is typically kept subordinate to sentiment areas in which no debate is permitted on policy matters. During a war or war crisis, for instance, the inhabitants of a region are overwhelmingly committed to impose certain policies on others. Since the outcome of the conflict depends on violence, and not debate, there is no public under such conditions. There is a network of sentiment groups that act as crowds, hence tolerate no dissent.[4]

From the foregoing analysis it is clear that there are attention, public, and sentiment areas of many degrees of inclusiveness in world politics. These areas are interrelated with the structural and functional features of world society, and especially of world power. It is evident, for instance, that *the strongest powers tend to be included in the same attention area,* since their ruling elites focus on one another as the source of great potential threat. The strongest powers usually pay proportionately less attention to the weaker powers than the weaker powers pay to them, since stronger powers

---

[4] The distinction between the "crowd" and the "public" was worked out in the Italian, French, and German literature of criticism that grew up around Le Bon's overgeneralized use of the crowd concept. For a summary of this literature by a scholar who later became one of the most productive social scientists in this field, see Robert E. Park, *Masse und Publikum; Eine methodologische und soziologische Untersuchung,* Lack and Grunau, Berne, 1904. (Heidelberg dissertation.)

are typically more important sources of threat, or of protection, for weaker powers than the weaker powers are for the stronger.[5]

The attention structure within a state is a valuable index of the degree of state integration. When the ruling classes fear the masses, the rulers do not share their picture of reality with the rank and file. When the reality picture of kings, presidents, and cabinets is not permitted to circulate through the state as a whole, the degree of discrepancy shows the extent to which the ruling groups assume that their power depends on distortion.

Or, to express the matter another way: If the "truth" is not shared, the ruling elements expect internal conflict, rather than harmonious adjustment to the external environment of the state. Hence the channels of communication are controlled in the hope of organizing the attention of the community at large in such a way that only responses will be forthcoming which are deemed favorable to the power position of the ruling classes.

THE PRINCIPLE OF EQUIVALENT ENLIGHTENMENT

It is often said in democratic theory that rational public opinion depends upon enlightenment. There is, however, much ambiguity about the nature of enlightenment, and the term is often made equivalent to perfect knowledge. A more modest and immediate conception is not perfect but equivalent enlightenment. The attention structure of the full-time specialist on a given policy will be more elaborate and refined than that of the layman. That this difference will always exist, we must take for granted. Nevertheless, it is quite possible for the specialist and the layman to agree on the broad outlines of reality. A workable goal of democratic society is equivalent enlightenment as between expert, leader, and layman.

Expert, leader, and layman can have the same gross estimate of major population trends of the world. They can share the same general view of the likelihood of war. It is by no means fantastic to imagine that the controllers of mass media of communication will take the lead in bringing about a high degree of equivalence throughout society between the layman's picture of significant relationships, and the picture of the expert and the leader.

[5] The propositions in this paragraph are hypotheses capable of being subsumed under the general theory of power, referred to in footnote 3. See also Harold D. Lasswell and Joseph M. Goldsen, "Public Attention, Opinion and Action," *The International Journal of Opinion and Attitude Research*, Mexico City, I (1947), 3-11.

SUMMARY

The communication process in society performs three functions: (a) *surveillance* of the environment, disclosing threats and opportunities affecting the value position of the community and of the component parts within it; (b) *correlation* of the components of society in making a response to the environment; (c) *transmission* of the social inheritance. In general, biological equivalents can be found in human and animal associations, and within the economy of a single organism.

In society, the communication process reveals special characteristics when the ruling element is afraid of the internal as well as the external environment. In gauging the efficiency of communication in any given context, it is necessary to take into account the values at stake, and the identity of the group whose position is being examined. In democratic societies, rational choices depend on enlightenment, which in turn depends upon communication; and especially upon the equivalence of attention among leaders, experts, and rank and file.

COMMUNICATION SYSTEMS AND
SOCIAL SYSTEMS[1]

BY DANIEL LERNER

Dr. Lerner is a professor of sociology at the Massachusetts Institute of
Technology and a member of the Center for International Studies. This
article appeared in *Behavioral Science* for October, 1957, and is reprinted here by permission of the author and the copyright holder, which
is the Mental Health Research Institute, University of Michigan.

PEOPLE WHO live together in a common polity develop patterned
ways of distributing information, as of distributing other commodities. These patterns of information flow interact at many points
with the patterns of power, wealth, status, and other values to form
a *system*, i.e., institutional variation in one is accompanied by regular and determinate variations in the others. This paper aims to
determine the degree of systemic relationship between communication and other institutions in most of the societies around the
world.

We have identified two main types of public communication systems—media and oral. These are differentiated according to the
paradigmatic question of communication research: who says what,
how, to whom? On these four variables the differences are as follows:

---

[1] I wish to thank R. S. Eckhaus, E. E. Hagen, B. F. Hoselitz, H. D. Lasswell
for suggestions which have been incorporated in this paper. Case studies of
the theoretical structure here outlined are reported in the author's book entitled *The Passing of Traditional Society*.

	Media Systems	Oral Systems
Channel	Media (Broadcast)	Oral (Point-to-Point)
Audience	Mass (Heterogeneous)	Primary (Homogeneous)
Source	Professional (Skill)	Hierarchical (Status)
Content	[Descriptive][2]	[Prescriptive][2]

Media systems have been described in detail by communication specialists. The main flow of public information is activated by a professional corps of communicators, skilled in producing descriptive messages ("news") for transmission through impersonal "media" (print, film, radio) to relatively undifferentiated mass audiences.

Oral systems we know mainly from the reports of anthropologists. Since preliterate networks are considerably more diverse than media systems (which have an "homogenizing" effect on behavioral styles), their public institutions exhibit much variation. In some oral systems, for example, power is not rigidly hierarchized. In the modal type, however, messages usually emanate from sources authorized to speak by their place in the social hierarchy, i.e., by status rather than skill criteria. These messages typically appear to be prescriptive rather than descriptive, i.e., announcing the regulations that are to govern audience behavior toward imminent events of community-wide interest, such as tax collections and military drafts. They are transmitted through oral channels to highly differentiated audiences, i.e., the "natural" primary groups of kinship, worship, work, or play. Each of these groups completes the diffusion pattern of an oral network by acting as a relay channel of mouth-to-ear communication within and between groups.[3]

If we accept this terse formulation as satisfactorily differentiating the characteristics of two general models of communication systems, we come next to the problem of describing their occurrence with sufficient accuracy to discriminate consistently between media

---

[2] These are bracketed because the only systematic evidence of content variation between the two types available to me is confined to a study made in the Middle East several years ago. I suspect, but cannot demonstrate, that there is regularity in this variation around the world.

[3] Comment by H. D. Lasswell: "One interesting variant is the role of drumming and similar media channels in predominantly oral systems. Such modes of communication are simply telegraphic devices more like conventionalized signposts than expressive or prescriptive statement-making. The sign-symbol ratio is high, by which I mean the physical events that serve as channel are rather extensive. A visual system seems essential to cut down the sign-symbol ratio and approach the 'pure' sign. Such visual systems may be 'manufactured' when they appear and copyists arise. The demand must be great—as at a dominant capital or at another urban locus."

and oral systems in the observable world. Here we run into trouble, for there are few societies that give a perfect fit to either of these idealized sets of paired comparisons. For example, in Britain, where public communication approximates most closely the model of a media system, people still talk to each other about public issues. Conversely, in Saudi Arabia, which corresponds to the oral system, there is a radio station. In most societies, as we move from the ideal types into empirical data, various elements in the patterns begin to shift. Most societies in the world appear to be in some stage of transition from one pattern to the other.

We notice, however, two general features that appear to be common to all societies. First, the *direction* of change is always from oral to media system (no known case exhibits change in the reverse direction).[4] Second, the *degree* of change in communication behavior appears to correlate significantly with other behavioral changes in the social system. These observations indicate that we are dealing with a secular trend in communication systems, a long-term process of historical change that is unilateral in direction. Moreover, this trend appears to be systemic, since it occurs interdependently with a variety of non-communication factors. From this we derive the proposition that a communication system is both index and agent of change in a total social system. Leaving aside the genetic question of causality (on the view that once the process is started, chicken and egg in fact "cause" each other), the hypothesis may be formulated in a suitable manner for testing as a correlation matrix, viz.:

	Type I	*Type II*
Communication	media	oral
Socioeconomic	urban	rural
Political	representative	nonrepresentative
Cultural	literate	illiterate

Associated with each communication system is a "profile" of economic, political, and cultural attributes. To sharpen the differences, they are stated above in dichotomous fashion. The dogmatic character of such a formulation need trouble no one, however, for

---

[4] This discussion excludes the new totalitarian systems, which have revived the ancient importance of the Agitator, using oral modes of communication. This special case appears to fill a "communication gap" created by the excessive development of capacity to produce messages through the media (especially print) over the capacity to consume mediated messages (e.g., by reason of illiteracy or lack of equipment).

empirically we treat them as continuous variables, on which differences are calibrated. Just as there is no perfect media system, so there is no perfectly urban or perfectly representative or perfectly literate society. Our model is probabilistic, our measures are distributive, and our test of fit is correlational.

The procedure was to determine the actual degree of correlation among these indices for all societies of the world which supplied data. These indices were defined in such fashion as to permit maximum use of the statistical data reported by UNESCO and other U.N. agencies. As the number of countries reporting varies from one index to another, our correlations apply to groups of nations ranging from 54 to 73 in number.[5]

Each index is considered a reliable guide to the state of public participation in its "sector" as a whole. Thus the literacy index, by specifying the proportion of population which can read in one language, is considered to give a fair picture of national participation in the whole cultural sector. Also, the proportion of population actually voting in national elections indexes participation in the whole political sector. Similarly, urbanization, computed as the proportion of population living in cities over 50,000, is taken as an index of participation in the whole economic sector. While urbanization is usually taken more narrowly, as a measure only of occupational distribution, a broader interpretation can be based on previous studies showing high intercorrelations between occupational distribution, per capita income, and literacy.[6]

These indices express degree of participation within four sectors which, in this discussion, can be taken to represent the whole social

[5] The statistics were used as reported by UNESCO. This was checked wherever possible against other UNESCO sources (for typographical errors) and against the U.N. *Statistical Yearbook* and *Demographic Yearbook* (for errors of information and computation). Wherever significant differences appeared which could not be reconciled, the case was excluded from our analysis. Otherwise all "self-governing territories" are included. The writer is unable to offer any definitive evaluation of these U.N. data, which are assembled from reports prepared separately by each nation. There are national differences in definition of indices and accuracy of reporting. Whereas magnitudes of "error" cannot be checked systematically, the direction of error, in those cases I have checked, always tend toward overstating one's progress in modernization—i.e., underdeveloped countries are likely to report larger rather than smaller estimates of urbanization, literacy, voting, etc.

[6] Literacy around the world correlated at .84 with per capita income, at .87 with industrialization measured by proportion of gainfully employed males in non-agricultural occupations.

system. What they differentiate is the participant style of modern democratic societies from the nonparticipant ways of traditional hierarchic societies. By "participant style" we mean here the *frequency*, not the quality, of participation by individuals. The point is simply that *more* individuals receive and use the opportunity to participate, regardless of the "value" of their participation. Accordingly, the items selected to form the communication index also focus on frequency of participation by the general population. These items are: (*a*) circulation of daily newspapers; (*b*) number of radio receivers; (*c*) seating capacity of cinemas. Each of these items was first correlated separately with the other indices. After their separate coefficients had been determined, the three items were handled jointly as a single index. (In all cases they were expressed, for comparability between items and countries, as proportion per 1,000 population.)

TESTING THE COMMUNICATION ITEMS

Each of the three communication items was correlated with the cultural index of literacy.[7] The coefficients, for a group of 73 self-governing countries, were as follows:

Item	Correlation with Literacy
Daily newspaper circulation	.75
Number of radio receivers	.74
Cinema seating capacity	.61

It is obvious that newspaper circulation should correlate better with literacy than does movie attendance, the enjoyment of which does not require literacy. The high correlation of radio receivers leads, for explanation, in another direction. Whereas building cinemas (in which *imported* feature films are shown) requires no advanced technology, the mass production of radio receivers does require a fair rate of industrialization on a high technological level.

The differential rate of industrialization is subsumed, up to a certain determinate point, under our index of urbanization. Having established that a high correlation exists between literacy and media, we now seek to establish that urbanization is interdependent with both. Rising production and distribution of the media usually

---

[7] Literacy is reported by UNESCO in five categories, each covering a range of 20 percentage points. All other items were handled as ungrouped data. The standard deviation for the literacy distribution is high (31.4).

occur only where and when there is the minimal urbanization required for modern industrial processes. By the same token, urbanization requires rising literacy for industrial participation. At a certain point, when urbanization has done its work, literacy becomes the independent variable in the process of growth and a new phase of modernization begins. But the growth of literacy itself, in this phase, soon becomes closely associated with the growth of media. The media teach literacy, and growing literacy develops the market which consumes the media product. The high coefficients correlating literacy with each of the media suggest that these may be considered as reciprocal causes and effects in a communication market whose locus can only be, at least in its historical inception, urban.[8]

The role of cities becomes clearer if we consider the further suggestion that sheer density of population, without countervailing urbanization, tends to operate as an anti-literacy force in most societies. This appears to be so despite the fact that education is cheaper when pupils live close together and hence, other things being equal, density should be associated with greater literacy. But, in the absence of significant urbanization, other things are *not* equal—i.e., the production, distribution, and consumption of wealth are much lower. This has a direct depressing effect on all public services, notably free public education. In dense nonurban societies, where national income is relatively small, few schools are maintained by public funds; also, since per capita income is lower and less widely distributed, fewer individuals can afford to attend school. Hence, the more people there are in a given area, the smaller is the proportion being educated and the harder it is to get a rising proportion of literates among them—until they begin to be redeployed into cities. In sparsely settled lands the influence of urbanization is less marked and literacy rates will probably respond directly to rises in per capita national income. But in populous societies urban-

---

[8] Comment by B. F. Hoselitz: "I tend to believe that literacy is the independent variable, at least in some cases, since the general experience in South Asia seems to be that the proportion of literates among migrants to cities is greater than among the rural population whence they came. In other words, people with a higher degree of empathy engage in migration to towns. On the other hand, the urban development, partly because of the availability of better schooling facilities, tends to produce a higher degree of literacy. One would, therefore, have to make a distinction between literacy rates of those who were born, or at least lived, in the urban environment since they were of school age, and those who migrated to the city as grownups."

ization is the intervening variable and is crucial for the "take-off" toward increasing literacy. It appears that only when dense populations show a significant rate of urbanization do literacy rates begin to rise. The rise of literacy levels off, however, after a certain degree of urbanization is present in the society. This means that the continued growth of literacy—say, after the society has become half-literate—depends upon some factor other than the continued growth of cities.

The counter-literacy force of sheer population density is evident in the populous Asian societies, such as India and Indonesia, where significant rates of urbanization have not yet occurred. The suggested interplay of density and urbanism as factors conditioning literacy may be represented as follows:

| | | *Urbanism* | |
		High	Low
	High	High (Literacy)	Low (Literacy)
Density			
	Low	High (Literacy)	High/Low (Literacy)

To facilitate testing of these relationships between density, urbanization, and literacy, we formulated three distinct hypotheses: (a) that literacy and population density, in areas of low urbanization, vary inversely and exhibit a negative correlation; (b) that the rate of literacy increases positively as the degree of urbanization increases (whether density is low or high); (c) that when urbanization exceeds a determinate figure then literacy will be high, regardless of population density, but will no longer be raised simply by rising urbanization. (No hypothesis is offered under the fourth set of conditions, where *both* urbanization and density are *low*, the impact of rising urbanization upon literacy being indeterminate in this case.)

A more complex formulation would take these three hypotheses together and would seek to determine the triadic conditions under which monotone relations actually obtain between urbanization, density, and literacy. Here we take the simpler course of testing the pairwise relationships by correlation. Our main interest here being to establish the crucial role of urbanization in the early phase of modernizing a social system, we suggest its differential functioning under conditions of low and high density only as a lead for future investigation. In computing these correlations, population density was defined as the number of persons per square kilometer of territory, and urbanization was defined as the proportion of total population living in cities over 50,000. Correlation of literacy with population density gave us a negative coefficient of — .60. Inspection of the two sets of figures showed that this inverse relationship was due to the massive nonurban societies— China, India, Indonesia, Egypt, etc. This may be regarded as confirmation of the first hypothesis that sheer density of population, in areas of low urbanization, is a counter-literacy factor—as density rates increase, literacy rates tend to decrease.

Confirmation of the second hypothesis, that literacy *increases* as urbanization increases, was also clear from the coefficient of correlation between these variables: + .64. (It should be noted that inaccuracies in the raw statistical data tend to bias the results against this hypothesis. Density is computed by formal territorial jurisdiction rather than effective area of habitation; since the densest countries tend to have the largest "waste" areas this minimizes their actual density. Also the cutting point of 50,000 excludes many cases of genuine urbanization in the less dense and populous countries, where cities of smaller size represent a significant degree of urbanization. Hence, making the raw data more accurate would tend to raise all coefficients in the direction hypothesized.)

Our third hypothesis, that after a certain point in urbanization has been passed literacy is high regardless of other demographic variables, was made more plausible (though not completely confirmed) when we ranked all 73 countries with respect to literacy and urbanization.

Number of Countries	Literacy	Urbanization (Mean)
22	Over 80%	28.0%
4	61-80	29.2
12	41-60	25.0
13	21-40	17.0
22	Under 20	7.4

Clearly, urbanization is an important factor up to the point at which one-fourth of the population lives in cities over 50,000. The direct and monotonic relationship between literacy and urbanization (the surplus of 1.2% in the second row, which contains only four countries is insignificant) is clearest from the time urbanization reaches 10% until it passes 25%. Beyond this point urbanization levels off, while literacy continues to rise "independently" (in countries of extremely high *and* extremely low population density).

If we take 10% and 25% as approximate cutting points in the scale of urbanization, we are able to classify societies into three categories which also discriminate quite consistently the degree of literacy and media participation in each society. Let us designate these three categories as Modern, Transitional, Traditional, to mean the following:

	Literacy	*Urbanization*	*Communication System*
Modern	Over 61%	Over 25%	Media
Transitional	21-60	10-25	Media-Oral
Traditional	Under 20	Under 10	Oral

These cutting points are somewhat arbitrary, of course, in the sense that their outcome is partly determined by the statistical input. (Had urbanization been indexed by cities over 20,000 rather than 50,000 population, for example, the upper cutting-point on this continuum might well be located at 20% rather than 25%.)

The results do enable us, however, to specify two main phases in the process of secular change toward a participant social system. The first phase, speaking summarily, is urbanization. It is the transfer of population from scattered hinterlands to urban centers that provides minimum conditions needed for "take-off" toward widespread participation. Only cities have developed the industrial complex of machines and skills which produces, among other things, newspapers and radio networks and motion pictures. In this first phase, accordingly, increases in urbanization tend in every society to be accompanied by increases in the production and availability of communication media. Once the basic industrial plant is in operation, however, the development of a participant society passes into a subsequent phase. Increasing urbanization, once having provided the initial conditions of production, no longer automatically assures equivalent increases in consumption. The need now shifts to increasing the conditions which govern consumption.

Of this next phase, literacy is both the index and agent, since literacy provides the basic skill required for operation of a media system. Only the literate produce the media contents which, as our literacy-media correlations showed, mainly the literate consume.

Hence, in societies which are about 25% urbanized, the highest correlation of media consumption is with literacy. We shall soon explain more clearly why literacy is the pivotal agent in the transition to a fully participant modern society. Here we wish to stress, in summary fashion, that by the time this modern phase gets well under way, a different social system is in operation than that which governed behavior in a society that was under 10% urbanized and under 40–60% (roughly, less than half) literate. With higher literacy and media participation comes also increasing availability and use of facilities for participation in all sectors of the social system. An index of this is political participation, which reaches its most developed expression in governance by representation.

.   .   .   .

THE DAY

BY HENRY JUSTIN SMITH

This eloquent description of a newspaper at work, by a famous editor of the old *Chicago Daily News*, is reprinted from his book *Deadlines*, published and copyrighted in 1922 by Covici-McGee, Chicago. It is used here by permission of Covici-Friede, publishers. Some features of the newspaper described are not modern, but the account is still basically true in spirit and in most details.

I

IT IS STILL DARK in the streets, still dark among the flat roofs of our block, when the day begins.

It is a winter morning before seven o'clock. Night clings to the city. Windows in some of the tall buildings burn with a radiance never extinguished; others spring into color ahead of the belated sun. On street cars and elevated trains that sail through the darkness like lighted ships the seven o'clock workers are arriving "downtown." They are shabbier, more morose, than those who come later. It is hard to be buoyant before seven o'clock in the morning.

In the newspaper office desks and long tables stand in a twilight due to glimmerings that penetrate through the windows. Typewriters, grotesquely hooded, lie in ranks. Waste-baskets yawn. The wires, clinging to the desks, are asleep; telephones have not yet found their tongues. The electric contact with the waking world is in suspension. What happened yesterday? What will happen today? The wires do not care.

A sleepy boy, shivering, his shoes trickling melted snow, enters the spectral room, carrying a bundle of morning newspapers which he lets fall upon a table. He sighs. He turns an electric switch, and the desks and tables spring into outline. The boy stares about him, stumbles over a waste-basket, kicks it away, sits in a battered chair in front of the mouth of a tarnished copper tube that runs through the ceiling, and drowses. He has barely settled down when he hears men coming in, and starts up. The men are two; young, but with greying hair. They have not much to say to each other. They do not even glance toward the boy. With a manner somewhat repressed, but alert enough, they go to desks, call out for the morning papers, and start slicing them up with scissors. Ten minutes go by, while the clock ticks serenely and the windows become grey with creeping daylight; daylight that sifts down among the roofs and through veils of smoke and fog, that comes cold and ashamed and reluctant. It envelops in new shadows the bowed shoulders of the two young men, touching their cheeks with its own pallor, casting pale reminders upon the papers they are cutting. One man glances over his shoulder at the clock. The clock presently strikes a puny but peremptory "Ping!" It is seven o'clock. The day has begun.

Now enter through the swinging door, which flies back and forth impatiently, the staff. For some time the tramping of their feet, the sound of their breathing, their low laughter, the swish and creak of the door, fill the room. There are ruddy, careless fellows in this company, sanguine youths to whom strain and difficulty are nothing. They tramp, tramp, past the desks and tables, doff overcoats, strip the typewriters of their hoods, whistle, wink at each other, take final puffs of forbidden cigarettes, chuckle together over amusing things in the morning papers, and meantime remain secretly alert —for what? Not merely for the calling of a name by the city editor (now established at his desk and scowling at clippings). Not merely for the chatter of a telephone bell, which may mean a day's work for some or all. The possibilities are vague. The tingling of blood means only that this is a new day. Something is bound to happen. They do not mention this to each other. It is against the code for one man to say to his mate: "John, this may be a momentous day. It may bring fame to someone. This may be our great opportunity." Instead, one reporter stretches and yawns: "Well, here we are again, boys; back in the old squirrel cage, to do a few more turns for the antique Press. What of it? Say, do you suppose such a thing could happen as that I'd get an interesting assignment? Where's the bird who said newspaper work was exciting? . . ."

They are like hunting dogs, pretending to be asleep, but with their ears cocked for the mysterious, the shapeless approaching event that is in the spirit of the day.

II

The room is now full. In this loft, some ninety feet long by thirty wide, place is found for nearly forty men. At one end, the end farthest from the thunder of "L" trains, sits the city editor, surrounded by assistants, tables, telephones, filing cases, wire baskets, spindles, and boys—in that order of usefulness. Within elbow distance are the copy-readers, whom the city editor both prizes and reviles. They bend over their long, battered desk, some of them chewing tobacco unobtrusively, and jab with their pencils at piles of manuscript, giving it an earnest and sardonic scrutiny. Just beyond them sit the telegraph editors, older men and more solemn of face, as befits those whose judgment grapples with majestic cables and Washington dispatches. The chief of these worthies presides at a roll-top desk upon which boys periodically dump a mess of Associated Press sheets, damp from their passage through the tube. The desk has pigeon-holes crammed with dusty reports, statistics, speeches not yet delivered, and biographies of men not yet dead. The telegraph editor is just now arguing with the head proofreader over the spelling of a Russian name. The argument waxes hot. We pass on.

There is a group of desks pertaining to the three men who attend to the "make-up," two of the armchairs vacant because their owners are in the composing room. And there is a large and excessively dusty desk before which, with his back to its intricate recesses, sits the news editor, from whom are supposed to issue ideas, solutions, and enthusiasm. None of them have issued from him thus far; but the day is still young.

Behind all this is the ampler space occupied by the staff. Three reporters, sprawled over their typewriters and strings of clippings, are doggedly pounding out "re-writes" of morning paper articles. Two more are deciphering notes of matters they have just heard over the telephone. Four others stand by a window, engaged in brisk discussion. Are they discussing politics, prurient plays, or prohibition? None of these things. One overhears: "I doubt if Wells is such a scream in England as he is in America. Now, when it comes to Compton Mackenzie—"

A boy approaches one of these reporters and says, triumphantly: "Wallace, Mr. Brown wants you."

"Right."

The literary causerie continues during Wallace's absence. He returns, pulling on his gloves. A stir among the unassigned.

"I've got to interview Sir Scammon Scammonton. LaSalle station."

"Sorry for you. Must be dull day."

"It is," grimaces Wallace, swaggering off.

A dark-haired reporter sits penciling lines upon rough paper, and looking out dreamily into the hurly-burly of traffic and over the chaos of cornices and water tanks visible from the window. He is far, far away from all this. The lines he scrawls are mystical, tender. He is a poet. And he is a very good reporter but his habits—

A stout man in a corner is writing: "It is understood that the non-partisan element in the county board—" but half his thoughts are upon Japanese prints. He is an amateur of Japanese prints.

In another corner a tall and slightly grey-haired reporter stabs with his cane at a vagrant cockroach, while shadows of reverie and discontent flit across his face. He was lately in Europe, whence he returned in disgust, shouting for the "good old life." Now he is yearning for Europe again. A novel that he began to write lies, yellowing, in a corner of his desk. He would like to go to Mexico, or to California. He applies every week for some trip or other. Meantime he meticulously does what he is told to do.

And then, there is a Cub, who sits bolt upright before his idle typewriter, eagerly, lovingly watching the distant city editor from whom today—yes, this very day—may come that "good assignment." Something exciting. Good Lord, if they would only let him—

It is a dull day, yet there is a resistless movement of the commonplace which at last pulls nearly all these men from their trifling or their brooding and sends them out into the city, out into the slushy and gloom-fast streets, out into the enormous glittering skyscrapers, to run down little events. They scatter, with their various moods of hope, disgust, scorn, or vivacity, to thread their way through the city.

The office, emptied of the staff, retains only the "desk men." These are now a little relaxed. Not only has the day's program been laid down, as far as possible, but the first edition, which has furnished a few minutes of tension, is on the presses. From regions far below there comes a muffled thunder, a jarring that faintly shakes the desks. In the news-room silence, compared with the recent pecking of typewriters and murmur of voices, prevails. The desk men straighten up in their chairs, sigh, and stretch. One of them pulls from a drawer a thick novel and reads.

It is a pause. But during this pause life goes on, climaxes prepare. Something draws nearer.

The managing editor, a heavily-built being with harsh spectacles, prowls into the room, gazes about and halts, watched apprehensively by a benchful of small boys. He disregards the juvenile array and swings heavily, thoughtfully, over toward the desk of the news editor.

"What's doing?" he demands, in that voice whose cadences can convey so much wrath, so much bitterness—and so much sweetness.

"Nothing special."

"Humph!" exclaims the Old Man, and retires to his den.

III

The Old Man has officially stigmatized the day as dull.

Boredom is the word.

Take a score of keenly sensitized men, confront them with routine, and the result is boredom. However, they can endure this, just as they are able to stand severe and long-continued excitement. To those who most tremble with suspense or burn with pride there comes the profoundest lethargy; but they have learned to swim in it without impairment of the spirit. Here is a faculty which they have in common with musicians, actors, and other artists. These men in the news-room have traces of the creative temperament, which hibernates, then springs up with new vigor. In some of them it is faded, grown old, or hidden behind stoicism. But in the oldest and most morose of the "desk men" there lives a spark of dramatic instinct, which lights the weariest face at the coming of a "good story."

Nothing of the kind now animates them. They labor on in an incessancy of tasks which must be done at once, even though scarcely worth doing. They must be rapid and skillful without being driven by interest. Throughout the newspaper plant a finely-timed engine, deftly blended of the human and mechanical, is turning,

turning. Everything must move: The grotesque arms of the linotypes, the lumpishly-moving tables of the stereotypers, the gigantic,
glistening coils of the presses, the rolling sidewalks upon which the
finished papers slide toward the delivery wagons. All must turn
with the clock-tick. It makes no difference whether the day be dull
or thrilling. The relentless machinery waits for its injections of human intelligence. The world waits for the news. And always, among
these men in the newsroom, there is a dim sense of the mechanisms forever at work below them, a tinge of fear lest, through
some fault, there be a break in the process, a dreadful pause in
the endless tune. So, driven by habit and by their sub-conscious
perception of their membership in the whole activity of the building, they contribute by pencil-strokes, by orders, by corrections on
proofs, to the flow of this activity.

As the half-hours pass and the day mounts to its meridian, there
is a tensing of effort. Almost casually, two editions have already
been issued, inspected, and forgotten. But now one can feel the
climb toward a greater enterprise, the "home edition," the daily
bugbear whose tradition is that it must be more comprehensive and
correct than either of its predecessors. There is no more lassitude
along the copy-desks; the piles of unread manuscript mount too
fast. The staff is back, for the most part, and the spatter of typewriters deluges the silence. Boys run by with clumsy steps. Bells
ring. The air hisses in the pneumatic tubes. The long, low room
echoes to a thousand movements, a thousand utterances. Yet, despite
the *forte* of the news-room, one is aware of the *fortissimo* of the
city itself. For outside of the newspaper office, as well as within
it, the day is at its height. Skyscrapers now are belching out lunch-
hour crowds, and the shopping streets are filled with joyous, vivid
streams of people. Messages from this turbulence reach the newspaper office; cries come across the roof tops; the symphony of the
city, with its roars, whistles, bellowings, arrives modified but clear.
And if one puts his ear to the wires he can fancy that he hears the
shrill and terrible voices of a hundred other cities where life seethes,
even though "nothing is happening." One has a vision of potentialities of achievement or of disaster in these agitated centers of
life. Straight out of the seeming commonplace of their movement
in pursuit of tasks or fun will emerge the dramatic shock that the
news-room is waiting for. Something is bound to happen.

IV

Something does happen.

First there is the sharp outcry of the Associated Press telephone, distinct from all the other bell-signals. The telegraph editor picks up the receiver and listens. Without a quiver of lips or eyebrows he reaches for paper, and scrawls. The vigilant news editor sees the rigidity of his shoulders, the slight gleam of his eyes, and rises. The copy-readers look up. An instinct awakened by tiny signs, too tiny for the eye of laity, warns "the desk" that this bulletin has a high voltage.

The news editor stands reading as the hand of the telegraph editor traces:

"Washtn . . . bomb on steps . . . treasury building . . . 2 killed."

The telegraph editor hangs up the receiver. For an instant he and his chief stare into each other's eyes. But nothing is said. The implications of this message are self-evident.

"Ask Mr. Barlow to come here," the news editor murmurs to a boy.

While the boy skates nonchalantly off, the editor, with a hand that cannot keep pace with his brain, is writing notes that fly from his pad to distant parts of the building. Simultaneously he is calling earnestly on the house telephone for the circulation department.

Barlow, the make-up editor, enters, heavy-set, frowning at being called from his nearly-complete pages of the home edition. At his heels treads easily but ominously the Old Man, whose presence pervades the room like fate.

The news editor flies at Barlow and mutters to him in a paraphrase of the bulletin, which by this time is being masticated by a linotype machine. Barlow's frown vanishes. He gives an eager nod, seizes a just-written sheet of paper headed "eight-column line, rush extra," and takes it with him as he makes long, heavy strides toward the composing-room door. His mind's eye has mapped out a new first page. At the door he stumbles against a boy and leaves behind him an echo of brief profanity.

The Old Man is told the news.

"I thought it would happen some day," he remarked. He eyes calmly the "telegraph desk" where now two men are working frantically, while another takes more bulletins from the telephone.

Elsewhere in the room there is little commotion. The usual group of reporters is arguing the usual topics. "Peck-peck" goes the Cub's typewriter, grinding out some trifle or other.

Suddenly the young city editor emerges from his nest of telephones and comes down the room at a half-trot.

"They've tried to blow up the federal building here," he snaps, with a half-joyous, half-bitter gleam in his eyes. He dashes back to his desk, followed by the shadowy bulk of the Old Man.

The news editor begins to swear, and laughs instead, having in mind Barlow and his forms. "This will finish him," he thinks, as he speeds toward the composing room. Out there he finds Barlow and his assistant under full steam "breaking up the paper," ordering gleaming stacks of type about, shouting at printers above the perpetual clackety-swish of the linotypes, crossing out and writing in words upon the "schedules" that name the leading articles for various pages. The coatless printers paw the type with their blackened fingers, chew tobacco, and register unconcern. Type lies strewn, in bundles of lines, all over the "stone." Long galleys of brass are piled up like cordwood. Up to the high, glass-roofed ceiling resounds the turmoil of the "stone." The battered clock points imperturbably to 12:05. And at 12:25 all this puzzle must be cleared.

Taking Barlow by the elbow, the news editor speaks in his ear. The color surges into Barlow's face. Still speechless, he darts to the half-complete first-page "form," and roars at the printer whose hands are flying over its columns. The printer hears and nods. He must change everything. What of it? All in the day's work. But the composing-room foreman, sauntering up, tosses in the remark, "Tearin' up again? You'll never make it," and with a wave toward the clock, passes on.

"We've got to make it, Jim," the news editor cries after him. Then, like a man watching two boiling kettles at once, he hastens back to the news-room.

Within the last two minutes the news-room has been transformed in spirit. Everybody has straightened; everybody has caught the stroke. Who said newspaper work was monotonous? seems to shine from the faces. It is gorgeous. The telegraph editor and the city editor are in two separate whirlpools of movement. Boys rush at the telegraph editor and slam sheets of copy upon his desk; the man at the telephone shoves scribbled slips toward him. He rapidly assembles and groups these, discarding some, piecing others

together, laboring with his whole mind to form a story sequential
and lucid. A series of flashes are passing through his mind: "Doubt
if they'll get this bulletin in. . . . There'll be an awful mess for the
next edition." And farther back in his mind occur thoughts more
private, such as: "That rumor the other day about the reds was
right," and "I suppose the wrong man will be caught, as usual."
But his routine brain cells, his hands, go on shaping, shaping. And
save for an out-thrust lower lip he betrays no agitation.

The city editor is twice as busy as this. He has had to scratch off
a dozen lines of copy for the home edition, to dispatch six men to
the federal building, answer (and get rid of) three persons wanting
to know if he was "posted," listen to general orders from the Old
Man, alter a headline that does not "fit," and map out a sort of program for the rest of the day. His mind is ablaze with enterprises
and pierced with apprehensions. Who knows but a rival paper
has already beaten him? He will not be beaten. He sends out to
every part of himself a desperate signal to function, to be alive.
His tongue is dry; his voice threatens to scream. He is at bay, fighting an invincible alliance of enemies: The clock, his rivals, the
tangle of things to do, his own rebellious nerves, the nerve reactions
of everybody else. He calls upon his uttermost reserve. He is four
men in one. He is enraged at life—but he is deliriously happy. And
there flits through him a wan joke: "I suppose the police will call
it a sewer-gas explosion." The joke, which goes unspoken, is extinguished by a wave of perception, vaguer than these words, but
suggesting to him that society is a brutal and turbulent thing, and
bringing to him, like a passing flash of the cinema, a picture of
the federal building portico in ruins, and the bodies lying there.

Through all this pierces the realization that the home edition
has gone to press. The turmoil around him is no less, but here is
the face of his friend, the news editor, emerging from the delirium.

"How's it goin', George?"

"All right," he hears himself reply.

Wallace, the reporter, leans up against the desk.

"Well, boss," inquires Wallace with a subdued twinkle, "how
much on the great Sir Scammon Scammonton? He says—"

The city editor becomes aware of Wallace, and halts him with:

"John, jump down to federal building . . . take taxi . . . forget
about that damned lord—"

Wallace is off, murmuring quaintly: "I obey, boss, I obey."

City editor to news editor: "They think there are six dead down there. A delivery wagon was blown up. There are pieces of horse all over the street. The district attorney says—"

"We'll have to make four separate stories of it for the First Final. At least four—"

"I know. It's a big plot, of course. Oh, is that Billy on the wire? Give him here."

The news editor moves on, devoting a glance to the bowed backs of the local copy-readers, to whom the fury begun with the telegraph desk has now been transmitted. Their eyes bulge with the interest, the horror, of what they are reading. One counts with his fingers the number of letters required for a certain heading. A book that another, a placid, grey-haired man, was reading, has fallen to the floor, and lies open at the title page, "Growth of the Soil."

Reporters who have come in already from the explosion are mauling their typewriters, slamming the cylinders back and forth with a rattle like rifle fire. A constant yell of "Boy!" Dust, colored by the pale noonday sunlight, swims, serene and beautiful above their heads. Murmurs, chucklings, imprecations mingle in a flow of sound; the expressions of the fever that has seized the staff. They are painting, painting. The picture will be hurled out into the streets, seen, and lost. All are artists now, co-operating on the big canvas of the First Final. They are instinctively making art of it, discarding, heightening and coloring. Yes, they color some things, so that the hasty reader can tell them as more important than others. Maybe they do not distort facts; they do not so much distort as rearrange. They suggest perspectives, and introduce good lighting for this tale of tales.

All the while, into their hands is being poured more material, and more. The wires say that the nation is aroused. "The White House has let it be known that. . . ." The wires sing with theories, conjectures, revelations. The tragedy here at the federal building is in the foreground. A notebook has been found among the rags of one of the corpses, with code words in it. Wallace is reading sentences from this book over the 'phone. The district attorney is giving out a long statement. Every minute a member of the staff enters with details which he regards as "bigger stuff than anything." Evidently the mystery of this story is deeper than we thought. It will be unraveling itself for days. We shall be pestered with it for days. What a plague! But what joy!

Meantime, behold it is two o'clock, and the First Final stares us in the face. Ah, here comes the Old Man. "The composing room is swamped." We thought so. "Throw away everything except explosion stuff." The market reports must go in uncorrected. The speech of a distinguished guest at a luncheon goes on the floor. The Cub has written five hundred words about scenes at hospitals and is told he is a fool.

The inexorable clock—the damnable, gliding clock. The waiting machines. The waiting world.

We are desperate men.

We go to the "stone" to make up the First Final. Once more, chaos; bigger heaps of galleys, greater muddles of type. Parts of stories are lost; parts of others are still lagging on the linotypes. We lose our heads, and quarrel. We become children, and say: "Who's blaming me for it?" "I told him to do it." "Good God, this gang is going to pieces."

The type pours to the "stone" from all sides. The pages lie, broken, hopeless.

This time we shall never "get out."

And suddenly we find that it is all done. The forms are full. The last one is being locked up, and slid into the outstretched hands of the stereotypers.

We glance at each other, wipe off sweat, and grin.

v

This is a splendid product of ours, after all. The boys are bringing in papers, staggering under the bundles. We spread them out on the desks, admire and criticize. It is scarcely possible we did this. Thirty minutes, twenty minutes, ago we were writing the words that now peer at us from the pages, faintly familiar creations that have arrayed themselves in a manner distinctively their own. It is all there as we planned it in our frenzy. The house has risen from that chaos at the "stone." The event that has shaken the country's nerves lies there embodied in types of varying blackness and size, making a structure with girders and gables, with foundations and flourishes. A structure nevertheless built to last but a day, to outlast scarcely even our pride in it.

Our pride in it is momentary. We are conscious that we have conquered. This feeling is confirmed when our rivals are brought in, and their paltry efforts to keep pace with us are seen. But we are too wise, or too weary, to gloat more than for that moment. Tomorrow may snatch this triumph away from us. And besides—

It is the Old Man's voice:

"Look here, we say in this head that three wheels of the wagon were blown off; but in the eye-witness account it says—"

And he lays a broad thumb upon the column.

Two or three men, among them the city editor, respectfully examine the discrepancy.

"There's always something to spoil it all," grumbles the Old Man, and bears his newspaper away, grasped in both hands, while the staff exchanges rueful winks. The city editor slips on his coat and says savagely to the news editor: "If I don't show up tomorrow you can guess why." His eyes burn in his pale young face. He flings himself out, biting off the end of a cigar. The eyes of the grey-haired copy-reader follow him humorously, tenderly.

The news editor turns to the disposal of matters for the afternoon. The greater part of the afternoon still remains. There are still "late developments." There will be a "rush hour extra." The news editor walks back through the room, remarking to the "desk" as he goes: "Nobody off early today. We'll need all hands."

They look up, unamazed. Were it to go on forever, they would still be unamazed.

VI

But at last it is five o'clock, and the very last extra of all has been patched up, and there is nothing more to do.

Darkness has come again. It seems now to have been scarcely ten minutes since the first of those alert figures entered through the swinging door; but the evidences of a complete day are all about: waste-paper ankle deep around the desks; waste-baskets crammed with torn newspaper sheets; pencil-butts, proofs, crumpled notes.

The men, the last of them, are putting on hats and coats and departing. They go wearily and sulkily. The emotional storm in which they have been tossed has left them chilled. The more thrilling the day, the more leaden its close. This product, conceived with such skill and speed and evolved with such a fury of zeal, is already scarcely more than waste-paper. The men tramp gloomily into the hall, turning up the collars of their overcoats and peering into the shadows of the gloomy corridor. They go down the elevator, grumbling, but still with a vestige of elation.

"Well, that was *some* day," they mutter.

"*Some* day," echo the dying voices of the linotypes.

"*Some* day," groan the presses from the basement.

The men, slackened in spirit, cynical about it all, exuding revolt, are happy in spite of everything. "*Some* day," to be sure. They will tell their wives and children about it. They will meet acquaintances who will respectfully ask their opinions, because they are newspaper men.

There are new furrows in their faces; but their youth is inextinguishable.

The grey-haired copy-reader, who is last to leave, watches them go, turns out a light or two, and slowly prepares for the street. And he thinks about these men, whom, in a way, he loves:

"I wonder what draws them into this game? I wonder why they keep at it, the game being what it is. I wonder what the fascination of news is. I wonder what news really is. . . .

"The continuousness of it all; the knowledge that no matter what we do today, we must do better tomorrow. . . .

"The unendurable boredom; the unendurable excitement. . . .

"Maybe we stay on because life is like that, and we get more of life here than somewhere else."

VII

The only lights remaining are two that burn dispiritedly at either end of the long room. The wires sleep again, oblivious of the sparkling but dreadful world. The battlefield is deserted.

Now enter two sad-faced, elderly males in soiled and shapeless clothing, carrying large sacks. Into these they dump contents of waste-baskets, and bundles of scraps. They seem very, very old and depressed. In and out among the desks they go, muttering to themselves, and clearing away the dull traces of the splendid task. These specters know nothing of the efforts or the victories just recorded. The voices of the city, the cries of newsboys, the tootings and tinklings of the streets, are nothing at all to these aged scavengers. Outlived . . . all outlived.

Having finished their funereal task, they go out, and the room is left to its memories, the wires to their slumber.

So ends the day.

A DAY IN THE MAKING OF A MOVIE

BY LILLIAN ROSS

This is a section from Chapter 2 of Mrs. Ross's book, *Picture* (1952), which describes the making of the motion picture, "The Red Badge of Courage." It is published and copyrighted by Rinehart and is reprinted here by permission of the author and publisher.

THE FIRST SCENE to be shot, No. 72, read:

MEDIUM SHOT—NEW ANGLE

The regiment encounters the body of a dead soldier and the ranks open covertly to avoid the corpse.

It was being set up on a dirt road running through the thickly wooded park. A couple of hundred Chicoans, many of them sporting five-dollar-bonus beards and all of them dressed in Union blues and carrying rifles or swords, were lined up on the road in a column of fours. Near the head of the column stood Dixon Porter, wearing the sword and red sash of a lieutenant; he was one of the extras. A long dolly track, with wooden rails, had been laid beside the road. The camera, fixed on a tripod, stood on a rubber-wheeled dolly at one end of the track. The trees lining the road arched high over the heads of the warlike array. Everybody in Huston's crew seemed, with a harassed awareness of the dollar value of every minute, to be rushing everyone else. Rosson, standing on the dolly and peering through the camera at the line of soldiers, gave hurried signals to assistants helping him get the camera in position. Huston and Reinhardt made a hasty inspection of the Chicoan army. Marton dashed at Mauldin, collared him, and thrust him into the Union ranks behind Murphy and Dierkes. The time was 8:38 A.M.

In the road, ahead of the troops, lay a soldier, face down, his uniform dishevelled, a rifle under his limp arm, his legs sprawled. Callow was arranging and rearranging the legs. A still photographer aimed a Speed Graphic at the dead man; his flash bulb popped, and he quickly turned his camera on the waiting troops. Band arrived and began to tag after Huston, who walked over to the camera.

"Good morning, boys," Huston said to Rosson and his assistants. "Good luck, gentlemen!"

Jack Aldworth was writing in a hard-covered notebook. The first page was headed "LOG—PROD. NO. 1512—HUSTON." Under the heading, he had already written:

    7:45–8:00—Travel to Location
    8:00–8:20—Spot Equip. and Unload Trucks
    8:20–8:32—Lineup Dolly Shot with Soldiers

He now wrote:

    8:32–8:40—Set up camera with it on dolly—meanwhile reh
    and drill soldiers.

Aldworth would submit his daily log to Reinhardt and to Callow, who would submit it to Lee Katz, who would submit copies of it to Joe Cohn, Dore Schary, and L. B. Mayer, in Culver City, and to Nicholas Schenck, in New York. (Along with the daily log would go a daily report on the time the crew left for location, the time shooting started and finished, and the number of scenes filmed, and the number of extras used.) Reinhardt was standing beside the camera, reading a letter that had just been handed to him by a messenger:

Dear Gottfried:

Well, we're off! And we're off to a good start. I'm certain it will be good, Gottfried, damned good. We'll make it so. Good luck and my best.

                    Sincerely,
                    Dore

The rehearsal began. Callow yelled, "Here we go, boys! Get in line!" The troops started marching toward the man lying in the road. Callow told them to pause and look down at the body as they passed it. Huston peered into the camera and watched the procession, then called to the troops that this was the first dead man they had ever seen, and told them to keep this in mind when they looked down at the body. The time was 8:56.

For all the tension, hurry, and confusion, it was very quiet. At Callow's command, the Union soldiers, having passed the body, moved back to their starting point. They were silent, and their silence was respectful. A smoke machine mounted on a truck, which had been hidden in the woods off the road, started up with a clatter, and smoke drifted slowly among the trees in the almost windless heat of the morning.

Huston moved about quickly and smoothly. He strode over to the dead man in the road and called for a bucket of water. A prop man scurried off, and was back with it in a few seconds. Huston quickly mussed the man's hair and sprinkled dirt over his hair, face, and knapsack. Reinhardt looked down with a cynical smile as Huston mixed a handful of earth and water and daubed mud over the man's face and hands. Huston stood up. Aldworth was holding out a clean white handkerchief. Huston wiped his hands on it and called for blood. A makeup man sprinted over with a tube of "panchromatic blood"—mineral oil with vegetable coloring. Huston, thumbs hooked in the back of his belt, directed the bloodying process. Callow rushed up and said, "Mr. Huston, have the troops lost their knapsacks by this time or haven't they?" Huston, thoughtfully staring at the dead man, said they still had knapsacks. He sprinkled another handful of dirt over the man. Marton hurried up and asked whether the troops still had their knapsacks on, and Huston gave him the same answer he had given Callow. It was 9:10.

Colonel Davison came up to tell Huston that the drummer boys in the column looked too naked with only their drums. Huston directed a prop man to put packs on the boys. Aldworth was writing:

8:40–9:12—Cont. line up Dolly Shot

A makeup man fussed with Mauldin's wig under his kepi until it covered the better part of his neck. Huston saw the wig and said it was all wrong. The wig was removed, and a smaller one was substituted. Smoke now lay over everybody and everything. The smoke machine sounded like a couple of steam shovels. "Kill that motor!" Callow bawled.

A man carrying a loudspeaker box on his shoulder and a microphone in his hand walked over to Huston. "All right," Huston said in a dramatically calm voice into the mike. "All right, boys." Everybody looked at him. "The idea is these troops are coming into a battle area," he said. "This is the first time you have heard gunfire. I'm going to fire a revolver. This will be the first shot you have ever heard. Each soldier as he passes the dead man will slow down. This is the first dead man you have ever seen. All right." The time was 9:26.

There was a brief silence—a lull before a battle. Huston told a smoke man not to make smoke, because this would be a rehearsal. Callow reminded the troops that they were not to step over the dead man but pass around him. Huston went over to the camera and called for action. Callow told the men to get going. They began to shuffle toward the dead man. The camera trained on them rolled on ahead, pulled along the dolly track by grips. Huston walked backward behind the dolly, looking intently at the faces of the troops. He gave the Chicoans a menacing look, and slowly raised the revolver over his head. He fired the revolver, still watching grimly, then fired again. The troops shuffled uneasily around the body of the dead man. Callow called "About face!" and the men returned to their starting position. Huston went over to the dead man and sprinkled more dirt on him. Reinhardt laughed. "How he loves to do that!" he said.

The time was 9:35. Jack Aldworth was writing:

    9:12–9:35—Reh

Katz said to Reinhardt, "Joe Cohn asked me last night when you were coming back."

"I wish I knew," Reinhardt said.

"Consider the whole thing unasked," said Katz. At the end of each day, he told Reinhardt, the film that had been shot would be flown back to Culver City for developing.

Reinhardt said he wanted to see each day's film—called rushes, or dailies—the following day. He didn't want to wait two or three days. "I don't care how they feel about spending the money," he added.

"May I quote you?" Katz asked, smiling.

"It's important," said Reinhardt.

"Let me just find my studio notes," Katz said, digging in his pockets.

"If we can get them two *hours* sooner, I want them," said Reinhardt.

Katz took out his notes and studied them. "It would mean a difference of ten or twelve dollars a night," he said. "I'll talk to Joe Cohn about it."

"All this for two lines in the script," Albert Band said. "Would television go to all this trouble for two lines in a script?"

Callow announced that everyone was to be very quiet, because they were going to start shooting. A prop man was chalking on a small slate:

| Huston | Scene 72 |
| Prod 1512 | Set 01 |

EXT ROAD AND DEAD SOLDIER

The smoke machine started again. Aldworth wrote:

9:35–9:40—Put in smoke effect in BG [background]

Pistol in hand, Huston knelt directly in front of the camera.

"Quiet and roll it!" Callow shouted.

The camera buzzed. The prop man held his slate in front of the camera for a moment.

"*Action!*" Huston said. The soldiers moved forward. The camera moved ahead of them.

Reinhardt looked at Huston with a long sigh. "Now there is no turning back," he said. "We are committed."

On their fourth encounter with the body since the shooting had begun, the troops apparently gave the performance wanted. "Cut! That's it," he said. "Print it!"

Aldworth wrote down:

9:40–10:00—Shoot four takes (Takes 1-2-3—NG [no good] action)

The dead man got up and wiped a muddy palm over his muddy face. He asked Band whether he would be paid extra for lying in the road a couple of hours.

"Over Joe Cohn's dead body," Band said.

At 2:30 P.M., the temperature in the woods was a hundred and eight. Eight Chicoans had collapsed while Huston was rehearsing a scene that required some troops to run off the road and into the forest and start digging ditches, as the Lieutenant of the Youth's platoon, played by Douglas Dick, walked toward the camera, smoothing his mustache, youthfully arrogant as he looked forward to his first taste of battle. At 2:32, Huston ordered his crew to print the shot of the troops.

At 4:02, Huston began working on a closeup of Dick smoothing his mustache. Huston lifted his own shoulder slightly to signify youthful arrogance, and encouraged Dick to imitate him. At 4:28, after seven takes, Huston said, "That's it."

At 4:45, Huston started working on closeups of the soldiers digging in.

"Do we expect an attack?" Dixon Porter asked him.

"You don't know what the hell to expect. That's why you're digging," said Huston.

Katz came over and said he didn't want to rush anybody, but the film had to be flown out of Chico at 6:30. Huston nodded curtly.

Huston directed the camera to be set up behind an elderly Chicoan who was digging in. The man had a long, deeply lined face. Kneeling alongside the camera, behind the man, Huston ordered him to relax and said he would tell him exactly what to do. "Action!" he called. "All right, sir. Move a little forward, sir. Now turn around and look behind you, slowly. That's right. Now dig. With your scabbard. Hard at it. Now with your plate! Hard. Harder. Very good. "Cut!" He thanked the man and looked very happy. It was a face he liked.

Huston was rehearsing a group of soldiers in a digging scene when Rosson told him that they were fighting a losing battle with the sun. In the scene, Arthur Hunnicutt, an actor with a care-worn face, was leaning on his rifle, watching half a dozen comrades dig a hole. "I don't hold with layin' down and shootin' from behint a little hill," he was saying. "I wouldn't feel a bit proud doin' it. I aim t' do my fightin' standin' up." One of the soldiers digging said, "If yeh want t' get shot that's yer own business." Hunnicutt said, "Well, I ain't goin' t' lay down *before* I'm shot—and that's all there is to it!"

"Light's going!" Rosson cried. "Let's take it."

Jack Aldworth wrote:

6:10–6:17—Moving camera and actor to get sunlight.

At 6:20, Huston took his last shot of the day. Then he walked over to a rotting log and sat down. He put his elbows on his knees and cupped his face in his hands.

Jack Aldworth noted in his report—a copy of which would be in Nicholas Schenck's New York office the next day—that eleven scenes had been shot for "The Red Badge of Courage," out of a total of three hundred and forty-seven.

HOW A TELEVISION COMMERCIAL IS MADE

GENERAL ELECTRIC REVIEW

This vivid description of the making of a brief television presentation was published in the *General Electric Review* for September, 1956, and is reprinted by permission of the magazine, which holds copyright.

ON SUNDAY EVENING, March 4, from 9 to 9:30 o'clock in the East, approximately one out of every five Americans saw and heard Paul Muni and Polly Bergen in a television play called "A Letter from the Queen."

Each of the 33-odd-million viewers paid nothing for this entertainment, except a few pennies worth of depreciation on his TV set (assuming he wasn't at the neighbors) and a tiny fraction of the month's power bill.

General Electric, on the other hand, paid a handsome sum of money for the services of the people needed to produce a complex collection of electronic impulses and distribute them to 152 stations throughout the land.

And for this weekly outlay, General Electric has the opportunity to talk about itself for three minutes—all the Federal Communications Commission allows for each half hour of program time.

If all 33 million people watch and listen—and understand—the program is a tremendous bargain. Reaching this audience, say, by direct mail would cost many times as much in postage alone.

If only a few watch and listen—and if they should fail to understand—the program is a colossal waste of money.

And just because 33 million people watch the entertainment portion of the show—occurring both before and after the three-minute commercial—is no assurance that they will be on hand during those middle three minutes. It's obviously an ideal time to go to the refrigerator, to make sure the kiddies are in bed, to prepare a quick Sunday-night snack, or to check the newspaper to see what will be on what channel at 9:30.

There's the problem. In only 180 seconds the commercial must tell in a dignified manner how and why, among other things, General Electric is a leader in research, engineering, and manufacturing skill. And because the audience would just as soon be doing something else, the presentation must hold their interest from its outset until the entertainment resumes.

The three-minute Progress Report for the March 4 program was devoted to electric motors, *The Universal Servants*. The steps that led from the conception of this commercial to its brief moment of glory beginning at 9:16:16 P.M. make an interesting story of the problems encountered in communicating a fairly intricate technical idea to a mass audience—and making it register.

Progress Reports are handled by a three-man operation—supervisor and two producers—in the Schenectady unit of General Electric's Public and Employee Relations Services. The New York advertising agency of Batten, Barton, Durstine, and Osborn (BBDO) provides the General Electric unit with a basic staff of five men: coordinator, agency producer, film producer, and two writers. The agency producer hires the directors, scene designers, cameramen, and talent, usually free-lance. This team of eight men plans, develops, and produces—week in and week out—180 seconds of entertaining education that will register the company's message and draw above-average survey ratings.

Progress Reports are planned in 13-week cycles at a meeting with BBDO. The group presents ideas—always comes up with a surplus, relegates some to a future series, and immediately discards others.

Even approved subjects hurdle a long series of difficulties before being firmly scheduled. For instance, live commercials are usually coupled with live entertainment, film commercials with film shows. The difference in quality between film and live makes a mixture of the two noticeable to viewers. Money and time are other factors: a film commercial costs about three times as much as a live one and usually must be shot at least a month before the release date.

While films lack the here-and-now spontaneity of live commercials, they do give some advantages. They offer the chance of newsreel coverage of an important event and can be rerun as many times as the sponsor chooses, thus amortizing the cost premium.

Timing introduces another problem: An electricity-on-the-farm commercial should be scheduled in the spring; the engineer's role in today's technology would tie in with Engineers' Week. Also commercials must give a balanced picture of General Electric's activities: research, engineering progress, manufacturing skill, and human relations, to name a few.

That educational and entertaining commercials are produced each week and receive high ratings—even allowing for the vast range of subjects offered by a company the size of General Electric—is a tribute to the GE-BBDO team.

Toward the end of November 1955, the group met and planned the second cycle of Progress Reports (January through March). They discussed—and scheduled—a live commercial on electric motors for March 4, bracketed by one on railroad progress and one on lightning research.

Soon after this team meeting, they released the production schedule: Charlie Keenan of General Electric would follow it with Al Book of BBDO as the writer.

Because ten of General Electric's product departments manufacture motors, each justifiably proud of its products and prerogatives, Keenan knew that the job ahead would take an unusual amount of patience and understanding. And so late in January, he slated a meeting with the primary contact, Harry E. Smith, Advertising Manager of General Electric's Medium Induction Motor Department, Schenectady. Other company advertising men would be reached by additional communication lines.

One morning early in February, Keenan and Book met in Smith's office. MIM, as his department is called throughout the Company, produces 7½- to 3000-hp. motors—sold by General Electric under its registered trademark of Tri-Clad motors.

Keenan roughed out the objectives of the Progress Report: explain how an electric motor works; point out progress in electric motors; show some significant motors of today; tell how motors benefit everyone.

Quickly, talk turned to the first objective—just how *does* an electric motor work.

"Make it simple," said Book. "I'm a typical layman. I'm a sounding board. I pass on what I hear to the audience. The simpler it is the better for our purpose."

Smith explained that a motor basically converts electric energy received over lines into rotating motion to drive machines. He suggested a simple demonstration: Put metal filings into a beaker of water, then place the beaker inside a rotating electric field. "For the transition," he said, "take out the beaker and replace it with the motor's rotor. It's that simple."

As the discussion warmed, such terms as stator, lines of force, magnetism, a-c and d-c, automation, dynamometer, and synchronous motor flowed freely. Keenan, sensing that the objectives were fading rapidly, called a halt, urging that they discard these technical terms. "I know they sound simple. But just because we use them doesn't indicate that we know their meaning or can even explain them. Remember, this must be understood by a *mass* audience. You're not talking to an AIEE group. And leave out automation. We'll cover that in a later commercial."

After the meeting in Smith's office, Keenan circulated a letter that read, in part: "The next meeting on our research activities concerning the upcoming Progress Report on electric motors will be held in New York City on Tuesday, February 14. We're going to get together with Don Herbert with a view toward developing some simple demonstration that will help get this story across better."

Don Herbert, General Electric's Progress Reporter, is known to small-fry viewers—and many adults, too—as Mr. Wizard, star of a half-hour weekly television show seen on more than 141 stations. There are hundreds of Mr. Wizard clubs, and his technique of "teaching science painlessly" has been cited in a score of special awards and scrolls now hanging in his office. Herbert is an expert at performing graphic demonstrations for television cameras. This ability plus a fine combination of a businesslike mien and an ingratiating air got him the job of General Electric's Progress Reporter.

Prism Productions, Herbert's office-workshop on 23rd Street in New York where the group met, has large airy offices and a well-equipped workroom.

Shortly after 10 o'clock, Al Book read his first rough to the group. Into the script he had written Billy Quinn—a 10-year-old actor who had served as the "questioner" on many of the Progress Reports. The commercial would open with Herbert and Billy demonstrating the way that a motor works, followed by Billy guessing the number of motors in his home. This, Book said, would show the importance of motors in the home. And then film clips would emphasize the importance of motors in industry.

"For the opening shot they could be examining a fan," Book suggested.

Someone doubted whether a fan was dramatic enough and asked, "How about an erector set?"

"Can't use that," Keenan remarked, "we used it last week."

"How much time do I have to show how a motor works?" Herbert inquired. Before anyone could reply, he laughingly answered, "Yeah, I know, 22 seconds. This will revolutionize physics teaching!"

"That looks too complicated." The agency producer nodded toward a small demonstration motor whirring in front of Herbert. "Can't we show how a motor works without all this . . .?" He pointed to the exposed magnets, core, and wires.

"You're just like my wife," Herbert said, smiling. "She's always saying to me, 'Can't you tell me how atomic energy works without going into all those details?'"

Because the commercial had no opening, Keenan steered the talk in that direction. He again outlined the objectives, suggesting that they concentrate on something difficult when done by hand but easy with a motor.

One approach had Billy polishing a chair, with an electric buffer finishing the job. Reflections from the chair made this idea impractical. Then, too, not enough people in the TV audience owned buffers.

"Why not have the kid sawing a board? I could finish the job with a power saw," Herbert volunteered. There were nods of agreement.

More discussion followed concerning the demonstration motor and whether the three-phase 110- or 220-volt power would be available in the studio. Then the meeting moved into Herbert's office to wrap up the sequence of the commercial's elements.

One item brought to the group's attention was Book's concern about having the boy in the script. "If he blows a line, then Don has to cover. It means that Don must learn not only his own lines but also the kid's. I know the kid is good, but he's only 10. That's a lot of responsibility for a 10-year-old."

"I agree," Keenan said. "It's something we've considered from every angle. But the advantages of having the kid on the show far outweigh any fluffs. He's got audience appeal. He's got a likable face—wholesome. The audience puts itself in the boy's shoes. They say to themselves, 'If that kid can understand it, so can I.' And it works, too. This is nothing new—only an adaptation of what the Greeks did centuries ago. It's the Greek chorus all over again. During a play the chorus became the 'audience,' registering the reactions of an audience. The boy does the same thing: he's the Greek chorus; he's the audience. Okay?"

At 12:25 the group broke up for lunch. Book now had a better idea of how to proceed: Billy would open sawing on a piece of wood and Herbert would complete the job with a power saw; an electric motor demonstration would follow, plus some discussion about motors in the home, film clips on motors in industry, and a windup showing today's General Electric motors. Book promised a script in a couple of days.

In the two and one-half weeks between the meeting at Herbert's workshop and March 4, Keenan maintained a wearing and abrasive schedule. He was closely following not only the electric motors commercial but also seven others that were in various stages of development.

Script changes were usually of a minor nature—a constant effort to get a more informative and polished presentation. At the same time he remained aware of the three-minute limitation on the copy. Words and phrases were altered: Billy's "Whews" were changed to "Wows," his "Gees" to "Boys," and his "Yep" to "Yes." "General Electric" was placed in front of the word "motors" at the proper places, and "washing machine" became "washer."

In one instance it was decided that Herbert should wear safety glasses while he operated the power saw. As Keenan expressed it, "We'd have every safety man in the Company jumping all over us if Herbert didn't wear them. And it might encourage some of the do-it-yourselfers in the audience to use them, too."

Another one of Keenan's duties was coordinating and ordering the various properties for the commercial: General Electric unit kitchen, clock, mixer, mural of a wind tunnel, and a pair of safety glasses. BBDO, meanwhile, looked for a power saw with a General Electric motor and a hand saw.

Five days before air time, scripts were distributed to interested

General Electric operating departments for their approvals. By late that afternoon the approved copies began trickling in. The reactions were uniformly satisfactory except for the description of how an electric motor works. Immediately, Keenan began preparing a revised version of just how an electric motor *does* work.

On Wednesday, February 29, Book arrived from New York to work with Keenan on the electric motors commercial and others for future shows.

With some cardboard models he had developed with an engineer, Keenan showed Book the new idea for demonstrating the principle of an electric motor: A bar magnet brought close to one end of a magnet pivoting on a vertical shaft was either repelled or attracted. "Now," Keenan said, "we lift off this magnet that spins, place it inside the stator of a motor, turn on the power, and the magnet should spin."

"Herbert," he explained, "will say: 'When electricity is put through the stator.' Only the word "stator" won't mean anything to the audience. What's a better word?"

Book thought a second, then said, "How about core?"

Keenan nodded. "Herbert will say something like: 'And when electricity is put through the core of an electric motor, it becomes a magnet and causes the other magnet to spin.' Then he'll turn on a switch, and the magnet should spin."

"You sure this is going to work?" asked Book. "Remember, this is live. We're on the air."

To cover all chances, Keenan planned to have two demonstrations written into the script. One would use the bar magnets; the other would use one of Herbert's science demonstration motors.

Next he tackled the problem of getting the "magnet" motor built and shipped to New York for the telecast. Harry Smith furnished the stator of a 7½-hp Tri-Clad motor, and a General Electric model shop assembled the demonstration. Getting the bar magnets proved to be a task. Finally, a physics professor at Union College solved this problem with two 6-inch demonstration compasses.

Book returned to New York to get the final version on paper and duplicated for the show. A meeting in New York at CBS Studio 56 on 58th Street between Park Avenue and Lexington was set for 2 P.M. Sunday—seven hours before air time.

CBS Studio 56 was once the Liederkranz Hall, acoustically one of the better halls in New York. It has since been chopped up into studios and today is used almost entirely for the production of live TV commercials.

A look inside Studio 56 on this particular Sunday morning reveals four gaunt walls plus lighting equipment and sundry gear associated with a TV studio. The pile of crates in the middle of the floor contains the General Electric unit kitchen, a refrigerator, and other props.

2 P.M.—The unit kitchen and refrigerator are in place, and all sets are erected. The four sets—workshop, kitchen, living room, and motor display—form an arc to make camera movement easier.

All the latent energy that the project quietly absorbed for five weeks now comes to the surface. Twenty-five people busily work on staging details: spraying wax on all the unit kitchen and refrigerator's shiny surfaces to reduce glaring reflections, or flare, in the camera; putting the demonstration motors in place; and lining up the tools for the workshop area.

The first time any self-styled reasonable man sees live television being produced, he says, "There must be an easier way." But logic —surrounded by pressures, authorities, conflicting talents, union regulations, and the relentless progress of the clock on the wall— can seldom be found in the mechanics of a TV studio. That the visible results are logical and coherent is a tribute to the performers who maintain equanimity through it all. Most people have the idea that men like Don Herbert are overpaid. But when the time arrives and responsibility for the job rests on his shoulders alone, not many envy him.

2:40—In the upper reaches of the Hall, the show's director meets with Don Herbert, BBDO representatives, including Al Book, and General Electric representative Charlie Keenan.

Herbert reads through the script for timing; the director takes the part of Billy who is rehearsing for another show. The first read-through clocks out at 2 minutes and 40 seconds.

The film clips don't agree with the script; it is rewritten.

3:45—The "camera fax" begins—a rehearsal using cameras that transmit pictures to the control room. Camera positions are plotted, and the director "blocks," or plans, the action for Herbert and Billy.

A union man clamps a 2 x 4 in the workshop vise. Which end should Herbert saw? If he saws the end that would give the best camera shot, it would offend all the home craftsmen in the audience, as well as not be quite safe. Keenan decides it shold be done the safe and most logical way; the director works with the cameras to get a satisfactory angle.

4:20—On the control-room screen, the position of the 7½-hp Tri-Clad motor looks awkward. To say that a motor is a handsome piece of equipment would be charitable, even though designers have tried to give it style and dignity. But with the distortions that occur on the tiny screen, conduit boxes suddenly grow to outlandish and grotesque proportions, and shafts project at odd angles. "If we show the General Electric monogram, then you can't see the shaft. Which is most important?" the director asks. Keenan says that it must look like a motor—never mind the emblem on the end shield.

5:15—Herbert goes through the commercial and an agency man takes the part of Billy. It times out to three minutes and six seconds. Number 3 camera conks out. The director calls a break.

There's a stir in the control room. The whirling magnets in the motor demonstration aren't visible enough; they blend into the background.

It is suggested they be painted white. No, someone else says that may ruin their magnetism. A technician solves the problem when he sticks a piece of masking tape on the magnets and trims the tape to size. The contrast looks good on the control-room screen.

Then Herbert complains that the power saw spews sawdust over his dark suit, giving it a tweedy appearance. Another piece of masking tape seals the exhaust port on the saw.

Next, the mixer on the unit kitchen can't be seen. Again, it's a question of a light color against a light color. Because masking tape or paint is out of the question, the director works in a close-up shot to identify the mixer.

5:45—The director calls an hour break for dinner.

7:15—Rehearsals continue, each one becoming smoother as the actors fall into the rhythm of the pace and the cameramen and director integrate their routines.

Between 7:15 and 7:45 each run-through incorporates the film clips. The film—handled in another CBS studio—is seen on a monitor in Studio 56.

For the first run-through with the film, Herbert's commentary and the film sequence don't match. Reproduction quality is poor. Keenan shakes his head and calls the agency representatives together. They decide to eliminate the film clips, remove the living-room set, and rewrite the script to include electric motors in various industries.

7:45—At a CBS studio on the third floor of Grand Central Terminal, 16 blocks away, Paul Muni and Polly Bergen begin the dress rehearsal.

8:00—The commercial is integrated into the dress rehearsal and times out to exactly three minutes.

8:15—Herbert, anxious to get some "business" (eye-catching hand action) into the final scene with the two display motors, suggests giving one of the motor shafts a slight spin. This is accepted and a technician cleans off the gummy protective coating.

At the unit kitchen, more wax is sprayed on the cabinets to kill flares.

Herbert breaks his collar stay and replaces it with one borrowed from a BBDO man.

8:27—Herbert leaves to have make-up put on; Billy talks with his mother in a corner of the studio; others drift out for coffee.

8:42—Herbert returns and once more walks through the commercial with Billy. Billy's mother gives her son's hair a final combing.

9:00—The master screen in the control room shows the General Electric monogram, and the announcer says: "For General Electric here is Ronald Reagan."

In Studio 56, cameras warm up and the floor is cleared. The assistant director quips, "Isn't it true Muni did this show because he has some General Electric stock?"

But the problems of Paul Muni or Polly Bergen don't concern the men in Studio 56. Their only worry is the middle three minutes, the important part, the part that pays off. Admittedly, the men in Studio 56 agree that without good entertainment nobody watches the sponsor's message. But there is also the unexpressed attitude that it's tougher to get people to watch a commercial than to watch some make-believe story. And when you get right down to it, the commercial is the reason for the whole enterprise.

9:07—Herbert and Billy go through the commercial once again. During the motor demonstration, Herbert keeps calling the magnets "needles" (which, of course, they are). Keenan asks the agency producer to request Herbert to say "magnets."

9:14—In the control room the assistant director calls the one-minute signal. Someone scrapes a chair along the floor and tension mounts.

A phone rings. The assistant director answers, listens, puts his hand over the mouthpiece, and says, "Central control says they're running over. They'll appreciate anything we can give them." He uncovers the mouthpiece and to central control reports, "I relayed the message," then hangs up.

9:16—Ronald Reagan says: "Y'know, many of the jobs that we have to do at home and at work would be a lot harder if it weren't for General Electric motors —as you'll see in Don Herbert's Progress Report."

At exactly 9:16:16 the commercial begins and 2 minutes and 50 seconds later Herbert concludes with, ". . . and as you know, at General Electric, progress is our most important product."

The members of the audience, assuming they hadn't gone to check the kids or get that sandwich, heard Don Herbert and Billy Quinn speak barely 500 words—mostly words of one syllable. As the professional performers they are, both carried it off in perfect fashion. The 2 x 4 was neatly sawed, the demonstration motor hesitated momentarily then spun wildly, no flare came from the unit kitchen, and the smallest General Electric motor looked small indeed in Herbert's hand.

The program, it was disclosed later, had a Nielsen rating of 33.5. This means that 33.5 per cent of the 35 million television homes in America saw the program. Each of the nearly 12 million sets tuned to the General Electric Theater was watched by an average of 2.78 persons, making a total audience of 33 million. Both the Nielsen and the Trendex surveys put the General Electric Theater for March 4 among the "top 10" for the week.

Having spent the money for the program, it is not hard to justify spending a little more to see how much of an impact the first investment produced. For this purpose, General Electric and BBDO obtain the services of Gallup and Robinson, a well-known Princeton, N.J., opinion-survey organization. Gallup and Robinson submit a weekly "Television Impact Report," a 30-page mimeographed document describing in detail the results of their Monday survey.

The term "Remember Commercial" used in the report is considered by General Electric and BBDO to be the key factor. In this regard, the commercials on the General Electric Theater almost invariably have done well. Gallup and Robinson say that the Re-

member Commercial norm for all one-half hour programs advertising one product (about three minutes devoted to a commercial)
is 55 per cent. The average for all General Electric Theater programs
during the past season was 65 per cent. On these commercials, men
do better than women by a 71 to 54 score.

The electric motors commercial on March 4 achieved a score of
67 per cent—above the norm for all programs and above the average for the General Electric Theater. Of the men interviewed who
qualified as viewers of the program, 73 per cent could recall the
commercial with reasonable accuracy; for women the figure was
60 per cent.

Of greatest interest to the novice reading a Gallup and Robinson
Impact Report are the verbatim statements, recorded in astounding
detail by interviewers.

The vast majority of recalls indicated that the audience understood the message and that a favorable impression of General
Electric was created. Here are some samples:

A man showed a little boy how a small, primitive motor operated. It
had an armature and a magnet. The one thing they always say is,
"Progress is our most important product." They showed all the different
types of motors that GE makes; one was a huge thing. The commercial
pointed out how important motors are in our daily lives and how different things would be if we didn't have any motors. I thought it was a
good idea to use the little boy to explain the fundamentals of the motors.
They had a reasonable approach and, the points were easy to understand.

Don Herbert was talking to a kid about motors. He said that electricity
and magnetism work together. He demonstrated how the magnetic
field in the motor was activated. Large and small motors were shown.
A Telechron clock was an example of a small motor. Motors can be
any size and still be practical. They said, "Progress is our most important product" and showed that they are more interested in progress
than anything else. The commercial was done in the simplest manner.
If the little kid could understand, then anyone could comprehend the
way the motor worked.

A man showed a little boy all the motors there were in the house. He
pointed out everything electric in the kitchen that had a motor. They
showed a motor bigger than a man in a tremendous room. Men were standing by it. They showed the coils and the magnet on the inside of a smaller
motor and explained how it turned. It was very interesting. I had never
heard the working of a motor explained. It was an instructive commercial,
and people like me who didn't know anything about motors could grasp

it. The commercials are not too long, and they are not always interrupting the story. They're not over-done. . . .

And people who have the story all wrong still indicate a favorable impression of General Electric:

They showed a cylindrical object on a platform. The little pin or needle in the contraption was spinning, showing how electricity was produced. They also showed some motors. I think the main idea was to show the centrifugal force of GE to produce electricity which is the main object of the country [Company]. The more electricity produced the more advancements there will be in the country. They also try to sell their products. The little boy added a family life touch to the commercial. Anything GE says is very true. They are a good company.

It was a stupid commercial because the average person doesn't know too much about motors. It was just a way to bring the name of GE before the public. They showed the different types of motors they handle and talked about the sizes and the jobs they do. GE is a good name, and their products and the fields into which they go are vast. It is a big company with great resources, and they are in there pitching.

Constant analysis of these playbacks, or recalls, leads to two general conclusions:

No matter how straightforward or oversimplified the presentation may be in the eyes of those preparing it, the average viewer cannot be expected to gain more than a general impression of what the message is all about.

Complete comprehension of the details presented is not essential to creating favorable impressions of the sponsor.

But was it worth the time, worry, and expense wrapped up in that brief interval of time from 9:16:16 to 9:19:06 P.M. on Sunday, March 4?

One factor explains the time and worry—and justifies the expense. This fabulous factor is the size of the audience: On this one Sunday evening in March, Paul Muni performed for more people than saw Sarah Bernhardt in a lifetime on the stage.

The correlation between *audience size* and *preparation effort* is an obvious example of human nature at work. It might be expected that *preparation effort* would reach an absolute maximum and level off at a point well below an *audience size* of 33 million people. However, the explanation for the maximum effort surrounding General Electric's Sunday night commercials rests in the fact that, if there *is* a *maximum preparation* effort, it isn't reached with an audience of a mere 33 million.

"You oughta see," one advertising man says, "how some poor guys stew and fret about the commercials for something like Peter Pan—when 60 million people are watching."

—PRH

THE GATEKEEPER:
A Memorandum[1]

THE ESSENTIAL structural elements of communication in society are the message and the chain. Beneath the message, of course, there is a "sub-atomic" universe of very small particles, some of which must be inferred from secondary evidence: the cues, the processes, the relationships which enter into the encoding, transmitting, receiving, decoding, and ultimate disposal of the message. And beyond the message and the chain there are the great communication networks and organizations of human society. But the network is merely a set of interlocking chains, and the communication organizations (like the newspaper or the political action committee) are merely networks with a specific communication purpose. The whole structure can be built out of messages and chains.

The simplest chain, of course, is a sender passing a message to a receiver. In social communication, however, a large proportion of the communication chains are longer than two persons. They may be interpersonal chains, by which a message is passed from individual to individual; or mass media chains, in which information comes into the network of a newspaper or a broadcasting station, and is passed into the network of the media audience. A society where literacy and industrialization are high, is likely to depend on mass media chains; where literacy and industrialization are low, most of the information will flow by interpersonal chains. It is interesting to notice that wherever the mass media are tightly controlled by a dictatorial government so that people begin to doubt the reliability of the media chains, then, even in a highly industrial

---

[1] From a memorandum on "Gatekeepers and the transmission of information."

society, very long and important interpersonal chains tend to develop side by side with the mass media. These interpersonal chains carry rumors, gossip, undercover information of all sorts by which to check and supplement the mass media.

One special characteristic of a chain is of the greatest importance in understanding how it works and how communication moves through society. This is the fact that at every point along the chain, someone has the right to say whether the message shall be received and retransmitted, and whether it shall be retransmitted in the same form or with changes. In other words, all along the chain are a series of *gatekeepers,* who have the right to open or close the gate to any message that comes along.

For example, any person can decide whether to repeat or not to repeat a rumor; and we know that when rumors are repeated they are often changed and colored by the particular interests and knowledge of the person who tells them. When the chain is long enough, the message that comes out of the end of it often bears little resemblance to the one that started.

Consider what happens in the chains which carry news around the world. Suppose we want to follow a news item, let us say, from India to Indiana. The first gatekeeper is the person who sees the news happen. He sees it selectively; notices some things, not others; reports some parts of the event, not others. The second gatekeeper is the reporter who talks to this "news source." Now, of course, we could complicate this picture by giving the reporter a number of news sources to talk to about the same news; but in any case he has to decide which facts to pass along the chain, what to write, what shape and color and importance to give the event. He gives his message to his city editor, who must decide how to edit the story, whether to cut or add or change. Then the message gets to the wire news service, where someone must decide which of many hundreds of items will be picked up and telegraphed to other towns, and how important the story is, and therefore how much space it deserves. At a further link in the chain, this foreign wire service copy will come to a United States wire news service, and here again an editor must decide what is worth passing on to the American newspapers and broadcasting stations. The chain leads on to a regional and perhaps to a state news bureau, where the same decisions must be made: always there is more news than can be sent on—which items, therefore, and how much of the items, shall be retained and retransmitted? And finally the item comes to a local newspaper, where the telegraph editor must go through the same process, deciding which items to print in the paper. Out of news stories gathered by tens of thousands of reporters around the world, only a few hundred will pass the gatekeepers along the chains and reach the telegraph editor, and he will be able to pass only a few dozen of those on to the newspaper reader.

The gatekeeper, saying "yes" or "no" to messages that come to him along the chain, obviously plays one of the most important roles in social communication. Some gatekeepers are more important than others. In society certain individuals identified as "influentials" are usually persons who have an uncommonly large number of message chains centering on them. They may read more widely than most people, or have more personal contacts than most people; and what they choose to pass along from those contacts and that reading is especially important because their opinions are respected. In the news chains, the news agency and the telegraph editor are especially important, because they are responsible for the greatest number of decisions as to whether news should or should not be passed along the chain.

The breadth of knowledge and the critical ability of persons whose opinions are sought and respected, and the integrity and the news standards of wire news agencies and telegraph editors, are therefore of extreme importance in determining our views of the world. A few studies of these gatekeepers have been made. Rumor chains and their distortions have been studied by Allport and Festinger. Influentials have been studied, among others, by Merton, who has distinguished "cosmopolitans," specializing in information from outside the community, from "locals," specializing in knowledge and contacts within the community. Telegraph editors have been studied by White and Gieber. White was somewhat surprised at how many irrational elements seem to enter into the choice of news; and Gieber observed that the telegraph editor is so caught in the system of newspaper production that his choices are greatly limited. In any case, it is clear that even the most important communication chains are far from perfect, and that, with communication organized as it is, a few important gatekeepers have an enormous power over our views of our environment.

SOCIAL CONTROL IN THE NEWS ROOM

BY WARREN BREED

Dr. Breed, a sociologist, is on the faculty of Tulane University. This article was published first in *Social Forces* for May, 1955. It is reprinted here by permission of the author and the magazine, which holds copyright.

TOP LEADERS in formal organizations are makers of policy, but they must also secure and maintain conformity to that policy at lower levels. The situation of the newspaper publisher is a case in point. As owner or representative of ownership, he has the nominal right to set the paper's policy and see that staff activities are coordinated so that the policy is enforced. In actuality the problem of control is less simple, as the literature of "human relations" and informal group studies and of the professions[1] suggests.

Ideally, there would be no problem of either "control" or "policy" on the newspaper in a full democracy. The only controls would be the nature of the event and the reporter's effective ability to describe it. In practice, we find the publisher does set news policy, and this policy is usually followed by members of his staff. Conformity is *not* automatic, however, for three reasons: (1) the existence of ethical journalistic norms; (2) the fact that staff subordinates (reporters, etc.) tend to have more "liberal" attitudes (and therefore perceptions) than the publisher and could invoke the norms to justify anti-policy writing; and (3) the ethical taboo

---

[1] See, for instance, F. J. Roethlisberger and William J. Dickson, *Management and the Worker* (Cambridge: Harvard University Press, 1947), and Logan Wilson, *The Academic Man* (New York: Oxford University Press, 1942).

preventing the publisher from commanding subordinates to follow policy. How policy comes to be maintained, and where it is by-passed, is the subject of this paper.

Several definitions are required at this point. As to personnel, "newsmen" can be divided into two main categories. "Executives" include the publisher and his editors. "Staffers" are reporters, re-write men, copyreaders, etc. In between there may be occasional city editors or wire editors who occupy an interstitial status. "Policy" may be defined as the more or less consistent orientation shown by a paper, not only in its editorial but in its news columns and headlines as well, concerning selected issues and events. "Slanting" almost never means prevarication. Rather, it involves omission, dif-ferential selection, and preferential placement, such as "featuring" a pro-policy item, "burying" an anti-policy story in an inside page, etc. "Professional norms" are of two types: technical norms deal with the operations of efficient news-gathering, writing, and editing; ethical norms embrace the newsman's obligation to his readers and to his craft and include such ideals as responsibility, impar-tiality, accuracy, fair play, and objectivity.[2]

Every newspaper has a policy, admitted or not.[3] One paper's policy may be pro-Republican, cool to labor, antagonistic to the school board, etc. The principal areas of policy are politics, busi-ness, and labor; much of it stems from considerations of class. Policy is manifested in "slanting." Just what determines any publisher's policy is a large question and will not be discussed here. Certainly, however, the publisher has much say (often in veto form) in both long-term and immediate policy decisions (which party to support, whether to feature or bury a story of imminent labor trouble, how much free space to give "news" of advertisers' doings, etc.). Finally, policy is covert, due to the existence of ethical norms of journal-

---

[2] The best-known formal code is The Canons of Journalism, of the American Society of Newspaper Editors. See p. 623.

[3] It is extremely difficult to measure the extent of objectivity or bias. One recent attempt is reported in Nathan B. Blumberg, One-Party Press? (Lincoln: University of Nebraska Press, 1954), which gives a news count for 35 papers' performance in the 1952 election campaign. He concluded that 18 of the papers showed "no evidence of partiality," 11 showed "no conclusive evidence of partiality," and 6 showed partiality. His interpretations, however, are open to argument. A different interpretation could conclude that while about 16 showed little or no partiality, the rest did. It should be noted, too, that there are dif-ferent areas of policy depending on local conditions. The chief difference occurs in the deep South, where frequently there is no "Republican" problem and no "union" problem over which the staff can be divided. Color becomes the focus of policy.

ism; policy often contravenes these norms. No executive is willing to risk embarrassment by being accused of open commands to slant a news story.

While policy is set by the executives, it is clear that they cannot personally gather and write the news by themselves. They must delegate these tasks to staffers, and at this point the attitudes or interests of staffers may—and often do—conflict with those of the executives.[4] Of 72 staffers interviewed, 42 showed that they held more liberal views than those contained in their publisher's policy; 27 held similar views, and only 3 were more conservative. Similarly, only 17 of 61 staffers said they were Republicans.[5] The discrepancy is more acute when age (and therefore years of newspaper experience) is held constant. Of the 46 staffers under 35 years of age, 34 showed more liberal orientations; older men had apparently "mellowed." It should be noted that data as to intensity of attitudes are lacking. Some staffers may disagree with policy so mildly that they conform and feel no strain. The present essay is pertinent only insofar as dissident newsmen are forced to make decisions from time to time about their relationship to policy.[6]

We will now examine more closely the workings of the newspaper staff. The central question will be: How is policy maintained, despite the fact that it often contravenes journalistic norms, that staffers often personally disagree with it, and that executives cannot legitimately command that it be followed? The frame of reference will be that of functional analysis, as embodied in Merton's paradigm.[7]

---

[4] This condition, pointed out in a lecture by Paul F. Lazarsfeld, formed the starting point for the present study.

[5] Similar findings were made about Washington correspondents in Leo C. Rosten, *The Washington Correspondents* (New York: Harcourt, Brace, 1937). Less ideological conflict was found in two other studies: Francis V. Prugger, "Social Composition and Training of the Milwaukee Journal News Staff," *Journalism Quarterly*, 18 (September, 1941), 231-44, and Charles E. Swanson, "The Mid-City Daily" (Ph.D. dissertation, State University of Iowa, 1948). Possible reasons for the gap is that both papers studied were perhaps above average in objectivity; executives were included with staffers in computations; and some staffers were doubtless included who did not handle policy news.

[6] It is not being argued that "liberalism" and objectivity are synonymous. A liberal paper (e.g., *PM*) can be biased too, but it is clear that few liberal papers exist among the many conservative ones. It should also be stressed that much news is not concerned with policy and is therefore probably unbiased.

[7] Robert K. Merton, *Social Theory and Social Structure* (Glencoe: Free Press, 1949), esp. pp. 49-61. Merton's elements will not be explicitly referred to but his principal requirements are discussed at various points.

The present data come from the writer's newspaper experience and from intensive interviews with some 120 newsmen, mostly in the northeastern quarter of the country. The sample was not random and no claim is made for representativeness, but on the other hand no paper was selected or omitted purposely and in no case did a newsman refuse the request that he be interviewed. The newspapers were chosen to fit a "middle-sized" group, defined as those with 10,000 to 100,000 daily circulation. Interviews averaged well over an hour in duration.[8]

There is an "action" element inherent in the present subject—the practical democratic need for "a free and responsible press" to inform citizens about current issues. Much of the criticism of the press stems from the slanting induced by the bias of the publisher's policy.[9] This criticism is often directed at flagrant cases such as the Hearst press, the *Chicago Tribune,* and New York tabloids, but also applies in lesser degree, to the more conventional press. The description of mechanisms of policy maintenance may suggest why this criticism is often fruitless, at least in the short-run sense.

HOW THE STAFFER LEARNS POLICY

The first mechanism promoting conformity is the "socialization" of the staffer with regard to the norms of his job. When the new reporter starts work he is not told what policy is. Nor is he ever told. This may appear strange, but interview after interview confirmed the condition. The standard remark was "Never in my —— years on this paper, have I ever been told how to slant a story." No paper in the survey had a "training" program for its new men; some issue a "style" book; but this deals with literary style, not policy. Further, newsmen are busy and have little time for recruit training. Yet all but the newest staffers know what policy is.[10] On

---

[8] The data are taken from Warren Breed, "The Newspaperman, News and Society" (Ph.D. dissertation, Columbia University, 1952). Indebtedness is expressed to William L. Kolb and Robert C. Stone, who read the present manuscript and provided valuable criticisms and suggestions.

[9] For a summary description of this criticism, see Commission on the Freedom of the Press, *A Free and Responsible Press* (Chicago: University of Chicago Press, 1947), chap. 4.

[10] While the concept of policy is crucial to this analysis, it is not to be assumed that newsmen discuss it fully. Some do not even use the word in discussing how their paper is run. To this extent, policy is a latent phenomenon; either the staffer has no reason to contemplate policy or he chooses to avoid so doing. It may be that one strength of policy is that it has become no more manifest to the staffers who follow it.

being asked, they say they learn it "by osmosis." Sociologically, this means they become socialized and "learn the ropes" like a neophyte in any subculture. Basically, the learning of policy is a process by which the recruit discovers and internalizes the rights and obligations of his status and its norms and values. He learns to anticipate what is expected of him so as to win rewards and avoid punishments. Policy is an important element of the newsroom norms, and he learns it in much the following way.

The staffer reads his own paper every day; some papers *require* this. It is simple to diagnose the paper's characteristics. Unless the staffer is naïve or unusually independent, he tends to fashion his own stories after others he sees in the paper. This is particularly true of the newcomer. The news columns and editorials are a guide to the local norms. Thus a southern reporter notes that Republicans are treated in a "different" way in his paper's news columns than Democrats. The news about whites and Negroes is also of a distinct sort. Should he then write about one of these groups, his story will tend to reflect what he has come to define as standard procedure.

Certain editorial actions taken by editors and older staffers also serve as controlling guides. "If things are blue-pencilled consistently," one reporter said, "you learn he [the editor] has a prejudice in that regard."[11] Similarly an executive may occasionally reprimand a staffer for policy violation. From our evidence, the reprimand is frequently oblique, due to the covert nature of policy, but learning occurs nevertheless. One staffer learned much through a series of incidents:

I heard [a union] was going out on strike, so I kept on it; then the boss said something about it, and well—I took the hint and we had less coverage of the strike forming. It was easier that way. We lost the story, but what can you do?

We used a yarn on a firm that was coming to town, and I got dragged out of bed for that. The boss is interested in this industrial stuff—we have to clear it all through him. He's an official in the Chamber. So . . . after a few times, it's irritating, so I get fed up. I try to figure out what will work best. I learn to try and guess what the boss will want.

In fairness it should be noted that this particular publisher was one of the most dictatorial encountered in the study. The pattern

---

[11] Note that such executives' actions as blue-pencilling play not only the manifest function of preparing the story for publication but also the latent one of steering the future action of the staffer.

of control through reprimand, however, was found consistently. Another staffer wrote, on his own initiative, a series about discrimination against Jews at hotel resorts. "It was the old 'Gentlemen's Agreement' stuff, documented locally. The boss called me in . . . didn't like the stuff . . . the series never appeared. You start to get the idea. . . ."

Note that the boss does not "command"; the direction is more subtle. Also, it seems that most policy indications from executives are negative. They veto by a nod of the head, as if to say, "Please don't rock the boat." Exceptions occur in the "campaign" story, which will be discussed later. It is also to be noted that punishment is implied if policy is not followed.

Staffers also obtain guidance from their knowledge of the characteristics, interests, and affiliations of their executives. This knowledge can be gained in several ways. One is gossip. A reporter said: "Do we gossip about the editors? Several of us used to meet—somewhere off the beaten path—over a beer—and talk for an hour. We'd rake 'em over the coals."

Another point of contact with executives is the news conference (which on middle-sized papers is seldom *called* a news conference), wherein the staffer outlines his findings and executives discuss how to shape the story. The typical conference consists of two persons, the reporter and the city editor, and can amount to no more than a few words. (Reporter: "One hurt in auto accident uptown." City editor: "Okay, keep it short.") If policy is at stake, the conference may involve several executives and require hours of consideration. From such meetings, the staffer can gain insight through what is said and what is not said by executives. It is important to say here that policy is not stated explicitly in the news conference nor elsewhere, with few exceptions. The news conference actually deals mostly with journalistic matters, such as reliability of information, newsworthiness, possible "angles," and other news tactics.

Three other channels for learning about executives are house organs (printed for the staff by syndicates and larger papers), observing the executive as he meets various leaders and hearing him voice an opinion. One staffer could not help but gain an enduring impression of his publisher's attitudes in this incident:

I can remember [him] saying on election night [1948], when it looked like we had a Democratic majority in both houses, "My God,

this means we'll have a labor government." [Q. How did he say it?]
He had a real note of alarm in his voice; you couldn't miss the point
that he'd prefer the Republicans.

It will be noted that in speaking of "how" the staffer learns policy,
there are indications also as to "why" he follows it.

REASONS FOR CONFORMING TO POLICY

There is no one factor which creates conformity-mindedness,
unless we resort to a summary term such as "institutionalized
statuses" or "structural roles." Particular factors must be sought in
particular cases. The staffer must be seen in terms of his status and
aspirations, the structure of the newsroom organization and of the
larger society. He also must be viewed with reference to the operations he performs through his workday, and their consequences for
him. The following six reasons appear to stay the potentially in-
transigent staffer from acts of deviance—often, if not always.[12]

1. INSTITUTIONAL AUTHORITY AND SANCTIONS. The publisher ordinarily owns the paper and from a purely business standpoint has
the right to expect obedience of his employees. He has the power
to fire or demote for transgressions. This power, however, is di-
minished markedly in actuality by three facts. First, the newspaper
is not conceived as a purely business enterprise, due to the protection of the First Amendment and a tradition of professional public
service. Secondly, firing is a rare phenomenon on newspapers. For
example, one editor said he had fired two men in 12 years; another
could recall four firings in his 15 years on that paper. Thirdly, there
are severance pay clauses in contracts with the American Newspaper Guild (CIO). The only effective causes for firing are excessive drunkenness, sexual dalliance, etc. Most newspaper unemploy-
ment apparently comes from occasional economy drives on large
papers and from total suspensions of publication. Likewise, only
one case of demotion was found in the survey. It is true, however,
that staffers still fear punishment; the myth has the errant star re-

---

[12] Two cautions are in order here. First, it will be recalled that we are discussing not all news, but only policy news. Secondly, we are discussing only
staffers who are potential non-conformers. Some agree with policy; some have
no views on policy matters; others do not write policy stories. Furthermore,
there are strong forces in American society which cause many individuals to
choose harmonious adjustment (conformity) in any situation, regardless of
the imperatives. See Erich Fromm, *Escape from Freedom* (New York: Farrar
and Rinehart, 1941), and David Riesman, *The Lonely Crowd* (New Haven:
Yale University Press, 1950).

porter taken off murders and put on obituaries—"the Chinese tor-
ture chamber" of the newsroom. Fear of sanctions, rather than their
invocation, is a reason for conformity, but not as potent a one as
would seem at first glance.

Editors, for their part, can simply ignore stories which might
create deviant actions, and when this is impossible, can assign the
story to a "safe" staffer. In the infrequent case that an anti-policy
story reaches the city desk, the story is changed; extraneous reasons,
such as the pressure of time and space, are given for the change.[13]
Finally, the editor may contribute to the durability of policy by
insulating the publisher from policy discussions. He may reason
that the publisher would be embarrassed to hear of conflict over
policy and the resulting bias, and spare him the resulting uneasi-
ness; thus the policy remains not only covert but undiscussed and
therefore unchanged.[14]

2. FEELINGS OF OBLIGATION AND ESTEEM FOR SUPERIORS. The
staffer may feel obliged to the paper for having hired him. Respect,
admiration, and gratitude may be felt for certain editors who have
perhaps schooled him, "stood up for him," or supplied favors of a
more paternalistic sort. Older staffers who have served as models
for newcomers or who have otherwise given aid and comfort are
due return courtesies. Such obligations and warm personal sentiments toward superiors play a strategic role in the pull to conformity.

3. MOBILITY ASPIRATIONS. In response to a question about ambition, all the younger staffers showed wishes for status achievement.
There was agreement that bucking policy constituted a serious bar
to this goal. In practice, several respondents noted that a good
tactic toward advancement was to get "big" stories on Page One;
this automatically means no tampering with policy. Further, some
staffers see newspapering as a "stepping stone" job to more lucra-

---

[13] Excellent illustration of this tactic is given in the novel by an experienced
newspaperwoman: Margaret Long, *Affair of the Heart* (New York: Random
House, 1953), chap. 10. This chapter describes the framing of a Negro for
murder in a middle-sized southern city, and the attempt of a reporter to tell
the story objectively.

[14] The insulation of one individual or group from another is a good example
of social (as distinguished from psychological) mechanisms to reduce the likelihood of conflict. Most of the factors inducing conformity could likewise be
viewed as social mechanisms. See Talcott Parsons and Edward A. Shils, "Values,
Motives and Systems of Action," in Parsons and Shils (eds.), *Toward a General Theory of Action* (Cambridge: Harvard University Press, 1951), pp. 223-30.

tive work: public relations, advertising, free-lancing, etc. The reputation for troublemaking would inhibit such climbing.

A word is in order here about chances for upward mobility. Of 51 newsmen aged 35 or more, 32 were executives. Of 50 younger men, 6 had reached executive posts and others were on their way up with such jobs as wire editors, political reporters, etc. All but five of these young men were college graduates, as against just half of their elders. Thus there is no evidence of a "break in the skill hierarchy" among newsmen.

4. ABSENCE OF CONFLICTING GROUP ALLEGIANCE. The largest formal organization of staffers is the American Newspaper Guild. The Guild, much as it might wish to, has not interfered with internal matters such as policy. It has stressed business unionism and political interests external to the newsroom. As for informal groups, there is no evidence available that a group of staffers has ever "ganged up" on policy.

5. THE PLEASANT NATURE OF THE ACTIVITY. a. *In-groupness in the newsroom.* The staffer has a low formal status vis-à-vis executives, but he is not treated as a "worker." Rather, he is a co-worker with executives; the entire staff cooperates congenially on a job they all like and respect: getting the news. The newsroom is a friendly, first-namish place. Staffers discuss stories with editors on a give-and-take basis. Top executives with their own offices sometimes come out and sit in on newsroom discussions.[15]

b. *Required operations are interesting.* Newsmen like their work. Few voiced complaints when given the opportunity to gripe during interviews. The operations required—witnessing, interviewing, briefly mulling the meanings of events, checking facts, writing—are not onerous.

c. *Non-financial perquisites.* These are numerous: the variety of experience, eye-witnessing significant and interesting events, being to first to know, getting "the inside dope" denied laymen,

---

[15] Further indication that the staffer-executive relationship is harmonious came from answers to the question, "Why do you think newspapermen are thought to be cynical?" Staffers regularly said that newsmen are cynical because they get close enough to stark reality to see the ills of their society and the imperfections of its leaders and officials. Only two of 40 staffers took the occasion to criticize their executives and the enforcement of policy. This displacement, or lack of strong feelings against executives, can be interpreted to bolster the hypothesis of staff solidarity. (It further suggests that newsmen tend to analyze their society in terms of personalities, rather than institutions comprising a social and cultural system.)

meeting and sometimes befriending notables and celebrities (who are well-advised to treat newsmen with deference). Newsmen are close to big decisions without having to make them; they touch power without being responsible for its use. From talking with newsmen and reading their books, one gets the impression that they are proud of being newsmen.[16] There are tendencies to exclusiveness within news ranks, and intimations that such near outgroups as radio newsmen are entertainers, not real newsmen. Finally, there is the satisfaction of being a member of a live-wire organization dealing with important matters. The newspaper is an "institution" in the community. People talk about it and quote it; its big trucks whiz through town; its columns carry the tidings from big and faraway places, with pictures.

Thus, despite his relatively low pay, the staffer feels, for all these reasons, an integral part of a going concern. His job morale is high. Many newsmen could qualify for jobs paying more money in advertising and public relations, but they remain with the newspaper.

6. NEWS BECOMES A VALUE. Newsmen define their job as producing a certain quantity of what is called "news" every 24 hours. This is to be produced *even though nothing much has happened.* News is a continuous challenge, and meeting this challenge is the newsman's job. He is rewarded for fulfilling this, his manifest function. A consequence of this focus on news as a central value is the shelving of a strong interest in objectivity at the point of policy conflict. Instead of mobilizing their efforts to establish objectivity over policy as the criterion for performance, their energies are channelled into getting more news. The demands of competition (in cities where there are two or more papers) and speed enhance this focus. Newsmen do talk about ethics, objectivity, and the relative worth of various papers, but not when there is news to get. News comes first, and there is always news to get.[17] They are not

---

[16] There is a sizable myth among newsmen about the attractiveness of their calling. For example, the story: "Girl: 'My, you newspapermen must have a fascinating life. You meet such interesting people.' Reporter: 'Yes, and most of them are newspapermen.'" For a further discussion, see Breed, *op. cit.,* chap. 17.

[17] This is a variant of the process of "displacement of goals," newsmen turning to "getting news" rather than to seeking data which will enlighten and inform their readers. The dysfunction is implied in the nation's need not for more news but for better news—quality rather than quantity. See Merton, *op. cit.,* "Bureaucratic Structure and Personality," pp. 154-55.

rewarded for analyzing the social structure, but for getting news. It would seem that this instrumental orientation diminishes their moral potential. A further consequence of this pattern is that the harmony between staffers and executives is cemented by their common interest in news. Any potential conflict between the two groups, such as slowdowns occurring among informal work groups in industry, would be dissipated to the extent that news is a positive value. The newsroom solidarity is thus reinforced.

The six factors promote policy conformity. To state more exactly how policy is maintained would be difficult in view of the many variables contained in the system. The process may be somewhat better understood, however, with the introduction of one further concept—the reference group.[18] The staffer, especially the new staffer, identifies himself through the existence of these six factors with the executives and veteran staffers. Although not yet one of them, he shares their norms, and thus his performance comes to resemble theirs. He conforms to the norms of policy rather than to whatever personal beliefs he brought to the job, or to ethical ideals. All six of these factors function to encourage reference group formation. Where the allegiance is directed toward legitimate authority, that authority has only to maintain the equilibrium within limits by the prudent distribution of rewards and punishments. The reference group itself, which has as its "magnet" element the elite of executives and old staffers, is unable to change policy to a marked degree because first, it is the group charged with carrying out policy, and second, because the policy maker, the publisher, is often insulated on the delicate issue of policy.

In its own way, each of the six factors contributes to the formation of reference group behavior. There is almost no firing, hence a steady expectation of continued employment. Subordinates tend to esteem their bosses, so a convenient model group is present. Mobility aspirations (when held within limits) are an obvious promoter of inter-status bonds as is the absence of conflicting group

---

[18] Whether group members acknowledge it or not, "if a person's attitudes are influenced by a set of norms which he assumes that he shares with other individuals, those individuals constitute for him a reference group." Theodore M. Newcomb, *Social Psychology* (New York: Dryden, 1950), p. 225. Williams states that reference group formation may segment large organizations; in the present case, the reverse is true, the loyalty of subordinates going to their "friendly" superiors and to the discharge of technical norms such as getting news. See Robin M. Williams, *American Society* (New York: Knopf, 1951), p. 476.

loyalties with their potential harvest of cross pressures. The news-room atmosphere is charged with the related factors of in-groupness and pleasing nature of the work. Finally, the agreement among newsmen that their job is to fasten upon the news, seeing it as a value in itself, forges a bond across status lines.

As to the six factors, five appear to be relatively constant, occurring on all papers studied. The varying factor is the second: obligation and esteem held by staffers for executive and older staffers. On some papers, this obligation-esteem entity was found to be larger than on others. Where it was large, the paper appeared to have two characteristics pertinent to this discussion. First, it did a good conventional job of news-getting and news-publishing, and second, it had little difficulty over policy. With staffers drawn toward both the membership and the reference groups, organization was efficient. Most papers are like this. On the few smaller papers where executives and older staffers are not respected, morale is spotty; staffers withhold enthusiasm from their stories, they cover their beats perfunctorily, they wish for a job on a better paper, and they are apathetic and sometimes hostile to policy. Thus the obligation-esteem factor seems to be the active variable in determining not only policy conformity, but morale and good news performance as well.

SITUATIONS PERMITTING DEVIATION

Thus far it would seem that the staffer enjoys little "freedom of the press." To show that this is an oversimplification, and more important, to suggest a kind of test for our hypothesis about the strength of policy, let us ask: "What happens when a staffer *does* submit an antipolicy story?" We know that this happens infrequently, but what follows in these cases?

The process of learning policy crystallizes into a process of social control, in which deviations are punished (usually gently) by reprimand, cutting one's story, the withholding of friendly comment by an executive, etc. For example, it is punishment for a staffer when the city editor waves a piece of his copy at him and says, "Joe, don't *do* that when you're writing about the mayor." In an actual case, a staffer acting as wire editor was demoted when he neglected to feature a story about a "sacred cow" politician on his paper. What can be concluded is that when an executive sees a clearly antipolicy item, he blue-pencils it, and this constitutes a lesson for the staffer. Rarely does the staffer persist in violating policy; no such case appeared in all the interviews. Indeed, the best-known cases of firing for policy reasons—Ted O. Thackrey and Leo Huberman—occurred on liberal New York City dailies, and Thackrey was an editor, not a staffer.

Now and then cases arise in which a staffer finds his anti-policy stories printed. There seems to be no consistent explanation for this, except to introduce two more specific subjects dealing first, with the staffer's career line, and second, with particular empirical conditions associated with the career line. We can distinguish three stages through which the staffer progresses. First, there is the cub stage, the first few months or years in which the new man learns techniques and policy. He writes short, non-policy stories, such as minor accidents, meeting activity, the weather, etc. The second, or "wiring-in" stage, sees the staffer continuing to assimilate the newsroom values and to cement informal relationships. Finally there is the "star" or "veteran" stage, in which the staffer typically defines himself as a full, responsible member of the group, sees its goals as his, and can be counted on to handle policy sympathetically.[19]

To further specify the conformity-deviation problem, it must be understood that newspapering is a relatively complex activity. The newsman is responsible for a range of skills and judgments which are matched only in the professional and entrepreneurial fields. Oversimplifications about policy rigidity can be avoided if we ask, "*Under what conditions* can the staffer defy or bypass policy?" We have already seen that staffers are free to argue news decisions with executives in brief "news conferences," but the arguments generally revolve around points of "newsiness," rather than policy as such.[20] Five factors appear significant in the area of the reporter's power to bypass policy.

1. The norms of policy are not always entirely clear, just as many norms are vague and unstructured. Policy is covert by nature and

[19] Does the new staffer, fresh from the ideals of college, really "change his attitudes"? It would seem that attitudes about socio-economic affairs need not be fixed, but are capable of shifting with the situation. There are arguments for and against any opinion; in the atmosphere of the newsroom the arguments "for" policy decisions are made to sound adequate, especially as these are evoked by the significant others in the system.

[20] The fullest treatment of editor-reporter conferences appears in Swanson, *op. cit.*

has large scope. The paper may be Republican, but standing only lukewarm for Republican Candidate A who may be too "liberal" or no friend of the publisher. Policy, if worked out explicitly, would have to include motivations, reasons, alternatives, historical developments, and other complicating material. Thus a twilight zone permitting a range of deviation appears.[21]

2. Executives may be ignorant of particular facts, and staffers who do the leg (and telephone) work to gather news can use their superior knowledge to subvert policy. On grounds of both personal belief and professional codes, the staffer has the option of selection at many points. He can decide whom to interview and whom to ignore, what questions to ask, which quotations to note, and, on writing the story, which items to feature (with an eye toward the headline), which to bury, and in general what tone to give the several possible elements of the story.

3. In addition to the "squeeze" tactic exploiting executives' ignorance of minute facts, the "plant" may be employed. Although a paper's policy may proscribe a certain issue from becoming featured, a staffer, on getting a good story about that issue may "plant" it in another paper or wire service through a friendly staffer and submit it to his own editor, pleading the story is now too big to ignore.

4. It is possible to classify news into four types on the basis of source of origination. These are: the policy or campaign story, the assigned story, the beat story, and the story initiated by the staffer. The staffer's autonomy is larger with the latter than the former types. With the campaign story (build new hospital, throw rascals out, etc.), the staffer is working directly under executives and has little leeway. An assigned story is handed out by the city editor and thus will rarely hit policy head on, although the staffer has some leverage of selection. When we come to the beat story, however, it is clear that the function of the reporter changes. No editor comes between him and his beat (police department, city hall, etc.), thus the reporter gains the "editor" function. It is he who, to a marked degree, can select which stories to pursue, which to ignore. Several cases developed in interviews of beat men who smothered stories they knew would provide fuel for policy—policy they personally disliked or thought injurious to the professional code. The

---

[21] Related to the fact that policy is vague is the more general postulate that executives seek to avoid formal issues and the possibly damaging disputes arising therefrom. See Chester I. Barnard, *Functions of the Executive* (Cambridge: Harvard University Press, 1947).

cooperation of would-be competing reporters is essential, of course. The fourth type of story is simply one which the staffer originates, independent of assignment or beat. All respondents, executives, and staffers averred that any employee was free to initiate stories. But equally regularly, they acknowledged that the opportunity was not often assumed. Staffers were already overloaded with beats, assignments, and routine coverage, and besides, rewards for initiated stories were meager or non-existent unless the initiated story confirmed policy. Yet this area promises much, should staffers pursue their advantage. The outstanding case in the present study concerned a well-educated, enthusiastic reporter on a conventional daily just north of the Mason-Dixon line. Entirely on his own, he consistently initiated stories about Negroes and Negro-white relations, "making" policy where only void had existed. He worked overtime to document and polish the stories; his boss said he didn't agree with the idea but insisted on the reporter's right to publish them.

5. Staffers with "star" status can transgress policy more easily than cubs. This differential privilege of status was encountered on several papers. An example would be Walter Winchell during the Roosevelt administration, who regularly praised the President while the policy of his boss, Mr. Hearst, was strongly critical of the regime. A *New York Times* staffer said he doubted that any copyreader on the paper would dare change a word of the copy of Meyer Berger, the star feature writer.

These five factors indicate that given certain conditions, the controls making for policy conformity can be bypassed. These conditions exist not only within the newsroom and the news situation but within the staffer as well; they will be exploited only if the staffer's attitudes permit. There are some limitations, then, on the strength of the publisher's policy.

Before summarizing, three additional requirements of Merton's functional paradigm must be met. These are statements of the consequences of the pattern, of available alternative modes of behavior, and a validation of the analysis.

CONSEQUENCES OF THE PATTERN

To the extent that policy is maintained, the paper keeps publishing smoothly as seen both from the newsroom and from the outside, which is no mean feat if we visualize the country with no press at all. This is the most general consequence. There are several special consequences. For the society as a whole, the existing system of power relationships is maintained. Policy usually protects property and class interests, and thus the strata and groups holding these interests are better able to retain them. For the larger community, much news is printed objectively, allowing for opinions to form openly, but policy news may be slanted or buried so that some important information is denied the citizenry. (This is the dysfunction widely scored by critics.) For the individual readers, the same is true. For the executives, their favorable statuses are maintained, with perhaps occasional touches of guilt over policy. For newsmen, the consequences are the same as for executives. For more independent, critical staffers, there can be several modes of adaptation. At the extremes, the pure conformist can deny the conflict, the confirmed deviate can quit the newspaper business. Otherwise, the adaptations seem to run in this way: (1) Keep on the job but blunt the sharp corners of policy where possible ("If I wasn't here the next guy would let *all* that crap go through . . ."); (2) Attempt to repress the conflict amorally and anti-intellectually ("What the hell, it's only a job; take your pay and forget it . . ."); (3) Attempt to compensate, by "taking it out" in other contexts: drinking, writing "the truth" for liberal publications, working with action programs, the Guild, and otherwise. All of these adjustments were found in the study. As has been suggested, one of the main compensations for all staffers is simply to find justification in adhering to "good news practice."

POSSIBLE ALTERNATIVES AND CHANGE

A functional analysis, designed to locate sources of persistence of a pattern, can also indicate points of strain at which a structural change may occur. For example, the popular recipe for eliminating bias at one time was to diminish advertisers' power over the news. This theory having proved unfruitful, critics more recently have fastened upon the publisher as the point at which change must be initiated. Our analysis suggests that this is a valid approach, but one requiring that leverage in turn be applied on the publisher from various sources. Perhaps the most significant of these are professional codes. Yet we have seen the weakness of these codes when policy decisions are made. Further leverage is contained in such sources as the professional direction being taken by some journalism schools, in the Guild, and in sincere criticism.

Finally, newspaper readers possess potential power over press performance. Seen as a client of the press, the reader should be entitled to not only an interesting newspaper, but one which furnishes significant news objectively presented. This is the basic problem of democracy: to what extent should the individual be treated as a member of a mass, and to what extent fashioned (through educative measures) as an active participant in public decisions? Readership studies show that readers prefer "interesting" news and "features" over penetrating analyses. It can be concluded that the citizen has not been sufficiently motivated by society (and its press) to demand and apply the information he needs, and to discriminate between worthwhile and spurious information, for the fulfillment of the citizen's role. These other forces—professional codes, journalism schools, the Guild, critics, and readers—could result in changing newspaper performance. It still remains, however, for the publisher to be changed first. He can be located at the apex of a T, the crucial point of decision making. Newsroom and professional forces form the base of the T, outside forces from community and society are the arms. It is for the publisher to decide which forces to propitiate.

.   .   .   .

Thus we conclude that the publisher's policy, when established in a given subject area, is usually followed, and that a description of the dynamic socio-cultural situation of the newsroom will suggest explanations for this conformity. The newsman's source of rewards is located not among the readers, who are manifestly his clients, but among his colleagues and superiors. Instead of adhering to societal and professional ideals, he redefines his values to the more pragmatic level of the newsroom group. He thereby gains not only status rewards, but also acceptance in a solidary group engaged in interesting, varied, and sometimes important work. Thus the cultural patterns of the newsroom produce results insufficient for wider democratic needs. Any important change toward a more "free and responsible press" must stem from various possible pressures on the publisher, who epitomizes the policy making and coordinating role.

TABLES ON MASS COMMUNICATIONS IN THE UNITED STATES

Number of Daily and Weekly Newspapers

Year	Number of Dailies	Total Daily Circulation (millions)	Number of Weeklies °
1790	8		83
1800	24		210
1850	387	1.5	2,048
1900	2,190	15.1	16,387
1910	2,433	24.2	16,899
1920	2,042	27.8	14,405
1930	1,942	39.6	11,407
1940	1,878	41.1	11,108
1950	1,772	53.8	10,103
1958 †	1,751	57.4	9,315

Source: Compiled by Chapin from Lee, Census, and Ayer. Last line of figures from *Editor and Publisher* and Ayer.

* Includes also semi-weeklies and tri-weeklies.

† Figures as of the end of 1958.

Number of Periodicals in the United States

Year	Daily	Tri-weekly	Semi-weekly	Weekly	Fort-nightly	Semi-Monthly	Monthly	Bi-Monthly	Quar-terly	Other	Total
1935											6,021
1940	138	13	56	1,366	210	196	3,501	261	564	163	6,468
1945	124	13	29	1,251	213	222	3,097	319	564	153	5,985
1950	157	5	50	1,434	211	216	3,655	487	594	168	6,977
1955	169	9	49	1,665	239	255	3,904	573	768	276	7,907
1957	161	10	54	1,619	257	267	3,925	632	841	308	8,074

Source: Figures through 1955 compiled by Chapin from Ayer; 1957, from Ayer.

Numbers and Types of Books Published in the
United States

Classification	Titles	
	1948	1958
Agriculture, gardening	162	160
Biography	513	697
Business	223	373
Education	199	331
Fiction	643	2,235
Fine arts	336	459
Games, sports	199	236
General literature and criticism	473	626
Geography, travel	214	339
History	503	901
Home economics	183	161
Juvenile	929	1,522
Law	231	318
Medicine, hygiene	433	532
Music	104	97
Philology	149	149
Philosophy, ethics	308	447
Poetry, drama	563	451
Religion	677	1,050
Science	592	1,000
Sociology, economics	461	568
Technical and military	466	548
Miscellaneous	336	262
Total	9,897	13,462

Source: *Publisher's Weekly.*

Size of the Radio Industry in the United States

Year	AM Stations on Air	FM Stations on Air	Sets in Use (millions)	Homes with Radio (millions)
1922	30		0.4	0.3
1925	571		4.0	3.5
1930	612		13.0	12.0
1935	585		30.5	22.9
1940	765		51.0	29.2
1945	933		56.0	34.0
1950	2,086	691	90.0	45.0
1955	2,669	552	138.7	52.0
1959	3,008	578	150.0 (est.)	52.5 (est.)

Source: Stations from FCC; sets and homes from *Telecasting.*

Size of the Television Industry

At End of Year	TV Stations on Air	TV Sets in Use (millions)	Homes with TV (millions)
1947	11	0.3	0.3
1948	29	1.0	1.0
1949	69	4.0	4.0
1950	104	10.5	10.4
1951	107	15.8	15.5
1952	108	21.0	17.3
1953	199	27.6	23.4
1954	408	33.0	28.2
1955	469	35.0	32.3
1956	482	42.7	36.7
1957	511	47.7	40.3
1958	544	50.3	43.0

Source: Stations from FCC Annual Report; sets from *Telecasting*.

Size of the Motion Picture Industry in the United States

Year	Number of Feature Pictures Released	Estimated Weekly Attendance (millions)	Number of Operating: Conventional Theaters	Drive-in Theaters
1935	766	80	12,024	
1940	673	80	15,300	40
1945	377	85	19,040	100
1950	622	60	16,904	2,202
1955	305	47	14,009	4,494

Source: Compiled by Chapin from industry sources; 1955 data by UNESCO.

CONTROL AND SUPPORT OF MASS COMMUNICATIONS

THE MARXISTS say that control of mass media belongs to whoever owns the physical facilities of the media. We say that editorial policy is the privilege of the owner or his representative, the publisher. But control of the mass media in our society is immensely more complicated than in a society organized along Marxist principles. For example, in the Soviet Union the government owns the facilities of mass communication and says, without dispute, who shall work for the mass media and what content they shall carry. In our society, we try to give government as little control as possible over mass communication, because we want to use the media to represent the people in checking on government. On the other hand, ownership does not mean absolute control either. As President Eisenhower said, the editorial columns belong to the owner, but the news columns belong to the people. In the same way, the people exercise a certain amount of control over the programs on television and radio, the stories and articles in magazines, the films that are made, and the books that are published—not directly, of course, but by virtue of what they choose to buy, to read, to listen to or see.

Thus, to an extent, control goes with support. If people decide not to see a certain kind of movie, the studios aren't likely to make that kind of movie. If audience ratings fall off too far, a television program isn't likely to have advertising support. This is understandable in a privately owned and supported system like ours, although it sometimes makes it hard for the media to program for elite or minority audiences: to get adequate support they must usually try to reach audiences as large as possible.

The cost of media service makes this doubly difficult today. Gone is the time when a New York newspaper could be started for $15,000, and when a few fonts of type and a few reams of paper were sufficient to start a small town paper. A newspaper of 50,000 circulation, as you will see in the tables at the end of this chapter, now does nearly three million dollars worth of business a year. Any commercial VHF television station is likely to be a multi-million dollar operation. If a man wants to start a newspaper in New York today, he must be prepared to lose, say, five million dollars before he makes any money. Costs in mass communication have risen so fast that monopoly is much more attractive financially than it used to be. That is why the number of newspapers has been decreasing for so long, and why 94 per cent of all the daily newspaper towns in the United States now have no competitive ownership of their newspapers.

Such problems as this are not new; only the size and centralized power of the media are new. Monopoly was actually more grievous in the Middle Ages, but we talk more about it now because our political and economic systems require a free exchange of fact and opinion through the mass media, and because in some countries the proved potency of government control, and in our country the enormously greater needs of the media for financial support, raise questions about who will control the exchange of fact and opinion, whom the media should serve, what kind of service they should provide, and how free they should be. Thus control and support are intimately related to freedom and public service.

In the following pages you will find this topic treated from a number of sides. Dr. Cheyney gives a brief account of the changing social balance between freedom and control. Then comes Professor Siebert's analysis of the fourfold relationship of government to communication. Dr. Casey's article is a practical newspaperman's viewpoint concerning newspaper propaganda—what it consists of, how it may be guarded against, and what pressures actually operate on newspapers to make them use their columns for propaganda purposes. Dr. Nixon takes up the problem of increasing newspaper monopoly and discusses its likely trend and results. Professor Borden's article is a summary of his classic study on the economic effects of advertising—does it really contribute to the economy, does it raise or lower prices, and so on. The section ends with a number of tables on the costs and support of U.S. mass communication.

FREEDOM AND RESTRAINT:
A SHORT HISTORY

BY EDWARD P. CHEYNEY

Dr. Cheyney was a distinguished professor of European history at the University of Pennsylvania. This essay is from the *Annals of the American Academy of Political and Social Science,* November, 1938, and is copyrighted by the Academy.

ON THE SEVENTH of May, 1773, a group of friends were dining at the house of a bookseller in the Poultry in London. It was an interesting company, including Dr. Johnson, Oliver Goldsmith, Boswell, who records the conversation, Dr. Mayo, a Dissenting minister, Toplady, the writer of hymns, and some others. The discussion turned to freedom of thought and speech. Dr. Johnson remarked, "Every society has a right to preserve public peace and order and therefore has a good right to prohibit the propagation of opinions which have a dangerous tendency. . . ." That is to say there must be no expression of opinions disapproved by authority. Neither prevailing thought or existing conditions must be disturbed. As a royal duke somewhat later declared, "Any change, of any kind, at any time is bad." This is the pure doctrine of conservatism. It is expressed not so much in law as in opinion; not so much formulated in terms as embodied in conventions, habits of thought, and settled institutions. To disturb these is to arouse conservative antagonism. It is an attitude of mind still widespread and influential. It is necessarily opposed to freedom of inquiry and the expression of new opinions.

Condemnation of the expression of unauthorized opinion was not, however, universal, nor was it the most characteristic mental attitude of eighteenth-century England, for Hume in a contemporary essay remarks, "Nothing is more apt to surprise a foreigner than the extreme liberty which we enjoy in this country of communicating whatever we please to the public, and of openly censuring every measure entered into by the king or his ministers." Indeed, Blackstone had already written in 1769, "The liberty of the press is essential to the nature of a free state"; and Lord Kenyon somewhat later declared that "the liberty of the press is dear to England," though, it is true, he proceeded to qualify it by saying, "The licentiousness of the press is odious to England." In 1776, less than three years later than the conversation quoted above, some thousand Englishmen living across the sea, in the constitution of their newly emancipated state of Virginia, declared that "the freedom of the press is one of the great bulwarks of liberty, and can never be restrained but by despotic governments." This became a familiar note in the constitutions of the American states, as for instance in that of Massachusetts, adopted four years later, which declared, "The liberty of the press is essential to freedom in a state. It ought not therefore to be restricted in this Commonwealth"; and that of Delaware, adopted in 1782, in which Section 5 declares, "The press shall be free to every citizen who undertakes to examine the official conduct of men acting in a public capacity, and any citizen may print freely on any subject, being responsible for the abuse of that liberty." Freedom of opinion when expressed in writing, therefore, bade fair to be a generally approved practice.

FREEDOM OF SPEECH

Freedom of the spoken word was a different matter. Freedom of speech was no doubt widely indulged in both in England and America, though often punished, but its actual legalization came by another route. It appears first as a privilege of members of a representative assembly, where freedom to express the desires of their constituents was a duty incumbent on them. The practice in the English House of Commons was clearly formulated by Speaker Williams in 1562. He petitions the queen, on his election to the speakership, in traditional terms, "that the assembly of the Lower House may have frank and free liberties to speak their minds, without any controlment, blame, grudge, menaces or displeasure." Elizabeth, it is true, was restive under this claim, and it was the subject of much dispute in her reign and that of the Stuarts. A privy councilor in 1576 draws the familiar contrast between liberty and license, and declares that "though freedom of speech hath always been used in this great Council of parliament . . . yet the power was never, nor ought to be, extended so far as though a man in the House may speak what and of whom he list." The old controversy was settled once for all, however, a century later, in the Bill of Rights of 1689, where it is provided that "the freedom of speech and debates or proceedings in Parliament ought not to be impeached or questioned in any court or place out of Parliament." This protection to freedom of speech in parliamentary debate reappears as Article I, Section 6, of the Constitution of the United States, which declares that Senators and Representatives, "for any speech or debate in either house . . . shall not be questioned in any other place."

But general freedom of speech for all members of the community, not merely for parliamentary and congressional representatives, like full freedom of the press, is a product of the rise and spread of the passion for liberty characteristic of the late eighteenth century. As such it is not peculiar to England or America, but belongs to the new age. The eleventh article of the French "Rights of Man and of the Citizen," adopted by the National Assembly August 4, 1789, affirms the freedom of all forms of expression then known: "The free communication of ideas and opinions is one of the most precious of the rights of man. Every citizen may, accordingly, speak, write and print with freedom." This declaration, with a few changes, was prefixed to the Constitution of 1791 and was thus widely promulgated.

UNITED STATES BILL OF RIGHTS

But it was in another Bill of Rights, the first ten amendments attached to the Constitution of the United States and proclaimed December 15, 1791, that the assertion of the rights of freedom of speech, of the press, of religion, and of assembly received their classic and, so far as the United States is concerned, their authoritative form. It is a formula that cannot be too often repeated:

AMENDMENT I. Congress shall make no law respecting an establishment of religion, or prohibiting the free exercise thereof; or abridging the freedom of speech, or of the press; or the right of the people peaceably to assemble, and to petition the Government for a redress of grievances.

Long afterward, when the supremacy of the federal government over the states had been challenged and determined by the Civil War, the prohibition of federal interference with freedom of expression was further developed and extended to the individual states by the Fourteenth Amendment:

AMENDMENT XIV, Section 1. . . . No State shall make or enforce any law which shall abridge the privileges or immunities of citizens of the United States; nor shall any State deprive any person of life, liberty, or property, without due process of law.

"Due process of law," as vague in its meaning as some of the equally famous expressions in Magna Charta ("To no one will we sell, to no one will we deny right or justice," for instance), has nevertheless, like them, served many times since as a defense of liberty of thought and speech.

FREEDOM IN OTHER COUNTRIES

It may be of interest to note how far and wide, expressed in terms almost identical, these provisions of the American Constitution have spread. They appear in the constitutions of forty-six of the states. It is not a matter of surprise, perhaps, that the Constitution of the Philippine Republic, adopted February 8, 1935, embodies all the more general and protective provisions of the Constitution of the United States, including the amendments, and that it entitles them a "Bill of Rights." The words of the first, seventh, and eighth paragraphs of Section 1 of the third Article of the Constitution of this antipodean republic could hardly be more familiar:

No person shall be deprived of life, liberty or property without due process of law. . . . No law shall be made respecting an establishment of religion or prohibiting the free exercise thereof. . . . No law shall be passed abridging the freedom of speech or of the press, or of the right of the people to assemble and petition the government for redress of grievance.

It is, on the other hand, somewhat surprising to find the new Turkish Republic not only guaranteeing the familiar immunities of free nations but basing them on the rather antiquated foundation of natural rights. The following wording is that of the Constitution of 1924:

ARTICLE 68. All Turks are born and live free. Liberty consists of being able to do anything that does not interfere with the rights of others.

ARTICLE 70. Natural rights of Turks include: inviolability of person, liberty of conscience, of thought, of speech, of publication, of travel. . . .

ARTICLE 75. No one can be molested because of his religious beliefs or his philosophical contentions.

The Constitution of the Spanish Republic proclaimed December 12, 1931, so far as its formal provisions go, and so far as it has been able to control its own destinies against internal rebellion and foreign intervention, professed to establish the most democratic of all modern nations, with a touch of Marxism withal:

ARTICLE 1. Spain is a democratic republic of workers of all classes, organized as a regime of liberty and justice.

ARTICLE 27. Freedom of conscience and the right to profess and practice freely any religion are guaranteed in Spanish territory.

ARTICLE 34. Every person has the right to express freely his ideas and opinions, making use of any method of diffusion without subjecting himself to prior censorship.

ARTICLE 38. The right of peaceable assembly without arms is recognized.

So in the Constitutions of the Irish Free State and Czechoslovakia (before the Communist take-over), as typical of newly emancipated nations, and of various older countries, even with many restrictions, as in that of Japan, there are clear echoes of the French Declaration of the Rights of Man and of the American First Amendment.

The Weimar Constitution of the German Reich, adopted August 11, 1919, is now . . . but a reminiscence. But it is of interest to observe that these are, or were, her fundamental ideals of liberty:

ARTICLE 118. Every German has the right within the limits of general laws, to express his opinion freely, by word of mouth, writing, printed matter or picture or in any other manner.

No censorship shall be enforced, but restrictions and regulations may be introduced by law in reference to cinematograph entertainment. Legal measures are also admissible for the purpose of combating bad and obscene literature, as well as for the protection of youth in public exhibitions.

ARTICLE 123. All Germans have the right without notification or special permission to assemble peaceably and unarmed.

ARTICLE 130. Officials are servants of the community and not of any party.

Freedom of political opinions and the free right of association are guaranteed to all officers.

The latest and most dubious recruit to nations guaranteeing to their citizens freedom of the kind under discussion is Soviet Russia.

Its new Constitution, laid before the people in June, 1936, and ratified by the Congress of Soviets in December of the same year, includes the following striking provisions:

ARTICLE 124. With the object of insuring to the citizens freedom of conscience, the church in the Union of Soviet Socialist Republics is separated from the state and the school from the church. Freedom of religious cult and freedom of antireligious propaganda is acknowledged for all citizens.

ARTICLE 125. In accordance with the interests of the toilers and with the object of strengthening the socialist system, the citizens of the Union of Soviet Socialist Republics are guaranteed by law:
a) freedom of speech
b) freedom of the press
c) freedom of assemblies and meetings
d) freedom of street processions and demonstrations.

What use Russia will make of this strange graft of democratic franchises on a totalitarian stock remains to be seen. In the meantime it represents perhaps the furthest migration in principle of the eighteenth-century invention of freedom of expression.

PRINCIPLES VERSUS PRACTICE

Returning from the pursuit of these principles of liberty of expression through space and time to a period and a world where they are being so widely controverted, it may be observed that even in the country of their first assertion they have been by no means always faithfully applied to the problems of government and society. The main tradition of American history has certainly been of freedom of speech, of the press, of assembly, of religion, of teaching, of proposal of change, of independent intellectual self-assertion. On the other hand there have been many intrusions upon this liberty by the law, by the courts, by the use of economic power, by public opinion—sometimes by mob violence. At certain times it has seemed that the history of freedom has been but the history of interference with freedom. In the turbid atmosphere of political and religious controversy, of war and of economic conflict, the ideal and even the constitutional requirement has often been obscured. As the country has gone through successive phases of its history, new violations of fundamental liberty of thought and speech have appeared. But the claims of freedom have even more constantly asserted themselves. A rapid sketch of some historic examples of this conflict of forces may make more clear our present state.

CASES UNDER THE SEDITION ACT

The best example is the earliest. In the year 1798, when the Constitution was not yet ten years old, the party which had been especially responsible for its adoption, stung by bitter criticism, carried through Congress a bill which, though it never received interpretation by the Supreme Court, in the view of many at the time and of most careful historians and political thinkers since, was a gross violation of the First Amendment. This was the Sedition Bill. It provided:

> That if any person shall write, print, utter or publish . . . any false, scandalous and malicious writing or writings against the government of the United States, or either house of the Congress . . . or the President . . . with intent to defame the said government . . . or to bring them . . . into contempt or disrepute; or to excite against them . . . the hatred of the good people of the United States . . . [he] shall be punished by a fine not exceeding two thousand dollars, and by imprisonment not exceeding two years.

Identifying the Government with the individuals who at the time were administering the Government, it was evidently a partisan measure. It was carried by a majority of but three or four in each house, and amidst a bitterness of political controversy unknown to more modern times, Alexander Hamilton, although himself of the majority party, protested against its passage, foreseeing what actually occurred, that the popular opposition would use the first opportunity to bring about the downfall of the Federalist party which was responsible for it.

Nevertheless immediate steps were taken by the leaders of that party to enforce it. The first and most famous of these cases was the arrest, trial, conviction, and sentence of Matthew Lyon, member of Congress from Vermont. He had published in the *Vermont Gazette* a letter criticizing the President and had read at a meeting and aided afterward in publishing a letter to another member of Congress suggesting that the President be "sent to a madhouse." Lyon was a contentious and unpopular member of the Unionist party, the judge before whom he was tried was harsh, he pleaded his own case unskillfully, a verdict of guilty was therefore returned, and he was sentenced to four months' imprisonment and a fine of a thousand dollars. He was badly treated in prison, and the President refused to release him when he showed himself too proud to sign the petition for his own pardon. Nevertheless he was re-elected to Congress by his constituents, a subscription was taken up to pay his fine and relieve his necessities, and long afterwards, in 1840, Congress by special act refunded his fine.

Another case under the Sedition Act was that of an agitator named Brown who was tried for reckless and abusive speeches, convicted, and sentenced to imprisonment for a year and half and to pay a fine of $400. Several newspaper editors were arrested, including the publisher of the *Vermont Gazette* and the influential editor of the *Philadelphia Aurora*. Altogether some twenty-four persons were arrested, fifteen or more indicted, and ten convicted and sentenced. There was much mutual crimination. Those out of power called the Federalists Tories, declared the Sedition law unconstitutional, complained that the President, a United States marshal, the judge, and a grand jury together could make anyone a seditious criminal. The legislatures of Kentucky and Virginia protested against such an assumption of power by the federal government. Those in power, on the other hand, called their critics Jacobins and all but traitors. In 1801 the law expired by limitation. In the meantime, at the election of 1800, the Federal party fell from power. When Jefferson was inaugurated he immediately pardoned all sufferers under the act. Indeed, he went further and declared the act null and void from the beginning. In a letter of July, 1804, he wrote, "I discharged every person under punishment or prosecution under the Sedition law, because I considered and now consider the law to be a nullity, as absolute and as palpable as if Congress had ordered us to fall down and worship a golden image."

The passage of the Sedition law of 1798 and of its companion statute, the Alien law, has always since been considered an indefensible action on the part of the President and the majority in Congress. They were not so much laws for the protection of the state, which was in no danger, as they were for the exemption of holders of office at the time from criticism and political and personal abuse. They have never been re-enacted, at least in time of peace. Nevertheless, they represent a thread in our national and state history that has, however slender, been continuous, a legislative, executive, or judicial deviation from the recognition of complete freedom of speech, under the claim or with the excuse of the need of protection of the administrators of the government.

THE ABOLITIONISTS

More often than President, Congress, or the courts, it has been popular passion that has interfered with freedom. Between 1830 and 1850 the Abolitionists, advocates of immediate abolition of slavery, were generally denied both in the North and the South the opportunity of advocating their principles of freedom to express their views. A Southern senator declared in the Senate, "Let an Abolitionist come within the borders of South Carolina, if we catch him we will try him, and notwithstanding all the interference of all the governments on earth, including the Federal Government, we will hang him." Contemporary records are full of instances, if not of quite such virulent threats of action, at least of denial of freedom of speech, of violence, and in at least a few cases, of murder.

Robinson, an English bookseller, in 1831, the year before all slaves were freed in the British Empire, was whipped and driven out of Petersburg, Virginia, for saying what was everywhere being said in England "that black men have, in the abstract, a right to their freedom." Five years later, in June, 1837, he went to Berlin, Mahoning County, to deliver some lectures in which he expressed Abolitionist views. He was dragged from the house of a friend with whom he was staying, carried several miles away, subjected to a coat of tar and feathers, and left lying in an open field. A young Irish stonecutter working on the statehouse at Columbia, South Carolina, casually remarked that slavery in the South degraded the position of even the white laborer. He was overheard, seized, put in jail, afterwards taken out, tarred and feathered, then, in only a pair of pants, put into a Negro car for Charleston and afterwards sent out of the state. Even the law in many parts of the South denied the right to express Abolitionist opinions. The Virginia Code of 1849 provides, "If a person by speaking or writing maintains that owners have no right of property in their slaves, he shall be confined in jail not more than one year and fined not exceeding $500."

Even in the North there was much interference with the expression of Abolitionist sentiment by mobs and by organizations of men of a somewhat higher class but of similar inclinations, that came to be known as "Committees of Vigilance." Meetings of antislavery societies and the houses and offices of antislavery leaders and even churches in Boston, Baltimore, New York, Utica, Worcester, and elsewhere in the North were attacked and their property destroyed. Many of these riots proved to have been arranged beforehand by men who had political or business reasons for opposing the antislavery agitation. They were none the less indications of popular responsiveness to propaganda for intolerance. The most famous instance was the burning by a mob in Philadelphia of "Pennsylvania Hall," erected by popular subscription, in $20 shares, in order "that the citizens of Philadelphia should possess a room wherein the principles of Liberty and Equality in Civil Rights could be freely discussed and the evils of slavery freely portrayed." Three days after it had been dedicated, May 14, 1838, before a large audience, to "Liberty and the Rights of Man," it was burned by a mob. The mayor gave but half-hearted protection, and a committee of council afterward, while acknowledging the "strict legal and constitutional right" of the managers of the building to hold their meetings there, condemned them for actions having a tendency to endanger public peace by condoning "doctrines repulsive to the moral sense of a large majority of the community."

So far as the "moral sense" of the community was concerned, less than twenty-five years later, in 1861, troops were marching through Philadelphia to support by military force the very principle whose advocacy by moral force had been in 1838 so bitterly condemned. The moral sense of the community has usually but by no means always been in favor of freedom, and it has, besides, often been misinterpreted. The destruction by mobs of the Abolitionist newspaper presses in Baltimore, Cincinnati, St. Louis, and other border cities culminated in the murder of Elijah Lovejoy, a newspaper editor, in Alton, Illinois, November, 1837. This occurrence precipitated a nation-wide protest from supporters of the tradition of freedom of discussion and led to a famous gathering in Faneuil Hall, Boston, to demand freedom of speech even for advocates of so unpopular a cause as was at the time the abolition of slavery.

VARIOUS CONFLICTS

The emergence of new occasions for differences of interest or belief has led to various forms of interference with the free expression of opinion. At one time it was the "Native American" wave of violence against Irish Catholics, with its denial to them of religious liberty and educational opportunity; at another it was the Mormons who were mobbed and deported because of their religious and social views. The Governor of Missouri in 1834 commented, in answer to a Mormon petition for protection:

That which is the case of the Mormons today may be that of the Catholics tomorrow, and after them any other sect that may become obnoxious to the majority of the people of any section of the State. . . . They have the right, constitutionally guaranteed to them, and it is indefeasible, to believe and worship Smith as a man, an angel, or even as the only true and living God.

Nevertheless, the same governor and even the courts gave them poor protection, and after much disorder, almost to the extent of civil war, the Mormons, when they had power showing themselves as intolerant as their persecutors, migrated to Utah.

The Civil War and later the World War led to public and private efforts to suppress all spoken or printed disapproval of the war policy of the government, but this was to be expected. Freedom of speech and of the press has never been long preserved, probably cannot be preserved, in war time.

The spread of scientific knowledge and the wide acceptance of the doctrine of evolution by teachers and writers roused the religious fears and opposition of many and led to a series of attempts to prohibit by law or administrative action the teaching in state-supported institutions of the scientific conclusions of scholars. In one year laws limiting this form of freedom of teaching were introduced in thirty-nine state legislatures, and such laws are still on the statute books of three. The same effort was made by boards of trustees or other authorities in many private schools and colleges. Fundamental opposition to freedom of the teaching of what is believed by the teachers to be scientific truth is still existent, although the period of especial activity of this opposition is now in the past.

CAPITALIST INTERFERENCE

The growth of great economic interests and the simultaneous development of a critical attitude toward some characteristics of the social system that was being so deeply influenced by this growth led to attempts to prevent the dissemination of such criticism. The university professor who expressed radical views concerning the desirability of social change before his class or in the community often found himself in the same position as the Abolitionist of half a century before who criticized the established institution of slavery, and often suffered from similar attempts to reduce him to silence. If such opinions were expressed extravagantly, as they unfortunately sometimes were, or if the man who expressed them was vulnerable on other grounds, as unfortunately was often the case, his expulsion from his position was practicable without the odium of seeming to suppress free speech. But it was observable that men of conforming habits of mind and speech could go far in incompetency without official protest. This difficulty will be the subject of special study in a later essay. There is no doubt that freedom of speech has been widely denied to university and college professors and high school teachers.

The growth of trade unions and the more vigorous efforts of the working classes to improve their position have brought up problems of freedom of speech as well as other questions of the limits of legal action by workingmen. The courts have sometimes prohibited discussion as well as punished violence. In communities where control by large corporations was practically complete, the so-called "company towns," no freedom of discussion of controversial matters was allowed by the authorities. A graduate in education of a university, appointed to take charge of the educational interests of a certain town of this character, immediately resigned when he found he had to submit all his educational arrangements to the company executives before putting them into effect. There was no educational freedom there. Some industrial corporations, in their effort to prevent the formation of trade unions, have made a practice of paying certain of their workmen to report upon the conversation of their fellow workmen. Employees of these companies, knowing that they were being watched and reported upon to their disadvantage, certainly did not enjoy freedom of speech. There are charges that trade unions, in their turn, have prevented or tried to prevent dissemination of information they considered to be to their disadvantage.

Approval of radical political and economic theories in the constitutions of certain labor organizations led, along with general opposition to trade unions, to the adoption in certain states of the so-called "Criminal Syndicalism" laws. These made the advocacy of "subversive" views or even membership in organizations supporting them a criminal offense. There are men and women still in prison in the state of California under this statute whose offense was the expression of approval of doctrines considered by the legislature or the courts subversive—not any overt act or appeal for action for the immediate carrying of such doctrines into effect. Punishment under these laws is apparently a denial of freedom of speech, of the press, and of assembly.

The dark history of lynching, though not primarily a chapter in the history of freedom of expression or of its denial, has involved refusal by the mob, and sometimes by the constituted authorities, to give to the victim the opportunity to state his case openly in court as guaranteed by the Constitution and the law. In South Carolina, Alabama, Georgia, Arizona, California, and elsewhere, within recent years, the maltreatment or deportation of those who have spoken against certain local conditions or practices, such as the condition of the sharecroppers or of the farm laborers or orange pickers, has approached the actual exercise of lynch law, and certainly has violated freedom of speech.

The agitation for women's suffrage, especially in the years 1917, 1918, and 1919, provided abundant examples of interference with freedom of speech by mobs, by the police, and by the lower courts. This opposition originated no doubt largely in mere conservative feeling; it was further provoked by a somewhat exasperating ingenuity shown in their campaign by the protagonists of this new claim. It was rather opposition to the form the demands of the suffragists took than any essential denial of their right to express their views that gave to the contest the character of interference with their freedom of speech.

THE GENERAL TREND

Thus each successive period and phase of our history has given occasion for greater or less interference with liberty of expression. There seems to have been a tradition of "abridgment," to use the Constitutional word, as well as one of allowance of liberty. It is true, as has been before stated, that the enumeration of instances of interference gives a false idea of the general character of our history in this respect. It has been on the whole one of large liberty. Interference has been the exception; the rule has been that Americans have been, except in war time, free to express themselves on all subjects, at all times; the press has been, generally speaking, restricted only by the familiar limitations of libel, obscenity, and

incitement to disorder, or by coercion by advertisers or other interested parties; freedom of assembly has seldom been interfered with;
religious freedom still more infrequently. Other forms of liberty
of expression have suffered only from occasional and momentary
interference, popular passions, self-interest, superstition, religious
fear, or general conservatism.

The present is no exception to either tradition, if two traditions
can be said to exist. Questions of freedom and restriction face us
now as in the past, perhaps even more insistently than in some
earlier and less troubled periods. Liberty is of course still dominant.
Compared with the wide domain in which citizens of the United
States, like those of other democratic countries, are at liberty to
express their opinions and to publish with absolute freedom the
results of their study or thought, the fields where restriction prevails
seem small indeed. But there are such fields. Evidences of restraint
are elusive, but restraint nevertheless exists. We may well rejoice
in our large liberty and utilize it for the free exchange of opinion
and the intelligent discussion of proposed action. On the other
hand, every restriction that is imposed, every source of knowledge
that is shut off, is to that degree a weakness and a derogation from
our liberty, and may well be sought out and dealt with.

The difficult task of discovering the traces, measuring the amount,
and discussing the disadvantages or possible defense of interference in the various fields of human interest is undertaken in later
studies in this volume. But there are certain tendencies of our time
too general, too apt to be disregarded, and too dangerous for the
immediate future not to be commented on here.

COMMUNISM AND FASCISM

The extreme denunciation of communism, approaching the
bounds of hysteria, which swept across the country in previous
decades, was a serious danger to our continued freedom of discussion. An exaggerated and largely artificial fear of communism has
been utilized in Germany, Italy, Greece, and other countries as a
reason or an excuse for the introduction of a system that still more
completely prohibits all free discussion of political and largely of
social questions. If our people do not understand communism, have
made no study of it, have not discussed it, are at the mercy of
exaggerated warnings against it, the same thing may occur here as
in Europe. In our ignorant or unnecessary fear we may without

due thought and to our great loss introduce a system equally destructive to our free institutions. We must weigh and measure communism in order to avoid such a catastrophe.

Why cannot communism be made a matter of free and informed discussion? At present there is but little study of the subject. The current condemnation is largely ill-informed and emotional, not based on knowledge or argument. It is not only in the Hearst press but in sermons, addresses, casual speeches, and, it is to be feared, in college classrooms, that communism is execrated without being described. Its advocates are given every advantage, for they understand it while others only abuse it. Communism is a body of doctrines, a series of proposals for economic and social change. It should be examined and discussed like any other group of proposals. There is abundant material in print, both for and against, and a growing body of foreign experience, to form the basis of discussion.

If the mass of the people are to be appealed to, it is giving an undue advantage to the Communists to be unable or unwilling to meet them on the ground of argument. Merely to charge them with planning to bring about a change in the government of the United States "by force and violence," a doubtful and frequently denied charge at best, is to surrender the traditional American way of argument to a propaganda of shadowy fear. . . .

Of fascism there has been little more of genuine discussion than of communism; but for different reasons. There is apparently little general fear of it; though it is more likely to be introduced into our country than communism, and it is quite as destructive to democratic institutions. It must be discussed before it is introduced or never, for once accepted it would, here as elsewhere, preclude all freedom of speech, at least of speech in opposition. The adoption of fascism as a prophylactic against communism, if both were openly discussed, would probably not commend itself even to those who fear the latter. Even should it be an American type of fascism, giving some leeway to liberty, the same might be said of an American type of communism; but it is difficult to conceive of either as including freedom of criticism of the form or personnel of government. Acceptance of the dominant power would seem to be a fundamental requirement of both. What form of either or whether any form is to be accepted as a substitute for our present democracy is still within our choice, but only within our choice so long as we possess that democracy and practice the free discussion it allows.

THREATS TO FREE DISCUSSION

The prominence of these two forms of opinion must not prevent the recognition that there are other though obscure limitations. Looked at closely, education, the pulpit, politics, medicine, the law, business are all hesitant in practicing for themselves or permitting to others freedom of criticism beyond the conventional limits of each profession. The restrictive tendencies of our time, so obvious in those countries which permit no freedom of discussion, are probably to a greater extent than we realize within and around us as well as across the seas. Absolute freedom in closely knit civilized society is probably not either practicable or desirable, but it is notable that in every one of the various aspects of the community that has been surveyed in these studies some restriction has been discovered that might well, in the interests of either justice or progress, be removed.

One thing more may be said. Our present degree of toleration of freedom of speech, when subjected to a sudden strain, may not last. There are in our community powerful economic and social and ecclesiastical and even political forces that may wish and be able, if their position is endangered, to place limitation on criticism of their present position. Or war may intervene, or threat of it, with its invariable limitation of freedom of speech and of publication. Or the astounding revelations of science, or the boldness of advanced social thought, may subject conservative opinion to such a strain as to tempt it to the old effort to keep things as they are by forbidding what they consider destructive criticism. Or the increased power through numbers and organization of the working classes may conceivably be used to censor opinion deemed by them to be injurious to their interests.

It is not true that "It Can't Happen Here." However unlikely, some influential group of our people, aroused by danger to their property or moved by the spirit of patriotism or inflamed by religious or social rancor or frightened by the shadowy dread of something unknown, so easily aroused by propaganda among uninformed people, or stirred by some eloquent leader intoxicated by power, may succeed in putting an end to our privilege of open discussion. There is only one way to secure its retention—that is, to place so high a valuation on freedom of expression in all its forms as never to practice or permit any interference with it.

COMMUNICATIONS AND GOVERNMENT

BY FRED S. SIEBERT

Professor Siebert is director of the Division of Mass Communications at Michigan State University. His paper is from *Communications in Modern Society*, copyright 1948 by the University of Illinois Press, and is reprinted by permission of the author and the publisher.

ALL MY SUBSEQUENT REMARKS on the complex problems of the relation of government to mass communications are annotated to what I consider the basic objective of communications media. I have stated that objective as follows:

To make available to the peoples of the world the kind of communications content which will enable them to maintain a peaceful and productive society and which will also provide them with personal satisfactions.

Government's relation to communications can be classified under four headings. In actual operation, the activities of government are seldom confined to one of these classifications. Most such activities in the field of communications will fall into two or more, but for purposes of presenting the problems I shall proceed to classify government activities into four groups: (1) government as a restrictive agency, (2) government as a regulating agency, (3) government as a facilitating agency, and (4) government as a participating agency.

GOVERNMENT AS A RESTRICTIVE AGENCY

As a matter of fact, this was probably the earliest function to be assumed by organized government in the field of communications. As a restrictive agency, the function of government has been to keep certain types of communications content from the minds of its subjects or citizens. The various types of restricted material have varied from century to century and from government to government, and the great battles for freedom of speech and freedom of the press have been fought in this area. These battles were fought to keep government restrictions or prohibitions within narrowly defined limits, to make certain that existing officers of that government did not use the power of government over communications to maintain either their principles or their offices. In the United States, our historical and traditional definition of the constitutional phrase, freedom of the press, is that government is limited in its power to restrict or prohibit the circulation of communications content. I use the word "limited." At no time has it ever been contended that the government has been stripped of all restrictive power over material distributed through communications media. Our government retains the right to restrict the distribution of obscenity, of libels on persons, of material tending to produce internal disorder. Our first problem is to determine if, in the light of the constitutional provisions, government today is exercising its restrictive function in the interests of society. This problem has two aspects. Is government keeping the media of communications from transmitting to the American public information and ideas which the public should have in order to maintain a peaceful and productive society? The second is, are there areas of communications content now made available to the public through communications media which should be restricted by government action?

An answer to the first aspect of the problem requires a complete review of all restrictive statutes, orders, rules, and practices of the various governmental units of our nation. Several analyses of this nature have been made in the past. The most recent is volume I of Professor Chafee's *Government and Mass Communications*. It must be admitted that our ancestors fought effectively against the restrictive activities of government. In only a few areas do serious problems remain. The operation of the obscenity restrictions is not always intelligent or consistent; the statutes on peacetime sedition have not always been enforced with the immediate needs of society in mind. Our greatest problem in this area is to keep vigilant and to remind ourselves that it is possible for a government, or more especially the officers of government, to revive old restrictions or set up new ones ostensibly in the interests of society but utilized for the perpetuation of either their principles or their jobs.

The Commission on Freedom of the Press made one recommendation in this field—to the effect that the constitutional guarantees of freedom of the press be recognized as including radio and motion pictures. A number of rereadings of this recommendation, together with the three paragraphs of explanation, leave me confused. The same limitations on government regulation of newspapers and books should, according to the Commission, be placed on radio. At the same time the FCC should retain the right to license and should exercise the right to review program performance as a consideration in renewing a license.

More serious and soul-searching problems exist when we consider the second aspect of the restrictive function of government. Are communications media in this country distributing material which does not contribute to the objective stated at the head of this paper, and if so should government exercise its restrictive function so as to limit the distribution of such material? Or pursuing the problem further, granted that certain types of communications content do not contribute to our communications objective, would activity of government in this area produce greater harm through its restrictive functioning than it would do good by the elimination of this type of content? This, to me, is one of the most serious problems in this field of communications.

Let us look for a moment at some of the specific situations. One of the serious problems today is the interference in the administration of justice caused by individual communications agencies which make a Roman holiday of some of our more startling crimes and subsequent judicial proceedings growing out of these crimes. In my opinion, such published material does not contribute to our general objective. As a matter of fact, it frequently works to defeat that objective. Law enforcement officials, judicial officers, and managers of media will all agree that the situation is frequently disgraceful, yet no solution has yet been found which shows any promise of success in operation and which is acceptable to both government and the mass media. Judges, where they have adequate powers to cite for contempt, seldom use them, usually because of fear of reprisals by the press. The press points out that as individual units in a competitive business it can do nothing to remedy the situation. The only remedy is an organized solution adopted and enforced by government. Here is one area in which further restrictive activity of the government should contribute to the general objective without at the same time producing new evils. And there are many other areas which need study and examination so that on the basis of this research effective restrictions can be put into effect.

Our laws for the protection of the individual are woefully inadequate. They are too clumsy for speedy effect, and speed is essential in this day of rapid communications; they are too complex for the rank and file of attorneys and judicial officers; they do not provide the type of remedy which the injured party most needs. Libel laws as they exist today are an invitation to the unscrupulous to harass the communications media and at the same time are an effective barrier against those individuals whose rights have been seriously injured. The Commission on Freedom of the Press recommends some modification of the French and German "right of reply" as a substitute remedy. Unfortunately neither the French nor the German remedy has proved any more successful than our own libel laws. What we need to do is to throw out the seventeenth-century English libel laws which we inherited and, with our traditional ingenuity, invent a new remedy which will fit American conditions and American needs.

Before leaving the subject of government as a restricting agency, I again want to emphasize a caveat. Although we are more than a hundred years removed from the great battles to limit the restrictive function of government and although those battles were largely fought against an oligarchic and autocratic government, there is still a danger that even a democratic government elected by the people and representative of those people will seek to place unwarranted restrictions on the information content of communications media. Forms of governments may change, but the operators of a government in the form of officials are still likely to be more interested in maintaining their official position than in protecting the rights of the people or even promoting the "interests of society."

GOVERNMENT AS A REGULATING AGENCY

The second group of problems involved in the relation of communications to government falls under government's function as a regulating agency. In the consideration of this problem, I raise this question: Can government lay down rules of the game which will promote rather than obstruct the achievement of our communications objective? The answer is difficult. During the past twenty years there has been much discussion of the theory of the "market place of information and ideas." Consideration of this theory has led to the conclusion that such a market requires regulation, "just as a free market for goods needs laws against monopoly, for proper branding and grading, and so on" (Chafee, II, 475). I have no quarrel with the idea of a free market place for information and ideas, and I am willing to consider what is the proper function of the government to provide and regulate such a center of exchange, but I am not willing to agree that government can exercise the function of "branding and grading," without either (1) making serious errors, or (2) producing ancillary evils greater than the original failure to grade and label. I do not think that we have yet developed a civil service personnel either immune to official pressure or capable of acting solely in the interests of the general public. Better no action than a wrong action.

However, it is possible for the government to engage in regulatory activities which give promise of assistance in achieving our communication objective, but these regulatory activities should give as wide a berth as possible to information content. The government can see that the participants in the market place behave as gentlemen, that they do not shout so stridently that they drown out their competitors, that they obey minimum rules of conduct, that they do not engage in subterfuge, that they stand behind their own warranty of their wares, and that new products have access to the market. Here is an intricate and confusing field for investigation. It is a field for research looking toward the recommendation of such governmental activity as will encourage the open market without official grading and labelling of the quality of information and ideas.

Here again a caveat. This is a dangerous area since so much is at stake. Historical wisdom should not be thrown aside lightly in the desire to achieve a temporary and limited social goal. Neither should the activities in this area remain static. Government is the function of organized society and is the proper agency to engage in limited activities in this field. New problems such as monopolies call for new remedies, but the achievement of the ages should not be lost in solving a particular problem.

GOVERNMENT AS A FACILITATING AGENCY

The third group of problems falls under the function of the government as a facilitating agency. Surprisingly, there appears to be less controversy concerning the activities of government in this area than in any of the other three which I am presenting for discussion, and also less discussion and fewer recommendations have been made in this area than in any of the others. Facilitating, as I use the term, is an aspect of subsidization. Granted that communications can directly contribute to maintenance of a peaceful and productive society, it is worth considering what help government can give to the media in achieving this objective. Such help in the past has been in the nature of postal subsidies and little else other than keeping its hands off. Communications media, both living, unborn, and even unconceived, could use government assistance. And government could well afford to give such assistance in the interest of a peaceful and productive society. An intelligent analysis should be made of the existing post office financial structure and correlated with a study of the distribution needs of communications media through that avenue. It is time to re-analyze the rate structure of the post office department to see if that branch of the government is actually promoting to the proper extent "information of a public character."

The Commission on Freedom of the Press recommended that the government facilitate new ventures in the communications industry, that it foster the introduction of new techniques. Unfortunately, in none of the publications of the Commission is this theme developed. It should be developed.

Another problem in this area is that of making government information readily available to the public. The first step would obviously be to remove whatever obstacles now lie in the path of the existing media. Instead we have witnessed . . . efforts to increase these obstacles and to restrict certain types of information now available. Granted that officers in the government must possess on occasion information which cannot be divulged to the public, extreme care should be taken that the types of restricted information and circumstances under which they are restricted are not used as excuses for withholding embarrassing or personally damaging information. The government can do much to help distribute necessary information by making it readily available and in a form which can be understood. The great need today is for a Dr. Flesch as editor of government bulletins, regulations, and orders. Even the Supreme Court justices could stand a little training in this field— at least to the extent that they consider as their primary objective informing the public rather than disputing with their colleagues.

Facilities should be provided for new media to assist in informing the public concerning government activities. Radio and television require new and different assistance from that given to the newspapers and magazines. The excuse that the dignity of government bodies and government officers would be affronted by facilitating the work of these new media merely re-echoes arguments which took place in Parliament 150 years ago concerning similar services on the part of the press. After all, dignity comes from performing a job well and not from maintaining an artificial aloofness.

GOVERNMENT AS A PARTICIPATING AGENCY

The last group of problems falls under the heading, government as a participant in communications. By this I do not mean the informational activities of the government designed to supply the private media with material which it may or may not transmit to the people. I mean direct contact between the government and the people through government instruments. The most direct contact which the government now has with the mass of people is through the privately owned radio. Should the government, either national, state, or local, seek to find means of reaching the people directly rather than through the privately owned media? This is an entirely new problem for the American people and the American government. The fact that it has never been done is not sufficient reason for not investigating the possibilities and effects of doing it. The danger that government media would drive private media out of business is, in my opinion, slight. The possibility that additional information and ideas may reach the public is great. I see no reason why a public institution, government supported, should not enter the communications field. I see no reason why a city should not own a radio station. I see no reason why the federal government should not own and promote a national network. I am afraid that by and large the program content would be generally dull. I am afraid in many cases it would be a waste of taxpayers' money. But theoretically I see no fundamental objection. I would rather that the government engage in direct communication activities than assume the power to "grade and label" information distributed by private media.

I offer some tentative conclusions. Let the government keep its hands off information content, let it be efficient but cautious in regulating the market place, let it be unhampered in facilitating the work of existing media, and let it use its own media where such use seems desirable.

THE PRESS, PROPAGANDA, AND PRESSURE GROUPS

BY RALPH D. CASEY

Professor Casey was for many years director of the University of Minnesota School of Journalism. His essay was written at the beginning of World War II, and some sections referring especially to that time have been omitted. The essay was published in the *Annals of the American Academy of Political and Social Science,* for January, 1942, and is reprinted by permission of the author and the copyright holder.

EVERY INTELLLIGENT PERSON will recall the pother of the public over propaganda between 1939 and 1941. While all must agree that propaganda is a highly significant social phenomenon worthy of serious investigation, study, and the setting up of safeguards against its misuse as a weapon of social control, we must also admit that the degree of confusion in the use of the term and the misunderstanding of the process itself, produced some fearful and wonderful results during those days when the interest in the subject was red hot.

PROPAGANDA AGAINST PROPAGANDA

One such result was the spread of a "propaganda against propaganda." Mr. Lawrence Hunt, a reader of the *New York Times,* attributed the excitement over propaganda to the attitude of isolationism prevailing in this country prior to and during the early months of the war. Perhaps this was too single-minded an explanation, yet anxiety was no doubt the result of the fear that European propagandists would lure a helpless America into belligerency. Mr. Hunt was correct in saying that many a citizen, confused and excited, threw up his hands and exclaimed, "What *can* I believe?"

Disillusionment and anxiety on the part of the public were understandable when the war broke out. A great tide of printed material dealing with the manipulations of the propagandists of belligerent nations had flowed from the publishing houses since World War I, and studies of propaganda in the domestic field had whetted interest in the phenomenon. Result: a preoccupation with the subject.

Unhappily, propaganda has been credited with too great results in many episodes of our contemporary history, at the expense of more fundamental economic and political causes. Moreover, too little attention has been given to the broader study of *public opinion*. The earlier cogitations of Bryce, Lowell, Lippmann, and others were outmoded and dated in the minds of forum speakers, who preferred to whittle down the subject to the fascinating and explosive "new" mechanism of social influence—propaganda. Since politicians and publicists, who have the ear of the public, are either incapable of defining or delimiting *propaganda*, or unwilling to go to the trouble of doing so, in many persons' minds everything read in the press or heard over the air becomes propaganda. Using the term "propaganda" in a moralistic sense has confused the issue still more.

MISUNDERSTANDING OF PROPAGANDA

Concern here, however, is with the effects on the press of this contemporary preoccupation with the phenomenon. Every journalist now recognizes that he is confronted with a problem of first magnitude in the unthinking failure of sections of the public to distinguish between propaganda, which is the deliberate and conscious effort to fix an attitude or modify an opinion as it relates to a doctrine or program, and, on the other hand, the conscientious effort of the agencies of communication to disseminate facts in a spirit of objectivity and honesty. Citizens of a democracy must tie themselves to some mooring. Informational service in our society is fundamental to all social action.

The assumption that we have not a sufficient body of honestly presented facts at our disposal as dispensed by the press ties in with the equally fallacious notion of the magical power of propaganda. It assumes that we have all become rabbits in a bag, awaiting the dreadful day when some enemy propagandist will pull us out by the ears. It is equally suicidal to assume that there are no great and genuine issues of national policy at stake, which will require the most careful reading of authoritative news sources for the grounding of one's opinion.[1] It is the practice for some politicians and publicists to besmirch the press, charging that news columns are full of distortions and untruths. Evidently they would prefer that the public should completely lose regard for information acquired by reading newspapers or listening to radio broadcasts. Then the public would be thrown back upon what? Upon rumor, upon innuendo, upon propaganda. And these same public figures are the most zealous denunciators of propaganda.

DEALING WITH PROPAGANDA

This is not deny that propaganda gets into the press. Hitler's speeches were propaganda. So were many Churchillian utterances. They were reported. President Roosevelt was a shrewd propagandist as well as an informer on public policy. Could the press edit out those of his remarks that are obviously propaganda? Some propaganda is so newsworthy as to deserve first-page display.

Criticism that the press carries propaganda will no doubt continue as long as readers have differing views and beliefs. What one group of intelligent citizens may believe is propaganda will be described by another as news. We are not concerned here over honest differences of opinion. We express, rather, some anxiety over the lack of information possessed by the public in the techniques used by newspapers in subjecting information to scrutiny and analysis before it appears in print, and the failure to discriminate between disinterested news reporting by trained journalists, on the one hand, and propaganda on the other. While the feverish interest in propaganda may have run its course, at least for the present, scars remain. Unjustified distrust of all information service remains in the minds of many lay persons.

A few years ago this writer sat as a visitor in a high school class to witness a demonstration in a course in propaganda detection.

---

[1] Some politicians, propaganda "experts," and members of the lay public imply that there were no important issues for America in World War I and that our behavior was the result of bemusement with propaganda.

The students had been schooled in the then popular catechism of "name calling," "glittering generality," "card stacking," and so on. They showed unusual ability to use these symbols. But their poster display of newspaper clippings did not live up to their oral responses. Trained to fear the hobgoblin "propaganda," they saw the specter riding like a witch on an October night through every news story and every feature article that a trained newspaper staff had put into print.[2]

This illustration is not given to condemn the training of American citizens in gaining awareness of propaganda but to drive home the point that present perceptions of the problem are incomplete and are often damaging, rather than helpful, to newspapers that strive to present disinterested information.

FACTORS AFFECTING OPINION

What are the factors that are important in the opinion-forming process? Is propaganda the only factor? Are the press, the radio, and the motion picture the only influences that prevail in forming attitudes, as the Wheelers, the Nyes, and the Clarks seem to think? Harwood L. Childs placed this problem in its framework in his volume, *An Introduction to Public Opinion.* Environment factors, the attitudes and opinions of our immediate associates, the racial character of the people with whom we associate, all are important. Age may be a factor, since a person's maturity or lack of it may determine what he reads and to what he listens. Childs points out that our views and opinions are affected by the character of the political, social, and religious institutions which surround us. *Events* will determine attitudes. What we read and hear is of great importance, and in this sense the channels of communication and "what comes through them—the news, reports, ideas that

---

[2] It is fair to say that well-trained teachers will recognize that emphasis on devices and methods of propaganda, such as "card stacking" and other promotional tricks, is not sufficient to arm the students to become citizens and voters. A knowledge of whether the cards are being stacked in a quarrel in the arena of foreign affairs may not be apparent without some knowledge of world history. Training in logical thinking will be more fruitful than providing youth with a packet of "propaganda" devices. This would involve approaching conflicting situations from a *problem-solving* point of view. Some knowledge of the workings of pressure groups is desirable. To rectify the balance in some of the current courses in propaganda detection, teachers should aid students in obtaining some knowledge of the machinery of newsgathering and the problems (and certainly the responsibilities) faced by the press in getting at the news.

constitute our world of verbal symbols"—must be counted as of great significance.

H. C. Peterson in his polemical work, *Propaganda for War*, stresses the thesis that the overpowering influence of propaganda brought us into the first World War. Since his volume is familiar to many, it is cited here as a typical example of commentary which overlooks other factors in the political, economic, and social areas. Peterson loses no opportunity to berate the press, and is guilty not only of misunderstanding its relation to the forces of public opinion, but of making sweeping generalizations frequently unsupported even by qualitative evidence.[3] This bias need not detain us here. The point is that Professor Peterson attributes too much to propaganda and minimizes the individual acts of our governmental leaders (particularly in the field of diplomacy) and slights the dynamic influence of events, the response to the pressures of organized groups, the effects of the censorship, and, lastly, the final determination by governmental leaders and the public of wherein our national interest appeared to lie.

The sinking of the "Lusitania" in May, 1915, almost two years before we declared war against Germany, occasioned our government's strong stand for the rights of nationals on the high seas. The doctrine that bankers, munition makers, and British propagandists channelized our opinion on this issue at that time is hardly tenable. In May, 1915, our war trade with the Allies had not assumed a formidable volume. Moreover, the big loans to the Allies came later. Enthralled by his major thesis, Professor Peterson neglects the effect of a crisis *event* on the country's attitudes, and laboriously

---

[3] A single extract will serve as an example. "During the first twenty months of the war American newspapers displayed attributes which made them suspect among educated people," writes Peterson, p. 168. Elsewhere, he declares the real native American propagandists were preachers, teachers, politicians, and journalists. Evidently three of these groups, aside from journalists, did not exercise the type of discrimination Professor Peterson attributes to "educated people." Of President Wilson he says (p. 9): "He was thoroughly honest, he was governed by a strong sense of right and wrong, and he was not unintelligent."

Dr. Ralph O. Nafziger in "The American Press and Public Opinion During the World War, 1914 to April, 1917" (unpublished Ph.D. thesis, University of Wisconsin, 1936) concludes that "the press tended to trail behind the government in the development of American policy regarding the issues that grew out of the war." In its attempts to report the war, the press was circumvented by (1) the rigid censorship abroad, (2) the limited and controlled overseas communications, and (3) interest groups controlling news at the source. Dr. Nafziger puts propaganda in its proper setting.

stresses the mitigating factors in connection with the German attack on the ship.[4]

While language, cultural, and similar factors predisposed us toward the Allied cause in the first World War, and while incessant British and French propaganda did have unquestioned influence, it is unfortunate that the diplomatic, military, and other overt acts of belligerent nations have not been given sufficient weight by either the experts on propaganda or the lay public. It is unfortunate, too, that a few specialists in the field of public opinion prefer to make the press a scapegoat or a whipping boy, and to slight the difficult task of integrating public opinion manifestations with the whole social and historical fabric of the day.

CASE EXAMPLE OF PUBLICITY

The problem every newspaper faces in separating news from propaganda is trying and difficult. Nowadays almost every organized group has some knowledge of publicity techniques, and the issues these groups seek to promote gain for their cause an advantage usually involving much greater matters than the trivial events reported by the press agents of an older generation.

Perhaps the problem can best be illustrated by describing a minor event in which an effort was made to manipulate the news. The reader will perceive at once that questions of greater importance for an editor arise when major events are stage managed by propagandists, especially when the latter are highly placed in government or industry.

In 1941, a chap named Hopkins, hitherto an obscure parachute jumper, dropped from a plane to the top of Devil's Tower, Wy-

---

[4] A careful and unemotional study of newspaper behavior in wartime, which should complement the reading of the numerous volumes on wartime propaganda, is Edwin Costrell's "Newspaper Attitudes Toward War in Maine, 1914-17," *Journalism Quarterly* (Dec., 1939). Costrell reveals that after the murder of the Archduke there was mild sympathy for Emperor Francis Joseph but that a spontaneous anti-German reaction developed when Germany declared war, and this reaction came *before* the Allied and German propaganda machines began to operate efficiently, and *before* the cutting of cables from Germany to the United States helped to isolate the German Empire. Costrell places great emphasis upon the effects on public opinion of the series of crises in the relations of America to the belligerents.

Dr. George H. Gallup has declared on occasion that the experience of the American Institute of Public Opinion reveals "the fact that events and actions are infinitely more potent factors in influencing the formation of opinion than mere desire to imitate one's fellow citizens."

oming, bailing out above the monolith and spilling his 'chute as required until he reached the top of his lofty goal. The jump was clearly a promotional stunt. The resulting mild controversy between a Rapid City, South Dakota, managing editor, and a Fairmont, Minnesota, editorial writer as to whether a photograph of the leap should have been sent to the press by a news association picture service, illustrates the dilemma faced by newspapers even in such an inconsequential item as this.

The Fairmont editor referred to the affair as "the cheapest kind of a purposeless publicity stunt, something quite different from a legitimate news happening." And he inquired, "If this conclusion isn't correct, how come the news writers and picture takers happened to be there just at the right moment?"[5] To which the *Rapid City Journal* replied a few days later:

There was no deception involved in the Devil's Tower affair. Hopkins did go aloft in a plane, did bail out, and did land on Devil's Tower. That was newsworthy and, of course, local newspapermen and photographers were on hand to record the event, just as the *Fairmont Sentinel* staff would have been on hand had Hopkins undertaken a similar stunt in that city.

Had everything gone according to schedule, Hopkins' leap would have been a story of local and minor interest, soon forgotten. But the unexpected happened. He couldn't get down. That was news . . . and as such it was given wide play in newspapers throughout the country.

INTEREST GOVERNS THE NEWS

Every editor has to determine whether an event is sufficiently interesting to warrant publication.[6] This is the real test. The *Fairmont Sentinel* probably had no compunctions in publishing the exciting adventure of Leonard Coatsworth in escaping from the toppling Narrows bridge near Tacoma, an episode not inspired by a publicity man; yet Hopkins' rescue was no less interesting than Coatsworth's mad scramble to safety. The benefit an individual or group receives as a result of publicity cannot, moreover, serve

---

[5] *Fairmont Sentinel*, Oct. 15, 1941.

[6] See the essay by Dr. John W. Cunliffe, "The Case for Publicity," in F. L. Mott and R. D. Casey (eds.), *Interpretations of Journalism*. Dr. Cunliffe, former director of the Columbia University School of Journalism, wrote: "On all except the gravest matters, the public wants to be enlivened and amused rather than seriously informed. . . . This is a psychological principle to which the publicity agent, as well as the newspaperman, is bound to adapt himself. . . ."

as a final test of its legitimacy. To reject all propaganda-inspired material at the threshold of the newsroom is hardly a satisfactory solution of the problem. The fact that a news story benefits someone, whether written by a reporter or a publicity man, is hardly a test, since much of the news is likely to have values for some persons or groups.[7]

Furtive sponging on the press is easy to circumvent, but newspapers cannot disregard interesting and important events simply because the master hand of a propagandist is behind the scenes pulling strings. Neither can they post a warning sign over what appears to be propaganda, since sometimes the journalist would run grave risks in judgment. Who is to determine, for example, the motive of President Roosevelt in describing the South American map in his possession as a symbol of Nazi ambitions in our own hemisphere? Certainly the President's disclosure was news. Would any editor on the telegraph desk have the temerity to decide that the item should be slugged "propaganda"?

CHECKS ON PROPAGANDA

Decisions on what to include in the day's budget of news must be left to trained and experienced newspapermen. The public should recognize the different functions of the journalist and the propagandist. Press agents, publicity men, and propagandists are *interested* informers. Reporters and editors are *disinterested* informers. Someone has aptly said that a newspaper's function is to seek news and serve its readers, while the propagandist serves the producers of news rather than the consumers of news.

The best check on propaganda is the employment by the news organization of able men, equipped to match their wits against those of the cleverest special pleader, men with disciplined and informed minds, quick to reject superficial plausibility, and possessing the moral courage and honesty to serve the public interest. The number of this type of newspaperman has steadily risen in American journalism in recent years.

Careful editing and evaluation of news constitute another check

---

[7] Herbert Bayard Swope, when editor of the *New York World*, remarked in an address to the American Society of Newspaper Editors: "We each of us have some standard of judgment whereby we can separate proper from improperganda. At least I have not been able to discover a certain method whereby we can resolve all our doubts. Every utterance that is devoted at all to special pleading is propaganda."

on propaganda, and this type of service is corollary to the staff of well-trained men who can deal intelligently and objectively with the facts. A third check is the refusal to print material "except under the name of the client on whose behalf and in whose interest it is offered for publication." A fourth is stronger insistence on the part of the press that its own reporters uncover the news. Walter Lippmann has stressed the point that when a person has direct access to the news, he will at least have the opportunity to see for himself. And it should be remembered that good reporters are trained to avoid misconceptions.

NEWS BUREAUS

Newspapers, however, often fall into the easy habit of permitting publicity men to cover news sources that should be within the scope of their own reportorial activity. The growth of news bureaus is a modern phenomenon. A somewhat narrow view of what constitutes news forced many legitimate and worth-while enterprises to fight their way into the the columns of the press by engaging publicity men to handle their interests. The limitation of newspaper staffs—no newspaper is financially able to report all human activity—was another cause, notably since society developed a whole web of new specializations and activities. Other bureaus were created to interpose a functionary between the inquisitive newspaper reporter and the individual or group, with the intention of presenting only the most *favorable* case to the public.

It is difficult to generalize on the social usefulness of these independent news bureaus. Those associated with education, science, social work, government, and many forms of business generally play fair with the press and widen the scope of the news. Others are either parasitic growths or outright obstacles to complete coverage of the news. The highest type of information specialist thinks of himself as an extension of the arm of the press, and the keen-witted news bureau man realizes that to co-operate with the press is to get the best results for his client. Others have a clear conception of the public service nature of their clients' work, even if the newspapers have failed to understand this at all times,[8]

---

[8] In addressing the news bureau heads of colleges of agriculture, Russell Lord, editor of *The Land*, apotheosized the vocation of his listeners: "You are not publicity men, but teachers working through the press. But all good teachers are propagandists of higher concepts as they see them. . . . College and farm bureau editors alike are variously opinionated, nonpartisan public service propagandists."

and some hold advanced concepts on the place of publicity in modern society.

Nevertheless, while press bureaus can usually be trusted to make routine news available, it goes without saying that such information services will not always divulge the whole truth of a client's activities. It is not to be supposed, for example, that the publicity man for a metropolitan school system will rush to the telephone and broadcast the tip that a school director is secretly selling coal to the school purchasing department at a corrupt price.

It is not to be assumed, moreover, that all press bureaus through familiarity with a client's affairs will be in a better position to interpret them to the public than will the newspapers. This may have been true when the sole conception of news was to signalize an event. Today, the larger and financially secure newspapers are able to engage specialists in the various fields of finance and business, public affairs, science, labor, and other areas where a report of surface happenings cannot alone tell the whole story. Interpretation is included in many news stories involving specialized activities, and journalists have begun to realize that getting the facts accurately may be only the first step in gathering and writing the news, since getting below the *event* and interpreting its *meaning* are equally important.

PRESSURE GROUPS

The problem of dealing with the ordinary news bureau is never so vexing and difficult, however, as that of coping with militant pressure groups. These groups are usually engaged in a controversy or have a single-minded devotion to a program or doctrine which may not be socially acceptable generally. Each of these groups first creates an active central organization with a body of zealous followers, and next organizes its inevitable press committee. The instability or insecurity of various social classes in our present changing social order produces various ideologies to which groups of persons cling with religious-like devotion. They seek by every method of agitation and propaganda to accomplish their ends. They establish their own propaganda journals, both for their own membership and for such sections of the public as they are able to reach. One experienced editor of my acquaintance has described the tactics and strategy of these pressure-group organizations:

The propaganda papers of these pressure groups are not sparing in their criticism of the newspapers. They tell their followers how to bring pressure to bear on the press and at the same time inform them that any lack of newspaper support is due to unworthy motives.

It is not hard to understand these tactics. The pressure group is organized on the basis of a common grievance, real or fancied, but in any event the technique is to keep the grievance alive and active. The basic grievance must have the agitating support of minor grievances, and the newspaper is valuable to the agitator, either as an agency of propaganda, if possible, or failing in this, the sense of injustice on which these groups live.

I am convinced that the multiplication of pressure groups demanding support is in part responsible for the present unthinking criticism of the press. The existence of these pressure groups and the existence of this antagonism toward the press may be coincidental in time and without any causative relation to each other, but I suspect there is a relationship.[9]

TYPES OF PRESSURE

The war in Spain, prior to the final Franco victory, was productive of much group pressure, and the press was bombarded with appeals and complaints from American sympathizers on both sides. For a time, the Townsendites and the Coughlinites were a thorn in editorial flesh. The boycott against Japan brought its coterie of zealous persons to editorial sanctums. Mild but insistent pressure comes when groups put on drives for money and support, and it is obviously impossible to fill news columns with publicity material from all headquarters of these minorities. Yet the press is faced as never before by the insistent demands of minority groups for space in the newspapers and also for editorial support. It is a rare body of pressure-group leaders that is content to let the editor judge news values and determine what it is in the public interest to publish.

The nature of the press places upon it the responsibility of presenting both sides to a controversy. Sections of the public, however, will resent equal-handed writing and display of the news, and the publishing of the propaganda of one action group in a controversial situation will, of course, anger and outrage the antagonist. Even in the field of foreign affairs, where less controversy could be expected than in the domestic field, the editor has his difficulties. In a dispatch transmitted from Rome by an American

[9] Thomas J. Dillon, editor of the *Minneapolis Morning Tribune* since 1920. Mr. Dillon has edited newspapers since 1906.

news service, Virginio Gayda replied to President Roosevelt's assertion that the Nazis had in mind a plan to suppress the world's religions. Gayda was permitted to say:

National Socialist Germany respects all faiths and recognizes and protects the necessary freedom for all.

Catholic churches like the Protestant in German Territory are still open and carry out their functions undisturbed.

The same cannot be said of the United States where Protestant propaganda has attempted to strike Catholicism and where Protestant agents and plots go forth for propaganda of conversion and corruption in various parts of the world.

This, of course, was a thinly veiled effort to sow distrust in the minds of American Catholics over the wisdom of our Russian policy, and Gayda was not willing to permit the subtlety of his propaganda to speak for itself; he added that Russia, rather than Germany, was seeking to destroy religion.

COPING WITH FOREIGN PROPAGANDA

That propaganda of this sort crept into cable dispatches from our own foreign correspondents and into the direct short-wave appeals from Nazis and Fascists greatly disturbed many supporters of the President's foreign program. It disturbed them to see extreme foreign propaganda statements from totalitarian countries go unchallenged. The dictators repeatedly captured the headlines. Four or five days later, when and if Secretary Hull or some other official made an answer, the American view lacked timeliness and got inside position in the newspapers with a paragraph or two of type.

Some will argue that it is the function of cable editors and telegraph desks to edit out the most obvious forms of foreign propaganda. Others, with a critical turn of mind, assert that some editors fail to recognize "what is being done to them" by wily propagandists abroad, and require a special education in propaganda detection.

One method of obviating the delay in replying to the propaganda of the dictators was found. The Foreign Broadcast Monitoring Service, under the aegis of the Federal Communications Commission, established listening posts to record and analyze all foreign radio propaganda. Essentially a reporting function, the monitoring service had nothing directly to do with propaganda or censoring in this country. But if it kept American officials informed of the types of appeals made from abroad, and kept them up to date on the propaganda moves of foreign governments, it justified its costs. Only by this watchfulness can counterpropaganda hope to meet the positive foreign appeals with a promptness that enables it to catch the same edition of the newspapers.

OFFICIAL PROPAGANDA

The problem of official propaganda in the domestic field is not without significance to the general public as well as to the press. While most of the information personnel in the federal government have a healthy attitude toward the press and are willing to co-operate fully with Washington reporters, the great expansion of the publicity services in the administrative arm of the government raises problems. E. Pendleton Herring discussed these in *Public Administration and the Public Interest.* He warned that, before official publicity work was developed much further, the other side of the picture should be presented to the public with something approximating the efficiency with which the administrative branch reported its accomplishments. His view found support in the report of Brookings Institution experts who surveyed the administrative agencies of the government.

The furnishing of facts is undoubtedly a proper duty of a government agency, but the expenditure of over $500,000 a year for personal services for publicity work and the issuance of 4,794 releases in 3 months seems to indicate that, if possible, some controlling mechanism should be set up.[10]

PRESS AND OFFICIAL PROPAGANDA

The press has a vital interest in any plans that are made. The press co-operated fully and wholeheartedly with the program of the government to maintain the morale of the nation in time of war. Newspapers scrupulously shielded military and naval information which might prove useful to the enemy. They expected and will continue to expect, however, not to be victimized by either government propaganda or censorship. In the first World War, Lord Northcliffe cabled the following from London to the *New*

---

[10] Investigation of Executive Agencies of the Government. Report to the Select Committee to Investigate the Executive Agencies of the Government, 75th Congress, 1st Session, No. 13, p. 12.

York World as late as October, 1915: "The really serious aspect of the affairs here is that, owing to the censorship, this democracy knows nothing about the course of the war." Sound morale is achieved when citizens of a democratic state are not cut off from the news. Citizens of a democratic nation can be trusted to accept the bad tidings as well as the good.

THE PROBLEM OF NEWSPAPER MONOPOLY

BY RAYMOND B. NIXON

Dr. Nixon is professor of journalism at the University of Minnesota and editor of the *Journalism Quarterly*. This paper is reprinted, with some omissions, from *Communications in Modern Society,* copyright 1948 by the University of Illinois Press.

AN ARTICLE OF MINE in the *Journalism Quarterly* for June, 1945, pointed out that the total of 1,744 general-circulation dailies in the United States on December 31, 1944, was the lowest since 1891, though total daily circulation was the highest on record. Total daily circulation has climbed from the beginning, with only a few easily explained slumps, while the total number of dailies reached a peak of 2,600 in 1909 and has been going down ever since almost as steadily as circulation has been going on. A tendency toward concentration of ownership has been manifesting itself since the 1890's in (1) the formation of newspaper chains, (2) the elimination of all except one daily in cities of less than 50,000 population, (3) the combination of two papers under one publisher in cities of 50,000 to 400,000, and (4) the survival of competition only in cities of more than 400,000. Allowing for 174 local combinations of two or more dailies each and for 76 chains involving 368 papers, the maximum number of daily newspaper ownerships in the United States had dwindled by 1945 to less than 1,300.

The trend toward the elimination of competition has continued since the end of World War II, despite a slight increase in the total number of papers. The number of dailies on December 31, 1947, was 1,770, as compared with 1,744 three years earlier—a net gain of 26. Of 74 new papers established in this period, 60 were in communities of less than 25,000 population. Most of the new dailies were in towns of less than 10,000, which previously had been served by weeklies. Only 28 new papers were started in cities that already had dailies. Of the 28 dailies facing competition, 15, or more than half, already have suspended publication. In cities of more than 25,000 population, only 14 dailies have been established during the last three years, whereas 22 have merged or suspended.

More striking still, perhaps, is the fact that no new daily of general content and circulation has been started in a city of more than 200,000 population since 1941. On the other hand, two old established dailies—the *Philadelphia Record* and the *Seattle Star*—suspended publication in 1947 alone. The tendency is still toward fewer and bigger papers in the metropolitan centers, with new dailies appearing only in the smaller cities and surviving only under non-competitive conditions.

The first purpose of my 1945 study was to bring some pertinent factors besides mere numbers of papers into the concentration picture. For example, statistics revealed that although the 368 chain dailies of the nation had 42 per cent of the total daily circulation, only 27.7 per cent of the total circulation was absentee-owned. Likewise, although 91.6 per cent of the 1,394 daily newspaper cities had a single publisher, only 40.2 per cent of the total daily circulation was non-competitive. The reason for this, of course, was that daily circulation is concentrated most heavily in the larger cities, where competition still exists and probably will continue to flourish.

Even in the 1,277 non-competitive cities, it was pointed out, there are factors which keep the situation from being as "monopolistic" as Mr. Ernst has painted it. In the first place, the great majority of one-daily cities are small communities which cannot decently support more than one paper. Even so, some of them do have competition from a local weekly or an independent radio station. In the second place, modern transportation and communication mean that most small-city dailies have competition, both for news and for advertising, from nearby big-city dailies and other non-local media. With national magazines of news and opinion—many shades of it—blanketing the country, and with 36,000,-000 families listening to an average of four and a half hours a day of broadcasting, no single medium of communication in the United States can possibly be said to enjoy a complete "monopoly." The readers of Horace Greeley's *Weekly Tribune,* most of whom probably received no other periodical of news and comment, suffered far more from a lack of diversification than do readers anywhere in America today.

The decline of locally competing units in the newspaper business, as in other phases of American life, has been due to economic factors for which no single individual or group of individuals can be held responsible. In the newspaper business these factors include the loss of advertising revenue to radio and television, the demand of readers for more expensive services, the preference of advertisers for fewer media, with larger circulations, and the rising cost of newsprint, ink, machinery, building, labor, taxes, and everything else that goes into the making of a newspaper. For many dailies it has been a case of "death or consolidation," even though the surviving paper or combination of papers usually has gained strength and stability through its inheritance of a non-competitive field.

I was aware in 1945, as I am now, of the great danger inherent in even a local press "monopoly": the danger that freedom of expression for minority views will be curtailed and the formation of a sound public opinion made more difficult. I quoted the late Dr. Willard G. Bleyer as having emphasized, as early as 1934, the same socio-political objections to one-publisher communities that Mr. Ernst and others more lately have stressed. But since it was agreed that the decline of competition had been brought about by economic forces, I set forth as my second major purpose to discover what counterforces, if any, the decreasing numbers of competitive papers might be generating. For if economic factors are basic, as they no doubt will be so long as the press remains free, it is to them we must look for the shape of things to come.

Newspaper chains concern us here only so far as they affect the extent of competition. Perhaps the most significant point is that the larger national chains have declined in numbers of papers since 1935 and only the smaller regional groups have tended to increase. The chain that has added the most units since World War II and now has the largest number of papers—the John H. Perry group—illustrates this point, as 18 of its 20 dailies are in Florida. The chain that has shown the largest growth in circulation—the McCormick-

Patterson group—is concentrated in two cities and until recently had an active owner living in each city. The relation of chain circulation to the total daily circulation of the nation has remained fairly constant for the last 15 years.

Whether the more extensive national chains have declined in number of papers because they had reached "the optimum point of efficiency in bigness" would be an interesting subject for research. There probably is a point at which the economic savings from group operation fail to compensate for the disadvantages of absentee ownership. Certainly the chains have not shown the growth following World War II that they displayed after World War I. No new Frank A. Munsey has arisen to propose a chain of 500 newspapers for "economic efficiency." On the political side, the time seems to have passed when a William Randolph Hearst would seek to promote his presidential ambitions by personally directing a nationwide chain of newspapers. Present-day conditions would be more likely to lead a journalist with a drive for that kind of power into a different type of ownership concentration—the ownership, for example, of a "communications empire," consisting of a group of national magazines, a radio-television network, and a film-producing company. Here one would not encounter the prejudice that frequently operates against the success of a local chain daily, particularly if its owner is absentee.

Generalizations about either chain or absentee ownership, however, are extremely dangerous. Anyone acquainted with contemporary American journalism can name chain papers, some with the owner living far distant, that rank high in quality and public service. We are also familiar with many locally owned papers that rank extremely low.

If local ownership means entanglement with local financial and political interests, absentee ownership can be an actual advantage. It all depends upon the owner and the amount of freedom he gives his local executives.

Inasmuch as the large national chains seem to be falling apart of their own weight, most Americans probably would agree with Dr. Zechariah Chafee, Jr., that we should "wait and see which way the tide is running" before resorting to legal measures to break up this type of ownership concentration. We may be in for further battles in the courts and in the FCC over "communications empires"—the interlocking ownership of various media, but even in this connection, as Dr. Chafee says, "The question still remains—what specific good will breaking up an empire accomplish? . . . The undue influence of one man over public opinion rests considerably on the uncritical attitude of his reader or listeners. Until that attitude is removed, how much is gained by handing them over to another spellbinder whose views may be less enlightened?"[1]

With the growth of large national chains apparently checked for the moment by economic causes, I turned my attention to one publisher communities. I was particularly interested in the 161 combinations and 13 partial combinations that have eliminated competition in 174 American cities. Here the trend has been unbroken since the 1890's, unless there is now beginning a new tendency to eliminate the less profitable of the two or more papers in a combination. But there seems to be no case on record of two papers which have come together—in a combination or partial combination—ever going back to separate operation. The critics who have cried for competing dailies as a means of presenting a diversity of views have had no effect. The forces of economics are against them.

But what of those economic forces? Might they not, in the manner of the Hegelian dialectic, be breeding counterforces which would check the trend toward "monopolies"? A study of advertising rates in 97 pairs of dailies, before and after they combined under a single publisher, was revealing. In 43 cases the combined rates of the two papers immediately after consolidation were lower than the sum of their old rates; in 31 instances the rates remained the same; and in 23 cases they were higher. In other words, in 54 out of 97 cases combination resulted in no savings to advertisers, although publishers admitted that their own savings were "substantial." An analysis by the American Association of Advertising Agencies showed that the advertising rates of 211 combination papers averaged higher than the rates of independent papers in all except the fourteen largest cities, where there is competition. Moreover, nearly all non-competitive combinations have an "enforced rate" which compels their national advertisers, and frequently their local advertisers also, to buy space in both papers in order to advertise in one. A sampling of national advertising agencies and local department-store advertising managers revealed vigorous opposition to this practice.

---

[1] Zechariah Chafee, Jr., *Government and Mass Communications* (Chicago: University of Chicago Press, 1947), II, 664-66.

On the basis of this survey, I commented that unless more combinations passed on part of their savings to their customers, the critics who had been urging governmental action to maintain multiple outlets of news and opinion might find their ranks reinforced by a powerful ally: the newspaper advertiser. I quoted Dr. Fred S. Siebert's statement that "freedom of the press" would hardly be an adequate defense in such a situation, since the courts have shown increasing reluctance "to extend the meaning of the constitutional guarantees of freedom of the press to cover social and economic regulations." What I had in mind, of course, was the possibility of a commission which might regulate the rates and earnings of "monopoly" newspapers in the same way that public utility monopolies are regulated. But where I merely pointed out the danger of such regulation and urged the publishers themselves to take steps to forestall it, Mr. Ernst and his followers have advocated the use of governmental powers and subsidies to break up ownership concentration of all kinds and to bring about an artificial stimulation of newspaper competition.

The evils inherent in such proposals—far more devastating to democracy than any that have resulted from the decline of competition—are exposed fully by Dr. Chafee in his admirable book on *Government and Mass Communications*. Possibly as a result of Dr. Chafee's influence, the Commission on Freedom of the Press as a whole almost completely discarded Mr. Ernst's line of reasoning and advocated that the anti-trust laws be only "sparingly used" to break up large units in the communications field. "When you look at the swirling human and material forces which bring about a broadcast or motion picture or one issue of a newspaper, the Sherman Act recedes," wrote Dr. Chafee. "You stop expecting that a few lawyers in the Department of Justice and a statute passed in 1890 can do much to make the press of 1950 what you desire."[2]

Forrest W. Seymour, editor of the *Des Moines Register*, reminds us in the January, 1948, issue of *Nieman Reports* that it is "precisely" the operation of Mr. Ernst's "beloved competition" that has brought about the elimination of so many independent papers. If we "rub out the score and start all over again," the same thing would happen once more unless the weaker papers were aided, as Mr. Ernst suggests, by the government. In that event, says Mr. Seymour, "government has so many of the competitive elements

---

[2] *Ibid.*, p. 653.

in its favor that the competition would soon disappear again—but leaving, this time, a monopoly which the critics really would have some cause to fume about!"

Mr. Seymour is a biased witness, since he works for a daily which is both a "monopoly" paper and a chain paper. It is one which, nevertheless, he might have cited in pointing out the further absurdities of Mr. Ernst's argument:

The large daily newspapers of the United States provide no pattern whatever of "goodness" or "badness" that coincides with the degree of competition in the home cities of publication. One of the most competitive newspaper cities in the country is Boston, which has not had (at least until very recently) a single daily of general circulation that measures up to anything like the standards of the "monopolistic" Louisville *Courier-Journal* or Minneapolis *Star* and *Tribune*. Did the character of the Chicago *Tribune* undergo any visible change because of the competition even from so resourceful a capitalist as Marshall Field? The Denver *Post's* competitive situation has not appreciably altered in twenty-five years, and yet under the wise and thoughtful guidance of a new editor, it is rapidly undergoing transformation into a dignified, socially responsive, trusted journal of real integrity.

Why, then, must our critics be so blind to the obvious fact that the character, the social conscience, and the ethical standards of the newspaper as an institution are a reflection of the individuals and groups who own and produce it—rather than of some superficial competitive condition over which the publishers and editors have little or no control?

What is far more important than artificially stimulating competition, Mr. Seymour concludes, is that "we find out how to lift the standards of the press faster, and without waiting for the tedious processes of an economic rat race."

Ralph W. Page and Ernest K. Lindley—two newspapermen of long experience in competitive cities—took essentially the same position as Mr. Seymour in addresses before the 1947 convention of the American Association of Teachers of Journalism at Philadelphia. Mr. Lindley, the Washington editor of *Newsweek*, argued further that a lack of competition does not necessarily imply either a lack of quality or a lack of diversification:

Competition is supposed to produce better products. But in the local newspaper field, I am not sure that it always has resulted in a better-informed public. It often has encouraged sensationalism and the multiplication of features designed to entertain, divert, or lull the mind rather than better reporting and interpretation of news. Many of the communities with newspaper monopolies seem to be fairly well served. Many of these monopolists seem to me to have recognized, at least up to a point, their obligation to serve as common carriers not only of news but of opinion.

The trend toward local monopolies could be carried even farther, I think, without serious consequences—and, if the right newspapers survived, with real benefit to the public . . . [one paper] might be enough, if through the addition of more signed columnists, and such a device as a daily forum or pro-and-con feature, it provided an adequate outlet for conflicting opinions.

In my own cautious observations in 1945 about the possibility of economic regulation, I remarked that the new electronic media— television, FM, and facsimile—and the perfection of cheaper methods of printing might multiply local channels of opinion and advertising to such an extent that the cries of "monopoly" would subside. That, of course, is exactly what is happening. As Vincent S. Jones, executive editor of the Utica (N.Y.) *Observer-Dispatch* and *Daily Press* (another chain-combination!), told the teachers of journalism at Philadelphia, the various media are now about to enter upon "the biggest, toughest, roughest, freest spending fight for a share of Mr. Average Reader's time than ever was dreamed up!" Consequently, the danger that "monopoly" newspapers might bring regulation on themselves by unfair rate practices seems far more remote than it did in 1945.

What, then, are the implications that reasonably may be drawn today from the decreasing numbers of competitive newspapers?

1. *The number of competitive daily newspapers will continue to decline.* Even though the total number of dailies may increase, through the establishment of new papers in the faster-growing small cities, the percentage of communities having more than one general-circulation paper or one publisher will not increase at any time in the near future. Spiralling costs, which affect the advertiser and the reader as well as the publisher, will discourage the establishment of new publishing ventures in the larger cities. A severe depression would have a similar effect, as it did in the thirties.

2. *The one-publisher town is not an evil in itself—it all depends on the publisher.* To quote Mr. Lindley again, "a community is no worse served by one poor newspaper than by several poor papers," but "certainly it is better served by one good newspaper than by two or three poor ones." We cannot improve the situation merely by multiplying mediocrity. But a responsible "monopoly" pub-

lisher, as I observed in my 1945 article, can dedicate his paper to the principles of intelligent and objective reporting, giving all groups a fair hearing. Extensive research is needed on this point. A preliminary report of an investigation at Columbia (published in the June, 1948, *Journalism Quarterly*) indicates that except in the very large cities competing papers tend to be merely "rivals in conformity."

3. *The "monopoly" omnibus daily is here to stay.* The new methods of "cold-type printing," which do away with expensive linotyping and stereotyping, will make it easier for many smaller communities to support local newspapers. Moreover, these cheaper processes will enable private groups in the larger cities to operate their own special-interest papers as outlets for minority views. It is doubtful, however, whether either such publications or facsimile papers will offer any serious competition to the established general-circulation dailies that do a good job of supplying the wide variety of expensive news, opinion, features, and advertising that readers have come to demand. "A young man could start a daily newspaper in New York City today along the lines of *The Sun* of 1833, a four-page one-cent sheet, and he could do this on small capital," writes Dr. Alfred M. Lee. "But . . . the whole job would attract few purchasers even at one cent in competition with today's *Daily News* (or) . . . *Times.* . . . Part of the press's institutionalism, a very powerful part, is in the minds of subscribers."[3]

4. *Competition from the new electronic media will increase.* The growing number of both AM and FM stations, together with the advent of television and facsimile newspapers, is filling the gap left by the "disappearing dailies." This new competition for the advertiser's dollar will tend to hold newspaper advertising rates at a reasonable level and thereby stave off any demand for regulation solely because of economic practices. Even "monopoly" publishers are having their troubles today in keeping revenue ahead of expenses, and readers and advertisers know it.

5. *This new competition does not necessarily promise any improvement in quality.* On the contrary, as the struggle for survival becomes more intense, the temptation may increase for the weaker units to accept border-line advertising and to attract readers or listeners through sensationalism and "sure-fire" features at the ex-

[3] A. M. Lee, "The Basic Newspaper Pattern," in the *Annals of the American Academy of Political and Social Science*, CCXIX (January, 1942), 52.

pense of good reporting and diversified opinion. Excesses of this kind might lead to a far more widespread demand for regulation than we have had up to now.

We are faced, then, by a curious paradox. Although we seem to be on the verge of getting the increased competition on which Mr. Ernst has pinned his faith, it actually may lead to more of the evils and dangers he deplores. We are back to the premise on which most teachers of journalism started long ago: namely, that if we wish to improve newspapers, regardless of their number, we must raise the social responsibility and professional competence of the men who run them. At the same time we must educate a more enlightened generation of newspaper readers, who will demand, and in turn receive, a better product.

The Trend toward Non-Competitive Situations in U.S. Cities with Daily Newspapers

	1880	1909–10	1920	1930	1940	1944–45	1953–54	
Circulation (thousands)...	3,093	22,426	27,791	39,589	41,132	45,955	54,472	(54,140)
Total General Dailies........	850	2,202	2,042	1,942	1,878	1,744	1,785	(1,760)
Total Daily Cities	389	1,207	1,295	1,402	1,426	1,396	1,448	
One-Daily Cities.	149	509	716	1,002	1,092	1,107	1,188	
% of Total..	38.3	42.2	55.3	71.5	76.6	77.3	82.0	
One-Combination Cities........	1	9	27	112	149	161	154	
Joint Printing Cities........	..	..	..	..	4	11	19	
Total Non-Competitive...	150	518	743	1,114	1,245	1,279	1,361	
% of Total..	38.6	42.9	57.4	79.4	87.3	91.6	94.0	
Cities with Competing Dailies..	239	689	552	288	181	117	87	

Source: Raymond B. Nixon in the *Journalism Quarterly*.

THE ECONOMIC EFFECTS OF ADVERTISING

BY NEIL H. BORDEN

This is the summary of Professor Borden's monumental book, *The Economic Effects of Advertising*, published and copyrighted in 1947 by Richard D. Irwin. This material is here reprinted by permission of author and publisher. Professor Borden is professor of advertising in the Graduate School of Business Administration at Harvard.

DOES ADVERTISING INCREASE DEMAND FOR TYPES OF PRODUCTS AS A WHOLE?

STUDY OF DEMAND for a wide range of products leads to the conclusion that basic trends of demand for products are determined primarily by underlying social and environmental conditions, and that advertising by itself serves not so much to increase demand for a product as to speed up the expansion of a demand that would come from favoring conditions, or to retard adverse demand trends due to unfavorable conditions. The demands for some products, for example, lettuce, sugar, green vegetables, and professional services, have grown even though the products are little advertised, for underlying social and environmental conditions have been favorable to expansion of their demand. Other industries for which there have been underlying conditions favorable to demand expansion have had their demand more rapidly expanded through use of advertising than would have occurred without such advertising. Among the products studied, this quickening of expansion has occurred in the case of cigarettes, dentifrices, oranges, automatic refrigerators, and other mechanical products such as automobiles, radios, and electric

251

washers. On the other hand, for certain products for which underlying conditions caused adverse demand trends, demand was found
to continue to contract in spite of considerable expenditures for
advertising and promotion. Such was the situation with cigars,
smoking tobacco, furniture, wheat flour, and men's shoes. In these
instances advertising was powerless to reverse underlying declining
trends, although it probably served to retard the declines. In other
instances, certain products have had relatively constant per capita
consumption over a period of years, even though substantial advertising was devoted to them. In short, such contrasting demand
situations as mentioned above led to the conclusion that consumers'
wants for products are determined by the character of consumers
and their existing environment. Advertising has not changed people's
characteristics; it has changed environment only as it has contributed indirectly over a long period in helping to bring a mobile
society and a dynamic economy. In speeding up demand for new
products it has contributed to the dynamic character of the
economy.

DOES ADVERTISING INCREASE DEMAND
FOR INDIVIDUAL CONCERNS?

Advertising can and does increase the demand for the products
of many individual companies, but the extent to which it does so
varies widely and depends upon the circumstances under which
an enterprise operates. An individual company can use advertising
profitably to increase sales only when it serves to stimulate a volume
of sales at prices which more than cover all costs including the
advertising outlay. Advertising's effectiveness in profitably stimulating sales for a concern depends upon the presence of a combination
of conditions, of which the following are important.

First, advertising is likely to be more effective if a company is
operating with a favorable primary demand trend than if it is
operating with an adverse trend. With the industry's sales expanding, each concern has opportunity to strive for part of an increasing
whole. Thus in the tobacco industry some companies in recent
decades have put much of their advertising and promotional effort
on cigarettes, because the demand for cigarettes has been expanding
and promotional effort given to them has been particularly promising of results in the form of increased volume of sales. On the
other hand, their advertising of cigars, smoking tobacco, and chew-

ing tobacco has not been carried on with such favorable trends; and although advertising has been profitably used, each producer has been seeking to get a share of a contracting total demand.

Secondly, advertising is particularly helpful to individual companies in stimulating demand when their products provide large chance for differentiation. Conversely, advertising is of smaller help when there is a marked tendency for the products of various producers to become closely similar. Product differentiation provides the opportunity for influencing consumers to prefer one brand to another brand. Advertising provides the means for pointing out to consumers the significance of differentiating qualities. Moreover, when differentiations of significance to consumers are found, the seller often can secure wider gross margins than when such differentiations are absent, for when significant differentiations are effectively advertised, consumer valuations are affected. Wide margins, in turn, provide funds with which to support advertising. Among the products studied, smoking tobacco, cosmetics, dentifrices, soaps, electric refrigerators, and automobiles are products which have provided opportunities for product differentiations, and these individualizing points have been advertised. Conversely, sugar, salt, canned fruits, and sheeting are illustrative of products which have tended to be closely similar, with consequent limitations upon the use of advertising to increase the demand of individual companies.

A third condition having a bearing upon the effectiveness of advertising in increasing selective demand is the relative importance to the consumer of hidden qualities of the products, as contrasted with external qualities which can be seen and appreciated. For example, consumers attach importance to the hidden qualities of mechanical products, such as automobiles, watches, and washing machines, for satisfactory operation of the machine depends upon these hidden qualities. Manufacturers of such products find advertising helpful in building mental associations regarding the dependability of their products. Likewise, consumers are apt to give great weight to the purity, potency, and other hidden qualities of such products as drugs and cosmetics. Conversely, one reason why advertising has not been valuable to producers of green vegetables is the fact that the buyer can inspect the articles and judge their worth at the time of purchase. The seller's trade-mark can stand for no hidden qualities of great significance to the buyer, particularly in view of the perishable nature of the product. Similarly, in the case of fashion merchandise the consumer can judge the elements of style, such as color and design, and tell whether the product suits his fancy. These external characteristics often are more important to the buyer than are hidden product qualities which may be associated with a seller's trade-mark. This fact accounts in considerable part for the relatively small use of advertising to influence the demand for the branded merchandise of producers of fashion goods.

A fourth condition having a highly important bearing upon the effectiveness of advertising in increasing the demand for products of individual concerns is the presence of powerful emotional buying motives to which the concerns can appeal in their advertising. Thus in the case of oranges effective appeals to maintenance of health have helped to build demand for the products of the California Fruit Growers Exchange. Similarly, manufacturers of cosmetics, drugs, and food specialties have found in their products bases for appeal to strong consumer buying motives. Cosmetics are bought because they promise personal beauty and romance; food and drugs are bought because they promise health. Often such emotional appeals have material effect on consumers' valuations of the advertised products, a fact clearly illustrated in drug and cosmetic products. In contrast to the above, sugar manufacturers, walnut growers, sheeting manufacturers, and numerous other sellers have found their products less adapted to the use of strong emotional appeals.

A fifth condition of prime importance to the use of advertising for increasing the demands of individual companies is whether the company's operations provide substantial sums with which to advertise and promote their products. The matter of an advertising fund for any period turns upon the number of units of the product which can be sold in the period and upon the margin available for advertising. The size of the margin depends very largely upon the effectiveness of advertising in influencing consumer valuations for a product. This influence of advertising is dependent upon the extent and significance of product differentiation present and upon the strength of appeals which may be employed to present differentiated qualities. The amount of margin available for aggressive selling work depends also upon conditions of competition within an industry. Cigarettes and dentifrices are illustrative of products which are purchased by large numbers of consumers at relatively frequent intervals and on which the margins available for advertising have been substantial proportions of selling prices. In consequence, many sellers in these fields have had large advertising appropriations. In contrast, although sugar has had large sales volume, its price has provided very narrow margins available for advertising. Again, the number of units of electric refrigerators sold is not large as compared with the above products, but the size of unit sale has been large enough to provide a relatively large margin per unit and, consequently, large total advertising appropriations to individual companies. In contrast, manufacturers of products of high price but of thin demand, such as expensive clocks and pipe organs for the home, have been small advertisers because they have not sold enough units to support substantial advertising programs.

The effectiveness of advertising in influencing selective demand depends upon the extent to which the five conditions outlined above are present. The combination of conditions which exist rather than any one condition determines the effectiveness of advertising in influencing selective demand. The possible combinations are almost innumerable, and each demand situation as it relates to advertising use must be studied separately. Of the conditions, those which are particularly important in rendering advertising an effective means for increasing the demands of individual companies are the chance for significant product differentiation, the opportunity to use strong emotional appeals, the existence of hidden qualities of importance to buyers, and the existence of circumstances favoring the accumulation of substantial sums to support advertising.

The study of demand shows that the opportunity for the use of advertising to increase demand varies markedly among different products. Although advertising for some products can be a very important means of increasing sales for the advertiser, yet, contrary to the view of many laymen, advertising does not always pay. Moreover, the use of advertising, like other business expenditures, involves risk for businessmen.

The study of demand shows further that even in product fields for which advertising may be used effectively by some concerns to increase their demand, other producers find opportunity to gain sales volume by other means. For example, by eliminating or greatly reducing the advertising and promotional functions, some manufacturers gain desired business by selling at a low price. Moreover, some sellers elect to use larger proportions of personal selling or other forms of promotion and less of advertising.

DOES ADVERTISING INCREASE DEMAND FOR ALL PRODUCTS?

The question of whether advertising has had any effect in increasing the demand for all products has meaning only as advertising may have played a part in increasing the size of national income. Demand for all products can increase only as income from production increases. Over the past 100 years real national income has increased fourfold, and during this period aggressive selling and advertising were increasingly used. The part which advertising may have played in helping to bring the increase in national income will be summarized in connection with the review of advertising's effect on investment.

DOES ADVERTISING AFFECT ELASTICITY OF DEMAND FOR PRODUCTS?

Now that the effect of advertising in increasing the demand for products and for individual companies, i.e., its effect in shifting demand curves, has been summarized, its effect on elasticity, or the shape of demand curves, is reviewed. The evidence regarding the effect of advertising on elasticity of demand is not comprehensive and complete, and conclusions must be based largely on inference from comparisons and contrasts of the demand behavior of different products.

DOES ADVERTISING INCREASE THE ELASTICITY OF PRIMARY DEMAND FOR PRODUCTS?

First is the question, does advertising make the demand for classes of products as a whole more or less elastic? That is, has it made the demand for products, such as sugar, cigarettes, and dentifrices, more or less responsive to price changes?

It appears likely that for products whose demand is inherently inelastic, i.e., whose consumption by individuals is limited by the character of the products, advertising does not materially affect the elasticity of demand. For example, although salt has been advertised to consumers, it seems unlikely that advertising has materially shifted or changed the shape of the demand curve for salt. Its demand is and has been inelastic. Again, although advertising has helped in greatly expanding the demand for cigarettes, i.e., in shifting the demand curve, advertising does not appear to have greatly changed the shape of the curve. The sales of cigarettes fell somewhat in the 1930 depression, when leading companies generally held cigarette prices firm, an action which was equivalent to a normal price rise. But the decrease was relatively slight as compared with the decrease for many other products. This behavior of cigarette demand is in keeping with what would be expected from the fact that cigarette use is habitual with most buyers and their purchases are not appreciably affected by price change. In short, while advertising has helped induce some persons to acquire the use habit and thus has influenced total cigarette demand, advertising has not affected the shape of the demand curve, that is, the responsiveness of demand to price change.

In contrast to the above examples, for certain products advertising not only has had the effect of increasing their demand, i.e., of shifting the demand curves, but has apparently altered the shape of the curves. For example, many new products give evidence, in their early stages of marketing, of having small and relatively inelastic demand. Consumers are usually skeptical of a new product. They are not responsive to a price appeal at such times because of this skepticism and lack of an aroused desire for the product. Moreover, limited use of a product prevents the important selling forces of emulation and imitation from coming into play. As advertising and aggressive selling are employed, however, to build public acceptance for a new product and widening use brings the force of emulation into play, the shape of the product's demand curve evidently is altered. Large numbers of people come to desire the product. In short, in such cases the advertising and promotion have the effect of making demand more elastic. When public acceptance is once established, lowering of price generally serves to bring a large number of buyers into the market. Mechanical refrigerators are an example of a product whose elasticity of demand was increased by advertising and aggressive selling. Demand was built up slowly at first by aggressive selling. After the introductory period, as prices dropped, large numbers of buyers were brought into the market. Other new mechanical products which have been heavily promoted are also believed to have had their demand curves thereby rendered more elastic, products such as automobiles, radios, oil burners, and a long list of electrical appliances. Likewise, in other fields, it is believed that advertising has had the effect of increasing the elasticity of primary demand. For example, in the food field advertising and promotion have probably increased the elasticity of demand for such products as prepared breakfast foods, prepared desserts, and numerous other food innovations which have enjoyed substantial expansion of demand following their introduction to the market.

While conceivably there are products whose total demand becomes less responsive to price rise as the result of the building of strong consumers' preference for the products through advertising, no examples of this kind were found during this study, and they are believed to be few, if any. Dentifrices are a product which from *a priori* reasoning was expected to behave in this way. It was thought that the strong health and beauty appeals employed for dentifrices would have built such a strong desire for the product that an increase in price would not materially affect consumption. This reasoning was not borne out in the 1930 depression, however. When the price structure for dentifrices generally was held quite rigid in the depression, an action equivalent to a price rise in that period of declining prices, per capita sales for dentifrices fell some 25%. The contraction of dentifrice demand on this equivalent of a price rise suggests that demand for the product might be stimulated in turn by a general reduction of price. That this would actually happen is not supported by evidence. Strangely enough, price appeal has not been highly effective to individual companies in attracting selective demand.

DOES ADVERTISING MAKE DEMAND FOR AN INDIVIDUAL COMPANY'S PRODUCT MORE OR LESS ELASTIC?

From the question of the effect of advertising upon the elasticity of demand for types of products as a whole (primary demand), the review is turned to the question of whether advertising makes the demand for products of individual concerns more or less elastic.

The evidence indicates that the advertising of brands tends to make their demands relatively inelastic for varying periods of time. The data which support this conclusion are found in the relatively rigid prices of many advertised articles. That brand advertising would have this effect is natural, for an objective of brand advertising is to build consumer preferences. Some consumers will stick by a brand even though its price relationships with competing brands are disturbed. Clearly the establishment of strong brand preference has led some manufacturers to act as though these preferences made the demand for their brands relatively inelastic. Rarely have they tested the inelasticity of their brands by raising and holding up their prices when competitors have failed to follow a similar procedure. Yet numerous examples were found in which manufacturers in periods of depression held their prices rigid while prices generally and the prices of some competitors were being lowered.

In all such instances price competition was found to come into play sooner or later, and either demand shifted to sellers with lower prices or a reduction of prices was forced. The quickness with which price competition comes into play varies in different product fields. In the fields of proprietary remedies, the highly individualized nature of branded products and the tendency of consumers to build strong attachments to brands have given these brands an inelastic demand over relatively long periods of time. Even in these instances, however, price competition eventually has developed. Proprietaries which have become popular have been copied by other manufacturers or by private branders, who have then used the same appeals as the imitated brands and also have featured the price appeal. Thus, for example, certain leading antiseptics have been imitated and forced to reduce price. In the aspirin field, the Bayer Company has held its prices relatively constant over long periods, but competing aspirins have gained ground.

The demands for individual brands of dentifrices, which are believed to follow a pattern of price behavior similar to that of many toilet goods and cosmetics, have been relatively inelastic. Prices have been held relatively rigid, and although consumers have been given opportunities to buy dentifrices at lower prices than those of leading advertised brands, demand has gone primarily to the advertised brands. Notwithstanding, price competition has entered this area and gives promise over a long period of gaining headway.

Similarly, the demand for cigarette brands has been relatively inelastic. Nevertheless, during the 1930 depression, 10-cent cigarettes became generally established when the price differences between leading advertised brands and 10-cent brands became substantial, and since that date 10-cent cigarettes have come to claim nearly one-fifth of the market.

In the food field, manufacturers of food specialties were found frequently to hold their prices relatively rigid with the onset of depression and thus to treat the demand for the products as inelastic, although there were numerous exceptions to this practice. The evidence indicates, however, that when this policy has been followed and private branders have adjusted their prices more rapidly than the manufacturers, demand has tended to flow to the private brands. In such instances manufacturers of advertised brands either have lost ground or have been forced to reestablish normal price relationships in order to hold sales volume. In these areas the effects of price competition were felt relatively quickly.

DOES ADVERTISING TEND TO INCREASE DISTRIBUTION COSTS?

The review of evidence and conclusions is directed now to the question of whether advertising has tended to increase the costs of distributing merchandise.

The answer to this question is indeterminate from the evidence available. One cannot be certain to what extent the increased distribution costs which have attended the growth of industrialism are attributable to advertising. Yet the evidence, though conflicting in some aspects, is complete enough to dispel certain misconceptions sometimes met in the literature relating to advertising regarding the effects of advertising upon distribution costs.

The rising trend of distribution costs which was concomitant with the Industrial Revolution was inevitable. In the simple village economy which preceded the growth of the factory system, the few purchases of consumers were made without appreciable marketing costs. With the exception of the limited number of items then in general commerce, the exchange of merchandise was effected by direct contact between the buyer and the maker. After the factory system was established, the growth of large-scale, specialized units producing a tremendous variety of merchandise necessarily was accompanied by increasing costs of bringing about exchange. In addition to such essential marketing costs as those for transportation, warehousing, and credit, it was necessary also to incur the costs of bringing buyers and sellers together in the market. Sellers had to be informed of buyers' wants, and buyers had to be informed of merchandise available, if exchange was to take place. The costs of the selling process, i.e., providing the information and persuasion needed to effect exchange, became larger as the industrial organization became more complex.

But sellers have incurred selling and distribution costs greater than the minimum which may be deemed necessary to effect exchange. They have resorted to competition in advertising personal selling, and other non-price forms of competition, all of which involve cost. The charge that advertising increases the costs of distribution is attributable in considerable part to the competition in advertising that occurs in some industries.

In a number of the product fields studied there was substantial competition in advertising and consequently these products had high advertising costs relative to certain other products. In fields in which such intensive competition in advertising has existed, the use of advertising, like the use of other forms of non-price competition, has increased the costs of distribution, or at least has held these costs at high levels. In many of these instances, however, consumers have shown a willingness to pay for the costs which attend the vigorously advertised products, for in large numbers they have not exercised the options open to them of buying lower-price, non-advertised merchandise. Instances of this kind were found in many fields, but especially clear were the instances in the dentifrice, cigarette, and grocery fields.

The sweeping generalization sometimes made that high advertising costs result in low personal selling costs and other marketing costs was not substantiated by the evidence of this study. Sometimes this statement is true, many times it is not. The managements of individual concerns frequently experiment to reduce their selling costs by using advertising instead of personal selling or other forms of promotion. Often in such instances advertising is an economical alternative, although in other instances it is not. Frequently advertising proves to be an economical and effective complement to personal selling. In other cases, sellers increase advertising costs per unit, not with the thought of reducing unit selling costs, but rather with the idea of increasing the volume of sales or of affecting consumer valuations in such a way that aggregate net profit may be increased. In short, sellers do not necessarily use advertising to attain the lowest possible costs of marketing, but to attain a desired marketing objective of selling certain volumes of merchandise at certain prices.

It is not possible to trace on a large statistical scale the full effects of advertising by manufacturers on the expenses and margins of distributors who handle advertised products. Whenever advertising builds a ready demand for a branded product, the costs of selling that product by the trade tend to be low. Thus, manufacturers' advertised brands of cigarettes, grocery products, and numerous other items have low costs of selling among distributors. Upon such items distributors ordinarily receive lower margins than they do on similar products bearing their own private brands or sold unbranded. But low selling costs apply to many staple commodities in ready demand which have relatively little advertising by producers, such as sugar, butter, potatoes, and so on. Moreover, distributors' private brands, once established, may enjoy low selling costs. Whether the reductions in trade margins of numerous advertised brands are more or less than sufficient to cover the manufacturers' costs of advertising is uncertain. The evidence is inadequate and conflicting.

Indication that high advertising costs do not necessarily entail low distribution costs was gained from a comparison of the costs of distributing merchandise under competing methods of marketing. It was found that those methods which involved highest advertising costs did not necessarily have lowest total costs of distribution. For example, in certain instances in which distributors sold under their own brands, the total selling and advertising costs and the total distribution costs incurred between factory and consumer were less than corresponding costs for competing marketing methods in which the manufacturers sold under their own brands. It should be pointed out, however, that in such cases the manufacturers primarily shouldered the burden of promoting and stimulating the demand for the products of their industries and that the private branders benefited from this promotion and advertising.

There was evidence in numerous cases that advertising has played a large part in contributing to the size of enterprises, but the data also showed that increased size does not necessarily mean lower distribution costs. In fact, there was evidence, though contradictory, that large concerns may have relatively high marketing costs. It should be recognized, however, that such a result is not undesirable, provided the increase in scale permits production costs that more than offset increased marketing costs.

While the evidence regarding advertising and distribution costs was adequate to warrant the conclusions outlined above, no answer was possible to the question of whether advertising has tended to increase distribution costs as a whole. The distribution cost picture is obscured by the fact that advertising and distribution cost data of business concerns relate to numerous combinations of products and of functional services and these combinations are subject to constant shifting. The over-all effects of advertising on total distribution costs cannot be traced.

The answer to the question of advertising's effects on production costs is indeterminate. While there is much affirmative evidence of striking economies in the costs of production which have attended the concurrent growth in size of industries and in use of advertising and aggressive selling, it is impossible from cost data to trace a clear causal relationship between decreased production costs and advertising. Only limited and tentative conclusions regarding advertising's effect on production costs are warranted by the evidence.

Over a long time span, aggressive selling and advertising have played a more or less important part in different industries in making possible the volume of demand necessary for the establishment of factories whose costs have been low as compared with the costs of handicraft methods of production. Advertising evidently has had an indirect effect in reducing production costs in numerous industries, not only through its contribution to growth in scale of operations but through its contribution to technological development, points which are summarized later.

In the study of specific industries, numerous instances were noted in which manufacturers employed advertising to help gain sales volume and in which the increase in size was attended by economies, which in varying degree offset advertising expenditures. In certain instances studied, advertising played a considerable part in building industry demand, and the economies gained through increased size of factories as industry demand grew were apparently greater than the promotional expenditures. Among products discussed at length, this condition evidently held in the early days of the cigarette industry and clearly in the case of mechanical refrigerators; less intensive study of numerous other industries indicates that the condition has frequently held true.

Not all industries, however, have had to rely upon the stimulus of advertising to build a demand sufficient to support low-cost manufacturing operations. The sugar, shoe, and sheeting industries, for example, grew to large size without much influence from advertising in stimulating primary demand, although aggressive selling in other forms was used.

Once industry demand has been established, it is possible for producers to seek a volume of sales large enough to permit low costs of manufacture without employment of a substantial amount of advertising. This generalization applies clearly to industries such as the sugar industry, which never has been a substantial user of advertising, but it applies as well to industries in which many producers are advertisers. Thus, not only do numerous sugar refineries attain low costs of production with little advertising, but the same is true of certain producers of cigarettes, mechanical refrigerators, dentifrices, and numerous other products, who are operating in industries which have relatively high average ratios of advertising costs. As pointed out elsewhere, in the latter instances the advertisers have assumed the burden of building demand for these products and the nonadvertisers have benefited therefrom.

Sweeping claims of production economies resulting from and maintained by advertising are not in accord with the facts given above. In many industries, concerns which are nonadvertisers or are relatively small users of advertising have low production costs. These concerns have been able to attain a profitable volume of sales through special contracts with large customers, through an appeal to consumers on the basis of price, or through some form of promotion and selling other than advertising.

Production economies, furthermore, do not always attend large-scale operations. In some industries relatively small plants may enjoy low production costs. This condition may be the result of the character of manufacturing processes, or it may be attributable to a type of demand which necessitates small runs of a product, as in the cutting-up trades and in the shoe industry. In these instances fashion has made the use of standardization of production runs and mass production methods beyond a certain point unprofitable. Accordingly in these industries relatively small firms often operate with production costs as low as those of large concerns.

Apart from the question of advertising's effect on production costs through economies that might be gained in size, there is the question of the value of advertising as a means of attaining low overhead costs. The question posed is whether advertising serves to bring stability of demand and relatively constant use of plant, with subsequent lowering of overhead costs.

The contribution of advertising as a means of attaining low overhead costs in this way has frequently been overstated. To begin with, advertising in itself does not insure stability of operations to a concern. While it helps many businesses to gain the relative stability of demand which comes when a firm builds strong consumer brand preference, nevertheless in an industry in which competition is carried on largely through advertising, the relative standing of sales of individual companies turns not so much on whether the concerns advertise, as on how skillfully they advertise in comparison with competitors. Moreover, stability of sales depends upon good merchandising and numerous factors other than advertising. In the next place, the importance of stability as a factor in costs depends upon the amount of fixed costs under which a concern operates. The study indicates that businessmen do not have uniform and clear-cut ideas of their fixed and variable costs. Accordingly, what some of them class as overhead costs are not always in accord with the economist's definition of fixed costs. When fixed costs are taken into consideration, the evidence shows that for many products substantial fluctuation in the output of manufacturing plants does not produce appreciable changes in overhead charges per unit, although in certain instances where fixed costs are large, variations in costs are appreciable with fluctuation of output.

While the evidence regarding production costs warranted the conclusions which have been stated in this section, the evidence relating to production costs is especially unsatisfactory. Advertising and production cost data concerning specific industries, whether drawn from primary or secondary sources, are not satisfactory because business firms do not keep their records in a form which fits the needs of such economic analysis. The cost data obtainable are usually nonuniform and incomplete and generally cover only a short time span. In addition, the variables which bear upon size of production costs are too many to permit a sure determination of causal relations between size of operations and size of production costs. Because of these difficulties it is doubtful whether adequate and satisfactory cost evidence will ever be available.

DO ALL ADVERTISING COSTS ENTER INTO EQUILIBRIUM COSTS?

In effect the question as to whether advertising costs enter into equilibrium costs is an inquiry as to whether all advertising costs are costs which are incurred in the maintenance of an equilibrium, or balance, between the forces of supply and demand. Or are some advertising costs to be looked upon as growth or innovation costs which have the effect not of maintaining an equilibrium, but of raising the level of demand and supply in an industry, i.e., in establishing a new equilibrium?

Analysis of evidence regarding the growth of industries leads to the conclusion that in some immeasurable degree advertising and selling costs, particularly those devoted to new products and product differentiations, should be looked upon as growth costs, costs incurred by entrepreneurs in raising the level of economic activity. From the standpoint of the individual enterprise, they represent costs to establish a business, and like research expenditures incurred in developing a new product, they contribute to the growth of an industry. Their outlay is made not to maintain an equilibrium but to facilitate investment necessary to establish an industry and reach a new equilibrium.

For many commodities, in order to build a large primary demand which will make profitable the investment in an enterprise, business concerns often spend large sums on advertising and aggressive selling. Like the sums spent on product research, the advertising and selling outlays for developing a market often are not included in the current prices, but managements expect temporary losses and anticipate their recovery from profits on the increased sales volume of later years. Case evidence shows that it is common experience for new product ventures to show losses for several years after being launched, losses due in considerable part to the advertising and aggressive selling efforts incurred.

In most industries which have been built by the aggressive selling efforts of innovators, imitators enter the market to profit from the demand that has been built up. Often these new entrants make small outlay either for product research or for advertising and selling effort by which to maintain the demand of an industry at existing levels, or to raise it to new levels. Frequently they make their bid for business on a price appeal made possible by low costs. Their entry into the market and the elasticity of demand which they exploit are made possible by the aggressive selling efforts of innovators. In short, the imitators often ride on the coat-tails of the innovators.

The extent to which growth costs enter into equilibrium costs and prices depends upon the date of entrance of the imitators and on the marketing strategy which they use. If they enter at an early point and employ price competition, the growth cost of the innovator may not be fully recovered. In short, under these conditions growth costs may not fully enter into equilibrium costs and prices. In a far larger number of cases the innovators recover their growth costs and then continue advertising and aggressive selling costs at a high level. In numerous instances a condition of competition in advertising and other non-price forms exists. Under these conditions the advertising costs tend to enter equilibrium costs and be borne by consumers in prices.

Because of the tendency of business firms to maximize profits and to compete in advertising and non-price forms, the imitator who enters the market and makes his bid for business on a price basis performs a significant social service. By keeping his selling and marketing costs low and by offering consumers the option of low prices, he serves to help hold down competition in advertising and other non-price forms. In short, he serves to help bring low costs and low prices in established industries. On the other hand, the innovator should be given credit for the important social service he performs. He develops improved products and builds for them a public acceptance and demand which calls into being the investment made by himself. Likewise he paves the way for imitators.

The innovator must have the prospect of recovering growth costs if advancement in the economy is to occur, and such recovery makes necessary some degree of monopoly, such as is provided in patents, secret processes, brands, and so on. If the prospect of recovering growth or innovation costs is present, enterprisers are more likely to take the risk of incurring such costs than if such prospect is absent. The prospect for recovering such costs is enhanced if the innovator has in view the protection afforded by some degree of monopoly elements such as patents, secret processes, or the establishment of strong brand preference from early and aggressive development of a market. In short, the chance to have such protection in some degree is a stimulant to investment, upon which economic progress depends.

DOES ADVERTISING TEND TO PROMOTE CONCENTRATION OF SUPPLY?

No clear-cut answer of general application can be given to the question of the degree to which advertising tends to promote concentration of supply. In certain industries advertising has been employed to bring concentration of demand upon a few suppliers. In bringing concentration of demand it has probably had some, though not strong, influence in keeping down the number of suppliers. Whenever advertising has been effective in building strong brand discrimination this buyer preference for established brands has been one factor to discourage the entry of new brands into the market, because it has required any new entrant to make considerable outlay for aggressive selling costs to secure substantial volume. A number of cases were found in which manufacturers or distributors decided against entry into certain product fields because of the entrenched positions of leading advertised brands. On the other hand, other forces appear to have a much more important bearing on concentration of supply than does advertising. In a number of fields in which advertising has played an important role in marketing and in which manufacturers' advertised brands have been dominant, the total number of brands in the market has been large because forces other than advertising have favored easy entry of suppliers. Thus there are many brands of dentifrices even though demand is concentrated among a dozen or so brands. Similarly, numerous brands and suppliers are to be found in cosmetic and grocery product fields in which there is a relatively high degree of concentration of demand. In such industries, not only a potentially but an actually large number of suppliers exist in spite of advertising's effectiveness in building brand leadership for a limited number of concerns.

In industries studied it was found that some entrants by using price competition have found it possible to establish themselves without the risk of advertising expenditure. Thus the 10-cent cigarette manufacturers entered the market with small advertising outlay, and similarly certain manufacturers of dentifrices and food products have obtained business from private branders without use of advertising. These are examples of a widespread phenomenon.

In some of the industries studied, in which there is concentration of supply, the leading companies are large advertisers, but forces other than advertising have an important bearing on the degree of concentration. Thus, in the cigarette field, the need of heavy capital outlay for tobacco inventories and for plant investment has tended to keep down entry probably as much as the risk of capital for the promotional outlay to establish new brands. Again, in the automobile, refrigerator, and petroleum industries, although the leading companies are advertisers, advertising does not appear to be among the more important factors in bringing about the concentration in those industries. The reasons for concentration of industries are numerous and have not been investigated in this study, except for an appraisal of the part which advertising has played in the instances studied. In numerous industries in which a TNEC study[1] shows relatively high concentration, such as the meat, copper, iron and steel, rayon yarn, sugar, and electric bulbs, advertising has played practically no part in bringing concentration. In short, although advertising has been a factor in the development of concentration in certain industries, it does not loom large among the causes.

DOES ADVERTISING TEND TO INJURE OR DESTROY PRICE COMPETITION, THUS IMPEDING NORMAL BEHAVIOR OF THE COMPETITIVE SYSTEM?

The evidence indicates that in many industries advertising tends to impede quickly-acting price competition, but in no case does it prevent it ultimately. Each of the industries studied has presented a different pattern of competition. The extent to which competition has turned upon price has varied from industry to industry; the extent to which individual brands have been free from meeting competing prices has also varied. In industries in which the opportunity for product differentiation has been great and for which buying motives other than price have been effective among consumers, brands have become important guides to buying; and competition has tended to turn toward advertising and aggressive selling rather than toward price. Thus in certain industries studied, notably the cigarette, smoking tobacco, cosmetics, and drug industries, most producers have elected to compete on product differentiation and non-price forms; and price competition in numerous instances has been postponed for a long time. The areas in which price competition has been least effective, in which advertising and aggressive selling have been most intense, and in which margins between manufacturing cost and selling cost have been widest are the drug, cosmetics, and toilet goods fields. Consumer buying here has been less influenced by price than in most product fields. The advertising appeals to motives of health, beauty, and romance have been powerful; and consumers generally have lacked a basis for appraising product quality or performance since results from usage have not been subject to close check. Demand has gone primarily to the advertised products, and the degree of price competition found in many other industries has not been present.

[1] Temporary National Economic Committee, Monograph No. 27, *The Structure of Industry* (Washington: U.S. Government Printing Office, 1941).

In contrast to the situation in the drug and cosmetics field, competition in advertising in many fields is limited, and competition in price acts more quickly. This effective price competition does not allow margins permitting extensive advertising. The evidence shows that each well-known brand in any product field has what may be termed a "reputation" value, which permits it to obtain from consumers a price somewhat above that obtained for merchandise which has comparable objective characteristics but which has not had the advantage of being made well known. In most instances brand reputation has been backed up by and built around product differentiation of some kind. Thus the price difference between the brands is associated with differences in product qualities as well as differences in reputation built through advertising. For most products the well-known brander can permit to the less-known brand a certain price advantage without losing his competitive position, but when he puts too high a value on reputation and product differentiation, then demand flows away.

The freedom of pricing by sellers and the opportunity to carry out competition on non-price forms rather than on price were found to be limited in all product fields. Even in industries in which consumers have been particularly susceptible to advertising influence and in which leading companies have been prone to battle in advertising rather than in price, competition in price ultimately has entered. For example, in the 1930 depression the 10-cent cigarettes entered a market long dominated by advertising competition, and in 18 months gained 25% of total consumer demand, when sold at a retail price differential of 4 cents to 5 cents a package under the prices of leading brands. In the case of dentifrices, toilet goods, drugs, and numerous other products in which advertised brands are dominant, consumers have been given the options of buying little-advertised private brands and manufacturers' brands at low prices, although they have not availed themselves of the opportunities in large numbers. In all such instances they have had the chance to balance price against the product differences and reputation offered in the advertised brands.

The evidence leads clearly to the conclusion that in the economic structure there are strong forces to counterbalance any tendency for competition to turn solely to non-price forms and for sellers to be free from price competition. In most fields in the course of time, sellers appear who elect to offer consumers opportunity to buy however, in which there has been high concentration of supply, there is no evidence that such a live-and-let-live pricing policy has been followed. The managements have apparently set their prices without particular reference to competitors' actions, but at the level they have felt necessary to gain desired business or to hold their positions in the market. Under conditions of relatively high degrees of concentration of supply, different pricing practices are encountered in different industries and among different concerns. Concentration is determined by numerous forces other than advertising, and advertising in itself apparently has little to do with the pricing practices followed. The evidence indicates that the assumption frequently made that sellers have a perfect knowledge of costs, of the character of the demand curves for their products, and of the behavior of other sellers, which permits them to set prices so as to maximize profits, is far from reality. Prices are often set with great ignorance on the part of sellers as to supply and demand conditions.

The study has led to the conclusion that for new industries some delay in adjustment to strict price competition may be socially desirable in order to provide profit opportunities that will attract investment. Managements are likely to make investment when their chances of recovering their growth costs and of making a profit are bright. Accordingly, some slowing down in price competition in early periods may in the long run help to bring an advance in the level of national income which more than offsets the prices which consumers pay as a result of the lack of active price competition. On the other hand, businessmen in their efforts to maximize profits often are inclined to try to put off entering into active price competition. For this reason the imitators who enter the market to exploit the elasticity of demand made possible by pioneers in the field perform an important social service.

DOES ADVERTISING TEND TO INCREASE PRICE RIGIDITY?

Attention is given to this question because of the emphasis placed by certain economists on price rigidity as a possible cause of failure of the economic system, particularly as it may be a possible cause of cyclical fluctuation or, at least, a force to accentuate cyclical maladjustments and to prolong cyclical depressions.

The evidence shows that advertising has contributed to price rigidity. The prices of many advertised items have been relatively insensitive. In many fields manufacturers have been slow to reduce prices in times of depression and, likewise, slow to raise prices in periods of upswing. Among the industries studied, this insensitivity of prices was found, particularly in the tobacco, drug, toilet goods, and cosmetics industries, but it was also present in varying degree in others. From studies made by the TNEC and other agencies it has generally become accepted that advertised goods have fewer price changes than unadvertised goods, although there are many exceptions to this rule. This relative stability of prices is to be expected, for advertisers generally make their appeal to buying motives other than price.

The lack of sensitivity of prices of advertised products indicates that manufacturers who have established consumer preferences for their products generally assume that advertising has made the demand for their brands inelastic and that they can hold prices relatively stable in times of general price decline without loss of volume. An impression gained from the study is that advertisers as a rule, although there are numerous exceptions, have become unduly wed to the notion of price rigidity and that they are loath to explore the possible degree of elasticity of demand for their products. In many instances they do not venture to experiment to determine the effect of lower prices as a means of gaining sales volume. The evidence indicates that many concerns which have held to rigid prices apparently have been mistaken in their assumption of the inelasticity of their brand demands, for competing private branders who have been more flexible in their pricing have generally gained business from these concerns in periods of depression.

DOES ADVERTISING AGGRAVATE THE FLUCTUATIONS OF THE BUSINESS CYCLE?

Advertising cannot be classed as an important causal factor in cyclical fluctuations, although the way in which businessmen have used advertising leads to the conclusion that it has tended to aggravate cyclical fluctuations. None of the students of cyclical fluctuation have named advertising as an important causal factor. Moreover, fluctuations occurred before advertising became an important factor in the economy.

Advertising as used has tended to accentuate cyclical fluctuations because expenditures for advertising have varied directly with business activity. As as considerable employer of men and materials, advertising has thus contributed to fluctuations in the use of economic resources. As a stimulant to demand for products and services advertising has been most extensively used in boom times and most lightly used in depressions. When thus employed it has tended to accentuate the swings of demand.

The potentiality of advertising as a tool to help reduce fluctuations is illustrated in the case of certain individual companies which have been farsighted or fortunate enough to develop merchandising and promotional plans which have permitted them profitably to go counter to the general practice of their industries. They have maintained or even expanded advertising activities at a time when other firms were contracting. They could do so because they were in a position to offer product improvements at prices which permitted them to gain large sales volume even though buying power was down. Such concerns, however, represent the exception rather than the rule. Again, in past depressions certain important industries whose demand was expanding at the time of the advent of depression employed advertising and aggressive selling during the depressions as one force among a number to help stimulate a demand that aided in bringing readjustment. For example, the automobile proved a highly valuable product in helping to bring about economic recovery after the depressions of 1907, 1914, and 1920. Likewise, mechanical refrigerators, whose demand had just begun to mount to large proportions in 1929, were extensively advertised throughout the depression and enjoyed an expanding demand during that period. The behavior of these industries is, however, an exception and is counter to the behavior of industries which did not have exceedingly favorable demand trends at those times.

One of the principal hypotheses according to which advertising might be deemed a possible indirect cause of cyclical fluctuation rests in its contribution to rigid prices. Although prices of advertised products have tended to be relatively inflexible, recent studies relating to price flexibility tend to disprove the thesis that price rigidities can be looked upon as a chief causal factor in cyclical fluctuations. Accordingly it was concluded that advertising as a causal factor through its effect upon price rigidities was not significant. The most that can be said is that advertising is an integral part of a business system subject to fluctuations. Many activities of businessmen have some bearing on cyclical fluctuation, and of these advertising is one; but there are numerous other parts of the economic system, such as the use of money and credit, which are much more important causes of fluctuations.

DOES ADVERTISING TEND TO IMPROVE THE QUALITY AND RANGE OF MERCHANDISE?

The answer to the question of whether advertising tends to improve the quality and range of merchandise is decidedly affirmative. Advertising and aggressive selling have made an important contribution to the satisfactions of consumers through their part in stimulating the development of a wide range of merchandise and of product improvement. The part of advertising and aggressive selling here has been indirect, but nevertheless real and important. These two forces have played an integral part in a free enterprise system that has given a growing, dynamic economy. Business managements have relied on these selling forces to speed up the adoption of important inventions and product improvements, not only to enable their enterprises to recover research expenses devoted to product development, but also to afford a basis for new investment from which to profit.

In the matter of new major inventions, advertising's part has been that of affording to enterprise a larger and more speedy profit than would occur without such selling methods. New inventions do not come into the world in full perfection, but as relatively crude, inefficient products which are gradually perfected through painstaking, laborious efforts. Business is spurred on to such development effort by the hope of profit, but profit on new products and improvements has generally been realized only as a result of aggressive cultivation of the market and of educating and influencing consumers to a realization of the satisfactions the new products would give.

Advertising and aggressive selling have led to much more rapid adoption of major inventions than would have come without their use. Consumer adoption is slow; it depends not only on stimulation by the producer but also on the perfection of the product and on low selling prices. Advertising and aggressive selling have contributed to fulfillment of all these requirements. In building consumer acceptance, they have led to a relatively quick establishment of large-scale demand, upon which low prices have often depended. In turn, they have been a stimulant to product improvement.

Advertising and aggressive selling have had their most direct and important influence in widening the range of merchandise through the part they play in stimulating product differentiation among brands. The desire of producers to offer under their specific brands products which will be preferred by consumers has led them to a constant experimentation with possible combinations of desirable product qualities. Technology has been called upon to develop new and improved products which some group of consumers might prefer. The quest is for the desirable product, but always management has in mind aggressively promoting the improved product and is influenced by its desires for ideas which it may use in its advertising and selling efforts. Thus, advertising and selling are an integral part of the system, and out of the system has come a tremendous range of merchandise.

As part of the process of stimulating product differentiation, advertising has contributed to progress in merchandise improvements. As a result of the process of constantly offering new differentiations, enterprise has placed on the market improved products which better fill consumers' desires and needs than did previous products. This product improvement has been rapid and striking in the case of relatively new products, such as automobiles, radios, refrigerators, washing machines, and other mechanical contrivances. Over a relatively short period of years such products have been made far more efficient and dependable than those which preceded them and have been offered at prices which generally have been but a small fraction of the prices of earlier years. But even for merchandise long on the market, the improvement has been substantial over a period of time; this is true, for example, of products such as gasoline and sheeting, which at any one time appear to critics to be relatively standardized. One must employ a time span to discern the full effect of the drive for differentiation on product improvement. Always the improvements of one manufacturer which have proved desirable have had to be matched by competitors. Competition has taken place on a higher level of quality from year to year.

In addition to its effect in stimulating improvement, advertising has also had an effect on product quality through its influence on maintenance of quality of products sold under brands. While brands are not necessarily a guarantee of uniformity of product quality, the desire of businessmen to profit from continued patronage usually has led them to maintain quality. Although maintenance of brand quality is not entirely dependent upon advertising, nevertheless advertising has some influence because the advertised brand usually represents a goodwill asset which has been built at considerable expense, and injury to which would represent a business loss.

In their practice of differentiation, businessmen have placed upon the market many product differentiations that have appeared trivial and foolish to many people, but out of the process has come a remarkable product advancement. What is significant in product differentiation can be determined in a free society only by the action of consumers in the market place. Differentiations criticized as meaningless often prove to be significant to some consumers. Only through trial and error in the market can progress be made in merchandise development.

DOES ADVERTISING TEND TO INCREASE OR DECREASE THE REAL NATIONAL INCOME?

Advertising and aggressive selling as integral parts of the free competitive system have been a significant force in increasing the investment in productive facilities and in advancing the technology of production, two developments which have largely accounted for the fourfold increase of real national income per capita during the past 100 years. The tremendous advance in material welfare which has come since the Middle Ages would have been impossible without the building of a large-scale productive machine employing improved technology and management skills. But such an improved productive machine was called into being only as the result of strong social forces. On the one hand, there were forces to increase the willingness and desire of people to consume at a high quantitative level, for this willingness is not inherent in a population. On the other hand, there were forces leading to investment in productive facilities and to improvement in technology.

The willingness and desire of peoples in Western countries to support a high level of consumption is basically attributable to social changes that have given these countries a mobile society in which individuals have been free to rise from the lowest to the highest class and have been able to aspire to the consumption of all types of products in the market. With the development of social mobility, the introduction of new wants and an increase in consumption were possible. Such changes were essential to the growth of industrialism and a dynamic economy.

From a long-range point of view, aggressive selling and advertising probably have played a considerable but undeterminable part in the formation of mental attitudes necessary for a high level of consumption. The study of demand in this volume has indicated that what people want is determined largely by their social backgrounds and habits. New products have been accepted by people, but the demand for them has grown relatively slowly. Once new products have been accepted by a few consumers, however, consumption usually has expanded through much of the social group. By helping to expand the use of products, advertising and selling have permitted the strong buying motives of emulation and imitation to come into play relatively quickly. They have played a particularly important part in bringing first sales, upon which emulative consumption depends. The new wants and new products, which they have helped to bring, in turn have become a part of environment influencing the further expansion of wants and desires of consumers.

While changes in social conditions and the forces of selling provide an explanation of growth of wants and willingness of the population to consume, this willingness could not have been satisfied had not the productive machine been called into existence. The productive machine which makes the products available provides the consumer income with which to purchase products. The existence of both the products and the income of consumers depends upon risk-taking by businessmen who see an opportunity for profit through making and selling goods which they think consumers will want. Their risk-taking activities bring the investment in factory and production facilities, which not only produce goods for consumption but employ labor and pay the wages and the return on capital upon which consumer income depends. In short, the activities of entrepreneurs create the markets for their own products.

Advertising and aggressive selling have an influence upon investment because they are important, integral parts of the system which leads to investment. Advertising and aggressive selling in themselves have not been the causes of the launching of new enterprises, or of the expansion of old, but they have been important elements whereby the new or enlarged enterprises might hope to gain a profitable demand. They frequently have been helpful in speeding up a demand which has called for increasing investment. They have promised the stability of demand and of profit to an enterprise which is attractive to investment. By such means have factories been built, men employed, and the products and incomes for increasing consumer satisfactions been established.

While advertising and aggressive selling have probably had greatest influence upon investment in new industries, they have also played a part in helping to increase the demand of established industries, which has called for investment to expand productive facilities. Even in the case of declining industries, the selling force has been employed to try to hold demand and thus to protect the investment in those industries against the inroads of the new industries. In some instances selling has also served to stimulate demand for new improvements in the products of declining industries and thus has served to give to the industry a new life cycle calling for investment.

Advertising and aggressive selling have also had a close relationship to the improvement in technology, which is one of the important explanations of the increase in national income. Technological improvements have come in considerable degree as the result of the activities of the producers of industrial goods. The spur to such producers to bring out improved machines has come from the opportunity to profit from meeting the desires of industrial buyers for more economical and efficient machines and materials. In turn, in the industrial goods field advertising and aggressive selling have played a part in promising to the enterpriser a profitable demand and thus have attracted investment.

In the free economy there have been frictions and resistances to technological advance and to investment in new enterprises producing improved goods; but the profit urge of enterprisers has been a force more than strong enough to overcome such resistances.

It is generally recognized that while the dynamic society which advertising and selling helps to produce has brought a high standard of living and in the main is desirable, it has serious shortcomings and drawbacks. Neither investment in plants to produce new products nor investment in labor-saving or capital-saving machines has brought unmixed gain to the consumer group, for the new has caused obsolescence of the old. It is believed, however, that the losses from obsolescence, though they sometimes seem large, are not to be overemphasized. Demand for a declining industry generally does not disappear all at once; nor are products in use either among consumers or among industrial users made useless thereby.

Consumers' goods are generally used through second-and third-hand markets until their usefulness has gone. New machines are not substituted for old until the new are certain to pay their way. Moreover, business has learned to adapt itself to rapid change when necessary. In spite of losses and dislocations that are incurred in the process of change and growth, the balance so far as consumer incomes and rising standards of living are concerned has clearly rested in favor of change.

Possible Dangers

Now that the answers to the more important economic questions have been reviewed, possible dangers associated with the use of advertising which the study has indicated are summarized. Counter-balancing forces which tend to offset some of these dangers are not discussed at length here, but are noted at a later point.

INSUFFICIENT FREEDOM OF CHOICE BY CONSUMERS

The first of these possible dangers is that in some product fields in which advertising has been particularly effective in building brand preferences it has probably been a factor in reducing the opportunity of wide choice by consumers among products, particularly in so far as the option of buying low-price merchandise is concerned. One of the criteria employed in this investigation into the economic effects of advertising has been that the consumer should have in the market place a wide freedom of choice and particularly that among choices there should be products of low price.

The evidence indicates that in most product fields consumers do have a wide freedom of choice, including opportunities to buy low-price merchandise in competition with higher-price merchandise which is differentiated in some way to command the higher price asked. In certain fields, however, advertising has been so powerful a force that many consumers have not had readily available choices of buying low-price merchandise. The brands generally available have been the extensively advertised brands. Most of the leading brands available in these fields bear considerable costs for advertising and for other non-price forms of competition. Price competition has been slow to gain a foothold. Among the products studied this situation has been true especially of certain drug, cosmetic, and grocery specialty items. Private branders and others seeking demand on a price basis have made little headway in establishing their brands. The consequence has been that consumers have had in those fields a limited choice because of the domination of advertised brands and the lack of an appreciable number of competing low-price brands which are well established and widely distributed.

It should be pointed out, however, that private branders or others who make an appeal for business on a price basis have failed to enter some of these fields because the prices of the advertised brands have been so low as to make the price appeal of the unadvertised brands ineffective. The saving which the private branders have been able to offer consumers has not been sufficient to overbalance in the minds of many consumers the differentiating qualities and reputation of the advertised brands. Some manufacturers have been well aware that prices containing an unduly wide margin for promotion and net profit invite the entry of competition. Hence they have followed the policy of lowering their margins to discourage the entry of competition. In these cases the threat of price competition has been effective in reducing margins. In those instances in which manufacturers have maintained their dominating positions as a result of a policy of price reduction, consumers have not suffered appreciably from the relative lack of nonadvertised brands in the market, for the prices of the advertised brands have contained relatively small advertising costs and net profit margins.

It was found also that opportunity for wide choice by consumers varies considerably by localities. In small-town and local communities the choice available is not so wide as it is in cities. The number of retail establishments is smaller and, consequently, the number of stores of private branders, who have widened the range of choice through the offering of low-price merchandise; moreover, private branders and other price competitors are not equally active in all sections of the country.

Undoubtedly in many instances consumers fail to realize the opportunities of choice open to them. Evidence indicates that in many of their purchases consumers are not well informed or careful. They are not aware of the qualities of products available to them or of the satisfactions that might attend their use. Again in certain product fields appeals which the advertisers use are so strong that they are particularly effective in attracting consumers who are not well informed regarding merchandise qualities. In short, the evidence indicates that there is need of consumer education regarding products beyond that attainable from the persuasive messages of advertisers. In a free economy consumers need to be equipped to look out for themselves and should be trained to be wary in their buying.

INSUFFICIENT FREEDOM OF ENTRY INTO INDUSTRIES

Closely related to the danger just noted above is another possible danger, namely, the insufficient freedom of entry of new concerns in certain fields in which competition is carried out largely through advertising. In these fields the entry of new producers or of new brands has been made difficult and expensive because of the dominant position of the extensively advertised brands. As has been pointed out previously, however, it is believed that the restriction attributable to advertising is not large. While entry of firms desirous of competing through advertising is made expensive and risky through the need for large advertising outlay, other firms willing to compete on a price basis usually have found opportunity to enter sooner or later without heavy risk in advertising. They have found this opportunity because large-scale distributors gradually have tended to seek out sources through which to get merchandise to establish themselves even in industries where advertised brands have been strongest. Moreover, in fields where there is an appreciable amount of sales, entry on a price basis is likely to occur if the prices of the dominating brands become high enough to afford opportunity for effective price appeal by those desiring to compete on price. It should be pointed out also that in many product fields in which there is concentration of demand and in which entry is difficult, the difficulty of entry is attributable not so much to advertising as to other causes.

The evidence indicates further that in most product fields where an entrant has a really superior product, that is, a differentiation worth promoting, he ordinarily can establish himself in the market. In such cases advertising is for him an essential tool with which to make his product known. He has little hope of gaining appreciable sales volume without its use.

TOO LITTLE PRICE COMPETITION

In some product areas, among them those discussed under the two previous headings, there has been evidence that demand has been concentrated among a limited number of producers and that there has been too little competition in price on the part of many concerns and too much reliance on competition in advertising and other non-price forms. The entry of effective price competition in some of these fields has been too long delayed.

The presence of active price competition in any product field, after primary demand has once been well established, is highly desirable from a social standpoint. It serves as a means of holding down competition in non-price forms with its attendant costs. The virtues of non-price competition are appreciable and are worthy of repeating in this connection. From it comes progress in product development. It encourages a wide range of merchandise. In addition, when there is competition in services, such as delivery and credit, consumers may choose these services, even if they must pay for them. Their option is widened by such choice. But alongside this competition in differentiation and other non-price forms should be competition based largely on price to afford the economy a check against increasing cost of non-price competition. Effective price competition tends to reduce or to hold down the costs of distribution when once the advantages of growth in an industry have been largely attained. While active price competition was found in most fields studied, in a limited number it was not present in appreciable degree.

DANGER OF WASTE IN DISTRIBUTION

The danger of too little price competition is, in effect, the danger frequently mentioned by critics, namely, waste in distribution attending the use of advertising. When competition is carried on to a large extent in advertising and other non-price forms, competitive waste may develop in that distribution costs become high or remain high. The point need not be developed further, for the conclusion is adequately reviewed above. In so far as advertising and selling costs incurred by a concern are more than offset by production economies which result from increased scale of operations, there can be no complaint that advertising and selling costs are high and lead to competitive waste. In certain product fields, however, where advertising and selling costs are high, there is no evidence that these high costs are offset by production economies of the concerns which incur them. The high costs persist because effective price competition has been prevented by the existence of other strong appeals which have affected consumers' valuations.

THE LACK OF SUFFICIENT CONSUMER INFORMATION

The long persistence of relatively high advertising and distribution costs in some fields is attributable in appreciable degree to the emotional and the uninformed character of the buying of consumers. In large part they have not made use of such information as has been available to them in advertising and other sources regarding objective product characteristics. To a large extent they have not been guided in their buying by a careful rationalization of objective product characteristics in terms of price, and this study has pointed out that the character of consumer satisfaction does not lead to the belief that for much of their buying they may be expected to follow such a behavior. The evidence indicates, however, that there is a substantial minority of consumers desirous of more information to guide their buying.

In this connection there is the danger from the consumers' standpoint that advertising in itself does not provide the information which will permit consumers wishing to buy on a logical, informed basis to do so. Advertising is influence, and it provides information only as information is effective to induce buying action. Since detailed factual information has not in itself been an effective means of stimulating large demand for many products, advertisers generally have not provided such information.

That it is desirable for consumers in an advanced economy to have extensive information and knowledge regarding the wide range of products available to them is axiomatic. If consumers are to get a maximum of satisfaction from their expenditures, they should have opportunity to appraise the probable satisfactions that will attend their choices. They should know what is on the market, for the greater their knowledge, the more enlightened can be their choice of goods. Moreover, since goods are not identical, consumers should have knowledge regarding the qualities of competing goods and the use and care of these goods. Since there is the danger that advertisers will fail to provide a sufficient amount of information to satisfy the consumers desiring to buy on a logical and informed basis, there is need of counterbalancing forces to meet this difficulty.

Counterbalancing Forces

Since advertising incurs the possible dangers summarized above, what forces exist in the economic system which tend to counterbalance these dangers? Attention is directed first to forces tending to counterbalance the dangers arising from intensive competition in advertising.

DEVELOPMENT OF CONCERNS ELECTING TO COMPETE
ON A PRICE BASIS

The evidence has indicated that the best protection against the dangers arising from intensive competition in advertising and other non-price forms of competition is the presence of concerns which elect to reduce advertising, selling, and other non-price competitive costs and to make their bid for patronage on the basis of price appeal. These concerns serve to give to consumers the option of low-price purchases; they reduce the danger of excessive competition in non-price forms and help to assure that the degree of non-price competition which persists is giving to consumers satisfactions for which they clearly are willing to pay.

Among the strongest forces in the economy serving as a corrective of this kind against excessive brand advertising are the large-scale distributors, who in recent decades have become increasingly active in establishing their own brands in various product fields and in offering them on a price basis. These include many, though not all, of the chains, mail-order houses, voluntary chains, and supermarkets, and a lesser proportion of department stores. Through an integration of marketing functions they often have been able when selling under their own brands to attain economies in over-all marketing costs not attained when the manufacturer carries out the advertising and promotional functions. Many of the chains, though not the department stores generally, have greatly reduced their competition in offering services to consumers. In instances in which they have followed this policy, they have generally made their bid for business on a price basis. In addition, because of their size they have had strong bargaining power, which has often enabled them to buy merchandise at favorable prices, which, in turn, they have passed on, in part at least, to consumers.

They have established their own brands first in those fields in which they have been able to get volume of sales readily and without undue promotional costs. Many of them have been desirous, however, of extending their brands into fields strongly dominated by manufacturers' brands. Gradually they have done so, although the number of private brands in some product fields dominated by

manufacturers' brands is still small. Once these brands have become
established, the effectiveness of their price competition has tended
to become greater. Thus they have become an increasingly strong
force to limit competition in advertising and non-price forms in all
the fields in which they have entered with their own brands.

THE COUNTERBALANCING FORCE OF CONSUMER EDUCATION

The danger that advertising will fail to give adequate information
to consumers desiring to buy on a logical and informed basis has
been counterbalanced in part by the development of the so-called
consumer movement, which includes a wide range of activities,
among them consumer education in schools and colleges and the
formation of organizations to advise consumers regarding product
choices.

From the standpoint of maximizing consumer satisfactions, such
movements and activities are deemed natural and desirable developments. As yet consumer education has made little headway, but it
is gaining in strength.

Ethical Aspects

The summary turns now to a brief review of the evidence and
conclusions upon ethical issues.

The evidence from reports both of the Federal Trade Commission
and of Better Business Bureaus leads to the conclusion that a relatively small percentage of advertising material is of such a character
as to be misleading or false under the standards applied by those
organizations. Yet the volume of such advertising has been great
enough to provide a basis for the feeling on the part of a substantial
minority of consumers that there is a considerable volume of undesirable advertising. Part of this adverse attitude is attributable
to a sentiment held by some persons that the use of influence by
businessmen is unethical. This attitude has been frequently reflected
in the writings of certain critics of advertising.

A postulate accepted for this study is that influence is an integral
part of a free system and that it is no more denied to men in their
economic transactions than it is to men in their educational, religious, political, and other social intercourse. The question involved
is one of determining what is to be deemed ethical in the use of
influence.

Ethics is a constantly evolving concept, and what is deemed

ethical in selling transactions has changed materially over the centuries. When a long time span is employed, the evidence indicates that an appreciably higher standard of honesty in selling relationships holds now than held in former times. Furthermore, there has been a growing attitude that the consumer shall be given more and more protection and that the seller shall be subject to increasing limitations on his use of influence. This change is attributable to the fact that since handicraft days, when exchange was limited and direct, sellers have gradually attained a relatively more powerful position than they held formerly. As the range of products bought by consumers has increased, consumers have become relatively weaker in the matter of using influence in the exchange process. The seller now knows his merchandise well, whereas the untutored buyer has to learn the merits of thousands of items. The consumer group consequently, has received more and more protection.

This tendency to greater protection of buyers does not mean a denial of the use of influence to sellers. It means merely that they must adapt themselves to this tendency in ethical concepts. The evidence indicates that the social group will accept a pragmatic test of honesty. The group will judge the goodness of the actions of sellers by their intent and by the end they attain. If business is to avoid restrictive legislation, however, it must find a way of curbing the unethical activities of the relatively few sellers who transgress consumers' sentiments regarding what is ethical, moral, and in good taste.

Constructive Criticism

Out of this study of the use of advertising by businessmen have come impressions regarding certain business practices and business attitudes which have been commented upon along the way and are reviewed here.

PRICE STRATEGY

One of these impressions relates to a tendency on the part of many advertisers to fail to give proper attention to the elasticity of demand either for the type of products which they sell or for their brands. Consequently, in the opinion of the author, they fail fully to realize the effect of price upon their sales volumes.

In the case of products which are relatively new on the market or which are important new differentiations, advertising often has the effect of greatly increasing the elasticity of demand. Hence, a tremendous increase in volume can be realized sometimes through price decreases. New buyers in lower income levels than have been reached theretofore can be brought into the market by low prices. While in many instances producers are fully cognizant of the effect of price and use it to bring expansion, in others they fail to appraise correctly the effect of price and do not take the risk of reducing price to test thereby the effect upon volume and profits. Again, they do not include in their lines of merchandise inexpensive models that might reach new buying strata. Often as a result of failure to bring prices down, the leading innovators have paved the way for relatively easy entry of the imitative concerns which come in and exploit the elasticity of demand which the innovators' activities have built. This study indicates the wisdom from the standpoint of the business concern of carefully considering the profits it could gain from greater attention to price strategy.

Attention has been called also at various points to the tendency of some advertisers to overestimate the extent to which advertising has made the demand for their brands inelastic, that is, the extent to which advertising has freed them from price competition. This fact accounts in part for the relatively high degree of rigidity in the prices of many intensively advertised items. While brand advertising does build consumer preferences which permit some freedom from price competition, every advertiser should realize that when he permits normal price relationships to become disestablished, he is likely to lose volume. Numerous cases were found of businesses which lost much ground in their industry standing by overestimating the inelasticity induced by the advertising of their brands.

SUPPLYING PRODUCT INFORMATION

Another point to which many business concerns might well give careful consideration is the supplying of further product information to consumers. This study has recognized that advertising is essentially influence and that the provision of information in advertising is determined largely by its effectiveness in inducing consumer purchases. In recent years an increasing number of consumers have given evidence of wanting increased information. To the requests of this group, among whom are militant advocates of informative advertising, some concerns have turned a deaf ear or have voiced opposition, thereby harming the consumer relations of business.

Other concerns have recognized that by adopting informative label-ing they have had an opportunity to win the favor of the group requesting it. Since a broad survey of advertising usage indicates that when detailed information is provided it is because buyers desire the data, concerns in many fields should give careful thought to furnishing the sort of information which consumers may want and from which they may benefit. Thereby the business firm itself may profit. Such a procedure need not detract from the interest, attractiveness, or persuasiveness of an advertising campaign, which is essential to low advertising costs.

Business concerns should realize that the consumer educational movement, which is relatively new and weak, is a natural develop-ment resulting from the growing complexity of merchandise avail-able. From an economic standpoint it is a desirable development because it promises to make consumers able to look after their own interests. Accordingly, as in the case of other broad social develop-ments, businessmen would do well to study this movement sympa-thetically and to adapt themselves to it.

The Place of Advertising In a Capitalistic Economy—A Final Statement

In the end, what role of social significance does advertising play in our capitalistic economy? On the whole, does it add to consumer welfare? The discussion has shown that its use is accompanied by certain dangers, particularly those attending the tendency of busi-nessmen to compete in advertising and thus to bring into prices a large amount of selling costs. On the other side of the ledger, what is advertising's offsetting contribution, if any?

Advertising's outstanding contribution to consumer welfare comes from its part in promoting a dynamic, expanding economy. Adver-tising's chief task from a social standpoint is that of encouraging the development of new products. It offers a means whereby the enter-priser may hope to build a profitable demand for his new and differ-entiated merchandise which will justify investment. From growing investment has come the increasing flow of income which has raised man's material welfare to a level unknown in previous centuries.

In a static economy there is little need of advertising. Only that minimum is necessary which will provide information regarding sources of merchandise required to facilitate exchange between buyers and sellers who are separated from each other. Clearly in a static economy it would be advisable to keep informational costs at a minimum, just as it would be wise to keep all costs at a minimum.

In a dynamic economy, however, advertising plays a different role. It is an integral part of a business system in which entrepreneurs are striving constantly to find new products and new product differentiations which consumers will want. Without opportunity to profit relatively quickly from the new products which they develop, entrepreneurs would not be inclined either to search for them or to risk investment in putting them on the market. Advertising and aggressive selling provide tools which give prospect of profitable demand.

The critic must realize that progress in product improvement comes slowly; merchandise does not come on the market in full perfection. The constant seeking for product improvements, with which advertising and aggressive selling are intimately related, has been essential to an ever-increasing variety of new merchandise.

For much of this new merchandise, advertising and other forms of aggressive selling play the significant role of aiding the expansion of demand and the responsiveness of demand to price reductions upon which widespread enjoyment of the products among the populace depends. Widespread usage is made possible by low prices, which in turn require low costs. For many industries low costs of production depend upon large-scale operations which are not possible until there is a large volume of sales not only for the industries, but also for individual producers. Advertising may make increased sales possible not only through shifting demand schedules but also through increasing the elasticity of demand for products. Thereby it provides business concerns with the opportunity to increase dollar sales volume through price reductions and makes it worth their while to do so as production costs decrease. In past years in industry after industry the economies which have come from large-scale operations and technological developments have been passed along in lower prices.

As an industry matures and new differentiations, upon which expansion rests, become less important, then it is particularly desirable that counterbalancing forces which tend to check and reduce competition in advertising, and which prevent innovators from profiting over long periods of time from their innovations, should have free opportunity to operate. Probably the most important of these counterbalancing forces is that provided in the competition of business firms which do not make substantial outlays in development work on which growth depends, either in product development or in promotion of new merchandise. The price competition of these concerns serves to hold down the costs of competition in advertising and other non-price forms. The price competition of such concerns is to be encouraged rather than discouraged by restrictive price legislation, such as has been embodied in recent years in price control acts of one type or another.

To the counterbalancing force of price competition may be added that of increased education of consumers permitting them to choose intelligently among the variety of goods offered them.

Since advertising has in large part been associated with the promotion of new and differentiated merchandise, a substantial part of advertising costs should be looked upon economically as growth costs. They are the costs incurred in raising the economy from one level to another. From the standpoint of social welfare these costs have been far more than offset by the rise in national income which they have made possible. Such costs should not be prevented or decried. In the future if man's material welfare is to be raised to higher levels in our free economy, the spark of enterprise must be kept glowing brightly; the chance to profit from the new should continue to exist. So long as individual enterprise flourishes and a dynamic economy continues, advertising and aggressive selling will play a significant social role.

merchandise on a price basis. For instance, numerous data relating to private branding practices of distributors show them to be an important counterbalancing force against those who choose to compete in product differentiation, advertising, and other non-price forms. They provide consumers with the option of buying on a price basis or of choosing the differentiated product with special characteristics made known through advertising.

There was considerable evidence to indicate that price competition tends to reassert itself particularly in periods of depression. Many manufacturers of advertised products have tended to hold their prices relatively rigid at a time when the value of money to the consumer is increasing. Such times have been fruitful for those sellers who make their appeal on a price basis. Thus it was found that large-scale distributors who have been more flexible in pricing their brands than manufacturers have increased the sales of their private brands in competition with advertised brands. Again, the 10-cent cigarettes provide an example.

One of the charges made against advertising as it affects prices is that it tends to bring concentration of supply, and that concentration leads sellers to set prices with reference to the potential retaliatory action of competitors. Thus normal price competition is said to be hindered because prices are not determined free from the influence of individual sellers.[2] Do large advertisers who provide a considerable share of the total supply follow a live-and-let-live policy in their pricing, that is, do they set prices with reference to competitors' actions and establish their prices at points which maximize profits? Direct evidence from advertisers upon this point is not available, and conclusions have to be drawn by inference from price data. In certain fields where competition has been carried out among a small number of companies largely through advertising, and in which consumers in large numbers have not been attracted by the price appeal of non-advertisers, pricing data give the impression that leading companies in numerous instances have been guided in their pricing policies with reference to the activity of competitors. In such instances, since competition in advertising rather than competition in price has given promise of greatest profit, these concerns have elected to compete on that basis. In other instances,

---

[2] It is recalled for the general reader that the theory of pure competition assumes that individual sellers and buyers have no appreciable influence on the determination of market price.

TABLES ON THE COST AND SUPPORT
OF MASS COMMUNICATIONS

Consumer Expenditures for Mass Media in the United States

Year	Newspapers, Magazines, Sheet Music	Books and Maps	Radio, TV Sets, Records, Musical Instr.	Radio and TV Repairs	Motion Picture Admissions	Other Admissions	Total All Media
			(figures in billions of dollars)				
1930	.51	.26	.92	.03	.73	.09	2.54
1935	.46	.18	.25	.02	.56	.04	1.51
1940	.59	.23	.49	.03	.74	.07	2.15
1945	.97	.52	.34	.09	1.45	.15	3.52
1950	1.50	.68	2.46	.28	1.37	.19	6.48
1955	1.92	.89	2.79	.52	1.22	.25	7.59
1957	2.17	1.03	2.99	.65	1.12	.30	8.26

Source: U.S. Department of Commerce.

Advertising Expenditures for Mass Media in the United States

Year	News-papers	Maga-zines	Farm Publi-cations	Busi-ness Papers	Out-door	Direct Mail	Misc. Print	Radio	TV	Audio-Visual	Total All Media
				(figures in billions of dollars)							
1935	.76	.14	.01	.05	.03	.28	.28	.11		.03	1.68
1940	.82	.20	.01	.08	.04	.33	.36	.22		.04	2.09
1945	.92	.36	.01	.20	.07	.29	.53	.42		.06	2.87
1950	2.08	.51	.02	.25	.14	.80	1.02	.61	.17	.11	5.71
1955	3.07	.72	.03	.42	.19	1.27	1.60	.55	1.01	.17	9.02
1957	3.28	.81	.03	.57	.21	1.47	1.82	.62	1.29	.20	10.31

Source: Compiled by Scripps-Howard from *Printer's Ink* estimates.

Expenditures on U.S. Mass Media as Percentages of Gross National Product

Year	Total Expenditures (billions)	Percentage from Consumers	Percentage from Advertisers	Percentage of Gross National Product
1930	5.15	49.3	50.7	5.7
1935	3.19	47.3	52.7	4.4
1940	4.24	50.7	49.3	4.2
1945	6.39	55.1	44.9	3.0
1950	12.19	53.2	46.8	4.3
1955	16.61	45.7	54.3	4.2
1957	18.57	44.5	55.5	4.3

Source: Scripps-Howard.

Average Expenditure per Household on Mass Media in the U.S.

Year	Number of Households (thousands)	Average Expend. per Household By Consumers	Average Expend. per Household By Advertisers	Average Expend. per Household Total	Average Income per Household	Percentage Spent on Media	Percentage Spent by Consumers Directly
			(dollars)				
1930	29,905	84.94	82.78	172.22	2,571	6.7	3.3
1935	32,427	46.57	51.81	98.38	1,856	5.3	2.5
1940	34,949	61.52	59.80	121.32	2,252	5.4	2.7
1945	37,500	93.87	76.53	170.40	4,565	3.7	2.1
1950	43,554	148.78	131.10	279.88	5,214	5.4	2.9
1955	47,788	158.83	188.75	347.58	6,401	5.4	2.5
1957	49,543	166.72	208.10	374.82	6,865	5.5	2.4

Source: Compiled by Scripps-Howard from Bureau of Census and Department of Commerce data.

Distribution of Consumer Expenditures among Mass Media

Year	Percentage of Consumer Expenditures for Printed Media	Radio, TV	Admissions
1930	30.3	37.5	32.2
1935	42.4	17.9	39.7
1940	38.1	24.2	37.7
1945	42.3	12.2	45.5
1950	33.6	42.3	24.1
1955	37.0	43.6	19.4
1957	38.7	44.1	17.2

Source: Compiled by Scripps-Howard.

Real Increase in Consumer Expenditures for U.S. Mass Media *

	Expenditures per Household in Constant Dollars		Per cent Change	Expenditure in Actual Dollars for 1957
	1929	1957		
ALL MEDIA	$91.80	$101.70	+10.8	$166.72
Printed media only	28.48	39.40	+38.3	64.59
Newspapers and magazines	18.09	26.72	+47.7	43.80
Books and maps	10.39	12.68	+22.0	20.79
Audio and audio-visual media	63.32	62.30	−1.6	102.13
Radio, TV receivers	33.84	36.81	+8.8	60.35
Radio, TV repairs	1.01	8.00	+692.0	13.12
Motion picture admissions	24.12	13.79	−42.8	22.61
Other admissions	4.36	3.70	−15.1	6.06

Source: Scripps-Howard.
* 1957 figures revised to take into account changed purchasing power of dollar.

Expenditures on Mass Media Compared to Other Recreational Expenditures and to Total Consumer Expenditures

Year	Consumer Expenditures on Mass Media	Other Recreation (billions)	Total Consumer Expenditures	Mass Media as Percentage of Total Consumer Expenditures
1930	2.54	1.45	70.97	3.56
1935	1.51	1.12	56.29	2.68
1940	2.15	1.61	71.88	2.99
1945	3.52	2.62	121.70	2.89
1950	6.48	4.80	194.03	3.34
1955	7.59	6.63	254.40	2.98
1957	8.26	7.65	282.40	2.92

Source: U.S. Department of Commerce.

Percentage of Support by Consumers and by Advertising

	Newspapers and Magazines			Radio and Television		
	Total	Percentage from		Total	Percentage from	
Year	(billions)	Consumers	Advertisers	(billions)	Consumers	Advertisers
1935	1.41	32.6	67.4	.38	71.1	28.9
1940	1.96	34.9	65.1	.74	70.3	29.7
1945	2.47	39.3	60.7	.85	50.6	49.4
1950	4.36	34.4	65.6	3.52	77.8	22.2
1955	6.16	31.2	68.8	4.86	68.1	31.9
1957	6.87	31.6	68.4	5.55	65.6	34.4

Source: U.S. Department of Commerce.

Revenue and Expenses of a Typical Daily Newspaper
of 50,000 Circulation: 1958

Operating Revenue		
Local advertising	$1,468,578	50.98%
National advertising	382,112	13.26
Classified	293,583	10.19
Total advertising	2,144,273	74.43
Circulation	736,654	25.57
Total revenue	$2,880,927	100.00
Operating Expenses		
Paper, ink	$ 592,823	21.98%
Composing room	581,267	21.56
Editorial department	412,645	15.30
Circulation department	317,258	11.77
Advertising department	243,043	9.01
Admin. and general	142,102	5.27
Building and plant	88,428	3.28
Business office	47,208	1.75
Business taxes	34,024	1.26
Stereotype department	67,662	2.51
Press room	79,052	2.93
Photo-engraving	36,339	1.35
Depreciation	46,406	1.72
Provided for doubtful accounts	8,452	.31
	$2,696,709	100.00
Operating profit	$184,218	
Other income	19,309	
Total income	203,527	
Other deductions	6,609	
Profit before income tax	196,918	
Provided for tax	102,000	
Net profit	94,918	

Source: *Editor and Publisher.*

THE COMMUNICATION PROCESS

THE ESSENTIAL ELEMENTS of the communication process are a sender, a message, and a receiver. In mass communication the sender is a communication organization (for example, a newspaper staff) working with a communicating machine (for example, the printing press) to send similar messages (for example, printed newspapers) at about the same time to large numbers of people. Thus everything is somewhat more complicated than in face-to-face communication, but the process is essentially the same.

When we talk about the process we are referring to what happens when a sender transmits a message to a receiver. It seems simple, but it isn't. Let's take the example of a television program. First it is an idea, then a script, then action in a studio, then electrical impulses on a wire, then electrical impulses in a receiving set, then light and sound impulses in a room, then perceived light and sound in the nervous system of some viewer, then meaning, then, perhaps, a stimulus to action. These are the changes a message goes through between the impulse to communicate and the moment the receiver nods his head in agreement.

To understand what goes on, we have to know the answers to questions like these: How does the sender decide what he is going to communicate? (The actual choice of a television program, as we know, may take many months or years.) How does he go about encoding the message? (What ideas does he put into it, what pictures, what symbols? How does he organize it? What is he trying to accomplish with it?) What does the message finally look like? (There is a point, as you know, when the message is only ink on paper, or electrical impulses in the air, and thus entirely separate from both sender and receiver.) How does the receiver happen to select it? (We can pay attention to only a tiny fraction of all the communication that tries to get to our eyes and ears; we pick out what we do, apparently, by balancing the degree something promises to satisfy our needs against the availability of the message. For example, other things being equal, we are more likely to see a good television program than walk six blocks to get an equally attractive book from the library.) When a message is received, what does it mean to the receiver? (What anything means depends on our experience. Since no two people have had exactly the same experience, there is always a good chance of misunderstanding.) And finally, what does the receiver do about the message? (Does he reject it as uninteresting or untrue? Does he accept it and store it away in his memory? Does he take some action—for example, turn off his television set or write a letter to the station?)

The myth and magic surrounding artistic communication have probably served to delay for so long the scientific study of the process by which symbols are communicated between men. Only in the last fifteen or twenty years has there been noteworthy progress in understanding this central aspect of mass communication. In that time we have been gradually filling in the answers to questions like those above.

The selections which follow represent quite different approaches to this process, which sounds so simple when we describe it as man communicating with man but so complex when we begin to analyze it. Professor Johnson is a psychologist and a general semanticist; his article follows that line. Dr. Daniel Katz is a social psychologist and public opinion specialist who discusses the nature of language and the semantic barriers to effective communication. Dr. Mead is a cultural anthropologist who throws the light of that discipline on intercultural misunderstandings. And finally Dr. Elihu Katz, a sociologist, traces the development of one of the newer hypotheses about mass communication—the so-called "two-step flow," by which the ideas and facts of mass communication are frequently transmitted to the broader public through influential individuals in the audience.

THE COMMUNICATION PROCESS AND GENERAL SEMANTIC PRINCIPLES

BY WENDELL JOHNSON

Dr. Johnson is professor of speech and psychology at the State University of Iowa. This is part of his paper, "Speech and Personality," in *The Communication of Ideas*, published and copyrighted 1948, by the Institute for Religious and Social Studies, of New York. The paper is here reprinted by permission of the author and the copyright holder.

COMMUNICATION reduces to the event, both commonplace and awesome, of Mr. A. talking to Mr. B. And most commonplace and strange of all—possibly the most distinctively *human* occurrence to found or imagined—is the case in which Mr. A. and Mr. B. are one and the same person: a man talking to himself.

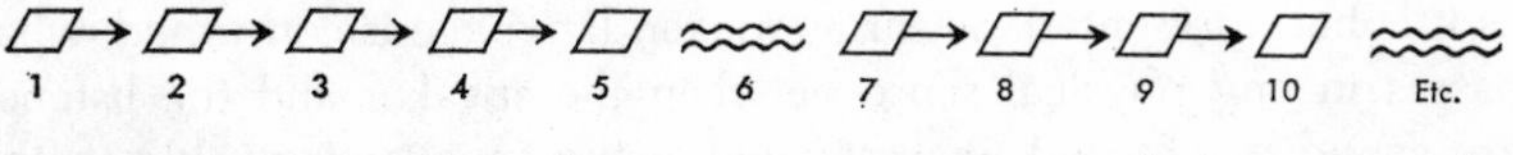

FIGURE 1. Schematic stage-by-stage representation of what goes on when Mr. A. talks to Mr. B.—the process of communication.

KEY:

1. An event occurs (any first order fact serving as a source of sensory stimulation)
2. which stimulates Mr. A. through eyes, ears, or other sensory organs, and the resulting
3. nervous impulses travel to Mr. A.'s brain, and from there to his

301

muscles and glands, producing tensions, preverbal "feelings," etc.,
4. which Mr. A. then begins to translate into words, according to his accustomed verbal patterns, and out of all the words he "thinks of"
5. he "selects," or abstracts, certain ones which he arranges in some fashion, and then
6. by means of sound waves and light waves, Mr. A. speaks to Mr. B.,
7. whose ears and eyes are stimulated by the sound waves and light waves, respectively, and the resulting
8. nervous impulses travel to Mr. B.'s brain, and from there to his muscles and glands, producing tensions, preverbal "feelings," etc.,
9. which Mr. B. then begins to translate into words, according to *his* accustomed verbal patterns, and out of all the words *he* "thinks of"
10. he "selects," or abstracts, certain ones, which he arranges in some fashion and then Mr. B. speaks, or acts, accordingly, thereby stimulating Mr. A.—or somebody else—and so the process of communication goes on, and on—with complications, as indicated in the accompanying text.

(Adapted from Wendell Johnson, *People in Quandaries*: *The Semantics of Personal Adjustment* (New York: Harper and Brothers, 1946), p. 472. For elaboration see accompanying outline of the process of communication, with discussion, *ibid.*, pp. 469-81.)

The restrictions and distortions of speech with which we are concerned can be particularly well appreciated in terms of the diagram of the process of communication shown in Figure 1. The diagram provides a convenient organizing scheme for dealing in an orderly manner with an exceedingly complex pattern of events. By breaking the pattern down into a series of stages it becomes possible to examine the functions and the possible disorders at each stage, as well as the conditions importantly related to these functions and disorders.

If we begin by having a look at stage 6, as represented in the diagram, and then work back toward stage 1, perhaps we shall gain most quickly the clearest possible view of the communicative process as it is here presented. So far as spoken language is concerned, what passes in any physical sense between the speaker and the listener are sound waves and, in cases where the speaker is visible to the listener, light waves. These waves may be sufficiently mysterious, but at least they set definite limits to such mystery as there may be in the transmission of whatever the speaker has to communicate to the listener. Anything in the way of "spiritual influence," "value," or "the intangibilities of personality" that Mr. A. may succeed in conveying to Mr. B. is to be described ultimately by the physicist conversant with optics and acoustics.

Undeniable as this may be, however, our understanding of communication is to be considerably abetted if we move back a step and examine the events of stage 6 in relation to the functions and the possible disorders involved in stage 5. Limiting our considerations to speech—rather than writing, musical performance, painting, etc. —we see that the functions at this stage are those involved in the use of appropriate symbol systems, such as the English language, for example, including words and the forms according to which they are arranged. The chief functions involved in speech at this stage are those of phonation and articulation of sounds. Auxiliary functions include gesture, posture, facial expression, and general bodily action. It is also to be considered that the manipulation of the situation is involved—the arrangement of background or setting for the spoken words. This may include the use of music, banners, sound effects, color, lighting, clothes, etc. Finally, the means of transmission are to be taken into account—the use of radio, television, motion pictures with sound, telephone, speech recordings, or face-to-face communication.

The possible disorders affecting these functions fall generally into the following categories: speech and voice defects; anxiety tension reactions, such as are involved in stage fright or feelings of inferiority, which noticeably affect speech; paralyses, diseases, or characteristics of physical appearance which interfere with expressive bodily action, or which tend to call forth unfavorable reactions on the part of listeners; lack of skill in the use of background or staging techniques, together with defects, such as radio static, in the means and conditions of transmission.

. . . .

GENERAL SEMANTIC PRINCIPLES AND DISTURBANCES

Certain other disorders of speech, which are more significant from a communicative standpoint than the ones we have discussed, are far less commonly known. In fact, until the recent development of semantics and general semantics many of these disorders were for practical purposes unrecognized; some had not even been named. The more important ones are to be most meaningfully discussed in relation to stage 4 of our diagram. This is the stage of preliminary verbal formulation, the stage at which the preverbal tensions resulting from a sensory stimulation are transformed into words. How vacuously we take speech for granted is to be sensed from a moment of intensive contemplation of this amazing transformation of non-verbal goings on within the nervous system, and throughout the organism, into the curiously codified motor responses that we so glibly refer to as "spoken words"!

One can at least be appropriately humble in recognizing the fact that no one understands very well just how this fateful transformation is brought about. But humility need not be carried to the point of swooning. The fact that does appear to be clear enough, although it is widely disregarded, is that what we verbalize is not—as the "practical minded" seem chronically to take for granted—anything that can be called "external reality." To say, for example, "The room is hot," is not, by any stretch of imagination, to make a statement about the room, as such, "in and of itself." As our diagram indicates, at least four discernible stages are passed through before we utter a statement at all. To stick with our homely example, there is first of all some source of sensory stimulation in what we call "the room"—some sort of "energy radiations" (stage 1) which play upon the sensory end organs in our skin. The effect of these "energy radiations" is that activity is aroused in the nerve endings, with consequent nervous currents which travel into the spinal cord and brain. This we represent in our diagram as stage 2. The resulting "disturbance" (stage 3), which we call "preverbal tensions," is determined in part by the character of the sensory nerve impulses coming into the nervous system and in part by the condition existing in the nervous system at the moment of their arrival. Moreover, the incoming impulses are relayed out to muscles and glands where the resulting activities give rise to proprioceptive stimulation, with subsequent incoming nerve impulses which complicate and intensify the effects of the original sensory stimulation. It is this whole complex process which we represent in our diagram as the preverbal tensions at stage 3. *And it is these preverbal tensions that we verbalize.*

The crucial significance of this fact is that basically we always talk about ourselves. Our statements are the verbalizations of our preverbal tensions. It is these organismic tensions—not the external reality of rooms, chairs, people, sound waves, light waves, and pressures—that we transform into words. What we talk about, then, is a joint product of reality (regarded as a source of sensory stimulation) and of the conditions existing within our nervous systems at the time of stimulation. This joint product is represented as stage 3 in our diagram. The preliminary verbalizations of it are represented as stage 4.

The basic function occurring in stage 4 is that of symbolic formulation. This function is affected in a determinative way by the structure of the speaker's available symbolic systems. In the case of speech, the symbolic system is the speaker's acquired language, or languages—his vocabulary and the rules according to which he uses it, the information it represents, the flexibility or rigidity with which he operates with it, and the insight and ingenuity with which he abstracts, from all the verbal formulations possible to him, those few statements which he actually utters.

The disorders to be considered in relation to stage 4 are to be identified accordingly. They fall roughly into three main categories. They are, first, deficiencies in vocabulary and grammatical form.

While a quite limited store of words, arranged in relatively simple sentences, might well serve for most purposes of common conversation and small talk, nevertheless present-day communal living and technological specialization require very considerable language skills of any citizen who presumes to maintain an intelligent grasp of the wide range of affairs by which his life is affected. Much can be done, of course, to simplify the discussion of even relatively complex social and scientific matters, as has been demonstrated by Rudolf Flesch in his provocative book, *The Art of Plain Talk,* and by I. A. Richards and C. K. Ogden in their publication concerning Basic English (for an unusually practical presentation see I. A. Richards' twenty-five-cent *Pocket Book of Basic English*). What these inventive students of language recommend as techniques of simplification, however, demand, for their adroit application, a degree of linguistic skill that is not to be come by without effort. The language skill of a school child who describes a movie, using short simple sentences and a limited vocabulary, is definitely to be contrasted with that of a university professor who manages to discuss psychoanalysis or atomic fission in equally short and simple sentences and with an equally limited vocabulary. In the case of the school child there is to be observed a deficiency, perhaps even a very grave deficiency, of language development, while in the simplified speech of the professor there is to be noted a linguistic subtlety and sophistication rarely achieved. It is probably as difficult for a highly trained scientific specialist to explain his work to a second grader as it is for the second grader to explain the scientist's work to the kid in the next seat.

Vocabulary deficiency, that is to say, works both ways; a vocabulary may be too limited or too elaborate for specific purposes of communication. One's vocabulary can be lacking in complexity— or in simplicity. The language used in the present discussion, for example, is probably lacking more in simplicity than in complexity, generally speaking.

The basic point to be emphasized in this connection is that the language, or languages, available to us are such that they tend to make for oversimplification and overgeneralization. Reality—that is, the sources of sensory stimulation—is, so far as we know, decidedly process-like, highly dynamic, ever changing. Our language, on the other hand, is by comparison quite static and relatively inflexible. The six hundred thousand or so words in the English language must serve to symbolize millions—indeed, billions—of individual facts, experiences, and relationships. Moreover, the average individual does not use or readily understand as many as ten per cent of the six hundred thousand words making up the English language. In a study by one of the writer's students (Helen Fairbanks, *The Quantitative Differentiation of Samples of Spoken Language*, Psychological Monographs 56, 1944, pp. 19–28), a total of thirty thousand words was obtained from a group of superior university freshmen, and the same size of speech sample was obtained from a group of mental hospital patients diagnosed as schizophrenic. Each individual talked, interpreting fables, until he had produced a sample of three thousand words. For the freshmen just forty-six different words made up half of the thirty thousand words in the total sample. For the schizophrenic patients the comparable figure was thirty-three words. (In fact, *one* word, the one most frequently used by the schizophrenic patients, which was the word *I*, made up over eight per cent of their entire thirty thousand words.)

Thus the magnitude of the discrepancy between reality and language, with respect to variability, is by no means adequately indicated by reference to the six hundred thousand words which make up the approximate total for the English language. The discrepancy is more meaningfully indicated by reference to the few hundred— at best, the few thousand—words which make up the practical daily use vocabulary of an ordinary person. In this general sense, we all suffer from vocabulary deficiency. The basic fact is that, at best, there are far more things to speak about than there are words with which to speak about them.

We have already noted that what a speaker has to verbalize is an organismic condition (stage 3) which is a joint product of the sensory stimulation arising from reality and the state of his organism at the moment of stimulation. We have now to add that what a speaker has to communicate (stage 5) is a joint product of this organismic condition (stage 3) and the language structure of the speaker, together with his habits of employing it (stage 4). What a speaker eventually says can hardly be anything but a far cry from the supposedly relevant first order facts (stage 1). And what the listener makes of what the speaker says is something else again! Anyone able to read a headline or twist a radio knob knows that there is no dearth of misunderstanding in the world—and anyone with even an elementary knowledge of the process of communication can only wonder that there is not more misunderstanding and confusion than there seem to be.

DISTURBANCES DUE TO IGNORANCE

We have so far considered only a part of the difficulty, however. A second considerable source of communicative inefficiency is sheer ignorance. The number of factual subjects which the average person is able to discuss in detail and with a thorough grasp of important relationships and implications has never been determined with statistical refinement, but it is doubtless lower than any college president would find to be gratifying. The "Quiz Kids" provide a thin ray of hope, but even that is dusted up a bit by the fact that we are seldom given an opportunity to find out whether they are thinkers or mere collectors of odds and ends of information. At best, of course, only a small portion of the little information most of us have is first hand; most by far of what we know we have gained verbally, and most of this has come to us in the form of relatively high order generalization rather than detailed descriptive report. Thus, we are not only drastically limited by our common verbal means of symbolizing fact and experience, but we are also appallingly limited in our reliable knowledge of fact and experience. There is almost always a significant degree of probability that discourse involving two or more individuals will result in misunderstanding, confusion, and the intensification of conflict. There is considerable hope of decreasing this probability, however, so long as the obstacles to communication are clearly recognized so that allowance can be made for them in a forthright, impersonal, and even good-humored manner. On the other hand, a naïve confidence in the constructive possibilities of discussion, an uncritical faith in the power of words, can be disastrously misleading and socially as well as individually disruptive. It obscures both the sources of misunderstanding and the possibilities of agreement and cooperative action.

DISTURBANCES DUE TO PRE-SCIENTIFIC ORIENTATION

A third large category of disorders affecting communication adversely are those due mainly to the generally pre-scientific orientation so common in our culture. It is this particular class of disorders that general semantics serves to highlight effectively. The disorders constitute violations of fundamental semantic principles. One is handicapped in discussing them briefly, however, because the principles themselves can hardly be presented in a few pages, and the particular frame of reference which they represent, so far from being generally familiar, constitutes in certain respects a major break from our traditional orientation. While a general suggestion of the relevant disorders can be given in the present discussion, any serious reader will insist upon a fuller knowledge of them and of general semantics itself than can possibly be provided in this chapter.

IDENTIFICATION

The most pervasive of these disorders is that which Korzybski first described systematically as undue identification. He gave this term a special meaning, which can best be approximated, perhaps, for our present purposes, by saying that undue identification involves a factually unwarranted degree of categorical thinking. Differences among individuals, and differences within given individuals from time to time, are relatively disregarded, because broad group trends and characteristics, and the general tendencies of individuals, are overemphasized. For example, no particular attention is paid to an individual Charles Brown, because he is evaluated by a process of identifying him with—of regarding him as identical with—all other "Negroes." The supposed attributes of the category "Negro" are taken as the basis of evaluation of each and every individual Negro. One who is grossly addicted to identification, therefore, thinks in terms of verbal fictions, or high order abstractions, rather than the extensional, or factual, sources of data and experience. Statements involving undue identifications constitute, therefore, overgeneralizations. It is to be emphasized, however, that generalization, as such, is not being indicted; it is unwarranted generalization, untested and uncorrected, to which reference is being made.

Class names—categorical nouns, verbs, adjectives, and adverbs— play a crucial role in the process of identification. The unreflective use of such class words makes automatically for identification, for overgeneralization and the relative disregard of individual differences and specific data. Discussions carried on in terms of such words as "Democrats" and "Republicans," "Communists" and "capitalists," "the Russian," "the Englishman," "the underprivileged," "the consumer," etc., tend, unless conducted with extraordinary semantic consciousness and care in qualification, to degenerate into almost meaningless manipulation of vacuous verbal forms.

Class names serve to lump together as identical indefinite numbers of different individuals. What this amounts to is the identification of—the failure to differentiate—high order abstractions and lower order abstractions. The principles of general semantics are principles of abstracting. In terms of our diagram (Figure 1), we abstract from the sources of sensory stimulation (stage 1) only so much as our sensory end organs and their functional connections within the nervous system are able to abstract. What we call an object, therefore, an orange, for example, as perceived by us, is a joint product of whatever the orange may be, independently of our perceptions of it, and whatever perceptions of it we are able to make. What appears to be the most reasonable assumption is that we leave out an indefinite number of details which we might be able to abstract if only we possessed different sensory and perceptive apparatus.

Going another step, any description we might make of this orange "manufactured by our nervous system" can be no more than an abstract of somewhat higher order. No matter how thorough we make it, our description can never be complete. Some details will be disregarded or left out of account. We seldom deal, however, with thorough descriptions. The statements we make about even first order experiences are usually partial to an extreme degree, mere summaries, often nothing but a word or two, or just names. A child experiences a complex experience of observation, for example, and we help him to verbalize it by saying, "That? Oh, that's a steamshovel." There should be no difficulty in noting in such an instance the process of abstracting. It is a process of leaving out details—of ignoring the unique in favor of the general, of putting the individual fact under the blurring dim light of the undifferentiating category, of identification.

One may speak of levels of abstraction: the levels, for example, of first order fact or direct experience (the non-verbal orange as seen, felt, or tasted), of naming or description, of inference from description, and of inference of higher order from inference of lower order practically without end. And the level of first order is made up of events which we cannot completely observe or experience, but about which we can imagine or infer as elaborately as we are able in such terms as electrons, protons, hereditary predispositions, immunities, and other hypothetical constructs.

Now, identification, as general semanticists use the term, refers most fundamentally to a failure to differentiate the levels of abstraction. Thus one may exhibit identification by reacting to a name as though it were an object—as in the word magic of certain primitive peoples, or in the reactions made by some persons in our own culture to such words as *syphilis, labor union,* or *expert.* Or, one may exhibit identification by reacting to the object, to what one sees or smells, for example, as though it were the event—as in the behavior of persons with food dislikes, many of whom have never eaten the foods in question, having always responded to the food, as seen, as though it were the food, as digested. Again, one may show identification by reacting to a high order verbal abstract, such as the present discussion, as though it were a highly detailed descriptive report. Having read the present chapter, for example, some readers might announce to their friends that they "know all about" general semantics, and even proceed to pass quite conclusive judgments one way or another concerning it.

The more highly conscious one is of the identifying tendencies of our language processes, the more effectively one may take them into account and even counteract them. Language necessarily involves varying degrees of identification, and for purposes of essential and fruitful generalization identification is indispensable. Precisely because it is both unavoidable and necessary, there is constant need for awareness of it. That is to say, since abstracting is a process of leaving out details, adequate abstracting, and so effective communication, necessitate an awareness of the details left out—and of those left in—in any act of observation or of verbal statement. This awareness is for practical purposes our only effective safeguard against undue and maladjustive identifications.

PROJECTION

Another basic aspect of the abstracting process, which can be misused with unfortunate effects, is that of projection. Since all we have to verbalize (stages 4 and 5) is an internal condition (stage 3), we are able to have any knowledge of, or to communicate anything about, reality (stage 1) only by projecting our internal condition "into" the external events. That is, if Mr. A. is to speak about an orange as a public event, so that Mr. B. might share his experience of it, or check his statements about it, he must project the orange as he experiences it, as "manufactured by his nervous system," into the orange as an object independent of himself. He must, in other words, speak about the orange (stage 3) "as if" it were outside himself (stage 1). If Mr. A. says, "There is an orange on the table," he is projecting, since all he has to verbalize is a condition inside his own nervous system. But if Mr. B. replies, "Yes, I see the orange," Mr. A.'s projection is thereby, to that extent, justified. If, however, Mr. A. says, "There is a green lizard on the wall," and Mr. B. replies, "I don't see a green lizard," we might, with sufficient evidence, conclude that Mr. A. is exhibiting the sort of illegitimate projection that we call hallucination.

There is nothing abnormal about projection, as such. In fact, it is like identification, unavoidable and necessary. It is an integral aspect of the process of abstracting. What is essential, for purposes of effective abstracting and communication, is that there be adequate consciousness of projection. We may, for practical emphasis, speak of consciousness of projection as "to-me-ness." That is to say, Mr. A. exhibits consciousness of his own projecting when he says, "It seems to me that there is a green lizard on the wall," or, "This orange tastes sour to me. How does it taste to you?" In this way he indicates an awareness that what he reports is a personal experience, not a universal truth—a personal experience, or evaluation, which depends for its reliability as a social fact on the degree to which others concur in it. Lack of "to-me-ness" is to be observed particularly in language that is highly "is-y"—in such statements as "This orange is sour," as though the sourness were in the orange rather than a quality of the experience of tasting the orange. To someone else the orange might taste sweet. Statements like "John is stupid," "Mary is beautiful," "Taxes are high," suggest, at least, a lack of consciousness of projection on the part of the speaker.

So long as the listener is aware of the speaker's projection, the listener, at least, can allow for it and respond accordingly. This is exemplified by a competent psychiatrist's manner of responding to the deluded statements of a patient who is indulging to an extreme degree in unconscious projection. The psychiatrist at least does not argue with the patient, and thereby sets us all an object lesson of great promise. He may go further, of course, and does whenever possible, to help the patient become sufficiently aware of his projecting to recapture a useful degree of self-critical ability. Participants in discussion groups and forums might well study closely the psychiatrist's techniques in bringing about such a beneficent transformation. If, in our schools, we ever get around to doing something systematically about teaching pupils how to listen, it would appear that one of the things most worth doing would be that of giving them a psychiatric attitude toward speakers who are relatively lacking in "to-me-ness."

Just so, in the teaching of speech, from the preschool ages on through graduate school and beyond, doubtless much can be done to improve communication by training speakers in consciousness of projection. This would amount to training speakers to listen effectively to themselves, out of due deference to the fact that every speaker is, as a rule, his own most affected listener. Such training would also involve attention to developing the speaker's skill in allowing for the lack, in those listeners in whom there is a notable lack, of awareness of the role of projection in verbal expression.

Unconscious projection would appear to be a mechanism fundamental in the development of delusional states, hysterical paralysis, fatigue and other symptoms, as well as prejudices of various kinds. It goes without saying that such reaction tendencies militate pervasively against effective communication. They limit the possibilities of adequate abstracting, and they make for systematic distortion of the verbal formulation of experience.

TWO VALUED EVALUATION

Undue identification and unconscious projection give rise to a considerable variety of disorders of abstracting and symbolic expression. One of the more common of these is to be seen as an excessive tendency to formulate issues and situations in a two valued, either-orish manner; people are evaluated as good or bad, policies as right or wrong, organizations as American or un-American, etc. With such an orientation, there are only two sides to any question, and one of them is to be rejected. This is the formula of conflict: The number of choices is reduced to two, and a choice is insisted upon. A two valued scheme of classification automatically enforces a vicious sorting of people into Jews and non-Jews, Americans and aliens, acceptable and nonacceptable. Identification without due regard to individual differences, together with unconscious projection of the resulting categorical evaluations, more or less inevitably results in an unrelenting either-orishness, conducive to conflict, prejudice, confusion, and injustice. It appears to be essentially futile to attempt to counteract specific prejudices, delusions, or fixed attitudes of any sort, so long as the underlying two valued orientation, arising out of relatively unconscious identification and projection, is left unexamined and undisturbed.

RELATED DISTURBING FACTORS

Further analysis of the semantic disorders operating particularly, though not exclusively at stage 4 of the communicative process, as diagrammed, would extend this discussion unduly. The more fundamental mechanisms of misevaluation have been indicated, unconscious identification and projection, and excessive either-orishness. The specific effects of these mechanisms are too numerous and varied to be catalogued readily and briefly. The effects are to be observed in an impressive variety of distortions and frustrations of the symbolic functions involved in speech and in interpretations of the spoken word. The consequences for personality development and for interpersonal relationships are disintegrative in varying forms and degrees.

At stage 3 of the process of communication the basic functions are those of the transmission of nerve currents from the sensory end organs (eye, ear, etc.) to the spinal, thalamic, and cortical levels of the central nervous system, and the relaying of these nerve currents out to muscles and glands, with consequent bodily changes from which further afferent nerve impulses arise to travel back to the central nervous system, elaborating and complicating the bodily condition later to be verbalized in stages 4 and 5.

Impaired transmission of nerve currents, the main disorder involved in stage 3, may manifest itself as failure of response, or as incoordination of response, to stimuli. The impaired transmission may be due to physical or semantic factors. That is, it may be due to damage to nerve tracts resulting from infections, tumors, inherited defects, etc. Or, it may be due to acquired or learned semantic blockages, as seen in inattentiveness, disinterest, aversion to colors, etc.; undelayed preverbal reactions of rejection, or overreactions of uncritical acceptance; fear responses, reactions of self-defensiveness, "bristling," etc.; fainting in response to certain odors, or in response to certain situations such as large crowds or small enclosures. Such reactions would appear to be dependent upon the characteristic identifications and projections discussed in relation to stage 4, but they are here identified with stage 3 because they are to be observed chiefly as highly conditioned organismic, preverbal responses to sensory stimulation. Perhaps they can best be characterized in a general sense as undelayed overreactions.

With respect to stage 2, the main function is sensory stimulation, and the chief disorder is that of sensory deficiency or defect, such as impaired vision, or blindness, and impaired hearing acuity, or deafness. Aside from the commonly recognized physical causes of such sensory defects, there are to be duly considered also the semantogenic (roughly psychological) factors responsible for hysterical or psychoneurotic blindness or deafness, for example. The mechanisms described in connection with stage 4 appear to have pervasive effects throughout the abstracting and communicative process.

It remains to be said of stage 1, the sources of sensory stimulation, that these sources play a less determinative role in most communication than might be commonly assumed. As we have noted, we do not verbalize in any direct or complete sense the "facts" of so-called reality. A relatively elaborate series of evaluative and transformative processes intervene between the sources of sensory stimulation (stage 1) and overt expression (stage 5). Nevertheless, it is the responsibility of the speaker to see to it that his statements mirror, as reliably as these intervening processes will allow, the facts to which his statements presumably refer. And reliability, in this case, is to be gauged in terms of the agreement among speakers and their listeners as to the factual dependability of given statements. Our common world of agreed-upon facts is a kind of average of the abstracting, evaluating, and reporting in which we all share. Public opinion, that fateful product of general communication, can be no more reliable than the common consciousness of abstracting, of identification and projection, will permit it to be. A population ignorant of the abstracting processes involved in communication can, with little difficulty, be led off in the fruitless or disastrous pursuit of red herrings and verbal mirages. Delusion can be made epidemic, as has been often and unfortunately demonstrated. Fifty million Frenchmen can be wrong—and never suspect it.

PSYCHOLOGICAL BARRIERS TO COMMUNICATION

BY DANIEL KATZ

Dr. Katz is professor of psychology and program director of the Survey Research Center in the University of Michigan. His article is reprinted by permission of the author and the publisher, from the *Annals of the American Academy of Political and Social Science*, March, 1947. It is copyrighted by the Academy.

ACCURATE AND ADEQUATE communication between groups and peoples will not in itself bring about the millennium, but it is a necessary condition for almost all forms of social progress. Physical barriers to communication are rapidly disappearing, but the psychological obstacles remain. These psychological difficulties are in part a function of the very nature of language; in part they are due to the emotional character and mental limitations of human beings.

THE NATURE OF LANGUAGE

Much of our communication in the great society must of necessity be by formal language rather than by visual presentation or by the explicit denotation or pointing possible in small face-to-face groups. Formal language is symbolic in that its verbal or mathematical terms stand for aspects of reality beyond themselves. Though onomatopoetic words are an exception, they constitute but a small fraction of any modern language. Because of its symbolic nature, language is a poor substitute for the realities which it attempts to represent. The real world is more complex, more colorful, more fluid, more multidimensional than the pale words or oversimplified signs used to convey meaning.

Nor is there any easy solution of the problem. A language too close to perceptual reality would be useless for generalization and would, moreover, ignore complex forms of experience. Language enables us to transcend the specificity of the single event and makes possible the analysis and comparison of experiences. But the abstraction and generalization through the use of symbols which has given man his control over the natural world also makes possible the greatest distortions of reality. Many language signs may in fact be completely lacking in objective reference. The semantic movement is the current effort to cope with the woeful inadequacies inherent in the symbolic nature of language. Thus far it has contributed more to exposing the inaccuracies and weaknesses in language than to developing a science of meaning.

The imperfection of language is not due solely to the weakness of its representational quality. Viewed realistically, language as a living process has other functions than accurate communication. It did not arise in the history of the race, any more than in the development of the child, solely in the interest of precise interchange of information. Language as it exists is not the product of scientists trying to perfect an exact set of symbols; it is the product of the arena of everyday life, in which people are concerned with manipulating and controlling their fellows and with expressing their emotional and psychological wants. The prototype of language as a functioning process can be seen in the child's acquisition of words and phrases to extend his control of environment beyond his limited physical reach. Similarly, adults use language to obtain sympathy, bulldoze their fellows, placate or embarrass their enemies, warm and comfort their friends, deceive themselves, or express their own conflicts. Language in operation is often intended to conceal and obscure meaning. Hence as an instrument for accurate communication it suffers from emotional loadings, polar words, and fictitious concepts.

Even the will to interchange factual information, therefore, is embarrassed by the heritage of a language developed for other purposes. This is one of the reasons for the slow growth of social science compared with natural science. Once the physical and biological sciences had got under way, their data were so far removed from everyday observation that they were free to develop scientific terminology and concepts. But this initial step is much more difficult in the social realm because we already have a well-developed popular language applying to social events and relationships. For example, F. H. Allport demonstrated some twenty years ago the scientific inadequacy of the popular concepts of "group" and "institution" through which we personify the group and, in the manner of the cartoonist, speak of a paranoid Germany, a schizophrenic France, or a megalomaniacal Russia.[1] But his warning went unheeded because social scientists have been unable to shed the habitual modes of thought arising from their language and their culture.

These general considerations concerning the psychological nature of language are the background against which more specific difficulties in communication can be understood. The following specific obstacles merit special attention: (1) the failure to refer language to experience and reality, (2) the inability to transcend personal experience in intergroup communication, (3) stereotypes: the assimilation of material to familiar frames of reference, and (4) the confusion of percept and concept: reification and personification.

RELATION OF SYMBOL TO FACT

Psychological research abounds with illustrations of the principle that analytic thinking occurs not as the prevalent mode of human response but as a limited reaction under conditions of block or need. Men think critically and precisely only under specific conditions of motivation, and then only in reference to the particular pressing problem. Ordinarily they respond according to the law of least effort. In the field of language behavior, this appears at the most fundamental level in the tendency to confuse words with the things or processes they name. The word and its referent are fused as an unanalyzed whole in the mind of the individual. Among primitives, for example, it is not permitted to mention the name of a person recently deceased. Since there is deep fear of the spirit of the departed, it is dangerous to bring up his name, fundamentally because the name and the person named are psychologically confused. Even in our society, many obscene and sacred words are taboo because the name is regarded as the equivalent of the object or process for which it stands.

[1] Floyd H. Allport, " 'Group' and 'Institution' as Concepts in a Natural Science of Social Phenomena," *Publications of the American Sociological Society*, XXII, 83-99.

This inability to grasp the difference between the symbol and its referent is one reason for the failure to check back constantly from language to experience and reality. Much has been said about the virtues of scientific method, but one unappreciated reason for the tremendous progress in natural science has been the constant referral of scientific language to the realities which it supposedly represents. Without such an interplay between symbol and experience, distortion in the symbol cannot be corrected.

Another difficulty is that the average man has little chance, even when motivated, to check language against the facts in the real world. In our huge, complex society the individual citizen often lacks the opportunity to test the language of the politicians, statesmen, and other leaders by reference to the realities involved. Walter Lippmann has presented this problem brilliantly in the *Phantom Public,* in which he shows how little possibility exists for the man on the street to participate intelligently in the political process. But it is also true at the leadership level that the individual official or leader accepts reports of the working of his policies which are gross oversimplifications and even misrepresentations of the facts. The leader lives in a world of symbols, as do his followers, and he comes to rely upon what appears in newsprint for the facts instead of upon direct contact with reality.

In the world of social action the newspaper has been the most important single medium in our culture for relating symbol to fact. In theory, the newspaper has a staff of trained observers and fact finders who constantly make contact with the real world to give accuracy to the symbols presented in news columns. Though the newspaper has functioned surprisingly well, its limitations for fact finding and presentation are obvious. On many problems, research has shown that there is a wide discrepancy between the real world and the world of newsprint. Up until the action of Congress in undercutting the Office of Price Administration in July, 1946, the history of price control is an interesting example of this point. The newspapers presented a story of public impatience with bureaucratic bungling during the very period when nation-wide polls, even those conducted by commercial agencies, indicated an overwhelming popular support for price controls and the OPA, and majority satisfaction with their actual functioning.

Polls and surveys have opened up new possibilities for leaders to refer words to the world of fact. During the war many governmental agencies discovered that they could learn more about the functioning of their policies through surveys using scientific samples and first hand accounts than through press clippings or through the occasional visit of a high official to the field.

EXPERIMENTAL LIMITATION

The important psychological fact that men's modes of thinking—their beliefs, their attitudes—develop out of their ways of life is not commonly and fully appreciated. Their mental worlds derive from everyday experiences in their occupational callings, and they are not equipped to understand a language which represents a different way of life.

Because language is symbolic in nature, it can only evoke meaning in the recipient if the recipient has experiences corresponding to the symbol. It will not solve the problem of the basic difficulties in communication between the peoples of the world to have them all speak the same tongue if their experiential backgrounds differ. The individual lives in a private world of his own perception, emotion, and thought. To the extent that his perceptions, feelings, and thoughts arise from similar contacts with similar aspects of reality as experienced by others, the private world can be shared and lose something of its private character. But language itself, even if exact and precise, is a very limited device for producing common understanding when it has no basis in common experience. The linguists who argue for a world language neglect the fact that basic misunderstandings occur not at the linguistic but at the psychological level.

A dramatic example of the inability of verbal symbols to bridge the gap between different experiential worlds was the lack of understanding between returned servicemen and civilians. Since foxhole existence has no real counterpart in unbombed America, American civilians were at a great disadvantage in understanding or communicating with returned combat servicemen. In the same way the peoples of the world living under different conditions and undergoing different types of experience live in worlds of their own between which there is little communication. Even in our own society, different groups are unable to communicate. The farmer, whose way of life differs from that of the coal miner, the steel worker, or the banker, is as much at a loss to understand their point of view as they are to understand him or one another.

Labor-management controversies illustrate the gap between

groups speaking different psychological languages as a result of following different ways of life. Granted that industrial disputes have as their bedrock real and immediate differences in economic interest, it is still true that these differences are augmented by the inability of each party to understand the opposing point of view. The employer, owner, or superintendent, through his executive function of making daily decisions and issuing orders and instructions, acquires a psychology of management. He can understand, though he may dislike, a union demand for more wages. But when the union requests, or even suggests, changes in the conditions of work or changes in personnel policy, he grows emotional and objects to being told by subordinates and outsiders how to run his own plant. For their part, the workers have little understanding of the competitive position of the employer. Since the employer enjoys a way of life luxurious in comparison with their own, they find his plea of inability to pay a higher wage laughable.

The role of imagination in bridging the gap is important. This, however, is largely the function of the artist, who has the sensitivity and the willingness to seek experience beyond his own original environment. By personalizing the experiences of people in plays, novels, and pictures, the artist often does more to develop mutual understanding between groups with divergent experiences than does the social scientist, the reformer, the politician, or the educator.

More and more, however, are psychologists and practitioners coming to realize the importance of common experience as the real basis of communication. Group workers and experimental educators are emphasizing the importance of role playing in true education. By assigning a person a new experiential role to play, it is possible to increase his understanding in a fashion which no amount of preaching or book learning could do. The modern trend in education, which emphasizes learning by doing, laboratory projects, and a mixture of work experience with book learning, is a recognition of the inadequacy of language divorced from experience to achieve much success in communication.

Surmounting the Difficulty

The difficulty of communication between people of different experiential backgrounds is augmented by the distinctive jargon which seems to develop in every calling and in every walk of life. Though groups may differ in their experiences, there is generally more of a common core of psychological reality between them than their language indicates. A neglected aspect of communication is the identification of these areas of common understanding and the translation of the problems of one group into the functional language of another. It is sometimes assumed that limitations of intelligence prevent the farmer or the worker from understanding the complexities of national and international affairs. Anyone, however, who has taken the trouble to discuss with the shipyard worker or the coal miner the economic and political factors operative in the worker's immediate environment will realize the fallacy of this assumption. Within his limited frame of reference, the coal miner, the steel worker, or the dirt farmer will talk sense. But he is unfamiliar with the language used by the professional economist or the expert on international affairs. He is capable of reacting intelligently to matters in this sphere if they are presented to him in terms of their specifics in his own experience. This translation is rarely made, because the expert or the national leader is as uninformed of the day-to-day world of the worker as the worker is of the field of the expert. And often the person most interested and active in talking to laymen in an understandable experiential language is the demagogue, whose purpose is to misinform.

STEREOTYPES

One aspect of the limitation imposed by one's own narrow experiences is the tendency to assimilate fictitiously various language symbols to one's own frame of reference. The mere fact we lack the experience or the imagination to understand another point of view does not mean that we realize our inadequacy and remain open-minded about it. Whether or not nature abhors a vacuum, the human mind abhors the sense of helplessness that would result if it were forced to admit its inability to understand and deal with people and situations beyond its comprehension. What people do is to fill the gap with their own preconceptions and to spread their own limited attitudes and ideas to cover all the world beyond their own knowledge.

In an older day it was popular to refer to this phenomenon through Herbart's concept of the *apperceptive mass*; later Lévy-Bruhl, in his anthropological interpretations, spoke of *collective* representations; twenty years ago psychologists embraced Walter Lippmann's notion of *stereotypes*; today we speak of assimilating material to our own frame of reference. Thus the farmer who knows little about Jews save from his limited contact with a single Jewish merchant in a nearby trading center will have an opinion of all Jews, and in fact of all foreigners, based on this extremely narrow frame of reference. In the same way he will feel great resentment at the high wages paid to the city worker, without any realization of the city worker's problems. The average citizen may assimilate all discussion of the Negro-white problem to the fractional experience he has had with Negroes forced to live in slum areas.

Nor need there be even a fragmentary basis in personal experience for the stereotype. The superstitions of the culture furnish the individual ready-made categories for his prejudgments in the absence of any experience. Research studies indicate that people in all parts of the United States feel that the least desirable ethnic and racial groups are the Japanese, the Negroes, and the Turks. When asked to characterize the Turk, they have no difficulty in speaking of him as bloodthirsty, cruel, and dirty; yet the great majority who make this judgment not only have never seen a Turk but do not know anyone who has. An Englishman, H. Nicolson, has written entertainingly of the stereotyped conception of his people held by the German, the Frenchman, and the American. He writes:

Now when the average German thinks of the average Englishman he . . . visualizes a tall, spare man, immaculately dressed in top hat and frock coat, wearing spats and an eyeglass, and gripping a short but aggressive pipe in an enormous jaw. . . . To him, the average Englishman is a clever and unscrupulous hypocrite; a man, who, with superhuman ingenuity and foresight, is able in some miraculous manner to be always on the winning side; a person whose incompetence in business and salesmanship is balanced by an uncanny and unfair mastery of diplomatic wiles. . . .

The French portrait of the Englishman . . . is the picture of an inelegant, stupid, arrogant, and inarticulate person with an extremely red face. The French seem to mind our national complexion more than other nations. They attribute it to the overconsumption of ill-cooked meat. They are apt, for this reason, to regard us as barbarian and gross. Only at one point does the French picture coincide with the German picture. The French share with the Germans a conviction of our hypocrisy. . . .

To the average American, the average Englishman seems affected, patronizing, humorless, impolite and funny. To him also the Englishman wears spats and carries an eyeglass; to him also he is slim and neatly dressed; yet the American, unlike the German, is not impressed by these elegancies; he considers them ridiculous. . . .[2]

---

[2] From *Time*, July 15, 1935, p. 26.

Though the oversimplified and distorted notions of racial and national groups are usually cited as examples of stereotypes, the process of assimilating material to narrow preformed frames of reference is characteristic of most of our thinking: of our judgment of social classes, occupational callings, artistic and moral values, and the characters and personalities of our acquaintances.

Motivation of the Stereotype

Stereotyping applies primarily to the cognitive weakness or limitation in our intellectual processes. But this stereotyped prejudgment has an emotional dimension as well. Many of our stereotyped labels or frames carry heavy emotional loading and so are the more resistant to fact and logic. Emotion attaches to them in many ways. Because they give the individual a crude and oversimplified chart in an otherwise confused universe, they afford him security. They tie in with his whole way of thinking and feeling and acting. To abandon them would be mental suicide. A famous British scholar, completely committed to spiritualism, enthusiastically witnessed a mind-reading performance by the magicians Houdini and Mulholland. When they tried to explain to him afterward that it was all a cleverly designed trick, he would have none of their explanation, and insisted that it was a clear instance of spiritualistic phenomena.

Emotion clings to words through association with emotional events which are never dissociated from the label itself. The feeling of dependence and affection that the child has for his mother saturates the words "mother" and "home" and related phrases. These conditioned words can then be used to call up the old emotions in logically irrelevant situations. In the same way the child acquires emotional content for the stereotypes of his group. If the hierarchy of social status is built on stereotypes about Negroes, foreigners, and the lower classes, then these stereotypes are not neutral but are invested with the emotional color associated with the superiority of the upper groups.

This last example suggests a further motivational basis of the stereotype. People cling to their prejudiced beliefs in labels because of the specific psychic income to be derived from the stereotype. If people the world over are to be judged solely on their merits as human personalities, there is little ego-enhancement in belonging to an in-group which bestows superiority upon its members merely through the act of belonging. The poor whites in the South are not going to abandon their notion of the Negro when this stereotyped belief itself makes them superior to every member of the despised group. The more frustrated the individual, the more emotionally inadequate and insecure, the easier it is to channelize his dissatisfaction and aggression against a stereotyped target.

REIFICATION AND PERSONIFICATION

The oversimplification of the stereotype is equaled by the extraordinary opportunities which language provides for reification and personification. We easily forget the distinction between words which refer to percepts, or aspects of perceived experience, and terms which designate concepts and abstractions. As a result, we take a concept like the state, which stands for many complexities of human interrelationships, and make that concept into a thing or person possessed of all the attributes of the object or person. Thus the state, like the individual, does things. It takes the life of a criminal, it glows with pride at the patriotic sacrifices of its citizens; it can grow old, become feeble, or wither away and die. When pressed, we readily admit that we do not mean to be taken literally, but are speaking metaphorically and analogically. Yet our thinking is so shot through with personification and analogy that the tendency is a serious impediment to our understanding and to our intelligent handling of important problems.

The problem of German war guilt is an interesting example. One school of thought made all German crimes the action of the German state; hence it was the state that should be punished, not individual Germans. The standard defense of high-ranking German generals, admirals, and officials was that they were mere servants of the state, who faithfully followed its orders. An opposed school of thought, likewise accepting the fallacy of a personified German nation, identified every German as a miniature of the German nation and so considered all Germans equally guilty. Our first treatment of the Germans was based on this logic. American troops, under the fraternization ban, were forbidden so much as to speak to any German man, woman, or child. This was mild treatment for leading Nazis, but relatively harsh treatment for German children.

In the same way, the original American information policy in Germany was to hammer away at German guilt and to make the German people feel guilty about concentration camp atrocities. But this blanket conception of German guilt took no account of the complex realities involved. It not only failed to take into account quantitative differences in guilt between high Nazis and lesser Nazis; qualitative differences between active leadership in atrocities and passive acceptance of or irresponsibility about them were also ignored. The type of guilt of the Nazi leaders who set up and ran the concentration camps was of one order. The social cowardice, political passivity, and irresponsibility of the German people, who were afraid to voice objection, or who were indifferent, is guilt of another order.

Distorted Pictures

In place, then, of communication through accurate descriptions and conceptions, we reinforce and magnify for ourselves a distorted picture of the universe by our tendency to reify and personify. Perhaps the most effective account of this process is in the following by Stuart Chase:

Let us glance at some of the queer creatures created by personifying abstractions in America. Here in the center is a vast figure called the Nation—majestic and wrapped in the Flag. When it sternly raises its arm we are ready to die for it. Close behind rears a sinister shape, the Government. Following it is one even more sinister, Bureaucracy. Both are festooned with the writhing serpents of Red Tape. High in the heavens is the Constitution, a kind of chalice like the Holy Grail, suffused with ethereal light. It must never be joggled. Below floats the Supreme Court, a black robed priesthood tending the eternal fires. The Supreme Court must be addressed with respect or it will neglect the fire and the Constitution will go out. This is synonymous with the end of the world. Somewhere above the Rocky Mountains are lodged the vast stone tablets of the Law. We are governed not by men but by these tablets. Near them, in satin breeches and silver buckles, pose the stern figures of our Forefathers, contemplating glumly the Nation they brought to birth. The onion-shaped demon cowering behind the Constitution is Private Property. Higher than Court, Flag, or the Law, close to the sun itself and almost as bright, is Progress, the ultimate God of America.

Here are the Masses, thick, black and squirming. This demon must be firmly sat upon; if it gets up, terrible things will happen, the Constitution may be joggled. . . .

Capital, her skirt above her knees, is preparing to leave the country at the drop of a hairpin, but never departs. Skulking from city to city goes Crime, a red loathsome beast, upon which the Law is forever trying to drop a monolith, but its Aim is poor. Crime continues rhythmically to rear its ugly head. Here is the dual shape of Labor—for some a vast, dirty, clutching hand, for others a Galahad in armor. Pacing to and fro with remorseless tread are the Trusts and Utilities, bloated unclean monsters with enormous biceps. Here is Wall Street, a crouching dragon ready to spring upon assets not already nailed down in any other section of the country. The Consumer, a pathetic figure in a gray shawl, goes wearily to market. Capital and Labor each give her a kick as she passes, while Commercial Advertising, a playful sprite, squirts perfume in her eye.[3]

The personified caricatures of popular thinking appeal not only because of their simplicity but also because they give a richness of imagery and of emotional tone lacking in a more exact, scientific description. Nor is the communication of emotional feeling to be proscribed. The problem is how to communicate emotional values without sacrificing adequacy and validity of description.

RESEARCH NEEDED

In brief, the psychological barriers to communication are of such strength and have such a deep foundation in human nature that the whole problem of social communication between individuals and groups needs to be re-examined in a new light. No simple formula will solve the problems arising from the many complex causes and widely ramifying aspects of the limitations of the symbolic mechanism and other psychological processes. The older attempt at an easy solution was the study of the dictionary. One instance of this type of thinking was the college faculty committee which tried to discover the dividing line between legislative matters of policy and executive matters of administration by looking up the words involved in the dictionary. The newer approach of the semanticists, though more sophisticated and more promising, sometimes ignores the psychological difficulties and sometimes begs the question in an uncritical operationalism.

Perhaps the whole problem of communication is inseparable from the larger context of the over-all social problems of our time. There might well be possibilities of significant advance, however, if we were to employ the research methods of science in attacking the many specific obstacles to communication. Procedures are already being worked out on the basis of research evaluation for the alleviation of minority group prejudice. Studies now in contemplation would provide functional dictionaries to supplement the standard etymological works. The process of interpersonal communication has been the subject of some research in studies of rumor.

---

[3] *Tyranny of Words* (New York: Harcourt, Brace, 1938), p. 23.

Though the importance to accurate communication of a maximum of objective reference in language symbols has experimental support, the fact remains that such complex and involved communication is much more feasible in science than in popular discussion. It is probable that precise scientific language, with its exact reference to the objective world and objective operation, will not solve the problem of communication in practical life, where short cuts in communication are essential. But it may be possible to determine the type of short-cut symbol which conveys meaning with minimum distortion. The problem invites research.

SOME CULTURAL APPROACHES
TO COMMUNICATION PROBLEMS

BY MARGARET MEAD

Dr. Mead is a well-known anthropologist and staff member of the American Museum of Natural History in New York. Her paper is reprinted by permission of the author and the copyright holder from *The Communication of Ideas*, published and copyrighted by the Institute for Religious and Social Studies, New York, 1948.

THE CULTURAL APPROACH to any problem is by definition so wide and all embracing that each separate discussion which invokes it must, of necessity, limit itself. In this paper, I shall, arbitrarily and for purposes of this discussion only, treat communication as those activities in which one or more persons purposefully communicate with a group of other persons. In this way all the simple interrelationships of everyday life, as a mother calls her child, or a husband a wife, a dog is whistled to heel, or a horse urged on to a gallop, will be excluded. So also will the simple message, the notched stick or the knotted bit of bark which is sent from one individual New Guinea native or American Indian to another, or the drum beat in which a single household in Manus calls the father home from the lagoon fishing grounds. All of these are of course communication and the whole mesh of human social life might logically, and perhaps, in other contexts, fruitfully, be treated as a system of human communications. But the considerations advanced in this article will be addressed to the problems which are facing us today, specifically in mass communications, when the words or images fashioned professionally by one group of people are sent out to influence, persuade, or merely inform many times the number of those responsible for creating the original communication. Within this expanding field of activity, we may distinguish three smaller questions (1) the way in which communication systems are related to given cultural values, (2) the particular ethical problems of responsibility raised by our current use of communication systems, and (3) problems of communication when cultural boundaries have to be transcended.

SOME PRIMITIVE CONTRASTS

In any consideration of the way in which formal communications fit into the values of a given culture, records of primitive societies provide useful contrasts. Our knowledge of these small societies, in which the whole culture must be carried in the memories and habits of a few hundred persons, is much more detailed and exact than our knowledge of our own or other great civilizations. Furthermore, the great civilizations of which we do have any first hand knowledge are becoming more and more part of one great world culture, where comparable techniques of communication are—to a degree—producing increasing uniformities. Primitive societies which for many centuries have been isolated by land and water barriers and by their own ignorance of transportation, developed sharper contrasts, each to each. They provide ready-made examples from which it is possible to glimpse the diversity of ways in which the communicator and his audience have been institutionalized.

I shall discuss here three cultures in which I have worked [1] where the attitudes are exceedingly different; all three, however, come from the same part of the world, the Southwest Pacific. Other orders of contrast could be developed by examining material from other great areas of the world, North and South America, or Africa.

Among the Arapesh [2] people of New Guinea, communication is

[1] The sacrifice of the widest amount of available contrast by restricting illustration to one area of the world seems justified because, when an anthropologist attempts to organize field results around a new problem, this can be done much better against a background of intimate knowledge of the culture.

[2] For accounts of this culture see:

Margaret Mead, *Sex and Temperament in Three Primitive Societies* (New York: William Morrow and Company, 1935).

Margaret Mead (ed.), *Cooperation and Competition among Primitive Peoples* (New York: McGraw-Hill, 1937), chap. I, "The Arapesh of New Guinea."

Margaret Mead, "The Mountain Arapesh," Part I, "An Importing Culture," seen primarily as a matter of arousing the emotions of the audience. This small group of two to three thousand mountain people, who do not even have a name for the whole group who speak their language, live in steeply mountainous country, with hamlets perched precariously on razor back ridges and stiff climbs intervening between one man's garden and another. Food is scarce and land is poor, and the people spend a great deal of time moving about from garden to garden, sago patch to sago patch, or hunting in small groups in the deep bush. Any unexpected event is likely to find them widely scattered, and a system of calls, with linguistic peculiarities, and slit-gong beats are used to attract the attention of those at a distance, and to convey a little imperfect information. Among the Arapesh the clue to the relationship between any communicator and the group is given by the behavior of a man or woman with a headache, or some other slight ailment, a burn from a fire stick thrown by an exasperated husband or wife, a scratch got out hunting. Such suffering individuals wind their foreheads or other affected parts in bark or scarify them slightly or daub them with paint and then parade up and down the village, invoking sympathy. The situation in which the wound was obtained, or the headache contracted, is irrelevant, but each individual turns his own personal state into a matter for group emotional involvement. So ready is this response that even the narration of some hurt, a finger crushed long ago in an accident in some other land, brings out a chorus of expressive vocalizations from any group of listeners. The communicator indicates a state of feeling, the group responds with a state of feeling, and a minimum of information is conveyed.

When, among the Arapesh, some event of importance occurs, a birth or a death, a quarrel of proportions, the visit of a government patrol, or a recruiting European, or the passage through the village of a traveling party of strangers who bring trade and the possibility of sorcery into each community they visit, there are shouts and drum beats from hilltop to hilltop. But all that the signals convey is that something has happened about which the listeners had better be-

Anthropological Papers of the American Museum of Natural History, 36 (1938), 141-349.

Ibid., Part II, "Supernaturalism," 37 (1940), 319-451.

Ibid., Part III, "Socio-Economic Life," 40 (1947), 171-231.

Ibid., Part IV, "Diary of Events in Alitoa," 40 (1947), 233-419.

R. F. Fortune, *Arapesh* ("Publications of the American Ethnological Society," Vol. 19 [New York: J. J. Augustin, 1942]).

come excited. A furious drumming on one hilltop starts off a series of shouted queries in a relay system from hilltops nearer to each other, or a child or a woman is dispatched to find out what has happened. The listeners immediately set about guessing what all the excitement can be about, speculating rapidly as to who may be dead, or traveling, whose wife may have been abducted, or whose wife sorcerized. A dozen explanations may be introduced and, according as they appear plausible, the movements of all the listeners will be altered or not. If no one can think of a plausible reason for the commotion, most of the listeners are likely to set off in the direction of the sounds.

There is some slight attempt to differentiate drum beats, but so contrary is specificity to the cultural emphasis of the Arapesh, that the distinctions are always getting blurred. The point of communication is to excite interest and bring together human beings who will then respond, on the spot, with emotion, to whatever event has occurred. They will also, once gathered, bury the dead, set out to find the sorcerer, or reluctantly line up to fulfil the requests of the visiting government official. But all specificity of information about the event, and of behavior appropriate to the event, follows after the emotional response has gathered them together.

So, when a group of people are working on a house, some individual, not necessarily the owner of the house to be, will come and shout out to a group that rattan is needed. His voice emphasizes the need for people to listen and the need for somebody to do something about it. Sooner or later, someone will go and get some rattan, but the initial request, in most cases, does not directly set such a purposeful series of acts in motion.

Interestingly also, when people tell stories about past events, they tend to impute to the moment when the drum beat was heard from a distant hilltop, a full knowledge of what they learned only after they had responded to the drum beat. So, a narrator will say, "when he was returning from a journey inland and still far away he heard the gongs being beaten and he *knew* that his brother had taken his wife," although he finds out only after he has reached his own village, his steps quickened in response to the sound.

This treatment of communication in which a state of readiness of excitement, a mixture of fear, dread, anxiety, and pleasant expectation, is aroused before any information is given or any action sought, is obviously always a possible theme in any complex communication system, and one which is sometimes involved in our culture. Walter

Winchell's strong punctuation of his broadcast with the word *Flash*, any radio program in which a strong signal is used first to awaken the audience, has this element in it. Some of the possible implications of such a theme become evident when it is seen writ large in the culture of a people; such as the extraordinary lack of precision which characterizes Arapesh thinking, their short attention span, their tendency to substitute emotional congruity for any sort of logical construct when each communicator seeks to evoke first undifferentiated emotional response, and only then to sharpen and specify events and action sequences.

Among the lagoon-dwelling Manus [3] people of the Southern Coast of the Admiralty Islands, there is a very different emphasis. The Manus are a hard-headed, puritanical, trading people, interested in material things, in economic activity, in continuously purposive behavior. Where the Arapesh seldom count to a hundred and then with units of a low degree of abstraction, the Manus count into the hundred thousands. Where the Arapesh set a day for a ceremony, and as likely as not the ceremony takes place a day earlier, or a week later, the Manus announce their plans weeks in advance and carry them out. Where the Arapesh set up traps and snares in the bush and then wait until game falls into them, often even depending upon a dream to direct their footsteps back in the direction of the trap, the Manus make their principal catches of fish each month in a timed relationship to the tide. Action is stimulated in Manus, not by creating an atmosphere of warm interdependent responsiveness, but by setting up exact instigating situations—a prepayment, a loan, an advance—to which other individuals respond, under penalty of supernatural punishment from their own exacting ghostly guardians, and the potentially hostile ghostly guardians of other people. Exact, effective, properly timed action, which is physically and ethically appropriate, is what the Manus are interested in.

In such a culture, communications take a very different shape. There are a series of drum signals, which include formal openings

---

[3] For accounts of this culture see:

Margaret Mead, *Growing Up in New Guinea* (New York: William Morrow and Company, 1930).

Margaret Mead, *Cooperation and Competition among Primitive Peoples* (New York: McGraw-Hill, 1937), chap. VII, "The Manus of the Admiralty Islands," pp. 210-39.

Margaret Mead, "Kinship in the Admiralties," *Anthropological Papers of the American Museum of Natural History*, 34 (1934), 183-358.

R. F. Fortune, "Manus Religion," *Transactions of the American Philosophical Society*, Philadelphia, 1935.

which set the stage, not in terms of excitement but of content, so that a certain pattern of beats means: "I am about to announce the date at which I will give a feast." Then, an intellectual readiness to listen for a piece of relevant information being established, the drummer goes on to beat out the number of days before his feast, accurately, carefully, and the listeners count and take note. Each houseowner has a special pattern of beats which is his signature, the same beat that his household use to call him home. Between villages, careful tallies and other accurate mnemonic devices are used to convey the same sort of information.

The other characteristic form of communication in Manus is oratory, used in most cases angrily, as a stimulant to economic activity. Some of this is purely ceremonial hostility, the accompaniment of some large-scale economic transaction of display and exchange, but some of it is argumentative and situational. Men inveigh against their debtors and battle bitterly over details in the calculations. This sort of behavior in which actual items of the number of dog's teeth or jars of coconut oil are at stake confuses the clarity with which the Manus habitually operate. And it is signficant that as soon as my pencil and notebook entered the scene, people began to try to substitute my records for this angry, confusing welter of accusation and refutation, which they had lacked the techniques to prevent. The Manus prefer action in a well-defined context, under the spur of past careful definition reinforced by guilt, with anger introduced as stimulus in ways which will not compromise the accuracy of the operations. This attempt to keep thought and action clear of immediate emotion, but reinforced by unpleasant emotions, of anger and fear of the reproaches of their own consciences and supernatural punishments from their ghosts, runs through the formal communications of the society.

Bali,[4] which is not a primitive society because writing is known,

---

[4] Gregory Bateson, "Bali: A Value System of a Steady State," in *Social Structure: Studies Presented to A. R. Radcliffe Brown* (Oxford: The Clarendon Press, 1948).

J. Belo, "A Study of Customs Pertaining to Twins in Bali," *Tijdschrift voor Ind. Tall., Land., en Volkenkunde,* 75, no. 4 (1935), 483-549.

Margaret Mead, "Administrative Contributions to Democratic Character Formation at the Adolescent Level," in *Personality in Nature, Society and Culture,* Henry A. Murray and Clyde K. Kluckhohn, chap. 37, part III (New York: Alfred A. Knopf, 1948).

Gregory Bateson and Margaret Mead, "Balinese Character," *Special Publications II,* New York Academy of Sciences, 1942.

but is a society with a culture exceedingly different from our own and perhaps comparable in political and economic organization to the early Middle Ages in Europe, presents a quite different picture. The Balinese live in closely knit village communities, in which the citizens are bound together by a very great number of shared tasks, both ceremonial and economic. Each such community has its own traditional law which was respected by the Balinese feudal rulers in the past, and by their Dutch successors in the colonial period. Citizens, whose names are arranged in a series of rotas, share in the work necessary to maintain the elaborate irrigation system, keep up the roads, repair the numerous temples, provide the materials for offerings and prepare them for the gods, maintain forces of watchmen, town criers, messengers between the village and extra village authorities.

An intricate calendar of several systems of weeks which turns on itself like the cogs in several different sized wheels, governs the recurring series of ceremonial events, and systems of trance and possession give the necessary slight pushes to the calendrical system to provide for emergencies, stimulate a sluggish community, or slow down an excessively active one. Residence in a given village, location in a given place in the status system, as to caste, age, sex, and marital status, the day of the week, position on a rota of citizens, and occasional formal instigation of action by a diviner or seer, provide the framework within which each individual acts. There is no oratory, no exhortation, no preaching. A day or so before the ceremony in a village like Bajoeng Gede, the man whose turn it is to be town crier will go through the streets, announcing the coming feast, and specifying what each household is to contribute, e.g., "rice, a large measure, betel pepper leaves five, grated coconut, a level container full." He may further specify what those who are on duty that month will give, e.g., "two woven square packets, eight bundles of white cooked rice meal, eight bundles of cooked black rice meal, five small containers of rice, eight items of red sugar meal, and one hundred units of pork." He will announce which groups in the population, as the full male citizens, full female citizens, the boys' group, the girls' group, are to appear at the temple at what time and for what services.

The people do not have the burden of remembering from day to day what is to be done, for remembering is the assigned duty of special officials, most of whom take turns over the years. It is assumed that all that is needed is information about the correct behavior which will then, in most cases, be forthcoming. For those who fail to make their appropriate contribution, in work or offering materials, or fail to accept their share when the offerings are redivided among the participants—for in Bali there is small distinction between obligation and privilege—there are small fines, well within the resources of every citizen. If the fine is not paid, it mounts, and if the citizen is seen as unwilling to pay the fine, it mounts at a tremendous rate and the individual is virtually cut off from the community until it is paid. But neither to the man who fails to perform a single duty, nor to the man who refuses to pay his fine, nor even to those who have violated some fundamental tenet of the caste or religious system, is anger shown. The system is impersonal, unyielding, and unequivocal. Those who run up against the laws of one community may, in most cases, leave it, but their choice is between a no man's land of vagrancy, beggardom and thievery, and casual labor, and again becoming members of another community that has and enforces a different but equally stringent set of laws.

In this system the communicator, whether he be rajah, Dutch official, or village council (which contains all the full citizens of the village), acts as if the audience were already in a state of suspended, unemotional attention, and only in need of a small precise triggering word to set them off into appropriate activity. The stimuli are as simple as red and green lights in a well-regulated traffic situation, where no policeman is needed to reinforce the effortless, uninvolved stopping and starting of groups of cars, driven by men who accept the traffic signals as part of the world. Communications, even from the gods, when, through the mouth of a possessed person, instructions are given to renovate a temple, repay some old village obligation, combine two clubs, or regularize an irregular marriage, have all the impersonality of the voice which tells the telephoning American, "When you hear the signal, the time will be . . . ," or "United States Weather Bureau report for New York and vicinity, eight o'clock temperature forty-two degrees, . . ." The voice that tells the time does not include in its note an urgency about trains to catch or children to get off to school, roasts to come out of the oven, or cows to be milked. People dial the correct number to find out what time it is so that they may act appropriately. Such a system, carried to the lengths to which Balinese culture carries it, in which there is a very deep personal commitment to maintaining a continuity and a steady state, can be maintained with a lack of either expressed emotion or expressed effortfulness. The communicator states a position; the people, conditioned throughout their development to find safety and reassurance in following well-established routines in company with others, respond.

Description of the cultural setting of communication, such as these three from Arapesh, Manus, and Bali, could be multiplied to sharpen appreciation of the variety of themes and their implications which are involved in our own communications system. They serve to point up the very great number of ways in which communicator and communicator's intent, audience and audience's responses, may be institutionalized in different cultural systems, and also in different facets of the same cultural system. In our own society, it is possible to distinguish the communication methods which rely on arousing emotion first and slipping in suggestions for action only after the individual members of the audience are suffused with feeling, those which are concerned with giving accurate information which will lead to indicated action, those which are concerned merely with giving information upon which individuals may act.

THE PROBLEM OF RESPONSIBILITY IN COMMUNICATIONS

The great contemporary concern with communication problems must be laid not only to the enormous advance in technology and the resulting shrinking of the world into one potential communication system, with all the attendant difficulties of communication across cultural boundaries, but also to the increase in social awareness on the one hand, and the disintegration of the institutionalized centers of responsibility on the other. It is true that, through the centuries, expanding movements and nations have used various methods of propaganda[5] to advance their causes, to convert the unconverted, bring in line the recalcitrant, reconcile the conquered to their lot and the conquerors to their conquering role. It is also true that secular and religious hierarchies have consciously used these methods to advance their avowed and unavowed ends. But the addition of modern technological methods, by which the ownership of one radio station may decide the fate of a local revolution,

---

[5] Margaret Mead, "Our Educational Emphasis in Primitive Perspective," in *Education and the Cultural Process*, Charles S. Johnson (ed.). Papers presented at Symposium commemorating the 75th Anniversary of the founding of Fisk University, April-May, 1941. Reprinted from the *American Journal of Sociology*, 48 (May, 1943), 5-12.

and a single film or a single voice may reach the whole of the listening and watching world, has changed the order of magnitude of the whole problem.

At the same time development of social science is making it possible for communications to change their character. Instead of the inspired voice of a natural leader, whose zestful "We shall defend our Island, whatever the cost may be. We shall fight on the beaches, we shall fight on the landing ground, we shall fight in the fields and the streets, we shall fight in the hills; we shall never surrender . . . " galvanizing people to action, the appeals can be, to a degree, calculated and planned. Instead of the politician's hunch as to how some program is going over, polls and surveys can be used to bring back accurate information to the source of the propaganda and introduce a corrective. Theories of human nature which are no longer the inexplicit emphases of a coherent culture, but instead the partly rationalized, partly culturally limited formulations of psychological research, can be used as the basis of planned campaigns.[6]

The thinking peoples of the world have been made conscious, during the past quarter of a century, of the power of organized and controlled communication, glimpsing that power both from the point of view of the victim or "target" and of the victimizer, he who wields the powerful weapon. Dissection of the methods of the enemy, the conscious cultivation of an immunity against appeals to one's own emotion, desperate attempts to devise methods appropriate to a democracy, while we envied totalitarian propagandic controls, have all contributed to the growth of this consciousness in the United States.

But consciousness of the potential power of communication has peculiar implications in the United States, in a country where no institution, neither Church nor State, has any monopoly of the organs of communication. The American, during the past twenty-five years, has seen systems of propagandic control develop in other countries, and even when propagandic moves of extreme importance have actually been promoted within the United States, they have usually been phrased as inspired by Berlin or Tokyo, London or Moscow, rather than as the expression of American attitudes.

---

[6] Ernest Kris, "Some Problems of War Propaganda," *Psychoanalytic Quarterly,* 12, no. 3, 381-99 (for a discussion of the way in which Nazi propaganda methods drew upon LeBon's psychology of the crowd).

The local American emphasis has thus been on resisting high-powered communication pressures, and this has been congruent, not only with the Americans' fear of playing the sucker role *vis-à-vis* other nations, more skilled in international necromancy, but also with the great importance of advertising in the United States. Those European peoples which have felt the impact of modern totalitarian communications had as a background for the experience a past in which Church and State traditionally controlled and manipulated the symbols which could move men to feel and to act. The American on the other hand has experienced instead the manipulation of the same sorts of symbols, of patriotism, religious belief, and human strivings after perfection and happiness, by individuals and groups who occupied a very different and far less responsible place in the social hierarchy.

In our American system of communications, any interest, wishing to "sell" its products or message to the public, is able to use the full battery of available communication techniques, radio and film, press and poster. It is characteristic of this system that the symbols used to arouse emotion, evoke attention, and produce action, have come into the hands of those who feel no responsibility toward them. In a society like Bali there is simply no possibility that such a symbol as "The Village," also spoken of as "Mr. Village" and as "God Village," could be used by a casual vendor or rabble rouser. The symbols which evoke responses are used by those whose various positions in the society commit them to a responsible use. But in the United States, most of the value symbols of American tradition are ready to the hand of the manufacturer of the most trivial debased product, or the public relations counsel of the most wildcat and subversive organizations.

The American is used to experiencing the whole symbolic system of his society, in a series of fragmented and contradictory contexts. These beget in him a continually heightened threshold to any sort of appeal (with a recurrent nostalgia for a lost innocence in which his tears could flow simply or his heart swell with uncomplicated emotion) and a casual, non-evaluative attitude toward the power wielded through any communication system. As he straightens his tie and decides not to buy the tie which is being recommended over the radio, or in the street car ad, he gets a sense of immunity which makes him overlook the extent to which he is continually absorbing the ad behind the ad, the deutero[7] contexts of the material which he feels he is resisting.

We may examine the types of learning which result from the various uses of symbols in the United States in terms of: Whose symbol is used? What is the order of relationship between the symbol-possessing group and the group which is using the symbol? What is the nature of the product or message for which the symbol is being used? Who benefits by its use?

As examples of various types of symbol usage, let us consider the use of the symbol of Florence Nightingale, devoted ministrant to suffering and dying humanity. In the first position, a maker of white broadcloth might put out an advertisement which said, "In the great tradition of Florence Nightingale, American nurses are to be found ministering to the suffering. And, needing the very best, in order to fulfill their devoted mission, they use *Blank's* broadcloth for their uniforms, because it wears—through sickness and death." The reader of this advertisement learns that Florence Nightingale is a name to conjure with, that she was admired and respected, and that *Blank's* broadcloth are using her to enhance *their* prestige. To this degree the value of Florence Nightingale's name is increased. But at the same time the reader or listener may also add a footnote, "Trying to tie their old broadcloth on to Florence Nightingale's kite," and the sense of a synthetic, temporary quality of all symbol association is strengthened in his mind.

In the second case, the advocates of a dishonest correspondence course in nursing might use the name of Florence Nightingale in a plea to individuals to rise and follow the lamp once carried aloft by the great Nurse, and prepare themselves, in only twenty lessons, money down in advance, to follow in her footsteps. Here, to the extent that the listener realized that the correspondence course was phony, Florence Nightingale's name would also be shrouded with some of the same feeling of the phonyness, bedraggled and depreciated.

In the third case, a nurses' association might decide to put themselves back of a public education program in chest x-rays for tuberculosis control, and develop a poster in which they placed their

---

[7] For a discussion of the concept of deutero learning see Gregory Bateson, "Social Planning and the Concept of 'Deutero-Learning,'" *Science, Philosophy and Religion, 2nd Symposium,* Conference on Science, Philosophy and Religion, New York, 1942, pp. 81-97.

great symbol, Florence Nightingale, beside an appeal for support for the local anti-tuberculosis committee. The reader and listeners here recognize that Florence Nightingale is a great and valuable symbol, because those to whom she is a value symbol have themselves used her name to advance some newer and younger cause. This last type is of course characteristic of the historical use of symbols in society. Even when groups which represented religious or political subversion from the point of view of those in power have appropriated to themselves the sacred symbols of those against whom they were fighting, such moves have been made seriously and responsibly by those who believed that their subversion and their heresy were neither subversion nor heresy but political justice and religious truth. Symbols which change hands between orthodox and heterodox, between conservative and liberal, do not suffer by the change as long as each group of users acts responsibly. Instead such exchange is an invaluable ingredient of continuity and consistency within a changing society.

But the advertising agency, the public relations counsel, as institutionalized in our culture, has no responsibility of this sort. An advertising agency, whatever the personal sense of conscientious rectitude of its staff, has one set of functions to perform, to sell the product successfully while keeping within the law. With sufficient sophistication, a refusal to spoil the market, either for the same product in the future, or for other products, might be included within its functions. But our society has no higher jurisdiction to which such agencies owe allegiance. The regulations formulated by patriotic societies to protect the flag have to be respected, or you get into trouble. Religious symbols can be used only if you are sure the churches will not get in your hair. Claims must be muted to the sensitivities of the Pure Food and Drug Administration. If you expect to keep the contract a long time, do not overplay a line which may go sour. If you do not want trouble from your other clients, or other agencies, do not take too obvious a crack at other products or organizations or causes. It is upon such disjointed rules of thumb that the day-by-day manipulation of the responsiveness, the moral potential of the American people, depends.

The National Nutrition Program, administered under federal auspices during the war, was one interesting attempt to deal with this contemporary situation. Agreements were worked out by which advertisers were permitted to use the name of the National Nutrition Program, if, and only if, they acceded to certain conditions, the final ethical sanction for which came from the best scientific knowledge of nutritionists. Advertisers were not permitted to misquote, quote in part, or add to, the gist of the Nutrition theme which had been agreed upon, nor could they use it in association with products of no nutritional value. In spite of the many small expediencies which clouded the issues, this was a genuine attempt to supply an ethical sanction, rooted in science and administered by government, to a whole mass of communications on the subject of food and its uses. On a very simple level, this program represented one possible direction in which a country like the United States might move to give ethical form to the almost wholly unregulated mass of communications which now serve the interests of such a variety of groups—one way in which control can be vested in those to whom the symbol belongs.

A continuation of the present state of irresponsibility is exceedingly dangerous because it provides a situation within which steps backward rather than steps forward are so likely to occur. One possible response to the confused state of our symbolic system and the dulling of our responsiveness is an artificial simplification, a demand for the return of control to central authorities who will see to it that there is no more of the haphazard and contradictory use of important symbols. If the only choice open to us appears to be this increasing immunization against any appeal, this increasing apathy and callousness, so that photographs of a thousand murdered innocents no longer have any power to move us, the temptation to swing back to authoritarianism may become increasingly great. If, however, we can go on and formulate a system of responsibility appropriate to the age in which we live, a system which takes into account the state of technology, the type of mixed economy, the democratic aspirations, and the present dulled sensibilities of the American people, we may prevent such a reaction and, instead, move forward.

Any theory of the way in which responsibility for communications must be developed must deal with the problem of intent, with the beliefs that the communicator has about himself, and about his audience, as well as with the particular constitution and situation of that audience. This facet of the problem is particularly important in America, where the average citizen still identifies his position as a minority one, and so always thinks of power as wielded by THEM, and not by himself or a group to which he belongs. All discussions of the locations of responsibility for the communication stream, in any positive or constructive sense, are likely to stumble over this feeling that responsibility means power, and power is always in the hands of someone else. A set of negative controls, such as the rule that a radio station must discuss both sides of a situation, no matter how imperfectly and destructively each side is presented, is more congenial than any set of positive controls. So also were the teachings of propaganda analysis: the American felt safer in learning how not to respond to a false appeal than in permitting any effective development of appeals which would be so good that he would respond to them.

It therefore seems that it is important to arrive at a phrasing of responsibility which will meet this fear of misused power and develop an ethic of communications within a democracy such as ours. Once a climate of opinion expressing such an ethic begins to develop, appropriate institutional forms may be expected to emerge, either slowly or under intensive cultivation.

Such an ethic might take the form of an insistence that the audience be seen as composed of *whole* individuals, not artificial cutouts from crowd scenes, such as are represented on the dust jacket of a book[8] on radio. It might take the form of insisting that the audience be seen as composed of individuals who could not be manipulated but could only be appealed to in terms of their systematic cultural strengths. It might include a taboo on seeing any individual as the puppet of the propagandist, and focusing instead on the purposeful cultivation of directions of change. It would then be regarded as ethical to try to persuade the American people to drink orange juice, as a pleasant and nutritional drink, by establishing a style of breakfast, a visual preference for oranges, and a moral investment in good nutrition, but not by frightening individual mothers into serving orange juice for fear that they would lose their children's love, or their standing in the community.

Probably the closest analogue for the development of such sanctions can be found in medical ethics, legal ethics, etc., in which a group of self-respecting practitioners constitute themselves as a final court of appeal upon their own behavior. To the extent that advertising, public relations, market research, and the various communication media experts come to hold themselves and be held by

---

[8] Paul F. Lazarsfeld and Harry Field, *The People Look at Radio* (Chapel Hill: University of North Carolina Press, 1946).

the public in greater respect, such internally self-corrective systems might be developed.

If the contention is justified that democratic institutions represent a more complex integration of society, in which greater or different possibilities are accorded to each individual, we must expect corresponding differences between the communication ethics of societies representative of different degrees of feudalism and capitalism in different political combinations. The wholly feudal state may be said to have localized responsibility for communications within a hierarchical status system, and avoided the problem of power over individuals or trends by regarding that system as fixed and immutable. The totalitarian system which has lost the sanctions of feudalism and cannot depend upon the character structure of its citizens, develops monopolistic communication systems which seek to establish a direction in the society, but which in the interval are seen as operating on identified individuals, playing upon their most vulnerable points to bring them in line with a dictated policy. Whether it is claimed that the availability of concentration camps influence the propagandist or merely makes the audience members vulnerable, the interrelationship is there.

Political democracies have, to date, by insisting on negative sanctions, maintained systems in which the individual was the target of many sorts of propagandic themes but in which he was protected by the existence of contradictions in the appeals made to him. Such negative sanctions are better than none, but the target of American advertising is not a dignified human figure.[9] The target of political campaigns in the United States is not a dignified human figure. The limitation on the sense of power of the advertising agency copy writer or the campaign manager has merely been the knowledge that they were opponents in the field, free to act just as irresponsibly as he and free to present an equally contradictory and destructive set of counterappeals.

This negative approach is challenged whenever the country goes to war and wishes to mobilize its citizens toward common goals. It is doubly challenged when branches of the United States Army or the United States government are charged with the task of re-educating peoples who have lived under totalitarian regimes. The

[9] Constantin Fitz Gibbon, "The Man of Fear," *Atlantic Monthly* (January, 1947), 78-81.

resistance of the Germans,[10] for example, to the sort of protection of freedom which is implied in the cultivation of a two-party system, challenges American culture to the development of a more positive ethic.

[10] Bertram Schaffner, *Father Land, A Study of Authoritarianism in the German Family* (New York: Columbia University Press, 1948).

THE TWO-STEP FLOW OF COMMUNICATION[1]

BY ELIHU KATZ

Dr. Katz is on the faculty of sociology of the University of Chicago. This report on the status of the "two-step flow" hypothesis is reprinted from the *Public Opinion Quarterly* for Spring, 1957, by permission of the author and the journal, which is the copyright holder.

ANALYSIS OF THE PROCESS of decision-making during the course of an election campaign led the authors of *The People's Choice* to suggest that the flow of mass communications may be less direct than was commonly supposed. It may be, they proposed, that influences stemming from the mass media first reach "opinion leaders" who, in turn, pass on what they read and hear to those of their everyday associates for whom they are influential. This hypothesis was called "the two-step flow of communication."[2]

The hypothesis aroused considerable interest. The authors themselves were intrigued by its implications for democratic society. It was a healthy sign, they felt, that people were still most successfully persuaded by give-and-take with other people and that the influence of the mass media was less automatic and less potent than had been assumed. For social theory, and for the design of communications

---

[1] This is an abridged version of a chapter in the author's "Interpersonal Relations and Mass Communications: Studies in the Flow of Influence" (unpublished Ph.D. thesis, Columbia University, 1956). The advice and encouragement of Dr. Paul F. Lazarsfeld in the writing of this thesis are gratefully acknowledged.

[2] Paul F. Lazarsfeld, Bernard Berelson, and Hazel Gaudet, *The People's Choice* (New York: Columbia University Press, 1948; 2nd edition), p. 151.

research, the hypothesis suggested that the image of modern urban society needed revision. The image of the audience as a mass of disconnected individuals hooked up to the media but not to each other could not be reconciled with the idea of a two-step flow of communication implying, as it did, networks of interconnected individuals through which mass communications are channeled.

Of all the ideas in *The People's Choice*, however, the two-step flow hypothesis is probably the one that was least well documented by empirical data. And the reason for this is clear: the design of the study did not anticipate the importance which interpersonal relations would assume in the analysis of the data. Given the image of the atomized audience which characterized so much of mass media research, the surprising thing is that interpersonal influence attracted the attention of the researchers at all.[3]

In the almost seventeen years since the voting study was undertaken, several studies at the Bureau of Applied Social Research of Columbia University have attempted to examine the hypothesis and to build upon it. Four such studies will be singled out for review. These are Merton's study of interpersonal influence and communications behavior in Rovere;[4] the Decatur study of decision-making in marketing, fashions, movie-going, and public affairs, reported by Katz and Lazarsfeld;[5] the Elmira study of the 1948 election campaign reported by Berelson, Lazarsfeld, and McPhee;[6] and, finally, a very recent study by Coleman, Katz, and Menzel on the diffusion of a new drug among doctors.[7]

---

[3] For the discussion of the image of the atomized audience and the contravening empirical evidence, see Elihu Katz and Paul F. Lazarsfeld, *Personal Influence: The Part Played by People in the Flow of Mass Communications* (Glencoe, Illinois: The Free Press, 1955), pp. 15-42; Eliot Friedson, "Communications Research and the Concept of the Mass," *American Sociological Review*, 18 (1953), 313-17; and Morris Janowitz, *The Urban Press in a Community Setting* (Glencoe, Illinois: The Free Press, 1952).

[4] Robert K. Merton, "Patterns of Influence: A Study of Interpersonal Influence and Communications Behavior in a Local Community," in Paul F. Lazarsfeld and Frank N. Stanton (eds.), *Communications Research, 1948-49* (New York: Harper and Brothers, 1949), pp. 180-219.

[5] Katz and Lazarsfeld, *op. cit.*, Part Two.

[6] Bernard R. Berelson, Paul F. Lazarsfeld, and William N. McPhee, *Voting: A Study of Opinion Formation in a Presidential Campaign* (Chicago: University of Chicago Press, 1954).

[7] A report on the pilot phase of this study is to be found in Herbert Menzel and Elihu Katz, "Social Relations and Innovation in the Medical Profession," *Public Opinion Quarterly*, 19 (1955), 337-52; a volume and various articles on the full study are now in preparation.

These studies will serve as a framework within which an attempt will be made to report on the present state of the two-step flow hypothesis, to examine the extent to which it has found confirmation and the ways in which it has been extended, contracted, and reformulated. More than that, the studies will be drawn upon to highlight the successive strategies which have been developed in attempting to take systematic account of interpersonal relations in the design of communications research, aiming ultimately at a sort of "survey sociometry." Finally, these studies, plus others which will be referred to in passing, will provide an unusual opportunity to reflect upon problems in the continuity of social research.[8]

FINDINGS OF *The People's Choice*

The starting point for this review must be an examination of the evidence in the 1940 voting study which led to the original formulation of the hypothesis. Essentially, three distinct sets of findings seem to have been involved. The first had to do with *the impact of personal influence.* It is reported that people who made up their minds late in the campaign, and those who changed their minds during the course of the campaign, were more likely than other people to mention personal influence as having figured in their decisions. The political pressure brought to bear by everyday groups such as family and friends is illustrated by reference to the political homogeneity which characterizes such groups. What's more, on an average day, a greater number of people reported participating in discussion of the election than hearing a campaign speech or

---

[8] Other authors who have drawn upon the concepts of opinion leadership and the two-step flow of communication, and developed them further, are Matilda and John Riley, "A Sociological Approach to Communications Research," *Public Opinion Quarterly,* 15 (1951), 445-60; S. N. Eisenstadt, "Communications Processes Among Immigrants in Israel," *Public Opinion Quarterly,* 16 (1952), 42-58, and "Communication Systems and Social Structure: An Exploratory Study," *Public Opinion Quarterly,* 19 (1955), 153-67; David Riesman, *The Lonely Crowd* (New Haven: Yale University Press, 1950); Leo A. Handel, *Hollywood Looks at its Audience* (Urbana: University of Illinois Press, 1950). The program of research in international communications at the Bureau of Applied Social Research has given considerable attention to opinion leadership; see Charles Y. Glock, "The Comparative Study of Communications and Opinion Formation," *Public Opinion Quarterly,* 16 (1952-53), 512-23; J. M. Stycos, "Patterns of Communication in a Rural Greek Village," *Public Opinion Quarterly,* 16 (1952), 59-70; and the recent book by Daniel Lerner, *The Passing of Traditional Society.* Forthcoming studies by Peter H. Rossi and by Robert D. Leigh and Martin A. Trow are also concerned with the interplay of personal and mass media influences in local communities.

reading a newspaper editorial. From all of this, the authors conclude that personal contacts appear to have been both more frequent and more effective than the mass media in influencing voting decisions.[9]

The second ingredient that went into the formulation of the hypothesis concerned *the flow of personal influence.* Given the apparent importance of interpersonal influence, the obvious next step was to ask whether some people were more important than others in the transmission of influence. The study sought to single out the "opinion leaders" by two questions: "Have you recently tried to convince any one of your political ideas?", and "Has anyone recently asked you for your advice on a political question?" Comparing the opinion leaders with others, they found the opinion leaders more interested in the election. And from the almost even distribution of opinion leaders throughout every class and occupation, as well as the frequent mention by decision-makers of the influence of friends, co-workers, and relatives, it was concluded that opinion leaders are to be found on every level of society and presumably, therefore, are very much like the people whom they influence.[10]

A further comparison of leaders and others with respect to mass media habits provides the third ingredient: *the opinion leaders and the mass media.* Compared with the rest of the population, opinion leaders were found to be considerably more exposed to the radio, to the newspapers, and to magazines, that is, to the formal media of communication.[11]

Now the argument is clear: If word-of-mouth is so important, and if word-of-mouth specialists are widely dispersed, and if these specialists are more exposed to the media than the people whom they influence, then perhaps "ideas often flow from radio and print to opinion leaders and from these to the less active sections of the population."[12]

DESIGN OF THE VOTING STUDY

For studying the flow of influence as it impinges on the making of decisions, the study design of *The People's Choice* had several advantages. Most important was the panel method which made it

---

[9] Lazarsfeld, Berelson, and Gaudet, *op. cit.*, pp. 135-52.

[10] *Ibid.*, pp. 50-51.

[11] *Ibid.*, p. 51.

[12] *Ibid.*, p. 151.

possible to locate changes almost as soon as they occurred and then to correlate change with the influences reaching the decision-maker. Secondly, the unit of effect, the decision, was a tangible indicator of change which could readily be recorded. But for studying that part of the flow of influence which had to do with contacts among people, the study design fell short, since it called for a random sample of individuals abstracted from their social environments. It is this traditional element in the design of survey research which explains the leap that had to be made from the available data to the hypothesis of the two-step flow of communication.

Because every man in a random sample can speak only for himself, opinion leaders in the 1940 voting study had to be located by self-designation, that is, on the basis of their own answers to the two advice-giving questions cited above.[13] In effect, respondents were simply asked to report whether or not they were opinion leaders. Much more important than the obvious problem of validity posed by this technique is the fact that it does not permit a comparison of leaders with their respective followers, but only of leaders and non-leaders in general. The data, in other words, consist only of two statistical groupings: people who said they were advice-givers and those who did not. Therefore, the fact that leaders were more interested in the election than non-leaders cannot be taken to mean that influence flows from more interested persons to less interested ones. To state the problem drastically, it may even be that the leaders influence only each other, while the uninterested non-leaders stand outside the influence market altogether. Nevertheless, the temptation to assume that the non-leaders are the followers of the leaders is very great, and while *The People's Choice* is quite careful about this, it cannot help but succumb.[14] Thus, from the fact that the opinion leaders were more exposed to the mass

[13] Strictly speaking, of course, if a respondent reports whether or not he is a leader he is not speaking for himself but for his followers, real or imagined. Furthermore, it ought to be pointed out for the record that it is sometimes possible for a respondent to speak for others besides himself. The voting studies, for example, ask respondents to report the vote-intentions of other family members, of friends, of co-workers, though this procedure is of undetermined validity.

[14] There is an alternative procedure which is something of an improvement. Respondents can be asked not only whether they have given advice but whether they have taken advice. This was done in the Decatur and Elmira studies which are cited below. Thus the non-leaders can be classified in terms of whether or not they are in the influence market at all, that is, whether or not they are "followers."

media than the non-leaders came the suggestion of the two-step flow of communication; yet, manifestly, it can be true only if the non-leaders are, in fact, followers of the leaders.

The authors themselves point out that a far better method would have been based on "asking people to whom they turn for advice on the issue at hand and then investigating the interaction between advisers and advisees. But that procedure would be extremely difficult, if not impossible, since few of the related 'leaders' and 'followers' would happen to be included in the sample."[15] As will be shown immediately, this is perhaps the most important problem which succeeding studies have attempted to solve.

DESIGNS OF THREE SUBSEQUENT STUDIES

To this point, two aspects of the original statement of the two-step flow hypothesis have been reviewed. First of all, the hypothesis has been shown to have three distinct components, concerning respectively the impact of personal influence; the flow of personal influence; and the relationship of opinion leaders to the mass media. The evidence underlying each has been examined. Secondly, the design of the study has been recalled in order to point up the difficulty that arises from attempting to cope with the fundamentally new problem of incorporating *both* partners to an influence transaction into a cross-sectional study.

From this point forward, the major focus will turn to those studies that have succeeded *The People's Choice*. We will first report the different ways in which three of the four studies selected for review approached the problem of designing research on interpersonal influence.[16] Thereafter, the substantive findings of the several studies will be reviewed and evaluated so as to constitute an up-to-date report on the accumulating evidence for and against the hypothesis of the two-step flow of communication.

1. *The Rovere Study.* Undertaken just as the 1940 voting study was being completed, the earliest of the three studies was conducted in a small town in New Jersey. It began by asking a sample of 86 respondents to name the people to whom they turned for

---

[15] Lazarsfeld, Berelson, and Gaudet, *op. cit.*, pp. 49-50.

[16] The Elmira study will be omitted at this point because its design is essentially the same as that of the 1940 voting study except for the important fact that it obtained from each respondent considerably more information about the vote-intentions of others in his environment, the kinds of people he talks with, etc., than was done in *The People's Choice*.

information and advice regarding a variety of matters. Hundreds of names were mentioned in response, and those who were designated four times or more were considered opinion leaders. These influentials were then sought out and interviewed.[17]

Here, then, is the initial attempt, on a pilot scale, to solve the problem of research design posed by *The People's Choice*. To locate influentials, this study suggests, begin by asking somebody, "Who influences you?" and proceed from the persons influenced to those who are designated as influential.

Two important differences between this study and the 1940 voting study must be pointed out. First, there is a difference in the conception of opinion leadership. Whereas the voting study regards any advice-giver as an opinion leader if he influences even one other person (such as a husband telling his wife for whom to vote), the leaders singled out by the criterion employed in Rovere were almost certainly wielders of wider influence.

Secondly, the voting study, at least by implication, was interested in such questions as the extent of the role of interpersonal influence in decision-making and its relative effectiveness compared to the mass media. The Rovere study took for granted the importance of this kind of influence, and proceeded to try to find the people who play key roles in its transmission.

A final point to make in connection with the design of this study is that it makes use of the initial interviews almost exclusively to *locate* opinion leaders and hardly at all to explore the *relationships* between leaders and followers. Once the leaders were designated, almost exclusive attention was given to classifying them into different types, studying the communications behavior of the different types and the interaction among the leaders themselves, but very little attention was given to the interaction between the leaders and the original informants who designated them.

2. *The Decatur Study*, carried out in 1945–46, tried to go a step further.[18] Like the voting study, but unlike Rovere, it tried to account for decisions—specific instances in which the effect of various influences could be discerned and assessed. Like Rovere, but unlike the voting study, it provided for interviews with the persons whom individuals in the initial sample had credited as influential in the making of recent decisions (in the realms of marketing, movie-

---

[17] Merton, *op. cit.*, pp. 184-85.

[18] Katz and Lazarsfeld, *op. cit.*, Part Two.

going, and public affairs). The focus of the study this time was not on the opinion leaders alone, but (1) on the relative importance of personal influence and (2) on the person who named the leader as well as the leader—the advisor-advisee dyad.

Ideally, then, this study could ask whether opinion leaders tended to be from the same social class as their followers or whether the tendency was for influence to flow from the upper classes downward. Were members of the dyads likely to be of the same age, the same sex, etc.? Was the leader more interested in the particular sphere of influence than his advisee? Was he more likely to be exposed to the mass media?

Just as the dyad could be constructed by proceeding from an advisee to his adviser, it was also possible to begin the other way around by talking first to a person who claimed to have acted as an adviser, and then locating the person he said he had influenced. The Decatur study tried this too. Using the same kind of self-designating questions employed in the voting study, persons who designated themselves as influential were asked to indicate the names of those whom they had influenced. By "snowballing" to the people thus designated, there arose the opportunity not only to study the interaction between adviser and advisee but also to explore the extent to which people who designated themselves as influential were confirmed in their self-evaluations by those whom they allegedly had influenced. Proceeding in this way, the researchers hoped to be able to say something about the validity of the self-designating technique.[19]

The authors of *The People's Choice* had said that "asking people to whom they turn and then investigating the interaction between advisers and advisees . . . would be extremely difficult if not impossible." And, in fact, it proved to be extremely difficult. Many problems were encountered in the field work, the result of which was that not all the "snowball" interviews could be completed.[20]

---

[19] About two-thirds of the alleged influencees confirmed the fact that a conversation had taken place between themselves and the self-designated influential on the subject-matter in question. Of these, about 80 per cent further confirmed that they had received advice. The extent of confirmation is considerably less in the realm of public affairs than it is in marketing or fashion. *Ibid.*, pp. 149-61 and 353-62.

[20] Partly this was due to inability to locate the designated people, but partly, too, to the fact that original respondents did not always know the person who had influenced them as is obvious, for example, in the case of a woman copying another woman's hat style, etc. See *Ibid.*, pp. 362-63.

In many parts of the analysis of the data, therefore, it was necessary to revert to comparisons of leaders and non-leaders, imputing greater influence to groups with higher concentrations of self-designated leadership. Yet, in principle, it was demonstrated that a study design taking account of interpersonal relations was both possible and profitable to execute.

But about the time it became evident that this goal was within reach, the goal itself began to change. It began to seem desirable to take account of chains of influence longer than those involved in the dyad; and hence to view the adviser-advisee dyad as one component of a more elaborately structured social group.

These changes came about gradually and for a variety of reasons. First of all, findings from the Decatur study and from the later Elmira study revealed that the opinion leaders themselves often reported that their own decisions were influenced by still other people.[21] It began to seem desirable, therefore, to think in terms of the opinion leaders of opinion leaders.[22] Secondly, it became clear that opinion leadership could not be viewed as a "trait" which some people possess and others do not, although the voting study sometimes implied this view. Instead, it seemed quite apparent that the opinion leader is influential at certain times and with respect to certain substantive areas by virtue of the fact that he is "empowered" to be so by other members of his group. Why certain people are chosen must be accounted for not only in demographic terms (social status, sex, age, etc.) but also in terms of the structure and values of the groups of which both adviser and advisee are members. Thus, the unexpected rise of young men to opinion leadership in traditional groups, when these groups faced the new situations of urbanization and industrialization, can be understood only against the background of old and new patterns of social relations within the group and of old and new patterns of orientation to the world outside the group.[23] Reviewing the literature of small group research hastened the formulation of this conception.[24]

---

[21] *Ibid.*, p. 318; Berelson, Lazarsfeld, and McPhee, *op. cit.*, p. 110.

[22] This was actually tried at one point in the Decatur study. See Katz and Lazarsfeld, *op. cit.*, pp. 283-87.

[23] See, for example, the articles by Eisenstadt, *op. cit.*, and Glock, *op. cit.*; the Rovere study, too, takes careful account of the structure of social relations and values in which influentials are embedded, and discusses the various avenues to influentiality open to different kinds of people.

[24] Reported in Part I of Katz and Lazarsfeld, *op. cit.*

One other factor shaped the direction of the new program as well. Reflecting upon the Decatur study, it became clear that while one could talk about the role of various influences in the making of fashion *decisions by individuals,* the study design was not adequate for the study of fashion in the aggregate—*fashion as a process of diffusion*—as long as it did not take account of either the content of the decision or the time factor involved. The decisions of the "fashion changers" studied in Decatur might have cancelled each other out; while Mrs. X reported a change from Fashion A to Fashion B, Mrs. Y might have been reporting a change from B to A. What is true for fashion is true for any other diffusion phenomenon: to study it, one must trace the flow of some specific item over time. Combining this interest in diffusion with that of studying the role of more elaborate social networks of communication gave birth to a new study which focused on (1) a specific item, (2) diffusion over time, (3) through the social structure of an entire community.

3. *The Drug Study.* This study was conducted to determine the way in which doctors make decisions to adopt new drugs. This time, when it came to designing a study which would take account of the possible role of interpersonal influence among physicians, it became clear that there were so few physicians (less than one and one-half per 1,000 population) that it was feasible to interview all members of the medical profession in several cities. If all doctors (or all doctors in specialities concerned with the issue at hand) could be interviewed, then there would be no doubt that all adviser-advisee pairs would fall within the sample. All such pairs could then be located within the context of larger social groupings of doctors, which could be measured by sociometric methods.

Doctors in the relevant specialties in four midwestern cities were interviewed. In addition to questions on background, attitudes, drug-use, exposure to various sources of information and influence, and the like, each doctor was also asked to name the three colleagues he saw most often socially, the three colleagues with whom he talked most frequently about cases, and the three colleagues to whom he looked for information and advice.[25]

In addition to the opportunity of mapping the networks of interpersonal relations, the drug study also provided for the two other

---

[25] See footnote 7.

factors necessary for a true diffusion study: attention to a specific item in the course of gaining acceptance, and a record of this diffusion over time. This was accomplished by means of an audit of prescriptions on file in the local pharmacies of the cities studied, which made it possible to date each doctor's earliest use of a particular new drug—a drug which had gained widespread acceptance a few months before the study had begun. Each doctor could thus be classified in terms of the promptness of his decision to respond to the innovation, and in terms of other information provided by the prescription audit.

Altogether, compared with the earlier studies, the drug study imposes a more objective framework—both psychological and sociological—on the decision. First of all, the decision-maker himself is not the only source of information concerning his decision. Objective data from the prescription record are used as well. Secondly, the role of different influences is assessed not only on the basis of the decision-maker's own reconstruction of the event, but also on the basis of objective correlations from which inferences concerning the flow of influence can be drawn. For example, doctors who adopted the new drug early were more likely to be participants in out-of-town medical specialty meetings than those who adopted it later.

Similarly, it is possible to infer the role of social relations in doctor's decision-making not only from the doctor's own testimony concerning the role of social influences but also from the doctor's "location" in the interpersonal networks mapped by the sociometric questions. Thus, on the basis of sociometric data, it is possible to classify doctors according to their integration into the medical community, or the degree of their influence, as measured by *the number of times* they are named by their colleagues as friends, discussion-partners, and consultants. They can also be classified according to their membership in one or another network or clique, as indicated by *who* names them. Using the first measure makes it possible to investigate whether or not the more influential doctors adopt a drug earlier than those who are less influential. From the second kind of analysis one can learn, for example, whether or not those doctors who belong to the same sub-groups have similar drug-use patterns. In this way, it becomes possible to weave back and forth between the doctor's own testimony about his decisions and the influences involved, on the one hand, and the more objective record of his decisions and of the influences to which he has been exposed, on the other hand.

Note that the networks of social relations in this study are mapped "prior" to the introduction of the new drug being studied, in the sense that friendship, consultation, and so on, are recorded independently of any particular decision the doctor has made. The study is concerned with the potential relevance of various parts of these sociometric structures to the transmission of influence. For example, it is possible to point to the parts of the structure which are "activated" upon the introduction of a new drug, and to describe the sequence of diffusion of the drug as it gains acceptance by individuals and groups in the community. While the Decatur study could hope to examine only the particular face-to-face relationship which had been influential in a given decision, the drug study can locate this relationship against the background of the entire web of *potentially* relevant relationships within which the doctor is embedded.

THE FINDINGS OF STUDIES SUBSEQUENT TO *The People's Choice*

Having examined the *designs* of these studies, the next step is to explore their *findings* insofar as these are relevant to the hypothesis about the two-step flow of communication. It will be useful to return to the three categories already singled out in discussing *The People's Choice:* (1) the impact of personal influence; (2) the flow of personal influence; and (3) opinion leaders and the mass media. Evidence from the three studies just reported, as well as from the 1948 Elmira study[26] and from others, will be brought together here; but in every case the characteristics of each study's design must be borne in mind in evaluating the evidence presented.

A. THE IMPACT OF PERSONAL INFLUENCE

1. *Personal and the Mass Media Influence.* The 1940 study indicated that personal influence affected voting decisions more than the mass media did, particularly in the case of those who changed their minds during the course of the campaign. The Decatur study went on to explore the relative impact of personal influences and the mass media in three other realms: marketing, fashions, and movie-going. Basing its conclusions on the testimony of the decision-makers themselves, and using an instrument for evaluating the rela-

---

[26] Berelson, Lazarsfeld, and McPhee, *op. cit.*

tive effectiveness of the various media which entered into the decisions, the Decatur study again found that personal influence figured both more frequently and more effectively than any of the mass media.[27]

In the analysis to date, the drug study has not approached the problem of the relative effectiveness of the various media from the point of view of the doctor's own reconstruction of what went into the making of his decision. Comparing mere frequency of mention of different media, it is clear that colleagues are by no means the most frequently mentioned source. Nevertheless, exploration of the factors related to whether the doctor's decision to adopt the drug came early or late indicates that the factor most strongly associated with the time of adoption of the new drug is the extent of the doctor's integration in the medical community. That is, the more frequently a doctor is named by his colleagues as a friend or a discussion partner, the more likely he is to be an innovator with respect to the new drug. Extent of integration proves to be a more important factor than any background factor (such as age, medical school, or income of patients), or any other source of influence (such as readership of medical journals) that was examined.

Investigation of why integration is related to innovation suggests two central factors: (1) interpersonal communication—doctors who are integrated are more in touch and more up-to-date; and (2) social support—doctors who are integrated feel more secure when facing the risks of innovation in medicine.[28] Thus the drug study, too, provides evidence of the strong impact of personal relations— even in the making of scientific decisions.

2. *Homogeneity of Opinion in Primary Groups.* The effectiveness of interpersonal influence, as it is revealed in the studies under review, is reflected in the homogeneity of opinions and actions in primary groups. The medium of primary group communication is, by definition, person-to-person. Both of the voting studies indicate the high degree of homogeneity of political opinion among members of the same families and among co-workers and friends. The effectiveness of such primary groups in pulling potential deviates back into line is demonstrated by the fact that those who changed their vote intentions were largely people who, early in the cam-

---

[27] Katz and Lazarsfeld, *op. cit.*, pp. 169-86.

[28] On the relationship between social integration and self-confidence in a work situation, see Peter M. Blau, *The Dynamics of Bureaucracy* (Chicago: University of Chicago Press, 1955), pp. 126-29.

paign, had reported that they intended to vote differently from their family or friends.[29]

The drug study, too, was able to examine the extent of homogeneity in the behavior of sociometrically related doctors, and was able to demonstrate that there were situations where similar behavior could be deserved. For example, it was found that, when called upon to treat the more puzzling diseases, doctors were likely to prescribe the same drug as their sociometric colleagues. The study also showed that, very early in the history of a new drug, innovating doctors who were sociometrically connected tended to adopt the new drug at virtually the same time. This phenomenon of homogeneity of opinion or behavior among interacting individuals confronting an unclear or uncertain situation which calls for action has often been studied by sociologists and social psychologists.[30]

3. *The Various Roles of the Media.* The 1940 voting study explored some of the reasons why personal influence might be expected to be more influential in changing opinions than the mass media: It is often non-purposive; it is flexible; it is trustworthy. It was suggested that the mass media more often play a reinforcing role in the strengthening of predispositions and of decisions already taken. Nevertheless, it was assumed that the various media and personal influence are essentially competitive, in the sense that a given decision is influenced by one *or* the other. The Decatur study tended toward this assumption too, but at one point the study does attempt to show that different media play different parts in the decision-making process and take patterned positions in a sequence of several influences. The drug study elaborates on the roles of the media even further, distinguishing between media that "inform" and media that "legitimate" decisions. Thus in doctors' decisions, professional media (including colleagues) seem to play a legitimating role, while commercial media play an informing role.

B. THE FLOW OF PERSONAL INFLUENCE

The 1940 voting study found that opinion leaders were not concentrated in the upper brackets of the population but were located in almost equal proportions in every social group and stratum. This

---

[29] Lazarsfeld, Berelson, and Gaudet, *op. cit.,* pp. 137-45; Berelson, Lazarsfeld, and McPhee, *op. cit.,* pp. 94-101, 120-22.

[30] That men, faced with an unstructured situation, look to each other to establish a "social reality" in terms of which they act, is a central theme in the work of Durkheim, Kurt Lewin, and his disciples, H. S. Sullivan ("consensual validation"), and in the studies of Sherif, Asch, and others.

finding led to efforts in subsequent studies to establish the extent to
which this was true in areas other than election campaigns and also
to ascertain what it is that *does* distinguish opinion leaders from
those whom they influence.

The first thing that is clear from the series of studies under review is that the subject matter concerning which influence is transmitted has a lot to do with determining who will lead and who
follow. Thus, the Rovere study suggests that within the broad sphere
of public affairs one set of influentials is occupied with "local" affairs
and another with "cosmopolitan" affairs.[31] The Decatur study suggests that in marketing, for example, there is a concentration of
opinion leadership among older women with larger families, while
in fashions and movie-going it is the young, unmarried girl who
has a disproportionate chance of being turned to for advice. There
is very little overlap of leadership: a leader in one sphere is not
likely to be influential in another unrelated sphere as well.[32]

Yet, even when leadership in one or another sphere is heavily
concentrated among the members of a particular group—as was
the case with marketing leadership in Decatur—the evidence suggests that people still talk, most of all, to others like themselves.
Thus, while the marketing leaders among the older "large-family
wives" also influenced other kinds of women, most of their influence
was directed to women of their own age with equally large families.
In marketing, fashions, and movie-going, furthermore, there was
no appreciable concentration of influentials in any of the three socio-
economic levels. Only in public affairs was there a concentration
of leadership in the highest status, and there was some slight evidence that influence flows from this group to individuals of lower
status. The Elmira study also found opinion-leaders in similar
proportions on every socio-economic and occupational level and
found that conversations concerning the campaign went on, typically, between people of similar age, occupation, and political
opinion.

What makes for the concentration of certain kinds of opinion
leadership within certain groups? And when influential and influencee are outwardly alike—as they so often seem to be—what,
if anything, distinguishes one from the other? Broadly, it appears
that influence is related (1) to the *personification of certain values*

---

[31] Merton, *op. cit.*, pp. 187-88.

[32] For a summary of the Decatur findings on the flow of interpersonal influence, see Katz and Lazarsfeld, *op. cit.*, pp. 327-34.

(who one is); (2) to *competence* (what one knows); and (3) to *strategic social location* (whom one knows). Social location, in turn, divides into whom one knows within a group; and "outside."

Influence is often successfully transmitted because the influencee wants to be as much like the influential as possible.[33] That the young, unmarried girls are fashion leaders can be understood easily in a culture where youth and youthfulness are supreme values. This is an example where "who one is" counts very heavily.

But "what one knows" is no less important.[34] The fact is that older women, by virtue of their greater experience, are looked to as marketing advisers and that specialists in internal medicine—the most "scientific" of the practicing physicians—are the most frequently mentioned opinion leaders among the doctors. The influence of young people in the realm of movie-going can also be understood best in terms of their familiarity with the motion picture world. The Elmira study found slightly greater concentrations of opinion leadership among the more educated people on each socio-economic level, again implying the importance of competence. Finally, the influence of the "cosmopolitans" in Rovere rested on the presumption that they had large amounts of information.

It is, however, not enough to be a person whom others want to emulate, or to be competent. One must also be accessible. Thus, the Decatur study finds gregariousness—"whom one knows"—related to every kind of leadership. The Rovere study reports that the leadership of the "local" influentials is based on their central location in the web of interpersonal contacts. Similarly, studies of rumor transmission have singled out those who are "socially active" as agents of rumor.[35]

Of course, the importance of whom one knows is not simply a matter of the number of people with whom an opinion leader is in contact. It is also a question of whether the people with whom he is in touch happen to be interested in the area in which his leadership is likely to be sought. For this reason, it is quite clear that the

---

[33] That leaders are, in a certain sense, the most conformist members of their groups—upholding whatever norms and values are central to the group—is a proposition which further illustrates this point. For an empirical illustration from a highly relevant study, see C. Paul Marsh, and A. Lee Coleman, "Farmers' Practice Adoption Rates in Relation to Adoption Rates of Leaders," *Rural Sociology*, 19 (1954), 180-83.

[34] The distinction between "what" and "whom" one knows is used by Merton, *op. cit.*, p. 197.

[35] Gordon W. Allport and Leo J. Postman, *The Psychology of Rumor* (New York: Henry Holt, 1943), p. 183.

greater interest of opinion leaders in the subjects over which they exert influence is not a sufficient explanation of their influence. While the voting studies as well as the Decatur study show leaders to be more interested, the Decatur study goes on to show that interest alone is not the determining factor.[36] In fashion, for example, a young unmarried girl is considerably more likely to be influential than a matron with an equally great interest in clothes. The reason, it is suggested, is that a girl who is interested in fashion is much more likely than a matron with an equally high interest to know other people who share her preoccupation, and thus is more likely than the matron to have followers who are interested enough to ask for her advice. In other words, it takes two to be a leader—a leader and a follower.

Finally, there is the second aspect of "whom one knows." An individual may be influential not only because people within his group look to him for advice but also because of whom he knows outside his group.[37] Both the Elmira and Decatur studies found that men are more likely than women to be opinion leaders in the realm of public affairs and this, it is suggested, is because they have more of a chance to get outside the home to meet people and talk politics. Similarly, the Elmira study indicated that opinion leaders belonged to more organizations, more often knew workers for the political parties, and so on, than did others. The drug study found that influential doctors could be characterized in terms of such things as their more frequent attendance at out-of-town meetings and the diversity of places with which they maintained contact, particularly faraway places. It is interesting that a study of the farmer-innovators responsible for the diffusion of hybrid seed corn in Iowa concluded that these leaders also could be characterized in terms of the relative frequency of their trips out of town.[38]

---

[36] Katz and Lazarsfeld, op. cit., pp. 249-52.

[37] It is interesting that a number of studies have found that the most integrated persons within a group are also likely to have more contacts outside the group than others. One might have expected the more marginal members to have more contacts outside. For example, see Blau, op. cit., p. 128.

[38] Bryce Ryan and Neal Gross, Acceptance and Diffusion of Hybrid Seed Corn in Two Iowa Communities (Ames, Iowa: Iowa State College of Agriculture and Mechanic Arts, Research Bulletin 372), pp. 706-7. For a general summary, see Ryan and Gross, "The Diffusion of Hybrid Seed Corn in Two Iowa Communities," Rural Sociology, 8 (1942), 15-24. An article, now in preparation, will point out some of the parallels in research design and in findings between this study and the drug study.

The third aspect of the hypothesis of the two-step flow of communication states that opinion leaders are more exposed to the mass media than are those whom they influence. In *The People's Choice* this is supported by reference to the media behavior of leaders and non-leaders.

The Decatur study corroborated this finding, and went on to explore two additional aspects of the same idea.[39] First of all, it was shown that leaders in a given sphere (fashions, public affairs, etc.) were particularly likely to be exposed to the media appropriate to that sphere. This is essentially a corroboration of the Rovere finding that those who proved influential with regard to "cosmopolitan" matters were more likely to be readers of national news magazines, but that this was not at all the case for those influential with regard to "local" matters. Secondly, the Decatur study shows that at least in the realm of fashions, the leaders are not only more exposed to the mass media, but are also more affected by them in their own decisions. This did not appear to be the case in other realms, where opinion leaders, though more exposed to the media than non-leaders, nevertheless reported personal influence as the major factor in their decisions. This suggests that in some spheres considerably longer chains of person-to-person influence than the dyad may have to be traced back before one encounters any decisive influence by the mass media, even though their contributory influence may be perceived at many points. This was suggested by the Elmira study too. It found that the leaders, though more exposed to the media, also more often reported that they sought information and advice from other persons.[40]

Similarly, the drug study showed that the influential doctors were more likely to be readers of a large number of professional journals and valued them more highly than did doctors of lesser influence. But at the same time, they were as likely as other doctors to say that local colleagues were an important source of information and advice in their reaching particular decisions.

Finally, the drug study demonstrated that the more influential doctors could be characterized by their greater attention not only to medical journals, but to out-of-town meetings and contacts as

[39] Katz and Lazarsfeld, *op. cit.*, pp. 309-20.
[40] Berelson, Lazarsfeld, and McPhee, *op. cit.*, p. 110.

well. This finding has already been discussed in the previous section treating the *strategic location* of the opinion leader with respect to "the world outside" his group. Considering it again under the present heading suggests that the greater exposure of the opinion leader to the mass media may only be a special case of the more general proposition that opinion leaders serve to relate their groups to relevant parts of the environment through whatever media happen to be appropriate. This more general statement makes clear the similar functions of big city newspapers for the Decatur fashion leader; of national news magazines for the "cosmopolitan" influentials of Rovere; of out-of-town medical meetings for the influential doctor; and of contact with the city for the farmer-innovator in Iowa[41] as well as for the newly-risen, young opinion leaders in underdeveloped areas throughout the world.[42]

CONCLUSIONS

Despite the diversity of subject matter with which they are concerned, the studies reviewed here constitute an example of continuity and cumulation both in research design and theoretical commitment. Piecing together the findings of the latter-day studies in the light of the original statement of the two-step flow hypothesis suggests the following picture.

Opinion leaders and the people whom they influence are very much alike and typically belong to the same primary groups of family, friends, and co-workers. While the opinion leader may be more interested in the particular sphere in which he is influential, it is highly unlikely that the persons influenced will be very far behind the leader in their level of interest. Influentials and influencees may exchange roles in different spheres of influence. Most spheres focus the group's attention on some related part of the world outside the group, and it is the opinion leader's function to bring the group into touch with this relevant part of its environment through whatever media are appropriate. In every case, influentials have been found to be more exposed to these points of contact with the outside world. Nevertheless, it is also true that, despite their

---

[41] Ryan and Gross, *op. cit.,* choose to explain "trips to the city" not so much as a source of influence but rather as another index of the non-traditional orientation of which innovation itself is also an index. The drug study, on the other hand, argues that out-of-town meetings, trips to out-of-town centers, etc., are key sources of advice for innovating and influential physicians.

[42] See Lerner's *The Passing of Traditional Society,* cited above.

greater exposure to the media, most opinion leaders are primarily affected not by the communication media but by still other people.

The main emphasis of the two-step flow hypothesis appears to be on only one aspect of interpersonal relations—interpersonal relations as channels of communication. But from the several studies reviewed, it is clear that these very same interpersonal relations influence the making of decisions in at least two additional ways. In addition to serving as networks of communication, interpersonal relations are also sources of pressure to conform to the group's way of thinking and acting, as well as sources of social support. The workings of group pressure are clearly evident in the homogeneity of opinion and action observed among voters and among doctors in situations of unclarity or uncertainty. The social support that comes from being integrated in the medical community may give a doctor the confidence required to carry out a resolution to adopt a new drug. Thus, interpersonal relations are (1) channels of information, (2) sources of social pressure, and (3) sources of social support, and each relates interpersonal relations to decision-making in a somewhat different way.[43]

The central methodological problem in each of the studies reviewed has been how to take account of interpersonal relations and still preserve the economy and representativeness which the random, cross-sectional sample affords. Answers to this problem range from asking individuals in the sample to describe the others with whom they interacted (Elmira), to conducting "snowball" interviews with influential-influencee dyads (Decatur), to interviewing an entire community (drug study). Future studies will probably find themselves somewhere in between. For most studies, however, the guiding principle would seem to be to build larger or smaller social molecules around each individual atom in the sample.[44]

[43] These different dimensions of interpersonal relations can be further illustrated by reference to studies which represent the "pure type" of each dimension. Studies of rumor flow illustrate the "channels" dimension; see, for example, Jacob L. Moreno, *Who Shall Survive* (Beacon, N. Y.: Beacon House, 1953), pp. 440-50. The study by Leon Festinger, Stanley Schachter, and Kurt Back, *Social Pressures in Informal Groups* (New York: Harper and Bros., 1950), illustrates the second dimension. Blau, *op. cit.*, pp. 126-29, illustrates the "social support" dimension.

[44] Various ways of accomplishing this have been discussed in a staff seminar on "relational analysis" at the Bureau of Applied Social Research. The recent study by Seymour M. Lipset, Martin A. Trow, and James S. Coleman, *Union Democracy* (Glencoe, Ill.: The Free Press, 1956), illustrates one approach in its study of printers within the varying social contexts of the shops in which they are employed. The study by Riley and Riley, *op. cit.*, is another good example.

THE CONTENT OF MASS COMMUNICATIONS

WHAT ARE the mass media saying to us? This is not a new question, nor is the study of content a new study, but the full social importance of content study has been realized only since the voice of mass communication became so loud and so pervasive.

Think back to what mass communications must have been like in, say, 1843 when the first telegraph line was built in this country. Newspapers, then, were tiny sheets, with little foreign news, and that very old. Magazines were few. Books were read by comparatively few people. There were no news agencies to cover the world's news for us. There was no rapid nation-wide delivery of periodicals. There was no motion picture, no radio, no television, to fill up our leisure hours with news and entertainment.

In the intervening years we have filled the air with sound, the newsstands and bookstores with print, and the time with expertly packaged messages from one mass medium or the other. We are directly connected to the theaters, the concert halls, the studios, the universities, and the newsgathering centers of the world. We are not at all surprised by a television program in which a topic is discussed by four men, on two sides of an ocean. We are rather irate if news of a battle 10,000 miles away comes to us a few hours late. We are not especially grateful to be invited to see in our living rooms a football game played on the other side of the continent, but likely to be critical of the network for not selecting *another* game.

But this very proliferation of opportunity has raised some disturbing questions. Our system requires that we have full, fair, and accurate information on political issues, and especially on candidates for office. Is this being provided? For example, it is undoubtedly true that a much larger group of newspapers are now Republican than are Democratic in their editorial policy. This is their right and privilege, but does their politics reflect itself in their news handling? The backers of Adlai Stevenson charged that their candidate did not get fair coverage in 1952. Senator Robert Taft charged in a memorandum recently disclosed that the majority of the newspapers and all the big magazines were for his primary opponent, Mr. Eisenhower, and that he stood no chance against that kind of opposition. These are serious charges, if true. But are they really true?

Take another example. A number of parents and social critics have been worried over the possible influence of television on children. What kind of myths, what kind of heroes, is television adding to the national tradition? Is television, for instance, teaching that a quick trigger finger is the only way to insure justice? Are programs too full of violence? Are they too low in level? What kinds of standards are they holding up to public taste? Obviously, the first step in answering such questions as these has to be a careful content study.

The study of content is not new, as we have indicated, but only since the late 30's have a group of scholars, largely motivated by Harold D. Lasswell, begun to try to answer mass media content questions scientifically, rather than impressionistically.

The following section contains some hard facts on the content of the media. It begins with Dean Mott's analysis of changes in newspaper content during thirty years. There follows an analysis of themes and plots in motion pictures. Rudolf Arnheim reports on the contents of daytime serial programs, and Messrs. Heine and Gerth on changing values in periodical fiction. Then come a number of tables which supplement what has been said about radio content, and fill in a picture of television content—in addition, providing an idea of what types of content are liked by the great masses of people. Finally, for convenience we reprint the "devices of propaganda" made famous by the Institute for Propaganda Analysis, and the much used and discussed formula of Dr. Rudolf Flesch for measuring readability.

TRENDS IN NEWSPAPER CONTENT

BY FRANK LUTHER MOTT

Frank Luther Mott is dean emeritus of the School of Journalism of the University of Missouri. His article is reprinted from the *Annals of the American Academy of Political and Social Science,* January, 1942, by permission of the author and the Academy, which holds copyright.

THE PUBLISHER is a merchant, and the editorial art is largely one of merchandising, as respects general newspaper content. In taking a position on a public issue, the editor and the publisher may be, to a certain extent and under certain conditions, individualists; but in providing the general menu spread in the 75 to 225 nonadvertising columns of a metropolitan daily, editors and publishers attempt to provide, as closely as possible, satisfaction for the desires and tastes of what they conceive to be their proper reader audiences.

Occasional newspaper failures testify that mistakes are sometimes made in this catering business, but the upward curve of aggregate circulations is evidence of the skill of newspaper makers in answering faithfully to the wishes of readers. The old "able editor," himself a part of the social group for which he prepared his paper, and united to it by economic, political, and institutional backgrounds and training, believed that he knew through a sixth sense what his readers wanted; and since he himself felt the same desires and responded to the same symbols, this was often true enough. But in a more complicated society, modern techniques for the study of reader interests have afforded helpful guidance. Even editors who are somewhat contemptuous of such supposedly "theoretical" devices are affected by them through their imitation of the successes of those who are less cynical, for imitation of successful newspaper practices is the oldest and most consistent secondary cause of general newspaper trends.

The existence of wide divergences in what has been called the socialization index[1] of a newspaper signifies only that reader audiences are different. The *New York Times,* the *New York Mirror,* the *Baltimore Sun,* and the *Boston Post* are all edited alike for newspaper readers; but their audiences are found on different economic and intelligence levels. All of them are subject to the weekly referendum and recall offered when the delivery boy collects his money and his stops.

THE RELATIVE STABILITY OF NEWSPAPER CONTENT

This intimacy with the popular audience which is the essence of journalism gives newspaper content high validity as an index of social desires and responses. What a nation of newspaper readers wants to read and what it finds pleasure in reading are shown pretty definitely in a sympathetic journalism.

But the student who begins to analyze and measure newspapers to discover trends in content—and thereby trends in popular tastes and desires—soon finds that his percentages change but little from year to year. Apparently there are two reasons for this comparatively static condition. In the first place, basic desires are essentially static; and in the second place, when circulation holds up, it seems like tempting fate to change the offering. But beyond these considerations, it is undeniable that newspapers in general are fairly conservative in policy. In studying the history of the evolution of any new technique—say the comic strip or the front-page banner—one is impressed by the caution and slowness with which it was adopted. There are always experimenters, but the great bulk of newspapers are slow to change. The accompanying table indicates few striking changes.[2]

---

[1] Susan M. Kingsbury, Hornell Hart, and associates, "Measuring the Ethics of American Newspapers," *Journalism Quarterly,* X (June, 1933), 93-108.

[2] The table is presented with the following warnings against improper reading. The categories are not mutually exclusive; pictures, for example, are included under both Illustration and the category of the story illustrated. The averages represent measurements of ten prominent newspapers (excluding tabloids) in New York, Chicago, Philadelphia, Boston, and Baltimore for the first week of each year named. Measurement of additional weeks in other parts

Average Number of Columns Given Certain Categories of Content in Each Issue in Ten Leading Metropolitan Newspapers at the Beginnings of Four Decade Years, with Proportions in Decimals on the Base of Total Nonadvertising Space

	1910		1920		1930		1940	
	Cols.	Prop.	Cols.	Prop.	Cols.	Prop.	Cols.	Prop.
Foreign News and Features	2.4	.031	6.2	.088	6.8	.048	14.0	.079
Washington News	4.7	.061	5.0	.071	5.7	.040	10.6	.060
Columns Dealing with Public Affairs			.4	.006	1.0	.007	2.5	.014
Original Editorials	3.0	.039	2.8	.040	3.0	.021	3.1	.018
Business, Financial, Marine, etc.	16.0	.211	11.4	.160	53.2	.375	56.6	.320
Sports	7.1	.094	10.4	.146	18.2	.128	20.9	.118
Society	1.4	.019	1.8	.026	4.5	.032	6.4	.036
Women's Interests	1.1	.015	1.4	.020	2.3	.016	6.7	.038
Theater, Movies, Books, Art, etc.	2.2	.029	2.2	.031	4.4	.033	7.4	.042
Radio Announcements and News					2.5	.018	2.5	.014
Comic Strips and Singles..	.8	.010	2.0	.028	5.1	.036	10.8	.061
Illustration (excluding comics)	4.0	.054	4.0	.057	8.5	.060	19.8	.112

War and Foreign News

During the past hundred years of American journalism, booms in foreign news have generally accompanied European wars; and the same rule holds good today. But the interest in foreign affairs following the Spanish-American War was not a wartime boom; the United States then for the first time found itself a recognized world power, and the enthusiasm called forth by the watchword "expansion," as well as a new concern for our international relations and

of the year, and of other papers would doubtless result in modifications of these figures. Indeed, southern and western papers, and three other midwestern papers, as well as ten papers for the last week in August 1941, have been measured in order to furnish checks, and the results will be referred to in the ensuing discussion. It must be kept in mind that the figures tabulated have little value except as they indicate marked changes in the proportion of space given to different kinds of content, and even then the measurements have not been extensive enough to give exact statistics on the extent of the changes. It is doubtful if any set of measurements, however extensive, would be valuable for more than general indications, on account of the differences in newspapers and in newspaper fields as we get outside the full-sized metropolitan group, and the resulting difficulties in the correlation of heterogeneous data.

responsibilities and for the commerce which "follows the flag," all stimulated the gathering and publication of foreign news. Thus in the decade and a half before the World War the average metropolitan paper carried from one to six columns of foreign news daily. This tripled and quadrupled during the war, never again dropped to former levels, and went up again as the second world conflict developed. This is a normal and predictable trend, dependent largely on events and on the news itself.

Washington News

Washington news, always important in American papers, has been furnished to metropolitan dailies by their own special correspondents, in addition to other services, for more than a hundred years; and for the past twenty years, by certain syndicate columnists also. The figures representing the proportion that this category bears to the total nonadvertising content are perhaps less significant than the record of the number of columns of Washington news.[3] The number of columns averaged about five in metropolitan papers until the beginning of the first F. D. Roosevelt administration and the New Deal. Since then it has virtually doubled. True, the papers in the smaller cities of the South, Midwest, and West carry much less; but even they commonly have from three to five columns under Washington datelines.

And this does not include the public-affairs "columns" unless they actually bear the Washington dateline. This material, usually syndicated, became prominent at about the same time we note the increase of Washington correspondence—in 1932. In several papers measured, it now occupies more space than the paper's own editorials.

Editorials and Economic News

Original editorial matter has kept to about the same space in the years 1910–40. Meantime, the increase in the size of papers made its proportion to the whole in 1940 about half of what it was in 1910.

Business and financial news measurements disclose some interesting facts. Individual papers vary greatly in the amount and in the proportion of their space given to this type of material. In 1910 some

---

[3] The total number of nonadvertising columns for the 1910 and 1920 papers varied from 60 to 90, and for the 1930 and 1940 papers from 90 to 225. Thus the proportion is lower in 1930 and 1940, though the number of columns is greater.

New York and Chicago papers were devoting about one-fourth of their space to the business and finance section, and the general average of metropolitan papers for the week measured was 21 per cent. This large allotment of space had been common for several years, reflecting the interests in the expansive years preceding the panic of 1907 and the ensuing hard times. But by 1920 this space was much reduced, only to leap upward in the late twenties under the impulse of the universal interest in a far greater debacle than that of 1907. Some New York papers were giving 40 per cent of their nonadvertising space to the business and finance section in 1930. The *Times* was still doing so in January 1940, though most big papers had cut the proportion to about 30 per cent, which commonly meant at least 50 columns. With sizes of newspapers shrinking in 1941, on account of the advertising situation, and a general feeling that too much space was being assigned to this type of content, the proportion dropped from about one-third in January 1940 to about one-fourth in August 1941. Of course, outside of the financial centers the finance space drops sharply, 10 per cent and 15 per cent being common.

Sports News

The increase of sports news has been slow but steady over many years. From the first sports "departments" of the latter nineties, comprising three or four columns, there was a gradual growth to the point reached by 1910, when the average large paper had a full page of such matter. It was in the twenties that the most striking increase occurred; it continued in the thirties, and by 1940 the big papers were printing, on the average, twice as many columns of sports as they had twenty years earlier[4]—not twice as large a proportion of the total content, however; it appears that when the papers doubled in number of pages, they doubled the size of the sports section. This was only reasonable, since reader-interest surveys rated certain features of the sports sections higher (for men, at least) than anything else except the most striking news story, the comics, cartoons, and picture pages. Gate figures also show an increase in American interest in the more spectacular sports in these years—an increase caused largely by the newspapers themselves.

---

[4] Sports news has seasonal variations, and about one-fourth should be added to January totals in the accompanying table to get the proper figures for September.

Of Interest to Women

Society news and women's interests (household features, fashions, cookery, child training, gardens, and the like) have been strong Sunday features since Pulitzer's "new journalism" of the eighties; but not until the expansion in newspaper sizes in the 1930's did the papers carry, on the average, more than a column or two of society and a similar amount of women's interests in their daily editions. By 1940 they were carrying nearly a page of each, and a check in the summer of 1941 showed no falling off in these classes because of shrunken papers.

The Arts and Radio News

The "critical" departments of the papers, comprising reviews and notes on books, music, art, drama, and the movies, owe their increase largely to Hollywood news and publicity releases on motion pictures. So far as criticism proper is concerned, it has kept to about the same proportions in the large metropolitan papers for the past fifty years.

Papers began to publish the day's radio program in the late twenties; they have given about the same average space to that category consistently. It varies from nothing to as much as five columns in various papers, but averages two and a half columns daily, including news and releases of the radio world.

Comics and News Pictures

Since the first six-days-a-week comic strip in 1907, the vogue of this entertainment feature has increased by leaps and bounds. Nearly half the papers measured in 1910 carried no comic strips at all in their daily editions; others carried one on the sports page and perhaps another somewhere else. By 1920 the average amount of comics had more than doubled; and ten years later, when the reader-interest surveys were pointing out that more people read a favorite comic than any other definite thing in the newspaper, the average grew to five columns—which commonly meant five or six strips. In the next decade some evening papers began giving two full pages of comics daily, and the space in the ten papers measured in 1940 was double that of ten years before. Thus it will be observed that the comics have doubled in each decade following 1910.

News pictures occupied on an average of four columns each day for many years—from shortly after the turn of the century to the coming of the tabloids in the early twenties. The flood of pictures in the tabloids affected the full-sized papers, and those measured for 1930 showed more than double the amount of illustration of ten years before—though, to be sure, the papers had doubled in total number of columns. In the next decade came improvements in news photography, cheaper engraving methods, wire-photo, and the picture magazines. Readers seemed to go picture-crazy. The proportion of picture space in the full-sized papers nearly doubled by 1940; including the tabloids, the average proportion of total space given to pictures by metropolitan papers reached about one-third.[5]

THE MAJOR TRENDS IN CONTENT

It appears, then, that foreign news, Washington correspondence, and the financial section have shown in recent years increases which are significant chiefly as reflections of increased news interest; while the even more striking growth of comics and news illustration represents the development of new techniques in enlisting reader interest.

In 1896 Edwin Lawrence Godkin declared that news pictures were "childish,"[6] and he would have none of them in his *New York Evening Post*. The *Times* stood out against them until 1925; and it is still a standout against comics—a lonesome standout since the desertion of such papers as the *Kansas City Star* and *Christian Science Monitor*. Undeniably the news angle of a majority of newspaper pictures is subsidiary to the feature angle, while the comics are wholly feature material. The comics and the feature element in news pictures represent the entertainment function in modern newspapers.

The chief recent change in the comics has now gone so far as to have passed beyond the stage of mere trend; at least, it is fully established on all the comic pages. This is the adventure strip without humorous angle. Earliest of this type of strip was "Tarzan," which was also the forerunner of the immensely popular "Superman" and others detailing the exploits of heroes who overcame their enemies by the exercise of supernatural powers—a relatively crude but imaginative manipulation of a symbol of the basic desire for power. Prominent as the Superman type has been in the adventure-strip field, it has not monopolized the new development.

---

[5] Surveys by Jack M. Willem, of the Stack-Gable Advertising Agency, quoted in *Editor & Publisher*, Feb. 25, 1939, p. 16, and Feb. 24, 1940, p. 20.

[6] Allan Nevins, *The Evening Post: A Century of Journalism* (New York: Boni and Liveright, 1922), p. 549.

Certain trends in the contemporary news story are easily discernible—notably the turn toward interpretive reporting, and the tendency to use feature leads.

Interpretive News

Mark Ethridge, of the *Louisville Courier-Journal*, one of the most thoughtful of American newspapermen, wrote in the midst of the economic depression of the thirties:

There is a demand on the part of the intelligent reader these days to know not only what is happening but why it is happening, and how what transpires fits into the general political and social pattern. The popular acceptance of these [background] columns and of such weekly reviews as *Time* and *Newsweek* are, I think, an indictment of the adequacy of news reporting and handling [in newspapers].[7]

This attitude, which has grown steadily, was primarily the result of the American feeling of confusion in facing the economic disasters of the depression and, a little later, the upset of world politics. In such a disordered world, the ordinary reader feels himself at a loss to understand the true meaning of the smallest objective fact. Newspapers, and their servants the news agencies, have therefore attempted during the past five or six years to interpolate more interpretive material in the objective news. For the most part this has been done very carefully, for it is easily apparent that biased interpretation would quickly impugn the reliability of news reports. Yet there are undeniably some strong and bigoted papers which have taken advantage of this license to comment in the news to give their reports the shape and hue of their own opinions. This abuse may conceivably lead to a reaction against interpretive reporting. Many papers, with that feeling for the sanctity of the direct news report which is characteristic of the honest journalist and of American newspapers in general, protect themselves by using such typographical devices as italics and brackets to indicate interpolated comment.

Changing Style and Departmentalization

The old-fashioned lead of the five W's and the H, crystallized largely by Pulitzer's "new journalism" and sanctified by the schools, is widely giving way to the much more supple and interesting feature lead, even on straight news stories. Radio newscasting and

---

[7] *Quill,* March, 1936, p. 3.

Time journalism have undoubtedly been effective in promoting this trend; but common sense alone was enough to reject in many cases a technique which made for repetition in head, lead, and body, and which also resulted in awkward and unwieldy introductions to many stories.

Stricter departmentalization is another trend noticeable in many papers and largely referable to the influence of the weekly news magazines. Frequently allied with this technique is that of the first-page news summary. These experiments have often been accompanied by so-called "streamlining"—a layout along modern typographical lines.

. . . .

So long as circulations remain fairly stable, we need not look for any violent changes in the trends of American newspapers. It is only when newspapers are themselves about to be submerged in the flood that they grasp at the straws of radical experimentation.

AN ANALYSIS OF THEMES AND PLOTS
IN MOTION PICTURES

BY MARTHA WOLFENSTEIN
AND NATHAN LEITES

Dr. Wolfenstein is a professor of psychology at the City College of New York. Dr. Leites is a professor of political science at Yale. Their article is from the *Annals of the American Academy of Political and Social Science,* for November, 1947, and is reprinted by permission of authors and publisher. The article is copyrighted by the Academy.

THIS PAPER presents part of a larger study of contemporary American movies in which we analyzed the content of 67 Hollywood movies released in New York City between September 1, 1945, and September 1, 1946. These were all the grade-A movies with a contemporary American urban setting. Our study intends to ascertain the Hollywood variants of the love and hostility themes which pervade the dramatic plots of western culture. The study also aims to relate these variants to actual patterns in American life.

Our interest is not to compare the movie world with the real-life world so as to ascertain to what extent the movies reproduce existing conditions or deviate from them. We are rather concerned with the ways in which movie plots express psychological dispositions of the culture in which they are produced and consumed. Limitations of space prevent us from presenting all the major recurrent movie plot structures in this vein. To illustrate our approach, we shall discuss only some aspects of the treatment of love in our films.

UNCONVENTIONAL MEETINGS

A major tendency in the treatment of love in contemporary American films is the attempt to combine the appeal of the conventional and unconventional in a single relationship. This is expressed in the manner in which the hero and heroine become acquainted. There is a marked preference for showing the first meeting, as a self-introduction, frequently occurring between the hero and heroine in complete isolation, or in an impersonal milieu surrounded by strangers. Such unconventional meetings are preferred in the pictures analyzed to formal introductions in a ratio of about three to one.

The manner and place of the first meeting underscore its unconventionality. One third of the self-introductions are pickups. Usually initiated by the man, they take place mainly on the street, in trains, or in cheap places of entertainment. Equally frequent is the sudden irruption of one partner into the life of the other. One third of the self-introductions take this form, again with a predominance of male initiative. The hero of "Somewhere in the Night," fleeing from his underworld pursuers, breaks into the dressing room of the startled heroine, a night-club singer. In "The Kid from Brooklyn," the hero rushes into the heroine's bedroom to telephone for a veterinary obstetrician for his parturient milk wagon horse. In one of the exceptional cases of female initiative, the heroine forces her way into the apartment of the hero, her favorite mystery story writer, to urge him to help her solve a mystery ("Lady on a Train").

Professional contacts also provide a basis for self-introduction. However, the professional contexts or incidents are usually out of the ordinary. For instance the hero may meet the heroine in the course of his work as a private detective, in an atmosphere of danger and pursuit. Other occasions for self-introduction are head-on collisions and rescues of women in distress. Least frequently self-introductions occur in a context of normal social life.

The isolation of the couple at their first meeting is emphasized by the fact that they are apt to be either entirely alone or in a milieu of complete strangers. In only about one third of the cases is anyone else present who is known to either member of the couple. Where such familiar persons are present, they are more frequently acquaintances of the heroine than of the hero, thus maintaining a vestige of conventionality. In several cases the bystanders are mutual acquaintances, but this is considerably less frequent than the cases where the bystanders are known to only one member of the couple. A social setting common to both is thus the least frequent.

Conventional Desires

The result of these many unconventional meetings is exactly the same as that of proper introductions. The man meets a sweet nice girl (though she may appear excitingly bad for some time), and the girl meets a fine young man whose intentions are entirely honorable. So, for instance, the sailor in "Deadline at Dawn" soon discovers that the dime-a-dance girl whom he has picked up yearns only to return to her home town while she fends off unattractive men for a living. The girl finds that the sailor, who at first aroused her suspicions, is a helpless child towards whom she soon feels quite maternal. In "Blue Dahlia," where the woman picks the man up on a highway at night, they both turn out to be sterling characters, though for some time he is suspected of murder and she appears to be a gangster's moll.

In several cases the hero and heroine might have been properly introduced if they had not saved themselves from it by an earlier unconventional approach. In "Because of Him," for instance, the couple are introduced by a mutual acquaintance shortly after the hero has tried to pick up the heroine on the street. In some cases the attempts of friends or family to introduce or to promote a proper acquaintance have a directly negative effect. In "Pride of the Marines," the hero, who boards with a family of old friends, is urged by his landlady to make the acquaintance of a nice girl whom she strongly recommends. The hero feels that he is being trapped and treats the girl very rudely at their first meeting. Later, when the girl has snubbed him, he picks her up at a street corner, forcing her to get into his car by telling the bystanders that she is his wife and has deserted their children. This unconventional approach removes the curse of the formal introduction, and the affair assumes a promising aspect.

The unconventionality of these pickup relations rarely extends beyond the first meeting. The movies express the longing not so much to depart from the conventional as to spice it up with unconventional details. The feeling seems to be that nothing is more dull than to meet as father and mother did; no one is less romantic than an old friend of the family. There is a longing for the exotic,

the new, the unfamiliar, the nonfamilial. At the same time this longing does not go very far. It is impeded by the opposite longing, that
for the nice girl and the fine, clean-cut young man. The characteristic American solution, as indicated by the films, is that we can
have both together. We can have the appearance of unconventionality, the stimulating beginning of picking up a stranger in an
alien locale. At the same time we feel relieved when this turns out
to be a mere appearance.

Contrasted with European Pattern

The illicit quality, which is given to the couple's relation by their
mode of meeting, is displaced from the major relationship to a
minor incident, and is safely confined to this detail. There is no
tendency for a small unconventional act to involve greater, unfore-
seen irregularities. The American movies seem to be in marked contrast in this respect to one of the traditions of continental European
films, which tended to use street pickups as preludes to danger, dis-
grace, and even death.[1] The difference in feeling here is perhaps
related in part to the greater social mobility in America. The danger of losing status by inappropriate associations is not felt to be
very serious. There also seems to be a denial of sexual dangers.
The strange man or woman is not really dangerous but only seems
so for a moment, evoking an old myth of sexual fatality which we
no longer believe.

THE BEGINNING AND THE END

If we compare the first meeting of the couple with the last view
which we have of them at the end of the film, we get further confirmation of the point that the relationship which begins unconven-
tionally ends in a conventional way. The couple are much less likely
to be left alone together for their final embrace than they were for
their first handshake. Where three out of four couples introduced
themselves, meeting for the most part either in complete isolation
or in an impersonal milieu where no one was paying any attention
to them, there is only a fifty-fifty chance that the couple will be
alone at the end. This is the more remarkable since it is more usual
in life, and more appropriate for love-making, for the couple to be

---

[1] Cf. Siegfried Kracauer, *From Caligari to Hitler: A Psychological History of
the German Film* (Princeton: Princeton University Press, 1947), pp. 119-20,
157-58, 194-95. A Swedish film, *Torment* (1946), had a similar theme.

increasingly by themselves as their relation progresses. However, of the couples whom we see together at the end of the film, only half are alone. Even of those that are alone, one third are last seen in a public rather than a private place. For instance, the hero and heroine of "Weekend at the Waldorf," who met when he smuggled himself into her bedroom, have their final encounter as he flies over New York in a plane and she waves a large handkerchief from the Waldorf tower.

Of the couples who are last seen surrounded by people, about half are in the company of common acquaintances. This is an interesting contrast to the tendency to eliminate common acquaintances from the first meeting. The common milieu of the couple is thus not one of a shared background, but rather one that they acquire in the course of their association. Or, in several cases, the friends of one partner become friends of the other also.

Sometimes, where the couple have both their first and last encounters in a relatively impersonal crowd, they are less alone in the crowd at the end than at the beginning. In "Because of Him," the hero first tried to pick up the heroine on a busy street where the passers-by were not particularly interested in them. In the final scene, the couple are embracing on the stage of a large theater (she has just had a successful debut in a play which he has written), and a large audience is watching and applauding them. There are, of course, several films which give the couple greater privacy at the end than they had at their first meeting, but the opposite tendency is much more prominent.

The recurrent final embrace before witnesses resembles a marriage ceremony, for which it is perhaps a substitute representation. Relationships which have begun in an unconventional way do not develop into anything which must be kept secret or out of sight. Also, from the American point of view, a considerable part of the satisfaction in having acquired an attractive partner comes from showing him or her off to the admiration and envy of others. A secret love does not fulfill this requirement. The scene of the happy couple embracing on a stage before a large applauding audience satisfies the need much better.

CONFLICT BETWEEN SACRED AND PROFANE LOVE

The combination of sacred and profane love in a single relationship constitutes one of the major pervasive themes of American films. The possibility of developing a conventional relation from un-conventional beginnings is one illustration of this theme. Of deeper significance is the emergence of a group of heroines who combine the charms of good and bad girls.

Freud has pointed out the the difficulty of choosing between a good and bad girl constitutes one of the major problems in the love life of western men. The difficulty is that of fusing two impulses in relation to the same woman. On the one hand, there are sexual im-pulses which a man may feel to be bad and which he may therefore find it hard to associate with a woman whom he considers fine and admirable. The image, and the actuality, of the "bad" woman arise to satisfy sexual impulses which men feel to be degrading. On the other hand, there are affectionate impulses which are evoked by women who resemble the man's mother or sister, that is to say, "good" women. A good girl is the sort that a man should marry, but she has the disadvantage of not being sexually stimulating.

SOLUTIONS TO CONFLICT

In Nineteenth Century

There are various possible solutions to this conflict. The attempt may be made to satisfy one of these impulses at the expense of the other, to satisfy them both but with different women, or to combine the two impulses in a single relationship. For instance, in Victorian England the major approved solution was to renounce profane love in favor of the sacred variety. A rebellion against this Victorian ideal is expressed in Swinburne's "Dolores," an attempt to go to the opposite extreme of sexual satisfaction unmingled with affection. A different solution was the pattern supposedly frequent in France and Italy, in which a man would keep both a wife and a mistress. The frequent nineteenth-century fantasy of the saintly prostitute, of the Camille type, represented an attempt to combine sex and affection, to imagine a woman toward whom both feelings could be expressed.

In Hollywood Films

The solution favored by current American films is another variant of the combination of sex and affection in a single relationship. The image of what we may call a "good-bad girl" has been created. The good-bad girl differs from the saintly prostitute of the last century in that she is not really bad, but only appears bad. After her apparent badness has been sufficiently established to make her sexually exciting, it is explained away as a false impression, created by ambiguous circumstances, and the hero is left with a warm-hearted, loving girl whom he can marry and settle down with. At the same time she retains the glamorous appearance and bold manners which made it so easy to believe in her wickedness.

Usually the good-bad girl appears to be promiscuous, or to be involved with a bad man (a gangster or Nazi). Occasionally she appears guilty of theft or murder. In "Gilda," the title character (after whom the Bikini bomb was named) is the most thoroughgoing example of a heroine who looks widely promiscuous through the greater part of the film, and who in the end turns out to be a faithful and devoted woman who has never loved anyone but the hero. Gilda and the hero had been lovers before the action of the film begins, and had separated because of his jealousy. When they meet again the hero has become the right-hand man of a big gambler and international schemer; Gilda has become the gambler's wife. The hero is tortured not only by seeing Gilda as his boss's wife, but also by her strenuous flirtations with other men. Eventually the boss disappears and is considered dead. Gilda has tried to persuade the hero of her continued love for him, and he now agrees to marry her. But he still does not believe in her. To punish her for her apparent infidelities to the boss and to himself, he holds her a virtual prisoner. His strong-arm men follow her wherever she goes and forcibly dissuade her admirers. One night Gilda appears at the swank night club adjoining the gambling casino which the hero now runs. She sings and dances with great seductiveness and finally begins stripping off her clothes (she doesn't get much farther than her long black gloves) while men from the audience rush forward to assist her. The hero, who enters just in time to get an agonizing glimpse of the climax of the performance, sends his men to carry her out. While episodes of this sort present vividly the image of the beautiful promiscuous woman, they are interspersed with other occasions when Gilda pleads with the hero to believe that she has never loved anyone but him. In the end it turns out that what the hero thought he saw was a deceptive appearance, and what Gilda told him was entirely true. An understanding police official, who interests himself in their affairs, persuades the hero of this. All of Gilda's carryings-on with other men have been motivated by her love for the hero, whom she wished to hold by making him jealous. Once this has been explained to the hero by an impartial observer, he finally recognizes her for what she is: a good girl who loves only him.

In other cases the good-bad girl is not so completely free from taint, but still she turns out to be less bad than she had seemed, or there are strong extenuating circumstances for a lapse which is in any case temporary. The heroine of "Strange Love of Martha Ivers" manifests a complicated combination of real badness, seeming badness, and goodness. The girl has just come out of jail, to which she had been sent for stealing a fur coat. She explains to the hero that the coat was given to her by a boy friend who later disappeared. Thus she did not really steal the coat, but wasn't she rather friendly with the thief? In another episode she is forced by the wicked district attorney, who is still pursuing her for the crime she did not do, to play a trick on the hero. She induces him to go with her to a café where, by prearrangement, a man comes up and claims to be her husband. The pretendedly outraged husband demands that the hero come outside and fight. The hero is then forced into a waiting car in which several thugs beat him up. The heroine later has a chance to explain the whole thing to the hero; she really has no husband, and so on. In this series of bad appearances and virtuous explanations, one or two bad things remain that are not explained away. However, since the girl repeatedly turns out to be so much better than she seemed, there is probably the illusion that with a few more explanations, for which perhaps the film did not have time, she could be shown to be completely good. An atmosphere is created in which both the affirmation and the denial of the girl's badness have a strong emotional impact. They do not entirely cancel each other out, since it is most satisfying to believe both.

In Foreign Films

The good-bad girl seems to be a peculiarly American solution to the problem of two types of women. A comparison with films of other countries seems to indicate certain marked differences. A British film, "Madonna of the Seven Moons," deals with the two-types problem in a different way. The heroine is a dual personality. Most of the time she is a rather prim and stately wife and mother, devoted to her family and to good works, but every so often her other personality takes possession of her. She completely forgets her usual life, assumes a gypsy-like costume and abandon, and runs away to join her lover, a dark and passionate underworld character. The development in this good woman of a wild character is attributed to a girlhood seduction at the hands of a dark vagabond. The British film seems to say rather gallantly that it is the fault of a bad man if the sexy potentialities of a good woman are brought to the surface. The same woman can be both good and bad, but she does not have both characters in relation to the same man. This contrasts with the American good-bad girl pattern, according to which the girl always appears to the same man in both her aspects. The bad component appears much more dissociated and alien in the British version than in the American. It is significant that the fiery lover is an Italian. There is much less feeling in the American films of the irretrievable harm that men can do to women if they are not careful. The American good-bad girl survives her adventures unharmed. The British heroine can only escape her double life by dying.

French films seem to persist in maintaining the separation of good and bad women. The hero, placed between a good and a bad woman, is more attracted to the bad one. Attempts at fusion tend to take the form of having the bad woman converted from perennial promiscuity to true love by the right man. In a French film, "Macadam" (1947), a young sailor is shown pursuing a promising friendship with a rather severely good girl. A young prostitute seduces the sailor, and he immediately loses interest in the good girl, even treating her quite rudely. The prostitute at the same time falls in love with the sailor, and a stable relationship is established between them. In this and other French films, the promiscuous woman is shown as not being bad at heart. This is what redeems her. No attempt is made, as in the American films, to explain away her promiscuity as merely apparent.

German pre-Hitler movies seem to have expressed an even stronger duality of good and bad women. The man moves between the good woman who is safe, domestic, and dull and the bad woman who will lure him to his destruction.[2]

THE DISAPPEARANCE OF THE VAMP

The good-bad girl of the recent American films has put the old-style vamp out of business. The vamps of the twenties were dan-

---

[2] Kracauer, *op. cit.*, pp. 119-20, 126, 216. Comparison with these German films is, of course, subject to the limitation that they are not contemporary.

gerous women who unscrupulously used their sexual appeal to ruin men. Men were fascinated and bound by these women who alone could offer them the dizzy excitement of sex. Sex in those days was more mysterious, a dark rite of which the wicked woman was the priestess. It retained some of the aura of Biblical sin. One has only to recall, for instance, Greta Garbo in "Flesh and the Devil," the story of the fatal woman destroying the friendship of two fine men by becoming the mistress of one and the wife of the other. As the old preacher explains to the hero, when the devil cannot find any other way to tempt a man, he sends a beautiful woman. This image of the dangerous woman has disappeared. In the good-bad girl the hero can find sex and a square deal at the same time. Bad girls still remain, but they have mainly lost their hold on men. They have become rather a pathetic lot, hankering after heroes for whom they have no appeal.

The issue between the two types of women appears mainly in the films which one may call "male melodramas," revolving around the love and hate problems of a central hero. In films of this type, 80 per cent have a good-bad girl as the main female character. In about 50 per cent of the cases, the good-bad girl is opposed to a straight bad girl, over whom she regularly wins out. In approximately 30 per cent, the good-bad girl occupies the center of the stage alone. In only 20 per cent is the issue one between a bad girl and a simple good girl, a contest in which the good girl does not always win.

The difference between the bad and the good-bad girls is mainly that the bad girls really are what the good-bad girls only seem to be, that is, promiscuous, involved with bad men, and criminal. In "Blue Dahlia," the hero returns from the war to find his wife drunk in the midst of a wild party, and on terms of obvious intimacy with an older man who later turns out to be a gangster. After the party has dispersed, she completes the alienation of her husband's affections by admitting that their baby was killed in an auto accident caused by her drunken driving. In "The Big Sleep," the bad sister of the heroine is a nymphomaniac who has killed a man who repulsed her advances. In "Strange Love of Martha Ivers," the bad woman has a long list of crimes to her credit, including murder and theft. In each of these cases, the bad girl loses out to a good-bad girl who is equally alluring and less harrowing to have around.

The majority of bad girls fail to win the love of the men they want. Frequently they experience the frustrating combination of being repulsed by the men they love and pursued by men whom they dislike. Only a small minority are happy in love. The good-bad girl, on the other hand, always gets her man. She is frequently pursued by other men as well, who help to provide an atmosphere of desirability.

The disappearance of the vamp is further evident if we compare movie spy types of World War I and World War II. The earlier beautiful spy, like Mata Hari, for instance, was an irresistible woman who lured men from the opposite side to betray their secrets to her. She was quite cold and ruthless until the day when she fell in love with one of her victims. At this point her employers always had to shoot her; like a horse that has broken a leg, she was no longer useful. This spy legend was another version of the prostitute ennobled by love. In contrast to this, World War II women spies are shown as clean-cut American girls doing a patriotic job. They do not have to be redeemed by love since they are good all along; and they are always in love with men on their own side. The enterprising girl from home is thus substituted for the alluring foreign woman.

MOVIE TRENDS AND OTHER CULTURE TRENDS

The tendency to combine all satisfactions in one relationship, symbolized by the figure of the good-bad girl, may be related to various other trends in American culture. The ideal of monogamy still persists, but hedonistic demands, developing in part from an economy of abundance, urge the satisfaction of every need. The combination of these two trends leads to the expectation of finding one person who will satisfy every wish. The strength of this expectation is attested by the high divorce rate. Disillusionment with a marriage partner cannot be mitigated by supplementary satisfactions on the side. The longing is to begin all over again and try to find the perfect person.

The uncompromising demand to have everything seems to be more marked in Americans than in Europeans. There is little readiness to accept compromises, much less to make renunciations. The more characteristically European solutions of the two-types problem seem to express an underlying resignation. There is more the feeling that one can't have everything, that life is necessarily haunted by regrets for missed opportunities, that a certain amount of frustration is inevitable, that the attempt to get too much is likely to involve fatal conflicts. The American feeling seems to be less tragic. The belief that you can eat your cake and have it still seems strong. The hero of the American films happily survives the conflicts of love and hate which have so often been fatal for dramatic heroes of other times and places.

The real-life counterpart of the good-bad girl has probably developed with the increasing sexual accessibility of good girls. Terman, for instance, pointed out the continuously increasing trend in women toward premarital sexual relations. With this development, the prostitute becomes less necessary, and the sheltered innocent less frequent. The two corresponding images tend to lose their hold on imagination. On the one hand, the seductress, more or less glorified, tends to fade out. On the other hand, the sweet helpless girl, whom the good man had to protect against the roué, also disappears.

Another real-life development, related to the disappearance of two-typism, seems to be that an increasing number of urban women try, and succeed more or less, to remain glamorous looking for an indefinite length of time. To have an appearance which proclaims the comfortable homey wife and mother is felt as a failure. The image of a mother is being transformed in the direction of a continuity between mother and glamour girl. This is illustrated in a series of advertisements featuring "model mothers," i.e., professional models who continue their careers after becoming mothers and who appear no less glamorous when they have one or two pretty children in the picture with them.

Another relevant real-life factor may be that educated parents have been trying to be more moderate in imposing sexual taboos on their children. Possibly the impression of the extreme badness of sex has been less firmly implanted in childhood than was formerly the case. This would weaken the adult tendency to conceive of sex as something shady, secret, and separate from the rest of life.

The movie image of the good-bad girl expresses the feeling that sexual needs can be satisfied by a good girl, that they no longer require involvement with a dangerous bad woman. However, the split in the good-bad girl image suggests that the sexual component is not entirely assimilated. In order to be sexually stimulating, the good girl must retain a semblance of badness, particularly in the form of seeming to be involved with other men. A lingering association of sex and wickedness remains.

THE WORLD OF THE DAYTIME SERIAL

BY RUDOLF ARNHEIM

Dr. Arnheim, now on the faculty of Sarah Lawrence College, was a Rockefeller fellow at Columbia when he wrote this study. It appeared in *Radio Research, 1942-43*, edited by Paul F. Lazarsfeld and Frank Stanton, published and copyrighted by Duell, Sloan and Pearce, New York, 1944. It is reprinted by permission of editors and publisher.

THE SOCIAL MILIEU

Locale

DO RADIO SERIALS choose the large centers of modern life as settings for the adventures of their characters, or do they prefer small towns or the village? Do they have their heroes escaping from civil community to solitude and the wilderness? A rough classification of the settings is given in Table 1. As two types of settings appeared in 5 of our samples, we present the results in terms of the number of serials and of settings.

Middle or small towns predominate over large cities, such as New York or Chicago. In only 10 per cent of all cases is the serial laid in a rural community. The preference for middle towns may reflect an intention of catering to listeners who belong to just that social setting. In this case, we would have to note that these listeners are believed to prefer plays which, at least outwardly, reproduce the framework of their own life rather than permitting access to the higher sphere of metropolitan life.

But whether a large or small place is chosen as a setting, there

TABLE 1. Locale of the Serials

Locale	Number of Serials	Number of Settings
Large cities	8	13
Middle or small towns............	16	20
Rural communities	4	5
Combinations	5	..
Doubtful (either large or middle town)	5	5
Other cases	5	5
Total	43	48

is certainly no tendency toward fleeing regular life in a community. Even the five "other" cases mentioned in Table 1 refer to fragments of this normal life rather than to exotic or fantastic backgrounds. These took place in the "most expensive sanitarium of the country," at a country college, in two cases on the estates of wealthy people, and on a pleasure cruise near Havana. With the exception of the latter, the episodes were all set in the United States. This again indicates that listeners are believed to enjoy a familiar environment rather than one which permits or demands that they imagine what may happen elsewhere.

Social Status of Main Characters

What are the social backgrounds of the people presented in the radio serials? Are they rich or poor? Are they individuals distinguished by social prestige and influence or are they representatives of the common folk? Table 2 shows the occupation of the central, plot-sustaining group of characters. Most of the categories in this table are self-explanatory. "Society people" comprise those characters whose status was described exclusively by their belonging to "society" (society matrons, the son of a millionaire, etc.).

If we accept the order of the categories as a rough social scale we find that the status of the main characters clusters at about the middle of the scale with professionals and housewives being most frequent.[1] The frequent appearance of housewives can be explained

---

[1] A breakdown according to size of community shows that the middle or small town setting follows this distribution closely, while in the large city setting the drop in the high occupational groups, and in the rural setting the drop in the low groups, is less pronounced.

by their predominance in the audience. The preference for the professionals seems less easy to explain. The physicians, lawyers, college teachers, artists, etc., who comprise this group are probably on a higher social level than the average listener, but they are not the highest class available for wish-dreams. Society people, high officials, and big businessmen do not appear more frequently than small business people and employees whose status can be supposed to correspond most closely to the average listener's. One might speculate that physicians and lawyers are indispensable in the troubles which are characteristic of the plots. In fact, the serials afford sufficient opportunity to lawyers for keeping busy. But there is not enough illness in serials to explain the large number of physicians. And quite often the lawyers and doctors appear mainly as husbands, friends, etc., rather than in the exercise of their professions. Can this result be explained by the attitude of lower middle class people towards other social classes? Do they consider the class of learned or artistically gifted men, who give help and advice or produce enjoyment and who live on a higher economic level, the object of admiration and aspiration; and does resentment dominate their attitude towards still higher social groups?

The complete absence of the working class proper is striking. The characters of serials include small shopkeepers, business employees, a taxi driver, even one garage mechanic, and then there is a jump to a small group of destitute outcasts: an ex-convict, a family of unemployed migrant workers, a senator reduced to vagabondage by amnesia. *There is no case of a factory worker, a miner, a skilled or unskilled laborer, playing an important role in any of the 43 serial*

TABLE 2. Occupational Status of Main Characters
(Proportion of 48 Settings in Which the Different
Occupations Appear)

Occupational Status	Number of Settings	Per Cent of All Settings
Society people	9	19
High officials	10	21
Big business	16	33
Professionals	35	73
Housewives	31	65
Small business	15	31
Wage earners	9	19
Destitute people	3	6

samples. Here again, social attitudes of the listeners, and possibly the policy of advertisers, might give an explanation.

Apart from the occupational scale, we examined how often people appeared who were equipped with the *splendor of wealth*: people who possess large houses and servants, who visit nightclubs, charter private planes, send orchids by wire, etc. This happened in 24 out of 48 settings; i.e., in 50 per cent, and specifically in 85 per cent of the large town settings; 30 per cent of the middle and small town settings; and 20 per cent of the rural settings. The occupational groups who contributed to this feature were the "society people," business, and, among the high officials, mainly senators, but also some of the doctors, lawyers, and artists.

About the relations between high-class and low-class people it can be said that while popular fiction of the European tradition often introduces the reader into the company of rich noblemen, the radio serials, an American product, present their heroes as illuminated by the upper sphere, but not necessarily identified with it. On the contrary, in many of the cases in which wealthy and socially highly situated people appear, they are shown paying courtship to the attractiveness or efficiency, or both, of the middle-class people. This may be an attempt to compensate the listener for her lack of social prestige and power in real life. Personal qualities, which are independent of the distribution of benefits in the community and therefore equally accessible to all are chosen to counteract social inequality.

The fiction of mutual intercourse on an equal level is stressed, e.g., in the case of a famous Broadway actor who consumes his time and nervous energy in helping the humble middle-class family next door. Marriage with a member of the upper-class conveys honor on the just plain people. There is the spectacular career of the "orphan girl who was reared by two miners and who in young womanhood married England's wealthiest, most handsome lord." Ma Perkins, an elderly housewife and lumberyard owner in the country, has her daughter married to a brilliant young congressman in Washington. Mrs. Stella Dallas, who is a lower middle-class woman and wants to remain one, was married to a diplomatic attaché in the Capital, and her daughter "went out of her mother's life" by marrying a man who is prominent in Washington society. At the same time, proud self-assertion and a certain resentment against people who draw high prestige from wealth or a professional position is often clearly expressed. A rich businessman's marriage proposal is rejected. A bankrupt real estate agent protests against his daughter's desire to marry an attractive young millionaire.

The elegant and rich physician courting a simple "government girl" is a "heel" who well deserves to be murdered by an equally rich "glamour girl." A taxicab driver writes a symphony worth $25,000 and receives but scarcely appreciates the attentions of an unscrupulous wealthy wangler and his elegant wife.

Leaders

Great importance is attributed to the quality of "leadership." *In 30 out of 48 settings, i.e., in 62.5 per cent, such "leaders" were found among the central characters.*

Table 3 shows the number of leaders in communities of different sizes, the "leaders" being broken down into those who excel by their professional position and those who do so by their personal qualities, such as intelligence, helpfulness, initiative. These "personal leaders" are further divided according to leadership in the whole community or in their private group (family, friends, etc.).

Leadership is due to personal qualities about as often as it is to a professional position. The leaders by personal merit exert their influence within their private group twice as often as in the whole community. In the large cities the professional leaders prevail. Most of them are people of a nationwide reputation, e.g., a president of the United States, senators, famous actors, a No. 1 debutante. In the middle or small towns this group of leaders is still predominant: a superintendent of schools, a city manager, a parson, an influential journalist of the local paper, etc. In the rural setting, personal efficiency and helpfulness enable individuals to become leaders in their community, although they are a barber, a garage mechanic, a small store owner, etc.

TABLE 3. Leaders in Communities of Different Size

Type of Leadership	Large cities	Middle or small towns	Rural communities	Others	Total Number
Professional	6	9	1	3	19
Personal	1	5	6	6	18
In community	..	1	5	..	6
In private group	1	4	1	6	12
Total	7	14	7	9	37 *

* 37 cases are given instead of the 30 indicated above because in seven settings two of the three leader categories were present.

An examination of the plots shows that often individuals of relatively low social standing, but great personal merits, are described as being more efficient leaders than those on whom society has conferred the prestige of official leadership.

David Harum, who is the owner of a small store, but first of all a "country philosopher," appears absorbed in a community garden project. Garage mechanic Lorenzo Jones is organizing a charity dance. The "leave-it-to-me" man, storekeeper Scattergood Baines, convicts the respected president of the local school of a grave professional error. Ma Perkins, the country woman, provides a senatorial committee with the decisive clues for the disclosure of a large scandal, and the owner of a small second-hand book store at the lower East Side of New York, an old Jew, gives philosophical advice to a famous physician, to his son, and to last year's No. 1 debutante, who, excited by their troubles, rather foolishly buzz among the book shelves.

THE PROBLEMS

The Role of the Problems

The narrative content of our samples consists almost entirely of problems created and solved by the characters. These problems stem from disturbances of static life situations, rather than from obstacles to the accomplishment of goals. One could imagine plays in which the characters were bent on achieving certain positive aims such as educating children, fighting for a social reform, solving a scientific problem. Then the "problems" would consist in conquering the forces opposed to the realization of the aim. The typical radio serial situation, instead, cannot be compared to a stream hampered by a dam, but rather to a stagnant lake which is troubled by a stone thrown into it. The attitude of the serial characters is essentially passive and conservative, possibly a reflection of the role which the average serial listener plays in the community.

Human existence is pictured as being continuously threatened by catastrophe. There is not just one problem which has to be faced by a character or a group of characters, but an uninterrupted chain of more or less severe nuisances. A total number of 142 problems was traced in 596 installments.[2] *The average number of problems per serial was 3.3 (average deviation: 1.6) for the test period, which comprised an average of only 12.7 fifteen-minute installments.*

---

[2] Sometimes during the analysis, one problem situation turned out to be a combination of several problems, which had to be treated separately.

Roughly speaking, there was one problem for every four installments.

Literature may seem to offer something similar in the great epics
such as the Odyssey or in the Bible story of Job. But in these epics
the succession of the episodes is as rigidly regular as the recurring
design of a frieze. The stylized composition and the unrealistic content of the stories are the reasons why the succession of disastrous
episodes appears not as a true-to-life picture, but as a symbol for a
high degree of suffering, intensity being expressed through repetition. Radio serials, instead, do their best to create the impression
that they present "real life." They interlace the episodes in an irregular, more "lifelike" manner. In the realm of such "realism," the
wave-after-wave attacks of evil cannot but have an unintended
humorous effect on the more discriminating listener. An unsophisticated serial listener who accepts these programs as convincing and
true must carry away the impression that human life is a series of
attacks to be warded off by the victims and their helpers.

Due to the briefness of the test period, no distinction was possible
between problems of major or minor weight. In order to get an idea
of the general structure of the serials, one would have to examine
them over a longer period. Roughly, two types of serial "composition" were distinguishable. In one, a leader, generally by personal
qualities, guides the other characters through their personal troubles. The "conflict-carriers" as well as the type of conflict involved
may vary from episode to episode. In other cases, there is a group
of people, generally a family, to whom disaster after disaster occurs.
If the family is large enough and has a fringe of fiancés and friends,
the victims of new troubles are never lacking. In some cases also a
constant setting helps to maintain the unity of the serial.

The Content of the Problems

What kinds of problems trouble the serial characters? An examination of the data suggested the nine content categories listed in
Table 4. The table shows in how many of the total 43 serials each
type of problem occurred. It also shows how the total number of
problems which were traced during the test period is distributed
among the nine categories.

Problems in the realm of "personal relations," i.e., problems occurring between lovers, marriage partners, in the family, or among
friends, account for 47 per cent of all problems. One or more of

TABLE 4. Distribution of Kinds of Problems
(Proportion of Serials in Which Each Type Occurred and Per Cent Distribution of Types of Problem)

Kind of Problem	Per Cent of 43 Serials *	Per Cent of All 159 Problems †
Personal relations	91	47
Courtship	49	16
Marriage	44	18
Family	33	10
Friends	12	3
Economic and professional.................	47	22
Crime	30	9
Illness, accidents	29	9
Public affairs	26	10
Others	9	3

* In 91 per cent of all 43 serials studied, a problem pertaining to personal relationships occurred. However, as one serial might contain different types of problems of personal relationships, the proportions for the subgroup "personal relations" adds up to more than 91 per cent. Percentages in the second column of the table add up to 100 because here the base is not the total number of serials, but the total number of problems.

† The increase from 142 problems (p. 397) to 159 is explained by the fact that some problems had to brought under more than one category.

them occurred in 91 per cent of all 43 serials studied for a three weeks' period. Most of the cases listed as economic, professional, crime, or illness problems, and even some of the public affairs problems could be classified under another master category, namely as "problems endangering the individual." This is obvious in the case of illness and accidents, but economic threats and crime might concern the community as a whole, and in the realm of public affairs one would certainly expect it to be so. Instead, the economic and professional problems deal mostly with the job or money difficulties of individuals, crimes are committed against individuals, and even the corrupt officials who dominate the public affairs group are shown mainly as damaging single persons—ambitious district attorneys trying to convict innocents, or a senator wanting to expose a colleague. This second master category of problems, related to the economic or professional standing, the physical integrity, and the reputation of the individual, is almost as large as the group devoted to "personal relations." Both of these categories together account for nearly all the problems traced during the test period. The world of the serials is thus quite clearly a "private" world in which the interests of the community fade into insignificance.[3]

What Causes the Problems?

Do people create trouble for themselves or are other people to blame? What role is played by non-personal forces such as natural powers or economic and political conditions? The distribution of the different kinds of causes is shown in Table 5.

Trouble is somewhat more often created by the very people who have to suffer from it ("sufferers") than by other persons.[4] In only 24 cases out of 159 (15 per cent), non-personal forces rather than individuals are described as creators of trouble.

Disturbances of a "personal relationship" are created by members of the group concerned almost three times as often as by other people outside the group, while the situation is reversed where the individual is endangered by crime, a professional problem, or a public affair. Non-personal forces are decisive in the illness and accident

Table 5. Causes of the Different Kinds of Problems

| Kind of Problem | Caused by | | | | Total Number |
	People Themselves	Others	Non-personal Forces	Doubtful	
Personal relations	52	19	1	3	75
Courtship	19	5	1	1	26
Marriage	24	3	..	1	28
Family	8	7	..	1	16
Friends	1	4	..	..	5
Economic and professional	8	16	7	4	35
Crime	2	10	..	3	15
Illness, accidents	1	..	13	..	14
Public affairs	2	11	2	1	16
Others	2	1	1	..	4
Total	67	57	24	11	159

[3] One might object that it is in the nature of dramatic representation to deal with the problems of individuals. But then it is significant in itself that the most popular form of narrative radio programs uses the dramatic form. And secondly, another type of drama is conceivable in which individuals appear as the representatives of a general cause (e.g., the inquisitors in G. B. Shaw's *Saint Joan*).

[4] If a husband creates trouble for his wife or a daughter for her father or a friend for a friend, the case is classified among the "sufferers" wherever the problem is described as disturbing the harmony of the group of which both persons are members. The disturbance of such a relation clearly affects both people.

cases, but for the rest, have some importance only in the economic category.

The problems of life are presented largely as caused by individuals, by their shortcomings or corruption, rather than by any general social, economic, or political conditions.

An examination of the plots shows that more than half of the "getting a job"-problems, for instance, dealt with being offered a job which the person did not care to accept rather than with the difficulties of finding work. Sons did not want to enter their fathers' business. A college professor refused a position in New York because country life suited him better. Intriguing women also caused difficulties in getting a job. As far as "losing a job" was concerned, two people wanted to get rid of their present occupation. Personal shortcomings, jealousy, professional rivalry, and political blackmailing furnished threats to people's employment. There were some instances of dishonest professional behavior. There was a profiteering landowner. A crooked businessman tried to profit by the sale of a symphony at the expense of the poor composer. A man was swindled into buying a manganese mine. And a dishonest renting agent intrigued against the appointment of an administrator who would reveal his frauds. In only two cases economic reasons for job problems were given: a man needed a job because he needed the money, and another one did not get a promised job because "business was bad." Other "non-personal forces" to interfere with business were an inundation, illness, an accident, etc.

Troubles in public administration were likewise attributed to the shortcomings of individuals. Senators tried to sell the government bad land for an army camp. District attorneys worked for their personal careers rather than for justice. High municipal officials were involved in intrigue, blackmailing, and fraud. And the president of a community garden was tempted to cheat. National Defense was used as a pretext to present private problems very loosely connected with public issues; a private, through carelessness, provoked an accident, which a woman friend of his was accused of; another private, on leave, visited a girl who fell ill with measles, and was prevented by quarantine from being back at the camp in time.

Crimes were rarely committed and by very bad people only. In 12 out of 15 total crime cases, innocent and virtuous people were accused of having committed murder or adultery; having embezzled the property of a bus company; having taken somebody's car, etc. This feature may be designed pleasantly to nourish the listener's feeling that she is often the victim of accusations which she does not deserve.

MORAL EVALUATION

Three Types of Characters

A significant relationship seems to exist between the kind of "problem" presented and the moral evaluation of the characters involved.

There is little difficulty in finding out for many of the leading characters whether they are meant to be good or bad people. The announcer, whose comments are to be considered as authoritative, often attributes to them precise traits which imply equally precise ethical evaluations. He will talk about "the kindly man walking down the stairs" or refer to "that half-gangster" who is trying to obtain the heroine's favor. Just as outspoken about their fellow-characters are the characters themselves. Especially the "reliable" people (present in almost every serial as a moral framework from which to judge the happenings) express the opinion of the authors. Besides, the actors generally do their best to distinguish, by the inflexions of their voices, the tough scoundrel or the suave intriguer from the considerate friend or the nervously lamenting victim of passion, fate, or villainy.

In addition to the "bad" and the "good" people we find a third group of characters, almost as neatly defined as those of the two other groups. They excel in unpleasant qualities such as jealousy, vindictiveness, lack of balance, deceitfulness, selfishness, but it is clearly stated that these defects do not spring from an evil nature, but are weaknesses resulting from bad experiences or lack of control. It is suggested that they may eventually be brought back to their better selves. For the sake of brevity we shall call this third type the "weak" people.

One might have expected a clear-cut black-and-white method of moral evaluation in radio serials. Instead, as is shown in Table 6, the "weak" people are most frequent among the creators of trouble. A further remarkable result is given by the large proportion of "good" people among the trouble makers.[5]

There is a clear difference between the moral evaluation of those

---

[5] Good people create trouble, e.g., by deceiving others for their own good: a wife "gives hope" to a blind husband by making him believe she is expecting a child; an actor plays the role of a blind girl's brother to save her from knowing that the brother is in prison under a murder charge; another actor offers his services to make a neglecting husband jealous. A "good" man may fall in love with somebody else's wife or, being married himself, with another woman, but such a love relation is never "consummated," and generally the third person's faultiness tends to justify the slip. Good people also accuse themselves of crimes in order to shield others. An exemplary woman was allowed to try keeping an adopted child from the real mother by dubious tricks, these being apparently excused by virtue of motherly affection.

TABLE 6. Moral Evaluation of Characters Who Create Troubles

Troubles Created for:	Moral Evaluation of Characters				
	Good	Bad	Weak	Doubt-ful	Total Number
Themselves	18	8	34	2	62
Others	5	30	12	6	53
Total	23	38	46	8	115 *

* To the 115 total problems caused by persons, 20 have to be added which were caused by non-personal forces and 9 in which the cause was undecidable. This leads to a total of 144 problems. The increase from 142 (cf. p. 397) to 144 problems is explained by the fact that in two cases good as well as weak creators of trouble were traced.

who create trouble to themselves or to their private group and those who do it to others. Weak characters prevail in the former group and good ones too are frequent. Those who create problems for others are mainly bad, sometimes weak, and good only in a few cases.

As far as the "sufferers" are concerned, Table 6 gives information only about those who create trouble to themselves. If *all* the sufferers are considered—those who create trouble to themselves as well as those who have to suffer from others—the good people are shown as doing most of the suffering (Table 7). Bad people are hardly ever the victims of trouble. To the 166 cases of Table 7, six are to be added in which the community is described as the sufferer— which low number shows again the privacy of the world of daytime serials.

The Characterization of Men and Women

As the serials cater mainly to a female audience it seemed worth while to look for differences in the presentation of men and women.

TABLE 7. Moral Evaluation of All Sufferers

Moral Evaluation	Number of Sufferers
Good	103
Bad	8
Weak	46
Doubtful	9
Total	166 *

* The increase of 142 to 166 sufferers is again explained by the number of cases which had to be classified under more than one category.

TABLE 8. Moral Evaluation of Men and Women Who Create Troubles

	Troubles Created for				Total Number *	
	Themselves		Others			
Moral Evaluation	M	W	M	W	M	W
Good	11	9	4	3	15	12
Bad	4	4	23	8	27	12
Weak....................	20	17	9	3	29	20
Doubtful	1	2	3	3	4	5
Total	36	32	39	17	75	49

* The increase from a total of 115 in Table 6 to 124 (75 men and 49 women) in Table 8 is explained by the fact that, e.g., the bad troublemaker in a problem-situation may actually be more than one person, sometimes a man and a woman. The same condition holds good for the sufferers in Table 9.

Table 8 shows that men appear considerably more often as troublemakers than women do. This refers particularly to the cases in which trouble is created for others. (A breakdown according to the kinds of trouble listed in Table 4 shows that men surpass women in doing harm to other people especially in the realm of public affairs, crime, and economic problems.) The male troublemakers are almost as often bad as they are weak and are considerably less often good. Among the women, the weak characters are almost twice as frequent as the good or the bad ones. Thus the difference in the sex distribution is most striking for the bad people: bad troublemakers are more than twice as often men as women.

The distribution and moral evaluation of men and women among *all* the sufferers is shown in Table 9. It can be seen that men and women are about equally often the victim of trouble-situations. Among the weak sufferers, men predominate.

Moral evaluation goes in favor of the women. Men create trouble more often than women, especially to other people. They are mostly weak and bad, the latter considerably more often than women. Among the people who have to suffer, men excel clearly in the group of the weak.

A few examples of marriage problems may show how this tendency comes out in the plots. Marriage disturbances through unfaithfulness are presented rarely and handled with care. The presentation goes in favor of the wife. In no case does a wife fall in love with another man. In three cases, husbands had a girl friend: two of these husbands were described as "selfish, suspicious, jealous" and "unstable, unbalanced"; the third succumbed to a "petty, selfish, quarrelsome, jealous" woman.

Table 9. Moral Evaluation of All Men and
Women Who Suffer from Problems

Moral Evaluation	Men	Women
Good	59	65
Bad	5	4
Weak	33	19
Doubtful	3	6
Total *	100	94

* See footnote to Table 8.

Where the marriage was imperiled by the shortcomings of one of the partners, there was usually something wrong with the husband. He was a tyrant or neglected his wife, or disgusted her by his laziness, or his being involved in political intrigues, etc. There were only two cases of thoroughly bad wives—one who defamed a colleague of her husband out of professional rivalry, and another whose husband, a plastic surgeon, refused after an accident to restore her "wickedly beautiful face through which she did every bad thing in her life." This latter was the only case of a man who wanted to get rid of an unsympathetic wife, and it seemed significant that her guilt was stated as springing from what is a woman's most desired asset—beauty.

The Solutions of the Problems

It has often been observed that in popular narrative art (novels, plays, movies) trouble-situations are solved according to conventional ethical standards. The stories are governed by perfect justice, thus providing the audience with reassurance and pleasant compensation.

Plans apt to create trouble to other people or to the trouble-makers themselves are permitted to develop, but hardly ever to be consummated. In a sample of 73 solutions, only about 12 per cent of the trouble-creating plans were carried through; all others were thwarted. The relatively largest measure of success was granted to the "good" troublemakers.

It seems interesting that while all the motives ascribed to good people were considered excusable or even praiseworthy, there was still a distinction—presumably also based on moral evaluation—as to whether the plans were allowed to succeed; they were not in cases in which they interfered with an institution like marriage, family, or the administration of justice. "Good" people were allowed: to leave a woman for the time being because of faithfulness to an insane wife; to refuse a better job because of preference for country life; to choose neither of two suitors; and to help a blind husband over a crisis by making him believe he would have a son. But they were prevented from such things as with-holding an adopted child from her real mother, making love to an honest girl while married to a disagreeable wife, or seducing an honest wife neglected by her husband; or accepting punishment for a murder committed by somebody else.

Earlier in this chapter it was stated that good people prevail among the sufferers and that the bad are hardly ever the vic-tims of trouble. While this is characteristic for the initial set-up of the problems, the solutions show that perfect justice is provided. No definitive harm is done to the victims; many of them are agree-ably indemnified for what they had to suffer. No good trouble-makers are punished, their motives being virtuous. But all the bad ones are. And as the weak troublemakers did wrong but are eligible for reform, about one half of them are punished, the rest not.

It may be added that the perfect justice which rules the serials is of a curious type. There is a reason for its existence, but it has no sufficient cause. Whether a person is punished or rewarded is ex-plained by the sort of ethical evaluation of his or her deeds which may be expected from the average listener. But there is no indica-tion in the serials of a principle which brings justice about. Virtuous and efficient persons are shown to help innocent sufferers and to fight malefactors. But who provides these helpers, who assists them in succeeding, who makes the honest invalids recover, who sends a paralytic stroke to the villain? God might be this principle, but He is hardly ever mentioned. There is no causal explanation for the high correlation between what people deserve and what they get. Radio serials procure the satisfaction created by a rule of ideal justice, but do not bother about explaining to whom we are indebted for such a perfect state of affairs.

A PSYCHOLOGICAL FORMULA OF SOAP OPERA

The Object of Identification

The listener's evaluation of the plot and the characters involved will largely depend on whom she identifies herself with. If she is presented, for instance, with the story of a woman who cheats her best friend, everything depends on whether the center of attention is the malefactor, the circumstances which led the woman to do what she should not have done and perhaps did not wish to do, her strug-gles of conscience, her repentance, and so on; or whether the plot is given the perspective of the victim. In the first case, the play reminds one of human imperfection. By eliciting identification with the sinner it warns that all people are sinners. It creates an attitude of melancholy humility, but at the same time enlightens by clarifying the mechanism that pushes people into guilt. In the second case it appeals to the Pharisee in man. It shows that decent people are treated badly even by those whom they have every reason to trust. It evokes the satisfaction of being good oneself while others, unfortunately, are bad. Instead of opening the road towards humble self-knowledge it nourishes the cheap pleasure of self-complacency.

Identification is invited in the radio serials by various means, most of which belong to the common technique of narrative art—novel, drama, film. The central position of a character invites the listener to perceive and to evaluate the plot situation from the point of view of this person.[6] Identification is furthered by the sheer quantity of time devoted to a character and by the amount of insight given into what the person thinks and feels. Physical, intellectual, and ethical perfection, social power, and prestige must also promote identification very strongly. Furthermore, there is the factor of resemblance: a middle-aged housewife will identify herself more readily with a middle-aged housewife, etc.

On the basis of these criteria, the objects of identification were sought. The crude and oversimplifying technique of characterization used by the average radio serial author made this task much more easy and reliable in practice than it might seem in theory. *For 118 out of 121 cases on whom there was sufficient detail, there was no doubt about the object of identification intended.* Twenty-one cases had to be omitted because of poor reports.

Identification tends toward a surprisingly uniform type. Moral perfection is the most constant feature of the group of symptoms which was used for establishing the "object of identification." With no exception these characters are spotlessly virtuous, good-hearted, helpful. They are intelligent, often physically attractive. They are

---

[6] This holds good for the heroine and the hero, who, as we explained, are not necessarily identical with the protagonists of the current episodes but are constant leading characters, generally mentioned in the daily theme announcement, as, e.g., "Kate Hopkins—the story of a beautiful and courageous woman who lives to serve others." Even if such a character is not one of those directly involved in the conflict he or she may become the object of identification. He or she may lead and advise the people involved; the whole conflict may be shown in the way it appears to him or her.

the "leaders by personal qualities," whose frequent appearance was discussed above (see p. 396). *In 101 out of 118 cases, the object of identification was a woman.* As to her main function in the plot, the "ideal woman" was presented as

An eligible woman	in 23 cases
A wife	21
A mother	16
A professional woman	14
A friend	13
A daughter	2
Unspecified	12
	101

The Psychological Structure of Radio Serials

We are now equipped to suggest a psychological formula which seems to underlie the outwardly varied plots of radio serials and which expresses itself in many of the previously discussed features characteristic of the serials. Three types of characters with significantly different roles sustain this psychological structure. They are suggested by and roughly correlated with the three types of moral evaluation which we were able to distinguish.

Moral evaluation	Role in plot	Listener's attitude
Weak	Helpless troublemaker, guilty sufferer, reformable	Resonance to portrait
Good	Helpful leader, innocent sufferer	Identification with ideal
Bad	Outside cause of trouble, personification of hostile forces, unreformable	Hatred towards enemy

The function of these three types can be described in the following way.

I. The "weak" characters have a large share of guilt in the uninterrupted series of catastrophes which—according to radio serials —form human life. But they are not bad by nature. The trouble they create though often directed against others makes them suffer themselves because they disturb the harmony of the private group to which they belong. They are selfish, jealous, vindictive, deceitful and need other people's help to get out of the conflict situations which they create. It is this type which may be expected to furnish an unvarnished *portrait of the average listener* herself. *Resonance* is the probable reaction provoked by the weak character, who faithfully mirrors the listener's own feelings and experiences. It is the presence of this type which we may expect to attract the listener to the radio serials as something which concerns herself.

II. However, the portrait offered by the "weak" characters is an unpleasant one. So if the listener is to enjoy the resonance which it provokes in her, she must be given the means of detaching herself from it. The second type, represented by the *good* people, fulfills this function. It keeps identification away from the weak type. It provides a safe platform from which to look down on the weak character's unfortunate adventures in an attitude of aloofness and complacency. It adds the embodiment of an *ideal* to the representation of the true-to-life portrait.[7] It allows the listener to *identify* herself with a woman who is always good and right, recommended by her virtue, energy, helpfulness, leader qualities, and by the outstanding position which is granted to her in the structure of the play and by her fellow-characters. She appears mostly as an "eligible" woman desired by desirable suitors, or as a wife, but quite often also as a mother, a friend, a professional woman. The weak character is the object of her helpful activity. The object of identification provides reparation for the essentially passive and subordinate role which in real life the listener plays as a housewife and as a member of the underprivileged classes.[8] She assumes government in a world of individuals in which the power and the function of the community are eliminated. An examination of the plots shows that she steers the destinies of afflicted people more often than she is herself involved in conflict. But if she is involved, then she appears prevalently as the innocently suffering victim of other people's failure, thus offering to the listener the opportunity to pity

---

[7] A mixture of goodness and badness has, ever since Aristotle, been considered, somewhat vaguely, a main characteristic of the dramatic character in literature. Thus, the high number of "weak" characters traced in our sample may lead to optimistic opinions about the literary qualities of the radio serials. By stressing the "mixed" character, the serials are, it is true, somewhat nearer to real life than the black-and-white characterization often found in other types of popular narrative art. But whereas the genuine dramatic character is always intended as the object of identification and produces in himself the forces which bring about the solution of the conflict, the "weak" character in the serials lacks the artistic and educational values offered by a truly dramatic spectacle.

[8] Passivity as a personality trait plays an important part in the psychology of radio listening in general. Cf. Rudolf Arnheim, *Radio* (London: Faber and Faber, 1936), pp. 260-73.

herself. If she creates trouble herself she does so as a praiseworthy
person for praiseworthy reasons.[9]

III. The third type is formed by the thoroughly *bad* people. They
come from outside to threaten the security of the characters to
whom the listener is linked by resonance and identification. Whereas
for the good woman the weak character is an object of help, the bad
one is the *enemy* against whom she has to defend others and herself. And it must be remembered that the bad people are mostly
men. In a world of individuals, the villains represent not only personal adversaries like a girl rival but also the anonymous forces of
politics and economics which in real life constantly afflict the listener's existence. No community is admitted between the bad people
and the listener, no understanding for their motives exists or is
desired. They are evil per se: they provoke nothing but resentment
and fear. They attack the innocent victim—as symbolized in so
many court trial episodes of the serials. By lending human shape
to the outside forces of disturbance and by painting these dis-
turbers in solid black, radio serials provide a confirmation of the
listener's attitude towards what she considers her enemies. Only in
the case of physical illness or accidents are impersonal forces recognized and allowed to join the ranks of the enemy.

Our *psychological formula* could then be stated in about the
following terms. Radio serials attract the listener by offering her a
portrait of her own shortcomings, which lead to constant trouble,
and of her inability to help herself. In spite of the unpleasantness
of this picture, resonance can be enjoyed because identification is
drawn away from it and transferred to an ideal type of the perfect,
efficient woman who possesses power and prestige and who has to
suffer not by her own fault but by the fault of others. This enables
the listener to view (and to criticize) her own personal shortcomings, which lead to trouble, as occurring in "other," less perfect
creatures. Still, these shortcomings, being her own after all, are
presented as springing from mere weakness of character; reform is
possible and often achieved. No such tolerance is needed for the
outside causes of the listener's suffering. Her resentment against

---

[9] Remarkably enough, the objects of identification sometimes, in a difficult
personal situation, forget their part and show a "weak" behavior which is quite
in contrast with the masculine energy they display while helping others. They
take fright at decisions, they burst into tears, they wail around in a hysterical
and pitiful way, they take refuge in the unwavering strength of male friends or
follow obediently.

them is confirmed and nourished by the introduction of the villain-type, who also personifies and assumes responsibility for any detrimental effects of non-personal forces (in whose immunity the listener is interested), such as the institutions of society.

The psychological scheme presented here is a hypothesis based on the evidence of our content analysis. It would be desirable to test it by investigating the reactions of listeners.

VALUES IN MASS PERIODICAL FICTION, 1921-1940

BY PATRICKE JOHNS-HEINE
AND HANS H. GERTH

These are tables from a longer study which appeared in the *Public Opinion Quarterly*, for Spring, 1949. They are here reprinted by permission of the authors and the magazine. Dr. Gerth was associate professor of sociology at Wisconsin, and Patricke Johns-Heine was a research assistant at Wisconsin when this study was made.

TABLE 1. Occupational Distribution of Heroes by Magazine and by Periods: (1) 1921-30, (2) 1931-40

Occupation	Ladies' Home Journal		True Story		Atlantic		Saturday Evening Post		Country Gentleman	
	(1)	(2)	(1)	(2)	(1)	(2)	(1)	(2)	(1)	(2)
Business-Industry	32%	25%	42%	38%	23%	16%	38%	32%	18%	35%
Professional	24	22	42	40	24	21	18	29	11	15
Agricultural	5	6	—	6	10	19	9	9	35	18
Public Service	3	4	17	2	6	4	6	9	6	8
None Specified	25	32	—	6	24	29	19	10	14	15
All Other	12	10	—	8	13	10	9	10	16	9
Total number of heroes	76	77	12	50	70	70	99	97	71	79

TABLE 2. Distribution of Locales by Magazine and by Periods:
(1) 1921-30, (2) 1931-40

Locale	Ladies' Home Journal		True Story		Atlantic		Saturday Evening Post		Country Gentleman	
	(1)	(2)	(1)	(2)	(1)	(2)	(1)	(2)	(1)	(2)
Farm	4%	11%	8%	2%	9%	18%	6%	10%	46%	20%
Country	11	10	—	8	15	12	12	5	10	15
Small Town	9	13	25	29	16	18	17	14	11	22
Town	56	42	25	44	12	26	26	31	16	16
Metropolis	9	16	42	10	16	8	30	31	3	9
Suburb	2	4	—	4	—	—	2	—	1	—
Indetermi- nate*	9	4	—	4	32	19	7	9	13	18
Total number of locales	80	79	12	52	75	74	100	100	71	80

* Includes settings on boats, on planes, in camps, in caves, and other.

TABLE 3. Distribution of Major Themes by Magazine and by Periods:
(1) 1921-30, (2) 1931-40 *

Theme	Ladies' Home Journal		True Story		Atlantic		Saturday Evening Post		Country Gentleman	
	(1)	(2)	(1)	(2)	(1)	(2)	(1)	(2)	(1)	(2)
Success	10%	12%	14%	7%	5%	12%	24%	33%	13%	21%
Nostalgia	4	2	—	—	6	2	4	2	18	7
Virtue	17	17	29	24	17	16	16	20	30	32
Love	42	48	48	44	26	21	36	25	17	21
Religion	1	—	—	—	17	1	—	—	2	—
Crime	2	2	10	11	—	2	9	7	7	10
Personal Portrayals	6	3	5	4	8	21	4	1	—	—
All Other†	18	15	—	8	20	25	7	11	12	9
Total number of themes	96	89	21	72	83	81	132	135	83	99

* Stories were classified in terms of major content, hence interlocking themes are classified as two distinct themes whenever a tangible reward, or rewards, was the outcome. The typical linkages are between love and success, love and virtue, or virtue and success.

† Includes adventure, animal, and "social issue" themes.

TABLES ON RADIO AND TELEVISION CONTENT

Top Ten Radio Network Shows and Their Ratings, February, 1959

World News Roundup (CBS)	4.3
Lowell Thomas	4.2
Arthur Godfrey	4.1
Ned Calmer News (7:45 A.M.)	4.1
Edward R. Murrow	4.0
Ma Perkins	4.0
Dallas Townsend News	4.0
Ned Calmer News (11:00 A.M.)	3.9
Whispering Streets	3.9
Young Dr. Malone	3.9

Source: Nielsen.

Ten Top Television Programs, and Their Ratings, Winter, 1958

Gunsmoke	45.0
Perry Como Show	41.4
Bob Hope Show	40.6
Tales of Wells Fargo	40.2
Cheyenne	38.6
Sugarfoot	38.1
Danny Thomas Show	37.6
Shirley Temple Storybook	37.1
Steve Allen Show	37.0
Wyatt Earp	36.3

Source: Nielsen ratings from *Broadcasting-Telecasting*.

Division of Television Viewing Times among Program Types
(Percentage of viewing time in average home)

	Winter, 1955-56	Winter, 1956-57	Winter, 1957-58	Winter, 1958-59
General, 30 min.	9	7	5	5
Drama, 60-90 min.	13	15	8	7
Variety, 30 min.	8	6	7	8
Variety, 60 min.	16	18	16	13
Western, 30 min.	4	6	10	14
Western, 60 min.	0	1	5	10
Adventure	4	6	6	5
Situation comedy	16	15	15	12
Quiz and audience participation	11	11	10	7
Suspense drama	5	5	10	8
Information	5	4	3	6
Miscellaneous	9	6	5	5

Source: Nielsen, reprinted in *Sponsor*.

Composition of Audiences to Different Types of Television Shows

	Viewers per set in 20 television communities			
	Men	Women	Children	Total
Drama, 30 min.	0.89	1.07	0.54	2.50
Drama, 60 min. or more	0.84	1.03	0.31	2.18
Variety, comedy, music	0.80	1.11	0.58	2.49
Situation comedy	0.63	0.97	1.01	2.61
Adventure	0.79	0.67	1.14	2.60
Mystery, crime, police	0.82	0.98	0.53	2.33
Sports	1.15	0.72	0.22	2.09
Westerns	0.86	0.92	0.80	2.58
Quiz, panel	0.77	1.07	0.36	2.20
Children's shows	0.58	0.70	1.46	2.74
Interview	0.88	1.09	0.32	2.29

Source: Trendex, reprinted in *Sponsor*, for February-March, 1959.

Four Years of New York Television: Time Devoted to Different Types
of Programs during Test Week

	Percentage of Total Time †			
	1951	1952	1953	1954
General drama	24.3	31.7	37.3	37.8 ‡
Children's drama	7.8	6.7	3.9	6.8
Domestic drama	1.1	4.0	5.8	1.6
Children's programs, not otherwise classified	0.1	0.1	0.0	0.1
Comedy, not in drama or variety format	*	*	*	0.4
Dance	0.1	0.0	0.1	0.0
Fine arts, all	0.1	0.1	0.3	0.2
Music, all	3.6	4.2	4.4	6.7
Personalities	4.2	2.3	2.7	4.8
Quizzes, stunts, contests	7.2	7.0	5.6	5.0
Recreation and participant sports	0.2	0.4	0.2	0.0
Sports events, spectator	9.2	6.8	5.3	3.4
Variety, all	18.4	10.9	11.8	11.0
Information, general	11.8	11.3	12.8	9.2
News, all	5.5	5.9	6.6	6.1
Sports news and interviews	0.7	1.2	1.3	1.5
Weather	0.4	0.4	0.5	0.7
Personal relations	0.2	1.0	0.5	0.7
Public events	0.9	1.0	0.0	0.0
Public institutional programs	1.1	1.6	1.2	0.6
Public issues	1.4	1.9	1.5	1.8
Religion	0.2	1.0	1.7	1.8

Source: The Purdue Opinion Panel, *Four Years of New York Television*, published by the National Association of Educational Broadcasters.

* Figures not available for these years.

† The over-all division of time for the most recent year is: Information time, 17.4%; Orientation time, 4.9%; and Entertainment time, 77.7%.

‡ Drama is divided as follows: Comedy drama, 11.1%; Crime drama, 13.5%; Western drama, 7.1%; all other drama, 14.5%.

THE DEVICES OF PROPAGANDA

BY ALFRED MC CLUNG LEE
AND ELIZABETH BRYANT LEE

This formulation of the devices of propaganda appears in *The Fine Art of Propaganda*, published and copyrighted, 1939, by Harcourt, Brace and Company. It is reprinted by permission of the publisher.

Name Calling—giving an idea a bad label—is used to make us reject and condemn the idea without examining the evidence.

Glittering Generality—associating something with a "virtue word" —is used to make us accept and approve the thing without examining the evidence.

Transfer carries the authority, sanction, and prestige of something respected and revered over to something else in order to make the latter acceptable; or it carries authority, sanction, and disapproval to cause us to reject and disapprove something the propagandist would have us reject and disapprove.

Testimonial consists in having some respected or hated person say that a given idea or program or product or person is good or bad.

Plain Folks is the method by which a speaker attempts to convince his audience that he and his ideas are good because they are "of the people," the "plain folks."

Card Stacking involves the selection and use of facts or falsehoods, illustrations or distractions, and logical or illogical statements in order to give the best or the worst possible case for an idea, program, person, or product.

Band Wagon has as its theme, "Everybody—at least all of *us*— is doing it"; with it, the propagandist attempts to convince us that all members of a group to which we belong are accepting his program and that we *must therefore* follow our crowd and "jump on the band wagon."

THE FORMULA FOR READABILITY

BY RUDOLF FLESCH

This, the best-known of the formulas for measuring readability, was developed by the author at Columbia a number of years ago, and was later simplified and revised. Dr. Flesch has had a long career as teacher, writer, and consultant on readability. His revised formula is explained in detail in his article, "A New Readability Yardstick," *Journal of Applied Psychology*, June, 1948. The double formula is reproduced here, with some explanation of its terminology and scoring, by permission of Dr. Flesch. Readers uncertain about its use should consult the article mentioned, or one of Dr. Flesch's books, or the book by Klare listed in the bibliography.

READING EASE equals 206.835 minus .846 WL minus 1.015 SL.

HUMAN INTEREST equals 3.635 PW plus 3.14 PS.

In these formulas,

WL means average number of syllables per 100 words.

SL means average sentence length in number of words.

PW means average percentage of personal words. Personal words include all nouns with natural gender, all pronouns except neuter pronouns, and the words *people* (used with the plural verb) and *folks*.

PS means average percentage of personal sentences. Personal sentences are defined as spoken sentences marked by quotation marks or otherwise; questions, commands, requests, and other sentences directly addressed to the reader; exclamations and grammatically incomplete sentences whose meaning has to be inferred from the context.

Table for Interpreting Reading Ease Scores

RE Score	Description of Style	Typical Magazine	Syllables per 100 Words	Average Sentence Length in Words
0–30	Very difficult	Scientific	192 or more	29 or more
30–50	Difficult	Academic	167	25
50–60	Fairly difficult	Quality	155	21
60–70	Standard	Digests	147	17
70–80	Fairly easy	Slick fiction	139	14
80–90	Easy	Pulp fiction	131	11
90–100	Very easy	Comics	123 or less	8 or less

Table for Interpreting Human Interest Scores

HI Score	Description of Style	Typical Magazine	Percentage of Personal Words	Percentage of Personal Sentences
0–10	Dull	Scientific	2 or less	0
10–20	Mildly interesting	Trade	4	5
20–40	Interesting	Digests	7	15
40–60	Highly interesting	New Yorker	11	32
60–100	Dramatic	Fiction	17 or more	58 or more

THE AUDIENCES OF MASS COMMUNICATION

IN FACE-TO-FACE COMMUNICATION or in communication within small groups, audience study really takes care of itself. The audience is close at hand, and the communicator gets constant feedback that tells him who is listening and who is understanding. But when mass media enter the picture, when circulations grow large and stations begin to broadcast over an area of many hundreds of square miles, when the communicator never sees the audience and rarely hears from them, then audience study becomes an activity of great importance.

Therefore the measurement of audience is a crucial, and sometimes a very difficult, problem for mass communications. The newspaper or magazine must know how large is its reading audience in order to attract advertisers and be able to set a proper advertising rate. The success or failure of a film is measured, of course, by the box-office admissions. The sponsorship of a radio or television program depends on how many are listening.

Whereas it is relatively easy to count subscribers or admissions, it is by no means easy to count broadcast audiences. In an attempt to do this accurately and quickly, a number of rating systems have been developed. All of them work with samples of the audience. Some of them have a sample of people fill out diaries of their television or radio use. Some send interviewers the next day to talk to the sample. Some make a considerable number of "coincidental" telephone calls while a program is on the air, trying to find out how many sets are turned on and to what station. One service attaches a little machine to the receiving set, to record on tape the hours the set is turned on, and the channel. Each of these methods has certain advantages and certain disadvantages. But when you hear that a program has a rating of x per cent, you will know that percentage came from one of these methods. And whether a program has a rating of x or a rating of x + 1, may cause heads to roll on the production staff, and an advertiser to cancel a contract.

Of course, the number of viewers is only one of the elementary facts mass communicators want to know about their audiences. They are anxious to know *who* is listening. For example, if a cosmetics firm is sponsoring a program, the firm wants the program to attract a lot of women. If the sponsor is a razor manufacturer, he wants lots of men. Certain newspapers and magazines can prove that their readers contain a larger-than-average proportion of high-income families, or opinion leaders, and this makes their advertising more valuable for certain products.

Another question that often concerns students of mass audiences is *why* people choose to be in a particular audience, and *what they think* of what they receive. Mass communication is often a rather lonely business for the people who write copy and even for some of the performers, because feedback from the audience is so late and scant. In many cases, they don't know exactly what people think of what they are getting. For example, a newspaper nearly cancelled feature A which had less readership than feature B, only to find out just in time that the people who read feature B didn't feel very strongly about it, whereas the readers of feature A felt very strongly about it, and many of them would have cancelled their subscriptions if A had been removed. One of the contributions of Paul Lazarsfeld to audience study was his realization that audience measurements can be used as readily to study the people as to study the media. What people select, what they like, what they seek, in the mass media, tell us a great deal about their values, tastes, and needs.

The following pages begin with Dr. Lazarsfeld's summary of the communication behavior of Americans—unfortunately, before television became widespread. The next paper is an analysis of newspaper reading patterns by sex, age, and economic status. Mr. Asheim analyzes the book reader. There follows a table showing the ages at which children begin to use the different mass media. Notice that over a third of all children are using television by age 3, and 90 per cent of them are using it by the time they come to school. Finally, there are a number of other tables describing the United States television and radio audience.

THE COMMUNICATIONS BEHAVIOR
OF THE AVERAGE AMERICAN

BY PAUL F. LAZARSFELD
AND PATRICIA KENDALL

Dr. Lazarsfeld was for many years director, Miss Kendall a staff member, of the Bureau of Applied Social Research of Columbia University. Miss Kendall is now Mrs. Lazarsfeld. This chapter is from *Radio Listening in America*, published by Prentice-Hall, New York, 1948, and is reprinted by permission of authors and publisher. The book is based on the second NAB survey of radio listeners, conducted by the National Opinion Research Center of the University of Chicago.

THE MASS MEDIA are a characteristic feature of present-day American life. From a few central agencies come the materials—the radio programs, the magazine stories, the films—which reach throughout the country. And for several hours of each day the average American finds himself a part of the audience for one or another of these mass media.

The present survey is essentially a study of the radio audience. However, it does provide an over-all picture of the general "communications behavior" of the American population. The nation-wide sample, reported on in these pages, was not asked only about radio listening: There were questions on book-reading, movie attendance, the regularity of newspaper and magazine readership. These latter questions were not intended to yield detailed information. They do enable us, however, to distinguish between the "fans," "average consumers," and "abstainers" for any of the mass media, and they do make it possible for us to characterize these different groups. As a result, we can relate radio listening to other types of communications behavior. We can determine whether there is any pattern of exposure, whether a "fan" of one medium is more or less likely to be a fan of other media as well. We can also study the relative importance of the various media for different subgroups in the population.

The classification of respondents into fans, average consumers, and abstainers is, of course, somewhat arbitrary. This can best be seen by comparing the information on movie-going and radio-listening given in Table 1. When we consider that a quarter of our sample saw four or more movies in one month, it does not seem unreasonable to consider a person who saw none as an abstainer, even though he may visit the movies six or seven times a year.

The classification of our respondents according to their amount of radio listening is more arbitrary.[1] Actually, only 5 per cent say that they never listen to the radio in the evening. An additional 21 per cent indicate that their evening listening is confined to less than an hour. Strictly speaking, then, this 21 per cent cannot be called abstainers, for they are reached by the radio. But, again, when we consider the more avid radio listeners, the persons who spend several hours an evening beside their radios, those who listen an hour or less can hardly be placed in the same category. They are light

TABLE 1. Movie-Going and Radio-Listening Behavior

Number of Movies Seen in Previous Month:	
No movies	39%
1-3 movies	37
4 or more movies...........................	24
Total	100%
Amount of Radio Listening on Average Weekday Evening:	
Less than 1 hour...........................	26%
1-3 hours	49
3 or more hours...........................	25
Total	100%

[1] In this as well as in following discussions, our analysis of radio-listening behavior is based on the 91% of our total sample who reported that they owned radios in working order.

TABLE 2. Book and Magazine Readership

Book reading:	
Read no books during past month...............	74%
Read at least one book during month............	26
	—
Total	100%
Magazine reading:	
Read no magazine regularly....................	39%
Read at least one magazine regularly............	61
	—
Total	100%

listeners, at least so far as evening listening is concerned. (Daytime radio listening will be discussed in a later section of this chapter.)

In both of these cases it is the extremes of behavior in our sample which enable us to distinguish between the fans and the abstainers. In neither case should the proportions within each category be taken too literally. Another classification scheme would yield a different distribution of "fans" and "abstainers."

There were no such problems of classification with regard to book and magazine readership. The respondents were asked only whether they read "any magazines regularly" and whether they happened to have read "any books during the last month." The information yielded by these questions is presented in Table 2. Incidentally, the figures reported here correspond fairly closely to those obtained in other surveys.[2]

Newspapers will not be included among the mass media to be discussed, for fully 90 per cent of the respondents in our sample say that they usually read a daily newspaper. It is true, of course, that newspaper reading may mean very different things for different people: Some readers just glance at the headlines; others carefully study the editorials, the feature articles, and so on. But a minimum reading of daily newspapers is so general a habit that no further analysis is possible here.

OVERLAPPING AUDIENCES

The four media with which we shall be concerned fall into two distinct groups. On the one hand there are those that require definite

[2] A review of other studies recently has been carried out for the Public Library Inquiry by Bernard Berelson, dean of the Graduate Library School at the University of Chicago.

TABLE 3. Relationship Between Book and Magazine Reading

Combinations of book and magazine reading:	
Read both books and magazines.................	20%
Read magazines but do not read books...........	41
Read books but do not read magazines...........	5
Read neither books nor magazines...............	34
Total	100%

skills: One must be able to read before he can join the audience for books or magazines. But the readers of the two printed media are not always the same people. Books are more difficult to read than magazines, and, since they are more expensive, they are less easily accessible. It is not surprising, then, that almost every book reader is also a magazine reader, whereas the reverse is by no means true. These facts are shown in Table 3. The total number of magazine readers are found in the first two rows of this table; these figures indicate that only about one-third of the total read books as well as magazines. The total number of book readers, on the other hand, is listed in the first and third rows of Table 3, and here we find that the great majority of book readers, 80 per cent, read magazines in addition to books.

The few respondents (5 per cent of the total) who say that they read books but no magazines pose an interesting problem, for their behavior runs contrary to all expectations. And yet there was nothing in our survey to distinguish them from other readers. There are a few of them in all occupational groups, a few of them on all educational levels, a few of them in all geographical areas. Perhaps they have unusual tastes in reading matter, or perhaps they interpreted our questions in some special manner.

The second group of media, the movies and radio, require no such skills as do books or magazines. They are more properly "spectator" media, in which the audience need do little more than watch or listen. Although there is a considerable number of people who prefer one of these forms of entertainment to the other, the audiences for movies and radio overlap to a large degree, much more than is the case with the printed media. From time to time there have been suggestions that the mass media might compete with

TABLE 4. Proportion of Light Radio Listeners According to
Movie Attendance

	NUMBER OF MOVIES SEEN IN PREVIOUS MONTH		
	No Movies	1-3 Movies	4 or More Movies
Proportion who listen to the radio less than one hour in the evening..............	31%	24%	18%

each other for their audiences;[3] but when actual data have been
available, they have indicated that the media tend to complement,
rather than compete with, each other. It is true, of course, that
television may change this situation in years to come.[4] But our
survey contains no information on this point.

In the present study we found once again that the audiences for
the different mass media are overlapping: A radio fan is likely to
be a movie fan also, while, conversely, those persons who rarely
go to the movies are likely at the same time to be light listeners.
This is indicated in Table 4.

There is a similar relationship even between the printed and the
spectator media. Table 5 shows that individuals who read no magazines regularly are likely to be light listeners and rare moviegoers.

We may speculate for a moment as to the meaning of this general
finding regarding communications behavior. What might account
for the fact that a radio fan tends also to be a frequent moviegoer
and a regular magazine reader? Two possibilities come to mind:
interest and opportunity. The man who is interested in world affairs
finds that the radio will keep him abreast of the most recent events,
that the newsreels will give him a pictorial summary of occurrences,
and that the magazines will provide him with editorial comment
and feature articles. Similarly, a woman interested in romantic
fiction will find stories to suit her liking on the air, in movies, and
in magazines. Or, to put it another way, the individual who is
interested in a particular content will find that he can satisfy his

---

[3] Hugh M. Beville, Jr., "The Challenge of the New Media: Television, FM,
and Facsimile," *Journalism Quarterly*, 25 (1948), 3-11.

[4] For some speculations about the possible effects of television, see "Facts
for the Future—The Broadcaster's Stake," a talk presented by Kenneth H.
Baker at the annual convention of the National Association of Broadcasters,
Los Angeles, May, 1948.

TABLE 5. Proportion of Light Radio Listeners and Rare Moviegoers
According to Magazine Readership

	Do Not Read Magazines	Read Magazines
Proportion who listen to the radio less than one hour in the evening......................	30%	22%
Proportion who saw no movies in the previous month	49	34

interests better by exposing himself to all media than he can by confining his attention to one or two of them. Thus, if he has the time, he will divide it among the various media.

This raises the problem of opportunity. People who are absorbed in a specific activity, whether it is homemaking, a demanding job, or a time-consuming hobby, will have little time to expose themselves to any type of mass medium. Accordingly, they will be the abstainers, not only with regard to one or two, but all media. There may be factors other than interest and opportunity which bring about this pattern of high exposure to all media or no exposure (relatively speaking) to any. But whatever these influences may be and whatever their relative weight in producing the pattern, the fact itself is of obvious general interest and practical importance.

When we consider the relation of book reading and exposure to the spectator media, however, the results are no longer so clear-cut. As we see from Table 6, book readers are more likely to be movie fans, but there is no relation between book reading and radio listening: There are exactly as many radio fans, average consumers, and abstainers among the book readers as there are among the non-readers. With only the material that we have at hand, it is impossible to interpret this result.

The relationship between book reading and movie attendance deserves further comment, however. Table 6 shows that the audiences for these two media are characterized by the familiar overlapping: Book readers are more often frequent moviegoers, and, conversely, nonreaders are more often non-moviegoers. Although this may seem difficult to understand at first glance, developments in the communications industry suggest an explanation. In recent years the film industry has tended more and more to produce movies

TABLE 6. Relationship Between Book Reading and
Exposure to Spectator Media

	Do Not Read Books	Read Books
Amount of Evening Listening		
None to 60 minutes....................	25%	25%
1-3 hours	50	48
Over 3 hours........................	25	27
Total..............................	100%	100%
Movies Seen During Previous Month		
No movies	44%	26%
1-3 movies	35	43
4 or more movies....................	21	31
Total..............................	100%	100%

based on best-selling works of fiction and nonfiction. This apparently
results in a kind of "double exposure": If people read a book which
is later filmed, they go to see that movie and, conversely, they want
to read the book on which a movie they have seen was based. This
mutual stimulation of book-reading and movie-going behavior deserves more detailed study than is possible in the present survey.

THE STRUCTURE OF THE MASS AUDIENCE

There is a tendency, then, toward "all or none" behavior in the
mass media field, but as is so frequently the case with such tendencies, there are a large number of exceptions. These exceptions, to
which we now turn, are due largely to the fact that preferences for
one or another of the media vary according to certain personal
characteristics. Except for radio, each medium draws its most devoted audience from a different sector of the total population.

We should expect formal education to be one of the characteristics distinguishing "fans" and "abstainers." It is unlikely that persons whose schooling does not enable them to read with ease will
be part of the audience for the printed media. These expectations
are borne out by the data in Table 7: As level of formal education declines, so does readership of either books or magazines.

TABLE 7. Proportion of Magazine and Book Readers
According to Education

	College	High School	Grade School
Proportion who read magazines regularly....	86%	68%	41%
Proportion who read at least one book in previous month	50	27	11

Nearly all of the college-educated respondents report that they are regular readers of magazines; less than half of the respondents with grade-school education make that claim. The same educational differences characterize book-reading behavior. But Table 7 indicates also how few book readers are found in a cross-section of the American population: Within each educational group there are fewer book readers than magazine readers.

For the two spectator media, movies and radio, education plays only a minor role. As we see in Table 8, there are only small and irregular differences between the various educational groups in amount of radio listening and movie attendance. It will be well to keep in mind, however, that so far as radio listening goes, the absence of educational differences refers only to the amount of time spent listening to the radio. . . . There are marked differences in *what* is listened to and in attitudes toward radio.

Although it is inherent in the nature of printed media that they will appeal primarily to highly educated people, it is not so immediately obvious what should characterize the audiences of the spectator media. Any observer of the American scene, however, who is asked to guess at the most distinguishing feature of the movie audience would at once think of age. And the materials in our survey would not disappoint him. Table 9 shows that the movie fans are found most generally among the young respondents, and that

TABLE 8. Proportion of Radio and Movie Fans According
to Education

	College	High School	Grade School
Proportion who listen to the radio three hours or more in the evening.................	21%	29%	22%
Proportion who saw four or more movies in previous month	25	28	16

TABLE 9. Movies Seen During Previous Month According to Age

Movie Attendance	21–29	30–39	40–49	50–59	60+
No movies	19%	31%	36%	51%	73%
One movie	15	18	16	15	9
Two or three movies	26	26	27	18	9
Four or five movies	23	16	14	11	6
More than five movies	17	9	7	5	3
	100%	100%	100%	100%	100%

frequent movie going becomes less common as we proceed from one age class to the next. In fact, once the age of fifty is reached, it is non-movie going which is most characteristic.

The relationship between age and movie attendance is probably one of the most spectacular findings in the whole field of communications behavior. Furthermore, it is a result which is confirmed in every study of movie going. For these reasons we have presented the data in considerable detail.[5]

It is not difficult to account for the fact that the movie fans are found among the young people. The teens and twenties are age periods of relatively few personal and social responsibilities, and therefore those people have more "free evenings." And since few young people have as yet developed definite intellectual goals, a free evening might just as well be spent at the movies as in any other type of activity. Furthermore, movie going is a social activity (more than magazine reading, for example) through which the young people make social contacts which are important to them. Movie going is thus much more than mere entertainment. Whatever the content of the film, the experience of attending a movie probably plays an important role in the daily lives of young people.

As people grow older, however, they find their evenings filled with duties and plans, either imposed or self-assigned. In addition, movie going becomes more and more of an effort with increasing age: Having to travel to a theater, perhaps stand in line, and not

---

[5] It might be relevant to point out here that none of our respondents was under 21 years of age. From other surveys of movie-going behavior, however, we know that the peak of movie attendance is at an even younger age—at about 19—so that, if anything, Table 9 underestimates the relationship between age and movie attendance.

TABLE 10. Movie Attendance According to Size of Community

Movies Seen During Previous Month	Metropolitan Districts Over One Million	Metropolitan Districts Under One Million	2,500 to 50,000	Rural Nonfarm (Under 2,500)	Farm
No movies	32%	36%	36%	49%	52%
1-3 movies	40	39	38	33	35
4 or more movies	28	25	26	18	13
Total	100%	100%	100%	100%	100%

return home until late are considerations which make movie going less enjoyable. Finally, older people, married and with a circle of friends of long standing, have less need for the kind of social activity represented by movie going.

There are additional data in our study to indicate the social context of movie attendance. We find, for example, that single people, whatever their age, are more likely to be movie fans than married people. Furthermore, there is a marked sex difference in this respect. The single men in each age group, those who initiate social contacts, are more frequent moviegoers than are single women. Among the married people there is no such sex difference. Further evidence is contained in the radio program preferences expressed by different segments of the movie audience. The fans, no matter what their age, choose popular and dance music, the kind of program suitable for social gatherings, much more frequently than do either the occasional or rare moviegoers.

The movies have an additional feature not characteristic of the other media. Magazines and radio programs come into the home; but we have to go to the movies. We should expect, therefore, that there will be fewer moviegoers where movies are less easily available. Table 10 shows that this is actually the case. We find less movie attendance in rural areas and in small towns than we do in the large cities where there is a movie theater around almost every corner.

This table confirms what many students of communications behavior have emphasized before: The more easily available a medium is, the more people will expose themselves to it. We know, for example, that people are more likely to read the books within easy reach than they are to spend any time or effort searching for books in which they might be more interested.[6]

If education is such an important characteristic of the audience for the printed media, and age and residence for the movie audience, what characterizes the radio audience? Its most outstanding characteristic, it develops, is that it has no special features. During the evening, when most people are at home, there are no marked differences in listening among the major social groups. It is true that people with college training listen somewhat less, but the differences are small compared to those discussed so far.

The term "mass," then, is truly applicable to the medium of radio, for it, more than the other media, reaches all groups of the population uniformly. As we have already indicated, this is true only in so far as *amount* of evening listening is concerned; we shall see presently that there are marked differences in what people listen to. Furthermore, we should remember that we have excluded newspapers from our discussion. Our data do not tell us how much time people spend reading the daily news, but if we take the mere fact of looking at a newspaper, of course, newspaper reading is as general as radio listening.

By confining our discussion to evening listening we have, so far, bypassed one very obvious fact. During the day most men are at work, and the large majority of married women are at home. Women, then, can more easily listen to the radio during the day, and they usually do. Because of this, one might modify the previous statements by saying that a sex difference is the outstanding characteristic of the radio audience. But this difference is due to the time schedules of men and women, rather than to any inherent appeals or characteristics of the medium.

We have data on the amount of time women spend listening to the radio in the morning and afternoon. This information permits us to return once more to the basic pattern of communications behavior. What should we expect from a comparison of women's listening during the three periods of the day? Is there a tendency to become satiated? If a woman listens a lot during one period of the day is she less likely to listen during another? Or does our law hold true here, too? Do women who listen a great deal during one part of the day also listen a lot at another?

[6] D. Waples and R. W. Tyler, *What People Want to Read About: A Study of Group Interests and A Survey of Problems in Adult Reading* (Chicago: American Library Association and the University of Chicago Press, 1931).

The latter possibility is the correct one. Table 11, which actually contains three separate tables, shows the relationship between morning and afternoon listening, between morning and evening listening, and between afternoon and evening listening. Examination of these figures shows again how strong the "all or none" tendency is in communications behavior. And, although the tendency exists in all three comparisons, it is particularly marked between morning and afternoon listening.

We can summarize our findings in this way: A radio fan in the morning is one in the afternoon and evening as well. Because of their psychological characteristics, their time schedules, and their lack of competing interests, women who are heavy listeners at one period of the day will tend to be radio fans throughout the day.

TABLE 11. Three Comparisons of Listening at Different Periods of the Day (Women Only)

a) Relation of Morning and Afternoon Listening	AFTERNOON LISTENING		
Morning Listening	Less than One Hour	1–3 Hours	3 Hours and Over
Less than 1 hour......................	74%	35%	9%
1-3 hours	23	51	34
3 hours and over......................	3	14	57
Total............................	100%	100%	100%

b) Relation of Morning and Evening Listening	EVENING LISTENING		
Morning Listening	Less than One Hour	1–3 Hours	3 Hours and Over
Less than 1 hour......................	70%	51%	39%
1-3 hours	22	37	37
3 hours and over......................	8	12	24
Total............................	100%	100%	100%

c) Relation of Afternoon and Evening Listening	EVENING LISTENING		
Afternoon Listening	Less than One Hour	1–3 Hours	3 Hours and Over
Less than 1 hour.....................	66%	53%	38%
1-3 hours	28	36	33
3 hours and over.....................	6	11	29
Total............................	100%	100%	100%

Conversely, those women who cannot or do not want to listen much at one period will be light listeners consistently.

This ends our brief survey of general communications behavior. . . . It is interesting to observe what happens, . . . when a variety of factors are combined and, thus, a variety of differences accumulated. We remember, for example, that three factors influenced movie attendance; ranked in the order of their importance these were age, residence, and sex. When we isolate the groups in which these three factors operate in combination, the differences in movie attendance become much greater. Among men between twenty-one and twenty-nine years of age living in large metropolitan areas, only 11 per cent fail to go to the movies; but among men fifty years or older living in rural areas, fully 75 per cent said they had seen no movie during the previous month. In the same way, the reader will find that age and education, when combined, make for interesting differences in exposure to the printed media. It is only in regard to radio listening that these various combinations of characteristics fail to distinguish the fans from the abstainers.

AGE, EDUCATION, AND ECONOMIC STATUS AS FACTORS IN NEWSPAPER READING

BY WILBUR SCHRAMM
AND DAVID M. WHITE

Dr. Schramm is director of the Institute for Communication Research at Stanford University. Dr. White is research professor of journalism, Boston University. This paper was first printed in the *Journalism Quarterly* for June, 1949, and is reprinted here by permission of the authors and the magazine.

[This is a brief report of a study made to establish tentative indices for the relation of newspaper reading patterns to the age, education, and socio-economic status of readers.

The conclusions and tables are based on data gathered by a readership study made on January 10 and 11, 1949, in an Illinois city of approximately 100,000 population. The survey dealt with the local evening paper which has approximately 65,000 circulation, half of it in the city. The sample of 746 readers was obtained by selecting home addresses throughout the city on a random basis. Technique is described more fully and implications of the data are discussed in the *Journalism Quarterly*, June, 1949, where this study was first reported.]

CONCLUSIONS

INSOFAR as these data are representative, the following conclusions seem to be indicated:

1. In general, the amount of news reading tends to increase with age, with education, and with economic status. News reading increases very rapidly through the teens, reaches a peak somewhere between the ages of thirty and fifty, and thereafter drops off slightly. High school educated persons read markedly more news in the paper than grade school educated persons, and college educated persons read a little more than high school persons (see Tables I, II, III).

2. A young reader seems to be introduced to the newspaper by its pictorial content. Among readers ten to fifteen, comics are by far the most read items in the paper, followed by news pictures and public affairs cartoons. Readership of news is far below the readership of these pictorial features. And in this entire sample, not one single person between the ages of ten and fifteen was found who had read *any* of the editorials (Table XV).

3. Men's reading of news seems to come to a peak at an earlier age than does women's (Table II).

4. Education seems to make a greater difference in women's reading than in men's (Table I).

5. Economic status seems to make a greater difference in men's reading than in women's (Table III).

6. Teen-agers, persons who have had only grade school education, and persons in the lower economic groups are more likely to read crime and disaster news than any other broad class of news. Reading of crime news increases with age until the decade of the thirties, after which it remains relatively level. It remains unchanged or slightly decreases with rising economic status, and decreases with more education (Table VIII).

7. Reading of public affairs and editorials increases with age, with education, and with higher economic status (Tables IX, X).

8. Reading of comics is at its height in the teens, and decreases steadily from the age of fifteen on. It decreases also with more education and with higher economic position (Tables XI, XVI).

9. Reading of news pictures apparently begins as early as comics, but increases (instead of falling off as comics do) after fifteen, reaches a peak in middle life, and remains relatively high. It increases slightly with education and higher economic status (Tables XII, XVI).

10. Reading of political and editorial cartoons begins strongly

in the teens, increases slightly, then tapers off. It seems to increase significantly with economic status (Table XIII).

11. Reading of society news is low in the teens and thereafter rises to a high plateau between the ages of thirty and sixty. In the case of women, it increases significantly with economic status (Table XIII).

12. Reading of sports news is at its height in the twenties, thereafter tapers off. It increases with economic status, and there is considerable increase between grade school and high school educated groups (Table XV).

13. Older readers are more likely than younger readers to read letters to the editor (Table XVI).

14. Dividing news into two classes—that which gives an immediate reward psychologically (crime, corruption, accidents, disasters, sports, society, human interest, etc., which we shall call Class I) and that which gives a delayed reward (public affairs, economic matters, social problems, science, education, etc., which we shall call Class II)—it appears that:

a. Reading of Class I news comes to a peak at an earlier age than reading of Class II (Table V).
b. Reading of Class I news is higher among the high school educated segment of the population than in the college segment; Class II, higher in the college educated group (Table IV).
c. Reading of Class II news is more likely than reading of Class I to increase with rising economic status (Table VI).

15. People tend to read farther into Class I news than into Class II news (Table VII). There seems to be no significant correlation of depth of reading with age, education, or economic status.

16. Summarizing reading patterns by age, it appears that a reader comes in later years to use a newspaper less and less for entertainment, more and more for information and serious viewpoints on public affairs. There are noteworthy declines of comics and sports with age, noteworthy increases in the reading of public affairs news and editorials. Editorials, which are near the bottom in the ten to twenty bracket, are second only to news pictures in the over-sixty bracket.

17. Summarizing reading patterns by education, it appears that readers on the lower end of the educational curve tend to use the newspaper for entertainment, sensational news, and pictorial mate-

rial. Those at the top of the educational curve tend to use it less for entertainment, more for information on public affairs.

18. Summarizing reading patterns by socio-economic status, it appears that as comic reading declines, so reading of editorials and public affairs news increases with higher economic status. However, in some important respects the pattern for reading by socio-economic groups is not like the two patterns just described in 16 and 17. There is no decline in picture and cartoon reading with higher economic status, and there is a marked increase, with higher status, in the reading of sports and society news.

TABLE I. Percentage of News Read, by Education[1]

	M:%	N	W:%	N	All:%	N
Grade school	17.7	67	12.7	68	15.2	135
High School	21.0	144	17.8	207	19.4	351
College	20.7	132	18.7	128	19.7	260

N (items) = 124

[1] The figures are mean percentages, and should be read as follows: The 67 men in the sample who had only grade school education read an average of 17.7 per cent of all the news in the paper. Since there were 124 news items, the average grade school educated man therefore read about 22 items; the average reader of the paper read a little over 23 items (18.7 per cent).

TABLE II. Percentage of News Read, by Age[2]

	M:%	N	W:%	N	All:%	N
10–19	9.5	37	8.8	61	9.3	98
20–29	21.3	84	15.2	91	18.3	175
30–39	23.4	60	20.1	74	21.8	134
40–49	21.5	60	20.9	86	21.2	146
50–59	22.8	67	19.9	59	21.4	126
60–	21.1	35	17.6	32	19.4	67

N (items) = 124

[2] This seems to be substantiated by earlier studies on time spent reading the newspaper. Henry C. Link, in 4000 interviews for the Psychological Corporation, found that persons 15-19 years of age spent an average of 22 minutes on the paper, whereas persons 40-49 spent an average of 44 minutes. A Minnesota study of a Sunday paper found that readers 15-21 spent 79 minutes (men) and 80 minutes (women), whereas persons 22 or over spent 122 minutes (men) and 100 minutes (women). It must be remembered that this was a Sunday paper, and the reading time therefore was longer. Eugene Liner, in an Illinois thesis, found that readers 20-30 spent 38.5 minutes on the paper as compared to 51 minutes for persons 40-50.

More direct evidence comes from Liner's study:

	Readers	
	20-30	40-50
Wire news	25.5%	28.5%
Local news	16.5	23.5

TABLE III. Percentage of News Read, by Economic Status

	M:%	N	W:%	N	All:%	N
1 (Highest)	25.3	52	19.1	63	22.2	115
2	20.8	129	19.1	144	19.9	273
3	18.3	132	15.4	154	16.9	286
4	18.1	30	14.3	42	16.2	72
			N (items) = 124			

TABLE IV. Percentage of Two Main Classes of News Read, by Education

	Grade School	High School	College	N (items)
Delayed Reward News (public affairs, social problems, economic matters, education, health)	17.1%	22.7%	25.3%	33
Immediate Reward News (crime and corruption, accidents, disasters, sports and recreation, social events, human interest)	14.8	18.2	17.7	91
	N = 135	N = 351	N = 260	

TABLE V. Percentage of Two Main Classes of News Read, by Age

	10–19	20–29	30–39	40–49	50–59	60–
Delayed Reward News	7.6%	20.3%	26.5%	26.1%	27.1%	27.8%
Immediate Reward News	9.9	17.8	20.1	19.5	19.3	16.3
	N = 98	N = 175	N = 134	N = 146	N = 126	N = 67

TABLE VI. Percentage of Two Main Classes of News Read, by Economic Status

	Highest	2	3	Lowest
Delayed Reward News	27.9%	24.0%	20.5%	18.8%
Immediate Reward News	20.1	18.4	15.5	15.3
	N = 115	N = 273	N = 286	N = 72

TABLE VII. Depth of Reading, by Two Main Classes[3]

	M	W	All
Delayed Reward News	64.7%	54.0%	59.7%
Immediate Reward News	85.6	85.9	85.7
All News	71.9	67.3	69.4
	N = 343	N = 403	N = 746
		N (items) = 50	

[3] These figures represent the percentage of persons who, after beginning to read a story, read all of it. They do not include the persons who rejected a story without beginning to read it. Therefore the third column of Table VII means that 85.7 per cent of the persons who began to read immediate reward stories finished them; whereas only 59.7 per cent of persons who began to read delayed reward stories finished them. The 50 items were obtained by selecting pairs of stories with the same length and display position. For a more complete description of this technique, see the article by Wilbur Schramm, "Another Dimension of Newspaper Readership," *Journalism Quarterly*, 24 (1947), 293-306.

TABLE VIII. Percentage of Crime and Disaster News Read[4]

By education:	M	W
Grade school	26.3%	29.6%
High school	27.9	33.2
College	25.7	28.7
By age:		
10–19	11.9	14.2
20–29	21.2	22.8
30–39	34.0	35.6
40–49	25.6	39.2
50–59	32.1	33.3
60–	31.2	31.0
By economic status:		
Highest	28.4	27.4
2	27.7	34.0
3	24.2	29.9
Lowest	28.7	31.8
N (items) = 18		

[4] Liner found that the reading of crime news was slightly higher in the 40-50 bracket than in the 20-30 range, and that the reading of death and hospital news was significantly higher. Chilton J. Bush and Darwin J. Teilhet ("The Press, Reader Habits, and Reader Interest," *Annals of the American Academy of Political and Social Science*, 219, 7-10) report that young adults (20-29) are as interested as older adults in news of crime.

TABLE IX. Percentage of Public Affairs News Read[5]

By education:	M	W
Grade school	23.4%	13.8%
High school	29.6	20.0
College	30.1	26.1
By age:		
10–19	6.8	8.3
20–29	25.1	18.9
30–39	31.5	26.2
40–49	30.7	27.1
50–59	35.6	25.5
60–	36.9	26.8
By economic status:		
Highest	35.8	27.9
2	29.2	23.5
3	27.3	18.1
Lowest	22.1	16.3
N (items) = 20		

5 A University of Minnesota survey of the *Minneapolis Star-Journal* for May 15, 1948, indicates that men are about one-third more likely than boys to read something on the front page. The survey of the *Minneapolis Sunday Tribune* for Oct. 28, 1945, has similar results. Liner found that his readers in the 40-50 age bracket were about 15 per cent more likely than readers in the 20-30 bracket to read political and international news.

TABLE X. Percentage of Editorials Read[6]

By education:	M	W
Grade school	23.0%	17.6%
High school	39.0	23.6
College	36.6	40.3
By age:		
10–19	2.1	7.6
20–29	26.5	22.6
30–39	43.3	36.3
40–49	44.3	36.0
50–59	47.6	33.0
60–	36.0	32.0
By economic status:		
Highest	54.0	45.3
2	38.6	30.0
3	31.3	21.3
Lowest	22.3	20.3

N (items) = 3

[6] Bush and Teilhet: "Elderly men, but not women, are (slightly) more interested in editorials."

Star-Journal survey May 15, 1948: 20 per cent increase in editorial page reading on part of readers over 21 as compared to readers 12-20.

Liner: 40 per cent increase in editorial reading between 20-30 age group and 40-50 age group.

Schramm: two Iowa weekly newspapers studied in 1946 and 1947 showed a doubling of editorial readership after the age of 20.

Continuing Study of Newspaper Reading, in its 100-study summary:

Editorial page reading by occupational groups:

	M	W
A. (executive and professional)	58%	44%
B. (junior executive)	52	38
C. (skilled workmen)	45	28
D. (unskilled labor)	38	24

TABLE XI. Percentage of Comics Read[7]

By education:	M	W
Grade school	55.5%	48.8%
High school	57.0	43.9
College	46.8	33.3
By age:		
10–19	76.5	71.0
20–29	66.3	54.4
30–39	60.3	42.6
40–49	59.4	35.5
50–59	32.1	21.8
60–	36.5	12.1
By economic status:		
Highest	49.1	30.2
2	49.3	35.5
3	55.2	46.5
Lowest	57.3	58.5

N (items) = 13

[7] Higher reading of comics among youth is confirmed by Bush and Teilhet, Liner, and the Minnesota surveys. George Gallup ("A Scientific Method for Determining Reader Interest," *Journalism Quarterly*, 7 (1930), 9-12 says, "Bankers, university presidents, professors, doctors, and lawyers read comic strips as avidly as truck drivers, waiters, and day laborers.") This is not confirmed by the present study, or by the *Continuing Study's* 100-study summary, which gives these figures:

Reading of comics by occupational groups:

	M	W
A. (executive and professional)	68%	66%
B. (junior executive)	74	73
C. (skilled workmen)	81	78
D. (unskilled labor)	81	81

TABLE XII. Percentage of News Pictures Read[8]

By education:	M	W
Grade school	56.0%	50.8%
High school	60.2	57.5
College	57.7	58.7
By age:		
10–19	46.8	44.6
20–29	61.2	59.6
30–39	65.3	62.5
40–49	67.6	59.3
50–59	46.7	51.7
60–	51.6	41.1
By economic status:		
Highest	57.7	63.1
2	57.6	57.5
3	57.8	56.7
Lowest	56.0	43.7
N (items) = 18		

[8] 200 interviews with children 6 to 16, made in 1946-47 by Schramm, indicated clearly that the first real interests of children in the newspaper are with comics and pictures.

TABLE XIII. Percentage of Cartoons Read

By education:	M	W
Grade school	32.5%	23.0%
High school	40.5	23.5
College	34.5	20.0
By age:		
10–19	41.5	15.0
20–29	39.4	20.1
30–39	39.0	27.0
40–49	42.5	26.0
50–59	29.0	23.5
60–	22.5	17.0
By economic status:		
Highest	39.5	29.5
2	39.0	21.0
3	36.0	20.5
Lowest	26.5	23.5
N (items) = 2		

TABLE XIV. Percentage of Society News Read[9]

By education:	M	W
Grade school	9.2%	10.3%
High school	8.4	17.1
College	8.6	18.5
By age:		
10–19	3.6	7.7
20–29	6.8	14.0
30–39	10.8	19.6
40–49	8.8	20.7
50–59	11.2	20.1
60–	11.0	15.3
By economic status:		
Highest	10.8	19.0
2	9.6	18.8
3	7.9	14.7
Lowest	8.9	9.3
N (items) = 29		

[9] The *Continuing Study's* 100-study summary confirms this greater interest in society news on the part of upper occupational groups.

TABLE XV. Percentage of Sports News Read[10]

By education:	M	W
Grade school	17.1%	2.8%
High school	23.0	15.3
College	21.8	16.3
By age:		
10–19	17.0	4.5
20–29	31.7	3.9
30–39	22.4	5.2
40–49	25.5	4.5
50–59	18.2	7.1
60–	14.1	4.9
By economic status:		
Highest	30.6	6.8
2	20.9	5.7
3	19.3	4.2
Lowest	16.4	3.8

N (items) = 33

[10] The *Minneapolis Sunday Tribune* survey of Oct. 28, 1945, gave these results for sports readership:

Boys	Girls	Men	Women
70%	49%	63%	17%

These figures are for *any* sports readership; the figures in the present study are for average readership of all sports items.

The *Continuing Study's* 100-study summary does not show an increase of sports readership in higher occupational groups.

TABLE XVI. Readership in Age Group 10–15

All News	5.7%
News Pictures	43.3
Cartoons	27.1
Comics	80.3
Editorials	0
Public Affairs News	3.6
Economic News	0
Crime and Disaster News	6.7
Sports News	9.2
Society News	3.8

N = 46

TABLE XVII. Readership of Letters to the Editor,
by Age[11]

Age	Readership
10–19	2.3%
20–29	19.0
30–39	30.1
40–49	31.0
50–59	37.2
60–	35.6

[11]Bush and Teilhet, in the article cited: "Elderly readers (those over 50 years) are more interested than the younger age groups in letters to the editor. . . ."

PORTRAIT OF THE BOOK READER
AS DEPICTED IN CURRENT RESEARCH

BY LESTER ASHEIM

Professor Asheim is dean of the Library School at the University of Chicago. He has adapted the following data from Bernard Berelson's *The Library's Public*, New York, 1949, on which he worked as a research assistant. The material is used by permission of the Columbia University Press, which holds copyright, and the Public Library Inquiry of the Social Science Research Council.

READING STUDIES have by now pretty well defined the reader of books in the usual ecological terms.[1] The major correlate of book reading has been definitely established as education: that the better-educated read more books is a consistent finding in all investigations of reading and under all patterns of factor control. The other distinguishing characteristics of the book reader—the younger adults read more books than the older; those with higher economic status more than those with lower; urban dwellers more than rural—are all allied, to more or less degree, with the education factor. Clearly, the special skill required to make book reading comparatively easy and

---

[1] See, for example, William S. Gray and Ruth Munroe, *The Reading Interests and Habits of Adults,* a Preliminary Report (New York: Macmillan, 1930); B. Lamar Johnson, "Adult Reading Interests as Related to Sex and Marital Status," *School Review,* XL (January, 1932), 33-43; Bernice K. Leary, "What Does Research Say About Reading?" *Journal of Educational Research,* XXIX (February, 1946), 434-44; Henry C. Link and Harry Hopf, *People and Books: A Study of Reading and Book-Buying Habits* (New York: Book Industry Committee, Book Manufacturers' Institute, 1946); *et al.*

enjoyable limits the number of potential book readers to those who have had the education which provides it.

Just how extensive, then, is the reading of books relative to the other major forms of communication exposure which make less stringent demands upon the user? The comparison can be made only in rough terms, but from several recent studies[2] the picture of public exposure to the major media of communication in the United States today may be described somewhat as follows: About 25 to 30 per cent of the adult population read one or more *books* a month; about 45 to 50 per cent of the adult population see a *motion picture* once every two weeks or oftener; about 60 to 70 per cent of the adult population read one or more *magazines* more or less regularly; about 85 to 90 per cent of the adult population read one or more *newspapers* more or less regularly; about 90 to 95 per cent of the adult population listen to the *radio* fifteen minutes a day or more. Of the five major public media of communication, book reading is the most limited in terms of total population. Almost everybody listens to the radio or reads a newspaper, but only one person in four reads a book a month.

Two of the recent surveys mentioned above, based upon national cross-sectional samples, reasonably well agree as to the incidence of monthly book reading in the adult population as here summarized. Their findings are reported in the following table:

Amount of Monthly Book Reading

Number of Books Read During One Month	Percentages, 1948	
	SRC	Lazarsfeld & Kendall
No books	70	74
One book	13	9
Two or three books	8	11
Four or more books	8	6
No answer	1	0
Total number of respondents	1,151	3,529

[2] For example: Paul F. Lazarsfeld and Patricia L. Kendall, *Radio Listening in America: The People Look at Radio—Again* (New York: Prentice-Hall, Inc., 1948); Survey Research Center, University of Michigan, "The Public Library and the People; a National Survey Done for the Public Library Inquiry" (S. R. C., April, 1948), (mimeographed); Magazine Advertising Bureau, Inc., *Nationwide Magazine Audience Study* (New York: M. A. B., 1948).

If the definition of book reader is extended to include everyone who has read one or more books in a year, then almost one-half of the adult population qualifies. The Survey Research Center reports the incidence of book reading per year as follows:

Amount of Yearly Book Reading

Number of Books Read in Past Year	Percentages
No books	48
One to four books	18
Five to fourteen books	16
Fifteen to forty-nine books	9
Fifty books or more	7
No answer	2
Total number of respondents	1,151

Because of the socially desirable and prestige-bearing status of book reading in this country, it seems fair to assume that the figures in both tables indicate an upper limit to the amount of such reading. The data for the longer period depend upon the respondent's memory and are thus subject to an additional inflation or other inaccuracy. In either case, then, book reading is clearly not an activity of the majority of Americans today.

BOOK READING AND OTHER TYPES OF COMMUNICATION

To what extent does book reading correlate with use of the other communication media? Do readers of books tend to use the other

Relationship of Book Reading to the Use of
Other Types of Communication [3]

Communications Behavior	Percentage of Book Readers [*]	Percentage of Non-readers of Books
Read one or more newspapers every day	91	76
Listen to the radio two or more hours a day	69	68
Read two or more magazines regularly	71	39
Attend two or more motion pictures a month	58	45
Hear one or more speeches or talks a year	29	14
Sometimes read government bulletins	58	37

[*] Book readers are defined as adults who have read one or more books during the past year.

[3] SRC, op. cit.

media more than nonreaders do, or do they tend to rely less on the other media because of their use of books? Are the other media rivals for the attention of book readers, or do they supplement and complement book reading?

According to the studies, book readers listen and see and read more than those who do not read books. This is true in the case of every major medium of communication except radio.

Almost every book reader, for example, is also a magazine reader. The reverse, however, is by no means true; every magazine reader is not a reader of books. Lazarsfeld and Kendall[4] report that whereas 41 per cent of Americans read magazines but not books, only 5 per cent read books but not magazines. Another 20 per cent read *both* books and magazines. Thus, only one-third of the magazine readers are also book readers, whereas 80 per cent of the book readers are also readers of magazines.

Book readers are also more likely to be movie fans. Lazarsfeld and Kendall[5] provide data on this aspect of overlapping communication behavior also. Their study shows that only 26 per cent of book readers, as opposed to 44 per cent of nonreaders, do not go to movies; and also that the percentage of book readers who attend movies at least once a week is one-fourth to one-third higher than the corresponding attendance figure for nonreaders of books. The use of novels as a source of motion picture scripts, if based upon the assumption that book readers will be enticed into theaters to see the film versions, would seem to be justified by the evidence of attendance by book readers. The novel's readers are definitely potential patrons of its motion picture adaptation.

In the realm of radio alone this pattern fails to appear. Again turning to Lazarsfeld and Kendall,[6] we see that book readers, although they are more likely than nonreaders of books to read newspapers, read magazines, go to movies, hear speeches, and order government bulletins, nevertheless are *not* more likely to listen to the radio. There are almost exactly as many avid radio fans, average consumers of its programs, and total abstainers from listening among the book readers as there are among the nonreaders.

[4] *Op. cit.*
[5] *Ibid.*
[6] *Ibid.*

OTHER CHARACTERISTICS OF BOOK READERS IN TERMS
OF COMMUNICATION BEHAVIOR AND ATTITUDES

The major implication of these findings is that the readers of the book are not limited to that one form of communication. Instead they also give a good deal of attention to the other forms. The book readers in any community are prominent members of the group who are interested in communications in general.

In addition they tend to be the heaviest users of the "serious" content of the communication media.[7] A survey of women in a middle-sized Midwestern community[8] supplies the following figures:

	Percentages	
Special Communication Behavior	Book Readers	Nonreaders
Read magazine articles discussing news events in more detail	62	40
Read biographical sketches in magazines	47	26
Saw a documentary film in last three months	41	27
Listen to discussion of public issues on air	34	23

Book readers are also among the more critically minded persons in the community, so far as the communication media are concerned. They are more likely than are the nonreaders of books to be dissatisfied with newspapers, magazines, and the radio. To some extent, perhaps, their dissatisfaction with the commercial mass media is responsible for their reliance upon or supplemental use of the more specialized medium of books. In any case, in any community, book readers tend to be particularly critical of the communication media available, as shown by Lazarsfeld and Kendall.[9]

The differences between readers and nonreaders in the matter of criticism hold when education is controlled, and the differences on the fee question hold with an economic level control. The fact of book readership, then, is a significant correlate of the attitudes expressed in reply to these questions.

[7] This may explain in part their comparative lack of interest in the usual radio fare.

[8] Bureau of Applied Social Research, Columbia University. "The Flow of Influence in an American Community," 1948 (manuscript).

[9] *Op. cit.*

CONCLUSION

Does book reading make people more serious and critical, or do the more serious and critically minded people tend to read books to supply the kind of content that will meet their needs? Does use of

Attitudes Toward Other Media of Communication	Percentages	
	Book Readers	Nonreaders
Sometimes feel like criticizing:		
Newspapers	80	64
Radio	78	63
Movies	72	52
Would prefer to pay $5 fee per year for present radio without advertising	29	17
Total number of respondents	830	2,320

one medium send people to others, or is the use of one medium of communication merely indicative of interest in communication in general? The question of the direction of the influence cannot, of course, be answered from these data. What we do know is that, whether as cause or effect or a combination of both, the readers of books are those who are, as Berelson[10] has pointed out, the "culturally alert" members of the community.

[10] Bernard Berelson, "The Public Library, Book Reading, and Political Behavior," *Library Quarterly*, XV (October, 1945), 281-99.

BEGINNINGS OF MEDIA USE AMONG CHILDREN

Percentage of Children Who Had Begun to Use Given Media by a Given Age

Age	TV	Radio	Maga-zines	Comic Books	Movies	Books Read to Them	Books They Read	Newspapers Read to Them	Newspapers They Read
2	14	11	3	1	1	38	0	0	0
3	37	20	11	6	8	58	0	0	0
4	65	27	20	17	21	72	2	4	0
5	82	40	33	35	39	74	9	9	0
6	91	47	41	50	60	75	40	12	9
7	94	53	53	61	70	75	73	12	44
8	95	62	59	68	76	75	86	12	59
9	96	65	62	70	77	75	89	12	71

Source: Schramm, San Francisco data, 1958.

TABLES ON TELEVISION AND RADIO AUDIENCES

Television Saturation by Region of the U.S.

Region	Homes	Saturation
Northeast	12,102,000	91%
East Central	7,815,000	89%
West Central	8,432,000	86%
South	9,390,000	77%
Pacific	6,261,000	86%

Source: Nielsen, March, 1959.

Average Hours of Television Viewing per Home

	Morning	Afternoon	Night	Total Day
Monday-Friday	39 min.	1 hr. 32 min.	3 hrs. 39 min.	5 hrs. 50 min.
Saturday	48	1:31	4.03	6:22
Sunday	16	1:44	3:43	5:43
All days	37	1:33	3:43	5:53

Source: *Sponsor*, from NTI, Jan.-Feb., 1959.

Radio and Television Use per Day Compared, for an Average Home

Year	Radio	Television	Total
1950	4 hrs. 19 min.	0 hrs. 35 min.	4 hrs. 54 min.
1955	2:27	3:39	6:06
1959	1:54	5:29	7:23

Source: *Telecasting.*

U.S. Television Viewing, by Hour and Season

(Average number of homes at a given minute using television)

Hour	Summer viewing: July-August, 1958		Winter viewing: January-February, 1959	
	Percentage	Thousands of homes	Percentage	Thousands of homes
Daytime, Monday-Friday:				
6-7 A.M.	0.5	215	0.8	352
7-8	4.4	1,892	6.6	2,904
8–9	8.9	3,827	13.1	5,764
9–10	12.7	5,461	15.6	6,864
10-11	14.8	6,364	19.4	8,536
11-12 noon	17.4	7,482	23.4	10,296
12 N-1 P.M.	20.4	8,772	25.8	11,352
1-2	18.0	7,740	21.7	9,548
2-3	16.9	7,267	20.7	9,108
3-4	19.0	8,170	22.8	10,032
4-5	21.6	9,288	32.5	14,300
5-6	23.8	10,234	42.4	18,656
Evening, Sunday-Saturday:				
6-7 P.M.	28.6	12,298	56.1	24,684
7-8	35.8	15,394	65.4	28,776
8-9	45.4	19,522	69.7	30,668
9-10	50.0	21,500	65.3	28,732
10-11	39.5	16,985	46.9	20,636
11-12 mid.	21.9	9,417	24.5	10,780

Source: Nielsen, tabulated by *Sponsor*.

U.S. Radio Listening Audience, by Hour and Season

(Thousands of homes)

Hour	Summer, 1958	Winter, 1959
Daytime, Monday-Friday:		
6-7 A.M.	3,622	4,945
7-8	6,020	9,593
8-9	6,362	9,148
9-10	6,362	7,665
10-11	6,313	6,478
11-12 noon	6,118	6,132
12 N-1 P.M.	6,705	6,725
1-2	5,775	5,143
2-3	5,188	4,599
3-4	4,845	4,401
4-5	4,405	4,500
5-6	4,894	5,192
Evening, Sunday-Saturday:		
6-7 P.M.	4,502	4,302
7-8	3,230	2,918
8-9	2,741	2,473
9-10	2,790	2,423
10-11	2,692	2,423
11-12 mid.	1,909	1,929

Source: Nielsen.

Television Audience Composition at Different Hours

Hour	Percentage of viewers who are			
	Men, 18 and over	Women, 18 and over	12-17	4-11
10-11 A.M.	12	49	5	34
(Total viewers: 10,956,000)				
2-3 P.M.	14	59	6	21
(Total viewers: 13,134,000)				
6-7 P.M.	21	30	14	35
(Total viewers: 38,623,000)				
8-8:30 P.M.	28	34	12	24
(Total viewers: 67,408,000)				
10-10:30 P.M.	36	43	10	11
(Total viewers: 56,463,000)				

Source: *Sponsor*, using Nielsen audience figures for November-December, 1958.

Radio Audience Composition by Time of the Day

(In millions of listeners, per average quarter-hour)

	Men, 18 or over	Women, 18 or over	12-17	4-11	Total
Morning, Mon.-Fri.	2.6	7.3	1.0	1.7	12.6
Afternoon, Mon.-Fri.	1.9	5.5	0.7	1.1	9.2
Evening, Sun.-Sat.	2.1	3.3	1.1	0.9	7.4

Source: NRI, November-December, 1958, reprinted in *Sponsor*.

Radio Listening by Region of the U.S.

(Average hours per home per day)

Northeast	1 hr. 50 min.
East Central	1:34
West Central	2:16
South	1:44
Pacific	1:52

Source: Nielsen (in home listening only), November-December, 1958.

EFFECTS OF MASS COMMUNICATIONS

THE EFFECTS OF COMMUNICATION are, of course, the chief reason for all other communication study. What does a given communication do to people? By what persons, under what conditions, is it likely to be attended to? By whom is it likely to be understood? By whom, favorably received? What attitudes or action will it lead to? Questions like these are in the mind of a communicator when he constructs and sends a message; and they are in the minds of scholars and critics when they think about communication.

One characteristic of communication study is that it tends to have exceedingly practical and important implications for us. The effects of communication are no "merely academic" question when we meet them in the form of propaganda effects, or effects of the mass media on children. This is why a great deal of communication effect study goes on in society as well as in the laboratory. Political candidates and parties are constantly trying to find out how they can communicate with people so as to win votes. Advertisers and advertising agencies conduct a great deal of research into people's buying habits, wishes, and needs, trying to find out what kind of ad will bring the most sales. Public-spirited organizations are trying to find out how best to communicate with people so as to persuade them to adopt better health or agricultural practices. Propaganda agencies of governments are studying the ways in which their messages may influence the attitudes and opinions of the people of other countries. School officials are studying how they can communicate with their students so as to make them learn as fast as possible. A great many kinds of communication effect studies like these are going on all the time, in addition to laboratory studies in universities; and we are gradually accumulating a body of useful knowledge as to how communication has an effect and how it may be put to use in service of man.

There are two extreme theories about mass communication effects. One is that they are extremely potent, and, in the hands of advertisers, political propagandists, and mass educators, are manipulating man against his will. This we might call the "1984" theory. In opposition to it is the kind of theory which you will read in the Lazarsfeld-Merton article which follows, and which argues that the very nature of the mass media leads them to be conservative, to oppose change rather than bring it about, and to stay close to the status quo ante even in matters of taste.

There is a great deal in each of these theories, and yet neither is the whole truth. You will have to decide, from reading the following selections and others, how much effect the mass media really have on society. But you can begin by supposing, at least tentatively, that the truth lies somewhere between the "1984" and the "status quo" theory, and probably a bit closer to the latter.

We know that people learn from the mass media. School children learn from television, and through their lives people learn much of their picture of the distant world from newspapers and other mass media. We know also that mass media have something to do with public taste. For example, we very quickly find out about the new popular songs and begin to whistle them, now that we have broadcast media. A few years ago, children all over the country broke out with Davy Crockett caps and sweaters, because Crockett programs were being broadcast. And we know also that mass communication can affect our attitudes and opinions and help to build up our pictures of candidates or of foreign relations—persons and places we seldom see except through the media.

But there are two other elements of great importance in determining what kind of effect the media have. For one thing, does one point of view have a monopoly of the media? This is what happens in totalitarian countries. Our intention has been to let the mass media compete in a "free market place of ideas," so that people could read opposing viewpoints on politics, foreign relations, and all other controversial issues—and decide for themselves. Therefore, if we ever find that our media are being monopolized by one viewpoint on a controversial issue, that is something worth worrying about. The other question has to do with what happens outside the media. The family, the school, the church, the kind of discussion that takes place in society, are very important influences. Anything that comes to us from the mass media is passed through that set of influences before it becomes a very important guide to our action. Therefore, unless these other institutions and relationships abdicate, the mass media are not likely to have any "1984" influence on us. We might say that what television does to children, for example, is less significant than what children do with television; and what children do with television, the needs they use it to meet, depend on their homes, their schools, their peer group relations, and many other factors quite outside the mass media.

This section begins with one of the classics of public opinion study, the first chapter from Walter Lippmann's *Public Opinion*. There follows a penetrating examination by Waples, Berelson, and Bradshaw of the social effects of reading. The article by Lazarsfeld and Merton, already mentioned, faces up to the question of whether the media really make for change or for retaining the status quo. The selection by Lazarsfeld, Berelson, and Gaudet, on the effect of mass media in a presidential campaign, is a chapter from their book, *The People's Choice*, which was the first intensive scientific study of communication and opinion in national politics. Dr. Berelson's paper, which follows, is a much admired study of how public opinion and communication affect one another. The Langs' paper is a stimulating, somewhat disturbing study of how television can alter political reality and, wittingly or unwittingly, contribute to a "landslide" of popular sentiment. And finally Dr. Wirth examines the idea of consensus, and points out that mass communications may be used either to divide humans from one another, or bring them together. They can contribute either to a will to fight or a will to cooperate. They can contribute, if used wisely, to "a social psychological integration of the human race commensurate with the interdependent far-flung and rich material resources and human energies of the world." Or they can simply waste time!

THE WORLD OUTSIDE AND THE PICTURES IN OUR HEADS

BY WALTER LIPPMANN

Walter Lippmann is the distinguished political columnist. This is the
first chapter of his book *Public Opinion,* copyright 1922, by the author.
It is used by permission of The Macmillan Company, publishers.

THERE IS an island in the ocean where in 1914 a few Englishmen,
Frenchmen, and Germans lived. No cable reaches that island, and
the British mail steamer comes but once in sixty days. In September
it had not yet come, and the islanders were still talking about the
latest newspaper which told about the approaching trial of Madame
Caillaux for the shooting of Gaston Calmette. It was, therefore, with
more than usual eagerness that the whole colony assembled at the
quay on a day in mid-September to hear from the captain what the
verdict had been. They learned that for over six weeks now those of
them who were English and those of them who were French had
been fighting in behalf of the sanctity of treaties against those of
them who were Germans. For six strange weeks they had acted as
if they were friends, when in fact they were enemies.

But their plight was not so different from that of most of the population of Europe. They had been mistaken for six weeks, on the
continent the interval may have been only six days or six hours.
There was an interval. There was a moment when the picture of
Europe on which men were conducting their business as usual, did
not in any way correspond to the Europe which was about to make

a jumble of their lives. There was a time for each man when he was still adjusted to an environment that no longer existed. All over the world as late as July 25th men were making goods that they would not be able to ship, buying goods they would not be able to import, careers were being planned, enterprises contemplated, hopes and expectations entertained, all in the belief that the world as known was the world as it was. Men were writing books describing that world. They trusted the picture in their heads. And then over four years later, on a Thursday morning, came the news of an armistice, and people gave vent to their unutterable relief that the slaughter was over. Yet in the five days before the real armistice came, though the end of the war had been celebrated, several thousand young men died on the battlefields.

Looking back we can see how indirectly we know the environment in which nevertheless we live. We can see that the news of it comes to us now fast, now slowly; but that whatever we believe to be a true picture, we treat as if it were the environment itself. It is harder to remember that about the beliefs upon which we are now acting, but in respect to other peoples and other ages we flatter ourselves that it is easy to see when they were in deadly earnest about ludicrous pictures of the world. We insist, because of our superior hindsight, that the world as they needed to know it, and the world as they did know it, were often two quite contradictory things. We can see, too, that while they governed and fought, traded and reformed in the world as they imagined it to be, they produced results, or failed to produce any, in the world as it was. They started for the Indies and found America. They diagnosed evil and hanged old women. They thought they could grow rich by always selling and never buying. A caliph, obeying what he conceived to be the Will of Allah, burned the library at Alexandria.

Writing about the year 389, St. Ambrose stated the case for the prisoner in Plato's cave who resolutely declines to turn his head. "To discuss the nature and position of the earth does not help us in our hope of the life to come. It is enough to know what Scripture states. 'That He hung up the earth upon nothing' (Job xxvi. 7). Why then argue whether He hung it up in air upon the water, and raise a controversy as to how the thin air could sustain the earth; or why, if upon the waters, the earth does not go crashing down to the bottom? . . . Not because the earth is in the middle, as if suspended on even balance, but because the majesty of God constrains it by the law of His will, does it endure stable upon the unstable and the void."[1]

It does not help us in our hope of the life to come. It is enough to know what Scripture states. Why then argue? But a century and a half after St. Ambrose, opinion was still troubled, on this occasion by the problem of the Antipodes. A monk named Cosmas, famous for his scientific attainments, was therefore deputed to write a Christian Topography, or "Christian Opinion concerning the World."[2] It is clear that he knew exactly what was expected of him, for he based all his conclusions on the Scriptures as he read them. It appears, then, that the world is a flat parallelogram, twice as broad from east to west as it is long from north to south. In the center is the earth surrounded by ocean, which is in turn surrounded by another earth, where men lived before the deluge. This other earth was Noah's port of embarkation. In the north is a high conical mountain around which revolve the sun and moon. When the sun is behind the mountain it is night. The sky is glued to the edges of the outer earth. It consists of four high walls which meet in a concave roof, so that the earth is the floor of the universe. There is an ocean on the other side of the sky, constituting the "waters that are above the firmament." The space between the celestial ocean and the ultimate roof of the universe belongs to the blest. The space between the earth and sky is inhabited by the angels. Finally, since St. Paul said that all men are made to live upon the "face of the earth" how could they live on the back where the Antipodes are supposed to be? With such a passage before his eyes, a Christian, we are told, should not 'even speak of the Antipodes.' "

Far less should he go to the Antipodes; nor should any Christian prince give him a ship to try; nor would any pious mariner wish to try. For Cosmas there was nothing in the least absurd about his map. Only by remembering his absolute conviction that this was the map of the universe can we begin to understand how he would have dreaded Magellan or Peary or the aviator who risked a collision with the angels and the vault of heaven by flying seven miles up in the air. In the same way we can best understand the furies of war and politics by remembering that almost the whole

[1] Hexaëmeron, i. cap 6, quoted in *The Mediæval Mind*, by Henry Osborn Taylor (London: The Macmillan Company, 1927), I, 73.

[2] Lecky, *Rationalism in Europe* (London: Longmans, Green, 1913), I, 276-78.

of each party believes absolutely in its picture of the opposition, that it takes as fact, not what is, but what it supposes to be the fact. And that therefore, like Hamlet, it will stab Polonius behind the rustling curtain, thinking him the king, and perhaps like Hamlet add:

> Thou wretched, rash, intruding fool, farewell!
> I took thee for thy better; take thy fortune.

2

Great men, even during their lifetime, are usually known to the public only through a fictitious personality. Hence the modicum of truth in the old saying that no man is a hero to his valet. There is only a modicum of truth, for the valet, and the private secretary, are often immersed in the fiction themselves. Royal personages are, of course, constructed personalities. Whether they themselves believe in their public character, or whether they merely permit the chamberlain to stage-manage it, there are at least two distinct selves, the public and regal self, the private and human. The biographies of great people fall more or less readily into the histories of these two selves. The official biographer reproduces the public life, the revealing memoir the other. The Charnwood Lincoln, for example, is a noble portrait, not of an actual human being, but of an epic figure, replete with significance, who moves on much the same level of reality as Aeneas or St. George. Oliver's Hamilton is a magnificent abstraction, the sculpture of an idea, "an essay" as Mr. Oliver himself calls it, "on American union." It is a formal monument to the statecraft of federalism, hardly the biography of a person. Sometimes people create their own façade when they think they are revealing the interior scene. The Repington diaries and Margot Asquith's are a species of self-portraiture in which the intimate detail is most revealing as an index of how the authors like to think about themselves.

But the most interesting kind of portraiture is that which arises spontaneously in people's minds. When Victoria came to the throne, says Mr. Strachey, "among the outside public there was a great wave of enthusiasm. Sentiment and romance were coming into fashion; and the spectacle of the little girl-queen, innocent, modest, with fair hair and pink cheeks, driving through her capital, filled the hearts of the beholders with raptures of affectionate loyalty. What, above all, struck everybody with overwhelming force was the contrast between Queen Victoria and her uncles. The nasty old men, debauched and selfish, pigheaded and ridiculous, with their perpetual burden of debts, confusions, and disreputabilities— they had vanished like the snows of winter, and here at last, crowned and radiant, was the spring."

M. Jean de Pierrefeu[3] saw hero-worship at first hand, for he was an officer on Joffre's staff at the moment of that soldier's greatest fame:

For two years, the entire world paid an almost divine homage to the victor of the Marne. The baggage-master literally bent under the weight of the boxes, of the packages and letters which unknown people sent him with a frantic testimonial of their admiration. I think that outside of General Joffre, no commander in the war has been able to realize a comparable idea of what glory is. They sent him boxes of candy from all the great confectioners of the world, boxes of champagne, fine wines of every vintage, fruits, game, ornaments and utensils, clothes, smoking materials, inkstands, paperweights. Every territory sent its specialty. The painter sent his picture, the sculptor his statuette, the dear old lady a comforter or socks, the shepherd in his hut carved a pipe for his sake. All the manufacturers of the world who were hostile to Germany shipped their products, Havana its cigars, Portugal its port wine. I have known a hairdresser who had nothing better to do than to make a portrait of the General out of hair belonging to persons who were dear to him; a professional penman had the same idea, but the features were composed of thousands of little phrases in tiny characters which sang the praise of the General. As to letters, he had them in all scripts, from all countries, written in every dialect, affectionate letters, grateful, overflowing with love, filled with adoration. They called him Savior of the World, Father of his Country, Agent of God, Benefactor of Humanity, etc. . . . And not only Frenchmen, but Americans, Argentinians, Australians, etc., etc. . . . Thousands of little children, without their parents' knowledge, took pen in hand and wrote to tell him their love; most of them called him Our Father. And there was poignancy about their effusions, their adoration, the sighs of deliverance that escaped from thousands of hearts at the defeat of barbarism. To all these naif little souls, Joffre seemed like St. George crushing the dragon. Certainly he incarnated for the conscience of mankind the victory of good over evil, of light over darkness.

Lunatics, simpletons, the half-crazy and the crazy turned their darkened brains toward him as toward reason itself. I have read the letter of a person living in Sidney, who begged the General to save him from his enemies; another, a New Zealander, requested him to send some soldiers to the house of a gentleman who owed him ten pounds and would not pay.

Finally, some hundreds of young girls, overcoming the timidity of

---

[3] Jean de Pierrefeu, *G. Q. G. Trois ans au Grand Quartier Général*, pp. 94-95.

their sex, asked for engagements, their families not to know about it; others wished only to serve him.

This ideal Joffre was compounded out of the victory won by him, his staff and his troops, the despair of the war, the personal sorrows, and the hope of future victory. But beside hero-worship there is the exorcism of devils. By the same mechanism through which heroes are incarnated, devils are made. If everything good was to come from Joffre, Foch, Wilson, or Roosevelt, everything evil originated in the Kaiser Wilhelm, Lenin, and Trotsky. They were as omnipotent for evil as the heroes were omnipotent for good. To many simple and frightened minds there was no political reverse, no strike, no obstruction, no mysterious death or mysterious conflagration anywhere in the world of which the causes did not wind back to these personal sources of evil.

3

World-wide concentration of this kind on a symbolic personality is rare enough to be clearly remarkable, and every author has a weakness for the striking and irrefutable example. The vivisection of war reveals such examples, but it does not make them out of nothing. In a more normal public life, symbolic pictures are no less governant of behavior, but each symbol is far less inclusive because there are so many competing ones. Not only is each symbol charged with less feeling because at most it represents only a part of the population, but even within that part there is infinitely less suppression of individual difference. The symbols of public opinion, in times of moderate security, are subject to check and comparison and argument. They come and go, coalesce and are forgotten, never organizing perfectly the emotion of the whole group. There is, after all, just one human activity left in which whole populations accomplish the union sacrée. It occurs in those middle phases of a war when fear, pugnacity, and hatred have secured complete dominion of the spirit, either to crush every other instinct or to enlist it, and before weariness is felt.

At almost all other times, and even in war when it is deadlocked, a sufficiently greater range of feelings is aroused to establish conflict, choice, hesitation, and compromise. The symbolism of public opinion usually bears, as we shall see, the marks of this balancing of interest. Think, for example, of how rapidly, after the armistice, the precarious and by no means successfully established symbol of

Allied Unity disappeared, how it was followed almost immediately by the breakdown of each nation's symbolic picture of the other: Britain the Defender of Public Law, France watching at the Frontier of Freedom, America the Crusader. And think then of how within each nation the symbolic picture of itself frayed out, as party and class conflict and personal ambition began to stir postponed issues. And then of how the symbolic pictures of the leaders gave way, as one by one, Wilson, Clemenceau, Lloyd George, ceased to be the incarnation of human hope, and became merely the negotiators and administrators for a disillusioned world.

Whether we regret this as one of the soft evils of peace or applaud it as a return to sanity is obviously no matter here. Our first concern with fictions and symbols is to forget their value to the existing social order, and to think of them simply as an important part of the machinery of human communication. Now in any society that is not completely self-contained in its interests and so small that everyone can know all about everything that happens, ideas deal with events that are out of sight and hard to grasp. Miss Sherwin of Gopher Prairie is aware that a war is raging in France and tries to conceive it. She has never been to France, and certainly she has never been along what it now the battlefront. Pictures of French and German soldiers she has seen, but it is impossible for her to imagine three million men. No one, in fact, can imagine them, and the professionals do not try. They think of them as, say, two hundred divisions. But Miss Sherwin has no access to the order of battle maps, and so if she is to think about the war, she fastens upon Joffre and the Kaiser as if they were engaged in a personal duel. Perhaps if you could see what she sees with her mind's eye, the image in its composition might be not unlike an eighteenth-century engraving of a great soldier. He stands there boldly unruffled and more than life size, with a shadowy army of tiny little figures winding off into the landscape behind. Nor it seems are great men oblivious to these expectations. M. de Pierrefeu tells of a photographer's visit to Joffre. The General was in his "middle class office, before the worktable without papers, where he sat down to write his signature. Suddenly it was noticed that there were no maps on the walls. But since according to popular ideas it is not possible to think of a general without maps, a few were placed in position for the picture, and removed soon afterwards."[4]

---

[4] *Ibid.*, p. 99.

The only feeling that anyone can have about an event he does not experience is the feeling aroused by his mental image of that event. That is why until we know what others think they know, we cannot truly understand their acts. I have seen a young girl, brought up in a Pennsylvania mining town, plunged suddenly from entire cheerfulness into a paroxysm of grief when a gust of wind cracked the kitchen window-pane. For hours she was inconsolable, and to me incomprehensible. But when she was able to talk, it transpired that if a window-pane broke it meant that a close relative had died. She was, therefore, mourning for her father, who had frightened her into running away from home. The father was, of course, quite thoroughly alive as a telegraphic inquiry soon proved. But until the telegram came, the cracked glass was an authentic message to that girl. Why it was authentic only a prolonged investigation by a skilled psychiatrist could show. But even the most casual observer could see that the girl, enormously upset by her family troubles, had hallucinated a complete fiction out of one external fact, a remembered superstition, and a turmoil of remorse, and fear and love for her father.

Abnormality in these instances is only a matter of degree. When an Attorney-General, who has been frightened by a bomb exploded on his doorstep, convinces himself by the reading of revolutionary literature that a revolution is to happen on the first of May, 1920, we recognize that much the same mechanism is at work. The war, of course, furnished many examples of this pattern: the casual fact, the creative imagination, the will to believe, and out of these three elements, a counterfeit of reality to which there was a violent instinctive response. For it is clear enough that under certain conditions men respond as powerfully to fictions as they do realities, and that in many cases they help to create the very fictions to which they respond. Let him cast the first stone who did not believe in the Russian army that passed through England in August, 1914, did not accept any tale of atrocities without direct proof, and never saw a plot, a traitor, or a spy where there was none. Let him cast a stone who never passed on as the real inside truth what he had heard someone say who knew no more than he did.

In all these instances we must note particularly one common factor. It is the insertion between man and his environment of a pseudo-environment. To that pseudo-environment his behavior is a response. But because it *is* behavior, the consequences, if they are acts, operate not in the pseudo-environment where the behavior is stimulated, but in the real environment where action eventuates. If the behavior is not a practical act, but what we call roughly thought and emotion, it may be a long time before there is any noticeable break in the texture of the fictitious world. But when the stimulus of the pseudo-fact results in action on things or other people, contradiction soon develops. Then comes the sensation of butting one's head against a stone wall, of learning by experience, and witnessing Herbert Spencer's tragedy of the murder of a Beautiful Theory by a Gang of Brutal Facts, the discomfort in short of a maladjustment. For certainly, at the level of social life, what is called the adjustment of man to his environment takes place through the medium of fictions.

By fictions I do not mean lies. I mean a representation of the environment which is in lesser or greater degree made by man himself. The range of fiction extends all the way from complete hallucination to the scientists' perfectly self-conscious use of a schematic model, or his decision that for his particular problem accuracy beyond a certain number of decimal places is not important. A work of fiction may have almost any degree of fidelity, and so long as the degree of fidelity can be taken into account, fiction is not misleading. In fact, human culture is very largely the selection, the rearrangement, the tracing of patterns upon, and the stylizing of, what William James called "the random irradiations and re-settlements of our ideas."[5] The alternative to the use of fictions is direct exposure to the ebb and flow of sensation. That is not a real alternative, for however refreshing it is to see at times with a perfectly innocent eye, innocence itself is not wisdom, though a source and corrective of wisdom.

For the real environment is altogether too big, too complex, and too fleeting for direct acquaintance. We are not equipped to deal with so much subtlety, so much variety, so many permutations and combinations. And although we have to act in that environment, we have to reconstruct it on a simpler model before we can manage with it. To traverse the world men must have maps of the world. Their persistent difficulty is to secure maps on which their own need, or someone else's need, has not sketched in the coast of Bohemia.

---

[5] James, *Principles of Psychology* (New York: Holt, 1950), II, 638.

4

The analyst of public opinion must begin then, by recognizing the triangular relationship between the scene of action, the human picture of that scene, and the human response to that picture working itself out upon the scene of action. It is like a play suggested to the actors by their own experience, in which the plot is transacted in the real lives of the actors, and not merely in their stage parts. The moving picture often emphasizes with great skill this double drama of interior motive and external behavior. Two men are quarreling, ostensibly about some money, but their passion is inexplicable. Then the picture fades out and what one or the other of the two men sees with his mind's eye is reënacted. Across the table they were quarreling about money. In memory they are back in their youth when the girl jilted him for the other man. The exterior drama is explained: the hero is not greedy: the hero is in love.

A scene not so different was played in the United States Senate. At breakfast on the morning of September 29, 1919, some of the senators read a news dispatch in the *Washington Post* about the landing of American marines on the Dalmatian coast. The newspaper said:

FACTS NOW ESTABLISHED

The following important facts appear already *established*. The orders to Rear Admiral Andrews commanding the American naval forces in the Adriatic, came from the British Admiralty via the War Council and Rear Admiral Knapps in London. The approval or disapproval of the American Navy Department was not asked. . . .

WITHOUT DANIELS' KNOWLEDGE

Mr. Daniels was admittedly placed in a peculiar position when cables reached here stating that the forces over which he is presumed to have exclusive control were carrying on what amounted to naval warfare without his knowledge. It was fully realized that the *British Admiralty might desire to issue orders to Rear Admiral Andrews* to act on behalf of Great Britain and her Allies, because the situation required sacrifice on the part of some nation if D'Annunzio's followers were to be held in check.

It was further realized that *under the new league of nations plan foreigners would be in a position to direct American Naval forces in emergencies* with or without the consent of the American Navy Department. . . . etc. (Italics mine).

The first senator to comment is Mr. Knox of Pennsylvania. Indignantly he demands investigation. In Mr. Brandegee of Connecticut, who spoke next, indignation has already stimulated credulity. Where Mr. Knox indignantly wishes to know if the report is true, Mr. Brandegee, a half minute later, would like to know what would have happened if marines had been killed. Mr. Knox, interested in the question, forgets that he asked for an inquiry, and replies. If American marines had been killed, it would be war. The mood of the debate is still conditional. Debate proceeds. Mr. McCormick of Illinois reminds the Senate that the Wilson administration is prone to the waging of small unauthorized wars. He repeats Theodore Roosevelt's quip about "waging peace." More debate. Mr. Brandegee notes that the marines acted "under orders of a Supreme Council sitting somewhere," but he cannot recall who represents the United States on that body. The Supreme Council is unknown to the Constitution of the United States. Therefore Mr. New of Indiana submits a resolution calling for the facts.

So far the senators still recognize vaguely that they are discussing a rumor. Being lawyers they still remember some of the forms of evidence. But as red-blooded men they already experience all the indignation which is appropriate to the fact that American marines have been ordered into war by a foreign government and without the consent of Congress. Emotionally they want to believe it, because they are Republicans fighting the League of Nations. This arouses the Democratic leader, Mr. Hitchcock of Nebraska. He defends the Supreme Council: it was acting under the war powers. Peace has not yet been concluded because the Republicans are delaying it. Therefore the action was necessary and legal. Both sides now assume that the report is true, and the conclusions they draw are the conclusions of their partisanship. Yet this extraordinary assumption is in a debate over a resolution to investigate the truth of the assumption. It reveals how difficult it is, even for trained lawyers, to suspend response until the returns are in. The response is instantaneous. The fiction is taken for truth because the fiction is badly needed.

A few days later an official report showed that the marines were not landed by order of the British Government or of the Supreme Council. They had not been fighting the Italians. They had been landed at the request of the Italian Government to protect Italians, and the American commander had been officially thanked by the Italian authorities. The marines were not at war with Italy. They had acted according to an established international practice which had nothing to do with the League of Nations.

The scene of action was the Adriatic. The picture of that scene in the senators' heads at Washington was furnished, in this case probably with intent to deceive, by a man who cared nothing about the Adriatic, but much about defeating the League. To this picture, the Senate responded by a strengthening of its partisan differences over the League.

5

Whether in this particular case the Senate was above or below its normal standard, it is not necessary to decide. Nor whether the Senate compares favorably with the House, or with other parliaments. At the moment, I should like to think only about the world-wide spectacle of men acting upon their environment, moved by stimuli from their pseudo-environments. For when full allowance has been made for deliberate fraud, political science has still to account for such facts as two nations attacking one another, each convinced that it is acting in self-defense, or two classes at war, each certain that it speaks for the common interest. They live, we are likely to say, in different worlds. More accurately, they live in the same world, but they think and feel in different ones.

It is to these special worlds, it is to these private or group, or class, or provincial, or occupational, or national, or sectarian arti-facts, that the political adjustment of mankind in the Great Society takes place. Their variety and complication are impossible to describe. Yet these fictions determine a very great part of men's political behavior. We must think of perhaps fifty sovereign parlia-ments consisting of at least a hundred legislative bodies. With them belong at least fifty hierarchies of provincial and municipal assemblies, which with their executive, administrative, and legis-lative organs, constitute formal authority on earth. But that does not begin to reveal that complexity of political life. For in each of these innumerable centers of authority there are parties, and these parties are themselves hierarchies with their roots in classes, sec-tions, cliques, and clans; and within these are the individual poli-ticians, each the personal center of a web of connection and mem-ory and fear and hope.

Somehow or other, for reasons often necessarily obscure, as the result of domination or compromise or a logroll, there emerge from these political bodies commands, which set armies in motion or make peace, conscript life, tax, exile, imprison, protect property or confiscate it, encourage one kind of enterprise and discourage another, facilitate immigration or obstruct it, improve communication or censor it, establish schools, build navies, proclaim "policies," and "destiny," raise economic barriers, make property or unmake it, bring one people under the rule of another, or favor one class as against another. For each of these decisions some view of the facts is taken to be conclusive, some view of the circumstances is accepted as the basis of inference and as the stimulus of feeling. What view of the facts, and why that one?

And yet even this does not begin to exhaust the real complexity. The formal political structure exists in a social environment, where there are innumerable large and small corporations and institutions, voluntary and semi-voluntary associations, national, provincial, urban, and neighborhood groupings, which often as not make the decisions that the political body registers. On what are these decisions based?

Modern society [says Mr. Chesterton] is intrinsically insecure because it is based on the notion that all men will do the same thing for different reasons. . . . And as within the head of any convict may be the hell of a quite solitary crime, so in the house or under the hat of any suburban clerk may be the limbo of a quite separate philosophy. The first man may be a complete Materialist and feel his own body as a horrible machine manufacturing his own mind. He may listen to his thoughts as to the dull ticking of a clock. The man next door may be a Christian Scientist and regard his own body as somehow rather less substantial than his own shadow. He may come almost to regard his own arms and legs as delusions like moving serpents in the dream of delirium tremens. The third man in the street may not be a Christian Scientist but, on the contrary, Christian. He may live in a fairy tale as his neighbors would say; a secret but solid fairy tale full of the faces and presences of unearthly friends. The fourth man may be a theosophist, and only too probably a vegetarian; and I do not see why I should not gratify myself with the fancy that the fifth man is a devil worshiper. . . . Now whether or not this sort of variety is valuable, this sort of unity is shaky. To expect that all men for all time will go on thinking different things, and yet doing the same things, is a doubtful speculation. It is not founding society on a communion, or even on a convention, but rather on a coincidence. Four men may meet under the same lamp post; one to paint it pea green as part of a great municipal reform; one to read his breviary in the light of it; one to embrace it with accidental ardour in a fit of alcoholic enthusiasm; and the last merely because the pea green post is a conspicuous point of rendezvous with his young lady. But to expect this to happen night after night is unwise. . . .[6]

[6] G. K. Chesterton, "The Mad Hatter and the Sane Householder," *Vanity Fair* (January, 1921), p. 54.

For the four men at the lamppost substitute the governments, the parties, the corporations, the societies, the social sets, the trades and professions, universities, sects, and nationalities of the world. Think of the legislator voting a statute that will affect distant peoples, a statesman coming to a decision. Think of the Peace Conference reconstituting the frontiers of Europe, an ambassador in a foreign country trying to discern the intentions of his own government and of the foreign government, a promoter working a concession in a backward country, an editor demanding a war, a clergyman calling on the police to regulate amusement, a club lounging-room making up its mind about a strike, a sewing circle preparing to regulate the schools, nine judges deciding whether a legislature in Oregon may fix the working hours of women, a cabinet meeting to decide on the recognition of a government, a party convention choosing a candidate and writing a platform, twenty-seven million voters casting their ballots, an Irishman in Cork thinking about an Irishman in Belfast, a Third International planning to reconstruct the whole of human society, a board of directors confronted with a set of their employees' demands, a boy choosing a career, a merchant estimating supply and demand for the coming season, a speculator predicting the course of the market, a banker deciding whether to put credit behind a new enterprise, the advertiser, the reader of advertisements. . . . Think of the different sorts of Americans thinking about their notions of "The British Empire" or "France" or "Russia" or "Mexico." It is not so different from Mr. Chesterton's four men at the pea green lamppost.

6

And so before we involve ourselves in the jungle of obscurities about the innate differences of men, we shall do well to fix our attention upon the extraordinary differences in what men know of the world.[7] I do not doubt that there are important biological differences. Since man is an animal it would be strange if there were not. But as rational beings it is worse than shallow to generalize at all about comparative behavior until there is a measurable similarity between the environments to which behavior is a response.

The pragmatic value of this idea is that it introduces a much

[7] Cf. Graham Wallas, Our Social Heritage (New Haven: Yale University Press, 1921), pp. 77 et seq.

needed refinement into the ancient controversy about nature and nurture, innate quality and environment. For the pseudo-environment is a hybrid compounded of "human nature" and "conditions." To my mind it shows the uselessness of pontificating about what man is and always will be from what we observe man to be doing, or about what are the necessary conditions of society. For we do not know how men would behave in response to the facts of the Great Society. All that we really know is how they behave in response to what can fairly be called a most inadequate picture of the Great Society. No conclusion about man or the Great Society can honestly be made on evidence like that.

This, then, will be the clue to our inquiry. We shall assume that what each man does is based not on direct and certain knowledge, but on pictures made by himself or given to him. If his atlas tells him that the world is flat he will not sail near what he believes to be the edge of our planet for fear of falling off. If his maps include a fountain of eternal youth, a Ponce de Leon will go in quest of it. If someone digs up yellow dirt that looks like gold, he will for a time act exactly as if he had found gold. The way in which the world is imagined determines at any particular moment what men will do. It does not determine what they will achieve. It determines their effort, their feelings, their hopes, not their accomplishments and results. The very men who most loudly proclaim their "materialism" and their contempt for "ideologues," the Marxian communists, place their entire hope on what? On the formation by propaganda of a class-conscious group. But what is propaganda, if not the effort to alter the picture to which men respond, to substitute one social pattern for another? What is class consciousness but a way of realizing the world? National consciousness but another way? And Professor Giddings' consciousness of kind, but a process of believing that we recognize among the multitude certain ones marked as our kind?

Try to explain social life as the pursuit of pleasure and the avoidance of pain. You will soon be saying that the hedonist begs the question, for even supposing that man does pursue these ends, the crucial problem of why he thinks one course rather than another likely to produce pleasure, is untouched. Does the guidance of man's conscience explain? How then does he happen to have the particular conscience which he has? The theory of economic self-interest? But how do men come to conceive their interest in one way rather than another? The desire for security, or prestige, or domination, or what is vaguely called self-realization? How do men conceive their security, what do they consider prestige, how do they figure out the means of domination, or what is the notion of self which they wish to realize? Pleasure, pain, conscience, acquisition, protection, enhancement, mastery, are undoubtedly names for some of the ways people act. There may be instinctive dispositions which work toward such ends. But no statement of the end, or any description of the tendencies to seek it, can explain the behavior which results. The very fact that men theorize at all is proof that their pseudo-environments, their interior representations of the world, are a determining element in thought, feeling, and action. For if the connection between reality and human response were direct and immediate, rather than indirect and inferred, indecision and failure would be unknown, and (if each of us fitted as snugly into the world as the child in the womb), Mr. Bernard Shaw would not have been able to say that except for the first nine months of its existence no human being manages its affairs as well as a plant.

The chief difficulty in adapting the psychoanalytic scheme to political thought arises in this connection. The Freudians are concerned with the maladjustment of distinct individuals to other individuals and to concrete circumstances. They have assumed that if internal derangements could be straightened out, there would be little or no confusion about what is the obviously normal relationship. But public opinion deals with indirect, unseen, and puzzling facts, and there is nothing obvious about them. The situations to which public opinions refer are known only as opinions. The psychoanalyst, on the other hand, almost always assumes that the environment is knowable, and if not knowable then at least bearable, to any unclouded intelligence. This assumption of his is the problem of public opinion. Instead of taking for granted an environment that is readily known, the social analyst is most concerned in studying how the larger political environment is conceived, and how it can be conceived more successfully. The psychoanalyst examines the adjustment to an X, called by him the environment; the social analyst examines the X, called by him the pseudo-environment.

He is, of course, permanently and constantly in debt to the new psychology, not only because when rightly applied it so greatly helps people to stand on their own feet, come what may, but because the study of dreams, fantasy, and rationalization has thrown light on how the pseudo-environment is put together. But he cannot assume as his criterion either what is called a "normal biological career"[8] within the existing social order, or a career "freed from religious suppression and dogmatic conventions" outside.[9] What for a sociologist is a normal social career? Or one freed from suppressions and conventions? Conservative critics do, to be sure, assume the first, and romantic ones the second. But in assuming them they are taking the whole world for granted. They are saying in effect either that society is the sort of thing which corresponds to their idea of what is normal, or the sort of thing which corresponds to their idea of what is free. Both ideas are merely public opinions, and while the psychoanalyst as physician may perhaps assume them, the sociologist may not take the products of existing public opinion as criteria by which to study public opinion.

7

The world that we have to deal with politically is out of reach, out of sight, out of mind. It has to be explored, reported, and imagined. Man is no Aristotelian god contemplating all existence at one glance. He is the creature of an evolution who can just about span a sufficient portion of reality to manage his survival, and snatch what on the scale of time are but a few moments of insight and happiness. Yet this same creature has invented ways of seeing what no naked eye could see, of hearing what no ear could hear, of weighing immense masses and infinitesimal ones, of counting and separating more items than he can individually remember. He is learning to see with his mind vast portions of the world that he could never see, touch, smell, hear, or remember. Gradually he makes for himself a trustworthy picture inside his head of the world beyond his reach.

Those features of the world outside which have to do with the behavior of other human beings, in so far as that behavior crosses ours, is dependent upon us, or if interesting to us, we call roughly public affairs. The pictures inside the heads of these human beings, the pictures of themselves, of others, of their needs, purposes, and relationship, are their public opinions. Those pictures which are

---

[8] Edward J. Kempf, *Psychopathology* (St. Louis: C. V. Mosby, 1920), p. 116.
[9] *Ibid.*, p. 151.

acted upon by groups of people, or by individuals acting in the name of groups, are Public Opinion with capital letters. And so in the chapters which follow we shall inquire first into some of the reasons why the picture inside so often misleads men in their dealings with the world outside. Under this heading we shall consider first the chief factors which limit their access to the facts. They are the artificial censorships, the limitations of social contact, the comparatively meager time available in each day for paying attention to public affairs, the distortion arising because events have to be compressed into very short messages, the difficulty of making a small vocabulary express a complicated world, and finally the fear of facing those facts which would seem to threaten the established routine of men's lives.

The analysis then turns from these more or less external limitations to the question of how this trickle of messages from the outside is affected by the stored up images, the preconceptions, and prejudices which interpret, fill them out, and in their turn powerfully direct the play of our attention, and our vision itself. From this it proceeds to examine how in the individual person the limited messages from outside, formed into a pattern of stereotypes, are identified with his own interests as he feels and conceives them. In the succeeding sections it examines how opinions are crystallized into what is called Public Opinion, how a National Will, a Group Mind, a Social Purpose, or whatever you choose to call it, is formed.

The first five parts constitute the descriptive section of the book. There follows an analysis of the traditional democratic theory of public opinion. The substance of the argument is that democracy in its original form never seriously faced the problem which arises because the pictures inside people's heads do not automatically correspond with the world outside. And then, because the democratic theory is under criticism by socialist thinkers, there follows an examination of the most advanced and coherent of these criticisms, as made by the English Guild Socialists. My purpose here is to find out whether these reformers take into account the main difficulties of public opinion. My conclusion is that they ignore the difficulties, as completely as did the original democrats, because they, too, assume, and in a much more complicated civilization, that somehow mysteriously there exists in the hearts of men a knowledge of the world beyond their reach.

I argue that representative government, either in what is ordinarily called politics, or in industry, cannot be worked successfully, no matter what the basis of election, unless there is an independent, expert organization for making the unseen facts intelligible to those who have to make the decisions. I attempt, therefore, to argue that the serious acceptance of the principle that personal representation must be supplemented by representation of the unseen facts would alone permit a satisfactory decentralization, and allow us to escape from the intolerable and unworkable fiction that each of us must acquire a competent opinion about all public affairs. It is argued that the problem of the press is confused because the critics and the apologists expect the press to realize this fiction, expect it to make up for all that was not foreseen in the theory of democracy, and that the readers expect this miracle to be performed at no cost or trouble to themselves. The newspapers are regarded by democrats as a panacea for their own defects, whereas analysis of the nature of news and of the economic basis of journalism seems to show that the newspapers necessarily and inevitably reflect, and therefore, in greater or lesser measure, intensify, the defective organization of public opinion. My conclusion is that public opinions must be organized for the press if they are to be sound, not by the press as is the case today. This organization I conceive to be in the first instance the task of a political science that has won its proper place as formulator, in advance of real decision, instead of apologist, critic, or reporter after the decision has been made. I try to indicate that the perplexities of government and industry are conspiring to give political science this enormous opportunity to enrich itself and to serve the public. And, of course, I hope that these pages will help a few people to realize that opportunity more vividly, and therefore to pursue it more consciously.

THE EFFECTS OF READING

BY DOUGLAS WAPLES,
BERNARD BERELSON, AND
FRANKLIN R. BRADSHAW

The authors are, respectively, two former deans and a former professor of the Graduate Library School of the University of Chicago. The selection is from their book, *What Reading Does to People,* published and copyrighted by the University of Chicago Press, 1940. It is here reprinted by permission of the publisher.

THE DISCUSSION as a whole seeks to identify and to interrelate the more important of the factors or conditions presumed to determine the effects of any reading experience. Such factors may be grouped in broad classes for easier description.

A reading experience involves a person who reads a publication and who is affected by the reading in various ways and in varying degrees. How he is affected depends both upon the publication and what he brings to it. Hence it becomes important to distinguish the content of the publication itself from the readers' predispositions and from such other factors as may be responsible for any inferred or observed effects of the experience.

The publication combines several distinguishable factors: the author's predispositions, the subjects discussed, the statements made (whether statements of fact or statements of preference), the simplicity or complexity of the idiom, the author's many psychological traits which give the work its individuality, the author's intent, and the "slanting." By slanting we mean the author's conscious and unconscious use of symbols which tend to sway the reader's sympathies and convictions in certain directions.

The reader's predispositions combine elements somewhat less readily identified than the elements of the publications are, because the predispositions may change. The predispositions that partially determine the effects of reading include the reader's sympathies with the various groups in which he is placed by his sex, age, income, education, occupation, and other traits—sympathies which combine to sway the reader toward or away from the direction in which the publication is slanted; the reader's motives for reading, or the satisfactions he expects the particular publication to furnish; his present beliefs, loyalties, opinions, prejudices, and other attitudes regarding the subjects read about, which may strengthen or weaken or completely reverse the flow of influence intended by the author; and the emotional and physical conditions in which the reading is done. Such conditions affect the quality of attention the publication receives and hence the number and character of the predispositions called into play.

The two major factors (the publication itself and the reader's predispositions) combine to produce reader responses and effects. The effects upon the individual reader extend through time, and the more remote effects are complicated by the publication's effects upon other readers, by what people are saying about it. They are also complicated, of course, by the effects of other communications (conversations, radio talks, newsreels, etc.). The range of time and space through which the social effects of a publication may be traced extends even to nonreaders; not merely to those who have not read the item in question—say, the *Federalist* papers or *Uncle Tom's Cabin*—but even to those who do not read at all. The initial effect upon a few readers may be so diffused by the currents of group interest and by the groundswells of public opinion at large that the effects of a single publication may carry far indeed.

The unrealistic character of present notions about the social effects of public communications may be due in large part to inadequate terms of description. The terms conventionally used, by popular writers and by students alike, are inadequate because they confine attention to but one or two of the many factors involved in the effect.

As the following chapters should explain, any "social effect" of reading may be attributed in part to several major factors, each of which needs to be duly considered; for example: (1) the social context (folkways and group conflicts and personal conditions), which explains the publication of some writings and the nonpublication of others; (2) the methods of distributing publications, which explain the variations between what different groups of people would prefer to read and what they do read; (3) the differences among the publications themselves, which explain why and how some are more influential than others; and (4) the different predispositions of readers, which explain why the same publication will incite one reader to revolutionary action, will be vigorously condemned by another, and will be ignored or read with apathy by a third. To these, for logical completeness, should be added a fifth; namely, the influence of other communications than reading, since the influence of radio, films, public speeches, or private conversation may either reinforce or offset the influences of reading as such.

. . . .

It is, of course, much harder to identify the several factors in the effects of reading upon groups. The student group effects should therefore begin with groups so chosen that as many as possible of the factors may be safely inferred. The choice of groups, other things equal, should be based *primarily* upon the type of effect which is assumed to be predominant. The more easily distinguishable types of group effect might include the following: (1) the instrumental effect (e.g., fuller knowledge of a practical problem and greater competence to deal with it); (2) the prestige effect (e.g., relief of inferiority feeling by reading what increases self-approval); (3) the reinforcement effect (e.g., reinforcement of an attitude or conversion to another attitude toward controversial issues); (4) the aesthetic effect (e.g., obtaining aesthetic experience from specimens of literary art); and (5) the respite effect (e.g., finding relief from tensions by reading whatever offers pleasant distraction).

Typical effects of about this degree of generality offer a useful frame of reference for group studies because they suggest effects upon which each of the more important factors converge. It is plain that each of these five types represents a large *amount* of publication; for example, (1) instrumental effects are served by factual reports of all kinds; (2) prestige effects are served by sentimental fiction, as in women's magazines, with characters expressly drawn to encourage readers to identify themselves with characters they would like to resemble; (3) reinforcement effects are served by the entire range of special pleading which seeks to influence votes or purchases; (4) aesthetic effects are served by all genuinely artistic writing which helps the reader to view reality through the author's more observing eyes, by writing which is innocent of "designs" upon the reader; and (5) respite effects are served by all sorts of writing —comic strips, joke columns, human interest stories, and other diverting items, which come between the reader and his worries.

It is equally plain that the system of distribution is well organized to supply each of these types of publication to some groups who demand them; for example, (1) textbooks to students; (2) women's magazines to housewives; (3) campaign literature to voters, journals of opinion to businessmen, and the equivalent in each occupation or special interest group; (4) belles-lettres to the sophisticated reader; and (5) newspaper supplements to everybody.

Each of these types of publication is abundantly supplied to several groups who are known to read it constantly. Hence we can select one or more groups sufficiently homogeneous to exhibit certain common predispositions toward the given type of publication; e.g., (1) the students' desire to learn what textbook information will pass the course, (2) the housewives' loneliness and desire for prestige, (3) the businessmen's desire to find support for their political opinions, (4) the readers of any first-rate novel, or (5) the readers of the New Yorker. In selecting housewives, for example, whose common predispositions would encourage their identification with the fiction characters of women's magazines, one would naturally seek housewives who are young, who have slender incomes, who have not attended high school, who belong to few organizations, and who for other reasons are likely to be lonely and feel inferior. Such women are likely to seek and obtain prestige effects from their reading.

A further step in describing the group effects of reading will be to identify the relevant content in each type of publication by making appropriate analyses. The categories to be used in the analysis will naturally be determined by the effects anticipated and the publications involved. Factual writing will require categories which distinguish differences in the veracity, organization, concreteness, etc., of the subject matter. Sentimental magazines will require categories distinguishing types of fiction characters by their social class, age, income, sophistication, deference to other characters, attitude toward authority, and the like. Controversial writing will invite attention to the symbols which show with which particular social or political interests the author sympathizes and to which he seeks to convert the reader. Belles-lettres would involve categories based on appropriate principles of aesthetic criticism. Merely diverting publications would require categories which differentiate the kinds and degrees of novelty they supply.

We should then have as sources of evidence a group suspected of common predisposition, toward a definable literary stimulus, which the agencies of distribution make easily available, and which we know the group seeks with some consistency, because it supplies a type of satisfaction this group wants more than most readers want it. The more important factors are thus accounted for in the situation available for study. We have them to examine the group's responses to the reading in relation to responses to other comparable experiences—e.g., other communications. While it is not possible to psychoanalyze the group, it is possible under such conditions to apportion responsibility for any assumed effects among the several factors involved. As the examples may suggest, reliable evidence concerning the several factors will serve to identify the stimuli supplied by the publications read by the group and to relate the stimuli to the personal and environmental conditions which give them meaning, which determine how much and in what directions the group is influenced by the reading experience. Analysis of such *typical* effects makes it easier to describe the social effects of *any* widely read publication when its modal readers have been identified. Such is the justification for intensive and synthetic study of the problem. This, in brief, is the burden of the present chapter.

As the result of our labors, the conclusion that the social effects of reading cannot be fairly described without due attention to each of their major factors is by no means dramatic. It smacks of the anticlimax. We wish the conclusion were instead a revolutionary idea, simple of statement and easy of application, from which we could expect the prompt clarification of our present notions on what reading does to people. But the plain facts are that the problem has been hitherto greatly oversimplified. Hence the pedestrian qualities of our conclusion are forced upon it by the nature of the problem. If a simpler prescription could accomplish the desired results, it would doubtless have been produced long ago by the efforts of each generation's best minds to describe the social consequences of contemporary writing.

MASS COMMUNICATION, POPULAR TASTE AND ORGANIZED SOCIAL ACTION

BY PAUL F. LAZARSFELD AND ROBERT K. MERTON

The authors are professors of sociology at Columbia University. This paper is reprinted from *The Communication of Ideas,* published and copyrighted 1948 by the Institute for Religious and Social Studies, of New York.

PROBLEMS ENGAGING the attention of men change, and they change not at random but largely in accord with the altering demands of society and economy. If a group such as those who have written the chapters of this book had been brought together a generation or so ago, the subject for discussion would in all probability have been altogether different. Child labor, woman suffrage or old-age pensions might have occupied the attention of a group such as this, but certainly not problems of the media of mass communication. As a host of recent conferences, books, and articles indicate, the role of radio, print, and film in society has become a problem of interest to many and a source of concern to some. This shift in public interest appears to be the product of several social trends.

SOCIAL CONCERN WITH THE MASS MEDIA

Many are alarmed by the ubiquity and potential power of the mass media. A participant in this symposium has written, for example, that "the power of radio can be compared only with the

492

power of the atomic bomb." It is widely felt that the mass media comprise a powerful instrument which may be used for good or for ill and that, in the absence of adequate controls, the latter possibility is on the whole more likely. For these are the media of propaganda and Americans stand in peculiar dread of the power of propaganda. As the British observer, William Empson, remarked of us: "They believe in machinery more passionately than we do; and modern propaganda is a scientific machine; so it seems to them obvious that a mere reasoning man can't stand up against it. All this produces a curiously girlish attitude toward anyone who might be doing propaganda. 'Don't let that man come near. Don't let him tempt me, because if he does, I'm sure to fall.' "

The ubiquity of the mass media promptly leads many to an almost magical belief in their enormous power. But there is another and, probably a more realistic basis for widespread concern with the social role of the mass media; a basis which has to do with the changing types of social control exercised by powerful interest groups in society. Increasingly, the chief power groups, among which organized business occupies the most spectacular place, have come to adopt techniques for manipulating mass publics through propaganda in place of more direct means of control. Industrial organizations no longer compel eight-year-old children to attend the machine for fourteen hours a day; they engage in elaborate programs of "public relations." They place large and impressive advertisements in the newspapers of the nation; they sponsor numerous radio programs; on the advice of public relations counsellors they organize prize contests, establish welfare foundations, and support worthy causes. Economic power seems to have reduced direct exploitation and turned to a subtler type of psychological exploitation, achieved largely by disseminating propaganda through the mass media of communication.

This change in the structure of social control merits thorough examination. Complex societies are subject to many different forms of organized control. Hitler, for example, seized upon the most visible and direct of these: organized violence and mass coercion. In this country, direct coercion has become minimized. If people do not adopt the beliefs and attitudes advocated by some power group —say, the National Association of Manufacturers—they can neither be liquidated nor placed in concentration camps. Those who would control the opinions and beliefs of our society resort less to physical force and more to mass persuasion. The radio program and the institutional advertisement serve in place of intimidation and coercion. The manifest concern over the functions of the mass media is in part based upon the valid observation that these media have taken on the job of rendering mass publics conformative to the social and economic *status quo*.

A third source of widespread concern with the social role of mass media is found in their assumed effects upon popular culture and the esthetic tastes of their audiences. In the measure that the size of these audiences has increased, it is argued, the level of esthetic taste has deteriorated. And it is feared that the mass media deliberately cater to these vulgarized tastes, thus contributing to further deterioration.

It seems probable that these constitute the three organically related elements of our great concern with the mass media of communication. Many are, first of all, fearful of the ubiquity and potential power of these media. We have suggested that this is something of an indiscriminate fear of an abstract bogey stemming from insecurity of social position and tenuously held values. Propaganda seems threatening.

There is, secondly, concern with the present effects of the mass media upon their enormous audiences, particularly the possibility that the continuing assault of these media may lead to the unconditional surrender of critical faculties and an unthinking conformism.

Finally, there is the danger that these technically advanced instruments of mass communication constitute a major avenue for the deterioration of esthetic tastes and popular cultural standards. And we have suggested that there is substantial ground for concern over these immediate social effects of the mass media of communication.

A review of the current state of actual knowledge concerning the social role of the mass media of communication and their effects upon the contemporary American community is an ungrateful task, for certified knowledge of this kind is impressively slight. Little more can be done than to explore the nature of the problems by methods which, in the course of many decades, will ultimately provide the knowledge we seek. Although this is anything but an encouraging preamble, it provides a necessary context for assessing the research and tentative conclusions of those of us professionally concerned with the study of mass media. A reconnaissance will suggest what we know, what we need to know, and will locate the strategic points requiring further inquiry.

To search out "the effects" of mass media upon society is to set upon an ill-defined problem. It is helpful to distinguish three facets of the problem and to consider each in turn. Let us, then, first inquire into what we know about the effects of the existence of these media in our society. Secondly, we must look into the effects of the particular structure of ownership and operation of the mass media in this country, a structure which differs appreciably from that found elsewhere. And, finally, we must consider that aspect of the problem which bears most directly upon policies and tactics governing the use of these media for definite social ends: our knowledge concerning the effects of the particular contents disseminated through the mass media.

THE SOCIAL ROLE OF THE MACHINERY OF MASS MEDIA

What role can be assigned to the mass media by virtue of the fact that they exist? What are the implications of a Hollywood, a Radio City, and a Time-Life-Fortune enterprise for our society? These questions can of course be discussed only in grossly speculative terms, since no experimentation or rigorous comparative study is possible. Comparisons with other societies lacking these mass media would be too crude to yield decisive results, and comparisons with an earlier day in American society would still involve gross assertions rather than precise demonstrations. In such an instance, brevity is clearly indicated. And opinions should be leavened with caution. It is our tentative judgment that the social role played by the very existence of the mass media has been commonly over-estimated. What are the grounds for this judgment?

It is clear that the mass media reach enormous audiences. Approximately forty-five million Americans attend the movies every week; our daily newspaper circulation is about fifty-four million, and some forty-six million American homes are equipped with television, and in these homes the average American watches television for about three hours a day. These are formidable figures. But they are merely supply and consumption figures, not figures registering the effect of mass media. They bear only upon what people do, not upon the social and psychological impact of the media. To know the number of hours people keep the radio turned on gives no indication of the effect upon them of what they hear. Knowledge of consumption data in the field of mass media remains far from a demonstration of their net effect upon behavior and attitude and outlook.

As was indicated a moment ago, we cannot resort to experiment by comparing contemporary American society with and without mass media. But, however tentatively, we can compare their social effect with, say, that of the automobile. It is not unlikely that the invention of the automobile and its development into a mass-owned commodity has had a significantly greater effect upon society than the invention of the radio and its development into a medium of mass communication. Consider the social complexes into which the automobile has entered. Its sheer existence has exerted pressure for vastly improved roads and with these, mobility has increased enormously. The shape of metropolitan agglomerations has been significantly affected by the automobile. And, it may be submitted, the inventions which enlarge the radius of movement and action exert a greater influence upon social outlook and daily routines than inventions which provide avenues for ideas—ideas which can be avoided by withdrawal, deflected by resistance and transformed by assimilation.

Granted, for a moment, that the mass media play a comparatively minor role in shaping our society, why are they the object of so much popular concern and criticism? Why do so many become exercised by the "problems" of the radio and film and press and so few by the problems of, say, the automobile and the airplane? In addition to the sources of this concern which we have noted previously, there is an unwitting psychological basis for concern which derives from a socio-historical context.

Many make the mass media targets for hostile criticism because they feel themselves duped by the turn of events.

The social changes ascribable to "reform movements" may be slow and slight, but they do cumulate. The surface facts are familiar enough. The sixty-hour week has given way to the forty-hour week. Child labor has been progressively curtailed. With all its deficiencies, free universal education has become progressively institutionalized. These and other gains register a series of reform victories. And now, people have more leisure time. They have, ostensibly, greater access to the cultural heritage. And what use do they make of this unmortgaged time so painfully acquired for them? They listen to the radio and go to the movies. These mass media seem somehow to have cheated reformers of the fruits of their victories. The struggle for freedom for leisure and popular education and social security was carried on in the hope that, once freed of cramping shackles, people would avail themselves of major cultural products of our society, Shakespeare or Beethoven or perhaps Kant. Instead, they turn to Faith Baldwin or Johnny Mercer or Edgar Guest.

Many feel cheated of their prize. It is not unlike a young man's first experience in the difficult realm of puppy love. Deeply smitten with the charms of his lady love, he saves his allowance for weeks on end and finally manages to give her a beautiful bracelet. She finds it "simply divine." So much so, that then and there she makes a date with another boy in order to display her new trinket. Our social struggles have met with a similar denouement. For generations men fought to give people more leisure time and now they spend it with the Columbia Broadcasting System rather than with Columbia University.

However little this sense of betrayal may account for prevailing attitudes toward the mass media, it may again be noted that the sheer presence of these media may not affect our society so profoundly as it is widely supposed.

SOME SOCIAL FUNCTIONS OF THE MASS MEDIA

In continuing our examination of the social role which can be ascribed to the mass media by virtue of their "sheer existence," we temporarily abstract from the social structure in which the media find their place. We do not, for example, consider the diverse effects of the mass media under varying systems of ownership and control, an important structural factor which will be discussed subsequently.

The mass media undoubtedly serve many social functions which might well become the object of sustained research. Of these functions, we have occasion to notice only three.

The Status Conferral Function

The mass media *confer* status on public issues, persons, organizations, and social movements.

Common experience as well as research testifies that the social standing of persons or social policies is raised when these command favorable attention in the mass media. In many quarters, for example, the support of a political candidate or a public policy by

The Times is taken as significant, and this support is regarded as a distinct asset for the candidate or the policy. Why?

For some, the editorial views of *The Times* represent the considered judgment of a group of experts, thus calling for the respect of laymen. But this is only one element in the status conferral function of the mass media, for enhanced status accrues to those who merely receive attention in the media, quite apart from any editorial support.

The mass media bestow prestige and enhance the authority of individuals and groups by *legitimizing their status*. Recognition by the press or radio or magazines or newsreels testifies that one has arrived, that one is important enough to have been singled out from the large anonymous masses, that one's behavior and opinions are significant enough to require public notice. The operation of this status conferral function may be witnessed most vividly in the advertising pattern of testimonials to a product by "prominent people." Within wide circles of the population (though not within certain selected social strata), such testimonials not only enhance the prestige of the product but also reflect prestige on the person who provides the testimonials. They give public notice that the large and powerful world of commerce regards him as possessing sufficiently high status for his opinion to count with many people. In a word, his testimonial is a testimonial to his own status.

The ideal, if homely, embodiment of this circular prestige pattern is to be found in the Lord Calvert series of advertisements centered on "Men of Distinction." The commercial firm and the commercialized witness to the merit of the product engage in an unending series of reciprocal pats on the back. In effect, a distinguished man congratulates a distinguished whisky which, through the manufacturer, congratulates the man of distinction on his being so distinguished as to be sought out for a testimonial to the distinction of the product. The workings of this mutual admiration society may be as nonlogical as they are effective. The audiences of mass media apparently subscribe to the circular belief: "If you really matter, you will be at the focus of mass attention and, if you *are* at the focus of mass attention, then surely you must really matter."

This status conferral function thus enters into organized social action by legitimizing selected policies, persons, and groups which receive the support of mass media. We shall have occasion to note the detailed operation of this function in connection with the con-

ditions making for the maximal utilization of mass media for designated social ends. At the moment, having considered the "status
conferral" function, we shall consider a second: the enforced application of social norms through the mass media.

The Enforcement of Social Norms

Such catch phrases as "the power of the press" (and other mass
media) or "the bright glare of publicity" presumably refer to this
function. The mass media may initiate organized social action by
"exposing" conditions which are at variance with public moralities.
But it need not be prematurely assumed that this pattern consists
simply in making these deviations widely known. We have something to learn in this connection from Malinowski's observations
among his beloved Trobriand Islanders. There, he reports, no organized social action is taken with respect to behavior deviant from a
social norm unless there is *public* announcement of the deviation.
This is not merely a matter of acquainting the individuals in the
group with the facts of the case. Many may have known privately
of these deviations—e.g., incest among the Trobrianders, as with
political or business corruption, prostitution, gambling among ourselves—but they will not have pressed for public action. But once
the behavioral deviations are made simultaneously public for all,
this sets in train tensions between the "privately tolerable" and
the "publicly acknowledgeable."

The mechanism of public exposure would seem to operate somewhat as follows. Many social norms prove inconvenient for individuals in the society. They militate against the gratification of wants
and impulses. Since many find the norms burdensome, there is
some measure of leniency in applying them, both to oneself and to
others. Hence, the emergence of deviant behavior and private toleration in these deviations. But this can continue only so long as one is
not in a situation where one must take a public stand for or against
the norms. Publicity, the enforced acknowledgment by members
of the group that these deviations have occurred, requires each
individual to take such a stand. He must either range himself with
the non-conformists, thus proclaiming his repudiation of the group
norms, and thus asserting that he, too, is outside the moral framework or, regardless of his private predilections, he must fall into
line by supporting the norm. *Publicity closes the gap between "private attitudes" and "public morality."* Publicity exerts pressure for

a single rather than a dual morality by preventing continued evasion of the issue. It calls forth public reaffirmation and (however sporadic) application of the social norm.

In a mass society, this function of public exposure is institutionalized in the mass media of communication. Press, radio, and journals expose fairly well-known deviations to public view, and as a rule, this exposure forces some degree of public action against what has been privately tolerated. The mass media may, for example, introduce severe strains upon "polite ethnic discrimination" by calling public attention to these practices which are at odds with the norms of non-discrimination. At times, the media may organize exposure activities into a "crusade."

The study of crusades by mass media would go far toward answering basic questions about the relation of mass media to organized social action. It is essential to know, for example, the extent to which the crusade provides an organizational center for otherwise unorganized individuals. The crusade may operate diversely among the several sectors of the population. In some instances, its major effect may not be so much to arouse an indifferent citizenry as to alarm the culprits, leading them to extreme measures which in turn alienate the electorate. Publicity may so embarrass the malefactor as to send him into flight as was the case, for example, with some of the chief henchmen of the Tweed Ring following exposure by *The New York Times*. Or the directors of corruption may fear the crusade only because of the effect they anticipate it will have upon the electorate. Thus, with a startling realistic appraisal of the communications behavior of his constituency, Boss Tweed peevishly remarked of the biting cartoons of Thomas Nast in *Harper's Weekly*: "I don't care a straw for your newspaper articles: my constituents don't know how to read, but they can't help seeing them damned pictures."[1]

The crusade may affect the public directly. It may focus the attention of a hitherto lethargic citizenry, grown indifferent through familiarity to prevailing corruption, upon a few, dramatically simplified, issues. As Lawrence Lowell once observed in this general connection, complexities generally inhibit mass action. Public issues must be defined in simple alternatives, in terms of black and white, to permit of organized public action. And the presentation of simple

---

[1] James Bryce, *The American Commonwealth*, Vol. 2, (New York: The Macmillan Company, 1910, 1914).

alternatives is one of the chief functions of the crusade. The crusade may involve still other mechanisms. If a municipal government is not altogether pure of heart, it is seldom wholly corrupt. Some scrupulous members of the administration and judiciary are generally intermingled with their unprincipled colleagues. The crusade may strengthen the hand of the upright elements in the government, force the hand of the indifferent, and weaken the hand of the corrupt. Finally, it may well be that a successful crusade exemplifies a circular, self-sustaining process, in which the concern of the mass medium with the public interest coincides with its self-interest. The triumphant crusade may enhance the power and prestige of the mass medium, thus making it, in turn, more formidable in later crusades, which, if successful, may further advance its power and prestige.

Whatever the answer to these questions, mass media clearly serve to reaffirm social norms by exposing deviations from these norms to public view. Study of the particular range of norms thus reaffirmed would provide a clear index of the extent to which these media deal with peripheral or central problems of the structure of our society.

The Narcotizing Dysfunction

The functions of status conferral and of reaffirmation of social norms are evidently well recognized by the operators of mass media. Like other social and psychological mechanisms, these functions lend themselves to diverse forms of application. Knowledge of these functions is power, and power may be used for special interests or for the general interest.

A third social consequence of the mass media has gone largely unnoticed. At least, it has received little explicit comment and, apparently, has not been systematically put to use for furthering planned objectives. This may be called the narcotizing dysfunction of the mass media. It is termed *dys*functional rather than functional on the assumption that it is not in the interest of modern complex society to have large masses of the population politically apathetic and inert. How does this unplanned mechanism operate?

Scattered studies have shown that an increasing proportion of the time of Americans is devoted to the products of the mass media. With distinct variations in different regions and among different social strata, the outpourings of the media presumably enable the twentieth-century American to "keep abreast of the world." Yet, it is suggested, this vast supply of communications may elicit only a superficial concern with the problems of society, and this superficiality often cloaks mass apathy.

Exposure to this flood of information may serve to narcotize rather than to energize the average reader or listener. As an increasing meed of time is devoted to reading and listening, a decreasing share is available for organized action. The individual reads accounts of issues and problems and may even discuss alternative lines of action. But this rather intellectualized, rather remote connection with organized social action is not activated. The interested and informed citizen can congratulate himself on his lofty state of interest and information and neglect to see that he has abstained from decision and action. In short, he takes his secondary contact with the world of political reality, his reading and listening and thinking, as a vicarious performance. He comes to mistake *knowing* about problems of the day for *doing* something about them. His social conscience remains spotlessly clean. He *is* concerned. He *is* informed. And he has all sorts of ideas as to what should be done. But, after he has gotten through his dinner and after he has listened to his favored radio programs and after he has read his second newspaper of the day, it is really time for bed.

In this peculiar respect, mass communications may be included among the most respectable and efficient of social narcotics. They may be so fully effective as to keep the addict from recognizing his own malady.

That the mass media have lifted the level of information of large populations is evident. Yet, quite apart from intent, increasing dosages of mass communications may be inadvertently transforming the energies of men from active participation into passive knowledge.

The occurrence of this narcotizing dysfunction can scarcely be doubted, but the extent to which it operates has yet to be determined. Research on this problem remains one of the many tasks still confronting the student of mass communications.

THE STRUCTURE OF OWNERSHIP AND OPERATION

To this point we have considered the mass media quite apart from their incorporation within a particular social and economic structure. But clearly, the social effects of the media will vary as the system of ownership and control varies. Thus to consider the social effects of American mass media is to deal only with the effects of these media as privately owned enterprises under profit-oriented management. It is general knowledge that this circumstance is not inherent in the technological nature of the mass media. In England, for example, to say nothing of Russia, the radio is to all intents and purposes owned, controlled, and operated by government.

The structure of control is altogether different in this country. Its salient characteristic stems from the fact that except for movies and books, it is not the magazine reader nor the radio listener nor, in large part, the reader of newspapers who supports the enterprise, but the advertiser. Big business finances the production and distribution of mass media. And, all intent aside, he who pays the piper generally calls the tune.

SOCIAL CONFORMISM

Since the mass media are supported by great business concerns geared into the current social and economic system, the media contribute to the maintenance of that system. This contribution is not found merely in the effective advertisement of the sponsor's product. It arises, rather, from the typical presence in magazine stories, radio programs, and newspaper columns of some element of confirmation, some element of approval of the present structure of society. And this continuing reaffirmation underscores the duty to accept.

To the extent that the media of mass communication have had an influence upon their audiences, it has stemmed not only from what is said, but more significantly from what is not said. For these media not only continue to affirm the status quo but, in the same measure, they fail to raise essential questions about the structure of society. Hence by leading toward conformism and by providing little basis for a critical appraisal of society, the commercially sponsored mass media indirectly but effectively restrain the cogent development of a genuinely critical outlook.

This is not to ignore the occasionally critical journal article or radio program. But these exceptions are so few that they are lost in the overwhelming flood of conformist materials. . . .

Since our commercially sponsored mass media promote a largely unthinking allegiance to our social structure, they cannot be relied upon to work for changes, even minor changes, in that structure. It is possible to list some developments to the contrary, but upon close inspection they prove illusory. A community group, such as the PTA, may request the producer of a radio serial to inject the theme of tolerant race attitudes into the program. Should the producer feel that this theme is safe, that it will not antagonize any substantial part of his audience, he may agree, but at the first indication that it is a dangerous theme which may alienate potential consumers, he will refuse, or will soon abandon the experiment. Social objectives are consistently surrendered by commercialized media when they clash with economic gains. Minor tokens of "progressive" views are of slight importance since they are included only by the grace of the sponsors and only on the condition that they be sufficiently acceptable as not to alienate any appreciable part of the audience. Economic pressure makes for conformism by omission of sensitive issues.

IMPACT UPON POPULAR TASTE

Since the largest part of our radio, movies, magazines, and a considerable part of our books and newspapers are devoted to "entertainment," this clearly requires us to consider the impact of the mass media upon popular taste.

Were we to ask the average American with some pretension to literary or esthetic cultivation if mass communications have had any effect upon popular taste, he would doubtlessly answer with a resounding affirmative. And more, citing abundant instances, he would insist that esthetic and intellectual tastes have been depraved by the flow of trivial formula products from printing presses, radio stations, and movie studios. The columns of criticism abound with these complaints.

In one sense, this requires no further discussion. There can be no doubt that the women who are daily entranced for three or four hours by some twelve consecutive "soap operas," all cut to the same dismal pattern, exhibit an appalling lack of esthetic judgment. Nor is this impression altered by the contents of pulp and slick magazines, or by the depressing abundance of formula motion pictures replete with hero, heroine, and villain moving through a contrived atmosphere of sex, sin, and success.

Yet unless we locate these patterns in historical and sociological terms, we may find ourselves confusedly engaged in condemning without understanding, in criticism which is sound but largely irrelevant. What is the historical status of this notoriously low level of popular taste? Is it the poor remains of standards which were once significantly higher, a relatively new birth in the world of values, largely unrelated to the higher standards from which it has allegedly fallen, or a poor substitute blocking the way to the development of superior standards and the expression of high esthetic purpose?

If esthetic tastes are to be considered in their social setting, we must recognize that the effective audience for the arts has become historically transformed. Some centuries back, this audience was largely confined to a selected aristocratic elite. Relatively few were literate. And very few possessed the means to buy books, attend theaters, and travel to the urban centers of the arts. Not more than a slight fraction, possibly not more than one or two per cent, of the population composed the effective audience for the arts. These happy few cultivated their esthetic tastes, and their selective demand left its mark in the form of relatively high artistic standards.

With the widesweeping spread of popular education and with the emergence of the new technologies of mass communication, there developed an enormously enlarged market for the arts. Some forms of music, drama, and literature now reach virtually everyone in our society. This is why, of course, we speak of *mass* media and of *mass* art. And the great audiences for the mass media, though in the main literate, are not highly cultivated. About half the population, in fact, have halted their formal education upon leaving grammar school.

With the rise of popular education, there has occurred a seeming decline of popular taste. Large numbers of people have acquired what might be termed "formal literacy," that is to say, a capacity to read, to grasp crude and superficial meanings, and a correlative incapacity for full understanding of what they read.[2] There has de-

---

[2] *Ibid.*, Part IV, Chapter LXXX, James Bryce perceived this with characteristic clarity: "That the education of the masses is nevertheless a superficial education goes without saying. It is sufficient to enable them to think they know something about the great problems of politics: insufficient to show them how little they know. The public elementary school gives everybody the key to knowledge in making reading and writing familiar, but it has not time to teach him how to use the key, whose use is in fact, by the pressure of daily work, almost confined to the newspaper and the magazine. So we may say that if the political education of the average American voter be compared with that of the average voter in Europe, it stands high; but if it be compared with the functions which the theory of the American government lays on him, which its spirit implies, which the methods of its party organization assume, its inadequacy is manifest." *Mutatis mutandis*, the same may be said of the gap between the theory of "superior" cultural content in the mass media and the current levels of popular education.

veloped, in short, a marked gap between literacy and comprehension. People read more but understand less. More people read but proportionately fewer critically assimilate what they read.

Our formulation of the problem should now be plain. It is misleading to speak simply of the decline of esthetic tastes. Mass audiences probably include a larger number of persons with cultivated esthetic standards, but these are swallowed up by the large masses who constitute the new and untutored audience for the arts. Whereas yesterday the elite constituted virtually the whole of the audience, they are today a minute fraction of the whole. In consequence, the average level of esthetic standards and tastes of audiences has been depressed, although the tastes of some sectors of the population have undoubtedly been raised and the total number of people exposed to communication contents has been vastly increased.

But this analysis does not directly answer the question of the effects of the mass media upon public taste, a question which is as complex as it is unexplored. The answer can come only from disciplined research. One would want to know, for example, whether mass media have robbed the intellectual and artistic elite of the art forms which might otherwise have been accessible to them. And this involves inquiry into the pressure exerted by the mass audience upon creative individuals to cater to mass tastes. Literary hacks have existed in every age. But it would be important to learn if the electrification of the arts supplies power for a significantly greater proportion of dim literary lights. And, above all, it would be essential to determine if mass media and mass tastes are necessarily linked in a vicious circle of deteriorating standards or if appropriate action on the part of the directors of mass media could initiate a virtuous circle of cumulatively improving tastes among their audiences. More concretely, are the operators of commercialized mass media caught up in a situation in which they cannot, whatever their private preferences, radically raise the esthetic standards of their products?

In passing, it should be noted that much remains to be learned concerning standards appropriate for mass art. It is possible that standards for art forms produced by a small band of creative talents for a small and selective audience are not applicable to art forms produced by a gigantic industry for the population at large. The beginnings of investigation on this problem are sufficiently suggestive to warrant further study.

Sporadic and consequently inconclusive experiments in the raising of standards have met with profound resistance from mass audiences. On occasion, radio stations and networks have attempted to supplant a soap opera with a program of classical music, or formula comedy skits with discussions of public issues. In general, the people supposed to benefit by this reformation of program have simply refused to be benefited. They cease listening. The audience dwindles. Researches have shown, for example, that radio programs of classical music tend to preserve rather than to create interest in classical music and that newly emerging interests are typically superficial. Most listeners to these programs have previously acquired an interest in classical music; the few whose interest is initiated by the programs are caught up by melodic compositions and come to think of classical music exclusively in terms of Tschaikowsky or Rimsky-Korsakow or Dvorak.

Proposed solutions to these problems are more likely to be born of faith than knowledge. The improvement of mass tastes through the improvement of mass art products is not as simple a matter as we should like to believe. It is possible, of course, that a conclusive effort has not been made. By a triumph of imagination over the current organization of mass media, one can conceive a rigorous censorship over all media, such that nothing was allowed in print or on the air or in the films save "the best that has been thought and said in the world." Whether a radical change in the supply of mass art would in due course reshape the tastes of mass audiences must remain a matter of speculation. Decades of experimentation and research are needed. At present, we know conspicuously little about the methods of improving esthetic tastes and we know that some of the suggested methods are ineffectual. We have a rich knowledge of failures. Should this discussion be reopened in 1976, we may, perhaps, report with equal confidence our knowledge of positive achievements.

At this point, we may pause to glance at the road we have traveled. By way of introduction, we considered the seeming sources of widespread concern with the place of mass media in our society. Thereafter, we first examined the social role ascribable to the sheer existence of the mass media and concluded that this may have been exaggerated. In this connection, however, we noted several consequences of the existence of mass media: their status conferral function, their function in inducing the application of social norms, and their narcotizing dysfunction. Secondly, we indicated the constraints placed by a structure of commercialized ownership and control upon the mass media as agencies of social criticism and as carriers of high esthetic standards.

We turn now to the third and last aspect of the social role of the mass media: the possibilities of utilizing them for moving toward designated types of social objectives.

PROPAGANDA FOR SOCIAL OBJECTIVES

This final question is perhaps of more direct interest to you than the other questions we have discussed. It represents something of a challenge to us since it provides the means of resolving the apparent paradox to which we referred previously: the seeming paradox arising from the assertion that the significance of the sheer existence of the mass media has been exaggerated and the multiple indications that the media do exert influences upon their audiences.

What are the conditions for the effective use of mass media for what might be called "propaganda for social objectives"—the promotion, let us say, of non-discriminatory race relations, or of educational reforms, or of positive attitudes toward organized labor? Research indicates that, at least, one or more of three conditions must be satisfied if this propaganda is to prove effective. These conditions may be briefly designated as (1) monopolization, (2) canalization rather than change of basic values, and (3) supplementary face-to-face contact. Each of these conditions merits some discussion.

MONOPOLIZATION

This situation obtains when there is little or no opposition in the mass media to the diffusion of values, policies, or public images. That is to say, monopolization of the mass media occurs in the absence of counterpropaganda.

In this restricted sense, monopolization of the mass media is found in diverse circumstances. It is, of course, indigenous to the political structure of authoritarian society, where access to the media of communication is wholly closed to those who oppose the official ideology. The evidence suggests that this monopoly played some part in enabling the Nazis to maintain their control of the German people.

But this same situation is approximated in other social systems. During the war, for example, our government utilized the radio, with some success, to promote and to maintain identification with the war effort. The effectiveness of these morale building efforts was in large measure due to the virtually complete absence of counterpropaganda.

Similar situations arise in the world of commercialized propaganda. The mass media create popular idols. The public images of the radio performer, Kate Smith, for example, picture her as a woman with unparalleled understanding of other American women, deeply sympathetic with ordinary men and women, a spiritual guide and mentor, a patriot whose views on public affairs should be taken seriously. Linked with the cardinal American virtues, the public images of Kate Smith are at no point subject to a counterpropaganda. Not that she has no competitors in the market of radio advertising. But there are none who set themselves systematically to question what she has said. In consequence, an unmarried radio entertainer with an annual income in six figures may be visualized by millions of American women as a hard-working mother who knows the recipe for managing life on fifteen hundred a year.

This image of a popular idol would have far less currency were it subjected to counterpropaganda. Such neutralization occurs, for example, as a result of preelection campaigns by Republicans and Democrats. By and large, as a recent study has shown, the propaganda issued by each of these parties neutralizes the effect of the other's propaganda. Were both parties to forgo their campaigning through the mass media entirely, it is altogether likely that the net effect would be to reproduce the present distribution of votes.

This general pattern has been described by Kenneth Burke in his *Attitudes Toward History* ". . . businessmen compete with one another by trying to *praise their own commodity* more persuasively than their rivals, whereas politicians compete by slandering the *opposition*. When you add it all up, you get a grand total of absolute praise for business and grand total of absolute slander for politics."

To the extent that opposing political propaganda in the mass media are balanced, the net effect is negligible. The virtual monopolization of the media for given social objectives, however, will produce discernible effects upon audiences.

CANALIZATION

Prevailing beliefs in the enormous power of mass communications appear to stem from successful cases of monopolistic propaganda or from advertising. But the leap from the efficacy of advertising to the assumed efficacy of propaganda aimed at deep-rooted attitudes and ego involved behavior is as unwarranted as it is dangerous. Advertising is typically directed toward the canalizing of preexisting behavior patterns or attitudes. It seldom seeks to instil new attitudes or to create significantly new behavior patterns. "Advertising pays" because it generally deals with a simple psychological situation. For Americans who have been socialized in the use of a toothbrush, it makes relatively little difference which brand of toothbrush they use. Once the gross pattern of behavior or the generic attitude has been established, it can be canalized in one direction or another. Resistance is slight. But mass propaganda typically meets a more complex situation. It may seek objectives which are at odds with deep-lying attitudes. It may seek to reshape rather than to canalize current systems of values. And the successes of advertising may only highlight the failures of propaganda. Much of the current propaganda which is aimed at abolishing deep-seated ethnic and racial prejudices, for example, seems to have had little effectiveness.

Media of mass communication, then, have been effectively used to canalize basic attitudes but there is little evidence of their having served to change these attitudes.

SUPPLEMENTATION

Mass propaganda which is neither monopolistic nor canalizing in character may, nonetheless, prove effective if it meets a third condition: supplementation through face-to-face contacts.

A case in point will illustrate the interplay between mass media and face-to-face influences. The seeming propagandistic success achieved some years ago by Father Coughlin does not appear, upon inspection, to have resulted primarily from the propaganda content of his radio talks. It was, rather, the product of these centralized propaganda talks *and* widespread local organizations which arranged for their members to listen to him, followed by discussions among themselves concerning the social views he had expressed. This combination of a central supply of propaganda (Coughlin's addresses on a nation-wide network), the coordinated distribution of newspapers and pamphlets and locally organized face-to-face discussions among relatively small groups—this complex of reciprocal reinforcement by mass media and personal relations proved spectacularly successful.

Students of mass movements have come to repudiate the view that mass propaganda in and of itself creates or maintains the movement. Naziism did not attain its brief moment of hegemony by capturing the mass media of communication. The media played an ancillary role, supplementing the use of organized violence, organized distribution of rewards for conformity, and organized centers of local indoctrination. The Soviet Union has also made large and impressive use of mass media for indoctrinating enormous populations with appropriate ideologies. But the organizers of indoctrination saw to it that the mass media did not operate alone. "Red corners," "reading huts," and "listening stations" comprised meeting places in which groups of citizens were exposed to the mass media in common. The 55,000 reading rooms and clubs which had come into being by 1933 enabled the local ideological elite to talk over with rank-and-file readers the content of what they read. The relative scarcity of radios in private homes again made for group listening and group discussions of what had been heard.

In these instances, the machinery of mass persuasion included face-to-face contact in local organizations as an adjunct to the mass media. The privatized individual response to the materials presented through the channels of mass communication was considered inadequate for transforming exposure to propaganda into effectiveness of propaganda. In a society such as our own, where the pattern of bureaucratization has not yet become so pervasive or, at least, not so clearly crystallized, it has likewise been found that mass media prove most effective in conjunction with local centers of organized face-to-face contact.

Several factors contribute to the enhanced effectiveness of this joining of mass media and direct personal contact. Most clearly, the local discussions serve to reinforce the content of mass propaganda. Such mutual confirmation produces a "clinching effect." Secondly, the central media lessen the task of the local organizer, and the personnel requirements for such subalterns need not be as rigorous in a popular movement. The subalterns need not set forth the propaganda content for themselves, but need only pilot potential converts to the radio where the doctrine is being expounded. Thirdly, the appearance of a representative of the movement on a nation-wide network, or his mention in the national press, serves to symbolize the legitimacy and significance of the movement. It is no powerless, inconsequential enterprise. The mass media, as we have seen, confer status. And the status of the national movement reflects back on the status of the local cells, thus consolidating the tentative decisions of its members. In this interlocking arrangement, the local organizer ensures an audience for the national speaker and the national speaker validates the status of the local organizer.

This brief summary of the situations in which the mass media achieve their maximum propaganda effect may resolve the seeming contradiction which arose at the outset of our discussion. The mass media prove most effective when they operate in a situation of virtual "psychological monopoly," or when the objective is one of canalizing rather than modifying basic attitudes or when they operate in conjunction with face-to-face contacts.

But these three conditions are rarely satisfied conjointly in propaganda for social objectives. To the degree that monopolization of attention is rare, opposing propagandas have free play in a democracy. And, by and large, basic social issues involve more than a mere canalizing of preexistent basic attitudes; they call, rather, for substantial changes in attitude and behavior. Finally, for the most obvious of reasons, the close collaboration of mass media and locally organized centers for face-to-face contact has seldom been achieved in groups striving for planned social change. Such programs are expensive. And it is precisely these groups which seldom have the large resources needed for these expensive programs. The forward looking groups at the edges of the power structure do not ordinarily have the large financial means of the contented groups at the center.

As a result of this threefold situation, the present role of media is largely confined to peripheral social concerns and the media do not exhibit the degree of social power commonly attributed to them.

By the same token, and in view of the present organization of business ownership and control of the mass media, they have served to cement the structure of our society. Organized business does approach a virtual "psychological monopoly" of the mass media. Radio commercials and newspaper advertisements are, of course, premised on a system which has been termed free enterprise. Moreover, the world of commerce is primarily concerned with canalizing rather than radically changing basic attitudes; it seeks only to create preferences for one rather than another brand of product. Face-to-face contacts with those who have been socialized in our culture serve primarily to reinforce the prevailing culture patterns.

Thus, the very conditions which make for the maximum effectiveness of the mass media of communication operate toward the maintenance of the going social and cultural structure rather than toward its change.

RADIO AND THE PRINTED PAGE
AS FACTORS IN POLITICAL
OPINION AND VOTING

BY PAUL F. LAZARSFELD,
BERNARD BERELSON, AND
HAZEL GAUDET

This is a part of the study of Erie County, Ohio, during the presidential campaign of 1940, made by Dr. Lazarsfeld and his associates in the Bureau of Applied Social Research, of Columbia University. Published as *The People's Choice,* and copyrighted by Duell, Sloan and Pearce in 1944, the book was republished by the Columbia University Press in 1948. It is here reprinted by permission of the authors and the original publisher.

A PRESIDENTIAL ELECTION means a presidential campaign, and that means a flood-tide of political propaganda. Campaign managers devise comprehensive strategies and ingenious tactics in an attempt to make their will the will of the electorate. Party workers adapt general policy to specific situations in an effort to corral the timid, lead the willing, and convince the reluctant. Partisan leaders of opinion—the newspaper editor, the columnist, the free lance writer and the syndicated cartoonist, the radio commentator, and the local sage—all edge into the campaign by placing the weight of their authority behind the cause of their favored candidate. Propaganda is let loose upon the land to control or inform, to constrain or tease potential voters into the appropriate decision.

Thus the *output* of campaign propaganda is tremendous. But

what of the *intake?* Unheard music may be sweeter, but unseen
or unheard propaganda is simply useless. How much actual attention is paid to it? By whom? In which media of communication?
In short, what about actual exposure to campaign propaganda?

Most people have several claims upon their attention and interest
which necessarily compete with one another. There is competition
between the problems of their "private world" and those of the
"public world." Preoccupation with personal problems does not
leave much time or energy for concern with such relatively remote
issues as the choice of a president. And even within the world of
public affairs, no single focus of attention remains unchallenged.
For example, the campaign of 1940 had to compete for attention
with a series of major events which have not marked a presidential
campaign since 1916—a European war.

As everyone knows, the intensity of a presidential campaign hits
its high point just before Election Day when all the media of mass
communication—newspapers, magazines, and radio—are filled with
political propaganda. If people are ever going to read about the
campaign or listen to political speeches, this is the time. How many
actually did? In Erie County, during the last twelve days of the
campaign, 54 per cent of the respondents had heard at least one
of five major political talks broadcast in the days just before the
interview, 51 per cent had read at least one campaign story which
had appeared on the front page of their favorite newspaper the
day before the interview, and 26 per cent had read at least one
campaign article in the current mass magazines. This is important.
At the peak of the campaign, in late October, about half the population ignored stories on the front pages of their newspapers or
political speeches by the candidates themselves, and about 75 per
cent of the people ignored magazine stories about the election. In
short, the flood of political material at that time, far from drown-
ing any of these people, did not even get their feet wet.

THE CONCENTRATION OF EXPOSURE

But this interpretation might miss the mark. Although half the
respondents were not exposed to any *one* source, perhaps all of
them, or nearly all, were exposed to *some* source. In other words,
perhaps the people *specialized* in their exposure to communication,
some reading but not listening and others listening but not reading.
And thus perhaps everyone was exposed to the campaign somewhere.

Actually, however, the opposite is the case. With remarkable consistency, political materials, distributed through the various media of communication reached the *same* group of potential voters. The people who were exposed to a lot of campaign propaganda through one medium of communication were also exposed to a lot in the other media; and those who were exposed to a little in one were also exposed to a little in the others. Most of the people above average in their exposure to political speeches over the radio were also above average in their exposure to political material in newspapers (Chart 1). The same relationship holds for newspapers and magazines and for radio and magazines. And conversely, the people who were low in exposure to one medium were also low in the others.

Exposure to the different media of political communications, then, is concentrated in the same group. But what of exposure at different times during the campaign? Perhaps some people read and listened during the first months of the campaign and others during the last months—and thus perhaps everyone was exposed to about the same

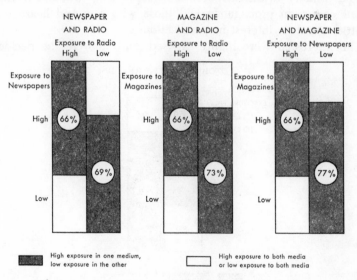

CHART 1

People highly exposed to one medium of communication also tend to be highly exposed to other media. There are relatively few who are highly exposed to one medium and little exposed to the other.

amount of political propaganda over the campaign as a whole. Again, however, this is just not so. Again the same group of people were highly exposed at different periods of the campaign and another group of people were little exposed at different periods in the campaign (Chart 2).

In sum, then, exposure to political communications during the presidential campaign is concentrated in the *same* group of people, not spread among the people at large. Exposure in one medium or at one time *supplements* rather than complements exposure in another medium or at another time. The large and increasing supply of political propaganda during the campaign leads primarily not to a wider base of informed voters but to a more intensive dosage of the same part of the electorate.

WHO READ AND LISTENED TO POLITICS?

Who were the people who did most of the reading about and listening to the campaign? What distinguished them from the people who paid little attention to politics?

The primary distinction between people who saw and heard a lot of campaign propaganda and those who saw and heard only a little was their interest in the election.

The interested were highly exposed, and so were the decided.

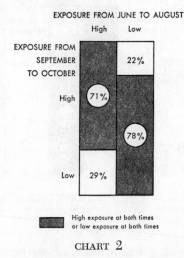

CHART 2

People highly exposed at one time also tend to be highly exposed at another time of the campaign.

At any one time, the people who already knew how they were going to vote read and listened to more campaign material than the people who still did not know how they would vote. In other words the group which the campaign manager is presumably most eager to reach—the as yet undecided—is the very group which is less likely to read or listen to this propaganda. Just as educational programs on the air attract an audience largely composed of those previously familiar with their contents, so does political propaganda tend to reach an audience that has already decided on its choice of a candidate.

In the chapter dealing with the role of interest in the election, we saw that interest serves as a synoptic index for an entire complex of personal characteristics. The most interested people were better-educated, better off, older, urban men. These same characteristics are associated with high exposure to political communications. There are good cultural reasons to explain this. The better-educated have more intellectual equipment and more civic training. The better off have a greater awareness about politics and think they have a larger stake in it. The older also think they have a bigger stake in politics; in addition, the younger people in this country, unlike the youth of Europe, are not particularly politically conscious. The urban find it easier to expose to communications, especially print, because there are more opportunities to do so in the city than in the country. And finally, men are compelled by the mores to pay attention to politics and women are not.

Obviously, the people who expose most to campaign communications are those who possessed all three factors: interest, decision, and the appropriate personal characteristics. But what about their relative importance? Cross-analysis reveals that exposure to campaign communications was determined primarily by interest in the election; secondly by a vote decision; and finally by education, economic status, and sex and to a lesser extent by age and residence.

In summary, then, the relative strength of these factors highlights an important fact about exposure to political communications. We will recall that the people with most interest were most likely to make their vote decision early and stick to it throughout the campaign. What we find now is that the people who did most of the reading about and listening to the campaign were the most impervious to any ideas which might have led them to change their vote. Insofar as campaign propaganda was intended to change votes, it was most likely to reach the people least susceptible to such changes. It was least likely to reach the people most likely to change.

In recent years, the radio has taken its place beside the newspaper as a distinctive medium of communication. Perhaps not just "beside"; perhaps in some instances the radio has taken the place *of* the newspaper. For example, has the radio cut into the neswpaper's sphere of influence in American politics? Did the two media serve the same function for the major parties? In short, what were their comparative political roles in Erie County in 1940?

Before attacking this question directly, we must digress for a brief methodological note. Suppose we asked the respondents themselves to indicate what sources were most effective in influencing their vote decision. Merely raising the question is enough to call to mind the dangers involved in such a procedure. Can respondents appraise the relative influences exerted upon them over an extended period of time? Any statement by them to the effect that they were "influenced" by the "radio" or "newspaper" may refer as much to the *amount* of listening or reading they have done as to the *actual influence* of the media. A direct self-estimate by respondents, then, will not serve our purpose.

Accordingly, a method of investigation was devised which rests on the following assumption: the more concrete and specific the respondent's account of the experiences which have modified his view, the more likely it is that the account is valid. General comments may inadvertently refer to amount of exposure and not to influence. But concrete and circumstantial reports of specific experiences tend to focus on decisive events and to eliminate the component of amount of exposure. Obviously, no single question can be expected to provide an adequate index of influence. But we can use a battery of questions which enable us to distinguish between general and vague replies on the one hand and concrete replies on the other. If we find that the influence attributed to one medium is consistently mentioned more frequently as we move from general to specific replies, then we conclude that this medium has actually exerted a preponderant influence and that we have arrived at a valid measure of influence.

With that procedure and that measure, what was the comparative influence of radio and newspaper in the 1940 campaign? Just after the election, voters were asked to name in retrospect the sources from which they obtained most of the information that led them to arrive at their vote decision. They were then asked to indicate which source proved most important to them. Although the radio and newspaper ranked about the same as general sources, the radio was mentioned half again as frequently as the single most important source of influence (Chart 3). Half of those who mentioned the radio at all considered it their most important source of information, whereas only a third of those who initially mentioned the news-paper regarded it as most important. Thus, as we move from the more general to the more specific indication of influence, radio plays a relatively stronger role than the newspaper. The same sort of distinction can be applied to another set of data.

RADIO AND NEWSPAPER AS SOURCES OF REASONS FOR CHANGE

Whenever a respondent indicated a vote intention different from the one mentioned in the previous interview, he was asked the reason for the change. In some cases the source of the new vote intention was stated in *general* terms, e.g., "I changed my mind as a result of my newspaper reading." In other cases, the source of the change was reported in *concrete* terms, with a medium of com-munications *directly linked* to the reason for change, e.g., "An edi-

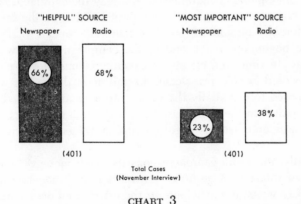

CHART 3

Asked which medium helped them to make their decision, the voters mention radio and newspaper about equally. When they are asked for the "most important" source, however, radio gets a clear lead.

torial in Wednesday's Sandusky *News* convinced me that the president's experience in international affairs was indispensable." (We should note here that whereas in the preceding section we dealt with the respondents as a whole, here we deal only with the crucial sub-group—the people who changed their minds during the campaign.) When the mentions of media making for changes in vote intention are classified as general and concrete, how did newspaper and radio compare?

Until the last period of the campaign, considerably more political material was available in the newspapers than on the radio. Although it is difficult to measure this factor of accessibility, only toward the close of the campaign could the amount of political material on the air be considered at all comparable to that found in the press. If we limit mentions of media in connection with reasons for change to the last two months of the campaign—the most active months of the campaign—what then?

At that time the radio was mentioned less frequently as a *general* source of influence but more frequently as a *concrete* source. Once again, the stronger role of radio becomes more conspicuous in the case of concrete ascriptions of influence.

In sum, to the extent that the formal media exerted any influence at all on vote intention or actual vote, radio proved more effective than the newspaper. Differences in the way the campaign is waged in print and on the air probably account for this. In the first place, a considerable amount of political material appears in the press from the beginning to the end of the campaign with few notable variations. In time, the claims and counterclaims of the parties as they appeared in cold print came to pall upon the reader who had been exposed to essentially the same stuff over an extended period. The campaign on the radio, however, was much more cursory in its early phases and became vigorous and sustained only toward the close.

Secondly, the radio campaign consists much more of "events" of distinctive interest. A political convention is broadcast, and the listener can virtually participate in the ceremonial occasion: he can respond to audience enthusiasm, he can directly experience the ebb and flow of tension. Similarly with a major speech by one of the candidates: it is more dramatic than the same speech in the newspaper next morning.

And thirdly, the listener gets a sense of personal access from the radio which is absent from print. Politics on the air more readily becomes an active experience for the listener than politics in the newspaper does for the reader. It represents an approach to a face-to-face contact with the principals in the case. It is closer to a personal relationship, and hence more effective.

A MEDIUM FOR EACH PARTY

In 1936 and even more in 1940, most of the country's newspapers supported the Republican candidate for the presidency (and the same was true in Sandusky). And in both campaigns, according to popular legend, Roosevelt's "superb radio voice" enabled him to exploit that medium far more effectively than either Landon or Willkie. Thus, broadly speaking, it would appear that each party had an effective hold on one of the two major media of communication.

This was actually the case. In exposure, in congeniality of ideas, in trust, and in influence—in all of these characteristics the Republicans inclined in favor of the newspaper and the Democrats in favor of the radio. Among people with the same amounts of formal education, the Republicans read the newspaper more than the Democrats and the Democrats listened to the radio more than the Republicans (Chart 4). When we recall the finding that the pro-Republican content of the newspapers was higher than that on the air, this suggests once more that people tend to seek out political

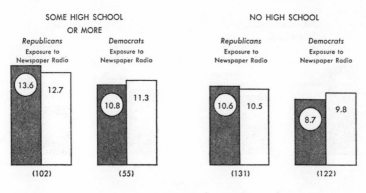

CHART 4

Republican voters expose themselves more to newspapers and Democratic voters more to radio, on each educational level.

views similar to their own. And our respondents were aware of the
facts in the case: when asked, in late October, where they found
"ideas on the coming election which agree most closely with your
own ideas," the Republicans favored the newspaper and the Democrats favored the radio, relatively speaking (Chart 5).

What about the implications? Again in late October, respondents
were asked which they thought was "closer to the truth (more impartial)—the news you get in the newspapers or what you hear on
the radio?" Again, relatively, the partisans ascribed "impartiality"
and "veracity" to the media which presented views similar to their
own (Chart 6). A transfer was effected from partisan value to
truth value.

This tendency was virtually confined to the better-educated
respondents. They were more sensitized to the partisanship of the
media and responded with distrust of the veracity of the "rival"
source of information. The less educated were less likely to detect
the partisan character of the media and hence less likely to discount
them accordingly.

And finally, the influence of the two media was different for
the two parties (Chart 7). People changing their vote intentions
favorably for the Republicans mentioned newspapers more frequently as the source of their reason for change and Democrats
mentioned the radio more frequently (taking the more reliable
concrete mentions only).

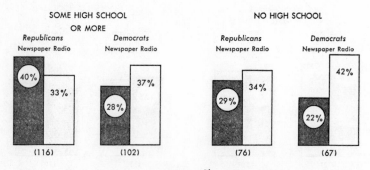

CHART 5

*Republicans find the newspaper relatively more consistent with
their own ideas and the Democrats the radio, on each educational
level.*

In summary, then, Republicans preferred the newspaper and Democrats the radio. Each party exposed more to "its own" medium, found it more congenial, trusted it more, and was more influenced by it.

In spite of the fact that the content of the radio favored the Republicans, the radio more often impressed people in favor of the Democratic party. Some of the reasons for this are clear. When radio commentators and newscasters were cited by our respondents, it was not so much because of their broadcasts on domestic politics but because of their reports on foreign affairs and war news. Under the circumstances, these worked to the advantage of the Democrats. Take, for example, the young woman who returned to a Democratic vote because of a newscast: "FDR knows the European situation as well as any man. *I heard a news report that Hitler and Mussolini want FDR defeated.* If they do, it's for their own benefit, so I will vote for FDR if only to spite the dictators."

The radio speeches of the candidates themselves also helped the Democrats. All three of the respondents who mentioned a Roosevelt speech in connection with a change in vote intention shifted toward the Democrats. Similarly, all four of the respondents who mentioned both Roosevelt and Willkie speeches were persuaded to vote Democratic. But of the eight respondents who mentioned speeches by Willkie, four decided to vote for Roosevelt. In other

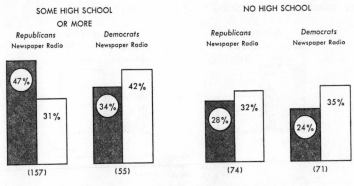

CHART 6

Republicans also thought the newspaper was relatively more impartial (closer to the truth) than the radio and the Democrats favored the radio, again on each educational level.

words, Willkie's speeches were as likely to boomerang against him as they were to operate in his favor. For example, this young man, after vacillating between the parties, finally decided for Roosevelt in October: "*I have heard some of Willkie's speeches and I don't like him. . . .* All he does is condemn Roosevelt. He doesn't say how he will do things if he gets elected. Roosevelt has never said anything against Willkie."

On the other hand, the speeches by the President did not affect any changers adversely. The typical reaction is illustrated in the case of this elderly woman who was undecided right up to the last days of the campaign: "*Since I heard President Roosevelt's speech from Philadelphia* I have decided that Willkie has not had enough experience to be president. He doesn't know enough about the war situation." And Roosevelt had much the better of it whenever the respondents listened to both men and compared them. For example, here is a young man who finally decided to vote Democratic: "*Willkie's and Roosevelt's speeches on Saturday night made me decide to vote for FDR. They were the first speeches I heard. Willkie is no speaker—he knocks too much.*"

Thus Roosevelt's "good" radio manner and Willkie's "bad" radio manner, often discussed during the campaign, actually paid off. One should remember that most of these changers were only activated and not converted by what they heard on the radio. Still, such experiences clarify why the radio was considered more the Democrats' medium as compared with the newspaper.

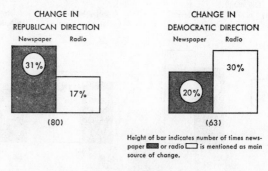

CHART 7

People changing towards the Republicans mention newspapers more often as an influence which led to the change and those changing towards the Democrats mention radio.

THE MAGAZINE—SPECIALIZED MEDIUM OF COMMUNICATION

Turning finally to the weekly and monthly journals, we find another picture. A presidential campaign provides American magazines with a central event around which articles can be planned and written for a period of months, and they take good advantage of it. Throughout the campaign, the mass magazines carried a good deal of political discussion of election issues and particularly of the candidates' personalities.

The possibility of magazine influence upon vote is limited at the outset by the relatively small numbers of magazine readers. It was found that only 15% to 25% of the respondents read magazine articles on the campaign at any one time.

But the small size of the magazine audience is somewhat offset by its characteristics. We found a small proportion of politically active and alert people in each social group who were likely to influence the decision of their fellow citizens—the opinion leaders. Among other differences, they read more about the campaign and also listened more. Such differences between the opinion leaders and the rest of the people are especially marked in regard to magazine reading. On our index of exposure we find that the average opinion leader has about twice as high a score as the ordinary citizen with reference to newspapers and radio. But with magazine reading, the difference is almost three to one.

The highpoint of the magazine's influence came relatively early in the campaign in question. At that time, the newspapers and radio are relatively free of campaign material because not much is going on, and the magazines fill the breach with "timeless" articles such as reviews of the challenger's career. Most of the mentions of magazines as sources connected with reasons for change came during the first half of the campaign. And the magazine is probably relatively more important during the preconvention period of late spring, before our interviewing began. But once the campaign reaches its height, in middle and late October, the magazine takes even more of a back seat to newspaper and radio.

Two tendencies in particular characterize the political role of magazines: (1) they deal largely with personalities, and (2) they have more space to devote to the elaboration of a point. The preceding chapter showed the extent to which magazines stressed the personalities of the candidates, particularly Willkie's. This emphasis on personality also came out in the citation of magazines in connection with the reasons for change in vote intention. More often than not, it was the character of the Republican candidate or his career or some other aspect of the man himself, rather than his program, which was cited. Such testimony appeared often: "Read a sketch of Willkie's life in the *Saturday Evening Post.* . . . Read about Willkie's life in the *Farm Journal.* . . ."

At the same time, there were suggestions in the citation of sources that the magazine was relatively more likely to supply elaborations of a point than either the newspaper or the radio. It is less tied to current events than the newspaper and it can take more time to develop a point than the usual political speaker, who tries to cover a good many topics within one talk. No definitive evidence is available on this matter, but hints of it appeared from time to time in the interviews. For example, here is a woman who decided to vote Republican in June because she thought Dewey would get the nomination: "I like Dewey, from what I have read—his *cleaning up the gangsters,* etc. I read an article in the *American* about *the life and background* of Dewey, and *his work on crime* in New York City."

As a source of influence, the specialized magazine designed for a special-interest audience rivalled the general mass magazine. The latter have many times the coverage of the former but they are relatively less effective in changing peoples' minds. The specialized magazine already has a foot in the door, so to speak, because it is accepted by the reader as a reliable spokesman for some cause or group in which he is greatly interested and with which he identifies himself. The general magazine tries to speak to everyone at once and as a result is less able to aim its shots directly at a particular target. In addition, the general magazine is ordinarily considered as an entertainment publication whereas specialized magazines are granted a serious turn. In Erie County in 1940, the *Farm Journal* was mentioned as a concrete influence upon changes in vote intention as frequently as *Collier's,* despite their great difference in circulation, and the Townsend publication as frequently as *Life* or the *Saturday Evening Post.*

COMMUNICATIONS AND PUBLIC OPINION

BY BERNARD BERELSON

Dr. Berelson is director of the Bureau of Applied Social Research at Columbia University. His paper was first published in *Communications in Modern Society*, copyright 1948 by the University of Illinois Press.

OF THE IMPORTANCE of this topic it is hardly necessary to speak. If the defenses of peace and prosperity, not to mention other desirable political conditions, are to be constructed in men's minds, then the critical position of communication and public opinion for that defense is evident. What is not so evident, perhaps, is why social scientists have given so little systematic attention to problems of the formation of public opinion with special reference to the role of the media of communication in that process. It was not evident to a "classical" writer on public opinion twenty-five years ago,[1] and it may be even less so today.

In any case, the field of interest is now developing and the line of development is reasonably clear. The political scientist's concern with political parties was generalized to a concern with the role of pressure groups in political life. The concern with pressure groups led directly into concern with propaganda, and that into concern with public opinion and the effect of propaganda upon it. At about this time, technicians began to develop scientific instruments by which to measure public opinion; a new medium of communication with great potentialities for popular influence came vigorously upon

---

[1] Walter Lippmann, *Public Opinion* (New York: The Macmillan Company, 1922), p. 243.

the scene; in a series of presidential elections people voted strongly for one candidate while their newspapers voted strongly for his opponent; and a World War made more visible as well as more urgent the battle for men's minds. Thus the background of academic interest was prepared just when dramatic events highlighted the urgency of the problem and when technical developments provided means for at least some solutions. As a result, interest in communication and public opinion is now at an all-time high.

The purpose of this paper is to discuss the relationship between communication and public opinion. "Discuss" here means to report on some (illustrative) research findings in the area and to propose relevant (and again illustrative) hypotheses for investigation. By communication is meant the transmission of symbols via the major media of mass communication—radio, newspaper, film, magazine, book—and the major medium of private communication—personal conversation. By public opinion is meant people's response (that is, approval, disapproval, or indifference) to controversial political and social issues of general attention, such as international relations, domestic policy, election candidates, ethnic relations.

The paper is organized into two parts because the relationship between communication and public opinion is twofold. The first section deals with the effect of public opinion upon communication and the second with the effect of communication upon public opinion. The second section is traditional, and there is more to say about it; the first is usually neglected.

EFFECT OF PUBLIC OPINION UPON COMMUNICATION

This problem is usually neglected in analyses of the relationship because it is not so obvious as the other and perhaps because it is more difficult to study. The problem deals with the extent to which, and the ways in which, communication content is determined to harmonize with the actual or presumed opinions of the actual or potential audience. It is clear that one factor, among others, that conditions what the media of communications say on social and political issues is the desire or expectation of the readers-listeners-seers to be told certain things and not others. The reporter or commentator or editor or producer may know or may think he knows "what his public wants" on a given issue, and to the extent that such knowledge affects what he communicates, to that extent public opinion becomes a determinant of communications. This aspect of the relationship between communication and public opinion is not always admitted, or even recognized, because of the immorality of suggesting that anything but "truth" or "justice" contributes to the character of communication content.[2] However, everyone knows that communication channels of various kinds tell people what they want to hear. In such cases, public opinion sets limits upon the nature of what is typically communicated.

This determination (or really, partial determination, since this is, of course, not the only factor responsible for communication content any more than communication content is the only factor responsible for public opinion) can operate in two ways, once the communication channel (newspaper, magazine, political writer, radio commentator, and so forth) has attracted to itself a distinguishable audience. The two ways are themselves interrelated and can coexist. First, it can operate through conscious and deliberate and calculated manipulation of the content in order to coincide with the dominant audience opinion. Sometimes this operates by rule of thumb, as when someone on the production line in the communication process decides that "our public won't take this, or won't like it." Sometimes it operates through elaborate machinery organized precisely for the purpose, as when thousands of research dollars and hours are spent in finding out what kinds of people the audience is composed of and what kinds of opinions they hold on controversial issues. Whether the decision to conform to audience predispositions is taken on the front line or in the front office is for the moment immaterial; so is the question of why it happens, e.g., the desire or need for constant and large audiences for economic reasons. The important point is that overt consideration of audience opinion does (help to) shape the social and political content of the mass media. Everyone recalls the story of the foreign correspondent who cabled a thoroughgoing analysis of a relatively obscure Hungarian crisis to the home office only to be told: "We do not think it advisable to print it because it does not reflect Midwestern opinion on this point."[3]

The other method by which public opinion can affect communi-

---

[2] However, some circles frankly acknowledge the power of the public to participate thus indirectly in the construction of communication content. This position is usually rationalized in terms of the presumed democratic ethic in which "the public is entitled to what it wants."

[3] Leo Rosten, *The Washington Correspondents* (New York: Harcourt, Brace, 1937), p. 231.

cations is implicit, through the sincere and more or less nonconscious correspondence of ideology between producers and consumers. The two groups often see the world through the same colored glasses. The correspondence is achieved through a two-way process: the audience selects the communications which it finds most congenial and the producers select people with "the right viewpoint" to prepare communications for other people with "the right viewpoint." Although this latter process also occurs through deliberate decision, it also happens through the most laudable and honest motives that people of the same general persuasion as their audience are found in influential positions in particular communication agencies. This is all the more true in specialized enterprises like trade papers or magazines like *Fortune* or *The Nation*. In such cases, producers react to new issues and events like the modal members of their audience; and their communications fit audience predispositions, not through a process of tailoring, but through correspondence in outlook. "The daily re-election of the editor" serves to make the editor quite sensitive to the wishes of the electors. Here again the economic necessity to hold an audience and the political desire to do so are relevant factors, as well as the "correctness" of outlook. The point is that the nature of one's audience places certain limits upon what one can say to it—and still have an audience. The need of the audience is not only to be informed but also to be satisfied, and the latter is sometimes evaluated more highly than the former.

It is important to take account of this direction in the flow of influence between communication and public opinion in order to appreciate the reciprocal nature of that influence, i.e., to recognize that it is not all a one-way process. It is also important to note that the total effect of this reciprocal process is probably to stabilize and "conservatize" opinion since ideologies are constantly in process of reinforcement thereby. The over-all picture, then, is that of like begetting like begetting like.

THE EFFECT OF COMMUNICATION ON PUBLIC OPINION

But the effect of communication on public opinion needs to be examined much more closely and directly than that. To speak roughly, in the 1920's propaganda was considered all-powerful—"it got us into the war"—and thus communication was thought to determine public opinion practically by itself. In the 1930's the Roosevelt campaigns "proved" that the newspaper had lost its influence and that a "golden voice" on the radio could sway men in almost any direction. Now, a body of empirical research is accumulating which provides some refined knowledge about the effect of communication on public opinion and promises to provide a good deal more in the next years.

What has such research contributed to the problem? By and large, do communications influence public opinion? By and large, of course, the answer is yes. But by-and-large questions and answers are not sufficient for a scientific theory of communication and public opinion. The proper answer to the general question, the answer which constitutes a useful formulation for research purposes, is this:

> Some kinds of *communication* on some kinds of *issues*,
> brought to the attention of some kinds of *people* under
> some kinds of *conditions,* have some kinds of *effects.*

This formulation identifies five central factors (or rather groups of factors) which are involved in the process, and it is the interrelationship of these variables which represents the subject matter of theory in this field. At present, students can fill out only part of the total picture—a small part—but the development of major variables and the formulation of hypotheses and generalizations concerning them are steps in the right direction. Theoretical integration in any full sense is not as yet possible, but descriptions of some ways in which these factors operate can be usefully made. Each set of factors will be discussed illustratively (*not* completely) in an effort to demonstrate how each of them conditions the total effect of communication on public opinion and thus contributes to the formulation of a general theory.

<h3 style="text-align:center">KINDS OF COMMUNICATION</h3>

The effectiveness of communications as an influence upon public opinion varies with the nature of the communication.

First let us deal with the effect of certain media characteristics. The more personal the media, the more effective it is in converting opinions. This means (other things being equal) that personal conversation is more effective than a radio speech, and that a radio speech is more effective than a newspaper account of it. The greater the amount of "personalism" the communication act contains, the more effective it presumably is. Recent analyses have confirmed the critical importance in opinion formation of personal contact between the individual and his fellows. The individual's opinions are formed in the context of his formal and informal group associations. College students become more liberal in political opinion over the period of their college attendance largely through the influence of the liberality of the college community, that is, the older students and the instructional staff.[4] Intensive case studies of current opinion toward the USSR held by adult men reveal the powerful influence of personal contacts: "The need to conform in one's opinion to the opinions of one's associates and of members of favored groups is an important motivational factor."[5] This effect operated in two ways: directly through the process of conformity as such and indirectly through the sharing of common values and information. The formation of political opinion during a presidential campaign was dependent upon personal influence to a large extent; the political homogeneity of social groups was strikingly high. "In comparison with the formal media of communication, personal relationships are potentially more influential for two reasons: their coverage is greater and they have certain psychological advantages over the formal media."[6] Personal contacts are more casual and nonpurposive than the formal media, they are more flexible in countering resistance, they can provide more desirable rewards for compliance, they offer reliance and trust in an intimate source, and they can persuade without convincing.[7]

The greater effectiveness of radio over newspapers derives to some extent from its greater "personalism." The radio speaks "to you" more than the newspaper does; it more closely approximates a personal conversation and can thus be more persuasive. The listener can "get a feel" of the speaker's personality, and this is often more effective a factor making for conversion of opinion than the content of the argument itself. The dominant characteristic which enabled Kate Smith to sell nearly $40,000,000 worth of war bonds in one day was the listener's image and evaluation of her personality

---

[4] Theodore M. Newcomb, *Personality and Social Change: Attitude Formation in a Student Community* (New York: Dryden Press, 1943).

[5] Mahlon Brewster Smith, "Functional and Descriptive Analysis of Public Opinion (Doctoral dissertation, Harvard University, 1947), p. 500.

[6] Paul Lazarsfeld, Bernard Berelson, and Hazel Gaudet, *The People's Choice: How the Voter Makes up His Mind in a Presidential Campaign* (New York: Duell, Sloan and Pearce, 1944), p. 150.

[7] For a full discussion of these factors, see chapter 16 of *The People's Choice*.

established over a period of time.[8] In other areas, too, the (radio) personality of such influencers of public opinion as Raymond Gram Swing or Gabriel Heatter or Franklin Delano Roosevelt contributed to their influence.

This discussion of the role of personal contact in opinion formation would not be complete without mention of the relationship between personal conversation and the formal media of communication. This relationship introduces the notion of the "opinion leader" or "opinion transmitter" who takes material from the formal media and passes it on, with or without distortion or effect, to associates who do not use the formal media so frequently in the particular area of concern. There are such people in all social groups and for all social topics, from politics to sports and fashions. This "two-step flow of communication" has been identified and is currently being studied intensively.[9] The concept is of central importance for the formation of a general theory of communication and public opinion.

Within a medium of communication, the particular channels specialized to the subject's predispositions are more effective in converting his opinion than the generalized channels. "The specialized magazine already has a foot in the door, so to speak, because it is accepted by the reader as a reliable spokesman for some cause or group in which he is greatly interested and with which he identifies himself. The general magazine tries to speak to everyone at once and as a result is less able to aim its shots directly at a particular target. . . . In Erie County in 1940, the *Farm Journal* was mentioned as a concrete influence upon changes in vote intention as frequently as *Collier's*, despite their great difference in circulation, and the Townsend publication as frequently as *Life* or the *Saturday Evening Post*."[10] Similarly farm programs on the air are probably more effective in influencing farmers' opinions than general radio programs dealing with the same issues.[11] Although there is little

[8] Robert K. Merton with the assistance of Marjorie Fiske and Alberta Curtis, *Mass Persuasion: The Social Psychology of a War Bond Drive* (New York: Harper and Brothers, 1946).

[9] See *The People's Choice*, pp. 49-51 and pp. 151-52; and the book by Elihu Katz and Paul Lazarsfeld, *Personal Influence* (Glencoe, Ill.: The Free Press, 1955). See also the article by Katz in this volume on "The Two-Step Flow of Communication."

[10] Lazarsfeld, Berelson, and Gaudet, *The People's Choice*, pp. 135-36.

[11] Some indirect evidence for this is available in William S. Robinson, "Radio Comes to the Farmer" in Lazarsfeld and Stanton (eds.), *Radio Research 1941* (New York: Duell, Sloan and Pearce, 1941), pp. 224-94.

direct evidence on this point, it is at least a plausible hypothesis that the specialized communication, per unit of exposure, is more effective in promoting opinion changes than the generalized communication. In a sense, then, this is an obstacle to the homogenizing influence of the mass channels in the mass media.

These are a few ways in which the distinctions among the media themselves are involved in the effect of communication upon opinion. What about communication content? Obviously it has a central position in this process. Perhaps the primary distinction in communication content as a factor affecting public opinion is the most primitive, namely, the distinction between the reportorial content and the editorial or interpretive content. Too often discussions of the general problem of the effect of communications upon public opinion is restricted to the latter kind of content. Yet the former is probably more effective in converting opinion. The events reported through the media presumably change more minds—or solidify more—than the comments of editorial writers, columnists, and commentators. "It was Sherman and Sheridan, and not Greeley and Raymond, who had elected him (Lincoln in 1864)."[12] And again, "Opinion is generally determined more by events than by words—unless those words are themselves interpreted as an 'event.'"[13] In addition events tend to solidify opinion changes produced by words, changes which otherwise would be short-lived; and the *fait accompli* crystallizes opinion in favor of the event even though words had not previously been able to do so.[14] Thus the reportorial content of the media is probably more influential than the interpretive.

However, it is necessary to make two remarks here. First, the distinction between "events" and "words" is not easy to make. Is a major speech by the President of the United States an "event" or just "propaganda"? Or a report issued by a pressure group? Or an investigation by a congressional committee? Or a tour of inspection? What about "propaganda of the deed"? Although the distinction is useful, the borderline is not always crystal-clear. And secondly, many events exercise influence not in and of themselves, but with active assistance from "words." Thus, for example, the relatively

[12] Frank Luther Mott, "Newspapers in Presidential Campaigns," *Public Opinion Quarterly*, VIII (1944), 354.

[13] Hadley Cantril, "The Use of Trends," in Cantril (ed.), *Gauging Public Opinion* (Princeton, N.J.: Princeton University Press, 1944), p. 226.

[14] *See ibid.*, pp. 227-28, for examples.

sharp changes in opinion on the interventionist-isolationist issue which occurred at the time of the fall of France in June, 1940, are often attributed to the event itself. However, it must be recognized that this event was strongly interpreted in one way (i.e., pro-interventionism) by most newspapers and radio commentators and by the pronouncements of the national administration. What if most communication channels and the official administration had taken another view of the event? At the least one might suppose that the effect of "the event" would have been different. More recently, the event represented by people's experience in the meat crisis in the fall of 1946 was sometimes credited with the Republican congressional victory at that time. Yet it must be remembered that the communication media gave that event a dominant interpretation (i.e., anti-administration) even though another was possible. In short, the interrelationship of "events" and "words" must be recognized in this connection. The fact is that the communication media are most effective when their reportorial and interpretive contents are in congruence.

Finally, to illustrate this aspect of the process, there is the hypothesis that emotional content of the media is more effective in converting opinions than rational content. There is some evidence for this. Votes for a Socialist candidate were increased more by "emotional" leaflets than by "rational" ones.[15] The highly effective bond broadcasts by Kate Smith even omitted two "rational" themes in favor of emphasis upon various "emotional" ones.[16] In the case of this distinction, of course, the need is not so much to test the finding as to refine it, especially for different population groups.

KINDS OF ISSUES

The effectiveness of communications as an influence upon public opinion varies with the nature of the issue.

Communication content is more effective in influencing public opinion on new or unstructured issues, i.e., those not particularly correlated with existing attitude clusters. The closer the opinion situation is to the *tabula rasa*, the easier it is for the communication media to write their own ticket. "Verbal statements and outlines

---

[15] George W. Hartmann, "A Field Experiment on the Comparative Effectiveness of 'Emotional' and 'Rational' Political Leaflets in Determining Election Results," *Journal of Abnormal and Social Psychology*, XXXI (1936), 99-114.

[16] See Merton, *op. cit.*, chap. III: "The Bond Appeals: A Thematic Analysis," pp. 45-69.

of courses of action have maximum importance when opinion is unstructured. . . ."[17] Again, with reference to opinion toward the USSR: "The object of the attitude is remote, the facts are ambiguous, and a person may fashion his own picture of Russia or fall in with the prevailing stereotypes"[18]—which are provided predominantly by the formal media.

Communication content is more effective in influencing opinion on peripheral issues than on crucial issues. That is, it is easier for the media to shape opinion on what to do about local courts than what to do about organized labor; and it is probably easier for them to shape opinion toward organized labor than on ethnic relations. The "relevance-quotient" or "intensity-quotient" of this issue is inversely correlated with the capacity of communication content to change minds.

Finally, communications are probably more effective in influencing opinion on "personalities" than on "issues." In the first place, Americans are an individualistic people. They like to have heroes; and the communications media do their best to supply heroes of various kinds to various groups in the population.[19] Secondly, Americans do not like to believe that there are deep-cutting political issues which have the potentiality of "class-ifying" the public so that they tend to resist the acceptance or even the recognition of some basic issues. As a result, the media probably can sway more people with "personality" arguments than with "issue" arguments.[20]

KINDS OF PEOPLE

The effectiveness of communications as an influence upon public opinion varies with the nature of the people.

In the first place, varying proportions of people simply do not read or see or listen to the different media. So far as direct effect of the media is concerned (and omitting considerations of indirect effects through such a process as opinion leadership), two-thirds of the adult population is not influenced by books, about one-half

---

[17] Cantril, op. cit., p. 226.

[18] Smith, op. cit., p. 195.

[19] For an example see Leo Lowenthal, "Biographies in Popular Magazines," pp. 507-48, in Lazarsfeld and Stanton (eds.), Radio Research, 1942-43 (New York: Duell, Sloan and Pearce, 1944).

[20] For a specific instance in which this was the case, see Bernard Berelson, "The Effects of Print upon Public Opinion," in Waples (ed.), Print, Radio and Film in a Democracy (Chicago: University of Chicago Press, 1942), pp. 55-56.

is not influenced by motion pictures, and so on. Direct effects of the media upon public opinion can be exercised only upon that part of the public which attends to the different media (and to different parts of them)—and that rules out distinguishable groups at the outset.

On one side of the coin is the distinction between peripheral and central issues; on the other side is the distinction between strong and weak predispositions. The stronger predispositions are on the issue, the more difficult it is for the media to convert opinions. Strong predispositions "compel" an opinion which the media only helps to rationalize and reinforce; in recent presidential elections very few people of high income, rural residence, and Protestant religion were *converted* to a Republican vote by the media of communication. Strong predispositions make for greater interest in the issue, an earlier decision on it, and fewer changes afterwards. All this is clear enough. What may or may not be so clear, however, is that the strongly predisposed on an issue actually manage not only to avoid contrary communication material, so that it just does not come to their attention, but also that they manage to misunderstand the material (which objectively is straightforward) when confronted by it. This has been particularly demonstrated in connection with communication material on ethnic relations, a topic on which predispositions run strong. Prejudiced people find several ways in which to evade the message of pro-tolerance propaganda: they avoid the intended identifications, they invalidate the message, they change the frame of reference, they "just don't get it."[21]

The less informed people are on an issue, the more susceptible they are to opinion conversion through the influence of the communication media. This means that the less informed are more mercurial in their opinions; the base of data upon which stable opinion is more securely founded[22] is simply absent from them, and the media (or more frequently, personal contacts) can more readily move them in different directions. "The compulsion of (media-supplied and other) stereotypes is great, particularly for persons with meager informational backgrounds."[23]

---

[21] Eunice Cooper and Marie Jahoda, "The Evasion of Propaganda: How Prejudiced People Respond to Anti-prejudice Propaganda," *Journal of Psychology*, XXIII (1947), 15-25.

[22] Cantril, *op. cit.*, p. 229.

[23] Smith, *op. cit.*, p. 195. In this connection, see also Herbert Hyman and Paul Sheatsley, "Some Reasons Why Information Campaigns Fail," *Public Opinion Quarterly*, XI (1947), 412-23.

KINDS OF CONDITIONS

The effectiveness of communications as an influence upon public opinion varies with the nature of the conditions.

Many mass communications on controversial issues in this country have to make their way in a competitive situation, i.e., under conditions in which alternative proposals are also available in the media. In some areas, such as the desirability of professing religious beliefs, this is not true: there is a virtual pro-religious monopoly on communications available to large audiences in America today. But it is the case in most areas of political and social concern, although here too various minority groups, e.g., the Communists, feel that their point of view is not given fair or proper attention in the mass media. It is necessary to recognize that the effect of communications upon public opinion must usually be exercised in this context of competing communication content and not in a context of monopoly. This is of central importance: communication has effects upon converting opinion under conditions of monopoly which are much greater than its effects under conditions of competition (even though that competition might be quite uneven). However, the effectiveness of formal communications is not unlimited; there are suggestions that the virtual monopoly exercised by the Nazis over communication content did not succeed in converting some large groups of Germans to their political philosophy.

That is one point—the greater but not absolute effectiveness of communication monopoly. Another deals with the problem of "balance" within competition. What does "balance" mean in the mass media? Does it mean a fifty-fifty division between pro and anti-content? What is a "fair" distribution of attention to the different sides on a public controversy? One approach to this matter is to consider what might be called "functional balance" in the media, i.e., the proportionate distribution of content which enables partisans on an issue to read or see or listen to their own side with reasonably equal facility. This does not necessitate an automatic fifty-fifty division of the content. In one presidential campaign, for example, the Republicans and Democrats in a community read and heard their own side about equally, even though there was about a two-to-one disproportion of content favoring the Republicans.[24] In any case, the

---

[24] Lazarsfeld, Berelson, and Gaudet, *The People's Choice*, chaps. XIII and XIV, pp. 110-36.

effect of the communication media upon public opinion is a function of the degree of competition on the issue within the media.

Another condition of communication exposure which affects opinion conversions is the purposiveness or non-purposiveness of the exposure. There is some slight evidence to suggest that non-purposive (or accidental) reading and listening is more effective in changing opinions than purposive (or deliberate).[25] In the first place, people see and hear more congenial material through deliberate communication exposure, and accidental reading and listening is more likely to bring diverse viewpoints to their attention. Secondly, in such exposure, defenses against new ideas are presumably weaker because preconceptions are not so pervasively present. Finally, there may be other psychological advantages centering around the gratification of "overhearing" something "not meant for you," a consideration that also weakens the resistance to "propaganda" (since "it would not be propaganda if it wasn't intended for you"). This factor of accidental-and-deliberate communication exposure corresponds to the factor of indirect-and-direct communication content, and the same hypothesis probably holds.[26] Direct content attacks the issue head-on (e.g., an article urging fairer treatment of the Negroes). Indirect content takes the roundabout approach (e.g., a story about Negro children without direct reference to the problem of race relations). The indirect content is more effective in converting opinions for much the same reasons which apply to accidental exposure.

KINDS OF EFFECTS

Finally, the media of communication have different kinds of effects upon public opinion.

First, a distinction should be made between the effect of the media upon the holding of certain opinions rather than others and their effect upon the holding of political opinions at all. Most attention has been given to the former problem, but the latter—the problem of the creation and maintenance of political interest or political apathy—is of considerable importance. The media have

---

[25] Based upon an unpublished manuscript by Paul F. Lazarsfeld.

[26] For recent discussions of other conditions affecting this relationship, see Samuel Flowerman, "Mass Propaganda in the War Against Bigotry," *Journal of Abnormal and Social Psychology*, XLII (1947), 429-39; and Ernst Kris and Nathan Leites, "Trends in 20th Century Propaganda," in *Psychoanalysis and the Social Sciences* (New York: International Universities Press, 1947), pp. 393-409.

a major influence in producing an interest in public affairs by constantly bringing them to people's attention in a context of presumed citizenly concern. The more the media stress a political issue, the less indecision there is on the issue among the general public.[27] At the same time, however, the communication media may also be promoting in actuality, but without intention, a sense of political apathy among some of its audience. This can occur in at least two ways.

In the first place, it is at least a plausible hypothesis that the attractive substance and easy accessibility of the entertainment or recreational or diversionary content of the mass media operate to minimize political interest for some groups in the population. Comedians, dramatic sketches, and popular music on the air; light fiction of the adventure, mystery, or romantic variety in magazines and books; comics and comic strips; feature films of "straight entertainment"—such "non-serious" content of the media may well serve to divert attention from political affairs directly and also to re-create the audience so that it is under less compulsion to "face up" to the general political problems which confront it and which shape its life. This is said with complete recognition of the psychological relief provided by such communication materials for many people; at the same time, their effect in lowering political interest and attention seems equally clear.

Secondly, the media may increase political apathy simply through presentation of the magnitude, the diversity, and the complexity of the political issues on which the responsible citizen is supposed to be informed. Some readers and listeners, conscious of their inability to become informed other than superficially on more than a few public problems, retreat from the whole area. How can one know what should be done about the Palestine partition, about inflation, about the Greek guerrillas and the Chinese Communists, about race relations in the United States, about the cold war with the USSR, about labor-management relations generally or the latest strike specifically, about "free enterprise" or "planning," about the atom—all at the same time? The media atmosphere of public responsibility for public actions may thus become a boomerang: the more the public is enjoined to exercise its duty to become an "informed citizenry," the less it feels able to do so. And, overwhelmed by the presentation of issues and problems of a public nature,

27 Berelson, *op. cit.*, p. 53.

part of the audience may withdraw into the relative security of their private problems and their private lives.

In any discussion of the effect of the media upon the *kinds of* political opinions held by people, an initial distinction should be made between long-run and short-run effects. The importance of the former is inversely related to the research attention which has been given them. The fact that it is easier to study short-run changes in attitudes produced by the communication media—not that that is easy!—should not divert attention from the pervasive, subtle, and durable effects of the media over long periods of time. For example, motion pictures undoubtedly affect the political attention of their audiences over the long run by strengthening certain "basic" values in terms of which political issues are later decided. The influence is remote and indirect, but it is nonetheless present and active. Or again, the communication media affect public opinion over the long run by providing a set of definitions for key political terms (of an affective nature) which come to be accepted through lack of adequate challenge. Thus, "freedom" in this country has mainly been defined in the media in terms of the absence of governmental intervention; and when the value of "freedom" is invoked in a political argument, it usually carries this meaning into the attitudinal battle. Other definitions are possible, but not so current. When it is suggested that "freedom of the press" be defined in terms of the ability of various population groups to secure the kind of communication they want (or someone thinks they should have) rather than in terms of governmental control, the proposal is confronted by the established definition—established through repetition over a long period of time.

Now for the short-run effects of the media upon opinion. Most is known about this area of the general problem, but not much is known. At the least, distinctions should be made among the various kinds of effects which the communication media can have upon public opinion. Usually the term "effect" includes only the conversion of opinions (i.e., changes away from a predispositional position or prior attitudes), but the (more frequent) reinforcement and activation effects should not be overlooked. The media are extremely effective in providing partisans with the deference and the rationalizations needed to maintain their position (i.e., reinforcement): "If the press follows a tenacious policy during an economic crisis, it may be able to retard or prevent shifts from one major party to another."[28] And they are also effective in bringing to visibility people's latent attitudes (i.e., activation).[29]

More than that, the media are effective in structuring political issues for their audiences. For example, there is a tendency for partisans on each side of a controversial matter to agree with their own side's argument in the order in which those arguments are emphasized in mass communications. Thus, the media set the political stage, so to speak, for the ensuing debate. In addition, there is some evidence that private discussions of political matters take their cue from the media's presentation of the issues; people talk politics along the lines laid down in the media.[30]

Finally, one thing must be made quite clear in this discussion of the effects of the media upon public opinion. That is that effects upon the audience do not follow directly from and in correspondence with the intent of the communicator or the content of the communication. The predispositions of the reader or listener are deeply involved in the situation, and may operate to block or modify the intended effect or even to set up a boomerang effect. This has been found time and again in studies of the effectiveness of materials promoting tolerance toward ethnic groups, on which topic predispositions run strong.[31] In another context—and under relatively favorable conditions—Communist propaganda provided a catharsis for its subjects, inefficiently for its own objectives, because its themes directly countered strong feelings of individualism and nationalism held by the audience.[32]

CONCLUSION

This brief discussion of communication and public opinion has indicated the reciprocal effects of the two major factors upon one another, and has presented a categorization in terms of which the effects of communication upon public opinion can usefully be investigated. In this latter analysis, five sets of variables were identified: communications, issues, people, conditions, effects.

---

[28] Harold F. Gosnell, *Machine Politics: Chicago Model* (Chicago: University of Chicago Press, 1937), p. 181.

[29] For a fuller description of these effects, see Lazarsfeld, Berelson, and Gaudet, *op. cit.*, chaps. VIII-X.

[30] For documentation of these points, see Berelson, *op. cit.*

[31] For example, see Cooper and Jahoda, *op. cit.*

[32] Harold D. Lasswell and Dorothy Blumenstock, *World Revolutionary Propaganda: A Chicago Study*, Section V: "The Influence of Propaganda," (New York: Knopf, 1939), pp. 247-358.

The interrelationships of these variables constitute the subject-matter of a scientific theory in this field. For example, illustrative hypotheses can be suggested which deal with these interrelationships:

The more specialized the media (communication), the greater reinforcement (effect).
The greater the competition in a communication system (conditions), the greater reinforcement (effect).
The "deeper" the predispositional affect toward the issue (people), the more effective the indirect content (communication) in converting opinion (effect).

And so on, within the formulation: some kinds of communication on some kinds of issues, brought to the attention of some kinds of people under some kinds of conditions, have some kinds of effects.

It is hypotheses of this sort that should be systematically explored as the next step in research in this field. Whatever the method of investigation (and some of these are better than others)—historical (Mott), trend analysis (Cantril), statistical correlation of ecological and voting data (Gosnell), case study (Smith), opinion survey and analysis (Cottrell),[33] experimental (I. and E. Division),[34] panel (Lazarsfeld, Berelson, and Gaudet)—this sort of propositional organization should be considered as the framework of study. In this way, a scientific theory of communications and public opinion can be developed for the enrichment not only of the field of communications research generally, but for social science as well.

---

[33] Leonard Cottrell, *American Opinion on World Affairs in the Atomic Age* (Princeton, N.J.: Princeton University Press, 1948).

[34] Information and Education Division, U.S. War Department, "The Effects of Presenting 'One Side' vs. 'Both Sides' in Changing Opinions on a Controversial Subject," in Theodore Newcomb and Eugene Hartley (eds.), *Readings in Social Psychology* (New York: Holt, 1947), pp. 566-79.

THE UNIQUE PERSPECTIVE OF TELEVISION AND ITS EFFECT: A PILOT STUDY[1]

BY KURT LANG
AND GLADYS ENGEL LANG

Mrs. Lang is a lecturer in sociology at Brooklyn College, and Dr. Lang is a lecturer at Queens College and a research sociologist for the Canadian Broadcasting Corporation.

THIS PAPER aims to investigate a public event as viewed over television or, to put it differently, to study in the context of public life, an event transmitted over video. The concern is not with the effects of television on individual persons, irrespective of the spread of this effect. Our assumption is, on the contrary, that the effect of exposure to TV broadcasting of public events cannot be measured most successfully in isolation. For the influence on one person is communicated to others, until the significance attached to the video event overshadows the "true" picture of the event, namely the impression obtained by someone physically present at the scene of the event. The experience of spectators may not be disseminated at all or may be discounted as the biased version of a specially interested participant. Or, again, the spectator's interpretation of his own experience may be reinterpreted when he finds the event in which he participated discussed by friends, newspapermen, and radio commentators. If the significance of the event is magnified, even casual spectatorship assumes importance. The fact of

---

[1] Condensation of the paper winning the prize for 1952 of the Edward L. Bernays Foundation.

having "been there" is to be remembered—not so much because the event, in itself, has left an impression, but because the event has been recorded by others. At the opposite extreme, privately significant experiences, unless revived in subsequent interpersonal relations, soon recede into the deeper layers of memory.

By taking MacArthur Day in Chicago,[2] as it was experienced by millions of spectators and video viewers, we have attempted to study an event transmitted over video. The basis of this report is the contrast between the actually recorded experience of participant observers on the scene, on the one hand, and the picture which a video viewer received by way of the television screen, and the way in which the event was interpreted, magnified, and took on added significance, on the other. The contrast between these two perspectives from which the larger social environment can be viewed and "known," forms the starting point for the assessment of a particular effect of television in structuring public events.

THE RESEARCH DESIGN

The present research was undertaken as an exploration in collective behavior.[3] The design of the communications analysis differs significantly from most studies of content analysis. The usual process of inferring effect from content and validating the effect by means of interviews with an audience and control group is reversed. A generally apparent effect, i.e., the "landslide effect" of national in-

---

[2] "MacArthur Day in Chicago" includes the following occasions which were televised: arrival at Midway Airport, parade through the city including the dedication at the Bataan-Corregidor Bridge, and the evening speech at Soldiers Field.

[3] This paper reports only one aspect of a larger study of MacArthur Day in Chicago. This writeup is limited to drawing together some of the implications concerning the role of television in public events, this particular study being considered as a pilot study for the framing of hypotheses and categories prerequisite for a more complete analysis of other such events in general. The present study could not test these categories, but was limited to an analysis of the television content in terms of the observed "landslide effect" of the telecast. The authors wish to express their indebtedness to Dr. Tamatsu Shibutani (then of the Department of Sociology, University of Chicago) for lending his encouragement and giving us absolute freedom for a study which, due to the short notice of MacArthur's planned arrival in Chicago, had to be prepared and drawn up in three days, and for allowing his classes to be used for soliciting volunteers. No funds of any sort were at our disposal. Dr. Donald Horton was kind enough to supply us with television sets and tape recorders. In discussions of the general problems involved in the analysis of television content, he has indirectly been of invaluable aid. Finally, we are indebted to the other twenty-nine observers, without whose splendid cooperation the data could never have been gathered.

dignation at MacArthur's abrupt dismissal and the impression of enthusiastic support, bordering on "mass hysteria," given to him, was used to make inferences on given aspects of the television content. The concern was with the picture disseminated, especially as it bore on the political atmosphere. To explain how people could have a false imagery (the implication of participant observational data), it was necessary to show how their perspective of the larger political environment was limited and how the occasion of Chicago's welcome to MacArthur, an event mediately known already, was given a particular structure. The concern is how the picture of the events was shaped by selection, emphasis, and suggested inferences which fitted into the already existing pattern of expectations.

The content analysis was therefore focused on two aspects—the selections made by the camera and their structuring of the event in terms of foreground and background, and the explanation and interpretations of televised events given by commentators and persons interviewed by them. Moreover, each monitor was instructed to give his impression of what was happening, on the basis of the picture and information received by way of television. The monitors' interpretations and subjective impressions were separately recorded. They served as a check that the structure inferred from the two operations of "objective" analysis of content were, in fact, legitimate inferences.[4] At the same time, utilizing the categories of the objective analysis, the devices by which the event was structured could be isolated, and the specific ways in which television reportage differed from the combined observations could be determined.

Thirty-one participant observers took part in the study. They were spatially distributed to allow for the maximum coverage of all the important phases of the day's activities, i.e., no important vantage point of spectatorship was neglected. Since the events were temporally distributed, many observers took more than one station, so that coverage was actually based on more than 31 perspectives. Thus the sampling error inherent in individual participant observation or unplanned mass-observation was greatly reduced. Observers

[4] That this check together with our observation of the general impression left by MacArthur Day constitutes only a very limited validation is beyond question. Under the conditions of the study—carried on without financial support and as an adjunct to other research commitments—it was the best we could do.

could witness the arrival at Midway Airport and still arrive in the Loop area long before the scheduled time for the parade. Reports were received from 43 points of observation.

Volunteers received instruction sheets which drew their attention to principles of observation[5] and details to be carefully recorded. Among these was the directive to take careful note of any activity indicating possible influences of the televising of the event upon the behavior of spectators, e.g., actions specifically addressed to the cameras, indications that events were staged with an eye towards transmission over television, and the like.

SUMMARY OF FINDINGS

The Pattern of Expectations

The mass-observation concentrated on discerning the psychological structure of the unfolding event in terms of present and subsequent anticipations. Certainly the crowd which turned out for the MacArthur Day celebration was far from a casual collection of individuals: the members *intended* to be witnesses to this "unusual event." One may call these intentions specific attitudes, emergent acts, expectations, or predispositions. Whatever the label, materials on these patterns of expectations were taken from two sources: (1) all statements of spectators recorded in the observer reports which could be interpreted as indicative of such expectations (coded in terms of the inferences therein); (2) personal expectations of the 31 study observers (as stated in the personal questionnaire).

Though not strictly comparable—since the observations on the scene contained purely personal, very short-range, and factually limited expectations—both series of data provide confirmation of a basic pattern of observer expectations. The persons on the scene *anticipated* "mobs" and "wild crowds." They expected some disruption of transportation. Their journey downtown was in search

---

[5] Analysis of personal data sheets, filled out by participants prior to MacArthur Day, revealed that "objectivity" in observation was not related to political opinion held, papers and periodicals subscribed to, and previous exposure to radio or TV coverage of MacArthur's homecoming. The significant factor in evaluating the reports for individual or deviant interpretation was found to reside in the degree to which individual observers were committed to scientific and objective procedures. Our observers were all advanced graduate students in the social sciences.

of adventure and excitement. Leaving out such purely personal expectations as "seeing" and "greeting," the second most frequent preconception emphasizes the extraordinary nature of the preparations and the entertaining showmanship connected with the spectacle.

As a result of an unfortunate collapsing of several questions regarding personal data into one, the response did not always focus properly on what the observers "expected to see." In some cases no evidence or only an incomplete description of this aspect was obtained. Of those answering, 68 per cent expected excited and wildly enthusiastic crowds. But it is a safe inference from the discussion during the briefing session that this figure tends to underestimate the number who held this type of imagery. The main incentive to volunteer resided, after all, in the opportunity to study crowd behavior at first hand.

To sum up: most people expected a wild spectacle, in which the large masses of onlookers would take an active part, and which contained an element of threat in view of the absence of ordinary restraints on behavior and the power of large numbers.

The Role of Mass Media in the Pattern of Expectations

A more detailed examination of the data supports the original assumption that the pattern of expectations was shaped by way of the mass media. For it is in that way that the picture of the larger world comes to sophisticated as well as unsophisticated people. The observers of the study were no exception to this dependence on what newspapers, newsreels, and television cameras mediated. They were, perhaps, better able than others to describe the origin of these impressions. Thus Observer 14 wrote in evaluating his report and his subjective feelings:

I had listened to the accounts of MacArthur's arrival in San Francisco, heard radio reports of his progress through the United States, and had heard the Washington speech as well as the radio accounts of his New York reception. . . . I had therefore expected the crowds to be much more vehement, contagious, and identified with MacArthur. I had expected to hear much political talk, especially anti-Communist and against the Truman administration.

These expectations were completely unfulfilled. I was amazed that not once did I hear Truman criticized, Acheson mentioned, or as much as an allusion to the Communists. . . . I had expected roaring, excited mobs; instead there were quiet, well ordered, dignified people. . . . The air of curiosity and casualness surprised me. Most people seemed to look on the event as simply something that might be interesting to watch.

Other observers made statements of a very similar content.

Conversation is the crowd pointed to a similar awareness. Talk repeatedly turned to television, especially to the comparative merit of "being there" and "seeing it over TV." An effort was consequently made to assess systematically the evidence bearing on the motives for being there in terms of the patterns of expectations previously built up. The procedures of content analysis served as a useful tool, allowing the weighing of all evidence *directly* relevant to this question in terms of confirmatory and contrary evidence. The coding operation involved the selection of two types of indicators: (1) general evaluations and summaries of data; and (2) actual incidents of behavior which could support or nullify our hypothesis.

Insofar as the observers had been instructed to report concrete behavior rather than general interpretations, relatively few such generalizations are available for tabulation. Those given were used to formulate the basic headings under which the concrete evidence could be tabulated. The generalizations fall into two types: namely, the crowds had turned out to see a great military figure and a public hero "in the flesh"; and—its logical supplement—they had turned out not so much "to see *him,* as I noticed, but to see the spectacle (Observer 5)." Six out of eleven concretely stated propositions were of the second type.

An examination of the media content required the introduction of a third heading, which subdivided the interest in MacArthur into two distinct interpretations: that people had come to find vantage points from which to see the man and his family; or, as the official (media and "Chicago official") version held, that they had come to welcome, cheer, and honor him. Not one single observer, in any generalized proposition, confirmed the official generalization, but there was infrequent mention of isolated incidents which would justify such an interpretation.

The analysis of actual incidents, behavior, and statements recorded is more revealing. A gross classification of the anticipations which led people to participate is given (according to categories outlined above) in Table 1.

A classification of these observations by area in which they were secured gives a clear indication that the Loop throngs thought of the occasion *primarily* as a spectacle. There, the percentage of

TABLE 1. Types of Spectator Interest

Form of Motivation	Per Cent
Active hero worship	9.2
Interest in seeing MacArthur	48.1
Passive interest in spectacle	42.7
Total	100.0

observations supporting the "spectacle hypothesis" was 59.7. The percentage in other areas was: Negro district, 40.0; Soldiers Field, 22.9; Airport, 17.6; University district, 0.0. Moreover, of the six generalizations advanced on crowd expectations in the Loop, five interpreted the prevalent motivation as the hope of a wild spectacle.

Thus, a probe into motivation gives a confirmatory clue regarding the pattern of expectations observed. To this body of data, there should be added the constantly overheard expressions—as the time of waiting increased and excitement failed to materialize—of disillusionment with the particular advantage point. "We should have stayed home and watched it on TV," was the almost universal form that the dissatisfaction took. In relation to the spectatorship experience of extended boredom and sore feet, alleviated only by a brief glimpse of the hero of the day, previous and similar experiences over television had been truly exciting ones which promised even greater "sharing of excitement" *if only one were present.* These expectations were disappointed and favorable allusions to television in this respect were frequent. To present the entire body of evidence bearing on the inadequate release of tension and the widely felt frustration would be to go beyond the scope of this report, in which the primary concern is the study of the television event. But the materials collected present unequivocal proof of the foregoing statements, and this—with one qualified exception—is also the interpretation of each one of the observers.

Moreover, the comparison of the television perspective with that of the participant observers indicates that the video aspects of MacArthur Day in Chicago served to *preserve* rather than disappoint the same pattern of expectations among the viewers. The main difference was that television remained true to form until the very end, interpreting the entire proceedings according to expectations. No hint about the disappointment in the crowd was provided. To cite only one example, taken from what was the high point in the video presentation, the moment when the crowds broke into the parade by surging out into State Street:

> The scene at 2:50 p.m. at State and Jackson was described by the announcer as the "most enthusiastic crowd *ever* in our city. . . . You can feel the tenseness in the air. . . . You can hear that crowd roar." The crowd was described as pushing out into the curb with the police trying to keep it in order, while the camera was still focusing on MacArthur and his party. The final picture was of a bobbing mass of heads as the camera took in the entire view of State Street northward. To the monitor, this mass of people appeared to be pushing and going nowhere. And then, with the remark, "The whole city appears to be marching down State Street behind General MacArthur," holding the picture just long enough for the impression to sink in, the picture was suddenly blanked out.

Observer 26, who was monitoring this phase of the television transmission, reported her impression:

> . . . the last buildup on TV concerning the "crowd" (cut off as it was, abruptly at 3:00 p.m.) gave me the impression that the crowd was pressing and straining so hard that it was going to be hard to control. My first thought, "I'm glad I'm not in that" and "I hope nobody gets crushed."

But observers near State and Jackson did not mention the event in an extraordinary context. For example, Observer 24 explained that as MacArthur passed:

> Everybody strained but few could get a really good glimpse of him. A few seconds after he had passed most people merely turned around to shrug and to address their neighbors with such phrases: "That's all," "That was it," "Gee, he looks just as he does in the movies," "What'll we do now?" Mostly teenagers and others with no specific plans flocked into the street after MacArthur, but very soon got tired of following as there was no place to go and nothing to do. Some cars were caught in the crowd, a matter which, to the crowd, seemed amusing.

The Structure of the TV Presentation

The television perspective was different from that of any spectator in the crowd. Relatively unlimited in its mobility, it could order events in its own way by using close-ups for what was deemed important and leaving the apparently unimportant for the background. There was almost complete freedom to aim cameras in accordance with such judgments. The view, moreover, could be shifted to any significant happening, so that the technical possibilities of the medium itself tended to play up the dramatic.

While the spectator, if fortunate, caught a brief glimpse of the General and his family, the television viewer found him the continuous center of attraction from his first appearance during the parade at 2:21 p.m. until the sudden blackout at 3:00 p.m. For almost 40 minutes, not counting his seven-minute appearance earlier in the day at the airport and his longer appearance at Soldiers Field that evening, the video viewer could fasten his eyes on the General and on what could be interpreted as the interplay between a heroic figure and the enthusiastic crowd. The cheering of the crowd seemed not to die down at all, and even as the telecast was concluded, it only seemed to have reached its crest. Moreover, as the camera focused principally on the parade itself, the crowd's applause seemed all the more ominous a tribute from the background.

The shots of the waiting crowd, the interviews with persons within it, and the commentaries, had previously prepared the viewer for this dramatic development. Its resolution was left to the inference of the individual. But a sufficient number of clues had already come over television to leave little doubt about the structure. Out of the three-hour daytime telecast, in addition to the time that MacArthur and party were the visual focus of attention, there were over two hours which had to be filled with visual material and vocal commentary. By far the largest amount of time was spent on anticipatory shots of the crowd. MacArthur himself held the picture for the second longest period; thus the ratio of time spent viewing MacArthur to time spent anticipating his arrival is much greater for the TV observer than for the spectator on the scene.

The descriptive accounts of the commentators (also reflected in the interviews),[6] determined the structure of the TV presentation of the day's events. The idea of the magnitude of the event, in line with preparations announced in the newspapers, was em-

---

[6] An analysis of televised interviews is omitted in this condensation. Interviews obtained for the study by observers posing as press representatives elicited responses similar to those given over TV. Without exception, those questioned referred to the magnitude, import, and other formal aspects of the event. These stand in contrast to results obtained through informal probes and most overheard conversation. One informant connected with television volunteered that television announcers had had specific instructions to emphasize that this was a "dramatic event." Another of Chicago's TV newsmen noted that throughout the telecast the commentary from each position made it sound as if the high points of the day's activity were about to occur or were occurring right on their own spot.

phasized by constant reference. The most frequently employed theme was that "no effort has been spared to make this day memorable" (eight references). There were seven direct references to the effect that the announcer had "never seen the equal to this moment" or that it was the "greatest ovation this city had ever turned out." The unique cooperative effort of TV received five mentions and was tied in with the "dramatic" proportions of the event. It was impossible to categorize and tabulate all references, but they ranged from a description of crowded transportation and numerical estimates of the crowd to the length of the city's lunch hour and the state of "suspended animation" into which business had fallen. There was repeated mention that nothing was being allowed to interfere with the success of the celebration; even the ball game had been cancelled.[7] In addition to these purely formal aspects of the event, two—and only two—aspects of the spectacle were *stressed:* (1) the unusual nature of the event; (2) the tension which was said to pervade the entire scene. Even the references to the friendly and congenial mood of the waiting crowd portended something about the change that was expected to occur.

Moreover, in view of the selectivity of the coverage with its emphasis on close-ups,[8] it was possible for each viewer to see himself in a *personal* relationship to the General. As the announcer shouted out: "Look at that chin! Look at those eyes!"—each viewer, regardless of what might have been meant by it, could seek a personal interpretation which best expressed, for him, the real feeling underlying the exterior which appeared on the television screen.[9]

It is against the background of this personal inspection that the significance of the telecast must be interpreted. The cheering crowd, the "seething mass of humanity," was fictionally endowed by the commentators with the same capacity for a direct and personal relationship to MacArthur as the one which television momentarily

[7] The day's activities at a nearby race track were not cancelled. At one point in the motorcade from the airport to the Loop, a traffic block resulted in a partially "captive audience." An irritated "captive" remarked, "I hope this doesn't make me late for the races."

[8] In a subsequent interview, a TV producer explained his conception of the MacArthur Day coverage as "being the best in the country." He especially recalled bracketing and then closing in on the General during the motorcade, the assumption being that he was the center of attraction.

[9] During the evening ceremonies, MacArthur's failure to show fatigue in spite of the strenuous experiences of the day received special notice. A report from a public viewing of the evening speech indicates the centering of discussion about this "lack of fatigue" in relation to the General's advanced years (Observer 24).

established for the TV viewer through its close-up shots. The net effect of television thus stems from a convergence of these two phenomena; namely, the seemingly extraordinary scope of the event together with the apparent enthusiasm accompanying it and personalizing influence just referred to. In this way the public event was interpreted in a very personal nexus. The total effect of so many people, all shouting, straining, cheering, waving in personal welcome to the General, disseminated the impression of a universal, enthusiastic, overwhelming ovation for the General. The selectivity of the camera and the commentary gave the event a personal dimension, non-existent for the participants in the crowds, thereby presenting a very specific perspective which contrasted with that of direct observation.

Other Indices of the Discrepancy

In order to provide a further objective check on the discrepancies between observer impressions and the event as it was interpreted by those who witnessed it over television, a number of spot checks on the reported amount of participation were undertaken. Transportation statistics, counts in offices, and the volume of sales reported by vendors provided such indices.

The results substantiate the above finding. The city and suburban lines showed a very slight increase over their normal loads. To some extent the paltry 50,000 increase in inbound traffic on the street cars and elevated trains might even have been due to rerouting. The suburban lines had their evening rush hour moved up into the early afternoon—before the parade had begun.

Checks at luncheonettes, restaurants, and parking areas indicated no unusual crowding. Samplings in offices disclosed only a minor interest in the parade. Hawkers, perhaps the most sensitive judges of enthusiasm, called the parade a "puzzler" and displayed unsold wares.

Detailed Illustration of Contrast

The Bridge ceremony provides an illustration of the contrast between the two perspectives. Seven observers witnessed this ceremony from the crowd.

TV perspective: In the words of the announcer, the Bridge ceremony marked "one of the high spots, if not the high spot of the occasion this afternoon. . . . The parade is now reaching its climax at this point."

The announcer, still focusing on MacArthur and the other participating persons, took the opportunity to review the ceremony about to take place. . . . The camera followed and the announcer described the ceremony in detail. . . . The camera focused directly on the General, showing a close-up. . . . There were no shots of the crowd during this period. But the announcer filled in. "A great cheer goes up at the Bataan Bridge, where the General has just placed a wreath in honor of the American boys who died at Bataan and Corregidor. You have heard the speech . . . the General is now walking back . . . the General now enters his car. This is the focal point where all the newsreels . . . frankly, in 25 years of covering the news, we have never seen as many newsreels gathered at one spot. One, two, three, four, five, six. At least eight cars with newsreels rigged on top of them, taking a picture that will be carried over the entire world, over the Chicagoland area by the combined network of these TV stations of Chicago, which have combined for this great occasion and for the solemn occasion which you have just witnessed."

During this scene there were sufficient close-ups for the viewer to gain a definite reaction, positive or negative, to the proceedings. He could see the General's facial expressions and what appeared to be momentary confusion. He could watch the activities of the Gold Star mothers in relation to MacArthur and define this as he wished —as inappropriate for the bereaved moment or as understandable in the light of the occasion. Taking the cue from the announcer, the entire scene could be viewed as rushed. Whether or not, in line with the official interpretation, the TV viewer saw the occasion as *solemn,* it can be assumed that he expected that the participant on the scene was, in fact, experiencing the occasion in the same way as he.

Actually, this is the way what was meant to be a solemn occasion was experienced by those attending, and which constitutes the crowd perspective. The dedication ceremony aroused little of the sentiment it might have elicited under other conditions. According to Observer 31, "People on our corner could not see the dedication ceremony very well, and consequently after he had passed immediately in front of us, there was uncertainty as to what was going on. As soon as word had come down that he had gone down to his car, the crowd dispersed." Observer 8 could not quite see the ceremony from where he was located on Wacker Drive, slightly east of the bridge. Condensed descriptions of two witnesses illustrate the confusion which surrounded the actual wreath-laying ceremony (three other similar descriptions are omitted here).

It was difficult to see any of them. MacArthur moved swiftly up the steps and immediately shook hands with people on the platform waiting to greet him. There was some cheering when he mounted the platform. He walked north on the platform and did not reappear until some minutes later. In the meantime the crowd was so noisy that it was impossible to understand what was being broadcast from the loudspeakers. Cheering was spotty and intermittent, and there was much talk about Mrs. MacArthur and Arthur . . . (Observer 2).

Those who were not on boxes did not see MacArthur. They did not see Mrs. MacArthur, but only her back, MacArthur went up on the platform, as we were informed by those on boxes, and soon we heard some sound over the loudspeakers. Several cars were standing in the street with their motors running. . . . Some shouted to the cars to shut their motors off, but the people in the cars did not care or did not hear. . . . The people in our area continued to push forward trying to hear. When people from other areas began to come and walk past us to go toward the train, the people in our area shrugged their shoulders. "Well, I guess it's all over. That noise must have been the speech." One of the three men who had stood there for an hour or more, because it was such a good spot, complained, "This turned out to be a lousy spot. I should have gone home. I bet my wife saw it much better over television" (Observer 30).

Regardless of good intentions on the part of planners and despite any recognition of the solemn purpose of the occasion by individuals in the crowd, the solemnity of the occasion was destroyed, if for no other reason, because officials in the parade were so intent upon the time-schedule and cameramen so intent upon recording the solemn dedication for the TV audience and for posterity that the witnesses could not see or hear the ceremony, or feel "solemn" or communicate a mood of solemnity. A crowd of confused spectators, cheated in their hopes of seeing a legendary hero in the flesh, was left unsatisfied.

Reciprocal Effects

There is some direct evidence regarding the way in which television imposed its own peculiar perspective on the event. In one case an observer on the scene could watch both what was going on and what was being televised.

It was possible for me to view the scene (at Soldiers Field) both naturally and through the lens of the television camera. It was obvious that the camera presented quite a different picture from the one received otherwise. The camera followed the General's car and caught that part of the crowd immediately opposite the car and about 15 rows above it. Thus it caught that part of the crowd that was cheering, giving the impression of a solid mass of wildly cheering people. It did not show the large sections of empty stands, nor did it show that people stopped cheering as soon as the car passed them (Observer 13).

In much the same way, the television viewer received the impression of wildly cheering and enthusiastic crowds before the parade. The camera selected shots of the noisy and waving audience, but in this case, the television camera itself created the incident. The cheering, waving, and shouting was often largely a response to the aiming of the camera. The crowd was thrilled to be on television, and many attempted to make themselves apparent to acquaintances who might be watching. But even beyond that, an event important enough to warrant the most widespread pooling of television facilities in Chicago video history, acquired in its own right some magnitude and significance. Casual conversation continually showed that being on television was among the greatest thrills of the day.

CONCLUSION

It has been claimed for television that it brings the truth directly into the home: the "camera does not lie." Analysis of the above data shows that this assumed reportorial accuracy is far from automatic. Every camera selects, and thereby leaves the unseen part of the subject open to suggestion and inference. The gaps are usually filled in by a commentator. In addition the process directs action and attention to itself.

Examination of a public event by mass-observation and by television revealed considerable discrepancy between these two experiences. The contrast in perspectives points to three items whose relevance in structuring a televised event can be inferred from an analysis of the television content:

(1) technological bias, i.e., the necessarily arbitrary sequence of telecasting events and their structure in terms of foreground and background, which at the same time contains the choices on the part of the television personnel as to what is important;

(2) structuring of an event by an announcer, whose commentary is needed to tie together the shifts from camera to camera, from vista to close-up, helping the spectator to gain the stable orientation from one particular perspective;

(3) reciprocal effects, which modify the event itself by staging it in a way to make it more suitable for telecasting and creating among the actors the consciousness of acting for a larger audience.

General attitudes regarding television and viewing habits must also be taken into account. Since the industry is accustomed to thinking in terms of audience ratings—though not to the exclusion of all other considerations—efforts are made to assure steady interest. The telecast was made to conform to what was interpreted as the pattern of viewers' expectations. The drama of MacArthur Day, in line with that pattern, was nonetheless built around unifying symbols, personalities, and general appeals (rather than issues). But a drama it had to be, even if at the expense of reality.

Unlike other television programs, news and special events features constitute part of that basic information about "reality" which we require in order to act in concert with anonymous but likeminded persons in the political process. Action is guided by the possibilities for success, and, as part of this constant assessment, inferences about public opinion as a whole are constantly made. Even though the average citizen does, in fact, see only a small segment of public opinion, few persons refrain from making estimates of the true reading of the public temper. Actions and campaigns are supported by a sense of support from other persons. If not, these others at least constitute an action potential that can be mobilized. The correct evaluation of the public temper is therefore of utmost importance; it enters the total political situation as perhaps one of the weightiest factors.

Where no overt expression of public opinion exists, politicians and citizens find it useful to fabricate it. Against such demonstrations as the MacArthur Day, poll data lack persuasiveness and, of necessity, must always lag, in their publication, behind the development of popular attitudes. For the politician who is retroactively able to counter the errors resulting from an undue regard for what at a given time is considered overwhelming public opinion, there may be little significance in this delay. The imagery of momentary opinion, may, however, goad him into action which, though justified in the name of public opinion, may objectively be detrimental. It may prevent critics from speaking out when reasoned criticism is desirable, so that action may be deferred until scientific estimates of public opinion can catch up with the prior emergence of new or submerged opinion.

Above all, a more careful formulation of the relations among public opinion, the mass media, and the political process, is vital for the understanding of many problems in the field of politics. The reports and telecasts of what purports to be spontaneous homage paid to a political figure assume added meaning within this context. The most important single media effect coming within the scope of the material relevant to the study of MacArthur Day was the dissemination of an image of overwhelming public sentiment in favor of the General. This effect gathered force as it was incorporated into political strategy, picked up by other media, entered into gossip, and thus came to overshadow immediate reality as it might have been recorded by an observer on the scene. We have labelled this the "landslide effect" because, in view of the widespread dissemination of a particular public welcoming ceremony the imputed unanimity gathered tremendous force.[10] This "landslide effect" can, in large measure, be attributed to television.

Two characteristics of the video event enhanced this effect (misevaluation of public sentiment. (1) The depiction of the ceremonies in unifying rather than in particularistic symbols (between which a balance was maintained) failed to leave any room for dissent. Because no lines were drawn between the conventional and the partisan aspects of the reception, the traditional welcome assumed political significance in the eyes of the public. (2) A general characteristic of the television presentation was that the field of vision of the viewer was enlarged while, at the same time, the context in which these events could be interpreted was less clear. Whereas a participant was able to make direct inferences about the crowd as a whole, being in constant touch with those around him, the television viewer was in the center of the entire crowd. Yet, unlike the participant, he was completely at the mercy of the instrument of his perceptions. He could not test his impressions—could not shove back the shover, inspect bystanders' views, or attempt in any way to affect the ongoing activity. To the participant, on the other hand, the direction of the crowd activity as a whole, regardless of its final goal, still appeared as the interplay of certain peculiarly personal and human forces. Political sentiment, wherever encountered, could thus be evaluated and discounted. Antagonistic views could be attributed to insufficient personal powers of persuasion rather than seen as subjugation to the impersonal dynamics

---

[10] It must be re-emphasized that there was no independent check—in the form of a validation—of the specific effect of TV. However, newspaper coverage emphasized the overwhelming enthusiasm. Informal interviews, moreover, even months later, showed that the event was still being interpreted as a display of mass hysteria.

of mass hysteria. The television viewer had little opportunity to recognize this personal dimension in the crowd. What was mediated over the screen was, above all, the general trend and the direction of the event, which consequently assumed the **proportion** of an impersonal force, no longer subject to influence.

This view of the "overwhelming" effect of public moods and the impersonal logic of public events is hypothesized as a characteristic of the perspective resulting from the general structure of the picture and the context of television viewing.

CONSENSUS AND MASS COMMUNICATION

BY LOUIS WIRTH

Professor Wirth, late of the University of Chicago, gave this paper as the presidential address before the annual meeting of the American Sociological Society in December, 1947. It was printed in the *American Sociological Review*, February, 1948, and is here reprinted by permission of author and publisher.

BEFORE EXPLORING the nature and conditions of consensus, it seems appropriate to indicate the salient characteristics of mass societies. As we look back upon previous social aggregations, such as those of the ancient kingdoms, or at their greatest extent the Roman Empire, we wonder how, given the primitive communications that obtained, such impressive numbers and territories could be held together under a common regime over any considerable span of time. If we discover, however, that these aggregations were not truly societies but were little more than administrative areas, creatures of military domination along the main arteries of communication from some center of power, and that the economic base of their cohesion rested on exploitation of the outlying territories and peoples by the power holders at a center through their representatives who were scattered thinly over the territory, the magnitude of these aggregations does not seem too impressive. Mass societies as we find them today, however, show greater marks of integration. They are aggregations of people who participate to a much greater degree in the common life, and, at least in democratic parts of the world, comprise people whose attitudes, sentiments, and opinions have

561

some bearing upon the policies pursued by their governments. In this sense mass societies are a creation of the modern age and are the product of the division of labor, of mass communication, and a more or less democratically achieved consensus.

II

Since we shall speak of our society as a mass society and of the communication that it involves as mass communication, it behooves us to depict the characteristics of the mass. Its most obvious trait is that it involves great numbers in contradistinction to the smaller aggregates with which we have become familiar through the study of primitive life and earlier historical forms of human association. Second, and again, almost by definition, it consists of aggregates of men widely dispersed over the face of the earth, as distinguished from the compact local groups of former periods. Third, the mass is composed of heterogeneous members, in that it includes people living under widely different conditions, under widely varying cultures, coming from diverse strata of society, occupying different positions, engaging in different occupations, and hence having different interests, standards of life, and degrees of prestige, power, and influence. Fourth, the mass is an aggregate of anonymous individuals, as may be indicated by the fact that though millions of individuals listening to a radio program, reading a newspaper, or seeing a movie, are exposed to the same images, they are not aware of who the fellow members of the audience are, nor are those who transmit these images certain of the composition of their audience. These anonymous persons who constitute the mass may be, and usually are, of course, aware that they are part of a mass and they make some assumptions as to who their fellow members are and how many of them there are. They are likewise capable of identifying themselves with their anonymous fellows who are exposed to the same images and may even gain some support from the knowledge of their existence. They may even act as if they had their unanimous support as is illustrated by the slogan "Fifty million Frenchmen can't be wrong," or by the much disputed bandwagon effect resulting from the publication of the results of public opinion polls. Fifth, the mass does not constitute an organized group. It is without recognized leadership and a well-defined program of action. If it acts collectively at all it does so only as a crowd or as a mob, but since it is dispersed in space it cannot even move as these elementary social bodies are capable of action, although it may be far from constituting, as Carlyle thought, "an inert lump." Sixth, the mass has no common customs or traditions, no institutions, and no rules governing the action of the individuals. Hence, it is open to suggestions, and its behavior, to a greater degree than that of organized bodies, is capricious and unpredictable. And, finally, the mass consists of unattached individuals, or, at best, individuals who, for the time being, behave not as members of a group, playing specific roles representative of their position in that group, but rather as discrete entities. In modern urban industrial society, our membership in each of the multiple organizations to which we belong represents our interests only in some limited aspect of our total personal life. There is no group which even remotely professes to speak for us in our total capacity as men or in all of the roles that we play. Although through our membership in these organized groups we become articulate, contribute to the molding of public opinion, and participate more or less actively in the determination of social policies, there remains for all of us a quite considerable range of ideas and ideals which are subject to manipulation from the outside and in reference to which there is no appreciable reciprocal interaction between ourselves and others similarly situated. It is this area of life which furnishes the opportunity for others to entrap us or to lead us toward goals with the formulation of which we have had little or nothing whatever to do. Hence, all of us are in some respects characterized in our conduct by mass behavior.

The fragmentation of human interests in heterogeneous, complex modern societies is so far advanced that as Robert E. Park put it, "What a man belongs to constitutes most of his life career and all of his obituary." The trend in group organization is not merely toward the multiplication and diversification of organizations, but also toward bodies of enormously increased size. We have witnessed in recent decades the development of numerous giant organizations in business and industry, in labor, in the professions, in religion, in government, and in social life which seem to dominate our existence and to characterize our civilization.

Many of these organizations have become so colossal that they themselves come to approximate masses. The sense of belonging and of participation which smaller and more compactly organized groups are able to generate is hence largely frustrated by the very size of the typical organizations of our time. This is perhaps a price we must be willing to pay for living in an interdependent and technologically highly advanced world. But it should also constitute a major challenge to the analytical skill and the inventive imagination of social scientists, especially sociologists, for it is to a large extent upon the ability to maintain effective contact between the members and two-way communication between the leaders and the membership of these giant structures that the future of democracy rests.

The problem is complicated by the fact that not only is mass democratic society enormous in scope and intricate in structure, but it presents a dynamic equilibrium in which one of the principal conditions of effective collective action is the accuracy and speed with which the shifting interests and attitudes of great masses of men, whether organized or unorganized, can be ascertained and brought to bear upon the determination of policy.

Another significant feature of modern mass society, and especially of mass democracies, is the instability of the interests and the motives of the members, and the correspondingly frequent changes in leadership and the consequent uncertainty as to the locus of decisive power at any one juncture of events. If the spokesmen in any group are to know whom they are speaking for they must be able to assess how strong or enduring the interests are that they profess to represent, and whether, indeed, the groups for which they speak are at all interested in the issue.

Mass societies, furthermore, involve vast concentrations of power and authority and complicated machinery of administration. Perhaps the most urgent need that goes unmet in such a society is the capacity for prompt decisions in the face of recurrent crises. The fact that concerted action in such societies, if they are to remain democratic, must take into consideration the shifting constellation of public opinion imposes upon them who guide its destinies a responsibility which can only be met by the utilization of all the relevant sources of knowledge and the perfection of very much more advanced techniques than we now seem to possess.

III

When a social philosopher of the previous generation, Herbert Spencer, undertook to compare human society with the biological organism, he thought he had found that the one thing which human society lacked to make it truly comparable to a biological organism, was a social sensorium which would serve as the equivalent of the central nervous system and "the mind" in the individual organism. Whatever we may think about such analogies, this alleged lack of a social mind to go with the social body is the deficiency that we must supply if organized social life, on the scale on which we must now live it, is to endure. The only reasonable equivalent of "mind" in the individual organism that we can think of as an essential in the social organism can be supplied through consensus.

A thoughtful student has described society as "a highly intricate network of partial or complete understandings between the members of organizational units."[1] Consensus is the sign that such partial or complete understanding has been reached on a number of issues confronting the members of a group sufficient to entitle it to be called a society. It implies that a measure of agreement has been reached. The agreement, however, is neither imposed by coercion nor fixed by custom so as no longer to be subject to discussion. It is always partial and developing and has constantly to be won. It results from the interpenetration of views based upon mutual consent and upon feeling as well as thinking together.

If men of diverse experiences and interests are to have ideas and ideals in common they must have the ability to communicate. It is precisely here, however, that we encounter a paradox. In order to communicate effectively with one another, we must have common knowledge, but in a mass society it is through communication that we must obtain this common body of knowledge. The resolution of this paradox seems to lie in the possibility that though men of diverse backgrounds, experiences, and interests, when they first come in contact, are incapable of communicating with and understanding one another, much less arriving at agreement, they must initially be content to grope haltingly for such elementary understandings as can be supplied on the basis of the scanty and superficial common experiences that even the most casual and superficial contact supplies. They must and do live in the hope that as that experience is widened and deepened there will take place a parallel improvement in effective communication.

We live on the assumption that human beings the world over are sufficiently alike in their basic nature and their life careers that even the most alien groups in contact with one another, no matter how indirectly and remotely, will have some elementary capacity to put themselves in the place of the other, that the common understanding

---

[1] Edward Sapir, *Encyclopedia of the Social Sciences*, "Communication."

that comes through communication will have a cumulative effect, and that every step toward understanding becomes the basis for a still broader and deeper basis of understanding.

Modern society exhibits two major aspects. On the one hand, it consists of organized groups, ranging from informally constituted intimate groups to highly formalized organizations, such as the modern corporation, the union, the church, and the state. On the other hand, there are the detached masses that are held together, if at all, by the mass media of communication. The analysis of consensus must necessarily take account of these phases.

On every level of social life calling for concerted action whether it be that of organized groups or the mass, we need a degree of consensus capable of mobilizing the energies of the members or at least of neutralizing their opposition or apathy. Wherever and whenever we seek to enlist the uncoerced cooperation and participation of numbers of diverse men in their pursuit of a common cause, "We need," as John Dewey has said, "one world of intelligence and understanding, if we are to obtain one world in other forms of human activity."[2]

IV

There are many ways that society has developed of inducing consent. We may first point to the kind of acquiescence induced by superior force. Power is not equally distributed among the members of most societies and there probably is no society where it is so equally distributed that all the members are equally capable of exerting their will upon the others. In its extreme form, this inequality of power and influence is exemplified by dictatorship. But even in a dictatorship, while the ultimate monopoly of violence rests with the dictator, the members of the society count for something, and the dictator does not enjoy unlimited opportunity to coerce his subjects. Although, for instance, in the case of the present Soviet regime we are convinced of the actuality of its dictatorial character, we recognize nevertheless that there are certain limits beyond which the dictators cannot go, and that if the conditions of life which they can provide for their people and the hopes that they can hold out to them fall below a certain minimum, there will be rebellion and counter-revolution. Similarly, we act, at least with reference to the

---

[2] John Dewey, "Liberating the Social Scientist: A Plea to Unshackle the Study of Man," *Commentary*, IV, No. 4 (October, 1947), 382.

Voice of America broadcasts to the Soviet people, as if even their public opinion were of some importance.

Though social cohesion in a dictatorship rests ultimately upon force and violence, it need not at all times exercise this force and violence brutally and arbitrarily. It can be held in reserve for occasions when it is absolutely necessary, and indeed the wise dictator knows this principle of prudence in the exercise of his unquestioned power. Suppression may be the first or last stage in the life cycle. It can, for instance, be translated into law, however authoritarian and arbitrary its character, and into a religious control which may rest upon fear. This attenuated form of the exercise of force has been the practice at least of modern dictators ever since Machiavelli offered his counsel to the dictators of his day. It should be noted, of course, that people may never know that they are exploited and oppressed until they see their own humble status juxtaposed to an actual condition of relative freedom and opportunity that exists in some other society with which they are in contact, or unless they can recall some previous condition of existence in which these forms of oppression did not prevail, or unless, finally, there is held out to them some ideal condition which is possible of achievement and to which they consider themselves entitled. The idea of natural rights is an example of injecting into the minds of men an ideology which serves as an ideal against which they can measure their actual condition, and the experience with this ideology in recent times shows that it has made dictatorship of any kind untenable in the long run. The notion of the inalienable rights of man and of the dignity of the human personality is at work in increasing measure over all the world to challenge autocratic rule in every realm of human life.

Closely related to the type of basis of consensus provided by force and authority is the consensus that rests upon a common identification with great heroes or leaders, of which the charismatic leader depicted by Max Weber is perhaps the fittest example. There are many roads that lead to leadership, although they are not the same roads in all societies. Force and ruthlessness, law and authority, the sacred sanctions of religion or of tradition, or the wisdom or personality of the leader himself, or even the belief in his wisdom or personal qualities, separately or in combination, may establish a man or a group in a position of leadership which can evoke consensus on the part of the followers. Whatever these original sources are, they may be reinforced by propaganda and education and thus come to have a symbolic significance far out of proportion to the original sources.

Just as leaders can serve as instruments for building consensus, so ideas and ideals and the symbols with which they become identified can create cohesion in the group. The Cross and the Crescent, the Stars and Stripes, and the Hammer and Sickle, the Magna Charta, the Declaration of Independence, and the Four Freedoms, not to speak of the popular stereotypes and the slogans which are the stock-in-trade of so much of our present-day propaganda and public relations, are and will continue to be potential forces for creating and maintaining consensus. The instrumentalities of mass communication lend themselves particularly well to the dissemination of these symbols on a scale hitherto thought impossible. We happen to live in a world in which, despite barriers of technology and of politics, the whole human race becomes potentially exposed to the same symbols. They are weapons of offense and of defense, and they are bonds of union or of discord, depending upon the purposes which those who use them have in mind.

Sociologists have long been accustomed to analyze in particular one of the bases of consensus, namely, the consensus that derives from the social heritage of a people, from a common culture, a common history and set of traditions, from the mores, which can make anything seem right, true, good, beautiful, and possible. It is this basis of common social life as patterned by these traditions that makes it possible in the last analysis for any group to think of itself and to act as a society, to regard itself as a "we" group and to counterpose this "we" experience to all that is alien. The extent to which force and authority, law, religious sanction and leadership, propaganda and education, and the apparatus of symbols can be used effectively depends in large part upon this substratum of a common basis of knowledge, belief, and standards molded by tradition and reinforced by the ongoing social life which embodies that tradition.

The fact that the instrumentalities of mass communication operate in situations already prepared for them may lead to the mistaken impression that they or the content and symbols which they disseminate do the trick. It is rather the consensual basis that already exists in society which lends to mass communication its effectiveness.

A number of changes have, however, occurred since the days of the primitive local and isolated group life of our ancestors which have profoundly affected the force of tradition. The movements of population and the contact between people from the ends of the earth, the opening of world markets, and the spread of modern technology, the growth of cities, the operation of mass media of communication, the increasing literacy of the masses of people over all the world, have combined to disintegrate local cohesion and to bring hitherto disparate and parochial cultures into contact with each other. Out of this ferment has come the disenchantment of absolute faiths which expresses itself in the secular outlook of modern man.

One characteristic of this secularism is the increasing skepticism toward all dogmas and ideologies. With this goes the reluctance to accept things on faith or on authority, and the substitution of more or less rational grounds for believing, and where reason fails, to seek legitimation for a belief in personal tastes, preferences, and the right to choose.

Another feature of this secularism is the change from naïveté to sophistication. One of the prime virtues on which the modern man prides himself is that he will not be taken in by anybody; that he offers sales resistance to those who offer him a pig-in-a-poke; that he suspects the motives of the salesman of goods or of ideas; that he wishes to see the evidence upon which the appeal rests; and that he claims the right to exercise independent judgment on the validity of that evidence. This has in turn led to a perfection of the means of persuasion through the invention of ways of making the irrational appear rational and of subtle means for making people interested in things that may not be to their interest. It has led to an enormous interest in discovering through scientific means what the interests, prejudices, and predilections of men are and how they can be manipulated by appropriate appeals.

This secularism carries with it the disintegration of unitary faiths and doctrines, on the one hand, and their blending into new syncretisms which seek to combine a variety of hitherto incongruous elements in such a way as to attract the greatest number of followers. The symbols and slogans that formerly were characteristic of one party become mingled with those of others in order to woo more effectively the greatest number of adherents. Ideas and ideals that formerly stood for one set of objectives come to be perverted and diluted until they can comprise objectives which formerly seemed incongruous and until it seems that the unambiguous labels under which men formerly united not only no longer differentiate parties but actually can come to have the most contradictory content in order to appeal to all parties.

In addition to force and authority, leadership and personal prestige, ideas, ideals, and the symbols into which they are incorporated, and social traditions, we must consider an aspect of the basis of consensus which, though it overlaps with others, is nevertheless so distinctive of our society as to require separate treatment. I refer to public opinion. This, of course, is not an independent force but is an aspect of every ongoing society.

Public opinion is formed in the course of living, acting, and making decisions on issues. It is precipitated through the clash of representative ideas reflecting more or less faithfully the positions confronting the respective groups that compose the society. Our society, and others comparable to it, are composed of varieties of constituent groups, occupational and economic, racial and ethnic, and religious. Each of these groups articulates its own interests, has its own powers, leadership, creed, political and corporate organization.

Not all members of each group have an equal share of influence nor is the strength of each group determined solely by the size of its membership. These groups are not loose aggregations of men, and it is not necessary for all members of each group to share the official view of the group to which they give their adherence. There will be some who are indifferent or even hostile to what the group stands for without rebelling, as can clearly be seen by looking at our present-day political parties or major economic or religious organizations. The role which the individuals play is not determined alone by their age, sex, race, occupation, economic or educational status, although these may significantly influence the character and policies of the groups to which the individuals belong. What counts, rather, is their power, prestige, strategic position, their resources, their articulateness, the effectiveness of their organization and leadership. Within the group those who make the decisions and who exercise the dominant influence are subjected to pressures from all sides and radiate influence upon their group. The old saying: "I am your leader, therefore I must follow you," suggests the extent to which independent judgment is limited even among the leadership. The decisive part of public opinion, then, is the organization of views on issues that exercise an impact upon those who are in a position to make decisions.

The characteristic feature of public opinion in our society lies both in the fact that so many human beings are affiliated with a variety of organized groups, each of which represents only a segment of their interest, and that another large proportion of our fellow men are unattached to any stable group and in that sense constitute unorganized masses and thereby leave the decision-making to those who are organized and can exercise their corporate power.

In modern democracies, and to some extent in all inclusive societies on the scale of modern states, men exercise their influence and voice their aspirations through delegated powers operating through functionaries and leaders, through lobbies, party organizations, religious denominations, and a variety of other organized groups having a complex internal organization of their own. This seems to be the characteristic way of representative democratic government. In the course of the flow of communication the interests and grievances, the sentiments, attitudes, and opinions of the people at the bottom may become grossly distorted, and the people at the top may find themselves so remote from their constituents that they may either be ignorant of their actual feelings or may seriously misinterpret the fragmentary knowledge that they do have. It is at this point that public opinion studies may prove significant. We have already witnessed in the United States the rise of what might be called government by Western Union, which is instanced by the story of the lady who went to the telegraph office and said, "I should like to send a telegram to my Congressman to use his own judgment."

v

The various bases upon which consensus rests are, of course, not unrelated to the ways in which consensus is reached. Of these only some of the principal channels may be alluded to here: persuasion, discussion, debate, education, negotiation, parliamentary procedure, diplomacy, bargaining, adjudication, contractual relations, and compromise are all means for arriving at a sufficient degree of agreement to make the ongoing life of society, despite differences in interest, possible. Ultimately, consent in the face of differences comes down to a contrast between force and fraud on the one hand, and persuasion and rational agreement on the other hand. In some cases, however, the march of events may bring agreement where previously none was possible. If consent does not precede action there is still a chance to obtain consent in the course of action itself. The submission that comes with coercion, it should be noted, however, does not truly give us consensus. It results rather in what the Nazis called *Gleichschaltung*.

As over against the use of violence and fraud to obtain the pseudoconsensus, which even in authoritarian regimes is a precarious basis of power and social solidarity, democracies must resort to the art of compromise which results in agreements more or less rationally arrived at—agreements, the terms of which neither party wants, but at the same time cannot refuse to accept. Whereas authoritarianism gives us a seeming unanimity, which has been described as the unanimity of the graveyard, democracies rest upon the ultimate agreement to disagree, which is the tolerance of a divergent view. Even democracies, when they are in a hurry or when they are threatened by imminent danger, may sometimes have to resort to the shortcut of coercion, as is typical of the military interludes in democratic history, whereas autocracies may be able to afford at times to allow freedom in considerable areas of living which do not threaten the basis of autocratic power. In general, however, we may say that where consensus exists, coercion is unnecessary and where continuous coercion must be resorted to it is a sign that the regime is either in its initial stages or nearing its end. If might is not right, then might has at any rate to cloak itself in the mantle of rightness to persist, for no authoritarian government can ultimately determine the thinking of people, including what the people think of those who govern them.

The more intelligent and earnest people are the less likely it is that they will agree on all subjects. Coercion can achieve spurious agreement on all issues, but consent can be obtained only provisionally and perhaps only on those issues which do not threaten too deeply the interests, the ideas, and ideals of the heterodox. We seem to have worked out quite pragmatically in our democratic society the limits beyond which we are reluctant to push the struggle for agreement. We have agreed that uniformity is undesirable. We have, for instance, through the Bill of Rights, exempted religion from the sphere of necessary agreement, and we have enlarged the area of political freedom up to a "clear and present danger" line.

We have recognized moreover that it is not necessary to obtain agreement on everything in order to operate as an effectively functioning society. There is embodied in our sense of good taste a sensitiveness to our differences, some of which it is not correct to translate into issues for public debate and discussion. We are willing, frequently, to let our silence count as consent on a good many issues which we think are either too trivial or too delicate to push the point. And above all, we have developed patience to endure heresies and sufferance to endure transitory annoyance in the hope that minorities can, under freedom, develop themselves into majorities, and we have come to believe that for most purposes of life it is more economical, though perhaps less interesting, to count noses than to break heads.

But modern societies, whether they are autocratic or democratic, have learned that in the face of their size and complexity and their internal heterogeneity, the engineering of public consent is one of the great arts to be cultivated. Democracies, as distinguished from autocracies, seem to have taken the longer view by recognizing, as did Machiavelli, that the pseudoconsensus that is achieved by force cannot long endure and weather crisis, when he said: "It cannot be called talent to slay fellow citizens, to deceive friends, to be without faith, without mercy, without religion; such methods may gain empire but not glory." Democracies proceed on the assumption that even if the contending parties fight it out violently there is no assurance that the problem over which they fought won't remain after the stronger has suppressed the weaker. Even military conquest uses the technique of undermining the will to fight of the enemy, and nowadays, even after the enemy has surrendered, we send public opinion pollers among them to learn how best to govern them. The believers in the democratic principle have learned not to be impatient in the process of reaching agreement and that society can go on as long as we agree not to settle our disagreements by resort to force. They have had to learn that society can remain democratic only as long as we recognize and respect that essential residue, the freedom and dignity of every personality, which is no less important than it was before merely because it seems to have become a cliché. They have come to know also, as a contemporary philosopher has put it, that "lacking the consensus a legal crime may be a social virtue and religious heresy a moral duty."

Consensus in mass democracies, therefore, is not so much agreement on all issues, or even on the most essential substantive issues, among all the members of society, as it is the established habit of intercommunication, of discussion, debate, negotiation, and compromise, and the toleration of heresies, or even of indifference, up to the point of "clear and present danger" which threatens the life of the society itself. Rather than resting upon unanimity, it rests upon a sense of group identification and participation in the life of a society, upon the willingness to allow our representatives to speak for us even though they do not always faithfully represent our views, if indeed we have any views at all on many of the issues under discussion, and upon our disposition to fit ourselves into a program that our group has adopted and to acquiesce in group decisions unless the matter is fundamentally incompatible with our interests and integrity.

Consensus is supported and maintained not merely by the ties of interdependence and by a common cultural base, by a set of institutions embodying the settled traditions of the people and the norms and standards that they imply and impose, not merely by the living together and dealing with one another, but also, and not least important, by the continuing currents of mass communication, which in turn rest for their meaningfulness and effectiveness upon the pre-existence of some sort of a society, which hold that society together and mobilize it for a continuous concerted action.

VI

To the traditional ways of communication, rumor, gossip, and personal contact, to the pulpit, the school, and the forum, we have added in our generation the mass media of communication, consisting of the radio, the motion picture, and the press. These new media represent giant enterprises, dependent upon and designed to reach a mass audience. By virtue of the fact that they are dependent upon mass patronage, these media transcend both in their content and in their mode of presentation the peculiar interests and preoccupations of the special and segmental organized groups and direct their appeal to the mass. To reach their mass audiences they are constantly tempted to reduce their content, whether it be to the lowest common denominator, to what is believed will interest the greatest number, if not everybody. Since these mass media are so often tied to a mass market for their sustenance, they tend furthermore to be as near everything to everybody and hence nothing to anybody as it is possible to be.

Those who manage the mass communication enterprises have, of course, also some incentives to counteract this levelling influence of the mass audience by appeals to the tastes and interests of special groups. The third program of the British Broadcasting Corporation is an experiment in bringing high cultural values to a selected audience and in the effort to enlarge the demand for programs of high quality.

It is upon these mass media, however, that to an ever increasing degree the human race depends to hold it together. Mass communication is rapidly becoming, if it is not already, the main framework of the web of social life. In retrospect we can see how shrewd Hitler and his cohorts were in recognizing that in these instrumentalities they controlled the principal means for moving great masses of men into at least temporary adherence to their objectives and in using them for their own purpose. That they almost succeeded and that the rest of the world had to pay a terrible price in blood and treasure at the last moment to avert their domination over the world might serve as a warning to those who minimize the importance of mass communication and to remind them that we live in an era when the control over these media constitutes perhaps the most important source of power in the social universe. It is interesting to note that modern dictators who espouse the doctrine of the elite and who profess to hold the masses in great contempt, have shown themselves frequently to be more sensitive to the whims of the mass which they profess to despise than have some leaders of democratic societies. They have recognized also that the mass media can be used to manipulate and exploit existing situations and opportunities.

Recent investigations by polling and interview techniques have revealed that despite the dense blanketing of our country with informal educational and propaganda appeals, despite the enormous ramification of organized groups which discuss and disseminate knowledge on issues of current importance, there are vast areas of ignorance on some of the most important issues confronting our society.

The National Opinion Research Center found that less than

half of the people had any reasonably clear meaning of what a tariff was. Other investigations have shown that on even the most central public issues of our time only a small fraction of our people have sufficient understanding to act intelligently. This suggests that the state of public opinion as an aspect of consensus in a society such as ours calls for an unrelenting effort for popular education and for access to reliable sources of information. This does not mean that everybody must be equally well informed on such questions as the tariff, but it does suggest the need for general education to enable the citizen to participate more intelligently and critically in general public discussion as well as to equip him to act with greater knowledge and responsibility in the special interest groups with which he is identified.

If we consider in addition to the vast areas of ignorance, the astonishing degree of apathy and indifference that prevails concerning even the issues of transcendent importance, it becomes clear why mass democracies so often appear incapable of competing effectually with authoritarian societies. Here, again, the price we must pay for the survival of a way of life that we cherish calls for the expenditure of an immensely greater share of our resources than thus far we have been willing to devote to information and education. This calls not merely for continual effort to dispel areas of ignorance, but also areas of indifference which may in part be based upon ignorance. The content of what is to be communicated must therefore be adapted to the audience to which it is addressed, and there must be awareness that we may be speaking over the heads of people or that the symbols that we use may mean entirely different things to others than they do to ourselves. The predominance of the entertainment feature particularly in such media as radio and motion picture does not preclude the appeal to intelligence. It suggests rather that information and education services to be effective must also be interesting.

Communication, as it is carried on largely through verbal intercourse, can be fortified by a body of common experiences shared by the many, and can be dramatized through art and literature and other means for vivifying ideas and ideals, in order to achieve a sounder basis of common understanding. In the world of science we come about as near to a world society as in any phase of human life, and this world-wide scope of communication which science exemplifies might well serve as a model to be approximated in other realms of human experience, for science, including perhaps even social science and philosophic scholarship, has proved its power to surmount local, national, sectarian, and class barriers, and even to infiltrate through the obstacles of official censorship. The same appears to be true of music and art.

There has been much discussion recently, more with reference to the radio and motion picture than the older medium of the press, concerning the concentration of control over these mass media of communication. The fact that the media of communication tend toward monopolistic control, as is evidenced by the building up of industrial empires in this field of enterprise, has serious implications for mass democracy. The concentration of such power in a few hands—whether through press associations, newspaper columns syndicates, radio networks, or motion picture combines may create great imbalance in the presentation of divergent, especially minority views. It may result in the danger of censorship no less real for being unofficial, and may threaten the free and universal access to the factual knowledge and balanced interpretation which under-lie intelligent decision.

In a society dominated by centers of unquestioned power and authority, reinforced by sacred traditions and rituals and capable of eliciting unquestioning loyalty to its norms and purposes, such mass communication devices would not constitute a serious prob-lem. They would reinforce, but would not greatly alter the social structure. But in a society where all men irrespective of race, creed, origin, and status claim and are to be granted an increasing share of participation in the common life and in the making of common decisions, the control of these media of mass communication consti-tutes a central problem. If it is consensus that makes an aggregate of men into a society, and if consensus is increasingly at the mercy of the functioning of the mass communication agencies as it is in a democratic world, then the control over these instrumentalities becomes one of the principal sources of political, economic, and social power. The harnessing of this power is an infinitely more complex and vital problem than any previous challenge that the human race has had to meet.

In mass communication we have unlocked a new social force of as yet incalculable magnitude. In comparison with all previous social means for building or destroying the world this new force looms as a gigantic instrument of infinite possibilities for good or evil. It has the power to build loyalties and to undermine them, and thus by furthering or hindering consensus to affect all other sources of power. By giving people access to alternative views mass communication does of course open the door to the disintegration of all existing social solidarities, while it creates new ones. It is of the first importance, therefore, that we understand its nature, its possibilities, and its limits and the means of harnessing it to human purposes.

VII

Before closing, I should like to allude to the problems of consensus as they arise in some of the more crucial spheres of human interaction in contemporary society. The first of these is the sphere of racial and cultural relations, the second is the field of industrial relations, and the third is the area of international relations. I do not mean to suggest that these are the only areas where we face the problems of consensus. I use them merely for illustrative purposes, recognizing that the same problems are also found in family relations, in informal associations, in local community life, and in the operations of government. These three, however, seem to reflect the most characteristic features of mass communication as it impinges upon consensus in modern mass democracies such as our own.

The spread of industrialism and of capitalism with its world markets and its free workers has given rise among other institutions to giant corporations and giant unions, involving great concentrations of power. The competition and conflicting interests within and between these organizations affects every aspect of social life and determines the level of living and the utilization of the resources of all society. Management and unions, aware of the crucial influence of public opinion upon their relative positions, have not been slow to utilize the instruments of mass communication, both internally and in relation to one another, and in the effort to mold the attitudes and to affect the decisions of society. Insofar as these decisions involve national policies, the effort of each side has been directed to rallying support for itself by molding the attitudes and opinions of the larger public.

The relationship between conflicting groups, such as these, illustrates the significance of consensus within the group for the capacity of each to deal with its opponent. From the standpoint of the larger society the need for a more inclusive consensus involving both of these constellations is indispensable for the maintenance of industrial peace. Propaganda appeals directed toward the larger public, the pressure of government and organized bodies in society, such as the churches and the political parties, are among the indispensable elements in the strategy of collective bargaining, arbitration, labor legislation, and the conduct of strikes. The means of mass communication play no less significant a role in the maintenance of mass production and mass markets.

The rise of self-conscious racial and cultural minorities which has proceeded parallel to the spread of the ideal of equality and the institutions of mass democracy through ever larger areas of the world, has accentuated the problems of racial and cultural relations. The contrast between contemporary society and primitive and earlier historical societies with respect to the contact between diverse racial and cultural groups is startling. Whereas everyone in a primitive, ancient, and medieval society had a more or less fixed place in the social structure, depending to a large extent upon the character and position of his ancestor, today all of us are men on the move and on the make, and all of us by transcending the cultural bounds of our narrower society become to some extent marginal men. More and more the relations of life that were formerly settled by sacred tradition and custom become subjects of discussion, debate, negotiation, and overt conflict. Many of the problems affecting our national solidarity through our loyalties, rest for their orderly adjustment upon the achievement of consensus across the lines of the diverse races and cultures of which America is comprised. The great obstacles encountered by those who attempted to achieve in the face of prejudice and discrimination a national solidarity sufficient to see our nation through the recent war, should recall to all of us the reality of the existence of minorities in our midst. If the experiment of America shows anything, it shows that, despite the many setbacks which the democratic ideal and practice have suffered, we are determined to achieve consensus and have found the road toward it without too much coercion through the idea of cultural pluralism, which is another expression for the toleration of differences.

Nowhere do the problems of racial and cultural relations present themselves more dramatically than they do in our great cities, where the people of varying stocks and cultures live in dense physical concentration. Whereas, in an earlier society it was unusual to meet a stranger, under the conditions of life in great cities, it is an equal rarity to meet someone who is familiar. Although our face may still light up when, in the crowds of the great cities, we see a friend, we have nevertheless learned to live with people of diverse background and character to a degree sufficient at least to achieve the requirements of a fairly orderly, productive, and peaceful society.

What is true of self-conscious minorities impelled by the ideal of the equality of man in our own communities and in our own nation, is increasingly true of the world at large. The so-called backward peoples are increasingly being brought within the orbit of a world society resting upon a world consensus. In this the numerous organized groups and movements, among dominant and minority groups alike, using the instruments of mass communication to bring their ideals before a world public, are increasingly evident.

And finally the question must have occurred to people who are not versed in the language of sociologists and in the serious subjects with which they are preoccupied, why it is that sociologists who claim as their vocation the study of social interaction have paid so little attention to interaction on the grandest scale of all, namely, the interaction between national states and what we call international relations, for in this sphere is exemplified the operation of consensus upon which the future of mankind depends.

We have been making some progress in the building of world consensus. We do have a fairly general recognition of economic interdependence on a world scale. We have a great deal more of traffic across the bounds of nations and of continents than the world has ever seen before. We have even some incipient international institutions whose strength is being tested by the increasing tensions brought about by the very fact that we live in an emerging single world in which we have contacts and conflicts of interest and of ideas with people of whom we were formerly oblivious. We even can see some semblance of emerging world loyalties which makes the expression "world citizenship" sound less utopian than it did before. The instruments of mass communication, particularly the radio, and, it seems soon, television, combining the faithful transmission of the voice with that of the visual image of the human face and gesture, are particularly well suited to supply the means for the furtherance of understanding across the borders of sovereign states.

As long as we do not have a monopoly of power to coerce all of the other nations and people of the earth into our way of life, the only road we can travel is that of continued negotiation, persuasion, and compromise. We should probably, even if we had the power of coercion, not be able to use it on others without destroying the very values which might tempt us to use it.

If our ways of thought and conception of freedom and democracy, our system of economy, and our political and social ideals seem to be, as I am sure they seem to many, irreconcilable with those of the only other remaining power constellation in the world, it is well to recall that there was a time when Catholics and Protestants felt very passionately that they could not live in peace in the same state. Time has fortunately proved them wrong. There have been other conflicts in the history of man which seemed at the time equally irresolvable. The uncomfortable but at the same time reassuring fact, however, is that today in this shrunken world there are more effective ways of interfering with the internal life of any society by those without through the instrumentalities of mass communication, which are no respecters of boundaries and which find ways of surmounting all barriers. What is more, these products of mass communication have a way of reaching the great inert masses of the world, for making them restless and mobilizing them for action, or at least for making the dominant groups in their respective societies more responsive to their pressure.

Mass communication will not, of course, by itself produce the minimum of world consensus requisite for world peace and world society. But it does not operate by itself. It operates through and in conjunction with existing and emerging institutions in a climate of opinion and ultimately through and upon human beings. There are other things in the world besides mass communication, but these other things, some of which I have indicated, are tied increasingly to mass communication and through this tie give it its strategic significance.

The media of mass communication, like all the technological instruments that man has invented, are themselves neutral. They can be used to instil a fighting faith or the will to reconciliation. At any rate, the relationship between nations and people that will allow the fullest use of the world's resources to meet human needs under freedom and order and in peace, calls today for nothing less than the building of a world consensus, for a social psychological integration of the human race commensurate with the interdependent far-flung and rich material resources and human energies of the world.

In mobilizing the instrumentalities of mass communication for the building of that consensus, we cannot fail to remind ourselves that along with the perfection of these means of human intercourse science has also perfected unprecedented means of mass destruction. But in the case of neither the instruments of mass communication nor of atomic energy do the inventors of the instrument dictate the uses to which they shall be put. As a contemporary historian has recently put it: "If our characteristic Western gift [by which he refers to technology] proves to have been a blessing for mankind, it will be a great blessing; and, if a curse, a great curse. If things go well, the epitaph of history on the Franks [by which he means us] may run: 'Here lie the technicians, who united mankind'; and if things go badly: 'Here lie the technicians, who exterminated the human race.'" Except that in the later case, Professor Toynbee, the author of these remarks, fails to point out that there may not be anybody left to carve that epitaph.

RESPONSIBILITY FOR MASS COMMUNICATIONS

WHO IS RESPONSIBLE for the quality of mass communications? If members of a society are not satisfied with the services they get from their mass media, what can they do about it? And what should people realistically expect from the mass media which, by definition, must serve such large and heterogeneous masses of people?

Questions like these have been asked more and more often as the media have grown larger and as they have begun to fill such large proportions of our leisure time. Television, for example, fills about one-sixth of all the waking hours of a school child. The television set in an average home in the United States is turned on over five hours a day. It is not surprising, then, that people should be concerned about what kind of material the media are bringing them. Is there too much violence to be good for children? Is there enough national and foreign news to make possible a well-informed electorate? Is it right to use most of radio time for cheap popular music? Is it right to permit so much commercial influence over programs? Is there too much sexy material on the newsstands? Questions of this kind are a deep concern of many people.

In primitive days, such questions could be handled directly. If tribe members didn't like the bard, they could fire the old one and get a new one. One can't fire television or motion pictures. One can't, in most cities, even find an opposition newspaper. And when dissatisfaction is expressed, an individual voice sounds very small indeed amidst the welter of sound in modern society. For this reason, the question of *who* is responsible, *who* can make a change if a change needs making, has become more and more important.

There are three groups in our society powerful enough to make a change, if they want to. These are the government, the media themselves, and the public. Our belief is that responsibility is shared among them.

Yet we are very loath to let the government have much to do with mass communication content. If the government is permitted to control programs, it seems to us that the government can control news. In our system, we ask the media to check on government for us, and report back when public officials, agencies, or parties are doing something the public ought to question. But if the government controls the news, the media can hardly report freely about the government. Therefore, we think of the government as only a last resort, to be called in if the other groups are unable to get satisfactory service out of their media.

We have always hoped that the media would police themselves, and there have been many public-spirited men among mass communicators who have done just that. The media have made progress toward professional training and professionalizing their standards, toward adopting codes of conduct (which are of less use than they might seem), and, in a few cases, toward self-criticism.

But it is generally agreed that the media cannot do the job alone. They are in business to make a profit and to serve their advertisers as well as serving the public; and the demands of business sometimes conflict with the demands of public service. Therefore, the public has to make itself heard. This may mean that the public will have to organize to make itself heard. But the important thing is to have an alert and articulate public. If the public knows what it wants from the media, and wants it badly enough, it can probably get it. If it doesn't make itself heard, it doesn't deserve any better than it gets.

So the general approach to communication responsibility in our society is that the government is responsible for keeping its hands off media content, except in matters of libel, misleading advertising, and so forth; that the media are responsible for keeping their own house clean and maintaining high professional standards of public service; and that the public itself is responsible for making its needs and wishes, its satisfactions and dissatisfactions known.

The following pages present, first, two scholarly critics of the mass media. Mr. Seldes challenges us to take charge of the mass media that are changing our own lives. Mr. Adorno examines some of the qualities that differentiate adult and responsible programs from infantile and irresponsible ones. Then follow the recommendations of the Commission on Freedom of the Press, a body of distinguished citizens who devoted two years in the late 40's to studying the mass media. The next selection is an editor's view on whether we need endowed or government-owned newspapers, or whether the media can police themselves. Then come three examples of the media's attempts to police themselves—the codes of the newspaper, motion picture, and television industries. The final selection is the concluding chapter of a much-discussed book on communication ethics.

THE PUBLIC ARTS:
OUR RIGHTS AND DUTIES

BY GILBERT SELDES

Mr. Seldes, a long-time critic and writer on radio, television, and films, now director of the Annenberg School of Communications at the University of Pennsylvania, here states what he considers to be the rights and duties of the public in relation to television. This is the concluding chapter of his book, *The Public Arts*, published by Simon and Schuster in 1956. It is reprinted here by permission of the author, who holds the copyright, and the publisher.

"THIS COUNTRY, with its institutions, belongs to the people who inhabit it," said Abraham Lincoln, and as he was then facing the possible dissolution of the United States, he added, "Whenever they [the people] shall grow weary of the existing government, they can exercise their Constitutional right of amending it or their revolutionary right to dismember or overthrow it."

I am suggesting that the cultural institutions of a country also belong to its inhabitants, and, not having the courage of Lincoln's radicalism, I do not insist upon the revolutionary right of the people to destroy whatever wearies them. Moderately I propose the idea that the people have valid rights over those cultural institutions which can be properly called "the public arts." In the previous chapter I have indicated that the quality of being "public" inheres in various degrees in all the arts, that oratory and drama in ancient Greece were more public than the art of history, just as in folk arts

587

ballads were more public than pottery, and, although the lively arts are most affected with the special public quality, the movies are more public than dancing. I now propose to bring together from various sections of this book the identifying characteristics of these public arts, knowing that to some degree the identification is shadowy, that by definition no communicative art can be totally private. I am, on the other hand, convinced that in some instances the degree of difference is so great that you can no longer compare the effect of the public and the non-public art, as if quantity—the mass of material offered or the mass of people accepting it—had resulted in a change in essence, a quality change. Also, in one single respect the public arts differ absolutely from all others. The major marks of identification are these:

The public arts are popular to the extent of being almost universally acceptable.

They tend to be more and more professionalized, less and less to be practiced privately.

They are often produced by teams rather than by individuals. They are commissioned, the patron-sponsor-executive providing the pattern.

They are by intention ephemeral, paying well initially, but not increasing in value with the passage of time.

These are I think entirely self-evident.

The public arts are offered to the public as a whole, not to any segment of it. This is, I believe, a new thing in the world, because these arts solicit the favor of the entire public (excepting the highly intellectualized fringe that turns its back on whatever is popular). This was not the case when a mural, commissioned by a ruling family, was exposed in a Renaissance church or when Shakespeare's plays were presented in the presence of "the groundlings."

Physically, the public arts have mass or velocity or both, and they tend to outstrip or displace all the other arts.

They touch large numbers of people simultaneously, and their effect is not limited to those whom they directly touch.

They interconnect and support one another, thus causing a sort of reverberation.

They are, to an extent, habit-forming, and their effect is contagious. The social reverberation produced when millions of people follow the same entertainment or receive the same communication at one time is something different from the imitation of a royal mistress's hairdo—the diffusion is immeasurably greater, the penetration deeper. The physical reduplication of comic books and phonograph records, the velocity of radio and television, the availability of the motion-picture film, and the way the various entertainments support one another create another kind of contagion: the public mind is crammed with details about them, so that the true significance of "the mass media" becomes, not their appeal to the mass audience, but their own dimensions, the size and weight and speed and force that the mass media possess. Among these physical properties is the simple one of occupying a certain space and thus preventing any other body from occupying that space. As the public arts occupy more and more of the public mind over longer and longer periods, they are an obstacle to the extension of the other arts.

The public arts popularize the classic arts. These classic arts they diffuse without substantial alteration, as in the broadcast of a symphony, or they adapt with respect for the original (Shakespeare, for instance), or they degrade. Whether this degradation is inevitable is a prime question. Are the public arts an illustration of "nature's tendency to degrade the organized and to destroy the meaningful"? I am not sure. In *The Human Use of Human Beings*, Dr. Norbert Wiener notes that in control and communication we always fight this entropic tendency, and he adds: "While the universe as a whole . . . tends to run down, there are local enclaves . . . in which there is a limited and temporary tendency for organization to increase. Life finds its home in some of these enclaves." I am not sure whether the parallel I observe is more than verbal. It appears to me that the degradation of the highly organized corresponds to the observed tendency of the popular arts to go steadily to lower levels of general intelligence and emotional maturity; and the enclaves would correspond to those experiments which oppose the tendency toward routine and try to bring individuality back to the mass media.

The public arts create, refuse to create, or destroy their own audiences.

They are, in varying degrees, governed by public law.

The unique element: broadcasting uses a portion of the public domain. These social factors are obviously connected with the physical items previously noted. Granted that there are no *wholly* private arts, we still perceive a difference between a poem printed on a page of a mass-circulation magazine and a song presented a dozen times a day by singers of intense popularity. There is a difference in effect between "D'ye Ken John Peel" and the singing commercial for Pepsi-Cola, which uses the same tune and whose diffusion is now so great that the original song has virtually ceased to exist. We will not understand *I Love Lucy* in the terms of Walter Pater on the Mona Lisa, nor Disney's Davy Crockett if we think he is "merely" a contemporary version of Leatherstocking.

The physical properties of the public arts give to their managers certain social powers, but the managers do not generally accept responsibility for the creation of audiences; they say they satisfy public demand. To abridge a long argument, let us say they cannot pretend, as they do, that they create audiences for Shakespeare and symphonic music but do not create an audience for crime serials. Public demand is diffused and generalized: for diversion, for escape, for excitement, for something like an emotional spree; it is not specific. The makers of entertainment satisfy demand in the ways they find most profitable—just as the processors of food satisfy a demand. It is not the only way, and it may not even be the best way. In turn, the demand must be stimulated and made specific: the public must be made to *want* split-pea soup and panel shows if the makers of these commodities are to prosper. It is, moreover, demonstrable that the producers suppress those demands which they cannot advantageously fulfill—as when programs, even popular ones, are dropped or shifted or supplied to one part of the country and not to another, to correspond to the marketing requirements of the sponsor. This power to create audiences and to manipulate demand is the least understood element in the structure of the entertainment business.

That the public arts are subject to law is well understood, but it is hard to discover a fixed principle in the shifts of opinion about censorship in the movies, pre-publication licensing of comic books, and programs for children in television. The position taken by Walter Lippmann reflects a willingness (which I suspect is common) to compromise the principle of absolute freedom of expression if necessary—but the necessity does not have to be demonstrated by any clear and present danger. The unproved but suspected link between horror books and delinquency is always available for headlines, and a quick hysterical reaction can get laws on the books which it may take years to revoke.

The last characteristic of the public arts—that they use part of the public domain—applies to the broadcasting arts only and is without complexities. The federal government lends part of the air to a corporation—obviously it can impose conditions. If the conditions are too harsh, the broadcasters will return their franchises, as they have done recently—the requirement that they transmit programs on the UHF channels in order to hold their rights, even though receivers for these frequencies do not exist in their area, is too harsh. On the other hand, if the conditions are too easy (as in the case of broadcasting, taken as a whole), the public may be short-changed until competitors (e.g., backers of pay-TV) offer better service when a station applies for a renewal of license. The only hidden factor in this special case is that the public seems totally unaware of its legal rights—and the broadcasters are not in any hurry to enlighten them.

But the concept of the public arts to which, I am confident, we must eventually come is not drawn from this single characteristic of the entertainment-and-communications enterprises. The base of this new concept is that, by their own nature, these arts are matters of public concern, subject to public opinion; that even *outside of law* the public has sovereign rights over them, since these arts, no less than the institutions of government, belong to the people.

They belong to the people and consequently the people have certain rights and duties in respect to them. I have not put this down as one of the prime characteristics of the public arts because it seems to me highly subjective—and a matter of morality. Here the bearing of the Innis approach becomes most significant. Because the moment we see that a transformation in the way we live is taking place, the right and the duty to direct that change become self-evident. This is not only an appeal to the self-interest of the intelligent, the mature, and the educated—like the appeal the Federalists made to "the rich and wellborn" to support a strong federal government when the structure of our country was shaped. There is a self-interest, obviously. But in the end I must fall back on the simple moral ground that no good citizen, no good man or woman, has the right to abandon ship while there remains a reasonable hope of steering it into safe harbor if all hands do their work. If we knew that our whole system of free education was being undermined, or the right of every citizen to vote, would any citizen have the moral right to indifference? Would any citizen have the right to remain silent if he knew that a vast power was—inadvertently or not—attempting to destroy that system?

I do not assert that either of these things is happening. I note that either or both may happen without our knowing it, that people using power, often enough unaware of the consequences of their actions, may preserve the *forms* of our educational or political system and nullify its *effects*.

I suggest that, as the fundamental values of our lives and those of our children will be affected by the revolutionary change in entertainment and communications which I have described, we have an obligation to control the speed and direction of this change. Our *right* has been a thousand times established in law and custom. What we lack is the will.

In my own mind, the defect of all attempts so far to influence the mass media has been an almost snobbish dislike for them and an exaggerated fear. We have to recognize a possible danger. We have no right to panic in front of an imaginary one. The next step, after a realistic appraisal of the incalculable social values of the public arts and of the ills—avoidable or not—they bring, is to gather together all those whose livelihood, whose freedom, whose peace of mind are threatened if substantially *all* communications are used for a single purpose. Fortunately, some extremely skillful users of mass communications are in this number: the publishers of the Luce and Cowles magazines have a stake in intelligence only slightly less than that of the publishers of *Harper's* and the *Atlantic;* within the broadcasting business are groups and individuals who are more secure if the level of intelligence in the audience rises slowly and steadily. The makers of nonfiction movies require a high degree of intelligent attention in their audiences, but Walt Disney also needs something above the lowest common denominator. Beyond these groups are the educators, the publishers of fiction and nonfiction and textbooks, the producers of plays and the managers of concert tours, the museums and art galleries and the manufacturers of reproductions of works of art. Also, the scientists and the great corporations who need scientifically trained personnel, our diplomatic service, and, finally, our statesmen. In simplest terms, all these need citizens of good habits of mind and emotional maturity, and already the lack of these—of teachers and of scientists in particular—is proof that you cannot devote the great part of our communications systems to trivialities and be secure in a world as complex and divided as our own.

I do not know what form the pooling of interests will take. The natural turn is toward the rich foundations for research, or organization, and for publicity. They are, in many cases, already under suspicion as being too intellectual and not patriotic enough, but they can still fight for intelligence and for the kind of patriotism that protects the fundamentals of our national life. One aspect of our common genius is our capacity to organize for action when the necessity becomes clear. It is clear now because the moment we see that the public arts are bringing about social change, the right and the duty to direct this change is in our hands. Between those who are not aware of the effect these changes can have on their inalienable rights and those who do not know that they have the right to control the changes, the managers of the public arts have had almost unlimited freedom. They are not entitled to it.

I have suggested that awareness can start with the people themselves, in small units, combining into greater. Parallel to this, I now suggest that the managers of all our cultural institutions enter into an open conspiracy to *use* the public arts in order to protect our heritage of national culture. They can command the attention of the public and can bring the discussion of our basic problems to those very channels which now are used to dissipate our intellectual energies. As long as the means of communication are not available for criticism of themselves, as long as we are prevented from thinking about the process by which we are hypnotized into not thinking, we remain at the mercy of our simplest appetites, our immediate and almost childish sensations, and these can be exploited—for the arts most useful to the public are essentially those which can be most effectively turned against the public good.

To know this, to know that we have the right to put them into our service, is the beginning of an intelligent approach to the problems and to the opportunities of the public arts.

TELEVISION AND THE PATTERNS
OF MASS CULTURE

BY T. W. ADORNO

Dr. Adorno, who was formerly on the faculty of the University of California where he was one of the authors of *The Authoritarian Personality*, is now a professor of sociology at the University of Frankfort, Germany. This article was published in the *Quarterly of Film, Radio and Television*, volume 8, 1954, and is reprinted by permission of the author and the copyright holder, The University of California Press.

THE EFFECT OF TELEVISION cannot be adequately expressed in terms of success or failure, likes or dislikes, approval or disapproval. Rather, an attempt should be made, with the aid of depth-psychological categories and previous knowledge of mass media, to crystallize a number of theoretical concepts by which the potential effect of television—its impact upon various layers of the spectator's personality—could be studied. It seems timely to investigate systematically socio-psychological stimuli typical of televised material both on a descriptive and psychodynamic level, to analyze their presuppositions as well as their total pattern, and to evaluate the effect they are likely to produce. This procedure may ultimately bring forth a number of recommendations on how to deal with these stimuli to produce the most desirable effect of television. By exposing the socio-psychological implications and mechanisms of television, which often operate under the guise of fake realism, not only may the shows be improved, but, more important possibly, the public at large may be sensitized to the nefarious effect of some of these mechanisms.

We are not concerned with the effectiveness of any particular show or program; but we are concerned with the nature of present-day television and its imagery. Yet, our approach is practical. The findings should be so close to the material, should rest on such a solid foundation of experience, that they can be translated into precise recommendations and be made convincingly clear to large audiences.

Improvement of television is not conceived primarily on an artistic, purely aesthetic level, extraneous to present customs. This does not mean that we naïvely take for granted the dichotomy between autonomous art and mass media. We all know that their relationship is highly complex. Today's rigid division between what is called "long-haired" and "short-haired" art is the product of a long historical development. It would be romanticizing to assume that formerly art was entirely pure, that the creative artist thought only in terms of the inner consistency of the artifact and not also of its effect upon the spectators. Theatrical art, in particular, cannot be separated from audience reaction. Conversely, vestiges of the aesthetic claim to be something autonomous, a world unto itself, remain even within the most trivial product of mass culture. In fact, the present rigid division of art into autonomous and commercial aspects is itself largely a function of commercialization. It was hardly accidental that the slogan *l'art pour l'art* was coined polemically in the Paris of the first half of the nineteenth century, when literature really became large-scale business for the first time. Many of the cultural products bearing the anticommercial trademark "art for art's sake" show traces of commercialism in their appeal to the sensational or in the conspicuous display of material wealth and sensuous stimuli at the expense of the meaningfulness of the work. This trend was pronounced in the neo-Romantic theater of the first decades of our century.

OLDER AND RECENT POPULAR CULTURE

In order to do justice to all such complexities, much closer scrutiny of the background and development of modern mass media is required than communications research, generally limited to present conditions, is aware of. One would have to establish what the output of contemporary cultural industry has in common with older "low" or popular forms of art as well as with autonomous art, and where the differences lie. Suffice it here to state that the archetypes of present popular culture were set comparatively early in the development of middle-class society—at about the turn of the seventeenth and the beginning of the eighteenth centuries in England. According to the studies of the English sociologist Ian Watt, the English novels of that period, particularly the works of Defoe and Richardson, marked the beginning of an approach to literary production that consciously created, served, and finally controlled a "market." Today the commercial production of cultural goods has become streamlined, and the impact of popular culture upon the individual has concomitantly increased. This process has not been confined to quantity, but has resulted in new qualities. While recent popular culture has absorbed all the elements and particularly all the "don'ts" of its predecessor, it differs decisively inasmuch as it has developed into a system. Thus, popular culture is no longer confined to certain forms such as novels or dance music, but has seized all media of artistic expression. The structure and meaning of these forms show an amazing parallelism, even when they appear to have little in common on the surface (such as jazz and the detective novel). Their output has increased to such an extent that it is almost impossible for anyone to dodge them; and even those formerly aloof from popular culture—the rural population on one hand and the highly educated on the other—are somehow affected. The more the system of "merchandising" culture is expanded, the more it tends also to assimilate the "serious" art of the past by adapting this art to the system's own requirements. The control is so extensive that any infraction of its rules is *a priori* stigmatized as "highbrow" and has but little chance to reach the population at large. The system's concerted effort results in what might be called the prevailing ideology of our time.

Certainly, there are many typical changes within today's pattern; e.g., men were formerly presented as erotically aggressive and women on the defensive, whereas this has been largely reversed in modern mass culture, as pointed out particularly by Wolfenstein and Leites. More important, however, is that the pattern itself, dimly perceptible in the early novels and basically preserved today, has by now become congealed and standardized. Above all, this rigid institutionalization transforms modern mass culture into a medium of undreamed of psychological control. The repetitiveness, the selfsameness, and the ubiquity of modern mass culture tend to make for automatized reactions and to weaken the forces of individual resistance.

When the journalist Defoe and the printer Richardson calculated the effect of their wares upon the audience, they had to speculate, to follow hunches; and therewith, a certain latitude to develop deviations remained. Such deviations have nowadays been reduced to a kind of multiple choice between very few alternatives. The following may serve as an illustration. The popular or semipopular novels of the first half of the nineteenth century, published in large quantities and serving mass consumption, were supposed to arouse tension in the reader. Although the victory of the good over the bad was generally provided for, the meandering and endless plots and subplots hardly allowed the readers of Sue and Dumas to be continuously aware of the moral. Readers could expect anything to happen. This no longer holds true. Every spectator of a television mystery knows with absolute certainty how it is going to end. Tension is but superficially maintained and is unlikely to have a serious effect any more. On the contrary, the spectator feels on safe ground all the time. This longing for "feeling on safe ground"—reflecting an infantile need for protection, rather than his desire for a thrill— is catered to. The element of excitement is preserved only with tongue in cheek. Such changes fall in line with the potential change from a freely competitive to a virtually "closed" society into which one wants to be admitted or from which one fears to be rejected. Everything somehow appears "predestined."

The increasing strength of modern mass culture is further enhanced by changes in the sociological structure of the audience. The old cultured elite does not exist any more; the modern intelligentsia only partially corresponds to it. At the same time, huge strata of the population formerly unacquainted with art have become cultural "consumers." Modern audiences, although probably less capable of the artistic sublimation bred by tradition, have become shrewder in their demands for perfection of technique and for reliability of information, as well as in their desire for "services"; and they have become more convinced of the consumers' potential power over the producer, no matter whether this power is actually wielded.

How changes within the audience have affected the meaning of popular culture may also be illustrated. The element of internalization played a decisive role in early Puritan popular novels of the Richardson type. This element no longer prevails, for it was based on the essential role of "inwardness" in both original Protestantism and earlier middle-class society. As the profound influence of the basic tenets of Protestantism has gradually receded, the cultural pattern has become more and more opposed to the "introvert." As Riesman puts it,

> . . . the conformity of earlier generations of Americans of the type I term "inner-directed" was mainly assured by their internalization of adult authority. The middle-class urban American of today, the "other-directed," is, by contrast, in a characterological sense more the product of his peers —that is, in sociological terms, his "peer-groups," the other kids at school or in the block.[1]

This is reflected by popular culture. The accents on inwardness, inner conflicts, and psychological ambivalence (which play so large a role in earlier popular novels and on which their originality rests) have given way to unproblematic, cliché-like characterization. Yet the code of decency that governed the inner conflicts of the Pamelas, Clarissas, and Lovelaces remains almost literally intact.[2] The middle-class "ontology" is preserved in an almost fossilized way, but is severed from the mentality of the middle classes. By being superimposed on people with whose living conditions and mental make-up it is no longer in accord, this middle-class "ontology" assumes an increasingly authoritarian and at the same time hollow character.

The overt "naïveté" of older popular culture is avoided. Mass culture, if not sophisticated, must at least be up to date—that is to

---

[1] David Riesman, *The Lonely Crowd* (New Haven: Yale University Press, 1950), p. v.

[2] The evolution of the ideology of the extrovert has probably also its long history, particularly in the lower types of popular literature during the nineteenth century when the code of decency became divorced from its religious roots and therewith attained more and more the character of an opaque taboo. It seems likely, however, that in this respect the triumph of the films marked the decisive step. Reading as an act of perception and apperception probably carries with itself a certain kind of internalization; the act of reading a novel fairly close to a *monologue interieur*. Visualization in modern mass media makes for externalization. The idea of inwardness, still maintained in older portrait painting through the expressiveness of the face, gives way to unmistakable optical signals that can be grasped at a glance. Even if a character in a movie or television show is not what he appears to be, his appearance is treated in such a way as to leave no doubt about his true nature. Thus a villain who is not presented as a brute must at least be "suave," and his repulsive slickness and mild manner unambiguously indicate what we are to think of him.

say, "realistic," or posing as realistic—in order to meet the expectations of a supposedly disillusioned, alert, and hard-boiled audience. Middle-class requirements bound up with internalization—such as concentration, intellectual effort, and erudition—have to be continuously lowered. This does not hold only for the United States, where historical memories are scarcer than in Europe; but it is universal, applying to England and Continental Europe as well.[3]

However, this apparent progress of enlightenment is more than counter-balanced by retrogressive traits. The earlier popular culture maintained a certain equilibrium between its social ideology and the actual social conditions under which its consumers lived. This probably helped to keep the border line between popular and serious art during the eighteenth century more fluid than it is today. Abbé Prévost was one of the founding fathers of French popular literature; but his *Manon Lescaut* is completely free from clichés, artistic vulgarisms, and calculated effects. Similarly, later in the eighteenth century, Mozart's *Zauberfloete* struck a balance between the "high" and the popular style which is almost unthinkable today.

The curse of modern mass culture seems to be its adherence to the almost unchanged ideology of early middle-class society, whereas the lives of its consumers are completely out of phase with this ideology. This is probably the reason for the gap between the overt and the hidden "message" of modern popular art. Although on an overt level the traditional values of English Puritan middle-class society are promulgated, the hidden message aims at a frame of mind which is no longer bound by these values. Rather, today's frame of mind transforms the traditional values into the norms of an increasingly hierarchical and authoritarian social structure. Even here it has to be admitted that authoritarian elements were also present in the older ideology which, of course, never fully expressed the truth. But the "message" of adjustment and unreflecting obedience seems to be dominant and all-pervasive today. Whether maintained values derived from religious ideas obtain a different meaning when severed from their root should be carefully examined. For example, the concept of the "purity" of women is one of the invariables of popular culture. In the earlier phase this concept is

---

[3] It should be noted that the tendency against "erudition" was already present at the very beginning of popular culture, particularly in Defoe, who was consciously opposed to the learned literature of his day, and has become famous for having scorned every refinement of style and artistic construction in favor of an apparent faithfulness to "life."

treated in terms of an inner conflict between concupiscence and the internalized Christian ideal of chastity, whereas in today's popular culture it is dogmatically posited as a value *per se*. Again, even the rudiments of this pattern are visible in productions such as *Pamela*. There, however, it seems a by-product; whereas in today's popular culture the idea that only the "nice girl" gets married and that she must get married at any price has come to be accepted before Richardson's conflicts even start.[4]

The more inarticulate and diffuse the audience of modern mass media seems to be, the more mass media tend to achieve their "integration." The ideals of conformity and conventionalism were inherent in popular novels from the very beginning. Now, however, these ideals have been translated into rather clear-cut prescriptions of what to do and what not to do. The outcome of conflicts is pre-established, and all conflicts are mere sham. Society is always the winner, and the individual is only a puppet manipulated through social rules. True, conflicts of the nineteenth-century type—such as women running away from their husbands, the drabness of provincial life, and daily chores—occur frequently in today's magazine stories. However, with a regularity which challenges quantitative treatment, these conflicts are decided in favor of the very same conditions from which these women want to break away. The stories teach their readers that one has to be "realistic," that one has to give up romantic ideas, that one has to adjust oneself at any price, and that nothing more can be expected of any individual. The perennial middle-class conflict between individuality and society has been reduced to a dim memory, and the message is invariably that of identification with the *status quo*. This theme too is not new, but

---

[4] One of the significant differences seems to be that in the eighteenth century the concept of popular culture itself moving toward an emancipation from the absolutistic and semifeudal tradition had a progressive meaning, stressing autonomy of the individual as being capable of making his own decisions. This means, among other things, that the early popular literature left space for authors who violently disagreed with the pattern set by Richardson and, nevertheless, obtained popularity of their own. The most prominent case in question is that of Fielding, whose first novel started as a parody of Richardson. It would be interesting to compare the popularity of Richardson and Fielding at that time. Fielding hardly achieved the same success as Richardson. Yet it would be absurd to assume that today's popular culture would allow the equivalent of a *Tom Jones*. This may illustrate the contention of the "rigidity" of today's popular culture. A crucial experiment would be to make an attempt to base a movie on a novel such as Evelyn Waugh's *The Loved One*. It is almost certain that the script would be rewritten and edited so often that nothing remotely similar to the idea of the original would be left.

its unfailing universality invests it with an entirely different meaning. The constant plugging of conventional values seems to mean that these values have lost their substance, and that it is feared that people would really follow their instinctual urges and conscious insights unless continuously reassured from outside that they must not do so. The less the message is really believed and the less it is in harmony with the actual existence of the spectators, the more categorically it is maintained in modern culture. One may speculate whether its inevitable hypocrisy is concomitant with punitiveness and sadistic sternness.

MULTILAYERED STRUCTURE

A depth-psychological approach to television has to be focused on its multilayered structure. Mass media are not simply the sum total of the actions they portray or of the messages that radiate from these actions. Mass media also consist of various layers of meanings superimposed on one another, all of which contribute to the effect. True, due to their calculative nature, these rationalized products seem to be more clear-cut in their meaning than authentic works of art, which can never be boiled down to some unmistakable "message." But the heritage of polymorphic meaning has been taken over by cultural industry inasmuch as what it conveys becomes itself organized in order to enthrall the spectators on various psychological levels simultaneously. As a matter of fact, the hidden message may be more important than the overt, since this hidden message will escape the controls of consciousness, will not be "looked through," will not be warded off by sales resistance, but it is likely to sink into the spectator's mind.

Probably all the various levels in mass media involve *all* the mechanisms of consciousness and unconsciousness stressed by psychoanalysis. The difference between the surface content, the overt message of televised material, and its hidden meaning is generally marked and rather clear-cut. The rigid superimposition of various layers probably is one of the features by which mass media are distinguishable from the integrated products of autonomous art, where the various layers are much more thoroughly fused. The full effect of the material on the spectator cannot be studied without consideration of the hidden meaning in conjunction with the overt one, and it is precisely this interplay of various layers which has hitherto been neglected and which will be our focus. This is in accordance with the assumption shared by numerous social scientists that certain political and social trends of our time, particularly those of a totalitarian nature, feed to a considerable extent on irrational and frequently unconscious motivations. Whether the conscious or the unconscious message of our material is more important is hard to predict and can be evaluated only after careful analysis. We do appreciate, however, that the overt message can be interpreted much more adequately in the light of psychodynamics—i.e., in its relation to instinctual urges as well as control—than by looking at the overt in a naïve way and by ignoring its implications and presuppositions.

The relation between overt and hidden message will prove highly complex in practice. Thus, the hidden message frequently aims at reinforcing conventionally rigid and "pseudo-realistic" attitudes similar to the accepted ideas more rationalistically propagated by the surface message. Conversely, a number of repressed gratifications which play a large role on the hidden level are somehow allowed to manifest themselves on the surface in jests, off-color remarks, suggestive situations, and similar devices. All this interaction of various levels, however, points in some definite direction: the tendency to channelize audience reaction. This falls in line with the suspicion widely shared, though hard to corroborate by exact data, that the majority of television shows today aim at producing, or at least reproducing, the very smugness, intellectual passivity, and gullibility that seem to fit in with totalitarian creeds even if the explicit surface message of the shows may be antitotalitarian.

With the means of modern psychology, we will try to determine the primary prerequisites of shows eliciting mature, adult, and responsible reactions—implying not only in content but in the very way things are being looked at, the idea of autonomous individuals in a free democratic society. We perfectly realize that any definition of such an individual will be hazardous; but we know quite well what a human being deserving of the appellation "autonomous individual" should *not* be, and this "not" is actually the focal point of our consideration.

When we speak of the multilayered structure of television shows, we are thinking of various superimposed layers of different degrees of manifestness or hiddenness that are utilized by mass culture as a technological means of "handling" the audience. This was expressed felicitously by Leo Lowenthal when he coined the term "psychoanalysis in reverse." The implication is that somehow the psycho-analytic concept of a multilayered personality has been taken up by cultural industry, and that the concept is used in order to ensnare the consumer as completely as possible and in order to engage him psychodynamically in the service of premeditated effects. A clear-cut division into allowed gratifications, forbidden gratifications, and recurrence of the forbidden gratifications in a somewhat modified and deflected form is carried through.

To illustrate the concept of the multilayered structure: the heroine of an extremely light comedy of pranks is a young schoolteacher who is not only underpaid but is incessantly fined by the caricature of a pompous and authoritarian school principal. Thus, she has no money for her meals and is actually starving. The supposedly funny situations consist mostly of her trying to hustle a meal from various acquaintances, but regularly without success. The mention of food and eating seems to induce laughter—an observation that can fre-quently be made and invites a study of its own.[5] Overtly, the play is just slight amusement mainly provided by the painful situations into which the heroine and her arch-opponent constantly run. The script does not try to "sell" any idea. The "hidden meaning" emerges simply by the way the story looks at human beings; thus the audience is invited to look at the characters in the same way without being made aware that indoctrination is present. The character of the underpaid, maltreated schoolteacher is an attempt to reach a com-promise between prevailing scorn for the intellectual and the equally conventionalized respect for "culture." The heroine shows such an intellectual superiority and high-spiritedness that identification with her is invited, and compensation is offered for the inferiority of her position and that of her ilk in the social setup. Not only is the central character supposed to be very charming, but she wisecracks con-stantly. In terms of a set pattern of identification, the script implies: "If you are as humorous, good-natured, quick-witted, and charming as she is, do not worry about being paid a starvation wage. You

---

[5] The more rationality (the reality principle) is carried to extremes, the more its ultimate aim (actual gratification) tends, paradoxically, to appear as "im-mature" and ridiculous. Not only eating, but also uncontrolled manifestations of sexual impulses tend to provoke laughter in audiences—kisses in motion pictures have generally to be led up to, the stage has to be set for them, in order to avoid laughter. Yet mass culture never completely succeeds in wiping out potential laughter. Induced, of course, by the supposed infantilism of sensual pleasures, laughter can largely be accounted for by the mechanism of repression. Laughter is a defense against the forbidden fruit.

can cope with your frustration in a humorous way; and your superior wit and cleverness put you not only above material privations, but also above the rest of mankind." In other words, the script is a shrewd method of promoting adjustment to humiliating conditions by presenting them as objectively comical and by giving a picture of a person who experiences even her own inadequate position as an object of fun apparently free of any resentment.

Of course, this latent message cannot be considered as unconscious in the strict psychological sense, but rather as "inobtrusive"; this message is hidden only by a style which does not pretend to touch anything serious and expects to be regarded as featherweight. Nevertheless, even such amusement tends to set patterns for the members of the audience without their being aware of it.

Another comedy of the same thesis is reminiscent of the funnies. A cranky old woman sets up the will of her cat (Mr. Casey) and makes as heirs some of the schoolteachers in the permanent cast. Later the actual inheritance is found to consist of the cat's valueless toys. The plot is so constructed that each heir, at the reading of the will, is tempted to act as if he had known this person (Mr. Casey). The ultimate point is that the cat's owner had placed a hundred-dollar bill inside each of the toys; and the heirs run to the incinerator in order to recover their inheritance. The audience is given to understand: "Don't expect the impossible, don't day-dream, but be realistic." The denunciation of that archetypical daydream is enhanced by the association of the wish for unexpected and irrational blessings with dishonesty, hypocrisy, and a generally undignified attitude. The spectator is given to understand: "Those who dare daydream, who expect that money will fall to them from heaven, and who forget any caution about accepting an absurd will are at the same time those whom you might expect to be capable of cheating."

Here, an objection may be raised: Is such a sinister effect of the hidden message of television known to those who control, plan, write, and direct shows? Or it may even be asked: Are those traits possible projections of the unconscious of the decision-makers' own minds according to the widespread assumption that works of art can be properly understood in terms of psychological projections of their authors? As a matter of fact, it is this kind of reasoning that has led to the suggestion that a special sociopsychological study of decision-makers in the field of television be made. We do not think that such a study would lead us very far. Even in the sphere of autonomous art, the idea of projection has been largely overrated. Although the authors' motivations certainly enter the artifact, they are by no means so all-determining as is often assumed. As soon as an artist has set himself his problem, it obtains some kind of impact of its own; and, in most cases, he has to follow the objective requirements of his product much more than his own urges of expression when he translates his primary conception into artistic reality. To be sure, these objective requirements do not play a decisive role in mass media, which stress the effect on the spectator far beyond any artistic problem. However, the total setup here tends to limit the chances of the artists' projections utterly. Those who produce the material follow, often grumblingly, innumerable requirements, rules of thumb, set patterns, and mechanisms of controls which by necessity reduce to a minimum the range of any kind of artistic self-expression. The fact that most products of mass media are not produced by one individual but by collective collaboration—as happens to be true with most of the illustrations so far discussed—is only one contributing factor to this generally prevailing condition. To study television shows in terms of the psychology of the authors would almost be tantamount to studying Ford cars in terms of the psychoanalysis of the late Mr. Ford.

PRESUMPTUOUSNESS

The typical psychological mechanisms utilized by television shows and the devices by which they are automatized function only within a small number of given frames of reference operative in television communication, and the socio-psychological effect largely depends on them. We are all familiar with the division of television content into various classes, such as light comedy, westerns, mysteries, so-called sophisticated plays, and others. These types have developed into formulas which, to a certain degree, preestablished the attitudinal pattern of the spectator before he is confronted with any specific content and which largely determine the way in which any specific content is being perceived.

In order to understand television, it is, therefore, not enough to bring out the implications of various shows and types of shows; but an examination must be made of the presuppositions within which the implications function before a single word is spoken. Most important is that the typing of shows has gone so far that the spectator approaches each one with a set pattern of expectations before he faces the show itself—just as the radio listener who catches the beginning of Tschaikowsky's Piano Concerto as a theme song, knows automatically, "Aha, serious music!" or, when he hears organ music, responds equally automatically, "Aha, religion!" These halo effects of previous experiences may be psychologically as important as the implications of the phenomena themselves for which they have set the stage; and these presuppositions should, therefore, be treated with equal care.

When a television show bears the title "Dante's Inferno," when the first shot is that of a night club by the same name, and when we find sitting at the bar a man with his hat on and at some distance from him a sad-looking, heavily made-up woman ordering another drink, we are almost certain that some murder will shortly be committed. The apparently individualized situation actually works only as a signal that moves our expectations into a definite direction. If we had never seen anything but "Dante's Inferno," we probably would not be sure about what was going to happen; but, as it is, we are actually given to understand by both subtle and not so subtle devices that this is a crime play, that we are entitled to expect some sinister and probably hideous and sadistic deeds of violence, that the hero will be saved from a situation from which he can hardly be expected to be saved, that the woman on the barstool is probably not the main criminal but is likely to lose her life as a gangster's moll, and so on. This conditioning to such universal patterns, however, scarcely stops at the television set.

The way the spectator is made to look at apparently everyday items, such as a night club, and to take as hints of possible crime common settings of his daily life, induces him to look at life itself as though it and its conflicts could generally be understood in such terms.[6] This, convincingly enough, may be the nucleus of truth in

---

[6] This relationship again should not be oversimplified. No matter to what extent modern mass media tend to blur the difference between reality and the esthetic, our realistic spectators are still aware that all is "in fun." It cannot be assumed that the direct primary perception of reality takes place within the television frame of reference, although many movie-goers recall the alienation of familiar sights when leaving the theater: everything still has the appearance of being part of the movie plot. What is more important is the interpretation of reality in terms of psychological carry-overs, the preparedness to see ordinary objects as though some threatening mystery were hidden behind them. Such an attitude seems to be syntonic with mass delusions such as suspicion of omnipresent graft, corruption, and conspiracy.

the old-fashioned arguments against all kinds of mass media for inciting criminality in the audience. The decisive thing is that this atmosphere of the normality of crime, its presentation in terms of an average expectation based on life situations, is never expressed in so many words but is established by the overwhelming wealth of material. It may affect certain spectator groups more deeply than the overt moral of crime and punishment regularly derived from such shows. What matters is not the importance of crime as a symbolic expression of otherwise controlled sexual or aggressive impulses, but the confusion of this symbolism with a pedantically maintained realism in all matters of direct sense perception. Thus, empirical life becomes infused with a kind of meaning that virtually excludes adequate experience no matter how obstinately the veneer of such "realism" is built up. This affects the social and psychological function of drama.

It is hard to establish whether the spectators of Greek tragedy really experienced the catharsis Aristotle described—in fact this theory, evolved after the age of tragedy was over, seems to have been a rationalization itself, an attempt to state the purpose of tragedy in pragmatic, quasi-scientific terms. Whatever the case, it seems pretty certain that those who saw the *Oresteia* of Aeschylus or Sophocles' *Oedipus* were not likely to translate these tragedies (the subject matter of which was known to everyone, and the interest in which was centered in artistic treatment) directly into everyday terms. This audience did not expect that on the next corner of Athens similar things would go on. Actually, pseudo-realism allows for the direct and extremely primitive identification achieved by popular culture; and it presents a façade of trivial buildings, rooms, dresses, and faces as though they were the promise of something thrilling and exciting taking place at any moment.

In order to establish this socio-psychological frame of reference, one would have to follow up systematically categories—such as the normality of crime or pseudo-realism and many others—to determine their structural unity and to interpret the specific devices, symbols, and stereotypes in relation to this frame of reference. We hypothesize at this phase that the frames of reference and the individual devices will tend in the same direction.

Only against psychological backdrops such as pseudo-realism and against implicit assumptions such as the normality of crime can the specific stereotypes of television plays be interpreted. The very standardization indicated by set frames of reference automatically produces a number of stereotypes. Also, the technology of television production makes stereotypy almost inevitable. The short time available for the preparation of scripts and the vast material continuously to be produced call for certain formulas. Moreover, in plays lasting only a quarter to half an hour each, it appears inevitable that the kind of person the audience faces each time should be indicated drastically through red and green lights. We are not dealing with the problem of the existence of stereotypes as such. Since stereotypes are an indispensable element of the organization and anticipation of experience, preventing us from falling into mental disorganization and chaos, no art can entirely dispense with them. Again, the functional change is what concerns us. The more stereotypes become reified and rigid in the present setup of cultural industry, the less people are likely to change their preconceived ideas with the progress of their experience. The more opaque and complicated modern life becomes, the more people are tempted to cling desperately to clichés which seem to bring some order into the otherwise ununderstandable. Thus, people may not only lose true insight into reality, but ultimately their very capacity for life experience may be dulled by the constant wearing of blue and pink spectacles.

STEREOTYPING

In coping with this danger, we may not do full justice to the meaning of some of the stereotypes which are to be dealt with. We should never forget that there are two sides to every psychodynamic phenomenon, the unconscious or id element and the rationalization. Although the latter is psychologically defined as a defense mechanism, it may very well contain some nonpsychological, objective truth which cannot simply be pushed aside on account of the psychological function of the rationalization. Thus some of the stereotypical messages, directed toward particularly weak spots in the mentality of large sectors of the population, may prove to be quite legitimate. However, it may be said with fairness that the questionable blessings of morals, such as "one should not chase after rainbows," are largely overshadowed by the threat of inducing people to mechanical simplifications by ways of distorting the world in such a way that it seems to fit into pre-established pigeonholes.

The example here selected, however, should indicate rather drastically the danger of stereotypy. A television play concerning a fascist dictator, a kind of hybrid between Mussolini and Peron, shows the dictator in a moment of crisis; and the content of the play is his inner and outer collapse. Whether the cause of his collapse is a popular upheaval or a military revolt is never made clear. But neither this issue nor any other of a social or political nature enters the plot itself. The course of events takes place exclusively on a private level. The dictator is just a heel who treats sadistically both his secretary and his "lovely and warmhearted" wife. His antagonist, a general, was formerly in love with the wife; and they both still love each other, although the wife sticks loyally to her husband. Forced by her husband's brutality, she attempts flight, and is intercepted by the general, who wants to save her. The turning point occurs when the guards surround the palace to defend the dictator's popular wife. As soon as they learn that she has departed, the guards quit; and the dictator, whose "inflated ego" explodes at the same time, gives up. The dictator is nothing but a bad, pompous, and cowardly man. He seems to act with extreme stupidity; nothing of the objective dynamics of dictatorship comes out. The impression is created that totalitarianism grows out of character disorders of ambitious politicians, and is overthrown by the honesty, courage, and warmth of those figures with whom the audience is supposed to identify. The standard device employed is that of the spurious personalization of objective issues. The representatives of ideas under attack, as in the case of the fascists here, are presented as villains in a ludicrous cloak-and-dagger fashion, whereas those who fight for the "right cause" are personally idealized. This not only distracts from any real social issues but also enforces the psychologically extremely dangerous division of the world into black (the outgroup) and white (we, the ingroup). Certainly, no artistic production can deal with ideas or political creeds *in abstracto* but has to present them in terms of their concrete impact upon human beings; yet it would be utterly futile to present individuals as mere specimens of an abstraction, as puppets expressive of an idea. In order to deal with the concrete impact of totalitarian systems, it would be more commendable to show how the life of ordinary people is affected by terror and impotence than to cope with the phony psychology of the big-shots, whose heroic role is silently endorsed by such a treatment even if they are pictured as villains. There seems to be hardly any question of the importance of an analysis of pseudo-personalization and its effect, by no means limited to television.

Although pseudo-personalization denotes the stereotyped way of "looking at things" in television, we should also point out certain stereotypes in the narrower sense. Many television plays could be characterized by the sobriquet "a pretty girl can do no wrong." The heroine of a light comedy is, to use George Legman's term, "a bitch heroine." She behaves toward her father in an incredibly inhuman and cruel manner only slightly rationalized as "merry pranks." But she is punished very slightly, if at all. True, in real life bad deeds are rarely punished at all, but this cannot be applied to television. Here, those who have developed the production code for the movies seem right: what matters in mass media is not what happens in real life, but rather the positive and negative "messages," prescriptions, and taboos that the spectator absorbs by means of identification with the material he is looking at. The punishment given to the pretty heroine only nominally fulfills the conventional requirements of the conscience for a second. But the spectator is given to understand that the pretty heroine really gets away with everything just because she is pretty.

The attitude in question seems to be indicative of a universal penchant. In another sketch that belongs to a series dealing with the confidence racket, the attractive girl who is an active participant in the racket not only is paroled after having been sentenced to a long term, but also seems to have a good chance of marrying her victim. Her sex morality, of course, is unimpeachable. The spectator is supposed to like her at first sight as a modest and self-effacing character, and he must not be disappointed. Although it is discovered that she is a crook, the original identification must be restored, or rather maintained. The stereotype of the nice girl is so strong that not even the proof of her delinquency can destroy it; and, by hook or by crook, she must be what she appears to be. It goes without saying that such psychological models tend to confirm exploitative, demanding, and aggressive attitudes on the part of young girls—a character structure which has come to be known in psychoanalysis under the name of oral aggressiveness.

Sometimes such stereotypes are disguised as national American traits, a part of the American scene where the image of the haughty, egoistic, yet irresistible girl who plays havoc with poor dad has come to be a public institution. This way of reasoning is an insult to the American spirit. High-pressure publicity and continuous plugging to institutionalize some obnoxious type does not make the type a sacred symbol of folklore. Many considerations of an apparently anthropological nature today tend only to veil objectionable trends, as though they were of an ethnological, quasi-natural character. Incidentally, it is amazing to what degree television material even on superficial examination brings to mind psychoanalytic concepts with the qualification of being a psychoanalysis in reverse. Psychoanalysis has described the oral syndrome combining the antagonistic trends of aggressive and dependent traits. This character syndrome is closely indicated by the pretty girl who can do no wrong, who, while being aggressive against her father exploits him at the same time, depending on him as much as, on the surface level, she is set against him. The difference between the sketch and psychoanalysis is simply that the sketch exalts the very same syndrome which is treated by psychoanalysis as a reversion to infantile developmental phases and which the psychoanalyst tries to dissolve. It remains to be seen whether something similar applies as well to some types of male heroes, particularly the super-he-man. It may well be that he too can do no wrong.

Finally, we should deal with a rather widespread stereotype which, inasmuch as it is taken for granted by television, is further enhanced. At the same time, the example may serve to show that certain psychoanalytic interpretations of cultural stereotypes are not really too far-fetched; the latent ideas that psychoanalysis attributes to certain stereotypes come to the surface. There is the extremely popular idea that the artist is not only maladjusted, introverted, and *a priori* somewhat funny; but that he is really an "aesthete," a weakling, and a "sissy." In other words, modern synthetic folklore tends to identify the artist with the homosexual and to respect only the "man of action" as a real, strong man. This idea is expressed in a surprisingly direct manner in one of the comedy scripts at our disposal. It portrays a young man who is not only the "dope" who appears so often on television but is also a shy, retiring, and accordingly untalented poet, whose moronic poems are ridiculed.[7] He is in love with a girl but is too weak and insecure

---

[7] It could be argued that this very ridicule expresses that this boy is not meant to represent the artist but just the "dope." But this is probably too rationalistic. Again, as in the case of the schoolteacher, official respect for culture prevents caricaturing the artist as such. However, by characterizing the boy, among other things by his writing poetry, it is indirectly achieved that the artistic activities and silliness are associated with each other. In many respects mass culture is organized much more by way of such associations than in strictly logical terms. It may be added that quite frequently attacks on any

to indulge in the necking practices she rather crudely suggests; the girl, on her part, is caricatured as a boy-chaser. As happens frequently in mass culture, the roles of the sexes are reversed—the girl is utterly aggressive, and the boy, utterly afraid of her, describes himself as "woman-handled" when she manages to kiss him. There are vulgar innuendos of homosexuality of which one may be quoted: the heroine tells her boy friend that another boy is in love with someone, and the boy friend asks, "What's he in love with?" She answers, "A girl, of course," and her boy friend replies, "Why, of course? Once before it was a neighbor's turtle, and what's more its name was Sam." This interpretation of the artist as innately incompetent and a social outcast (by the innuendo of sexual inversion) is worthy of examination.

We do not pretend that the individual illustrations and examples, or the theories by which they are interpreted, are basically new. But in view of the cultural and pedagogical problem presented by television, we do not think that the novelty of the specific findings should be a primary concern. We know from psychoanalysis that the reasoning, "But we know all this!" is often a defense. This defense is made in order to dismiss insights as irrelevant because they are actually uncomfortable and make life more difficult for us than it already is by shaking our conscience when we are supposed to enjoy the "simple pleasures of life." The investigation of the television problems we have here indicated and illustrated by a few examples selected at random demands, most of all, taking seriously notions dimly familiar to most of us by putting them into their proper context and perspective and by checking them by pertinent material. We propose to concentrate on issues of which we are vaguely but uncomfortably aware, even at the expense of our discomfort's mounting, the further and the more systematically our studies proceed. The effort here required is of a moral nature itself: knowingly to face psychological mechanisms operating on various levels in order not to become blind and passive victims. We can change this medium of far-reaching potentialities only if we look at it in the same spirit which we hope will one day be expressed by its imagery.

social type seek protection by apparently presenting the object of the attack as an exception, while it is understood by innuendo that he is considered as a specimen of the whole concept.

TOWARD A FREE AND RESPONSIBLE PRESS

RECOMMENDATIONS OF THE COMMISSION ON FREEDOM OF THE PRESS

These recommendations are set forth and discussed in *A Free and Responsible Press*, published and copyrighted by the University of Chicago Press, 1947.[1]

WHAT CAN BE DONE THROUGH GOVERNMENT

1. WE RECOMMEND that the constitutional guarantees of the freedom of the press be recognized as including the radio and motion pictures.

2. We recommend that government facilitate new ventures in the communications industry, that it foster the introduction of new techniques, that it maintain competition among large units through the anti-trust laws, but that those laws be sparingly used to break up such units, and that, where concentration is necessary in communications, the government endeavor to see to it that the public gets the benefit of such concentration.

---

[1] Members of the Commission were Chancellor Robert M. Hutchins, University of Chicago, chairman; Zechariah Chafee, Jr., professor of law, Harvard, vice-chairman; John M. Clark, professor of economics, Columbia; John Dickinson, general counsel, Pennsylvania Railroad; William E. Hocking, professor of philosophy, *emeritus*, Harvard; Harold D. Lasswell, professor of law, Yale; Archibald MacLeish, professor of rhetoric, Harvard; Charles E. Merriam, professor of political science, *emeritus*, Harvard; Reinhold Niebuhr, professor of ethics and philosophy of religion, Union Theological Seminary; Robert Redfield, professor of anthropology, University of Chicago; Beardsley Ruml, chairman, Federal Reserve Bank of New York; Arthur M. Schlesinger, professor of history, Harvard; and George M. Shuster, president of Hunter College.

3. As an alternative to the present remedy for libel, we recommend legislation by which the injured party might obtain a retraction or a restatement of the facts by the offender or an opportunity to reply.

4. We recommend the repeal of legislation prohibiting expressions in favor of revolutionary changes in our institutions where there is no clear and present danger that violence will result from the expressions.

5. We recommend that the government, through the media of mass communication, inform the public of the facts with respect to its policies and of the purposes underlying those policies and that, to the extent that private agencies of mass communication are unable or unwilling to supply such media to the government, the government itself may employ media of its own.

We also recommend that, where the private agencies of mass communication are unable or unwilling to supply information about this country to a particular foreign country or countries, the government employ mass communication media of its own to supplement this deficiency.

WHAT CAN BE DONE BY THE PRESS

1. We recommend that the agencies of mass communication accept the responsibilities of common carriers of information and discussion.

2. We recommend that the agencies of mass communication assume the responsibility of financing new, experimental activities in their fields.

3. We recommend that the members of the press engage in vigorous mutual criticism.

4. We recommend that the press use every means that can be devised to increase the competence, independence, and effectiveness of its staff.

5. We recommend that the radio industry take control of its programs and that it treat advertising as it is treated by the best newspapers.

WHAT CAN BE DONE BY THE PUBLIC

1. We recommend that nonprofit institutions help supply the variety, quantity, and quality of press service required by the American people.

2. We recommend the creation of academic-professional centers of advanced study, research, and publication in the field of communications. We recommend further that existing schools of journalism exploit the total resources of their universities to the end that their students may obtain the broadest and most liberal training.

3. We recommend the establishment of a new and independent agency to appraise and report annually upon the performance of the press.

ENDOWED, GOVERNMENT-OWNED, OR RESPONSIBLE NEWSPAPERS?

BY NELSON ANTRIM CRAWFORD

Mr. Crawford was for many years editor of *Household Magazine,* later of *Author and Journalist.* This selection is from his book *The Ethics of Journalism,* published and copyrighted in 1924 by Alfred A. Knopf, New York. It is reprinted here by permission of the copyright holder.

THOSE WHO MAINTAIN that the press is essentially and consciously corrupt look for no improvement in the conditions of journalism from within the press itself. If they are sufficiently realistic in point of view to recognize the futility of legal measures as a corrective of evils in journalism, they are nevertheless prone to seek some other remedy, the impetus for which comes from outside the profession of journalism. Such an origin does not necessarily mean that a given proposal is unwise, but should lead the unprejudiced observer to regard it with caution, since it can hardly be presumed that any institution is wholly unwilling to be improved or unable to improve itself.

Aside from laws governing a privately owned press, the two suggestions most commonly made call respectively for endowed newspapers and for newspapers owned by the government, federal, state, or municipal.

Against both the endowed newspaper and the government-owned newspaper, one objection is commonly urged by practicing journalists; namely, that they would be too dull to appeal to the general public. Weight is given to this objection by a reading of government publications in general. Few of them possess interest except to the technical reader. *The Official Bulletin,* issued by the United States government during the recent war, was, although edited by a professional newspaperman, one of the dullest publications ever circulated. There are in this country no endowed newspapers, in the strict sense of the word, so that one cannot definitely pass judgment as to the probable interest of such publications. There are several magazines of opinion, however, which are practically endowed. However enjoyable and stimulating these may be to the intellectual reader, their small circulation proves their lack of appeal to the general public. If a publication is supported by the government or by private endowment, the staff does not feel strongly the necessity of interesting a large number of readers. While this might be beneficial in eliminating the ultra-sensational from a newspaper, it would at the same time reduce the value of the publication as a means of disseminating facts.

As to the endowed newspaper, another objection arises. Endowments are likely to be instituted for the purpose of advancing a particular cause rather than for the purpose merely of disseminating objective facts. Moreover, no matter how much care is taken to prevent it, there is a tendency for endowments to represent and perpetuate the mental attitude of the donors regardless of what the stated purpose of the endowment may be. This fact has been complained of time and again in the case of educational institutions, justly and unjustly; there is no reason to assume that the same complaints would not arise in the case of endowed newspapers. Once the complaint developed, whether well founded or not, much of the influence of the newspaper would be lost.

The government-owned newspaper is open to the objection that it would certainly be used for propaganda. Indeed, it seems astonishing that government newspapers should be seriously advocated by those who are familiar with the politician's attitude toward facts, and particularly by those who complain of current political conditions. The unreliability of purported facts furnished to newspapers by government officials has been emphasized again and again. The inability to reason from facts to conclusions and the practice of basing opinions purely on preconceived notions are apparent to any one who will read *The Congressional Record* or listen, as a newspaper reporter, to the press statements made by executive officials.

The theory that politicians would not take advantage of the opportunity of a government-owned newspaper to advance their own fortunes and those of their groups and parties, is untenable. The attempts of politicians to influence newspapers, privately owned, to misrepresent or suppress the facts, afford sufficient clue to what would happen were these same politicians in control of the financial support of the press. The method of the politician, even when he evidently considers he is acting for the best interests of the country, is illustrated by the following circular, issued when both Canada and the United States were engaged in the World War:

Circular No. C. P. C. 57a
CONFIDENTIAL CIRCULAR FOR CANADIAN EDITORS
(Not for Publication.)
(1) Owing to the shortage of agricultural labourers in Canada, consequent upon the absence of such a large proportion of Canadian manhood on military service, and in view of the supreme importance of securing the highest possible production in natural products, the Government is making an effort to bring in from the United States to the Western Provinces as much farm labour as possible. Editors are asked to suppress references to this particular matter, as it is feared that publicity may seriously interfere with the plan.

Ernest J. Chambers,
Chief Press Censor for Canada.
Office of the Chief Press Censor for Canada,
Department of the Secretary of State,
Ottawa, January 19, 1918.

Where the private interests of the politician or his party, rather than apparently those of his country, are involved, he employs much less obvious, but for that reason more sinister, methods.

Furthermore, unless the government newspapers were given exclusive rights, they would fail of their purpose. The best journalists would still be found on privately owned papers, and the public would prefer the latter. This was found to be true when even semi-official newspapers existed in Washington, in the first half of the nineteenth century.[1] To give exclusive rights to government newspapers would restore the abuses of seventeenth-century England, when the government endeavored to control all dissemination of news and all expression of opinion on public matters. At that time,

---

[1] See George Henry Payne, *History of Journalism in the United States* (New York: Appleton, 1920), pp. 238-39.

of course, there was a clandestine press, just as there was in Belgium during the German occupation in 1914–1918, and eventually government control was done away with. The same thing would undoubtedly occur in the United States were the government to attempt to take over the press.

The one thing which can be done by the government to improve the press is to develop certainty of record on a greater number of matters, comparable to the certainty of record that now exists on court proceedings, the acts of legislative bodies, and some other events. Particularly may this be wisely developed in social and economic problems. Mr. Lippmann's suggestion of intelligence bureaus, organized to supply facts but neither to render decisions nor take action, presents a plan which, if efficiently carried out, would mean a decided advance for the newspaper in its capacity as a disseminator of objective facts. Such a system would have to be removed from direct political control, and it should, in turn, have no control over politics or over the press, but should be exclusively a fact-finding agency, as distinguished from a fact-disseminating, a policy-advocating, or an executive agency.[2]

So far as other governmental steps are concerned, they would in all probability be worse than useless. A government-controlled press would be essentially a propaganda press, whereas one of the chief accomplishments which newspapers of themselves can hope to make is freedom from propaganda.

.   .   .   .

Aside from reducing the amount of propaganda, what, if anything, can the press as an institution do, toward raising the standards of journalism? The first step is to recognize that not all is well with the profession. This step has already been taken. While the universal tendency of the professional man to defend his profession against the laity still exists in journalism, the number of editorials in newspaper trade journals and even newspapers themselves about the faults of the press proves that the intelligent editor is not complacent. Too many publishers, who are not themselves editors, are complacent, but they are not likely to remain so indefinitely.

The second step is self-analysis. This is not an easy matter. The best plan, manifestly, would be an analysis of representative ex-

---

[2] An outline of the plan, which should be read by every student of the press, is to be found in Mr. Lippmann's *Public Opinion* (New York: Harcourt, Brace, 1920), pp. 369-410.

amples of the American press by a committee of whose objective-mindedness, fairness, and familiarity with journalistic practice there could be no doubt. Such an investigation should cover various sections of the country and should include various types of newspapers, from the metropolitan daily to the country weekly. The few studies that have been made cover only large city dailies, whereas the vast majority of American newspapers and probably the weight of journalistic influence are found in the papers published in small towns. Furthermore, reports made by persons strongly opposed to the press or strongly in sympathy with it are useful in drawing public attention to conditions, but do not carry great evidential weight; indeed, in most cases they contain too little authenticated evidence to sustain any conclusions. An investigative project such as has been suggested would require a large endowment, but the results would more than justify it. The mere publication of the findings of the investigators would put the indubitable concrete facts about American journalism into the arena of public discussion, and this of itself would result in a speedy improvement. If a group of public-spirited publishers—or for that matter a group of any sort —would endow such an investigation, it would produce incalculable results for the betterment of journalism.

Until this is done, each newspaper must make its own analysis. A few newspapers are already doing so. *The Detroit News* employs an editorial secretary whose duties include investigation of the accuracy of statements in the paper. In 1913, Ralph Pulitzer established the Bureau of Accuracy and Fair Play of *The New York World*. The purpose, as stated by the founder, is "to promote accuracy and fair play, to correct carelessness, and to stamp out fakes and fakers." Every complaint made concerning an item in *The World* is investigated. If the complaint is justified, a correction is published, and the blame for the error is also fixed. The complainant is invariably informed of the results of the investigation. Faking or gross carelessness on the part of a reporter or correspondent subjects him to dismissal.[3] Some other newspapers follow similar practices on a less formal and elaborate scale. The better newspapers quite generally correct errors that are called to their attention, some in a "Beg Your Pardon" column established for the purpose, others in the regular news columns. This is a marked advance over the older practice of refusing to make corrections on the ground that

[3] See Biennial Reports of the Bureau for details.

they destroyed confidence in the press. There are still, it should be remarked in passing, newspapers which refuse to make corrections except of matters which they deem "important," and thus lead the public to utter disbelief in their integrity.

While it may seem at first glance that these methods constitute merely a negative method of self-analysis on the part of the newspapers, reflection will show that a publication could hardly initiate investigation of all the stories that it publishes, because of their vast number and the numerous lines of investigation that must be followed in tracing down the accuracy or inaccuracy of each. A newspaper might, however, initiate investigation of a certain number of stories each week, choosing those written by various members of the staff. A newspaper might also, still more practicably, publish in a prominent place in each issue an invitation to readers to complain of inaccuracies in any story. Undoubtedly many errors occur to which attention is never called but which would perhaps be brought to the notice of the paper were readers assured of the desire for their co-operation in the promotion of accuracy.

The third step that may be taken by the newspaper, the attempt to eliminate the faults which self-analysis shows, is illustrated in the practice of *The New York World*, heretofore mentioned. So far as the reporter is concerned, he will in most cases try to be accurate and fair if he knows that accuracy and fairness are wanted, and particularly if he knows that a penalty will be exacted for their violation. Many newspapers publish codes of ethics for the guidance of their staffs, which fact alone indicates a genuine interest in improving journalism. The same thing may be said of codes adopted by state press associations and similar bodies. Unless the code is enforced, however, unless the reporter or other staff member, indeed, feels that there is behind it a vigorous moral purpose, it is likely to lead to few results. It is of course to be recognized that any code of ethics represents ideals rather than merely contemporary practice, but if the code is to be useful the practice must make an effort in the direction of actual conformity with the ideals set up.

So much for the newspapers as newspapers. Can the newspaper worker, reporter, copy-reader, or editorial writer, himself accomplish anything in the direction of maintenance of sound standards? He cannot, of course, do as an individual what a powerful organization of journalists could do. But he can do something. He can adopt a practical working code of ethics for himself. He can decide, for instance, that he will never intentionally write anything untrue or unfair, that he will never use any dishonorable means in securing news, that he will never violate a confidence, that he will never accept money or any other gratuity for writing or refraining from writing any item, that he will never knowingly give readers a false impression concerning any matter, however trivial. Having adopted a code, he can stand ready to be "fired" rather than violate it. He is not, it is true, very likely to be "fired," for intentional, studied dishonesty on the part of newspapers, it has been pointed out, is not the chief reason for their deficiencies.

Such betterment of conditions as can be accomplished by the various individualistic means suggested reaches mainly, it is evident, the more casual deficiencies of the press—inaccuracy, general carelessness, so-called "harmless" faking, and the like. The underlying causes can be reached by no such application of palliatives. They will be eliminated slowly, chiefly by organization and educational agencies in co-operation with the press itself.

CANONS OF JOURNALISM

AMERICAN SOCIETY OF NEWSPAPER EDITORS

THE PRIMARY FUNCTION of newspapers is to communicate to the human race what its members do, feel, and think. Journalism, therefore, demands of its practitioners the widest range of intelligence, of knowledge, and of experience, as well as natural and trained powers of observation and reasoning. To its opportunities as a chronicle are indissolubly linked its obligations as teacher and interpreter.

To the end of finding some means of codifying sound practice and just aspirations of American journalism, these canons are set forth:

I

Responsibility—The right of a newspaper to attract and hold readers is restricted by nothing but consideration of public welfare. The use a newspaper makes of the share of public attention it gains serves to determine its sense of responsibility, which it shares with every member of its staff. A journalist who uses his power for any selfish or otherwise unworthy purpose is faithless to a high trust.

II

Freedom of the Press—Freedom of the press is to be guarded as a vital right of mankind. It is the unquestionable right to discuss whatever is not explicitly forbidden by law, including the wisdom of any restrictive statute.

III

Independence—Freedom from all obligations except that of fidelity to the public interest is vital.

1. Promotion of any private interest contrary to the general welfare, for whatever reason, is not compatible with honest journalism. So-called news communications from private sources should not be published without public notice of their source or else substantiation of their claims to value as news, both in form and substance.

2. Partisanship in editorial comment which knowingly departs from the truth does violence to the best spirit of American journalism; in the news columns it is subversive of a fundamental principle of the profession.

IV

Sincerity, Truthfulness, Accuracy—Good faith with the reader is the foundation of all journalism worthy of the name.

1. By every consideration of good faith a newspaper is constrained to be truthful. It is not to be excused for lack of thoroughness or accuracy within its control or failure to obtain command of these essential qualities.

2. Headlines should be fully warranted by the contents of the articles which they surmount.

V

Impartiality—Sound practice makes clear distinction between news reports and expressions of opinion. News reports should be free from opinion or bias of any kind.

1. This rule does not apply to so-called special articles unmistakably devoted to advocacy or characterized by a signature authorizing the writer's own conclusions and interpretations.

VI

Fair Play—A newspaper should not publish unofficial charges affecting reputation or moral character without opportunity given to the accused to be heard; right practice demands the giving of such opportunity in all cases of serious accusation outside judicial proceedings.

1. A newspaper should not invade private rights or feelings without sure warrant of public right as distinguished from public curiosity.

2. It is the privilege, as it is the duty, of a newspaper to make prompt and complete correction of its own serious mistakes of fact or opinion, whatever their origin.

VII

Decency—A newspaper cannot escape conviction of insincerity if, while professing high moral purposes, it supplies incentives to base conduct, such as are to be found in details of crime and vice, publication of which is not demonstrably for the general good. Lacking authority to enforce its canons, the journalism here represented can but express the hope that deliberate pandering to vicious instincts will encounter effective public disapproval or yield to the influence of a preponderant professional condemnation.

THE PRODUCTION CODE

MOTION PICTURE ASSOCIATION OF AMERICA

PREAMBLE

MOTION PICTURE PRODUCERS recognize the high trust and confidence which have been placed in them by the people of the world and which have made motion pictures a universal form of entertainment.

They recognize their responsibility to the public because of this trust and because entertainment and art are important influences in the life of a nation.

Hence, though regarding motion pictures primarily as entertainment without any explicit purpose of teaching or propaganda, they know that the motion picture within its own field of entertainment may be directly responsible for spiritual or moral progress, for higher types of social life, and for much correct thinking.

During the rapid transition from silent to talking pictures they realized the necessity and the opportunity of subscribing to a Code to govern the production of talking pictures and of reacknowledging this responsibility.

On their part, they ask from the public and from public leaders a sympathetic understanding of their purposes and problems and a spirit of cooperation that will allow them the freedom and opportunity necessary to bring the motion picture to a still higher level of wholesome entertainment for all the people.

GENERAL PRINCIPLES

1. No picture shall be produced which will lower the moral standards of those who see it. Hence the sympathy of the audience shall never be thrown to the side of crime, wrong-doing, evil, or sin.

2. Correct standards of life, subject only to the requirements of drama and entertainment shall be presented.

3. Law, natural or human, shall not be ridiculed, nor shall sympathy be created for its violation.

PARTICULAR APPLICATIONS

I. CRIMES AGAINST THE LAW

These shall never be presented in such a way as to throw sympathy with the crime as against law and justice or to inspire others with a desire for imitation.

1. *Murder*
   a) The technique of murder must be presented in a way that will not inspire imitation.
   b) Brutal killings are not to be presented in detail.
   c) Revenge in modern times shall not be justified.

2. *Methods of crime* should not be explicitly presented.
   a) Theft, robbery, safe-cracking, and dynamiting of trains, mines, buildings, etc., should not be detailed in method.
   b) Arson must be subject to the same safeguards.
   c) The use of firearms should be restricted to essentials.
   d) Methods of smuggling should not be presented.

3. *The illegal drug traffic* must not be portrayed in such a way as to stimulate curiosity concerning the use of, or traffic in, such drugs; nor shall scenes be approved which show the use of illegal drugs, or their effects, in detail (as amended September 11, 1946).

4. *The use of liquor* in American life, when not required by the plot or for proper characterization, will not be shown.

II. SEX

The sanctity of the institution of marriage and the home shall be upheld. Pictures shall not infer that low forms of sex relationship are the accepted or common thing.

1. *Adultery and illicit sex,* sometimes necessary plot material, must not be explicitly treated or justified, or presented attractively.
2. *Scenes of passion*
    a) These should not be introduced except where they are definitely essential to the plot.
    b) Excessive and lustful kissing, lustful embraces, suggestive postures and gestures are not to be shown.
    c) In general, passion should be treated in such manner as not to stimulate the lower and baser emotions.
3. *Seduction or rape*
    a) These should never be more than suggested, and then only when essential for the plot. They must never be by explicit method.
    b) They are never the proper subject for comedy.
4. *Sex perversion* or any inference to it is forbidden.
5. *White slavery* shall not be treated.
6. *Miscegenation* (sex relationship between the white and black races) is forbidden.
7. *Sex hygiene* and venereal diseases are not proper subjects for theatrical motion pictures.
8. Scenes of *actual childbirth,* in fact or in silhouette, are never to be presented.
9. *Children's sex organs* are never to be exposed.

III. VULGARITY

The treatment of low, disgusting, unpleasant, though not necessary evil, subjects should be guided always by the dictates of good taste and a proper regard for the sensibilities of the audience.

IV. OBSCENITY

Obscenity in word, gesture, reference, song, joke, or by suggestion (even when likely to be understood only by part of the audience) is forbidden.

V. PROFANITY[1]

Pointed profanity and every other profane or vulgar expression, however used, is forbidden.

---

[1] As amended by resolution of the Board of Directors, November 1, 1939.

No approval by the Production Code Administration shall be given to the use of words and phrases in motion pictures including, but not limited to, the following:

Alley cat (applied to a woman); bat (applied to a woman); broad (applied to a woman); Bronx cheer (the sound); chippie; cocotte; God, Lord, Jesus, Christ (unless used reverently); cripes; fanny; fairy (in a vulgar sense); finger (the); fire, cries of; Gawd; goose (in a vulgar sense); "hold your hat" or "hats"; hot (applied to a woman); "in your hat"; louse; lousy; Madam (relating to prostitution); nance; nerts; nuts (except when meaning crazy); pansy; razzberry (the sound); slut (applied to a woman); S.O.B.; son-of-a; tart; toilet gags; tom cat (applied to a man); traveling salesman and farmer's daughter jokes; whore; damn, hell (excepting when the use of said last two words shall be essential and required for portrayal, in proper historical context, of any scene or dialogue based upon historical fact or folklore, or for the presentation in proper literary context of a Biblical, or other religious quotation, or a quotation from a literary work provided that no such use shall be permitted which is intrinsically objectionable or offends good taste).

In the administration of Section V of the Production Code, the Production Code Administration may take cognizance of the fact that the following words and phrases are obviously offensive to the patrons of motion pictures in the United States and more particularly to the patrons of motion pictures in foreign countries:

Chink, Dago, Frog, Greaser, Hunkie, Kike, Nigger, Spig, Wop, Yid.

VI. Costume

1. *Complete nudity* is never permitted. This includes nudity in fact or in silhouette, or any licentious notice thereof by other characters in the pictures.
2. *Undressing scenes* should be avoided, and never used save where essential to the plot.
3. *Indecent or undue exposure* is forbidden.
4. *Dancing costumes* intended to permit undue exposure or indecent movements in the dance are forbidden.

VII. Dances

1. Dances suggesting or representing sexual actions or indecent passion are forbidden.
2. Dances which emphasize indecent movements are to be regarded as obscene.

VIII. Religion

1. No film or episode may throw *ridicule* on any religious faith.
2. *Ministers of religion* in their character as ministers of religion should not be used as comic characters or as villains.
3. *Ceremonies* of any definite religion should be carefully and respectfully handled.

IX. Locations

The treatment of bedrooms must be governed by good taste and delicacy.

X. National Feelings

1. *The use of the flag* shall be consistently respectful.
2. *The history,* institutions, prominent people, and citizenry of all nations shall be represented fairly.

XI. Titles

Salacious, indecent, or obscene titles shall not be used.

XII. Repellent Subjects

The following subjects must be treated within the careful limits of good taste:
1. *Actual hangings or electrocutions* as legal punishments for crime.
2. *Third-degree* methods.
3. *Brutality* and possible gruesomeness.
4. *Branding* of people or animals.
5. *Apparent cruelty* to children or animals.
6. *The sale of women,* or a woman selling her virtue.
7. *Surgical operations.*

REASONS UNDERLYING THE GENERAL PRINCIPLES

1. No picture shall be produced which will lower the moral standards of those who see it. Hence the sympathy of the audience
should never be thrown to the side of crime, wrong-doing,
evil, or sin.

   This is done:

   1. When *evil* is made to appear *attractive* or *alluring,* and
good is made to appear *unattractive.*

   2. When the *sympathy* of the audience is thrown on the side
of crime, wrong-doing, evil, sin. The same thing is true of
a film that would throw sympathy against goodness, honor,
innocence, purity, or honesty.

   Note: Sympathy with a person who sins is not the same as
sympathy with the sin or crime of which he is guilty. We
may feel sorry for the plight of the murderer or even understand the circumstances which led him to his crime. We may
not feel sympathy with the wrong which he has done.

   The *presentation of evil* is often essential for art or fiction or
drama. This in itself is not wrong provided:

   a) *That evil is not presented alluringly.* Even if later in the
film the evil is condemned or punished, it must not be
allowed to appear so attractive that the audience's emotions are drawn to desire or approve so strongly that later
the condemnation is forgotten and only the apparent joy
of the sin remembered.

   b) That throughout, the audience feels sure that *evil is wrong*
and *good is right.*

2. Correct standards of life shall, as far as possible, be presented.
A *wide knowledge of life and of living* is made possible through
the film. When right standards are consistently presented, the
motion picture exercises the most powerful influences. It builds
character, develops right ideals, inculcates correct principles,
and all this in attractive story form.

   If motion pictures consistently *hold up for admiration high types
of characters* and present stories that will affect lives for the
better, they can become the most powerful natural force for the
improvement of mankind.

3. Law, natural or human, shall not be ridiculed, nor shall sympathy be created for its violation.

By *natural law* is understood the law which is written in the hearts of all mankind, the great underlying principles of right and justice dictated by conscience.

By *human law* is understood the law written by civilized nations.

1. *The presentation of crimes* against the law is *often necessary* for the carrying out of the plot. But the presentation must not throw sympathy with the crime as against the law nor with the criminal as against those who punish him.

2. *The courts of the land* should not be presented as unjust. This does not mean that a single court may not be represented as unjust, much less that a single court official must not be presented this way. But the court system of the country must not suffer as a result of this presentation.

REASONS UNDERLYING PARTICULAR APPLICATIONS

1. *Sin and evil* enter into the story of human beings and hence in themselves *are valid dramatic material.*

2. In the use of this material, it must be distinguished between *sin which repels* by its very nature, and *sins which often attract.*

   a) In the first class come murder, most theft, many legal crimes, lying, hypocrisy, cruelty, etc.

   b) In the second class come sex sins, sins and crimes of apparent heroism, such as banditry, daring thefts, leadership in evil, organized crime, revenge, etc.

   The first class needs less care in treatment, as sins and crimes of this class are naturally unattractive. The audience instinctively condemns all such and is repelled.

   Hence the important objective must be to avoid the hardening of the audience, especially of those who are young and impressionable, to the thought and fact of crime. People can become accustomed even to murder, cruelty, brutality, and repellent crimes, if these are too frequently repeated.

   The second class needs great care in handling, as the response of human nature to their appeal is obvious. This is treated more fully below.

3. A careful distinction can be made between films intended for *general distribution,* and films intended for use in theatres restricted to a *limited audience.* Themes and plots quite appropriate for the latter would be altogether out of place and dangerous in the former.

Note: The practice of using a general theatre and limiting its patronage during the showing of a certain film to "Adults Only" is not completely satisfactory and is only partially effective.

However, maturer minds may easily understand and accept without harm subject matter in plots which do younger people positive harm.

Hence: if there should be created a special type of theatre, catering exclusively to an adult audience, for plays of this character (plays with problem themes, difficult discussions, and maturer treatment) it would seem to afford an outlet, which does not now exist, for pictures unsuitable for general distribution but permissible for exhibition to a restricted audience.

I. Crimes Against the Law

The *treatment of crimes* against the law must not:
1. *Teach methods* of crime.
2. *Inspire potential criminals* with a desire for imitation.
3. *Make criminals seem heroic* and justified.

Revenge in modern times shall not be justified. In lands and ages of less developed civilization and moral principles, revenge may sometimes be presented. This would be the case especially in places where no law exists to cover the crime because of which revenge is committed.

Because of its evil consequences, *the drug traffic* should not be presented in any form. The existence of the trade should not be brought to the attention of audiences.

The use of liquor should never be excessively presented. In scenes from American life, the necessities of plot and proper characterization alone justify its use. And in this case, it should be shown with moderation.

II. Sex

Out of regard for the sanctity of marriage and the home, the *triangle*, that is, the love of a third party for one already married, needs careful handling. The treatment should not throw sympathy against marriage as an institution.

Scenes of passion must be treated with an honest acknowledgment of human nature and its normal reactions. Many scenes cannot be presented without arousing dangerous emotions on the part of the immature, the young, or the *criminal classes.*

Even within the limits of *pure love,* certain facts have been universally regarded by lawmakers as outside the limits of safe presentation.

In the case of *impure love,* the love which society has always regarded as wrong and which has been banned by divine law, the following are important:

1. Impure love must not be presented as *attractive and beautiful.*

2. It must *not* be the subject of *comedy or farce,* or treated as material *for laughter.*

3. It must *not* be presented in such a way as *to arouse passion* or morbid curiosity on the part of the audience.

4. It must *not* be made to seem *right and permissible.*

5. In general, it must *not* be *detailed* in method and manner.

III. Vulgarity; IV. Obscenity; and V. Profanity hardly need further explanation than is contained in the Code.

VI. COSTUME

General principles:

1. *The effect of nudity or semi-nudity* upon the normal man or woman, and much more upon the young and upon immature persons, has been honestly recognized by all lawmakers and moralists.

2. Hence the fact that the nude or semi-nude body may be *beautiful* does not make its use in the films moral. For, in addition to its beauty, the effect of the nude or semi-nude body on the normal individual must be taken into consideration.

3. Nudity or semi-nudity used simply to put a *"punch"* into a picture comes under the head of immoral actions. It is immoral in its effect on the average audience.

4. Nudity can never be permitted as being *necessary for the plot.* Semi-nudity must not result in undue or indecent exposures.

5. *Transparent* or *translucent materials* and silhouette are frequently more suggestive than actual exposure.

VII. DANCES

Dancing in general is recognized as an *art* and as a *beautiful* form of expressing human emotions.

But dances which suggest or represent sexual actions, whether performed solo or with two or more; dances intended to excite the emotional reaction of an audience; dances with movement of the breasts and excessive body movements while the feet are stationary violate decency and are wrong.

VIII. RELIGION

The reason why ministers of religion may not be comic characters or villains is simply because the attitude taken toward them may easily become the attitude taken toward religion in general. Religion is lowered in the minds of the audience because of the lowering of the audience's respect for a minister.

IX. LOCATIONS

Certain places are so closely and thoroughly associated with sexual life or with sexual sin that their use must be carefully limited.

X. NATIONAL FEELINGS

The just rights, history, and feelings of any nation are entitled to most careful consideration and respectful treatment.

XI. TITLES

As the title of a picture is the brand on that particular type of goods, it must conform to the ethical practices of all such honest business.

XII. REPELLENT SUBJECTS

Such subjects are occasionally necessary for the plot. Their treatment must never offend good taste nor injure the sensibilities of an audience.

THE TELEVISION CODE OF THE NATIONAL ASSOCIATION OF BROADCASTERS

PREAMBLE

TELEVISION IS SEEN and heard in every type of American home. These homes include children and adults of all ages, embrace all races and all varieties of religious faith, and reach those of every educational background. It is the responsibility of television to bear constantly in mind that the audience is primarily a home audience, and consequently that television's relationship to the viewers is that between guest and host.

The revenues from advertising support the free, competitive American system of telecasting, and make available to the eyes and ears of the American people the finest programs of information, education, culture, and entertainment. By law the television broadcaster is responsible for the programming of his station. He, however, is obligated to bring his positive responsibility for excellence and good taste in programming to bear upon all who have a hand in the production of programs, including networks, sponsors, producers of film and of live programs, advertising agencies, and talent agencies.

The American businesses which utilize television for conveying their advertising messages to the home by pictures with sound, seen free of charge on the home screen, are reminded that their responsibilities are not limited to the sale of goods and the creation of a favorable attitude toward the sponsor by the presentation of entertainment. They include, as well, responsibility for utilizing television to bring the best programs, regardless of kind, into American homes.

Television, and all who participate in it are jointly accountable to the American public for respect for the special needs of children, for community responsibility, for the advancement of education and culture, for the acceptability of the program materials chosen, for decency and decorum in production, and for propriety in advertising. This responsibility cannot be discharged by any given group of programs, but can be discharged only through the highest standards of respect for the American home, applied to every moment of every program presented by television.

In order that television programming may best serve the public interest, viewers should be encouraged to make their criticisms and positive suggestions known to the television broadcasters. Parents in particular should be urged to see to it that out of the richness of television fare, the best programs are brought to the attention of their children.

ADVANCEMENT OF EDUCATION AND CULTURE

1. Commercial television provides a valuable means of augmenting the educational and cultural influences of schools, institutions of higher learning, the home, the church, museums, foundations, and other institutions devoted to education and culture.
2. It is the responsibility of a television broadcaster to call upon such institutions for counsel and cooperation and to work with them on the best methods of presenting educational and cultural materials by television. It is further the responsibility of stations, networks, advertising agencies and sponsors consciously to seek opportunities for introducing into telecasts factual materials which will aid in the enlightenment of the American public.
3. Education via television may be taken to mean that process by which the individual is brought toward informed adjustment to his society. Television is also responsible for the presentation of overtly instructional and cultural programs, scheduled so as to reach the viewers who are naturally drawn to such programs, and produced so as to attract the largest possible audience.
4. In furthering this realization, the television broadcaster:
   (a) Should be thoroughly conversant with the educational and cultural needs and desires of the community served.
   (b) Should affirmatively seek out responsible and accountable educational and cultural institutions of the community with a view toward providing opportunities for the instruction and enlightenment of the viewers.

(c) Should provide for reasonable experimentation in the development of programs specifically directed to the advancement of the community's culture and education.

ACCEPTABILITY OF PROGRAM MATERIALS

Program materials should enlarge the horizons of the viewer, provide him with wholesome entertainment, afford helpful stimulation, and remind him of the responsibilities which the citizen has toward his society. Furthermore:

(a) (i) Profanity, obscenity, smut, and vulgarity are forbidden, even when likely to be understood only by part of the audience. From time to time, words which have been acceptable acquire undesirable meanings, and telecasters should be alert to eliminate such words.

(ii) The Television Code Review Board shall maintain and issue to subscribers, from time to time, a continuing list of specific words and phrases which should not be used in keeping with this subsection. This list, however, shall not be considered as all-inclusive.

(b) (i) Attacks on religion and religious faiths are not allowed.

(ii) Reverence is to mark any mention of the name of God, His attributes, and powers.

(iii) When religious rites are included in other than religious programs, the rites are accurately presented, and the ministers, priests, and rabbis portrayed in their callings are vested with the dignity of their office and under no circumstances are to be held up to ridicule.

(c) (i) Contests may not constitute a lottery.

(ii) Any telecasting designed to "buy" the television audience by requiring it to listen and/or view in hope of reward, rather than for the quality of the program, should be avoided (see Contests, page 647).

(d) Respect is maintained for the sanctity of marriage and the value of the home. Divorce is not treated casually nor justified as a solution for marital problems.

(e) Illicit sex relations are not treated as commendable.

(f) Sex crimes and abnormalities are generally unacceptable as program material.

(g) Drunkenness and narcotic addiction are never presented as desirable or prevalent.

(h)   The administration of illegal drugs will not be displayed.

(i)   The use of liquor in program content shall be de-emphasized. The consumption of liquor in American life, when not required by the plot or for proper characterization, shall not be shown.

(j)   The use of gambling devices or scenes necessary to the development of plot or as appropriate background is acceptable only when presented with discretion and in moderation, and in a manner which would not excite interest in, or foster, betting nor be instructional in nature. Telecasts of actual sport programs at which on-the-scene betting is permitted by law should be presented in a manner in keeping with federal, state, and local laws, and should concentrate on the subject as a public sporting event.

(k)   In reference to physical or mental afflictions and deformities, special precautions must be taken to avoid ridiculing sufferers from similar ailments and offending them or members of their families.

(l)   Exhibitions of fortune-telling, astrology, phrenology, palm-reading, and numerology are acceptable only when required by a plot or the theme of a program, and then the presentation should be developed in a manner designed not to foster superstition or excite interest or belief in these subjects.

(m)   Televised drama shall not simulate news or special events in such a way as to mislead or alarm (*see News, pages 641-42*).

(n)   Legal, medical, and other professional advice, diagnosis, and treatment will be permitted only in conformity with law and recognized ethical and professional standards.

(o)   The presentation of cruelty, greed, and selfishness as worthy motivations is to be avoided.

(p)   Unfair exploitation of others for personal gain shall not be presented as praiseworthy.

(q)   Criminality shall be presented as undesirable and unsympathetic. The condoning of crime and the treatment of the commission of crime in a frivolous, cynical, or callous manner is unacceptable.

(r)   The presentation of techniques of crime in such detail as to invite imitation shall be avoided.

(s)   The use of horror for its own sake will be eliminated; the use of visual or aural effects which would shock or alarm the viewer, and the detailed presentation of brutality or physical agony by sight or by sound are not permissible.

(t)   Law enforcement shall be upheld, and the officers of the law are to be portrayed with respect and dignity.

(u)   The presentation of murder or revenge as a motive for murder shall not be presented as justifiable.

(v)   Suicide as an acceptable solution for human problems is prohibited.

(w)   The exposition of sex crimes will be avoided.

(x)   The appearances or dramatization of persons featured in actual crime news will be permitted only in such light as to aid law enforcement or to report the news event.

RESPONSIBILITY TOWARD CHILDREN

1. The education of children involves giving them a sense of the world at large. Crime, violence, and sex are a part of the world they will be called upon to meet, and a certain amount of proper presentation of such is helpful in orienting the child to his social surroundings. However, violence and illicit sex shall not be presented in an attractive manner, nor to an extent such as will lead a child to believe that they play a greater part in life than they do. They should not be presented without indications of the resultant retribution and punishment.

2. It is not enough that only those programs which are intended for viewing by children shall be suitable to the young and immature. (*Attention is called to the general items listed under Acceptability of Program Materials, page 638.*) Television is responsible for insuring that programs of all sorts which occur during the times of day when children may normally be expected to have the opportunity of viewing television shall exercise care in the following regards:

   (a) In affording opportunities for cultural growth as well as for wholesome entertainment.

(b) In developing programs to foster and promote the commonly accepted moral, social, and ethical ideals characteristic of American life.

(c) In reflecting respect for parents, for honorable behavior, and for the constituted authorities of the American community.

(d) In eliminating reference to kidnapping of children or threats of kidnapping.

(e) In avoiding material which is excessively violent or would create morbid suspense, or other undesirable reactions in children.

(f) In exercising particular restraint and care in crime or mystery episodes involving children or minors.

DECENCY AND DECORUM IN PRODUCTION

1. The costuming of all performers shall be within the bounds of propriety, and shall avoid such exposure or such emphasis on anatomical detail as would embarrass or offend home viewers.

2. The movements of dancers, actors, or other performers shall be kept within the bounds of decency, and lewdness and impropriety shall not be suggested in the positions assumed by performers.

3. Camera angles shall avoid such views of performers as to emphasize anatomical details indecently.

4. Racial or nationality types shall not be shown on television in such a manner as to ridicule the race or nationality.

5. The use of locations closely associated with sexual life or with sexual sin must be governed by good taste and delicacy.

COMMUNITY RESPONSIBILITY

A television broadcaster and his staff occupy a position of responsibility in the community and should conscientiously endeavor to be acquainted fully with its needs and characteristics in order better to serve the welfare of its citizens.

TREATMENT OF NEWS AND PUBLIC EVENTS

News

1. A television station's new schedule should be adequate and well balanced.

2. News reporting should be factual, fair, and without bias.

3. Commentary and analysis should be clearly identified as such.
4. Good taste should prevail in the selection and handling of news:
   Morbid, sensational, or alarming details not essential to the factual report, especially in connection with stories of crime or sex, should be avoided. News should be telecast in such a manner as to avoid panic and unnecessary alarm.
5. At all times, pictorial and verbal material for both news and comment should conform to other sections of these standards, wherever such sections are reasonably applicable.
6. Pictorial material should be chosen with care and not presented in a misleading manner.
7. A television broadcaster should exercise due care in his supervision of content, format, and presentation of newscasts originated by his station, and in his selection of newscasters, commentators, and analysts.
8. A television broadcaster should exercise particular discrimination in the acceptance, placement, and presentation of advertising in news programs so that such advertising should be clearly distinguishable from the news content.
9. A television broadcaster should not present fictional events or other non-news material as authentic news telecasts or announcements nor should he permit dramatizations in any program which would give the false impression that the dramatized material constitutes news. Expletives (presented aurally or pictorially) such as "flash" or "bulletin" and statements such as "we interrupt this program to bring you . . ." should be reserved specifically for newsroom use. However, a television broadcaster may properly exercise discretion in the use in non-news programs of words or phrases which do not necessarily imply that the material following is a news release.

PUBLIC EVENTS

1. A television broadcaster has an affirmative responsibility at all times to be informed of public events and to provide coverage consonant with the ends of an informed and enlightened citizenry.
2. Because of the nature of events open to the public, the treatment of such events by a television broadcaster should be effected in a manner to provide for adequate and informed coverage as well as good taste in presentation.

CONTROVERSIAL PUBLIC ISSUES

1. Television provides a valuable forum for the expression of responsible views on public issues of a controversial nature. In
keeping therewith the television broadcaster should seek out and
develop with accountable individuals, groups, and organizations,
programs relating to controversial public issues of import to its
fellow citizens; and to give fair representation to opposing sides
of issues which materially affect the life or welfare of a substantial segment of the public.
2. The provision of time for this purpose should be guided by the
following principles:
   (a) Requests by individuals, groups, or organizations for time
       to discuss their views on controversial public issues should
       be considered on the basis of their individual merits and in
       the light of the contribution which the use requested would
       make to the public interest and to a well-balanced program
       structure.
   (b) Programs devoted to the discussion of controversial public
       issues should be identified as such and should not be pre-
       sented in a manner which would mislead listeners or viewers
       to believe that the program is purely of an entertainment,
       news, or other character.

POLITICAL TELECASTS

Political telecasts should be clearly identified as such and should
not be presented by a television broadcaster in a manner which
would mislead listeners or viewers to believe that the program is
of any other character.

RELIGIOUS PROGRAMS

1. It is the responsibility of a television broadcaster to make available to the community as part of a well-balanced program schedule adequate opportunity for religious presentations.
2. The following principles should be followed in the treatment of
such programs:
   (a) Telecasting which reaches men of all creeds simultaneously
       should avoid attacks upon religion.
   (b) Religious programs should be presented respectfully and
       accurately and without prejudice or ridicule.

(c) Religious programs should be presented by responsible individuals, groups, and organizations.

(d) Religious programs should place emphasis on broad religious truths, excluding the presentation of controversial or partisan views not directly or necessarily related to religion or morality.

3. In the allocation of time for telecasts of religious programs it is recommended that the television station use its best efforts to apportion such time fairly among the representative faith groups of its community.

PRESENTATION OF ADVERTISING

1. Ever mindful of the role of television as a guest in the home, a television broadcaster should exercise unceasing care to supervise the form in which advertising material is presented over his facilities. Since television is a developing medium involving methods and techniques distinct from those of radio, it may be desirable from time to time to review and revise the presently suggested practices:

(a) Advertising messages should be presented with courtesy and good taste; disturbing or annoying material should be avoided; every effort should be made to keep the advertising message in harmony with the content and general tone of the program in which it appears.

(b) A sponsor's advertising messages should be confined within the framework of the sponsor's program structure. A television broadcaster should seek to avoid the use of commercial announcements which are divorced from the program either by preceding the introduction of the program (as in the case of so-called "cow-catcher" announcements) or by following the apparent sign-off of the program (as in the case of so-called "trailer" announcements). To this end, the program itself should be announced and clearly identified before the sponsor's advertising material is first used and should be signed off after the sponsor's advertising material is last used.

(c) Advertising copy should contain no claims intended to disparage competitors, competing products, or other industries, professions, or institutions.

(d) Since advertising by television is a dynamic technique, a television broadcaster should keep under surveillance new advertising devices so that the spirit and purpose of these standards are fulfilled.

(e) Television broadcasters should exercise the utmost care and discrimination with regard to advertising material, including content, placement, and presentation, near or adjacent to programs designed for children. No considerations of expediency should be permitted to impinge upon the vital responsibility toward children and adolescents, which is inherent in television, and which must be recognized and accepted by all advertisers employing television.

(f) Television advertisers should be encouraged to devote portions of their allotted advertising messages and program time to the support of worthy causes in the public interest in keeping with the highest ideals of the free competitive system.

(g) A charge for television time to churches and religious bodies is not recommended.

ACCEPTABILITY OF ADVERTISERS AND PRODUCTS—GENERAL

1. A commercial television broadcaster makes his facilities available for the advertising of products and services and accepts commercial presentations for such advertising. However, a television broadcaster should, in recognition of his responsibility to the public, refuse the facilities of his station to an advertiser where he has good reason to doubt the integrity of the advertiser, the truth of the advertising representations, or the compliance of the advertiser with the spirit and purpose of all applicable legal requirements. Moreover, in consideration of the laws and customs of the communities served, each television broadcaster should refuse his facilities to the advertisement of products and services, or the use of advertising scripts, which the station has good reason to believe would be objectionable to a substantial and responsible segment of the community. The foregoing principles should be applied with judgment and flexibility, taking into consideration the characteristics of the medium and the form and content of the particular presentation. In general, because television broadcasting is designed for the home and the family, including children, the following principles should govern the business classifications listed below:

(a) The advertising of hard liquor should not be accepted.

(b) The advertising of beer and wines is acceptable only when presented in the best of good taste and discretion, and is acceptable subject to federal and local laws.

(c) Advertising by institutions or enterprises which in their offers of instruction imply promises of employment or make exaggerated claims for the opportunities awaiting those who enroll for courses is generally unacceptable.

(d) The advertising of firearms and fireworks is acceptable only subject to federal and local laws.

(e) The advertising of fortune-telling, occultism, spiritualism, astrology, phrenology, palm-reading, numerology, mind-reading, or character-reading is not acceptable.

(f) Because all products of a personal nature create special problems, such products, when accepted, should be treated with especial emphasis on ethics and the canons of good taste; however, the advertising of intimately personal products which are generally regarded as unsuitable conversational topics in mixed social groups is not acceptable.

(g) The advertising of tip sheets, race track publications, or organizations seeking to advertise for the purpose of giving odds or promoting betting or lotteries is unacceptable.

2. Diligence should be exercised to the end that advertising copy accepted for telecasting complies with pertinent federal, state, and local laws.

3. An advertiser who markets more than one product should not be permitted to use advertising copy devoted to an acceptable product for purposes of publicizing the brand name or other identification of a product which is not acceptable.

ADVERTISING OF MEDICAL PRODUCTS

1. The advertising of medical products presents considerations of intimate and far-reaching importance to the consumer, and the following principles and procedures should apply in the advertising thereof:

(a) A television broadcaster should not accept advertising material which in his opinion offensively describes or dramatizes distress or morbid situations involving ailments, by spoken word, sound, or visual effects.

(b) Because of the personal nature of the advertising of medical products, claims that a product will effect a cure and the indiscriminate use of such words as "safe," "without risk," "harmless," or terms of similar meaning should not be accepted in the advertising of medical products on television stations.

CONTESTS

1. Contests should offer the opportunity to all contestants to win on the basis of ability and skill, rather than chance.
2. All contest details, including rules, eligibility requirements, opening and termination dates should be clearly and completely announced and/or shown, or easily accessible to the viewing public, and the winners' names should be released and prizes awarded as soon as possible after the close of the contest.
3. When advertising is accepted which requests contestants to submit items of product identification or other evidence of purchase of product, reasonable facsimiles thereof should be made acceptable.
4. All copy pertaining to any contest (except that which is required by law) associated with the exploitation or sale of the sponsor's product or service, and all references to prizes or gifts offered in such connection should be considered a part of and included in the total time allowances as herein provided.

PREMIUMS AND OFFERS

1. Full details of proposed offers should be required by the television broadcaster for investigation and approval before the first announcement of the offer is made to the public.
2. A final date for the termination of an offer should be announced as far in advance as possible.
3. Before accepting for telecast offers involving a monetary consideration, a television broadcaster should satisfy himself as to the integrity of the advertiser and the advertiser's willingness to honor complaints indicating dissatisfaction with the premium by returning the monetary consideration.
4. There should be no misleading descriptions or visual representations of any premiums or gifts which would distort or enlarge their value in the minds of the listeners.
5. Assurances should be obtained from the advertiser that premiums offered are not harmful to person or property.
6. Premiums should not be approved which appeal to superstition on the basis of "luck-bearing" powers or otherwise.

WHO IS RESPONSIBLE FOR THE QUALITY
OF MASS COMMUNICATIONS?

BY WILBUR SCHRAMM

This selection, by the editor of this volume, was published as the concluding chapter of his book, *Responsibility in Mass Communication*,
published by Harper and Brothers in 1957. It is published here by permission of the publisher, who holds copyright.

THERE ARE only three great instruments which society may use to
encourage or prod the mass media to responsible performance.
These are government and its various regulatory bodies, national,
state, and local; the media themselves, their individual personnel,
and their formal and informal associations and administrative organizations; and the general public, with its formal and informal
organizations and associations.

If we ask where, among these, responsibility lies for the kind of
mass communication we have in this country, and for any change
we want to bring about in mass communication, then quite clearly
the answer is that responsibility is shared. Neither government, nor
the media, nor the public can be counted on to do the job alone,
and on the other hand, none of them is exempt from responsibility
for doing it. What we are looking for . . . is a desirable balance of
responsibility among them. . . .

Let us now consider the responsibility of the public.

The Commission on Freedom of the Press concluded that the
more the media and the public are willing to do toward insuring a

free and responsible communication system, the less the government will have to do; and that in general the "outside forces" of law and public opinion can check bad aspects of media performance, but only the media themselves can bring about good performance.

It is hard to disagree with these statements, but I depart somewhat from the Commission's emphasis. It seems to me quite clear that the media have the chief responsibility. If they do not assume it, if they do not voluntarily provide us with the public service on a high professional level which our society requires, then I do not see how our communication problem can be solved without to some extent going out of bounds, as we have defined the bounds of desirable action.

What the media do not do for us they invite the government to step in and do or cause to be done. This, in our view, is a dangerous, an ominous kind of action. For that reason, I have urged that the government "keep its hands off" wherever it can, that it put down the temptation to step in and set things right, that it set strict limits on the kind of actions it will take with reference to mass communication, and that these actions should be chiefly facilitating, rather than restrictive ones.

I have therefore tended to put somewhat more responsibility on both the media and the public than did the Commission. Whereas the media must assume the central responsibility and do the job, I envisage the public as being prime movers in the communication dynamic. It is my firm belief that the public can come pretty close to having whatever kind of mass communication system it wants. Of course, this requires that it know what it wants and say what it wants. I do not accept the old idea that the mass-media public is a vegetable. I think that the "great audience" can be active rather than passive, that it can assay its needs and be articulate in getting them. Granted those assumptions, then it seems to me that the people hold the balance of power in determining the shape of their system and the service it gives them.

The listening, viewing, reading public underestimates its power. The media heads do not underestimate it. I have seen very few media men who look on the public as a mass to be molded and say, "This year we shall teach them to like thus and so." Rather, they are deeply concerned with what the public will be interested in, what the public wants and *will* like, and one of their greatest problems is trying to find out these things.

Anyone who looks at mass communication as a social institution cannot fail to note the tremendous push and pull of public interests and tastes on the institution. The program pattern of the networks vibrates like a windharp to the breeze from the monthly program ratings. New films go out to "sneak" previews, sample public reaction, and go back to the cutting room. One hundred letters to a network will often bring a review of policy; even fewer letters to a station will lead it to review a program or a program structure. One visit of a serious committee to a newspaper editor will make him think hard about what he is doing, even though he will be crusty about making promises. The motion picture industry has been in greater fear of boycotts than of censorship. Its code is spotted throughout with "special legislation" intended to appease this or that group and avoid boycott or public criticism.

In an earlier part of the book we mentioned how a comparatively slight outpouring of public indignation forced a network to take a well-known personality off the air because he had offended the friends of "Silent Night." Letters to the Federal Communications Commission get into station files, and they have a way of turning up embarrassingly in hearings. Listeners' councils have been able in many cases to exert a real and salutary influence on the kind of programs a local station carries. And underneath all this is the great groundswell of audience and attention, which none of the media can ignore. A newspaper publisher, who may resist what he considers a special interest group or special pleading, will pay attention if his circulation begins to fall off. A network or a station will perk up when the ratings begin to drop. A film studio is keenly aware what kind of business its pictures are doing. A magazine is compelled to worry when its newsstand sales fall off, or its readership studies indicate little interest in a certain part of its content.

Ultimately, therefore, the audience calls the tune. The people hold the trumps. And the only question is whether they will play their cards.

Is it realistic to hope that the public, the great audience, will seize this opportunity? This, of course, is the fundamental problem posed by the coming of bigness and fewness to the media. When media were many and audiences were small; when only a small percentage of the population could read, and only a small elite group formed the reading audience for most newspapers, magazines, and books; when the entertainment media were small and intimate—then there was a close connection between the men who made the media and their audience. There was a quick and vigorous feedback of demands and judgments. The audiences themselves felt the closeness of their relationship and took a lively interest in what the media were doing. The readers knew the editors. The performers knew some of their audiences. But now that audiences have grown so large that they include almost the whole population, when a great anonymity has settled over them, and they become known to the media only in terms of program ratings or percentages of readership or circulation figures—is there a realistic hope that some of this liveness and intimacy can be recaptured?

Of course, CBS or Metro-Goldwyn-Mayer or the *Reader's Digest* is unlikely ever to recapture the relationship which the *Dial* maintained with its audience when that influential magazine had 200 subscribers, most of them known personally to the editor, Margaret Fuller. It is certainly unrealistic to expect that situation to recur except in the case of a little magazine subsidized to serve a coterie. But between that situation and the far end of the scale, at which audiences are a kind of anonymous mass, I think it is clearly realistic and possible for the audience of mass communication to move a long way up the scale from anonymity toward personality. It seems to me clearly possible for the great audience to become a live, responsive, discriminating audience, to make its opinions and wishes known to the media, and in its own quiet way to enforce those opinions and wishes on the media. And if it should appear that in this audience there are a number of levels of taste and kinds of need, then I think it is clearly possible for the audience to insist that the media serve those different tastes and needs, instead of ladling up an insipid common-denominator broth which appeals somewhat to each and satisfies none.

The basic responsibility of the public, therefore, is to make itself, as far as possible, an alert, discriminating audience. This may require a somewhat different habit of mind from the one we most commonly see on the part of many individuals who by virtue of position or education might be expected to be the leaders of and spokesmen for the public in their demands upon the media. This common attitude—"Oh, I never watch television except when there's something like a political convention on—it's just trash!"—is fundamentally an irresponsible attitude. It neglects the fact that television doesn't *have* to be all trash, if indeed, it is. Television is potentially one of our greatest windows on the world. It is one of the best ways in which we could expand our horizons, bring a sense of reality to faraway events, make a more informed judgment on public figures, share the lectures and demonstrations at our greatest universities, see the kind of opera, ballet, drama, museums, and concert artists formerly available only to a few fortunate people, most of them in great cities. If television isn't being used that way, what a great social waste it is! What a loss we are suffering! And whose fault is it? Basically, it is the fault of the people who don't watch it and don't do anything about improving it.

The greatest newsgathering services man has ever devised are connected to our home-town newspapers. Through wire services these newspapers are connected to every corner of the world where news is being made. A statement by Nasser in Egypt is perhaps twenty minutes away from each of our newspapers. An incident beside the Iron or the Bamboo Curtain is, at the most, thirty minutes away from our newsrooms. A full interpretation of Mr. Dulles' latest statement is available if a few persons in Washington or New York or on a university campus are given a few hours to think about it. In that situation, have we any right to say, as so many of us do: "I can't get any picture of what's happening in the world, from our paper; it carries only six or seven foreign news stories a day"? Or, "I can't understand what's really going on in national politics or this international situation. We never get any background." Have we any right to say that, if we never complain to the editor? He has the space to put in more world news, more background, if he thinks his audience wants it. He is putting that space into sports, or features, or society, or some other news. If he thought there was a serious demand for more world news or background, he would carry it.

The first requisite, therefore, is an alert, interested audience. This implies that we pay some attention to our media. We read, view, listen. We find out what is in the media. We don't wash our hands of the media in the supposition that they are being patterned for somebody else.

Then we try to make ourselves a discriminating audience. We give some thought to what the media *might* be giving us. We talk about the media with our friends. Perhaps we organize listeners' councils or readers' groups to talk about what we find in the media. We try to see that our schools give some attention to the question how to use the media intelligently; there are good textbooks now on such subjects as "How to read a newspaper," and many schools are helping their students to make best use of the mass media, just as they prepare them to make use of other parts of human experience. After all, these young people will be giving perhaps five hours a day, or nearly a third of their waking time, to mass media. This is too large a segment of life to use wastefully. And so we try to see that our young people have a systematic introduction to the media. We try to read newspaper or magazine criticism of the other mass media, just as we read book reviews. And in every way we try to build into ourselves some standards for judgment of what we see, hear, and read.

Another way in which we can develop discrimination is by controlling our attendance upon the media. If we don't want all movies to be made as though for children, we can keep our children away from *some* movies. If we don't want all television to be filtered out so as not to be above the sensibilities and sensitivities of *any* member of the family, then let us exercise some discrimination about what members of the family watch television at a given time. This is partly our responsibility. We can't expect the media to serve the interests of all kinds of people and displease or offend none unless we do so something about getting the right kind of people to the media at the right time.

Then the next step in our responsibility is to make our views known to the media. One way to do this is simply by reflecting in our patronage our discrimination in what we subscribe to, what we attend, what we view or listen to. If enough of us do this, it will have an effect. But this method sometimes cuts off our nose to spite our face. For example, if we stop buying our home-town newspaper because it carries only seven foreign news stories a day, that will lose us *all* the local news. The big stick is not the best way. A better way is to tell our media what we do and don't like about them, and what would make us like them better.

This we can do through letters—to the editor, to the station, to the network, to the theater, or to the studio. The more individual these letters are, the better. The media tend to fill their wastebaskets with letters which are all written in about the same words and therefore reveal that they are inspired by some pressure group. But individual letters are read and valued. So are individual contacts, when those are possible. These help to tell media employees, and especially media heads, what you think of their product. If you feel seriously enough about it, you can call on the editor or the station manager or the theater owner. You can certainly take advantage of meetings or social events or casual contacts to talk to media people. They appreciate these little feedbacks, and over the course of weeks such contacts add up to a picture of what the public wants and thinks.

Things like this you can do informally and individually. Or you can organize and go about it more formally. We have occasionally in this book said unkind things about pressure groups, but there is nothing in our political philosophy to keep audiences from organizing whenever and however they wish, to communicate more effectively with the media. Listeners' councils, where they have been organized, have been very effective in this way. Organizations like the League of Women Voters or the Association of University Women have sometimes made the media their chief discussion topic and have sent delegations or resolutions to represent their opinions and needs to media heads. Sometimes community groups, or student groups, or church groups have arisen spontaneously because of dissatisfaction with some aspect of the media. Often these groups have asked newspapermen or broadcasters or theatre operators, or magazine salesmen, to speak to their meetings, in order to get their side of the story and convey the feelings of the group.

There are already a number of well-organized groups active in the field, many of them with professional staffs watching the media, trying to keep out of them material offensive to the particular group. Such are, for example, the Legion of Decency, the Chamber of Commerce, the American Legion, et cetera. There is nothing wrong with this. Any group has a right to organize and tell the media what it thinks of them. But remember that our communication system is built on the theory of a free market place of ideas. It will not work right unless *all* viewpoints on a controversial question are freely presented.

Therefore, there is a kind of pressure-group activity which is as clearly out of bounds as is government interference with the media. I mean the kind of informal censorship which tries to remake the shape of the media in the image of one group's needs and sensitivities, at the cost of all other groups. The news about Christmas time, 1956, contained what may be an example of this kind of activity. Station WGN-TV, of Chicago, canceled the world première showing on television of the film *Martin Luther*. The station said the film was canceled because of the "emotional reaction" of the public to its plan to show the picture. This "emotional reaction," said the *Christian Century*, took the form of a telephone blitzkrieg "organized by Roman Catholics to keep WGN telephones humming with protests." The Chancellor of the Chicago archdiocese said that the Church had made no official representations to WGN-TV whatsoever, and that if any Catholics had protested it was an individual matter. It was claimed that the film was "down-right insulting" to Catholics.

Now I have neither investigated behind these facts nor seen the picture. It is a fact, however, that the film was shown in many theaters without any substantial opposition. If the facts are as suggested—an organized campaign by members of one religious sect to keep off the air a film about the founder of other religious sects—then this is a questionable kind of pressure-group activity. There could be no possible objection to one church exerting discipline over its own members and keeping them away from a theater or from watching a television program. But when such a group acts to deprive other groups of opportunities they very much desire in the mass media, and which are not obscene or otherwise clearly censorable, then it would seem that this is restricting the free market place, and should be resisted both by the media and the public.

As I say, the Chicago incident may or may not be an example of this kind of action; I have not thoroughly investigated it. And the particular religious group mentioned is by no means the only group, religious or political, which has been accused of such activity. But whoever does it, it doesn't fit into our system.

Pressure groups, like government, are usually on less dangerous ground when their activity is facilitating, rather than restrictive. That is, they are more helpful when they try to represent the needs of the public than when they speak for the sensitivities of particular groups. But even here caution is needed. We can't expect mass communication to meet all our needs if we depend on a few well-organized groups, each with a special interest, to speak for us. These groups may keep the media free of material which disturbs, and encourage the media to present material which pleases, the Legion, the Chamber, the Roman Catholic Church, or some other organization; but they will not necessarily be concerned that the media carry what the rest of the public wants or needs. The remedy for this situation is not to complain about "pressure groups," but to organize groups to represent our own interests, if these are not being represented. And when the media heads see the full spectrum of public needs and wishes, they will be better able to plan their product.

A further responsibility of the public, it seems to us, is to encourage intelligent criticism of the media. This is not an attack on the media; it is rather a service to media and public alike. Book reviews, for many years, have served not only to sharpen the standards of taste on the part of writer, reader, and editor, but also to call the attention of the public to new books of interest. It is amazing that so little criticism of broadcasting and newspapers has come into being. The influential daily critics of radio and television number less than a handful. No sustained regular criticism of newspapers has ever proved feasible. Yet criticism of this kind is surely a part of the professionalizing and general growing up of the media.

The Commission on Freedom of the Press recommended that "a new and independent agency" should be established to "appraise and report annually upon the performance of the press." By *press* the Commission meant all the mass media. This proposal was received with undisguised horror by the newspapers, and was equated with all sorts of dire threats to press freedom. Yet it is hard to see how such an agency, given a board of distinguished citizens and a competent staff, could really threaten freedom of the press. And it might do a great service, both in scrutinizing the media for the public and in representing to the media the dissatisfactions and unmet needs of the public. Such an agency would, of course, have no governmental connection and would represent the public in general rather than any segment of it. The Commission listed a long series of services such an agency might undertake, among which were the following:

Helping the media "define workable standards of performance";
"Pointing out the inadequacy" of media service in certain areas;
Investigating areas and instances "where minority groups are excluded from reasonable access to the channels of communication";
Examining the "picture of American life" presented abroad by the media;
Investigating charges of "press lying," with particular reference to the persistent misrepresentation of the data required for judging public issues;
Appraising "governmental action affecting communications";
Appraising the "tendencies and characteristics of the various branches of the communications industry";
Encouraging the "establishment of centers of advanced study, research, and criticism in the field of communications at universities";

Encouraging projects which give hope of meeting the needs of special audiences;

Giving "the widest possible publicity and public discussion" to all its findings.

For any one agency, this might be an overambitious assignment. Yet the objective of all of it is simple enough—an agency to represent the interest of the public as a whole, as distinguished from the special interest of groups; to speak for the whole public in a way that the public could never speak as individuals; to observe the work of the media and think about it in terms of the needs and interests of the American public; and finally to report both ways, to the media and to the public, and thus to serve as a valuable communication link between them. To choose the board and staff of such a public agency would be difficult. To outline and restrict its tasks to realistic goals and limits would take a great deal of thinking and some trial. But the result might be very salutary, might result in a much better mutual understanding between the media and their publics, and on the whole would be an excellent project on which a foundation might bet some money.

If such an agency of communication and observation is ever established, it is a responsibility of the public to do it. It should not be established by the government nor by the media, although it should counsel with both the media and government. It should represent public interest at the highest level. So far as the newspaper objection is concerned, it is a good guess that, after the first mechanical reaction of resistance, most of the newspapers and the other media would respect and welcome the new agency.

We said in the preceding chapter that it is a responsibility of the media to help in the establishment of adequate schools for prospective members of the profession, and also university research centers in mass communication. It is certainly a responsibility of the media to concern themselves with these problems and help with them, but the basic responsibility is the public's. The public has to found such organizations at universities, and send able young people to them. Over the next two or three decades the schools of journalism and their related training and research centers can make a profound difference in the level of media personnel. They can do so, that is, if they are used at their full potential which, as we tried to say in the last chapter, is not for vocational training, but for training of a breadth and depth which very few other occupations require.

Another way to say it is that journalism school and other mass communication curricula are not best used when they train students for the first six months of their employment; they should rather prepare their graduates for the years that follow the first six months: not in the skills which enable the young employee to do well at first, but rather in the understandings which enable him to do well throughout his career. There is no reason why he should not learn some skills, too; but, whenever there has to be a choice of time between learning the vocational skills and gaining the broad understanding of society and mass communication's place in it, the time should always be used for the broader and less immediately useful studies. The schools should aim for the long, not the short term; for on his job the new man can much more easily learn the skills of his job than he can learn to understand human beings, social organization, government, economics, and science.

Schools of journalism have been moving in this direction, but they are handicapped by a tradition which began in the land-grant colleges under the example of service to agriculture, and the early leadership of weekly newspapermen who wanted employees they would not have to train. Even now the schools of journalism are unlike other professional or quasi-professional schools in that *they* do not necessarily train the new members of the profession as do medical or law schools; their graduates have to compete on a level with graduates of every other curriculum in the university and with nongraduates of universities. Indeed, the fact that university graduates expect more salary gives an advantage to nongraduates on smaller papers and other media. Therefore, the school of journalism has felt some need to stress, by teaching journalistic techniques, its uniqueness in the university and its close relationship to the newspapers and the broadcasters. Even so, the best schools now build their curricula on a broad grounding of liberal studies in other departments, and this is a tendency which the public should certainly encourage.

Another healthy development is the establishment of research centers and programs in connection with a few schools of journalism and elsewhere in a few universities. This is a long step on the road to professionalization. Without strong research programs in connection with and feeding into schools of medicine, we should still be letting blood for various diseases and treating mental diseases with chains and dungeons. It should be pointed out that both the schools and the research centers in mass communication are essentially a public responsibility.

Another important way in which the public can demonstrate its discriminating concern with mass communication is in the encouragement of new ventures. It is increasingly hard to start anything new in mass communication because of the costs involved. Yet there is increasing need for new ventures, not only to provide a variety in viewpoint, but more important, to serve the needs of groups within the great audience who are not sufficiently served by "common denominator" media content. If the public, or segments of it, want these special services they must make their wants known, and be alert to support, or at least try out, new ventures when they come.

There could be more newspapers covering public affairs in somewhat the way *The New York Times* does, but in other parts of the country, if publishers thought people in sufficient numbers would buy them. There could be more and better community television stations, covering local public affairs and carrying the best in local entertainment and information, if audiences would give them a few dollars per viewer per year. The university radio and television stations would furnish a better service—indeed, they could give a very exciting service—if the public made known to administrations and legislatures that they wanted these activities adequately supported with budgets. There would be more theaters specializing in high-quality films, and more studios making such films for such theaters, if the public would patronize them. The possibility of endowed newspapers or broadcasting stations is a fascinating one, but it is not necessary to have financing from a foundation or a wealthy man in order to bring about superior communications. The thing most needed in order to have new ventures in mass communication is assurance that there is a discriminating public waiting for them, willing to support them.

In another way, too, the public has a peculiar responsibility in regard to mass communication. More nonprofessional members of the public must learn to use the media. There is no excuse for religious broadcasting being less skillful than entertainment broadcasting. There is no reason why the public should permit educational broadcasting to be any less skillful than entertainment broadcasting; yet the educational stations are starved for funds and are therefore unable to train and keep skilled performers. There is no reason why local broadcasting, radio or television, could not be more of a force than it is; for leaders in any community to acquire the basic skills of broadcasting would not be a great task. This implies also that more members of the nonprofessional public should come to understand the media—to learn what can be expected of the newspapers and the broadcasters especially, and how to work with them and make use of their media in the best way.

All this comes back to the question whether we can realistically expect to have a live, articulate, discriminating public concerning itself with mass communication. If so, great things are possible. If not, progress will be slow. For, as I have tried to indicate, responsibility in mass communication is a delicate balance between the media, the government, and the public. The chief responsibility for doing what needs to be done with mass communication is that of the media, but in a sense the basic obligation is with the public. The public's responsibility is to be an active, discriminating audience, to make its needs known to the media, to be helpful as the media try to meet these needs—in other words, to be full partner in the task of making the kind of communication society needs. To the extent that the public is less than a full partner, government and media will fill the gap, and we shall be less sure that we get what we want. For it is the public's own responsibility that is controlling in this case, and if we do not exercise it we deserve only what we get.

In a radio address to America in 1931, and in his usual salty tongue-in-cheek manner, George Bernard Shaw startled some of his listeners with the following proposition: "Every person who owes his life to civilized society," he said, "and who has enjoyed since his childhood its very costly protections and advantages should appear at reasonable intervals before a properly qualified jury to justify his existence, which should be summarily and painlessly terminated if he fails to justify it."

I am not advocating such summary justice. But I should like to suggest that all of us who enjoy the protections and advantages of a free communication system do indeed have some obligation to justify our existence under it. I have been suggesting what that obligation consists of. And if we are not doing enough to justify such protections and advantages, then we certainly face the possibility in this fateful century of having our existence under them summarily but not painlessly terminated.

APPENDIXES

APPENDIX A

MASS COMMUNICATIONS IN OTHER COUNTRIES

IN THE MAIN PART of this book, we have had to concentrate on mass communications in the United States. This should not, however, blind us to the fact there are well-developed systems of mass communication in many other countries of the world. Indeed, in some respects some of these systems are better developed than corresponding media in the United States. For example, a number of countries publish more new book titles per year than does the United States, and a number of countries circulate more copies of newspapers per capita than circulate in the United States. But the United States uses more than half of all the world's supply of newsprint, has about a third of all the radios in the world, and more than half of all the television sets.

What makes the mass media different in different countries? Three characteristics seem to be more useful than others in distinguishing one system from another. These are the national values, the political system, and the degree of economic development of the country.

NATIONAL VALUES

All we need say about national values here is that mass media reflect what people in a nation think is important. For example, for a number of years now one of the most important goals in the Soviet Union has been the socialization and industrial development of the country. Day after day, this has been the subject of the Soviet media. As one travels over the world, one hears on the radios of different countries the kinds of entertainment which are enjoyed and approved by people of those countries; and from place to place, these are often quite different. The national value system, then, will have a lot to do with the *content* of mass media in any given country.

POLITICAL SYSTEMS

The political system will determine what the media are used for, what control is imposed on them, and who owns them and has the right to use them. There are three large groups of nations, according to the kinds of political controls they impose on, and political uses they make of, their mass media. One of these is represented by the United States, most of the countries of Western Europe, Japan, and a few others. This system of political control is sometimes called the *libertarian* system, because its purpose is to keep the mass media as free as possible from government—in fact, to use the media to represent the people in checking on government and criticizing the actions of public officials when they seem to deserve criticism. Therefore, in libertarian countries, the media are usually privately owned (except, sometimes, the radio and television), and almost no government restrictions are put on them except the usual legal constraints on libel, obscenity, and so forth.

The libertarian countries are, for the most, highly industrialized, wealthy, and highly literate nations. It is much easier to maintain a libertarian system in a highly developed civilization of this sort. Most of the less industrialized, less wealthy countries of the world, and some of the more industrialized ones also, maintain what we can call an *authoritarian* political control over their mass media. This often accompanies a national policy of swift economic development, and sometimes a shaky political situation. In these authoritarian systems, the media are ordinarily privately owned (except radio and television) but either formal or informal controls are maintained over them so that they are not able to carry information which might be harmful to the party or individuals in power. Thus, the media do not so directly represent the people as in the libertarian countries. Sometimes permission is required before an individual may start a newspaper or magazine or publish a new book. Sometimes censorship is used to suppress what has been printed, and in some of these countries newspapers have been suppressed, copies of publications confiscated, and editors, publishers, and broadcasters punished by fines, jail terms, or exile. In a number of cases, also, the media are compelled to carry material which the government wants them to carry. This is by no means an uncommon political control over mass communications; indeed, it has been the most common and widespread system since the invention of printing. It was universal until the political changes of the eighteenth and nineteenth centuries in the presently libertarian countries.

The third kind of political control is represented today by the countries of Eastern Europe, the Soviet Union, and mainland China. This we can call the *Soviet totalitarian* system. This is an authoritarian kind of control, but the media are owned by the government and used by the government and the party in power to bring about their objectives. Thus, if the objective of the Soviet Union is to industrialize and socialize the country, the mass media will be used for that purpose just as will any other arm of the state. The people can use some of the media to criticize relatively minor government officials, but not to attack the basic policy or the chief leaders. The content is carefully watched, much of it approved before publication, and any deviations from policy censored.

ECONOMIC DEVELOPMENT

If the national values have a lot to do with media content, and the political system has a lot to do with what the media are used for and who uses them, the economic development of the country determines in large part the *size* of the mass communication system. In a rich country the people will have more money to buy radio and television receivers, publications, and admission tickets. A highly industrialized country will have the expert technicians needed for modern mass media. An industrialized country usually has large urban populations, which are easier to reach by mass media. A wealthy and industrialized country usually has a very high proportion of literates, able to read and interested in news and literature. Therefore, if you will look in the tables below for countries with high income and high literacy you will ordinarily find well-developed mass communication systems.

To illustrate some of the development of mass communications in other countries we have selected 20 nations from the more than 100 which currently report such information. If you look down the following tables, you will see that the first four represent the highly industrialized nations of Western Europe. The next four are Communist countries of Eastern Europe and Asia. Then follow four developing countries of South Asia, three nations of Latin America, three from Africa (including a very new country, Ghana, and the Belgian Congo, which is still a colony), and, from the Western Pacific, Japan and Australia. For all these countries we have collected the latest available figures, which are, for the most part, for 1956 and 1957. In order to make a comparison possible with the United States, we have inserted U.S. figures from the same sources. In the earlier parts of this book, you will have seen data on the United States which is, in many cases, more recent than these figures; but the 1956 and 1957 data make it possible to view the mass media development of all these countries at approximately the same time.

Here, then, are some basic figures. You will be interested to notice how the higher income and literacy figures in the first table are reflected in the size of the systems shown in the second and third tables. In particular, notice the differences among the countries that represent the three general types of political control, and, in the third tables, the striking differences among the per capita figures.

Twenty Countries: Population, Income, and Literacy

	Population (millions)	Per capita National Income * (dollars)	Literacy (percentage)
United Kingdom	50.2	918	99
France	42.8	817	96
West Germany	47.6	567	99
Sweden	7.0	862	99
U.S.S.R.	170.4	†	92
China	582.6	†	65
Poland	25.0	†	93
Bulgaria	7.6	†	75
India	356.9	57	20
Indonesia	60.4	63	20
Thailand	17.4	36	50
Pakistan	75.8	51	20
Argentina	15.9	446	90
Ecuador	3.2	43	50
Mexico	25.8	276	60
Egypt	19.0	131	25
Belgian Congo	12.2	81	30
Ghana	4.1	50	25
Japan	89.3	288	98
Australia	9.0	779	98
United States	**150.7**	**2,280**	**98**

Source: Computed from UN Statistical Yearbook. The figures are for the last year in which comparable data were available from these countries. They are therefore not current, as the reader will notice in the case of the U. S. population figures.

* Figures in this column are highly approximate, because of the different ways of estimating national income, the difficulties in expressing exchange realistically, and the different levels of prices. About all these say is that per capita income in some nations is very low, in others very high, and in still others neither very high nor very low.

† Figures for these countries not available.

Size of Mass Communication Systems

	Daily Newspapers Number	Circulation (millions)	Newsprint Used per Year (thousands of tons)	Radio Number of transmitters	Radio Number of receivers (thousands)	Television Number of transmitters	Television Number of receivers (thousands)	Motion Pictures New feature pictures made per year	Motion Pictures Number of cinemas	Books New titles per year
United Kingdom	114	29.1	972	60	14,434	19	6,570	108	4,325	19,107
France	137	10.7	444	45	10,158	16	442	129	5,756	1,416
West Germany	481	14.7	393	294	14,051	63	703	123	7,108	16,396
Sweden	139	3.4	170	35	3,548	1	2	33	2,396	4,891
U.S.S.R	385	21.5	313	130	20,000	10	700	38	33,312	59,530
China	776	8.0		225	1,500	†	*	12	815	*
Poland	40	4.1	51	24	3,310	1	†	*	654	7,012
Bulgaria	13	1.3	16	6	350	†	†	1	335	2,900
India	330	2.5	83	29	1,076	†	†	286	2,933	18,559
Indonesia	101	0.6	13	25	326	†	†	3	470	1,304
Thailand	30	0.08	14	17	108	1	7	48	120	*
Pakistan	79	0.7	4	13	100	†	†	47	284	*
Argentina	346	3.1	113	64	2,900	1	75	36	1,657	2,435
Ecuador	24	0.2	3	70	50	†	†	1	240	*
Mexico	162	1.3	81	236	1,500	7	100	99	2,460	923
Egypt	50	0.5	25	6	405	†	†	41	358	1,037
Belgian Congo	7	0.03	1	8	17	†	†	*	6	*
Ghana	5	0.1	2	2	21	†	†	*	32	*
Japan	255	35.2	485	186	13,254	15	328	514	5,184	24,541
Australia	53	3.7	266	160	2,051	5	27	4	1,792	596
United States	1,824	56.6	6,380	3,504	150,000	511	42,000	337	19,003	12,589

Source: UN Statistical Handbook, supplemented in a few cases by figures from UNESCO, *World Communications*.

* Figures not available.

† At the time these figures were gathered, no television was listed for these countries. In most of them, however, at least experimental television is under way now.

Per Capita Communication Figures

	Daily Newspaper Circulation (copies per 1,000 people)	Radio Receivers (per 1,000 people)	Movies Attended Per Year (per capita)
United Kingdom	580	288	22
France	250	237	10
West Germany	310	295	15
Sweden	486	507	9
U.S.S.R.	126	117	13
China	14	3	2
Poland	164	132	8
Bulgaria	171	5	5
India	7	3	2
Indonesia	10	5	†
Thailand	5	6	*
Pakistan	9	2	†
Argentina	195	182	7
Ecuador	6	15	*
Mexico	50	58	4
Egypt	26	21	3
Belgian Congo	2	1	†
Ghana	24	5	1
Japan	394	148	10
Australia	411	227	15
United States	**375**	**1,000**	**15**

Source: Computed from the UN Statistical Handbook and UNESCO, *World Communications*.

* Figures not available.   † Less than 0.5.

APPENDIX B

SUGGESTIONS FOR FURTHER READING

GENERAL TITLES

Berelson, Bernard, and Janowitz, Morris. *Reader in Public Opinion and Communication*. Glencoe, 1953. (Collection of scholarly articles and chapters.)

Bryson, Lyman. *The Communication of Ideas*. New York, 1948. (Series of lectures by Lasswell, Mead, others.)

Chapin, Richard. *Mass Communications: A Statistical Analysis*. East Lansing, 1957. (A critical look at the data on the communication industry. Many tables.)

Henry, Nelson. *Mass Media and Education*. Chicago, 1954. (Yearbook written largely by communication scholars.)

Lazarsfeld, Paul, and Stanton, Frank. *Radio Research, 1941*. New York, 1941.

———. *Radio Research, 1942-43*. New York, 1944.

———. *Communications Research, 1948-49*. New York, 1949. (Important collections of research on the media, their audiences, and effects, done mostly at the Bureau of Applied Social Research, Columbia.)

Rosenberg, Bernard, and White, David M. *Mass Culture*. Glencoe, 1956. (Readable collection; criticism and interpretation of the media.)

Schramm, Wilbur. *Communications in Modern Society*. Urbana, 1948. (Papers given at a symposium by Berelson, Nixon, Hovland, others.)

Seldes, Gilbert. *The Great Audience*. New York, 1950.

———. *The Public Arts*. New York, 1956. (Stimulating criticism and interpretation.)

Smith, Bruce, Lasswell, Harold D., and Casey, Ralph. *Propaganda, Communication, and Public Opinion*. (The chief bibliography in the field, but now out of date. Many of the titles have been retained in a new bibliography by Bruce and Chitra Smith, *International Communications*, New York, 1956. Somewhat more limited bibliographies appear every three months in the *Journalism Quarterly*.)

A note on periodicals:

Among the scholarly journals that carry frequent articles on communication are these from the United States: *Journalism Quarterly, Public Opinion Quarterly, Audio-Visual Communications Review, Quarterly of Film, Radio and Television, Journal of Marketing, American Sociological Review, American Journal of Sociology, Journal of Applied Psychology, Social Forces, Behavioral Science,* and others. There are a number of journals in other countries specializing in mass communications, of which the following are examples: *Études de Presse* (Paris), *Echo de la Presse et de la Publicité* (Paris), *Publizistik* (Bremen), *Gazette* (Leiden), *Zeitungs-Verlag* (Bad Gotesberg), *Kwartalnik Prasoznawczy* (Warsaw), *Novinarsky Sbornik* (Prague). There is also the trade press, such as *Editor and Publisher* (newspapers), *Broadcasting-Telecasting* and *Sponsor* (television and radio), *Film Daily* and *Film Almanac* (motion pictures), *Publisher's Weekly* (books), *Printer's Ink* (advertising and general). The yearbooks of these trade publications are annual sources of current data on the industry. *Niemann Reports* is a journal of cogent criticism of the press, written mostly by Niemann Fellows at Harvard. *IPI Reports* (Zurich) is valuable for its materials on the world press and news exchange. There is also a mass communication trade press and trade yearbooks in a number of countries beside the United States.

DEVELOPMENT OF MASS COMMUNICATIONS

Gramling, Oliver. *AP: The Story of News.* New York, 1940. (One of the most readable accounts of the development of news agencies. Viewpoint is, of course, that of the Associated Press.)

Hogben, Lancelot. *From Cave Painting to Comic Strip.* London, 1948. (There is no social history of mass communication. This book, which is readable and well illustrated, deals more with early centuries of human communication than with mass media.)

Jacobs, Lewis. *The Rise of the American Film.* New York, 1939. (Convenient history of American film in its first four decades.)

Kracauer, Siegfried. *From Caligari to Hitler.* Princeton, 1947. (Psychological study of rise of German film.)

McMurtrie, Douglas. *The Book: The Story of Printing and Bookmaking.* New York, 1937. (Approach is technical, esthetic, and antiquarian, rather than social.)

Mott, Frank Luther. *American Journalism.* New York, 1941. (Together with Smith and Emery, best one-volume histories of the American press.)

———. *History of American Magazines.* New York, 1933- (Standard history, now in its fourth volume, carrying the account to about 1900.)

Peterson, Theodore B. *Magazines in the Twentieth Century.* Urbana, 1956. (Social and economic currents in publishing.)

Shurick, E. P. J. *The First Quarter Century of American Broadcasting.* Kansas City, 1946. (In the absence of a good history of radio, this tabulation of dates is useful.)

Smith, Henry L., and Emery, Edwin. *The Press and America.* New York, 1954. (Good one-volume history of newspapers.)

White, Llewellyn. *The American Radio.* Chicago, 1947. (A good place to begin reading the history of radio.)

Wood, James Playstead. *Magazines in the United States.* New York, 1956. (The only one-volume history of American magazines.)

Wroth, Lawrence. *A History of the Printed Book.* Third number of *The Dolphin,* New York, 1938. (Usable short treatment, from same general viewpoint as McMurtrie's.)

A note on media histories and biographies:

There are literally hundreds of biographies of editors and publishers, and histories of newspapers and magazines, of this and other countries. Some of these are very useful in filling in the story of developing mass communications, but because of their number and specialness are not listed here. If on that score we have an embarrassment of riches, it must be recorded on the other hand that there is nothing approximating a full history of television; the medium is too young to have sat for its portrait.

STRUCTURE AND FUNCTION OF MASS COMMUNICATIONS

Breed, Warren. "Social Control in the News Room." *Social Forces,* 33, 326-35. (Dr. Breed is one of the few scholars who has turned the observational tools of social science on the inner workings of the media. See also his article in *Journalism Quarterly,* 32, 277-84, and others.)

Federal Communications Commission. *Annual Reports,* and *Economic Study of Standard Broadcasting, 1947.* (Standard reference source for economic data on broadcasting.)

Huettig, Mae D. *Economic Control of the Motion Picture Industry.* Philadelphia, 1943. (Economic basis of the former film monopoly.)

Lawrence, Raymond D. "Kansas Publishers—A Professional Analysis." *Journalism Quarterly,* 15, 337-48. (Their social characteristics and training.)

Lerner, Daniel. *The Passing of Traditional Society.* New York, 1958. (A study of communications' part in the great social changes under way in the Middle East.)

Miller, William. *The Book Industry.* New York, 1949. (Standard source.)

Nixon, Raymond B. "Trends in Daily Newspaper Ownership since 1945." *Journalism Quarterly,* 32, 1, 3-14. (Brings up to 1953 the figures on growing non-competitive situation of daily newspapers.)

Prugger, Francis. "Social Composition and Training of the Milwaukee Journal News Staff." *Journalism Quarterly,* 18, 231-44. (Pioneer study of newsroom personnel.)

Ross, Lillian. *Picture.* New York, 1952. (Account of the making and remaking of the picture "The Red Badge of Courage.")

Rosten, Leo C. *Hollywood: The Movie Colony, The Movie Makers.* New York, 1941. (Exceedingly readable account by a sociologist who is also a professional writer.)

Sabine, Gordon. "Oregon Editorial Writers: A Study of Characteristics."

Journalism Quarterly, 28, 69-73. (Another study of news personnel.)

White, David M. "The 'Gate Keeper': A Case Study in the Selection of News." *Journalism Quarterly,* 27, 383-90. (A study of the telegraph editor of a newspaper. See also Walter Gieber's later study in the *Journalism Quarterly* of a number of telegraph editors.)

White, Llewellyn, and Leigh, Robert D. *Peoples Speaking to Peoples.* Chicago, 1946. (Organization of international communication facilities.)

UNESCO. *News Agencies.* Paris, 1954. (Useful data on the wire news services of the world.)

CONTROL AND SUPPORT OF MASS COMMUNICATIONS

Borden, Neil H. *The Economic Effects of Advertising.* New York, 1947. (Standard book on advertising's effect on the economy.)

Chafee, Zechariah. *Government and Mass Communication.* Chicago, 1947. (Standard work on this topic.)

Communications Media: Legal and Policy Problems. Ann Arbor, 1954. (Series of lectures at University of Michigan.)

Cross, Harold L. *The People's Right to Know.* New York, 1953. (The case for freedom of access to news.)

Ernst, Morris. *The First Freedom.* New York, 1946. (Hard-hitting argument for freedom of speech and of the press.)

Gerald, J. Edward. *The Press and the Constitution.* Minneapolis, 1948. (Study of the definition of freedom of the press developing out of Supreme Court decisions.)

Haight, Anne. *Banned Books.* New York, 1955. (On an unpleasant aspect of control.)

Hocking, William E. *Freedom of the Press: A Framework of Principle.* (Twentieth-century philosophy of press freedom.)

Inkeles, Alex. *Public Opinion in Soviet Russia.* Cambridge, 1950. (Best American statement of Soviet position on communication control.)

Mill, John Stuart. *On Liberty.* Many editions. (This, together with Milton, Siebert on the English history of press freedom, and Mott on Jefferson, gives the basis of the libertarian view of communication freedom and control.)

Milton, John. *Areopagitica.* Many editions. (Libertarian philosophy of communication freedom.)

Mott, Frank Luther. *Jefferson and the Press.* Baton Rouge, 1943. (On an American's libertarian ideas about press freedom.)

Robinson, Thomas P. *Radio Networks and the Federal Government.* New York, 1943. (Background of government regulation of broadcasting.)

Siebert, Fred S., Peterson, Theodore B., and Schramm, Wilbur. *Four Theories of the Press.* Urbana, 1956. (Good starting place for reading about different philosophies of mass communication. Siebert on libertarian and authoritarian approaches; Peterson on social responsibility; Schramm on totalitarian approach.)

Terrou, Fernand. *Legislation for Press, Film, and Radio.* Paris, 1951.

(Most complete treatment of legal position of mass communication in different countries.)

A note on economics references:

There is no satisfactory book on the economics of mass communication. A few articles appeared in the journals about ten years ago, but unfortunately the data in most of those articles are now outdated. The FCC provides a certain amount of economic data on broadcasting, and the trade press frequently carries current data. Such sources as these, an occasional article, a few pamphlets issued by the industry, a publishing house, newspaper chain, or network, is what we shall have to depend on until a definite book is written.

THE COMMUNICATION PROCESS

Cherry, Colin. *On Human Communication.* London and New York, 1957. (An attempt to combine some of the different scholarly approaches to communication. Author is a telecommunications engineer.)

Hartley, Eugene, and Hartley, Ruth. *Fundamentals of Social Psychology.* New York, 1952. (Approximately the first 200 pages devoted to communication, "the basic social process.")

Hayakawa, S. I. *Language in Action.* New York, 1941. (From viewpoint of general semantics.)

Hovland, Carl. "Psychology of Communication Process." In Schramm, *Communications in Modern Society.* Urbana, 1948. (Brief, readable exposition by a leading communication psychologist.)

Morris, Charles. *Signs, Language, and Behavior.* New York, 1946. (One of the classics of semantic study.)

Ruesch, Jurgen. *Non-Verbal Communication.* Berkeley, 1957. (Useful corrective for everyone who tends to think of communication as being chiefly words.)

────── and Bateson, Gregory. *Communication: The Matrix of Psychiatry.* (Especially interesting for its treatment of implied and non-overt communication.)

Schramm, Wilbur. "How Communication Works." First chapter in *Process and Effects of Mass Communication.* Urbana, 1955. (Good place to begin reading about the communication process.)

Westley, Bruce, and MacLean, Malcolm. "A Conceptual Model for Communication Research." *Audio-Visual Communication Review,* 3, 3-12. (Introduces mass media into the model.)

Wiener, Norbert. *Cybernetics.* New York, 1948. (Communication as a control device.)

A note on information theory:

The standard book is by Claude Shannon and Warren Weaver, *The Mathematical Theory of Communication.* Urbana, 1949. An easy introduction is Wilbur Schramm, "Information Theory and Mass Communication," in the *Journalism Quarterly,* 32, 2, 131-46. Cherry (see above) also has an extensive treatment of it.

CONTENT OF MASS COMMUNICATIONS

Alpert, Hollis. "Sexual Behavior in the American Movies." *Saturday Review*, 39, 9-10. (Biting analysis of sex on the screen.)

Asheim, Lester. "From Book to Film" in Berelson and Janowitz, *Reader in Public Opinion and Communication*. (What happens to book content when the story is made into a film.)

Auster, Donald. "A Content Analysis of Little Orphan Annie." *Social Problems*, 2, 26-33. (What kinds of mores are being portrayed here?)

Battin, Robert. "San Francisco Newspapers' Campaign Coverage: 1896, 1952." *Journalism Quarterly*, 31, 297-303. (Attempt to measure bias in political coverage.)

Berelson, Bernard. *Content Analysis as a Tool of Communication Research*. Chicago, 1953. (Most inclusive book on the techniques.)

—— and Salter, Patricia. "Majority and Minority Americans: An Analysis of Magazine Fiction." *Public Opinion Quarterly*, 10, 168-90. (Magazine fiction population isn't like U.S. population.)

Bush, Chilton R. "The Analysis of Political Campaign News." *Journalism Quarterly*, 28, 250-52. (A tested method.)

Childs, Harwood, and Whitton, John B. *Propaganda by Short Wave*. Princeton, 1942. (Analysis of wartime propaganda messages.)

Dale, Edgar. *Content of Motion Pictures*. New York, 1935. (Still has more than historical interest.)

Doob, Leonard. *Propaganda: Its Psychology and Technique*. New York, 1935. (Psychological analysis of propaganda techniques.)

Gottlieb, Lillian. "Radio and Newspaper Reports of the Heirens Murder Case." *Journalism Quarterly*, June, 1947. (Comparative study of accuracy and objectivity.)

Head, Sydney. "Television and Social Norms." *Quarterly of Film, Radio and Television*. 9, 175-94. (What television is teaching.)

Jones, Dorothy. "Quantitative Analysis of Motion Picture Content." *Hollywood Quarterly*, Fall, 1942.

——. "The Hollywood War Film, 1942-44." *Hollywood Quarterly*, October, 1945. (Analyzes themes, plots, and characters.)

Kingsbury, Susan, and Hart, Hornell. *Newspapers and the News*. New York, 1937. (Attempt to develop content measure on which to make judgments as to ethical performance of newspaper.)

Klapper, Joseph T., and Glock, Charles Y. "Trial by Newspaper." *Scientific American*, 180, 16-21. (The relations of newspaper coverage to justice.)

Klare, George. *Know Your Reader*. New York, 1953. (Summary and criticism of different readability techniques.)

Kracauer, Siegfried. *Propaganda and the Nazi War Films*. New York, 1942. (Propaganda themes and techniques.)

Kris, Ernest, Speier, Hans, and others. *German Radio Propaganda*. New York, 1944. (What came over the air waves in World War II.)

Lasswell, Harold D. *Propaganda Technique in the World War*. New York, 1927.

———— and Blumenstock, Dorothy. *World Revolutionary Propaganda: A Chicago Study.* New York, 1939. (Two early content studies using the methods of social science.)

Lowenthal, Leo. "Biographies in Popular Magazines." In Lazarsfeld and Stanton, *Radio Research, 1942-43.* (Whose lives, how treated?)

Nixon, Raymond, and Jones, Robert L. "The Content of Competitive vs. Non-Competitive Newspapers." *Journalism Quarterly,* 33, 3. (What does "monopoly" do to newspaper content?)

Pool, Ithiel de Sola, and others. *Trends in Content Analysis.* Urbana, 1959. (New techniques and approaches in content analysis.)

Price, Granville. "A Method for Analyzing Newspaper Campaign Coverage." *Journalism Quarterly,* 31, 447-58. (Also contains bibliography of recent studies of newspaper performance in campaigns.)

A note on the NAEB studies of television content:

In the first half of the 50's, the National Association of Educational Broadcasters, whose headquarters is at Urbana, Illinois, sponsored and published a series of detailed content studies of one week of television in several large cities. New York, Chicago, and Los Angeles were among these cities, New York being studied in four consecutive years, 1951-54. Dallas W. Smythe was principal author of the majority of these studies, Donald Horton directed the Chicago study, and H. H. Remmers made the fourth New York study.

AUDIENCES OF MASS COMMUNICATIONS

Advertising Research Foundation. Continuing Study of Newspaper Reading. (Approximately 150 studies of newspaper reading, with a convenient study of the first 100. There are many other studies of readership. C. R. Bush studied the readership of a number of Pacific Coast dailies, and R. O. Nafziger the readers of several Minnesota newspapers. Other readership studies of newspapers were made by the schools of journalism at Iowa, Northwestern, Missouri, Minnesota, and Syracuse.)

Berelson, Bernard. *The Libraries' Public.* Chicago, 1952. (Who reads books and uses libraries.)

Handel, Leo. *Hollywood Looks at Its Audience.* Urbana, 1950. (Most complete analysis of movie-going.)

Herzog, Herta. "What Do We Really Know about Daytime Serial Listeners?" In Lazarsfeld and Stanton, *Radio Research, 1942-43.* (Why do they listen?)

Himmelweit, Hilde. *Television and the Child.* London, 1958. (Full and excellent account of the youthful audience in Great Britain.)

Lazarsfeld, Paul, and Kendall, Patricia. *Radio Listening in America.* New York, 1948. (Best treatment of the radio audience, but before television.)

Lazarsfeld, Paul, and Wyant, Rowena. *Magazines in 90 Cities: Who Reads What?* (Excellent insight into the magazine audience.)

Link, Henry C. *Books and Their Readers*. New York, 1946. (Report of a national survey of book reading.)

Ludeke, Herbert, and Inglis, Ruth. "A Technique for Validating Interviewing Methods in Reader Research." *Sociometry*, 5, 1942. (A test of the common method for readership study.)

Schramm, Wilbur. "Another Dimension of Readership." *Journalism Quarterly*, December, 1947. (How far people read into news.)

Wilson, Edmund. "Why Do People Read Detective Stories?" In *Classics and Commercials*. New York, 1950. (Another study of how members of the audience happen to be there.)

Wolfe, Katherine, and Fiske, Marjorie. "The Children Talk about Comics." In *Communications Research, 1948-49*. New York, 1949. (What are the children seeking and finding in comics?)

EFFECTS OF MASS COMMUNICATIONS

Berelson, Bernard, Lazarsfeld, Paul, and McPhee, William. *Voting*. New York, 1956. (Panel study of a presidential election.)

Blumer, Herbert, and Hauser, Philip. *Movies, Delinquency, and Crime*. New York, 1933. (Payne Fund study of movies.)

Cantril, Hadley. *The Invasion from Mars*. Princeton, 1940. (A study of the reasons why Orson Welles' broadcast of a radio play caused a panic.)

Cartwright, Dorwin. "Achieving Change in People; Some Applications of Group Dynamics Theory." *Human Relations*, 4, 381-92. (Analysis of communication techniques that worked for the Treasury during war.)

Charters, W. W. *Motion Pictures and Youth*. New York, 1933. (Summary of Payne Fund conclusions as to effects of movies on young people.)

Cooper, Eunice, and Jahoda, Marie. "The Evasion of Propaganda." *Journal of Psychology*, 23, 15-25. (The famous "Mr. Biggott" study.)

Fearing, Franklin. "Influence of the Movies on Attitudes and Behavior." *The Annals*, 254, 70-79. (By a psychologist who has specialized on study of communication and especially movies.)

Festinger, Leon. *The Theory of Cognitive Dissonance*. Chicago, 1957. (Theory which helps to explain why people seek certain kinds of information.)

Himmelweit, Hilde. *Television and the Child*. London, 1958. (Previously mentioned. Most intensive study yet made of television's possible effect on children.)

Hoban, Charles, and Van Ormer, Edward. *An Inventory of Instructional Television Research, 1918-1950*. Port Washington, Long Island, 1951. (Summaries of studies on teaching films.)

Hovland, Carl I. "Mass Communications." In Lindzey, *Handbook of Social Psychology*. New York, 1954. (Excellent chapter which makes a good starting point for reading about communication effects.)

Hovland, Carl I., Lumsdaine, Arthur A., and Sheffield, Fred D. *Experiments on Mass Communication*. Princeton, 1949. (Report of the Army Information and Education studies of mass communication during the war.)

Hovland, Carl I., Janis, Irving, and Kelley, Harold. *Communication and Persuasion.* New Haven, 1953.

Hovland, Carl I., and others. *The Order of Presentation in Persuasion.* New Haven, 1956.

Hovland, Carl I., and others. *Personality and Persuasibility.* New Haven, 1958. (This group of books is one of the most important series in the field of communication research. It represents one of the few continuing and systematically programmed research activities in the field: the program headed by Hovland at Yale.)

Hyman, Herbert, and Sheatsley, Paul. "Some Reasons Why Information Campaigns Fail." *Public Opinion Quarterly,* 11, 412-23. (Analysis by two experts in the measurement of public opinion.)

Jumata, Hideya. *An Inventory of Instructional Television Research.* Ann Arbor, Michigan, 1956. (Abstracts studies to 1956.)

Katz, Elihu, and Lazarsfeld, Paul. *Personal Influence.* Glencoe, 1956. (Importance of interpersonal communication that surrounds mass media.)

Lang, Kurt, and Lang, Gladys Engel. "The Unique Perspective of Television and Its Effect." *American Sociological Review,* 18, 1, 3-12. What television showed of the MacArthur parade looked different than the parade looked to its face-to-face watchers.)

Lazarsfeld, Paul, Berelson, Bernard, and Gaudet, Hazel. *The People's Choice.* New York, 1944. (First of the large panel studies of presidential elections.)

Lippmann, Walter. *Public Opinion.* New York, 1921. (A classic in its field.)

Maccoby, Eleanor. "Why Do Children Watch Television?" *Public Opinion Quarterly,* 18, 239-44. (Child psychologist on effect of television.)

Merton, Robert. *Mass Persuasion.* New York, 1946. (Study of the reasons for Kate Smith's highly successful radio talkathon to sell war bonds.)

Schramm, Wilbur. *The Process and Effects of Mass Communication.* Urbana, 1955. (Most representative collection of articles on effects.)

Waples, Douglas, Berelson, Bernard, and Bradshaw, Franklin. *What Reading Does to People.* Chicago, 1940. (Effects of reading.)

Wertham, Frederic. *Seduction of the Innocent.* New York, 1946. (Impressionistic treatment of possible effect of comics on children.)

RESPONSIBILITY FOR MASS COMMUNICATION

Becker, Carl. *Freedom and Responsibility in the American Way of Life.* New York, 1945. (By a distinguished historian.)

Brucker, Herbert. *Freedom of Information.* New York, 1949. (What is required to have freedom.)

Commission on Freedom of the Press. *Toward a Free and Responsible Press.* Chicago, 1947. (General report of the Commission. See also the reports of the British and Canadian Commissions on the Press and Broadcasting.)

Crawford, Nelson Antrim. *The Ethics of Journalism.* New York, 1924. (By a former editor.)

Flint, L. N. *The Conscience of the Newspaper.* New York, 1925. (Practical ethics, illustrated by cases and examples.)

Hocking, William E. *Freedom of the Press: A Framework of Principle.*
(A philosopher writing on the rights and responsibilities of the press.)

Inglis, Ruth. *Freedom of the Movies.* Chicago, 1947. (What the public
can expect its movie makers and movie owners to do.)

MacDougall, Curtiss. *Newsroom Problems and Policies.* New York, 1941.
(Practical problems in ethics and responsibility.)

Reid, Richard. *The Morality of the Newspaper.* South Bend, 1938. (A
Roman Catholic viewpoint on press ethics and responsibilities.)

Schramm, Wilbur. *Responsibility in Mass Communication.* New York,
1957. (The first extensive treatment of communication ethics in thirty
years.)

Siepmann, Charles. *Radio, Television, and Society.* New York, 1950.
(Shortcomings, responsibilities, opportunities of broadcasting.)

Svirsky, Leon. *Your Newspaper: Blueprint for a Better Press.* New York,
1948. (Niemann Fellows writing on responsible journalism.)

A note on bibliography for mass communications in other countries:

Space prohibits us from compiling a bibliography for each country,
but let us at least mention a few general books. UNESCO's *World Communications* (Paris, 1956) is the best roundup of information on mass
communication systems of different countries. UNESCO's *News Agencies*
(Paris, 1954) is the best roundup of information on wire news services.
The best available book on legislation affecting the media in various
countries is Terrou's *Legislation for Press, Film, and Radio* (Paris, 1951).
Among other useful books in this field published by UNESCO is Kayser's
One Week's News (Paris, 1950), which is an analysis of the news content of newspapers in a number of different countries. Another good
source for material of this sort is the International Press Institute, which
has its headquarters in Zurich. This organization not only issues the
IPI Report, which regularly carries information about what is happening
to and in the press of many countries, but also issues from time to time
studies on the flow of the news between countries. These are based on
content studies, and on the opinions and judgments of newsmen in the
various countries. A book by Daniel Lerner, *The Passing of Traditional
Society* (New York, 1958), deals with the changes that are taking place
in the communication systems and the societies of the Middle East.
Scratches on Our Minds by Harold Isaacs (New York, 1957) is a study
of how American images of India and China have been formed. *One Day
in the World's Press,* edited by Wilbur Schramm (Stanford, 1959)
translates fourteen prestige papers from fourteen countries into English,
and reprints them in the original format. Finally, it should be mentioned that a number of periodicals in other countries specialize in
articles and news about mass communication. Examples of these were
given early in this bibliography. There are such journals in many countries, and a number of countries also have a trade press for the mass
media.

INDEX